Within a few days of Katharine Hepburn's death in June of 2003, a tastefully whitewashed biography of the screen goddess was rushed "with unseemly haste" into print.

In September of 2003, in a review (*"Kate Selectively Remembered"*) by David Ehrensten, **The Advocate** referred to that biography as a "mixture of cautious disclosure and obsequious deference" and asked why that biography "does nothing to question the public persona (that) Hepburn had carefully constructed over the years."

In the same review, **The Advocate** issued a challenge to the writers and publishers of America: "One can only hope there's someone out there who remembers Kate a bit better (than A. Scott Berg), and has a manuscript at the ready."

To **The Advocate**, and to the readers of America, we at Blood Moon Productions proudly announce:

"Here it is."

D1531332

Katharine Hepburn (1907-2003)

There's a carload of other biographies about Hepburn that either got the facts wrong or whitewashed them to the point where there's almost been a consistent act of academic sabotage. But here at last is a biography that isn't afraid to wrestle with the outrageous ego and ferociously guarded privacy of Hollywood's most mysterious *über-*diva, **Katharine the Great.**

James Stafford

Ah, poor Katie....A victim, post-mortem, of the illusion-shattering mania of celebrity biographer Darwin Porter. But frankly, America's understanding of its own cultural origins is better off for having opened some of her closet's tightly sealed windows and doors.

Between the Covers

"You can say or write anything about me you like...
Just don't, for any reason, ever tell the truth."

A favorite declaration of Katharine Hepburn,
delivered to many journalists

We've all **Remembered Kate.** And many of us have shed genuine tears over her demise, and reverentially paid her the homage that was her due.

But now that the requisite period of mourning is over, here's the REAL story about what and who motivated Hollywood's holy terror with the Bryn Mawr diction.

The Georgia Literary Association

KATHARINE THE GREAT

(1907-1950)

SECRETS OF A LIFETIME...REVEALED

by Darwin Porter

ISBN 0-9748118-0-7
All Rights Reserved
Copyright 2004, Blood Moon Productions, Ltd.

302A West 12th Street, #358
New York, NY 10014
www.BloodMoonProductions.com

First Edition published February 2004
Cover Art by Howard Zucker (www.SylvesterQ.com)
Photos courtesy of Photofest (www.photofestnyc.com)
and The Haggart Collection
Corporate logo by Ed Husser

BLOOD
MOON
Productions, Ltd.

WHO IS DARWIN PORTER?

Darwin Porter, one of the most prolific writers in the world, has keenly observed the Hollywood scene since he worked, beginning at the age of 20, as an entertainment columnist for *The Miami Herald.*

Referring to himself as a "social historian," he specializes in sagas, some of them brutal, all of them artful, showcasing some aspect of the history of America during the 20th century. Many of his insights derive from extensive interviews with eyewitnesses to situations that Hollywood publicists sometimes worked hard to suppress.

Porter's writing is edgy, courageous, and extremely well-crafted. It's definitely not for the prudish, the squeamish, or the faint-hearted. Sensational and occasionally outrageous, his works are grounded in fact, using respected journalistic techniques based on decades of experience. In many cases, the revelations they contain, although sometimes commonly traded among Hollywood insiders, have never been revealed to the general public before. For more on the research techniques used during the compilation and crafting of this biography, please refer to *"A Cast of Thousands"* beginning on page 537 of this book.

Other biographies by Darwin Porter include *The Secret Life of Humphrey Bogart: The Early Years (1899-1931)*, which went a long way toward shattering the overused cliché of the strong but silent trenchcoat. Its release in June of 2003 earned either rave reviews or bitter condemnations from at least a hundred publications, and about a dozen different radio stations, throughout the US and Europe.

Porter's spin on the early days of Hollywood, *Hollywood's Silent Closet*, originally released in 2001, was defined by a London-based critic as "a brilliant primer" for the *Who's Who* of early filmmaking. Based on interviews with eyewitnesses, and years of tapping into the inexhaustible supply of entertainment industry gossip, it presents a steamy but accurate portrait of pre-Talkie Hollywood, which had a lot to be silent about, and where many of the sins were never depicted on the screen.

Aside from his writing about the entertainment industry, Porter is the highly visible creator and co-author of more than 800 editions of the *Frommer Travel Guides* to destinations that include most of Europe, the Caribbean, the Carolinas, and Georgia. When not traveling, which is rare, he lives in New York City, with frequent excursions to California. For thumbnail descriptions of some of Darwin Porter's other recent works, please refer to the endpages of this biography.

WHAT IS BLOOD MOON PRODUCTIONS?

Blood Moon Productions, Ltd. is administered and staffed by writers who were formerly associated with *The New York Times, United Press International,* and *The Miami Herald*, and who are presently involved with the production of editorial copy for many of ***The Frommer Guides***.

It was established as a "type S Corporation" in 2003 as a spinoff of another publishing venture, ***The Georgia Literary Association (The GLA)***. The GLA was conceived in 1997 in the rural hamlet of Washington, Georgia, quickly evolving into a small but commercially viable publishing enterprise that eventually moved to New York City, a more appropriate venue.

Blood Moon Productions is devoted to mainstream literary treatments of hardcore revelations about the history of Hollywood, always with an abiding respect for the creative talent that fueled Hollywood's Golden Age.

The name we gave to our organization derives from the title of one of the Georgia Literary Association's most successful novels, ***Blood Moon***, by Darwin Porter, an artfully brutal thriller packed with cinematic images. It's about love, psychosis, a deviant evangelist, sexual obsession, money, power, pornography, and evangelical Christianity in America today. It contains, in the words of one critic, "erotica that's akin to Anaïs Nin on Viagra with a bump of meth."

When we originally negotiated with Darwin Porter for the distribution rights to ***Katharine the Great***, we were keenly aware of the reams of sometimes trivial material that had been previously published about Katharine Hepburn. Frankly, if we hadn't had access to so much incendiary, never-before-published material about her, we would never have attempted to re-define such a shopworn subject.

But now that the child (i.e., this book) has been birthed, we freely admit that we nearly drowned in the deep and murky lake associated with the life and psyche of Katharine Hepburn. EVERYONE who ever met her seemed to have a strong, and sometimes violent, opinion or anecdote about her. So, in synch with our role as social historians, we're honored to have been the first to publish the revelations contained within this book.

Thanks for your interest in our organization, and happy reading. We wish you good fortune and joy.

Sincere best wishes,
Danforth Prince
President, Blood Moon Productions

The author dedicates this book

to Danforth Prince

CHAPTER ONE

It was April 2, 1921, in New York City, with spring bursting out in Central Park. It had been the greatest day of thirteen-year-old Kate Hepburn's life.

A five-day Easter holiday break had left her head spinning with delight. The parade along Fifth Avenue with her handsome, athletic brother, Tom, on her arm was worth the trip in from Hartford, Connecticut.

But that had not been all. They'd roamed Central Park, gone to shops and cafés, and had even seen the great Anna Pavlova dance in *The Dying Swan.* The only real discomfort had come when Tom and Kate had gone alone to see the silent film, Mark Twain's *A Connecticut Yankee in King Arthur's Court*, on April Fool's Day.

Tom had become extremely agitated during a hanging scene in the film. Only last year he had been seriously reprimanded when he'd attempted to perform this same dangerous stunt.

Although her brother had started to shake violently during that particular scene, he'd recovered quickly and had gone walking that night with her among the bright lights of Broadway. Buying her a big ice-cream cone, her brother had taken her to see the dazzling Broadway marquees, announcing the stars and their plays, including Laurette Taylor in *Peg O' My Heart* and Jeanne Eagles in *In the Night Watch.* After they'd had their fill of the bright lights, Tom and Kate had journeyed down to the art-filled house at 26 Charlton Street in Greenwich Village. They were the guests of an attorney, Mary Towle, whom they called "Aunty." Mary had been a classmate of their mother's at Bryn Mawr, and was Tom's godmother.

Mary had invited eight teenagers, both boys and girls, over to meet Kate and Tom that night. Although Kate was shy and didn't mingle freely, Tom had been an instant hit with the young Villagers, especially when he brought down his banjo from his garret bedroom and had launched into an impromptu concert, singing his own songs.

After the music, the girls had teased Tom, one young lady calling him "too handsome for your own good." Another found him "artsy," yet another taunted him for eating three big helpings of coconut cake, and a final girl pronounced Tom as "too sensitive." He'd blushed at the chiding but had told Kate that he'd thought "the girls really like me."

After the guests had gone, Tom had thanked Aunty for "memories I will treasure forever." Kate had run up to kiss him good night on both cheeks as he stood on the stairs. Uncharacteristically, he'd grabbed her in his arms and held her real close before kissing her gently on the lips. "You're my girl, aren't you?" he'd asked her.

"You're the only man who'll ever own me," she'd predicted. She slowly watched his mass of tousled blond curls bound up the steps to his garret bedroom before turning in for the night in her ground-floor chamber next door to Aunty's. Kate had checked the clock in the hallway. It was exactly 10:15pm.

No sound was heard from Tom's bedroom the rest of the night, although Kate did not sleep well. She would later tell her family that in the middle of the night she'd experienced a "gut-wrenching feeling in the pit of my stomach," which she blamed on all the rich food she'd consumed in New York.

The next morning at breakfast, Kate devoured a large plate of bacon and eggs with Aunty. Both had agreed that the sensible thing to do was to let Tom sleep to recover from a heady holiday. By 8:30am, Kate grew alarmed that they might miss the ten o'clock train back to Hartford if Tom didn't get up soon. Bounding up three flights of steps just like Tom had the night before, Kate pounded on his door. "Rise and shine, sleepyhead!" she shouted at him. There was an ominous silence from the other side. Since the bathroom door was opened nearby, she could tell he wasn't in there. After her second pounding went unheeded, she opened the door and barged in.

At first, the garret looked empty, her brother's cot barely disturbed. Suddenly, she looked up. Tom's body was hanging by his neck from one of the exposed wooden beams. Amazingly, his feet touched the floor, his knees bent. Kate screamed hysterically as she looked up into the pop-eyed face of her brother. He was a hideous shade of reddish-purple, his arms and bare chest blue.

Her screams brought Aunty Mary running up the stairs. She too screamed when she saw her godson. Mary quickly ran for help next door, seeking the aid of her closest friend and law partner, Bertha Rambaugh. Bertha immediately called an ambulance.

With Mary gone for help, Kate in her delirium felt that Tom might still be alive. Desperately she tried to untie the tight noose, finding it far too tight. Giving up, a sobbing Kate crawled under her brother's already stiff body. With Herculean strength, she lifted him from the floor, hoping to relieve the pressure on his neck.

This was "my Tom, my big brother," as she'd always called him. He'd been her champion. Hadn't he taken her to her first school dance at the age of twelve? Shy and intimidated, she'd retreated to the far corner of the dance hall while he'd gone to get her some red fruit punch. At the punch bowl, he'd heard a guy ask, "Who is that freckle-faced, gangling-limbed, stringbean wallflower?" For that probing question, Tom punched the boy right at the punch bowl.

As she waited for help to arrive, Kate took in the garret of this old-fashioned red-brick town house. It was a spooky, haunted place with its web-laced exposed beams, scattered—often broken—antiques, two steamer trunks, various crates, and even a discarded hatbox or two from the 1890s. Tom had spread out his clothes from the night before, placing his trousers on the dresser with his suitcase on top to keep their crease. On the night stand were two rail tickets back to Hartford.

Peter O'Rourke and John Taylor were the first two Greenwich Village patrolmen to arrive on the scene. Taylor quickly pushed Kate aside, as O'Rourke cut down Tom's body. The two policemen laid Tom's body on a cot. They did not bother to check for signs of life, as it was obvious that the victim was dead.

Within minutes, an ambulance pulled up, carrying Dr. Bradford Cody of St. Vincent's Hospital. After examining the body, he ordered it removed from the house.

Kate stood crying as she watched Tom's sheet-covered body carried down the steps in a stretcher. Then it was time for a lot of questions to be answered. Both Taylor and O'Rourke vigorously grilled Kate, Mary, and Bertha, as if they were suspects. They even contacted the teenagers who'd attended the party the night before.

Kate repeatedly told the police, "I don't know why Tom killed himself. He was a great athlete. On the football team. A great future ahead of him. He was going to attend Yale just like his great-grandfather did. At Kingswood School in West Hartford, he'd been nominated for the Citizenship Medal. That's the highest honor."

When Taylor and O'Rourke later returned to police headquarters, both men claimed they thought the girl was concealing something, even though the patrolmen felt it was "an obvious case of suicide."

Only the next day would there be an accusation of murder.

***

Arriving in New York's Grand Central the following afternoon, Dr. Thomas Hepburn and his wife, Katharine (Kit) Houghton Hepburn, were immediately besieged by the press. Even before he knew any of the facts, Dr. Hepburn charged that his son had been murdered by an intruder. This was in direct contrast to the report of Dr. Juan Gonzales, assistant medical examiner. After examining the cadaver, Dr. Gonzalez claimed that the cause of death was "asphyxia by hanging."

Kit was in a state of shock. Her own father, Alfred Houghton, had committed suicide in a fit of melancholia, and there had been other suicides in the family as well. Now her eldest son had hanged himself, too.

Dr. Hepburn claimed that his son was normal and healthy, having suffered only nervous twitches in the face which had been diagnosed as chorea or "St. Vitus's Dance." The symptoms were rapid contortions of the upper lip and nose and a quick winking of the eyes. The disease was said to have been brought on by excessive worry and too much stress.

Newspapers that day carried headlines about Tom's death, accurately listing his birth date as November 8, 1905, the first child of the Hepburn family. The *Hartford Courant* claimed that Tom's body had been discovered by his sister Catherine (sic), and *The New York Times* identified her as "Clara."

When Dr. Hepburn could find no sign of an intruder at Mary's house, and certainly none of murder, he backed down from his original statement, claiming that Tom killed himself because he'd "suddenly developed insanity."

The medical examiner's report was explicitly clear. Tom, it appeared, had committed suicide at three o'clock that morning. He'd taken off his bedsheets and ripped them into strips of cloth, from which he then crafted a "hanging rope." He'd fashioned a noose which he'd attached to a rafter, and had taken an old packing case loaded with pots and iron skillets and had stood on the case and placed the noose around his neck. He'd then jumped to his death only to find that he'd severely miscalculated, as the rope had stretched and he found himself standing upright on the floor.

The medical examiner assumed that to strangle himself, Tom had been forced to bend his knees and pitch his weight forward, swinging back and forth. The report concluded that at any time, he could have touched the floor with his feet.

The police investigators reported that the teenager's death must have been a "horrendous one of slow strangulation," as he'd used the last of his fading energy to hurl his weight forward into death.

Still wavering about his son's suicide, Dr. Hepburn offered what he thought was a "logical explanation," blaming it on "a foolish stunt gone wrong." He cited the film that Kate and Tom had seen only the day before, *A Connecticut Yankee in King Arthur's Court,* which had featured a hanging stunt.

Dr. Hepburn recalled to the press an event from his undergraduate days at Randolph-Macon in Virginia. A black man in his forties had known how to tighten his neck muscles to prevent his windpipe from being cut off "in case the white men come to string me up." As an undergraduate, Dr. Hepburn had hired the black man to perform this stunt in front of an unsuspecting football team visiting from the North. The performer was successful, and the visiting team went back to the North and told their families that they had actually seen a black man lynched.

Without the doctor's knowledge, Tom had already perfected this stunt to entertain his brothers and sisters. Tom could fix a bow-knot in the rope which he could untie just in time to prevent strangulation. When Dr. Hepburn had eventually caught him one afternoon attempting this stunt at their home at 133 Hawthorne in Hartford, he had immediately cut the rope and had warned Tom that if he continued with this stunt, he would surely kill himself one day.

Dr. Hepburn's final version as revealed to the press completely ignored the medical examiner's report that Tom had to deliberately swing back and forth to kill himself because his feet were too close to the ground.

Kate's own autobiography, *Me*, published in 1991, continued the misinformation. Amazingly, in her book, Kate claimed that she cut Tom down and laid his body on the cot, which was hardly the case. She was supporting Tom's body on her back when the two Greenwich Village patrolmen arrived. It was Mary Towle—not Kate—who'd gone for help. Yet Kate in *Me* reported that she'd gone along the street herself trying to find a house with a doctor's sign out front. Claiming to have found one, she said she'd rung the bell and the door had been opened by a maid but just by a crack. "My brother's dead," Kate quotes herself in *Me*. "Then the doctor can't help him, can he?" Kate quotes the maid as having said before slamming the door in her face.

This apocryphal story, which first appeared in an erroneous 1921 newspaper account, has frequently been reported in various books devoted to Hepburn's life and career. It never happened. Kate had read the account in a newspaper herself and reported it as fact in her memoirs.

Within a few days of Tom's suicide, his body was being prepared for cremation. Kate, who was very close to both her parents, had been tempted to share a secret with them, but in the rush of events that followed his death, she was either unwilling or unable to express it.

Yet another family tragedy blasted its way into the psyche of the Hepburns. It was revealed that Dr. Hepburn's brother, Sewell Hepburn, had committed suicide in a garage in Annapolis, Maryland. Sewell had crawled behind the wheel of his car and had turned on the ignition after sealing the garage doors shut. His wife, Annie, found him dead of monoxide poisoning the following morning. Sewell had fought severe depression for years and had suffered the debilitation of syphilis.

After cremation, Tom's ashes were taken to Cedar Hill Cemetery in Hartford and laid to rest. Only the ashes were laid to rest, not the controversy that still surrounds his death.

The memory of Tom and the way he died would plague Kate for the rest of her life. As her best friend, Laura Harding, once told director George Cukor, "Kate never got over Tom's suicide."

***

There is no evidence that Kate ever shared her secret about Tom's death with her parents. When her father returned from burying Sewell, she found him in such denial about Tom's suicide that she didn't want to "burden the poor man with anything else." In time, Kate would share the secret with a few trusted friends , including Kenneth MacKenna, George Cukor, and Laura Harding, no doubt Spencer Tracy himself.

But as the decades went by, Kate rarely referred to Tom's suicide. The only time she came even close to revealing the reason behind the suicide was in a conversation with A. Scott Berg, the biographer.

"I had heard that maybe a girl rejected him—who knows, maybe a boy. Whatever it was, he simply could not cope."

Such a revelation had never been made by her before. In all the stories about Tom's suicide, no member of her family had ever ventured forth with the suggestion that a rejection in love might have been the real reason behind the suicide. Kate had opened a revealing window into the past, if only by a tiny crack.

During their short years together, Tom and Kate shared all their secrets together, usually concealing "the really big ones" from the rest of the Hepburn clan.

Only the year before, tomboy Kate, who liked her family to call her "Jimmy," had told Tom that she had "hopelessly fallen in love" with Cathy Watson, her mannish gym instructor. Watson was no beauty and wore men's clothing and had a rather squarish figure—"no curves at all," as one of Kate's classmates recalled. In the same class with Kate, Jill Davids said Watson "was a monster, always blowing the whistle at the girls, always chastising us for not playing harder, and always comparing our sports skills unfavorably with the boy athletes at school."

Yet twelve-year-old Kate seemed to see Watson with some rosy glow, speaking of her "soft, gentle smile, her kind face, her lovely sandy hair, her graceful movements."

Since Kate had come clean with him, Tom too shared the secret of his own crush. He'd fallen in love with a boy named Tracy Walker, who just seemed to appear out of nowhere. He was believed to have traveled north with his mother from Georgia. His mother was said to have been one of the prostitutes who worked in the many bordellos in the Hartford area at the time, spreading syphilis among the young men of the town, who often passed it on to their wives. Many of Dr. Hepburn's patients had contracted syphilis this way.

Tracy was seventeen at the time Tom met him. The circumstances of how they met aren't known. A high-school drop-out, Tracy stood more than six feet tall and weighed about one hundred and eighty pounds "of pure muscle." Although never known to play sports, he had an athlete's frame, with a muscular chest and arms, broad shoulders, a narrow waist, and tennis player legs on which golden brown hair glistened. His hair was slightly reddish, and he kept it parted in the middle and brilliantined. His skin was deeply tanned, perhaps from the Southern sun, when he first arrived in Hartford. The only time Kate saw him, she claimed that Tracy's brownish eyes "twinkled with devilish mischief," and that "he had unnaturally white teeth against dark skin."

Soon Tom was giving Tracy all his spending money and buying gifts for him. It was believed that Tom was so smitten that he stole from the Hepburn household to provide for Tracy.

Eventually Tom must have pressed his sexual needs, although Tracy was notoriously heterosexual, having said to be the "deflowerer" of half the comely lasses of Hartford. As the benefactor of Tom's gifts and money, however, Tracy agreed to meet him in the woods after school let out at three o'clock. Overly eager, Tom headed into the woods hoping to consummate his love. Stories differ as to what actually happened that day.

But what is known is that "at a compromising moment," when Tom was on his knees in front of Tracy, three boys from Tom's school burst out from behind the bushes to taunt him and call him a faggot. As Tom rose to defend himself, this set-up became clear to him. As he was able to relate to his sister, Tracy had deliberately lured him to the woods to be humiliated in front of his classmates. Although he fought back, Tom was easily overpowered and had been held down to the ground as he'd received some severe blows to his face and body. Since Tom was often involved in fistfights at school, Dr. Hepburn wasn't surprised and quickly treated Tom's wounds and bruises. This encounter had taken place only two weeks before Tom embarked on his Easter holiday in Greenwich Village with Kate.

As Kate later told her friends, she had given Tom all the love and sympathy she could muster, but feared at the time that his humiliating experience in the woods had "cut a deep gash into his soul."

"For all I know," Kate later told friends, "Tom was already planning to kill himself as the train neared New York for what was supposed to have been a carefree holiday."

"Flattened emotionally," as Kate put it, by Tom's death, she was pushed deeper and deeper into the world of make-believe.

***

Throughout her long life, Katharine Hepburn always claimed that whatever she became, she owed to her parents, although she often expressed a fear that she'd been a disappointment to both of them. "I think they expected a lot more from me—perhaps wanting me to become a great surgeon, something like that."

Katharine Hepburn's capable and strong-willed mother, Katharine (Kit) Martha Houghton was the first born of Alfred Augustus Houghton and Caroline Garlinghouse, coming into the world one bitterly cold morning on February 2, 1878. Her parents would eventually produce two more children: Edith born in 1879 and Marion in 1884. Katharine Hepburn's grandfather, Alfred, was the younger brother of Amory Bigelow Houghton, an early chairman of the Corning Glass Company. Partly because of his own efforts, and partly because of cash bequests made to him by his richer older brother, the Houghtons led a genteel life of the upper-middle class—but not rich—gentry of their day. Of "nervous temperament," Alfred eventually took a revolver and wandered into a deserted lumberyard where he fatally shot himself in the temple on October 29,

1892.

More family tragedy was to follow. At the age of thirty-three, Katharine Hepburn's maternal grandmother Caroline, discovered that she had cancer which led to her hasty death. Orphaned at thirteen, Kit, along with her two younger sisters, was sent to Boston under the guardianship of their very strict and parsimonious uncle, Amory Houghton.

A striking, chestnut-haired beauty, with a stubborn streak, renegade spirit, and an indomitable will, Kit, in spite of her uncle's objections, was determined to go to Bryn Mawr to fulfull her dead mother's dreams. Bryn Mawr represented the epitome of Main Line Philadelphia posh, attracting some of the most prominent daughters of East Coast families in spite of its notoriously rigid and draconian entrance exams.

After graduating from Bryn Mawr, Kit met and in 1904 married a handsome young man from Virginia, Tom Hepburn, during his last year in medical school. "He was the most beautiful creature I'd ever seen," she'd told her sisters. What she saw was a man who stood five feet, eleven inches and weighed one-hundred and seventy-five pounds, with thick, mahogany-red hair, a finely chiseled jaw, and prominent cheekbones.

Having played on his college football team, he had rock-hard muscles and powerful shoulders. His eyes were as "blue and as brilliant as an alpine lake." "But it was the arms that did it for me," Kit later told her sisters. Good for a future surgeon, he had long, elegantly tapered fingers on smooth, white, manly hands.

Born December 18, 1879, the boy who would become Dr. Thomas Norval Hepburn was the youngest child of the Reverend Sewell Snowden Hepburn and Selina Lloyd Powell. Tom had four brothers and sisters: Charles, Selina, Sewell and Lloyd. They lived on six-hundred dollars a year that their father earned as the minister at the local Episcopal Church. The Hepburn family traced their Scottish ancestors back to James Hepburn, Earl of Bothwell, third husband of Mary Queen of Scots. Later, Kate would play the queen in a 1936 movie.

Once married, Tom and Kit began producing what eventually became an awesome brood of children in spite of her strong and public advocacy of birth control. In a period that stretched out for fifteen years, six children were born, beginning with Tom (named after his father) in 1905, then Katharine (named after her mother) in 1907, followed by Dick in 1911, Bob in 1913, Marion in 1918, and Margaret (Peg) in 1920. Kate for years insisted that she was born in 1909, and many biographers took her at her word, but the records in Hartford show differently.

***

It was the strangest family in town. Neighbors or acquaintances often

8

crossed over to the other side of the street when they saw one of the Hepburns coming their way. Instead of turning to the Lord to save their souls, "the Hepburns are always soaping and showering, putting cleanliness above godliness," as one irate neighbor put it.

On the surface, the Hepburns seemed like the comfortable bourgeois of their day, with a large manse, five servants, and even a shingled summer cottage at Fenwick, Connecticut, opening onto Long Island Sound. They were Protestant, which should have made them suitable company, as many Hartford citizens at the time despised Catholics. They were teetotalers, perhaps bringing out a small glass of sherry if a guest arrived. But it was what they talked about at their dinner parties, however, that sent most neighbors scurrying, never to return again.

Kit was a rather militant suffragette. When not talking about birth control, she'd force a give-women-the-vote pamphlet into your hand.

Tom was a noted urologist and surgeon and discussed the prevention of venereal disease with anyone who would listen. "Back in those days, people, especially men, got syphilis and a lot more than that," local resident Phil Kilmore said, "except that it was mentioned only in the deadly stillness of a doctor's office." Dr. Hepburn talked about anything in front of his family, and not one of his children was ever asked to leave the table. It was a cultured household. Sinclair Lewis might drop in for dinner, or else Dr. Hepburn would read a letter that he'd just received from George Bernard Shaw.

At one of her notorious tea parties, Kit might entertain the most reviled feminists of her day, including Charlotte Perkins Gilman, Emmeline Pankhurst, or the notorious Emma Goldman when Emma wasn't in jail on a charge of advocating anarchy. Young Kate grew up in a world where such subjects as social hygiene and sexual relations, even male homosexuality and lesbianism, were commonly discussed, as was Goldman's type of anarchy, along with the various movements of the day including Fabianism, Marxism, and socialism.

Of all the visitors to the Hepburn household, none impressed young Kate more than the arrival of Margaret Sanger, America's pioneer advocate of birth control. Sanger had witnessed her own mother die from child-bearing and a too large family. As a nurse in the overpopulated Lower East Side of New York, she'd watched the desperate measures used by tenement women with too many children to prevent subsequent pregnancies. Their crude methods of abortion often led to the deaths of these young mothers. As a nurse she also saw what the butcherers "did to the guts of these poor souls who entrusted them with their abortions," Sanger said. The unsanitized conditions often led to infections and deaths.

Although arrested and jailed for her beliefs, Sanger continued to fight. In the 1920s she even imported the first diaphragms into the United States from Japan.

Sanger was a bit dismayed by the size of Kit's family, but was pleased to see that Kit had kept her youthful face and figure and that she was a "playmate and companion, almost like a sister to her children, including the actress, Katherine (*sic*)," as noted in Sanger's autobiography.

Kate later would amuse friends with stories of her first "performance." At the age of four, she was taken by Kit to Washington to join women protesters in their sweeping skirts parading along Pennsylvania Avenue demanding the vote for women. Kate liked to fancy that President Woodrow Wilson himself peered out the windows of the White House "to see who was scaring the horses. I'm sure he noticed a spindly, tall little girl with unruly red hair who was more militant than all the older suffragettes."

***

After brother Tom's death, a despondent Kate fared poorly in school, her marks dropping off. Her parents feared that with such poor scholarship, she'd never be able to pass the entrance exams for Bryn Mawr, much less become a surgeon.

She began to exhibit some strange behavior. At Fenwick, the Hepburn's summer home, Katharine had befriended a young girl, Allie Barbour, with whom she embarked on what Kate called "a life of crime."

Allie and Kate began to break into a series of summer homes which had been closed down for the season by their owners. Their intention wasn't robbery but the "thrill of discovery." Kate usually did the breaking in, often through one of the windows on an upper floor. In those days of lax security, she would look for an unlocked window. She would then walk through the house and let Allie in through the front door. Mostly Allie and Kate would "sightsee," then depart through the back door. Kate remembered taking only one item: a nutcracker shaped like a crocodile. She had such guilt over her theft that she broke into the same house two afternoons later and returned it.

These break-ins almost led to her death. One afternoon, she and Allie conspired to raid the house of the Newton-Brainard family. Slipping, Kate lost her footing and fell headlong right through a skylight in the roof. In desperation she reached out to clutch anything. She grabbed onto "something" —she could never remember what—and looked down to find herself precariously perched over an atrium that extended down three floors onto a marble floor. Escaping the "jaws of death," she managed to pull herself up and out of the house. In her memoirs, *Me,* Kate recalled that she landed in the third floor hallway. Allie offered a different account and claimed that Kate almost died that day—"or else she might have ended up never able to walk again with spinal injuries."

Allie acquired a new boy friend, Robert Post. More daring than Allie, Robert offered to join in their crime spree, and then began urging them to become the "vandals of Fenwick." On their first mission, the trio battered down the door of a large Edwardian summer cottage. In the bathroom the teenagers found talcum powder which, on a whim, they proceeded to spread all over the house. From the house next door, a maid spotted what was going on and called the police. Kate, Allie, and Robert were taken to the station but not officially charged. Dr. Hepburn showed up and agreed to pay damages to the owner of the vandalized house.

Dr. Hepburn neither scolded nor punished Kate for her crime spree but had seemed to understand her desperate "need for discovery." Out of respect for her father, Kate gave up the criminal life. But it was only temporary.

***

When not breaking into houses, Kate sneaked away by herself to see flickers on the silent screen. Poker-faced cowboy William S. Hart was her favorite actor, but she also thrilled to the antics of Pola Negri, Clara Bow, Gloria Swanson, Charles Chaplin, Lilian Gish, and Rudolph Valentino. To her sisters she confided her secret desire about becoming a screen vamp, but she didn't tell either of her parents. Instinctively, she knew that both Kit and Dr. Hepburn would regard a film career as an "unworthy ambition." Both of her parents viewed show business careers as "only slightly more elevated than prostitution." A brilliant future in medicine was planned for their daughter.

It was a blistery day in September of 1924 when Kate set foot on the campus of exclusive Bryn Mawr, in a suburb of Philadelphia. She was no longer the tomboy who demanded to be called, "Jimmy," and the famous cheekbones of the future screen and stage actress, Katharine Hepburn, were just beginning to emerge. With all her swimming and athletics, her legs had developed—or, as she put it, "my gams were leggy enough for me to put on a burlesque show."

Freckles still covered her body, but she was no longer ashamed of them as she once was. Dr. Hepburn had convinced her that Jesus Christ had freckles—and "he made his way in the world all right, or at least the Afterworld."

She walked onto campus with a slightly loping gait—or, in the words of one of her first critics, "like a wounded antelope." Her tall and lanky figure was considered "unfeminine." Brick-red hair framed a face with gray-blue eyes that looked at one with unusual intensity. She wore that hair in a bun, as it was deemed uncontrollable.

Her most distinctive feature was her high-pitched and very penetrating voice which struck some classmates as strange and rather nasal, part New England schoolmarm and part Southern belle, the latter sound no doubt from the heritage of her father, a Virginian.

If she were insecure and uncertain, and indeed she was in 1924, she masked it with a false bravado which tended to alienate people instead of attract them

11

to her.

***

Within two months of her arrival as a freshman, Kate was the most gossiped about student at Bryn Mawr. If one of the young women in the dormitory went to the bathroom at midnight, she was likely to find Kate there taking a shower. The same situation might prevail at four in the morning as well. Throughout the rest of her life, Kate was to take five or six showers a day, always cold as Dr. Hepburn had prescribed them. Her father believed that icy plunge baths drove negative thoughts from the mind.

Her clothes were mannish and unconventional. Most of that first winter she was seen around campus wearing a tacky bright green overcoat with its buttons missing. Kate fastened it together with a giant safety pin.

Kate's unconventional behavior provided almost daily fodder for gossip in the school dining room. If Kate found that a classmate had a steady boyfriend, she'd lecture her on the "fraud of monogamy." That term, which referred to the enslavement potential in women who bonded themselves exclusively to one man, had come from social historian Havelock Ellis, and had been introduced into the Hepburn household by both Sanger and Goldman.

Kate's politics, viewed as extreme left wing, and definitely socialist, took second place to her tendency to take off her clothes at the most inopportune times. Kate had been brought up in a family where Dr. Hepburn and Kit walked around nude in front of their family, especially in the "too hot" summer months at the sea-bordering house at Fenwick.

When she was growing up, Kate noticed that both her father and her mother had an extreme physical attraction for each other. If they were sitting on the sofa, and wanted to kiss deeply and passionately, they did. If Dr. Hepburn produced a big erection, he viewed that as nothing to be ashamed of. He would walk around the living room and into the kitchen with his erection protruding before him before it deflated. "As a urologist, the problem I see in my office every day are men, for whatever reason, who can't produce an erection," Dr. Hepburn told Kate.

In spite of their passionate love-making, Dr. Hepburn never had sex with his wife in front of other family members. The walls of the old house were so thin, however, that everything going on in another room could be overheard. Kate, who slept in an adjoining bedroom, was awakened many a night to hear her parents in the throes of passion. Kit often screamed out her delight when her husband was particularly ardent in his love-making.

Kate's classmate, Alice Palache, recalled visiting Fenwick. Kate took two chairs and placed them in the bathroom where Dr. Hepburn was taking a bath. She then invited Alice to come in and meet her father. "We sat and conversed with Dr. Hepburn as he went through his ablutions," Alice said. "Up to that time, I don't think I'd seen my own father, a college professor, without a jacket, tie, and white shirt."

Having heard too many stories about Kate, many of her hallmates at Pembroke West Dormitory rarely spoke to her. Kate was used to that. Back in Hartford, the Hepburn family often suffered rocks being tossed through their windows because of political opinions espoused.

One day Kate showed up on campus wearing a hand-me-down ensemble inherited from Kit. It included tightly fitting black satin pants with a scarlet red jacket. On it Kate wore a sign, OATS FOR WOMEN, which was meant to suggest that the emerging Women's Liberation movement was also about personal and sexual freedom.

Kate's exhibitionism shocked the campus in January when she pulled off all her clothes and jumped into the icy fountain of the library cloister, rolling around in the snow later to dry off. On a dare, during a blizzard in February, she stripped again and stood on the roof of her dormitory in the snow, sleet, and wind. She tried to get three of her dormitory classmates to take nude pictures of her in her room but each woman refused. One of the classmates thought that Kate was trying to seduce her. The other two didn't seem to know what lesbian overtures were.

Kate had been eating off-campus at the College Inn ever since she'd made her first appearance in the school dining room dressed in a French blue flared skirt buttoned up the front with large ivory buttons as well as an Iceland blue-and-white sweater in vogue at the moment. One of the women had called out, "Oh, my, a self-conscious beauty!" Kate never dined there again but took her meals at the inn nearby when she didn't eat in her room.

At the restaurant, she befriended an older waitress in her early twenties who agreed to take the nude pictures of her. She slipped the waitress into the dormitory after the eleven p.m. curfew. Kate always climbed an ivy-covered trellis outside her second-story dorm window, and had never been caught.

When Kate took the pictures to the local drugstore for development and returned later to pick them up, she was told that the manager had refused to develop them after "being horrified" when he viewed the negatives. "Prudes!" Kate shouted at the beleaguered pharmacist. "Self-righteous prudes! There is nothing wrong with the human body." She stormed out of the drug store.

At the end of her freshman year, Kate had done poorly in school. When she couldn't master chemistry 101, her future as a doctor appeared unobtainable. It didn't help when Dr. Hepburn reminded her that if Tom had lived, "he would have made a finer surgeon than me." Bitterly disappointed in herself for having failed her father, Kate confided to her classmate, Allie, in April of that year that she'd actually contemplated suicide like her brother Tom.

Having barely made it through her freshman year, Kate faced her sophomore term with even more trepidation. Just as the school term began, she suffered an appendix attack. In spite of the hospital rule about doctors not operating on relatives, Dr. Hepburn insisted on performing the appendectomy on Kate himself. "I know how bad the other surgeons in this hospital are," Dr. Hepburn told his colleagues. "I've lost my oldest son. I don't plan to lose my oldest daughter." His operation on her was successful, and she recovered quickly.

Back at Bryn Mawr, Kate's friend and fellow houseburglar, Allie Barbour, dropped out after her freshman year. Kate was lonelier than ever. Dean Helen Taft Manning advised Dr. Hepburn that he should withdraw Kate from college as her grades continued to plummet. He struck back, claiming that in a hospital he didn't release a patient who was sick. Kate offered fierce resistance to the idea of abandoning Bryn Mawr and at long last confided in Dr. Hepburn her secret ambition: "to become an actress—no, a great actress!" He ridiculed her dream.

By her junior year, Kate decided to buckle down and her grades improved. She told friends that "I'm tired of being an embarrassment to my father. He'll be proud of me—just you wait and see." She switched her major from history to English.

Because of the improvement in her academic standing, she was eligible to try out for the Bryn Mawr College Varsity Dramatics group, securing the lead role in A.A. Milne's *The Truth About Blayds.* She played a man named Oliver— and "I was a damned attractive male animal at that." For the role, she had cut and straightened her red hair and parted it on the left, plastering it down with brilliantine.

The role marked a turning point in Kate's life. She decided that "from now on," she was going to wear trousers just like a man, finding them far more natural and comfortable than dresses "where the wind can blow up and chill your bloomers."

After a two-night performance on April 8 and 9, 1927, Kate boarded a train alone for Manhattan where the troupe was to appear at the Colony Club to raise money for the New York Alumnae Regional Scholarship Fund. Slipping off to travel by herself, she dressed as Oliver, a character in the play, masquerading as a man.

On the train to Manhattan, she met an attractive, if slightly vulgar, young woman in her early twenties. Kate later told friends that the "girl not only thought I was a man, perhaps a virgin, but flirted shamelessly with me. At one point she kissed me deeply on the lips." Kate claimed that when they got to Manhattan they went to see a movie together. In the dark theater, the young woman took Kate's hand and put it inside her blouse "so I could fondle her breasts." Kate confided to Allie that she became very excited but afraid when the girl began to fondle her. Kate feared that she'd be discovered to be a female. Kate said that she'd excused herself to go to the men's room but in reality had ducked out of the theater and had raced down the street. Back at her hotel, she changed into women's garb before joining the rest of the troupe that night.

***

In her junior year, Kate became more popular and excelled in sports, winning a trophy as a golfer and joining the 1927 championship swim team. She was still a misfit, however, and found four other young women who were also known as the "campus misanthropes." Kate preferred to call her cabal "The Tenement," a name that contrasted with the rich Main Line women at Bryn Mawr who lived in grand mansions. "I've made a comeback," Kate proudly announced to Dr. Hepburn on her first trip back home for the holidays.

The following summer Dr. Hepburn gave Kate a check for $500—she later claimed "I earned it picking potato buds." With that money, she set off on a tour of England with Alice, staying in cheap pub hotels "and taking whores' baths." At night they propped a chair in front of their bedroom door to keep the drunken Brits from the pub below from coming upstairs and raping these two American girls.

Back for her senior year, Kate continued to appear in college plays, notably in the role of Teresa in *The Cradle Song* by G. Martinez Sierra. Even though the college paper spelled her first name wrong, the reviewer pronounced her "extraordinarily lovely to look at."

***

In late February, attending a prom for Yale men, Kate met her first real beau, as she called men she dated. He was a handsome, "rather dashing" graduate art student, Robert J. McKnight, the son of a prominent family in Springfield, Ohio. A year older than Kate, he was graduating that year from Yale with a degree in economics, after which he planned to study sculpture at the Yale Art School.

When he danced with her and held her tightly in his arms, Kate captivated McKnight. Before the night was over, McKnight confided to her that he was going to become the world's greatest sculptor.

In time, he would become, if not the greatest, certainly one of the world's most distinguished sculptors. When she spoke of him to friends in the coming decades, Kate also claimed that "Bob did other wonderful things as well, like design the very best refrigerators, thermostats, and believe this, forty-two different kinds of riding lawn mowers. He even designed the glasses that were used to view 3-D movies during the Fifties." McKnight had never met any woman like Kate, and he told his friends at Yale, "I've fallen madly for the gal, with that untrained red mop, those freckles, and those dancing eyes."

Kate even invited McKnight home to meet her family, letting him share a room with her brothers, Bob and Dick. McKnight later recalled Kate slipping into the bedroom, as Bob and Dick slept, and giving him "deep, passionate kisses and leaving him a state of great arousal."

As the months went by, McKnight became so enamored of her that he planned to ask her to marry him. Eager to consummate their relationship, he asked her to pose nude for him and she readily agreed, since nudity was hardly a problem for her.

When he interrupted his sculpture and tried to seduce her, she refused his request for intimacy. "I understand that men have needs, however," she told McKnight. She agreed that he could masturbate himself while admiring her nude figure, and she also granted him permission to feel her breasts. "I have felt the breast of another woman," she confided in him," but no man has ever played with my breasts. I don't know if I'll like it or not."

The nude Hepburn breasts, revealed to the public for the first time, were on display when McKnight exhibited a selection of his works at the Carnegie Institute in Pittsburgh.

***

On October 20, 1927, Kate was caught smoking a perfumed cigarette in her room and was suspended for five days from Bryn Mawr. She'd been nabbed in her new tower room in the dormitory, Pembroke East, where she'd been relocated. President Marion Edwards Park had virtually created a revolution among women college presidents by permitting classmates to smoke in restricted areas that did not include their dorm rooms. The smokers seemed greatly relieved at such a compromise, and many of Kate's Bryn Mawr classmates were furious at her for violating the rules, lest their sacred privilege be revoked.

While on suspension, Kate decided to go to the King of Prussia Inn on her own, even though it was off-limits to Bryn Mawr girls. Since Kate reasoned that she wasn't technically a student during her suspension, she wouldn't have to obey school rules at that time.

While enjoying a hamburger and a cup of tea in the restaurant section, Kate became aware of a tall, lanky, blond-haired man staring and smiling at her whenever he caught her eye. At first she felt that she must have met him somewhere, perhaps at a Yale party. On closer examination, he looked too old to be a Yale undergraduate. Perhaps he was a graduate student, or even a young professor in his late twenties.

When Kate got up to pay the bill and leave the inn, the young stranger did too. As she'd later tell her cabal, "I found him a bit brash—but oh, so good looking—and there's nothing wrong with brash young men, now is there?"

At the door, he introduced himself as John G. Clark, but he told her she could call him Jack. "You can call me Kate," she said. "That's short for

Katharine. Oh, that's Katharine with an a in the middle."

He offered to drive her back to the Bryn Mawr campus, saying he lived right near by. Having decided to toss McKnight aside, she was eager to meet a new beau, in spite of her own mixed feelings about her sexuality, as she didn't know if she liked men or women better.

The thought occurred to her that she liked both sexes in equal measure. Dr. Hepburn told her that was entirely possible. He'd even had a label for it: bisexuality, which he claimed "was perfectly normal, existing in all men and women in one measure or another."

In his car, Kate was astounded that Jack so quickly invited her for dinner at his family home on Saturday night. She later told members of her trusted cabal that she fully expected to be asked to spend an evening with Jack in one of the "hot bedrooms" above the King of Prussia Inn.

To return his hospitality, she invited him to a school dance in three weeks. He told her he'd love to take her. "Mind if I bring Luddy? He's my best friend."

"Of course not," she said. "I'll get a ticket for him as well." She eyed Jack skeptically. "Is this Luddy coming along on our date next Saturday night?"

"No, but I'd invite him if he were in town," Jack said. "He won't be back until Sunday morning. Say, I have a swell idea. Why don't you, me, and Luddy go for a drive in the country Sunday afternoon and perhaps have a picnic lunch somewhere even though it's cold. We could bundle up."

"Fine with me," she said. "In Connecticut, I sometimes go swimming in January, so I'm not afraid of the cold."

"My kind of gal," Jack said. "Luddy will be impressed when I tell him that. He takes baths only in very hot water."

"This Luddy sounds like a real special person," she said. "When I tell my friends about bringing both of you to the dance, I'll be the envy of every girl on campus."

"How so?" Jack asked, looking puzzled.

"While many of them are sitting around the dorm wondering how they will get some young man to ask them out, I'll have a date with not one, but two young men." A doubt seemed to cross her face. "Luddy is handsome, isn't he? I mean he's not fat or deformed?"

"He's very handsome and very charming," Jack claimed, "and I'm sure you'll like him a lot. I sure do."

"You're not so bad yourself," Kate said, getting out of the car by herself, as she didn't like men to open doors for her. "What time Saturday night?" she asked.

"I'll meet you here at the gate at six-thirty," Jack promised. "That way, we'll have plenty of time. I'm going to call Luddy tonight and tell him the big news."

"What big news?" Kate asked.

"That he and I have a date Sunday afternoon with the most beautiful girl in the world."

CHAPTER TWO

Exactly on time, Jack Clark was waiting for Kate as she came through the gates of Bryn Mawr. Before visiting his home for dinner, he invited her for a drive in the country, and Kate gladly accepted.

On the drive, Kate was completely relaxed and comfortable with this handsome young war veteran, and felt that before the weekend was over, he would become her next beau. All he had to do was ask.

Four miles from the campus of Bryn Mawr, Jack came to a stop near a country meadow and invited Kate for a long walk before dinner—"good for the appetite." Following an old path carved out by cows, he showed her a spot in the meadow which sloped toward a fast-running mountain stream. "Luddy and I bought this little plot of land," he said, "and come spring we plan to build a hut here for escapes on the weekend. It'll be just our private place, although I'm sure Luddy will ask you to come and visit."

"It's a beautiful place," Kate said, surveying the bucolic setting. "Hell, I'll even help you guys build it." She looked at him with a quizzical expression on her face. "This Luddy must mean a lot to you."

Without hesitation, he turned to face her. "He's my life! I thought after Phil died, there would never be anyone else for me. When Luddy came along, he changed all that."

"Who was this Phil?" she asked.

Jack told her the story of having served on the battlefields of Europe in trench warfare during the closing months of World War I. Phil was born Phil Berry on the "wrong side of the tracks" in Philadelphia. Jack had met him in the army. "We were as close as two men could ever get. From the first day we met, we started talking to each other, and we never stopped sharing life together until the day a sniper's bullet did him in. As he lay dying in my arms, I kissed him and told him I loved him, and I didn't give a God damn who was looking or what in hell they might be thinking."

"Good for you," Kate said. "That's the way love should be."

"Then you're not shocked?" he asked.

"Not at all!" she said. "I understand such love. What I don't understand is how I fit into this picture. It seems like three might be a crowd."

"Luddy and I adore women," he said. "As dear, dear friends. We just don't like to sleep with them."

"Sex is vastly overrated," she said.

He took her hand and walked her back through the meadow. "It's getting late. We don't want to miss dinner."

To Kate's surprise, Jack lived with his father and two sisters right next door to the Bryn Mawr campus. Their three-story Victorian house, called Robindale and built in 1896, looked haunted in the cold gray twilight but it was warm inside, with brightly burning fireplaces.

Jack's father was distant and reserved, and Kate kept looking around for the mother to appear but she never did. A formally dressed maid came and offered her a sherry before dinner. Jack's sisters, Louise and Agnes, were a delight— outgoing, friendly, welcoming, and quick to take Kate into their confidence.

"You're not like the usual girls Jack and Luddy bring home from the campus to the tool shed," Agnes said. She showed Kate into the parlor where she pulled back heavy draperies to reveal a large shed, almost as big as a garage, set about two hundred yards from the main building. "It's heated inside. A lot of the gals from Bryn Mawr come here with their beaux. They smoke cigarettes, drink hooch, and go all the way. But Jack and Luddy sometimes come inside the house and go to Jack's bedroom before the fun and games begin. They like the smoking and drinking, though. Sometimes they stick around because Luddy is a crazed nut when it comes to photography. He likes to take pictures of some of the young men and women in the nude. He might even ask you to pose nude for him."

"Nothing I haven't done before," Kate said. The Clark family mystified her.

Over a big roast beef dinner with Yorkshire pudding and all the trimmings, Jack Clark, Sr. had little to say and looked rather foreboding. Finally, in exasperation, Kate asked, "Will Mrs. Clark be joining us for dinner or is she indisposed?"

"My mother's been committed to an insane asylum," Louise piped in. Her indiscreet remark was met with such an icy stare from Jack Sr. that she immediately shut up.

"Both my sisters and I have agreed never to marry and have children," Jack Jr. said. "We fear it's too dangerous. Our kids might grow up to become insane too."

"Insanity in a family is better than suicide," Kate said, asking for another hefty slice of blood-rare roast beef.

***

Ludlow Ogden Smith—nicknamed "Luddy"—lived up to Jack's advance billing. Aged twenty-nine when Kate first met him, Luddy struck her as suave and sophisticated, a "true man of the world," as she would write back to Dr. Hepburn and Kit. "He stands tall like a man should," wrote Kate, and "he always misses one main meal a day so that he is lean and mean like me. His profile is so fascinating that he could easily become a budding John Barrymore—no, no, there is no cause for alarm—he doesn't want to be an actor himself." Pictures of Luddy taken at the time suggest that even though good looking when judged by the standards of his day, he was no matinee idol. Actually, most people found Jack "the pretty one."

Like Jack, Luddy was a veteran of World War I. After the war, he'd stayed in France where he'd studied at the University of Grenoble, learning French and other romance languages and pursuing his love of classical music and art. His main pursuit was photography. Jack claimed Luddy took pictures all the time.

"I'd like to photograph you too," Luddy told Kate.

Remembering what Jack's sister had told her, Kate replied, "In the nude, of course."

"Of course," Luddy said matter-of-factly.

His pose of sophistication was a bit shaken when he showed her a trick he'd perfected. "I can touch the tip of my nose with my tongue." Instead of being thrilled at witnessing that trick, Kate was rather taken back by it and asked him not to do it anymore.

She was more impressed with his broad shoulders—"like a swimmer's build"— and hair "as black as Edgar Allan Poe's Raven." "To keep your shape, you must swim a lot," she told him. "I do," he said, "and I'm also a bit of a boatman." "And a great skier," Jack chimed in.

In the excitement of meeting Luddy, she had almost forgotten Jack existed. She couldn't help but notice that Jack's star shone only when Luddy wasn't around. When Luddy appeared in the sky, Jack's star dimmed. Jack struck her as strangely submissive to Luddy—or, as she put it to her cabal, "Jack acts more like Luddy's wife than his friend."

When Luddy asked Kate what she planned to do after Bryn Mawr, she told him she wanted to become an actress. Instead of reacting in horror as her father had, he seemed delighted with the choice. He told her that he and Jack knew many people in the world of the theater and, if she were really serious about becoming an actress, they might arrange an introduction for her. Delighted at Luddy's response, she reached over and kissed him affectionately on the tip of his nose now that he'd stopped licking it.

***

In the days to come, it was a rare afternoon that Kate didn't spend some time with Jack and Luddy who lived right off the campus in a rustically decorated but somewhat ramshackle house. They affectionately called it "The Grange." On her first visit, she was mildly surprised to see their living room walls covered with nude pictures.

21

She recognized many of her classmates and were amazed that they'd disrobed for Luddy's cameras. When Luddy and Jack showed her their bedroom, she arched an eyebrow when she studied two large blow-ups of each of the men, completely nude, over the double bed.

Luddy had brought some wine "from God knows where," and the trio sat around in front of their fireplace, laughing and drinking the wine. Luddy was fond of inserting French phrases into his conversation, and was a bit of a namedropper, relating anecdotes about famous people he'd met in the theater world. He also knew painters, singers, sculptors, and even a novelist or two, including F. Scott Fitzgerald.

His favorite poet was H. Phelps Putnam, and his favorite lines from Putnam had a crude Restoration-era wit. Phelps had written an ode to the male sex organ, ending it with this couplet: "You lead us, master, sniffing to the hunt/In quest forever of the perfect cunt."

All the rage among collegiates of his day, Putnam was a friend of Luddy's parents. Jack said he was staying off campus as the guest of Fred and Helen Manning in their home. As dean of Bryn Mawr, Helen Manning had suspended Kate from classes for five days when caught smoking in her room.

Luddy had a grand idea. His parents were entertaining Putnam Saturday night at their home, and Luddy included Kate in the invitation. She looked over at Jack. "Will Jack be invited too?" she asked. "Without Jack, I wouldn't be there," Luddy said.

That Saturday night, Jack drove Kate to the home of Luddy's parents, since he was already there helping his parents get ready for the evening. Jack made no comment on Kate's mannish dress or her wearing of trousers. When Kate was introduced to Luddy's father, Lewis I. Smith, and his wife, Gertrude Clemson Smith, they were formally dressed. Since Gertrude was known for manners called "enchanting," she had far too much Main Line breeding to make Kate feel uncomfortable in any way. She graciously showed Kate around Sherraden, their art-filled family mansion on Deepdale Road, the setting for many a lavish party for *le tout* Philadelphia.

Before coming face to face with the great man himself, Kate had read all of the published poems of Putnam, and, like Luddy, she too had fallen under his faddish spell. A graduate of Exeter and Yale, and eleven years older than Kate, Putnam had been hailed as one of the country's leading young poets by Edmund Wilson, the leading critic of his day. Wilson had said more, claiming that like e.e. cummings, Putnam was "fatally irresistible to women: the women's ideal poet, attractive and unreliable."

Even though Putnam arrived late and drunk at the Smith *soirée*, Kate, as she was to tell her friends later, found the poet "positively Byronic, dark and exceedingly handsome." She quickly came under his spell, ignoring Luddy and Jack for the rest of the evening. She told the poet how much she'd enjoyed his first volume of poetry, *Trinc*, published in 1927.

Like a creature from Montmartre in the Paris of the *belle époque*, Putnam wore a large Dracula-like black cape and a broad-brimmed charcoal hat which he did not remove all evening. When he learned that the Smiths did not serve hard liquor, he removed a large silver flask from his pocket, inviting the entire family to join him in this "bottled firewater which tastes better than the dew-covered breast of a virgin on a field of spring green against the same morning light that da Vinci used to paint the *Mona Lisa*." Somehow during the course of the evening, Kate learned that a wife, Ruth, waited for Putnam in some dreary Boston suburb. But that did not diminish Kate's enchantment for him. "Marriage is like sending ourselves to prison with no passport out," he told Kate.

Later in the evening, Kate's ardor dimmed when Putnam began sharing some of his poetic Gothic nightmares with her. He had a particular fear of nooses and hanging and told her that death by strangulation was the worst possible way to die. Putnam was horrified to see that he'd reduced Kate to tears, not knowing of the death by strangulation of her brother Tom.

Embarrassed by her breakdown, Kate retreated with Mrs. Smith to the bathroom but returned with a stiff back and a brave face about fifteen minutes later. With typical Hepburn pride, she seemed determined not to let Putnam reduce her to tears again. In fact, she stood in the room and recited the final lines of *Trinc*. In the poem an emotionally troubled young girl stands beneath a noose and cries out for the world to help her. "Come, lift me up, I too will hang, I shall be sisterly." After reciting that, she asked for a hefty swig from Putnam's silver flask.

At the end of the evening, Kate, still embarrassed to have shown such strong emotion in front of Putnam and Luddy's parents, triumphantly invited the poet, Mr. and Mrs. Smith, Luddy, and Jack to see her perform at the May Day revels at Bryn Mawr. All of them gladly accepted her invitation. Before departing that night, Kate stood in the foyer and said, "I'm going to be a star!"

***

In her unreliable memoirs, *Me*, Kate erroneously remembers meeting Putnam at a luncheon in the house of the Mannings, forgetting that Helen Taft Manning, the dean, heartily disapproved of her and didn't even want her at Bryn Mawr—much less as a luncheon guest. Helen was also on a mission to keep Fred's houseguest, the hard-drinking, hard-living, and totally womanizing Putnam away from her virgins—at least those remaining virgins—completing their senior year at Bryn Mawr.

What Kate did remember accurately, at least according to her friends at the time, was that meeting Putnam caused her to fly "up onto a pink cloud and I was literally sailing through those last weeks at college."

Although not completely forgotten, Jack and Luddy no longer occupied her free time. Luddy was to get used to his coming in and out of favor with Kate. He often told Jack, "Kate is our friend between engagements."

Midnight found Kate climbing down the vines from her second-floor tower to go on long midnight walks with the poet. He would cite his latest "verses from the workshop" to her, and she often gave him strong, candid opinions about his poetry. Once her negative reaction so infuriated Putnam that he refused to speak to her for five days.

When they got back together again, he'd written a poem for her called "The Daughters of the Sun." In the poem, he claimed that Kate was "my nourishment, my sister, and my child, My lust, my liberty, my discipline."

She might have been all those things except lust. Although, as she related to Jack and Luddy, Putnam would take her in his arms and feel all parts of her body, "including some plumbing handled before only by me in the shower," he had not made love to her.

She expressed a fear that Putnam might be impotent and felt that the following summer she should set up a meeting with her father for a physical examination. Luddy doubted Putnam's impotence, claiming his conquests of young women were legend. Although she pressed Putnam "to take my virgin blood" (she had begun speaking like Putnam herself), he adamantly refused to "deflower" her, as he called it.

***

For the May Day festivities at Bryn Mawr, Kate, with her firecracker-red mane, was selected to star in the Elizabethan pastoral, *The Woman in the Moone,* by John Lyllie, the 16th-century playwright, who described her character as "sometimes sullen, sometimes vain, and sometimes martial." She appeared barefoot and bare-armed in spite of her somewhat fleshy limbs. The play had not been presented since its *première* in front of Elizabeth I in 1597.

Putnam found her high-pitched, scratchy voice "evocative of a sandstorm," and Dr. Hepburn was horrified every time his daughter sat down and bared her dirty feet to the audience. Luddy and Jack told Kate later that she came out "looking like a goddess."

That weekend Putnam had a speaking engagement in Philadelphia, leaving Kate alone with Luddy and Jack Clark. It was one of the hottest days that May when Kate visited the young men at "The Grange." When Luddy suggested that both she and Jack strip for nude poses, Luddy encountered no objection from her at all. There was already a trunk filled with nude studies of Jack, so he was long used to disrobing before the probing eyes of Luddy's camera.

Luddy posed Kate on his living room sofa. Having posed before with McKnight, Kate felt she was a veteran nude model at this point. As Jack later recalled, we learned that Kate "was a natural redhead." Kate might have been a little awkward in the posed nudes with Jack, but she put up a brave front.

Two weeks later when Luddy gave her eight-by-ten glossies of the nudes, Kate shocked friends at Bryn Mawr by showing the photographs and even asking for their candid appraisals of herself blithely posing "jaybird nekked."

"It was no big deal," Kate told some of her classmates who expressed great shock at her daring. "Much worse," she claimed, "was going and getting yourself pregnant," as some of the young women had done on campus that lusty spring.

***

So impressed was Jack with Kate's performance as Pandora that he wrote her a letter of introduction to Edwin Knopf, the manager of a theater company in Baltimore. She was hoping to be cast in some roles for his season of summer stock productions. Knopf's brother, Alfred Knopf was already a big name in New York publishing circles.

As soon as Kate received her diploma at Bryn Mawr on the morning of June 7, 1928, she set out for Baltimore.

With a school friend, Elizabeth Rhett, Kate drove to Maryland in her car and stayed at the home of Edith Houghton, Kate's aunt.

Kate showed up to meet Knopf in dirty tennis shoes, a faded forest-green sweater borrowed from Luddy, baggy men's tweed trousers, and with uncontrollable reddish hair sticking out from under a battered russet-red felt hat used for deer hunting in the wilds of Pennsylvania. Knopf found her "awkward, green and freakish."

Nevertheless, maybe because of Jack's letter, he hired her to be one of six ladies-in-waiting in the comedy, *The Czarina,* based on the life of the empress, Catherine the Great. "No lines—plenty of curtsies," Knopf told Kate. "Maybe it will teach you some humility to be an attendant. You're far too arrogant for your own good."

The star of the play was the beautiful and popular Mary Boland, a leading Broadway actress. One of her most recent hits on Broadway had been *Cradle Snatchers*, in which she'd appeared with a young actor, Humphrey Bogart, whose career she had threatened to destroy because he was constantly forgetting his lines.

At first Boland befriended young Kate, even showing her how to make up her face to conceal "all those horrible freckles." "When you walk on stage," Boland instructed her, "you need not approach it like some enraged elephant in

Africa attacking helpless villagers." Boland showed her how to glide across the stage "in ladylike strides."

After only three days, Boland turned on Hepburn the way she had on young Bogart. She complained to Knopf, "when I'm on stage, she's standing there in the wings, her eyes boring in on me, watching my every move, my every speech inflection, the way I move my hands. I have this spooky feeling she's waiting for me to break a leg so she can step in and be me."

***

Gone were thoughts of Putnam the day she met the stage manager for Knopf. To her, Kenneth MacKenna was dashing and handsome with a *savoir-faire* that far surpassed that of Luddy. Kenneth, she knew, had appeared in silent films, including the 1926 *The American Venus* which had starred Louise Brooks and Douglas Fairbanks, Jr.

A fellow New Englander like herself, Kenneth offered her every encouragement with her stage career. When Kate was overcome with fright, she tended to speed up her speech, her voice cracking, jumping from contralto to castrato in a moment's notice. He taught her to speak slower and to breathe deeply for more presence. "Don't be frightened," he told her, offering the kind of help a director might. Boland had stopped speaking to Kate within the first week.

Kenneth represented the bohemia of New York, a society Kate so desperately wanted to belong to. He was also the first openly bisexual she'd ever known, freely admitting to her that he was sleeping with one of the "ladies-in-waiting" in the court of Catherine the Great in the play, *The Czarina*, as well as a handsome stagehand, Joe Quinn, from Chester, Pennsylvania.

One night over drinks back in his hotel room, she asked him pointedly, "Don't you have a preference—I mean, men over women or vice versa?"

"Not that I can discern," he said. "The experience is different. I can enjoy the soft contours of a woman's breasts but can also enjoy the hard-rock muscles of a manly chest."

"I see what you mean," she said. "I'm sorry to ask such questions, but, you see…"

"Don't tell me that any woman who knows H. Phelps Putnam is still a virgin?" he asked.

"I've had plenty of experiences with men," she said defensively. "I've posed nude for Robert McKnight and also for two beaux I have, Luddy Smith and Jack Clark. I'm far from innocent."

"You're a virgin!" he said, getting up and walking toward her. "No wonder you can't get the acting thing right. No virgin should be allowed on the stage."

"I don't see what virginity and acting have in common," she said.

26

"An actress must draw on her experiences," he said. "You're playing a lady-in-waiting to Catherine the Great. Do you know what ladies-in-waiting had to do for the empress?"

"Curtsy, I suppose," she said, "since that's all I seem to do around Boland."

"Catherine the Great used her ladies-in-waiting to audition prospective beaux," he said. "First, the stallion in her court slept with one of the ladies-in-waiting. Only when he got a favorable report did he get to sleep with the empress herself. With so many men in her kingdom, and so little time, Catherine didn't want to waste her time with men who were unsatisfactory lovers."

"They didn't teach that bit of history at Bryn Mawr," she said.

"At least you've kissed a man," he said, moving toward her and taking her in his arms.

"Of course, I have—many times and very deeply," she said.

He kissed her passionately and fondled her.

"Oh, what the hell!" she said, getting up and starting to pull off her clothes in front of him. "I thought it was going to be Putnam, maybe Luddy, but some man has to be first. Might as well be you."

He looked up at her in astonishment.

"What are you waiting for?" she asked. "Get on with the bloody deed."

***

In the glorious summer after graduation, Kate's newly acquired "gang" assembled in New York. Jack and Luddy transferred their business interests to the city and rented an apartment. Kenneth MacKenna decided to seek work on Broadway after the Baltimore summer stock season ended, and H. Putnam Phelps showed up looking for a good time but with no money.

Kate went to live with Putnam on Fifty-Fourth Street East on the river in a railroad flat, the tenement owned by Russell Davenport of *Time.* He was out of town. Although Putnam still hadn't made love to her, Kate remembered romantic evenings sitting out on the fire escape watching the river traffic.

In her attempt to seduce him, she even walked around the tenement in the nude after she emerged from one of her innumerable showers. Just as she was beginning to believe that Putnam was a homosexual, in spite of his reputation as a womanizer, he told her the truth. At the graduation ceremonies, Dr. Hepburn had approached him and warned him that his daughter would make "every effort to seduce you, as I can only compare her to a young bull about to charge." As a final warning, her father had told Putnam, "If you lay your hands on her, I shall shoot you!" Putnam was absolutely convinced that Dr. Hepburn was a man of his word.

Putnam must have had the power of steel in his reserve not to seduce Kate. To his friend, Robert Benchley, at Tony Soma's smoke-filled speakeasy on West

49th Street, he spoke glowingly of her "porcelain white and Venus-like nude body." Although a poet and totally aware of his symbolism, he surprisingly used a phallic image to Benchley, comparing Kate to "a dagger from the tales of Arabia, unsheathed and glimmering in my trembling hands."

He even told his friend, the very witty and sophisticated Dorothy Parker, that although he'd kissed every inch of Kate's body, he had never actually penetrated her. Apparently one night he had "driven her crazy." She'd made deep flesh wounds in his back by the digging in of her fingernails. "She could no longer contain her sexual frustration," Putnam claimed.

Benchley, Robert and Dorothy Parker were anxious to meet this "young sprig of an actress." On Putnam's arm, Kate paraded into Tony's speakeasy, wearing no makeup, her freckle-spotted face brightly gleaming after an alcohol rub.

She waved at Kenneth who was sitting with a group known as the "pussy posse," but didn't go over to the table to meet his friends. Posse members included the young actor, Humphrey Bogart, Bill Brady Jr. (son of the famous Broadway producer, William Brady Sr.), and Stuart Rose, Bogart's brother-in-law.

Parker took an instant dislike to Hepburn, and finally asked why she kept jumping up all night to go to the bathroom. "My father is a urologist," Kate said. "He insists that I drink massive quantities of water every day." Benchley, Parker, and Putnam regarded fresh water with great distaste, preferring Tony's bootleg booze.

Kate was a bit shocked when Benchley suggested that they end the evening with a nightcap at Polly Adler's bordello, the most famous in America. Although Kate had heard of this place, she was afraid to go there, but didn't want to appear the country bumpkin, especially in the presence of Parker, whom she regarded as far more sophisticated than herself. Trying to appear more worldly that she was, Kate asked Dorothy Parker, "Do they rent out male prostitutes at Polly's place, or only women for the men?"

Parker looked astonished at the question but chose not to answer it.

At the house run by the notorious Polly Adler on West Fifty-Fourth Street, America's most famous madam held forth nightly. She entertained in her downstairs parlor, the sex between her customers and her carefully selected "gals" going on in the neatly kept and comfortably furnished upstairs bedrooms.

Polly's downstairs parlor had become such a "literary salon" that men often brought their dates here to be entertained by the conversation. Everybody showed up from mobsters like Al Capone in days gone by—Polly had found him "very pleasant." Boxer Jack Dempsey was a frequent guest, as was bad guy Dutch Schultz. Big-shot politicians like Jimmy Walker had a charge account, as did Robert Benchley himself.

When Kate found that sex was not to be part of the evening, she relaxed and even switched from water to some of Polly's illegal hooch, enjoying her first-ever orange blossom. She was astonished to learn that Benchley often lived at the bordello, and Polly kept a neatly pressed black Japanese kimono waiting for him at all times.

Later, Kate drank Staten Island champagne at twenty dollars a bottle with the best of them. Putnam joined in a game of backgammon with Polly. Since he didn't have the twenty dollars to pay for one of the women, he gambled with Polly for the services of one of her gals—and, amazingly, he won. He excused himself in front of a heartbroken Kate and disappeared upstairs with a prostitute who looked amazingly like Mae West but wasn't.

Kate tried to conceal her rejection by Putnam but was on the verge of tears. A drunken Parker told Polly that she didn't like the "vulgar" choice of reading material in her sitting room and that she would send over a more classical list of books so that her customers would have more uplifting material to read while waiting for one of the whores to become available. Kate found that very amusing and was prepared to like Parker who did not return her affection.

Benchley told Kate that he was going to spend the night, claiming that Polly's personal maid, a woman incongruously called "Lion," even pressed his clothing and washed out his underwear—"skid marks and all. I get breakfast in bed and all the loving I want."

When Benchley disappeared, Parker excused herself, having been summoned to one of the upper rooms to watch "an exhibition." For some reason, Kate was not invited.

Sitting alone in Polly's parlor, the madam confided that "Benchley lights up my life just like the sun in the morning." When no one was in the room, Polly took Kate's hand and held it affectionately. "Dorothy tells me you want to be an actress. That's fine but it's a hard life. There will be many times when you are hungry and broke and walking the streets wondering where your next meal is coming from. Don't worry. Just come to Polly's. I can always use a gal like you although you're a special type. Would you consider wearing a nurse's uniform?"

***

In tears because of the way Putnam had treated her at Polly Adler's bordello, Kate fled to the apartment shared by Jack and Luddy even though it was early in the morning. In his pajamas, Luddy answered the door, telling her that Jack had gone to Philadelphia with his two sisters.

She threw herself into Luddy's arms and begged him to make love to her. Claiming she was a virgin, she asked him to "deflower me." At first reluctant to accommodate her, he finally did his duty, "'cause you know I love you so—and so does Jack."

Perhaps Kate would always suspect that Luddy found inspiration for his love-making by looking at the frontal nude of Jack over the bed they shared together.

The next morning when Kate woke up first and prepared breakfast for Luddy, she told him that she wouldn't require him "to perform like a stallion with me again." She shook hands and even decided to kiss him on the cheek. "Let's be friends—forever and always, and friends can ruin relationships by going to bed together."

Fresh from the bed Luddy shared with his lover, Jack, Kate retreated back to the tenement she occupied with Putnam. She found him fully packed and leaving. "I was just going to write you a note," he claimed. "I'm off to visit a Supreme Court justice friend who's vacationing in Nova Scotia." He gave her a good-bye kiss and a promise to write. At the door, he told her she'd have to move, since the owner of the apartment was returning that afternoon.

After frantic calls to friends, she found herself installed later that day in a large apartment at 925 Park Avenue. It belonged to the family of a Bryn Mawr friend, "Megs" Merrill. Since the Merrills were away for the summer, she was allowed to use the apartment until they returned home on Labor Day.

She called Kenneth, who was going out that night with Humphrey Bogart and his new bride, Mary Philips, the Broadway actress. Kenneth was very open in revealing that he too was bedding Bogart's new wife—"and should have married her myself"—but claimed that he could always make time for Kate.

He came over that night to "deflower" her again and to give her a letter of introduction to Frances Robinson-Duff, one of the grand old ladies of the theater. Kenneth felt that this matronly woman was just the right teacher to help Kate with any voice problems she'd experience on the stage.

***

It rained the day that Kate made her way across town to call on Frances Robinson-Duff's studio on the fourth floor of a walk-up building at 235 East Sixty-Second Street between the Second and Third Avenue Els. The apartment was decorated in the style of Louis XVI. In her late fifties, this gray-haired dowager of intimidating hauteur and ample girth was hailed as "the greatest acting teacher in America" by David Belasco, the theatrical impresario.

Running an advertisement in the newspapers, she claimed to have taught diction to the likes of Clark Gable, Miriam Hopkins, Osgood Perkins (later father of the actor, Tony Perkins), Cornelia Otis Skinner, Ina Claire, Ruth Chatterton, and Helen Hayes.

Arriving dripping wet on Miss Robinson-Duff's oriental carpeting, and earning a sneer from her snooty French butler, the bedraggled Kate sat down in front of the rather startled voice coach. "I hear you were friends with Sarah

Bernhardt," Kate gushed. "I want to be the American Sarah Bernhardt."

"What has Kenneth MacKenna sent to me?" the portly woman asked, sitting ramrod stiff like the Queen Mum on a gilt-painted "throne" upholstered in red velvet. "My darling, you don't evoke Bernhardt, but you might be the American equivalent of Eleanora Duse, who was, perhaps, an even better actress."

Thus, began one of the great student-teacher relationships in the American theater.

The afternoon ended not with a voice lesson but with an introduction. Kate had overstayed her time, listening to the great teacher tell fascinating stories of her involvements with Libby Holman, Dorothy Gish, and Mary Pickford.

The French butler ushered the next student into the salon, where Robinson-Duff made the introductions. "Miss Katharine Hepburn, meet Laura Harding!"

Standing before a rather bedraggled Kate was one of the most elegantly dressed young women she'd ever seen, a pert brunette with bright hazel eyes. Laura was attired in the latest Paris *haute couture*, a stunningly tailored violet-colored suit with a mauve lace blouse, purple shoes, and accessories that included gloves and purse in a subtle heather. Kate remembered Laura looking "like a spring meadow I'd discovered on my trip to Scotland."

Laura was rather disdainful of Kate, later confiding to Robinson-Duff that "the Hepburn girl isn't my type at all." She heartily disapproved of Kate's dress of a brownish tweed skirt and a man's ratty sweater pinned at the back with a giant safety pin. Laura felt that Kate's hair style was more suitable for a shaggy horse. "If I recall," she said some years later, "Kate wore her red hair long and it was unappetizingly pulled back in a ghastly knot."

As Kate took in the sight of the suntanned, athletic, and broad-shouldered Laura, her hair cut short in a bob, it was love at first sight.

***

To Laura's astonishment, she found Kate waiting downstairs in the rain for her when Laura had finished her voice lessons with Robinson-Duff. The ever-cool Laura asked, "Can I drop you off somewhere?"

"I'd like to take you to dinner but I don't have much money," Kate said. "It's going to take all my money to pay the ten dollars per lesson to Miss Robinson-Duff."

Laura was to remember taking a close second look at Kate. "Beneath that ugly duckling façade, I suddenly saw a beautiful white swan with a long neck. A young woman of great beauty and sexual vitality who had successfully concealed it from the world in her Apple Annie drag." Impulsively, Laura invited Kate to dinner that night with her family. But first, she extended an invitation for Kate to accompany her to Bergdorf Goodman's elegant department store.

Kate was astonished when Laura ushered her into the back seat of a large, black, chauffeur-driven limousine. In spite of Laura's fine clothes, Kate at first had assumed that she was a struggling actress like herself. Before that rainy afternoon ended, Kate was to learn that the beautiful, elegant, and oh, so cultured Laura Harding was one of the richest heiresses in America.

***

A former East Coast debutante, Laura was the daughter of brokerage heiress Dorothy Barney and her husband, J. Barclay Harding, a multi-millionaire New York banker and art collector who was both the founder and chairman of the board of American Express.

When Kate arrived at eight o'clock that night at the Fifth Avenue stone-built mansion of Laura Harding, her hair had been styled and her wardrobe drastically changed. She wore a stylish pink suit from Paris with a ruffled, ivory-colored lace blouse and high heels in a subtle beige with silk stockings that accentuated her shapely legs.

"I don't think I ever saw Kate look more beautiful than she did on that night," Laura later recalled. "The transformation, in spite of Kate's protests, had been remarkable. Later as we got to know each other, Kate reverted back to her sloppy dressing. But on the night of our first dinner, there was no more beautiful woman in all of New York than Miss Katharine Hepburn of Hartford, Connecticut. My parents were impressed with what I had dragged home for dinner, and they were not easy to impress. Only that afternoon, the new president of the United States, Herbert Hoover, had called my father for advice about the U.S. economy."

In fact, the tycoon had been a delegate-at-large to the 1928 Republican national convention that had nominated Herbert Hoover.

Not knowing the left-wing politics of the Hepburn family, Mr. Harding was misled by Kate's newly acquired wardrobe. As Kate later told Jack and Luddy, "He thought I was a Republican."

He dazzled Kate, however, by sharing his art collection with her that included paintings—most of them acquired in Spain—by El Greco and Goya.

As Kate was to remember, Mr. Harding was more impressed with what the paintings cost than what the paintings were. He advised her to invest her money in art by the Old Masters. "Since you're young, a painting that now sells for $50,000 will sell for five, maybe seven, million by the time you are sixty years old." Although Mr. Harding would not live to see that, his financial forecast was right on target.

Throughout the dinner, Kate restrained herself and held her political views in check. Both of Laura's parents liked Kate and even invited her to spend the night, as the rains had turned into a violent storm with gale-like winds. Laura virtually demanded that Kate stay over. Mrs. Harding offered Kate one of the guest rooms, but Laura invited her to share her own bedroom. "That way," Laura told her father, "Kate and I can have pillow fights and talk about girl things."

"I don't know if I know much girl talk," Kate said, "but I'm sure we'll find something to do."

After Kate and Laura had gone upstairs, Mr. Harding invited his wife into his study for a brandy and a cigar, neither of which she enjoyed. She indulged him in his bad habits, even though drinking and smoking had been forbidden by his doctors.

Apparently, Mr. Harding that night sensed something "strange and different" about Kate, but "I can't put my finger on it." Throughout the few remaining months of his life, he expressed that opinion to several friends and colleagues and even to Laura herself. "I don't know what it is, but I think that Kate Hepburn is a queer fish," he said, using the jargon of his day.

Before morning came to the Harding household, Katharine Hepburn, aspirant actress, had embarked on the most important and longest running relationship of her life. Her affair with Laura Harding would span the decades, even dwarfing her troubled relationship with Spencer Tracy.

***

After Kate's second class with Robinson-Duff, the matron concluded, "I note that as an actress you only have two gestures—arms held stiffly at attention like a soldier in the army, or bent at waist level with fists clenched. In addition to my voice lessons, I'm signing you up to work on stage movement and dance with Michael Mordkin."

When not studying with Robinson-Duff or Mordkin, Kate was actually working in the theater, where her career would take one giant leap forward, only to fall back fifty paces.

Once again, Kenneth MacKenna came through for her when the Edwin Knopf company mounted a production of *The Big Pond,* co-authored by George Middleton and A. E. Thomas. Kenneth was cast in the lead, playing a Frenchman, Pierre de Mirande. Knopf hired Kate as an understudy for the actress, Lucile Nikolas. But when the leading lady quit after "an artistic dispute" with Knopf, Kate was hired to go on in her place. As Kenneth later said, "Knopf needed a lot of convincing before he agreed to that, as he still had grave doubts about Kate as an actress."

Knopf's concerns proved well grounded. On a late summer evening at a playhouse, The Great Neck Theatre, Kate was to appear in her first professional starring role in a legitimate theater production, playing "an innocent American abroad," a character called Barbara, who falls for a dashing Frenchman as portrayed by Kenneth in white pants and navy blue blazer. After the preview of *The Big Pond* on Long Island, it was slated to open in September at Broadway's Bijou Theater.

On opening night, Kate delayed her entrance at the theater until ten minutes before curtain time, which caused panic among the staff. To overcome stage fright, she had wandered off and found a lonely spot along Long Island Sound where she'd gone to breathe the salt air and to eat her supper of a carton of milk and a box of freshly picked blackberries, which severely blackened her teeth, making them look rotten.

Accounts differ about what actually happened that night on stage. Kenneth later claimed that Kate appeared in a dress purchased for her by Laura at Bergdorf Goodman. Apparently, Kate was wearing a pair of lace panties from the same store. At one point, the elastic loosened, and her panties began to slide down her legs. Kenneth said that Kate rather nonchalantly slipped off the panties in front of the audience and blithely walked over and handed them to the stage manager in the wings. That bravado act brought wild, cheering applause from the first-night audience.

Although initially heartened by the cheering, the thunderous applause seemed to throw off her timing. Perhaps unconsciously she began to imitate Kenneth's French accent that he'd adopted for the play, even though Kate, as Barbara, was supposed to be an American. This brought more applause from the audience.

Kate came unglued and began to move about the stage awkwardly, her voice rising into a falsetto. She began to feed Kenneth all the wrong lines, and though he struggled to rescue the play, the task was too daunting. Toward the end, Kate was speaking in such a rapid-fire delivery that the audience could not understand her lines. A bewildered Kenneth, as he was later to write, felt he was in the wrong play with the wrong actress.

When the curtain rang down on the final act, there was mild applause and one loud boo as the audience silently filed out. Only one man was clapping hysterically as if overjoyed by her performance. His name was Arthur Hopkins.

In the wings, Kate burst into hysterical sobbing, throwing herself into Kenneth's arms and begging him to forgive her. At that point Knopf came up and interrupted her. In his rage, he grabbed Kate by her shoulders and spun her around. "You're fired, you Park Avenue lesbian!" he shouted at her before turning and stalking out of the theater.

When the show finally arrived on Broadway, Lucile Nikolas, "a real actress" in Knopf's words, had returned to her original part before Kate had taken it over. Knopf sent word to Robinson-Duff to tell Kate that "you're now a footnote in the history of the theater."

***

To Kate's amazement, the celebrated producer, J.J. Shubert, had witnessed her opening night and was willing to offer her a five-year contract, beginning at two-hundred and fifty dollars a week and with yearly options going up to the then astounding price of fifteen hundred dollars a week. Although virtually broke and with no prospects, Kate turned him down when she went with Laura to visit him at Shubert Alley.

Laura pronounced Kate as insane, as did Kenneth who called Shubert's offer "the sweetheart of sweetheart deals—would that I could be so lucky."

Even Dr. Hepburn claimed that an actress would give her "eye teeth for an offer like that." In her arrogance at the time, Kate told Shubert that he might offer her a role that she found unacceptable. "If that happens, a contract with you would be like the bondage of marriage."

When she returned to her apartment with both Kenneth and Laura, after having lunch with them, she found yet another offer from a Broadway producer. That wildly cheering and madly clapping fan in the audience of *The Big Pond* turned out to be Arthur Hopkins, who had found "something magical" in her disastrous debut. Later, Kenneth wandered off, claiming that he was going "to give the worst performance of my life so that I too will have Broadway producers clamoring at my door."

Hopkins, or even Shubert, had seen something the opening night audiences hadn't—a "diamond in the dross," as Hopkins put it. Shubert told his associates that Kate's performance was a walking nightmare on stage but that "in some strange way she possessed the fire of life like few actresses do—you could literally hear her heart beating up there."

Once again the chicly dressed Laura accompanied Kate to the offices of Hopkins, where they found a short, rotund, and portly little piece of sausage with piercing brown eyes and pudgy hands ready to cast her immediately in the role of a schoolgirl called Veronica. The play was *These Days* by Katharine Clugston, and it was slated to open at the Cort Theater in November of 1928.

The little Welshman quickly became "Hoppy" to Kate, and he had only one offer and one play—no longterm contract—calling for a salary of one-hundred and twenty-five dollars a week. Kate adored Hoppy and was impressed with his theatrical credentials, as he'd worked with all the Barrymores and had produced such prestigious hits as *Richard III, Hamlet*, and *Anna Christie.*

Unlike *The Big Pond*, the carefully rehearsed Kate pulled off the opening night of *These Days.* She was delighted with John Anderson's appraisal of her in *New York Evening Journal,* where he found her "perfect passage of repressed devilry done gorgeously." Regrettably, the play closed after only eight performances. Although a flop on Broadway, *These Days* was filmed at Kate's studio,

35

RKO, in 1934. Retitled *Finishing School*, it starred Frances Dee and Kate's future rival as the queen of RKO, Miss Ginger Rogers.

Laura, Luddy and Jack celebrated her opening night. After meeting Laura, Jack and Luddy had become fast friends with her. Bryn Mawr classmates assumed that Laura was dating Jack and that Kate and Luddy had become "a serious item." Seen about town, the foursome did nothing to correct that impression.

***

Undaunted, Hopkins made Kate yet another offer, this time to understudy the popular actress, Hope Williams, in Philip Barry's comedy, *Holiday.* Ironically, it was that very play that in ten years would be turned into one of Hepburn's most famous roles for RKO when she co-starred with Cary Grant. Back in 1928 the play had begun its pre-Broadway tryout in New Haven.

Her appearance in *Paris Bound*, a mild-mannered comedy also by Philip Barry, had won instant acclaim for Williams, who was hailed in the press as "the Park Avenue swagger girl." With her closely cropped hair, a sort of taffy color, she had an emphatic arm-swinging stride.

Several people in the theater, notably Lynn Fontanne, had tried to get Williams to walk in a way that was more ladylike and less mannish. Fontanne suggested that Williams walk naked in a room of mirrors. But after a long day of that, Williams confessed to her fellow actress that "all that did was get me sexually aroused at the sight of my own nude body."

When Williams walked across the stage, her stride, like an athlete stalking a golf course, was met with thunderous applause, and the actress decided to retain her flat-footed charge "as part of my image."

Of course, Williams was more than just a walk. With her upturned nose, she had a deadpan delivery even when saying something funny. Upon first hearing her, Noël Coward found her speaking voice "startling with its beguiling state of tone-deafness."

Upon seeing Williams for the first time, Kate was overcome with awe and admiration when she took in the skinny and rather androgynous figure of the woman. She later told Laura that Hope Williams was a "boy-woman." Kate had merely studied Mary Boland. She practically devoured Williams both on and off stage, hawkeying her every move, mannerism, and body movement. The 1950 film, *All About Eve*, in which an aspirant actress, Eve Harrington, studies established actress Margo Channing so that she could become Margo could have been based on the careers of Hope Williams and Katharine Hepburn.

At one point during production, Williams complained to Hopkins that "the damn bitch is trying to steal my very soul, my essense." Years later, Kate did admit that she created both her own stage and screen persona by imitating this Park Avenue socialite-turned-actress.

Kate based two of her greatest screen roles—that of Linda Seton in *Holiday*

36

and that of Tracy Lord in *The Philadelphia Story*—directly on the personality and stage movements of Williams.

But there was a major difference between Hope Williams and Katharine Hepburn: Kate was ambition crazed, whereas Williams was much more insouciant about the theater. Williams told Kate, "You take the theater far too seriously. I feel it's a mere game of charades—all make-believe, totally meaningless."

Around town, especially on the arm of Laura Harding and "two rich men from Philadelphia," Jack and Luddy, Kate deliberately left the impression that she too was "born to society's grace" and the social register just like her idol, Hope Williams.

Waiting in the wings every night, Kate was both falling in love with Williams and at the same time wanting her to get sick so she could go on in place of the star.

Of course, it didn't help when Williams found Kate waiting outside her dressing room door every night. "Feeling fine tonight, are we?" Kate would invariably ask. Williams was so determined that Kate would never step in for her that she once arrived with a burning fever one night and went on anyway almost to despite her understudy.

Williams seemed in "constant conspiracy" with two of her female co-stars, Beatrice Stewart and Barbara White. They found Kate "just too impertinent with a kind of colossal arrogance." Each of the actresses vowed that Kate was not going to achieve her obvious goal, which was to go on in Williams's place one night as Laura Seton.

According to one cast member, Donald Ogden Stewart, who later became a friend of Kate's, Kate pursued Williams aggressively and at one point, propositioned her. "In those days, if Kate saw something she wanted, male or female, she went after them," Stewart said. "She was not modest or shy when it came to her sexual pursuits." Apparently, according to Stewart, Williams must have slapped her face and ordered Kate from her dressing room.

Very early into her affair with Kate, Laura became "sickeningly jealous" of Kate's devoted attention to Williams. One night after rehearsals, Kate and Laura had a big fight in Kate's dressing room that was overheard by stagehands. "If you want and expect monogamy from me," Kate shouted, "you've got the wrong woman. I will go after any woman—or man—I want, and there's nothing you can do about it."

Laura had stormed out of the theater, vowing never to speak to Kate again, although the two women were planning to drive with Luddy and Jack to Fenwick to meet Kate's parents that weekend.

Williams's rejection wasn't on moral grounds. She was, in fact, a lesbian herself and was actively involved in a torrid romance at the time with Tallulah Bankhead.

It was backstage one night that Stewart introduced Kate to the dynamic and colorful Alabama belle, Miss Bankhead herself, who had arrived to pick up her date for the evening, Hope Williams, for a late night party in Harlem. Kate and Tallulah did not spark on their first meeting, although they would know each other "as sort of friends" for decades.

There was a certain irony to their meeting. Kate would win her first Oscar playing the stage-struck actress, Eva Lovelace, in the 1933 RKO picture, *Morning Glory*. The author of the play, Zöe Akins, would base the Lovelace character on Tallulah herself.

Tallulah returned the favor. Throughout her life she was known for her brilliant impersonations of famous actresses of her day, especially Ethel Barrymore, who once slapped Tallulah's face after watching Bankhead's brilliant, albeit cruel, impersonation of the grand lady herself. After seeing Kate on the screen in *Morning Glory*, Tallulah added her to her clever impersonations. Her fans always claimed that Talullah impersonated Katharine Hepburn better than Kate did herself, and better than any female impersonator.

On the night of their first meeting, Kate was treated to Tallulah's raw brand of "potty humor." After kissing Kate on both cheeks and wishing her well in the theater, "providing you're no competition to me," Tallulah stalked over to Williams's dressing room. Before entering, she called back to Kate who was waiting in the wings. "Give me a ring one rainy night, darling. Maybe we'll get together and suck each other's cocks!"

***

Somehow, some way, Laura made up with Kate in time to join Luddy and Jack for the drive to Fenwick. Without actually saying so, Kate planned to present Jack and Laura as a couple. They would be booked in a nearby inn, whereas Luddy would be assigned a room in the Hepburn manse.

Although Laura and Jack did not unduly impress Kit and Dr. Hepburn, Luddy was immediately taken into the intimacy of the family even though "he'd made the grave mistake of voting for the reactionary Herbert Hoover" in the recent election. Kit told Kate that she fully expected "to convert" Luddy and after a few days around her the young Philadelphian would see the error of his ways.

On the afternoon of his arrival, Luddy fixed three broken appliances for the unmechanical Hepburns, winning their gratitude and respect. Always with camera in hand, Luddy had insisted on taking endless pictures of the Hepburn brood. When Dr. Hepburn came out of his bathroom and paraded nude into the living room, Luddy tried to take a picture of him. But Dr. Hepburn, although he tended to be casual about nudity, did not want his privates photographed, viewing it as cheap exhibitionism, the same way he viewed anyone who wanted to go on stage like his daughter.

During an afternoon sail, Luddy plunged into the waters at five o'clock to prevent Marion and Peg from crashing their boat into a lighthouse breakwater. His place in the hearts of the Hepburns was virtually won. Marion even started confiding in him before the day was out.

The next morning over breakfast, Kit told her family that having Luddy in the house was in some way like having Tom reborn. This was one of the very few occasions she'd spoken of her dead son.

In front of her family, Kate assumed an imperial attitude with Luddy, bossing him around and even demanding such favors as hot tea served by him whenever she wanted some. Kate seemed to like showing off her control over him.

"Don't treat the man like a damn servant," Dr. Hepburn told her. "Give him some dignity." Usually Kate listened to her father, but in this case, she didn't. She continued to order Luddy about.

Marion told Luddy that she felt he was far too sensitive a man for Kate. Luddy was overly attentive to Kate's every movement, constantly hugging and holding her affectionately. The family wrongly assumed that they were passionately in love the same way that Dr. Hepburn was with Kit. The Hepburns were completely unaware that Luddy confined his love-making to his beloved Jack at night, while Kate slipped away to find comfort and also passion in the arms of Laura Harding, to whom she was now pledging "loyalty but not fidelity."

After a weekend with the Hepburns, Jack, Luddy, Laura, and Kate drove to a little inn on Cape Cod. No one involved ever revealed exactly what happened at the inn over that three-day period.

But some agreement among the friendly quartet was reached, and their actual reasons can only be guessed at. A deal was struck and it seemed that all parties left Cape Cod in complete agreement.

On December 12, 1928 in West Hartford, the Reverend Sewell Stavely Hepburn, at the age of eighty-three the oldest Episcopal minister in Virginia, presided over the wedding of his grand-daughter, Katharine Hepburn, eldest daughter of Dr. and Mrs. Hepburn, to one Ludlow Ogden Smith. The private ceremony was held at 201 Bloomfield Avenue, the Hepburn home.

The next day, Kate's parents announced to their Hartford friends that the newlyweds, "so madly in love," had departed at once for a honeymoon in Bermuda.

As the ship set sail from New York Harbor, Jack Clark slept in the arms of the just-married groom, Luddy Smith, and Laura Harding spent the night cuddling the bride, Katharine Hepburn.

CHAPTER THREE

After an idyllic honeymoon for four in Bermuda, domesticity reigned. Bowing temporarily to Laura's strenuous protests, Kate agreed to be "more restrained" in her relationships. In Bermuda, disappointed with the lack of progress in her career, she decided to abandon her plans to become an actress. Before leaving on her honeymoon, she'd called Arthur Hopkins with the news that she could no longer understudy for Hope Williams. "My career in the theater is over. *Adieu*, Hoppy. I'll love and miss you so—and thanks for all your encouragement."

Stepping ashore in New York upon her return from Bermuda, Kate parted for a few days from Laura, who had urgent family business. Kate took the train with Jack and Luddy, where the very next day they went house-hunting in the environs of Pennsylvania, Luddy promising to buy a mansion in which to install "wife number one and wife number two," although he never specified who one and two were. If they found their dream house, Laura planned to arrange her schedule to spend three nights a week in New York, the rest of the time with Luddy, Jack, and her beloved Kate.

It took only three days of house-hunting before the "Bermuda agreement" began to crumble. Kate was the reason. Without warning, she announced that there was no way she was going to live in Pennsylvania. She told Luddy that if he wished to stay married to her, she could live only in New York and with her family in Connecticut. As a final warning, she said, "This is my first and last offer."

A distraught Laura waited to meet the trio as their train pulled into New York City's Grand Central. Kate told Laura that she planned a return to a stage career. "I have to act or else I'll wither and die on the vine. Acting is in my blood."

Giving in to her wishes, Luddy abandoned the house-hunt. Instead, he found a modestly furnished walk-up apartment at 146 East Thirty-Ninth Street in Manhattan where he installed Jack and himself in the master bedroom, assigning the smaller bedroom to Kate. Laura, during her frequent visits, could share the bedroom with Kate. Luddy, as was his habit, set about decorating the walls with nude pictures of himself, Kate, and Jack. Laura proceeded to move in some of her own elegant clothing "so I won't be seen arriving with a suitcase all the time like some hotel-hopping prostitute."

Soon after her arrival at her new home, Kate rushed over to the offices of

Arthur Hopkins, begging him to reinstate her as the understudy for Hope Williams in *Holiday.* "I knew you'd be back," Hopkins told her. "You'll have a few mishaps, but you're going to become the biggest star on Broadway one day, bigger than Ethel Barrymore. You're already a better actress than Tallulah."

Once installed in the apartment, Kate had another demand. She wanted Luddy to change his name from Ludlow Ogden Smith to S. Ogden Ludlow. Even though it broke his parents' hearts, Luddy agreed. "I refuse to have the same name as that fat singer Kate Smith," she told him. At the time another performer named Kate Smith was an overweight, sentimental singer and one of the most popular recording artists of her day.

Those nights not spent understudying for Hope Williams were passed alone at the small apartment Kate shared with Luddy, Jack, and most often Laura visiting from her family mansion. Even though all three of her friends liked to dine out and go to nightclubs, Kate had developed her lifelong distaste for going to such places. She could not stand other people watching her eat and drink. She said restaurants "cause me to faint," and indeed they did for some amazing reason.

Fortunately, they had a landlord, Herbert Brice, an expatriate Londoner, and also a good cook, specializing in such classic English dishes as bangers and mash, steak-and-kidney pudding, and Bubble & Squeak. He had installed a dumbwaiter in all the apartments. Like a hotel offering room service, he sent up meals to his tenants who requested them.

Luddy didn't like the radio but insisted on playing classical records on his Victrola every night. Jack told his stockbroker friends, "I've had my fill of Bach, Beethoven, and Brahms." Laura too grew tired of constantly listening to Stravinsky, Wagner, and Debussy and longed to go with Kate to a Broadway musical. Kate claimed, "I'd never be caught dead going to a leg show on Broadway—no Broadway musicals for me."

By day, Luddy was a stockbroker, and on weekends he continued to photograph any nude male or female who would disrobe for him. He had long ago grown tired of taking pictures of Kate and Jack. But in spite of frequent requests, Laura adamantly refused to pose for one of his figure studies.

In private moments with Jack and Laura, Kate frequently attacked the institution of marriage. "No actress—or actor, for that matter—should marry. We belong to our public. More to the point, we belong to ourselves. Actors by their very nature are self-absorbed. We think of no one but *me, me*. You might call us pigs, and you'd be right on the mark."

In other candid moments, she speculated as to why she'd married Luddy in the first place. She claimed that in some ways, Luddy reminded her of her dead brother Tom. "He has the same anxieties, the same conflicts over his sexual identity. He's not comfortable being a homosexual, and he wants at least some semblance of a stable married life. He yearns to be Main Line respectable like his parents, not part of some Greenwich Village Bohemia fringe element."

Luddy always insisted that he was not a homosexual, "although I love Jack more than life itself." His relationship with Jack was not platonic, as both Laura and Kate, sharing the bedroom next door, could hear through thin walls.

Kate told Jack and Laura that she'd failed Tom and didn't want to make the same mistake with Luddy. "Another suicide on my hands might push me over the edge of a cliff." At her happiest moments, and there were only a few of those, Kate proclaimed that Luddy "filled the vacuum in my life left by Tom."

When the courts notified Luddy that his name had been officially changed, he rushed home to celebrate his victory with Kate. After studying the document, she abruptly told Jack and Laura, and even Luddy himself, that for the rest of her life, despite the efforts he had taken to legally change his name, she'd sign her name Katharine Houghton Hepburn.

On her frequent visits to her family home in Connecticut, she informed her parents that, "At least with Luddy as my husband, I don't have to endure proposals of marriage from men I can hardly tolerate."

"Aren't you having your cake and eating it, too?" Dr. Hepburn asked.

"Call it what you like," she said, "But I have purchased my freedom even though I'm stuck with a marriage contract. How many women can say that?"

***

No sooner had Kate settled in with Luddy and Jack at their New York apartment, than a hysterical Laura arrived at their door. Seeing Kate, she burst into tears and held her close. Her father, the tycoon, J. Horace Harding, had contracted a cold on New Year's Day. Three days later he was found dead in his bed. The doctor defined that the cause of death was influenza complicated by blood poisoning.

In his will, he'd left his family the Fifth Avenue townhouse and the family mansion, Thornton, at Rumson, New Jersey, as well as one of the great private art collections in America, which was eventually sold off.

After Kate calmed Laura down, and Jack rushed to get her a sherry, Laura recovered sufficiently to tell them that her attorneys had informed her that morning that her share of her father's estate came to seven-million dollars. She cautioned that that was only a "conservative estimate."

Overnight she'd become one of the wealthiest heiresses in America, keeping good company with "The Gold Dust Twins," Woolworth heiress Barbara Hutton and tobacco heiress Doris Duke.

With Laura tending to family business, and Jack involved in his new post as a stockbroker, Luddy invited Kate to go with him to France. He wanted to show her his favorite country, which he'd discovered as both a warrior and a student.

Unknown to Jack and Laura, and even to Kate herself, Luddy was actually planning the ocean voyage as a second honeymoon—"a real one this time."

On the second night of the sea voyage, Luddy's intentions became all too clear to Kate when he'd come to bed and had tried to seduce her. She kicked him out of her bedroom and accused him of "not fully coming to terms with your homosexuality." Throughout the rest of the trip, Kate stayed sick in her cabin, and Luddy had to bunk with two other men on the overcrowded vessel.

When they finally got to Paris, Kate hated the city and didn't want to travel any deeper into France. She still hadn't forgiven Luddy "for tricking me into this damn trip." She informed him that she was eager to sail back to America and into Laura's arms, and she promised never to tell Jack how Luddy had attempted to betray him. "I'm your wife in name only, and don't you ever forget that."

Two weeks later, Kate and Luddy sailed back to America occupying separate cabins. Kate stayed locked in her cabin reading plays throughout most of the trip. Even though Jack awaited him in New York, Luddy became momentarily enamored of a handsome bus boy from Trenton, New Jersey, although he confessed to Kate that the young man demanded one-hundred dollars for the services he'd rendered during the sail back to the port of New York. Kate urged Luddy to "pay up because pleasure has its price."

***

Kate was soon back in her job of understudying Hope Williams in *Holiday.* One night Kate received an urgent call claiming that Williams was far too ill to go on, and she was to come at once to the theater. Waiting for the curtain call, Kate was so nervous that she vomited in her dressing room. Even though taller than Williams, Kate was forced to wear her ill-fitting wardrobe.

During the performance, Kate was met with stony silence from the audience during scenes where Williams had elicited thunderous laughter, even applause.

The reaction to Kate's performance that night was mixed. Many patrons who viewed Kate in the role claimed that she was "totally lackluster." Others found her acting "highly polished." Jimmy Hagen, the stage manager, claimed that, "She truly amazed us—dazzled us even." The theatrically astute Hopkins told Kate the next day that her performance was "more vigorous and compelling than Hope herself." There was only one problem with Hopkins' appraisal. Kate later learned that the producer was actually watching another Broadway show the night she went on as Laura Seton.

The next day Kate told Laura, Jack, and Luddy that playing the role made her realize just how brilliant Williams had been in the part. "She brought a light tap and I wielded a sledgehammer."

Years later, Kate was to tell director George Cukor that, "If Hope Williams had not existed, I would have had to invent her. Without Hope Williams, there would be no Katharine Hepburn."

A few days later, Hopkins called another producer, Theresa Helburn of the Theatre Guild, urging her to hire Kate for the *ingénue* role in *Meteor,* the S.N. Behrman play slated to star Alfred Lunt and Lynn Fontanne, the two greatest names in American theater at the time. The salary was to be two-hundred and twenty-five dollars a week, considered incredibly high at the time.

Kate accepted the role, but before the play could go into rehearsals, she backed out. When Kenneth MacKenna took her to his apartment "to deflower " her again, he could not believe that she'd turned down the chance to work with Lunt and Fontanne. He claimed that he'd even gone to bed with homosexual Lunt "but I still didn't get a part."

Another almost simultaneous offer intrigued Kate more. She'd been pre-sented with the female lead in the fantasy-drama, *Death Takes A Holiday* by Alfredo Casella who'd written its original version in Italian. Translated into English, it was to be directed by Lawrence Marston. In this bizarre play, Death arrives at an Italian *palazzo* and eventually carts off its most glamorous occu-pant. According to the plot, Kate, playing an impressionable young woman, was to fall in love with this Prince of Darkness.

Evoking her young girl past as "Jimmy" back in Hartford, Kate demanded to play the role of Grazia as a rough-and-tumble tomboy. Marston however, wanted her to be more ladylike and alluring.

Throughout the five-week, pre-Broadway rehearsal period, they battled constantly until the play's producer, Lee Shubert, presented her with a letter of resignation which she refused to sign, claiming he'd have to fire her. He did just that. While he was at it, he also fired Marston.

To catch her last performance, Kit and Dr. Hepburn drove down from Hartford. When the curtain fell, Dr. Hepburn led the charge backstage. "Shubert is right to have fired you. You were galumphing on stage like a wild thing. Besides, who would believe that a big strong horse of a woman like you would be stupid enough to fall in love with Death? Get out of the theater before you drive me insane."

That night, he drove Luddy and Kate back to West Hartford, with Laura and Jack following on the train the next day.

It was a gloomy Christmas. The Great Crash had devastated Wall Street, and Luddy's job as a stockbroker was in peril. Dr. Hepburn predicted that most Broadway shows would soon close. Over Christmas turkey, he warned both his daughter and his son-in-law. "Now is the time to abandon the stock market and find some more worthwhile career."

In despair, Kate called the Theatre Guild Monday morning, claiming that she was ready to take on the role in *Meteor* with the Lunts after all. The direc-tor, Helburn, flatly turned her down. "You had your chance," Helburn said.

When *Death Takes a Holiday* opened at the Ethel Barrymore Theater, Kate asked Laura to go see it with her. Later that night, Kate told Laura that she was "horrified" at how Rose Hobart had played her former role of Grazia. The play would eventually be turned into a film starring Fredric March, who would find himself in 1936 co-starring with Kate in the John Ford film, *Mary of Scotland.*

With actors out of work all over New York, Kate was offered a minor job to understudy the *ingénue* lead in Ivan Turgenev's *A Month In The Country,* scheduled for presentation by the Theatre Guild. With no other prospects, she accepted the position, viewing it as a "comedown since I'd already appeared on Broadway as a star."

The job brought her into contact with the Russian-Armenian director, Rouben Mamoulian, who was to become an innovative film director, eventually producing such classics as *Dr. Jekyll and Mr. Hyde* with Fredric March, *Song of Songs* with Marlene Dietrich, and *Queen Christina* with Greta Garbo.

Mamoulian found Kate too green and not yet ready for a big part, yet he was intrigued by her. "There's a certain luminosity about her freckled face," he said. He introduced her to Cheryl Crawford, then serving as casting director for the Guild. In time, Cheryl Crawford would go on to become a producer herself of many famous plays, including two by Tennessee Williams: *Rose Tattoo* in 1951 and *Sweet Bird of Youth* in 1959. Crawford offered Kate only thirty dollars a week, which she accepted, although in her autobiography, *Me,* Kate remembered it as twenty-five dollars.

Once again Kate found herself an understudy for another actress, this time Eunice Stoddard in the role of Viera Aleksandrovna. The star of the play was the great Alla Nazimova, once queen of Metro pictures in the early Twenties. Now a faded movie star with a dwindling bank account, Nazimova had returned to the stage. A lover of hers, Lynn Fontanne, had intervened with the Guild to get Nazimova cast in the leading role in *A Month in the Country.* She played an aristocrat who falls in love with the tutor of her ten-year-old son. The tutor was played by Alexander Kirkland.

Kate was already familiar with Nazimova, the legendary Russian-born actress who had brought Stanislavsky and Chekhov to the American theater. Kate's own mother, Kit, had raved about Nazimova in a play by Ibsen, claiming that through her stage roles Nazimova was "portraying women hell-bent on independence." Night after night, Kate studied the slight, short, pale Nazimova with her tar-black curly hair and tragic, violet-blue eyes, just as she had studied another lesbian actress, Hope Williams.

Kate was thrilled when Nazimova took her aside and told her stories about the theater, including how she'd "discovered" a movie extra, Rudolph Valentino, and had cast him opposite her in *Camille,* and how she'd insisted on producing Oscar Wilde's *Salome* with an all-gay cast. In time, Nazimova would become the godmother of Nancy Davis Reagan.

The play opened to decent reviews on March 17, 1930. Kate stayed with the production as understudy until Hortense Alden dropped out as Katia the maid. As a footnote to theatrical history, Alden, in time, would create the role of Violet Venable in Tennessee Williams's off-Broadway production, *Suddenly, Last Summer*. Years later, Kate would bring Violet Venable to the screen in a role she detested, although it brought her an Academy Award nomination.

Remembering his earlier enthusiasm for Kate, Mamoulian cast her as the maid, although refusing her request for a five-dollar-a-week increase in salary. After seeing her on stage for the first time, Mamoulian told Kate, "You could go to Hollywood and become a film star, perhaps as a thinking man's Clara Bow." Kate laughed off the suggestion, claiming that she hadn't struggled through Bryn Mawr to become "some Hollywood floozie like Jean Harlow." When Kate eventually went on stage as the maid, the Guild billed her as Katharine Hapburn (sic).

***

Coming to see Nazimova on stage were some of the world's most famous lesbians, none more notable than author Djuana Barnes who arrived backstage attired in a midnight blue cape, purple lipstick, and chartreuse eye shadow. Alexander Kirkland introduced Kate to Barnes, who was suitably impressed, pronouncing Kate a "natural beauty who has not fully emerged into the dawn but when morning light strikes will illuminate like the Mona Lisa."

Before leaving to call on Nazimova, Barnes gave Kate a passionate kiss on the lips. Although Barnes at the time was years from writing her masterpiece, *Nightwood*, she'd anonymously authored *Ladies Almanack*, with its coded portraits of such Paris lesbian expatriates as Gertrude Stein, Radclyffe Hall (author of *The Well of Loneliness*), and Dolly Wilde (Oscar Wilde's niece). Even though not admitting to its authorship, Barnes nonetheless gave Kate an autographed copy, which Kate took back to Luddy's apartment and didn't put down until dawn came.

For one week in New York, Kate took to dressing like Djuana Barnes until Laura persuaded her to abandon such "outrageous clothing."

Slowly, very slowly, Nazimova began to take an interest in Kate, perhaps reacting to the rave review she'd heard from Barnes. Although not inviting Kate into her dressing room at first, she often deposited words of wisdom with the ingénue waiting in the wings. Lighting a long Russian cigarette, the actress who had been hailed as "the new Duse" told Kate that the thrill was not in playing a character on stage but in creating that character.

Kate was joyous when Nazimova invited her to accompany her on Sunday night, when the theater was dark, to a private party on New York's Upper East Side. Kate arrived in baggy clothes at Nazimova's apartment. Having seen her only in makeup before and elegantly dressed, Kate was startled to encounter an old lady—tired, a bit sad, with tear-streaked eyes wearing a dog-eared sweater with cigarette burns and shabby pants. After a drink with Kate, Nazimova excused herself and went to her bedroom.

When she emerged thirty minutes later, she was wearing a gown designed by the French *couturier*, Charles Frederick Worth, the same costume she'd appeared in when she'd starred in the play, *The Cherry Orchard.* Kate was stunned at the transformation.

Nazimova told Kate that she could not go to the party with her if she insisted on dressing as she did. She took Kate into her dressing room and told her to try on a peacock dress that had been designed and worn by Natacha Rambova, second wife of Valentino. After looking at herself in the mirror, Kate claimed she felt she was going to a masquerade.

At the party, Nazimova soon deserted her for a position in the center of the room, where she became the focus of attention. Exotically dressed women—no men—filled the room, drinking hard liquor cocktails. Many of the women were attired in black leather.

With a drink in hand, Kate in her peacock costume felt awkward and out of place. She retreated to the far corner of the salon to observe the party alone and from afar.

Feeling she'd stumbled into the wrong crowd, Kate looked up as a stunningly dressed woman approached her. With a swirling cloak, she was a vision in black and white with pointed shoes and a gold buckle. Cut short, her jet-black hair was mostly concealed by a tricorne hat.

"I know that peacock gown," the woman said with a slight Continental accent. But was it French or Spanish? "It could have been worn only by Natacha Rambova, and Natacha would just die if she thought the wearer of the gown would be sulking away like a retreating wallflower. That dress was meant to occupy center stage with Nazimova."

"I don't dare compete with her," Kate said.

"I have a talent," the woman said, "for spotting and discovering great figures before they become illustrious. The Barrymores, Pavlova, Eva Le Gallienne, Isadora Duncan. I feel I'm in such a presence tonight."

"I fear I'm a nobody playing a maid's part in Nazimova's play. I'm Katharine Hepburn."

"And, I my dear, am Mercedes de Acosta." She took her hand and reached inside Kate's gown, placing it over her breast. "When I was but a young girl, the great Spanish painter, Ignacio Zuloaga, told me 'All people born to greatness are ruled by their heart. I can feel your heart beating. Always remember to think with it, to feel with it, and, above all, to let it rule your life.'"

***

Without announcing her departure, Kate left the party with Mercedes. Before the night was over, Mercedes had promised to get Kate a part in her play *Prejudice*, which was to have its *première* in London at the Arts Theatre. "Tallulah loved London, and so will you. I'll go over with you. John Gielgud and Gwen Ffrangçon-Davies will play the leads, but I'll build up your part. After the play closes, I promised Clifton Webb and his mother, Mabel—he takes her everywhere—that I'd join them and Libby Holman for a motor tour of Bavaria. I'll introduce you to wonderful friends. John Becket in Munich. We'll have dinner with Prince Agoutinsky and Tamara Karsavina in Paris. Diaghilev has died in Venice, and Nijinsky is locked away in an insane asylum somewhere in Switzerland or else I'd introduce you to them, too."

By four o'clock that morning, Mercedes was still talking. "Let's go onto my terrace and watch the dawn come up just like I used to do with Isadora—what a great dancer!"

"Is there anybody you don't know?" Kate asked, growing impatient with the endless name-dropping.

"A few," Mercedes said. "It's true I've spent most of my life with celebrated people. But I have this amazing gift for spotting young women who will someday be celebrated."

"Surely you don't include me in that category?" Kate asked.

"Only time will tell," Mercedes said. "But there are two women I currently have my eye on. Both are actresses and both are European. Marlene Dietrich in Germany and Greta Garbo who's arrived from Sweden. I'm going to Hollywood, and I've got my hat set for both of those beautiful creatures."

"How do I fit into the picture?" Kate asked, still mesmerized by Mercedes.

"To that list of future screen goddesses, I will add the name of Katharine Hepburn," Mercedes said.

"No, not me," Kate said. "I might become anything in life but not a screen goddess. I'm not the type. I don't know about those other women. The acting is not so important to me. I just want to be famous."

"Who knows what will happen to you?" Mercedes said. "You do have a remarkable face and body. Why not show all of it to me?"

***

When Kate went home sometime after noon the next day, the phone was ringing hysterically. It was Laura, demanding to know where she'd been all night. Kate refused to tell her, and Laura slammed down the phone on her, but only after calling her a whore. Jack and Luddy called later, voicing their concerns. "I was a pig not to let you know," Kate said.

At six that evening, when she thought Mercedes might be awake, she called her apartment. Some woman answered the phone. "Didn't she tell you?" the woman asked. "Miss de Acosta left on the train for Chicago this morning. She's going to California."

"That bitch!" Kate said, slamming down the phone.

At the theater, almost an hour later, Kate encountered an enraged Nazimova. "That God damn Mercedes has done it to me again. How could you leave the party without me? You came as *my* escort."

"I guess I don't know all the rules about how you women play the game," Kate said defensively. "I'm new at this."

Nazimova whirled around as a young woman approached. "This is Glesca Marshall. She's replacing you in the maid part. You're fired!"

In stunned disbelief, Kate watched Nazimova head for her dressing room with Glesca. This was Kate's first exposure to the lavender casting couch in the American theater. She was heartbroken.

***

Laura once again made up with Kate and forgave her her indiscretions the following afternoon when they both attended voice lessons with Frances Robinson-Duff. Beginning in June, the teacher had gotten them summer stock jobs at the Berkshire Playhouse in Stockbridge, Massachusetts. Both Laura and Kate were hired, and the two women arrived in Stockbridge driving a LaSalle convertible, with Laura loaded down with money. For some reason, the multi-millionaire Laura had decided to arrive with a horde of jewelry, mostly diamonds, rubies and sapphires, and she and Kate caused instant envy among the other struggling actors by having such obvious wealth in the midst of a world-wide depression. For the first three weeks, the two women wore "tons of jewelry" at the most inappropriate occasions. They found a shared room in an old-fashioned, clapboard-sided boarding house that belonged to some British minister whom they knew only as "Bradley." The minister was married to an Alabama belle with three wild daughters who finished off at least three bottles of hooch a night and changed boy friends as often as some people change their underwear.

Fellow actor Osgood Perkins—future father of another actor, Tony Perkins—avidly pursued both Kate and Laura, getting nothing but turndowns. Richard Hale, another actor, shared the house, as did George Coulouris, who later appeared in *Citizen Kane*. Kate argued and fought constantly with Coulouris, who called her a "flibbertigibbet."

Osgood was an exhibitionist and often paraded nude in the upper hallways. One night he came into the bedroom occupied by Kate and Laura. He was completely naked. He pleaded to be allowed to seduce each of them in the same bed because he had had a premonition of his early death. Neither Kate nor Laura accepted that as an excuse. True to his word, Osgood did die at the age of forty-five.

Every Friday night Jack and Luddy arrived, staying at the nearby Red Lion Inn.

"It was the oddest thing," Perkins would later say. "We didn't know until later that Kate was married to Luddy. She treated him like a servant. As soon as he got to the boarding house, she'd order him into the bathroom to wash her hair. Then she demanded that Luddy go with Jack into the village for two quarts of chocolate ice cream for them to share. Luddy never slept over at the boarding house. Kate always bedded with Laura. I wondered at the time what kind of marriage it was. Finally, I figured out what was going on and stopped chasing after either Laura or Kate."

Both Kate and Laura mounted the boards for *The Admirable Crichton*, playing a pair of British girls left abandoned on an uninhabited island. Their director was Alexander Kirkland, who had co-starred with Nazimova in *A Month in the Country*. Kate refused to take direction from him, and the two fought bitterly. Kirkland would later marry the stripper Gypsy Rose Lee. Both Luddy and Jack came up for the opening bringing flowers.

Kate unsuccessfully demanded the lead in the next production, *A Romantic Young Lady,* a play written under a pen name by a husband-and-wife team who called themselves "G. Martínez Sierra." To her disappointment, the actual lead went to Edith Barrett, an actress who was later to marry the gay film star, Vincent Price.

Barrett won rave reviews, and Kate got no attention at all, even though she did everything she could to upstage Barrett. One night Kate came onstage with her dress on backward. When that didn't get the attention she wanted, she wore her hat backward.

Kate once again lobbied hard for the lead of the third production of the season, *The Torch Bearers,* a farce by George Kelly. When the role went to Aline MacMahon, Kate was furious. In 1944 Kate would be the star of an MGM film *Dragon Seed.* Ironically, MacMahon appeared in a supporting role in the same film, for which she would be nominated for the Oscar.

When she didn't get the part, Kate resigned before the season was out. Although Laura at first objected, Kate demanded that her friend quit too. "Good riddance!" Kirkland had said. He told Perkins that he had planned to fire both of them anyway.

Even though Kate was on bad terms with each of the cast members, she insisted on making the rounds and shaking everyone's hand to say good-bye. Prophetically, she announced to each member of the startled cast, "I'll be a star before any of you!"

To make sure they were really going, some of the occupants of the boarding house stood on the porch, watching "Miss Moneybags," as they called Laura, get behind the wheel of her LaSalle. Kate got in on the passenger seat.

With their jewelry and too much luggage, both Kate and Laura headed back to New York City. Kate later pronounced the summer "a God damn disaster."

***

Kate and Laura resumed their life in New York, although there were no roles waiting for either of them. Both of them jointly took their lessons with Robinson-Duff. While the summer lasted, weekends were reserved for Fenwick. The foursome of Luddy, Jack, Laura, and Kate became inseparable. Friends called them "The Four Musketeers."

The always poised, always well-groomed, and always elegantly attired Laura used this slow period in her life to try to make a lady out of Kate. In Laura's view, Kate "dressed like an itinerant handyman going door to door looking for work." Luddy too joined in the hopeless battle to put frilly dresses on Kate, likening her appearance to "a relic of the Depression. She could sell apples on the street and no one would be the wiser."

Robinson-Duff continued to try "to harness the unharnessable" in Kate's voice. At the end of every session, the voice teacher lobbied Kate to abandon her baggy trousers and ratty sweaters—"more suitable as horse blankets"—and attire herself in the stylish feminine adornments of her day. Instead of bare legs, Robinson-Duff suggested garter belts and stockings, the type of clothing worn at the time by Kay Francis and Ruth Chatterton on the screen.

The more her friends protested, the baggier Kate's pants became. Jack claimed that, "You could fit Fatty Arbuckle in those pants with room to spare for Alaska."

Robinson-Duff finally gave up the battle but made one final request. "No self-respecting scarecrow would dress as you do. But if you must wear that floppy green felt hat, why not one without a hole in it?"

Kate responded by attacking the lack of imagination in people. "A first-rate mind could easily conjure up a little bit of cloth to fill in the hole."

Kate was adamant, shouting down her critics. "I don't follow fickle fashion. I set it! When the women of America come to their senses, they'll be dressing like I do." Aided in no small part by the changing role of women in World War II, Kate proved to be a prophet.

In one of her first newspaper interviews, Kate discussed her mode of dress with Bradford Fenton, a newspaper reporter in Hartford. "Should we award sainthood to women for putting on garter belts to hold up their stockings? Ridiculous fiddle-faddle. I don't wear pants to conceal my legs. My gams are spectacular. I'm sure I could win any bathing beauty pageant. I don't even wear lipstick, much less makeup."

Much of what she said was true, but from this early interview, Kate began her custom of deceiving, or outright lying, to the press. Not at Fenwick, but everywhere else, Kate always carried a stick of orange-hued lipstick, having abandoned Djuana Barnes's purple as too vampirish. As the Twenties drew to a close and the bleak Thirties dawned, Laura and Kate solidified their relationship, a friendship that Kate tested time and time again. Kate became the forever errant child, Laura the forgiving parent who took her back after Kate wandered off into an almost continuous series of indiscretions.

Although not revealing her lesbianism to Dr. Hepburn, she told him, "If I see a man and I desire him, I will go after him."

"Even though the idea horrifies me, I know you will," Dr. Hepburn said. "Just do as I instructed so you won't have any unwanted babies with God-only-knows-who-the-daddy-is running around Fenwick."

"If I get pregnant," Kate told him, "I fully expect you to perform one of those neat, sanitized abortions on me. And from time to time, I'm sure I'll call on you for just such a service."

Among their friends, Laura and Kate became the Odd Couple as they dashed around New York. They could sometimes be seen walking arm in arm along Fifth Avenue and at other times emerging from the back seat of Laura's chauffeur-driven limousine.

During this period, Kate was rash and filled with a raw vitality. Uninhibitedly energetic, she lacked restraint to the point of arrogance. She basically said whatever she felt and delivered her judgments in a piercingly sharp voice likened to a "squeal of brakes."

Laura, in contrast, wrote the book on decorum. She was the model of propriety and good taste in both her conduct and appearance. She never went out for a cup of coffee but what she was "photographer ready." Kate's voice cracked, squeaked, and rose into an alarming falsetto at moments of peak excitement. Laura spoke in perfectly modulated Robinson-Duff tones, a virtual style setter in the rich post-debutante world of the East Coast Establishment. Had she pursued her career as an actress, she could have appeared on the screen and no doubt would have been the darling of every sound engineer.

After fruitless weeks of trying to change Kate, Laura confided to Jack and Luddy that she had virtually given up the challenge. "In spite of Kate's family background, and all of them are decent people, Kate washed up on the shores of Bohemia." Laura spoke at the time in such phrases. "I will never get rid of her *gaucheries*. At times she behaves like Miss Hayseed at a formal Park Avenue party, and she does so willingly and with malice. I could take the sharpest file and grate her roughest edges. But in the morning I would once again confront a jagged edge. Kate Hepburn, I have concluded, is a total iconoclast. An American original. Maybe she knows what she's doing. Sometimes an original can attract world attention, and Kate is so offbeat she might pull it off. Every time we go out together, she embarrasses the hell out of me. But no one but myself is forcing me to stay glued to her. She might be unconventional in every sense of the word, but I'm madly in love with the woman. No one provides me with the excitement she does. She's reason enough for me to live."

Kenneth MacKenna continued to take Kate secretly to his apartment "to deflower her," and he also continued to help advance her stage career. He tipped her off that Joseph Verner Reed and Kenneth MacGowan were producing a play, *Art and Mrs. Bottle* as part of their repertoire at the Maxine Elliott Theatre on Thirty-Ninth Street. The play was about a fallen society woman and her bohemian daughter. Kenneth felt that Kate would be perfect in the role of the *ingénue*.

Staging the play was Clifford Brooke. After Kate read for him "in very WASP tones," he hired her for one-hundred and twenty-five dollars a week, and that was in the midst of the Depression when lines formed around the block along Broadway whenever a role became available in a show.

The star of the play was Jane Cowl, an actress known for her bovine eyes and a slight catch in her voice. She seemed delighted with the casting of Kate in the minor role. The soft-spoken Cowl, born in 1887, had been one of the great stars of the American theater, and twenty years earlier she'd been acclaimed on Broadway for her portrayal of Juliet. Now aging, with her career in decline, Cowl feared being cast opposite an actress "too young and too pretty," as she confided to G.P. Huntley Jr., playing the role of Michael Bottle.

Kate showed up at the theater, looking like Raggedy-Ann, although actors in those days dressed for rehearsals. The British author of the "rose-tinted comedy," Benn W. Levy, was horrified to learn that Kate had been cast in the part. He found her "most unattractive, lacking talent, and dressing like a bum." He constantly compared her unfavorably to "the love of my life," the famous actress and blonde-haired beauty, Constance Cummings, who not only would become Mrs. Benn W. Levy, but who would also achieve screen immortality opposite Rex Harrison in *Blithe Spirit*. "My God!" Levy shouted at Kate, interrupting rehearsals. "What have you got on your face? Vaseline?" After a break, Cowl rushed to Kate's rescue, teaching her how to paint her face. Although Cowl transformed Kate into an *ingénue* of stunning, chiseled beauty, Kate ruined the effect by swabbing her face with alcohol before facing Levy on stage again. That left her face streaked, her makeup running. He denounced her appearance as "gauchely hideous" and fired her on the spot.

After producers auditioned fourteen other actresses, each of them beautiful and with painted faces, no one was suitable. Brooke was ordered "to rehire Hepburn." To save face, she demanded and got, through "clever Yankee trading," as she put it, another twenty-five dollars a week, though with Laura's millions at her disposal, Kate was not hard up financially.

Levy still hated Kate in the role, but gave in because the cast, including Cowl and the producers, liked her.

It was Jane Cowl herself who caused the next problem. In the middle of a rehearsal, Cowl was having a hard time remembering her lines. It was rumored that she was drinking heavily in her dressing room before coming on stage. In the middle of a scene with Kate, Cowl suddenly sat down on the floor and started to sob violently. When Brooke rushed over to pick her up, she shouted. "Someone's put the Evil Eye on me!" Impulsively, she fingered Kate. "It's you!" Although she'd never been known to utter even a *damn* before, Cowl shouted obscenities at Kate. In dismay, Brooke ushered Kate from the theater.

The next afternoon when Kate showed up with trepidation at rehearsals, Cowl was just as solicitous as before, making no mention of her outburst of the day before. Playing Sonia Tippet, Joyce Carey, a charming British actress, also befriended Kate, although telling Cowl that she felt Kate was badly miscast. "She was just desperately shy and uncertain," Carey recalled years later. "She looked eccentric and somehow very much like a star. I thought she was wonderful." Carey told Kate that she'd invited her best friend, Noël Coward, for opening night and that the playwright/actor had accepted. Privately, Carey had informed Coward that she felt that Kate "was really a boy—a cross-dresser for sure."

As President Hoover promised prosperity around the corner, the comedy opened on November 18, 1930 at the Maxine Elliott Theatre. There was a scene in the play where Kate had to kiss Cowl on the cheek. Throughout rehearsals of the scene, Kate wore no lipstick. But on opening night, Kate's lips were painted a scarlet red. She gave Cowl a big smack, leaving a lipstick imprint on her cheek, which caused a murmur in the audience. Only when the curtain fell, did Cowl discover what the murmur was all about. "I looked like a clown out there on stage." She flew into a rage, demanding that Kate wear indelible lipstick. For subsequent performances, and in spite of Cowl's kindness toward her, Kate defiantly refused to wear that indelible lipstick. In future performances, Cowl backed away every time Kate tried to kiss her, Kate having to settle for an air kiss instead.

That same opening night, Coward climbed five flights of steps to Kate's dressing room to congratulate her. He didn't tell her she was good. "You show remarkable promise and carry on and keep at it. Who knows? If Tallulah can do it, so can you." With that enigmatic review, he descended the five flights of stairs with Joyce Carey on his arm.

Later, Coward and Hepburn were to become the dearest of friends.

Mercedes de Acosta also showed up that opening night to congratulate Kate, but because of de Acosta's hasty departure to California, Kate turned down her request for "an evening on the town."

With Luddy, Jack, and Laura, Kate stayed up late to read the reviews. The *News* was the first paper to hit the streets. Jack retrieved one of the first copies and rushed back with the review. The critic found Kate "too gangling and affected."

Kate burst into tears and vowed she'd never again read another review of her work.

***

The following June both Kate and Laura signed on to appear in summer stock for producers Julian Anhalt and Milton Stiefel at the Ivoryton Playhouse in Connecticut, the theater lying only fifteen miles from her beloved Fenwick. There Kate could spend lots of time with the Hepburn brood.

Laura had agreed to go along to keep Kate company, her roles being incidental. Laura was rapidly losing her fascination with the acting profession, preferring to be known as an "heiress" instead of an "actress."

The star power for that summer was generated by a reed-thin Kentuckian, Henry Hull, already a well-known actor. Forty years old at the time, his furrowed brow was ideal for his stage specialty—crochety roles. Hull was to become celebrated in 1933 for appearing as Jeeter Lester in Erskine Caldwell's *Tobacco Road,* although he was later skipped over for the film version.

Privately, Kate told Laura that she found Hull "garrulously self-important," but outwardly she maintained a good working relationship with the actor, driving to his home in Lyme, just across the Connecticut River for rehearsals. Whether needed at the rehearsal or not, Laura played chauffeur to Kate.

Hull always liked to brag that he seduced all his leading ladies. By the time he appeared as the kindly pawnbroker who helped Spencer Tracy finance *Boys Town*, Katharine Hepburn was but one of the vast list of actresses Hull claimed he'd seduced. Kate always maintained, however, that she admired Hull as an actor but that he was "sexually repulsive to me."

The repertoire that summer included such plays as *Just Married* by Adelaide Matthews and Anne Nichols and *The Cat and the Canary* by John Willard. *The Cat and the Canary* had been a hit on Broadway when it had previously opened as *Let Us Be Gay*. In it, Kate played a forty-five year old sophisticate. Hull and Kate co-starred in *The Man Who Came Back* by Jules Eckert Goodman. Ironically, both Kenneth MacKenna and his friend, Humphrey Bogart, were later lured to Hollywood with the promise that each could play the lead in the film version of *The Man Who Came Back,* although the part eventually went to Charles Farrell.

Unlike previous directors, Julian Anthalt at Ivoryton was not only aware of Kate's talents but was sympathetic to her suggestions. He pronounced her a hit in all the plays that summer. Years later she was to give him great credit for "finely tuning my stage technique."

***

Unknown to Kate at the time, Philip Barry, the playwright of *Holiday*, was working in Bermuda on a new script, containing a role he was "tailor-making" for Kate. He saw his young heroine, Daisy Sage, as made of "platinum wire and sand," and he envisioned Kate in the role as "slim, lithe, a stripling, but with dignity beyond her years and a rare grace to accompany it."

In the script, the character of Tom Collier is the male lead, a conflicted man torn between a wife and a mistress. The character of Tom tells his mistress that their relationship should be spiritual and based on a platonic love, evoking Kate's own ill-fated sexual relationship with the poet Phelps Putnam who had abandoned her.

After reading Barry's play, Gilbert Miller agreed to produce it. However, he objected violently when Barry demanded Kate for the role. "That beanpole!" Miller said. Barry was so insistent that Miller finally agreed and called Kate at Ivoryton, offering her the role of Daisy Sage.

The play was set to open at the Broadhurst Theatre in New York in January of 1932 and rehearsals were to begin in November of 1931.

Waiting for her to be called, Kate retreated with Jack, Laura, and Luddy to The Lodge, a posh mountain retreat owned by the Hardings. There, with her three friends helping her with her cues, Kate rehearsed her role of Daisy for weeks, wanting to be letter perfect when she showed up for rehearsals with the star of the play, heartthrob Leslie Howard.

Eventually the telephone call came in. Kate was needed for rehearsals. Laura drove her to Boston where she met Howard. Once again, it was "love at first sight" for fickle Kate. She dumped Laura in a Boston hotel that night, claiming that Howard wanted her for private rehearsals.

He appeared handsome and charming to Kate, though with her five feet, seven inches of height, she was a bit tall for him. Upon being introduced to Howard by Gilbert Miller, the co-producer of the play (along with Howard), Kate said, "Perhaps I'm a little tall for you, Mr. Howard." Without missing a beat, Howard responded, "I'll cut you down to my size." These lines later became a famous but apocryphal story in Hollywood lore. Allegedly, they were the first lines exchanged when Katharine Hepburn met Spencer Tracy, except they were never said, at least not by Spencer Tracy.

No one knows for sure what happened that first night that Howard asked Kate back to his hotel room. A compulsive womanizer and serial seducer, Howard was a premature ejaculator, as has been rumored for years by some of his sexual conquests.

If Howard's sexual performance that night had been inadequate, the rather outspoken Kate might well have informed him. There remains speculation that Kate advised the actor that he should consult with Dr. Hepburn, her urologist father, about the ejaculation problem. Howard was said to have slapped her face and to have ordered her from his hotel suite.

Over the years the only time she mentioned Howard again was when her best friend, George Cukor, cast him as Ashley Wilkes in *Gone With The Wind*. At the time thinking she was going to play Scarlett O'Hara in the same film,

Kate told Cukor: "You must fire him. I can't play opposite the beast."

Kate was so desperate to succeed in the part of Daisy that she showed up for rehearsals in high heels and a dress, as previous directors had objected to her sloppy attire. Seeing Howard, she felt she'd made a mistake, because in her heels, she towered over him. She uttered some apology and promised to go back to her hotel that afternoon and get some flat shoes. She might have apologized to him for her outspoken words of the night before, although he made no reference to what had transpired, treating Kate as if he were being introduced to her for the first time.

The rehearsals went badly. Although Howard had initially been attracted to her, by that afternoon he was finding her "too tall, too arrogant, and with too many unbearable mannerisms." As co-producer, he had a lot of clout.

Kate told Laura that she desperately tried to please Howard "as the part of Daisy meant the world to me. It was, after all, God damn it, written for me." She tried to be sweet and almost girlish, but nothing she did seemed to please him. "At one point," Kate said, "Howard looked at me with such hostility, I begged him to tell me what I was doing wrong." He rose from his chair on the stage, looked at her with contempt, and said, "Frankly, my dear, I don't give a damn." That line was eerily evocative of Rhett Butler's closing remark to a distraught Scarlett O'Hara in *Gone With The Wind,* except it was uttered by Clark Gable playing Rhett Butler, not Leslie Howard playing Ashley Wilkes.

On the second day of rehearsals, no longer giving in to him, Kate encountered the "icily effete" Howard in her normal dress of baggy pants and an ill-fitting sweater. When he objected to her reading of a line, she attacked his "cultivated sensitivity" which Kate claimed belonged to another era in the theater. That infuriated him.

In her criticism, Kate had been wrong because it was Howard's cultured sensitivity that later brought him his greatest success as Ashley Wilkes. Kate had the last word, however. After George Cukor had taken her to see *Gone With the Wind*, a film from which he'd been fired as director, Kate said, "What woman in her right mind would turn down Clark Gable for Leslie Howard?"

After five days of rehearsing with Kate and Howard, a dress rehearsal for *The Animal Kingdom* was called. Some backers had come up from New York to see how their money was being spent. The performance went beautifully, Kate feeling "I've never been better." At curtain call, when Howard stepped up for his star bows, one of the backers called out, "Bring back Hepburn. She's the star!"

An infuriated Howard graciously extended his hand toward the wings, beckoning Kate forward and into the footlights. Then he hurriedly left the stage.

Backstage, Howard was furious for being upstaged by "this little Bryn Mawr schoolgirl." He told Miller that he was going to demand Barry rewrite the play, removing some of Kate's best lines and shortening her part. "In the new version, Leslie Howard will be the star, not Miss Katharine Hepburn."

Not fully aware of what was going on, Kate was driven back to her hotel by a character actor, Walter Abel.

When she got to her hotel, she was handed a telegram from Miller. "You are hereby given notice of the termination of your contract thereof."

In her hotel room, she broke down in Laura's arms and sobbed hysterically. "I'm only twenty-one and finished in the theater. It's been nothing but backstage dismissals. I'm giving up the theater and going into medicine—maybe law. My parents will be proud to know that finally I've decided to do something worthwhile with my life."

***

Although she'd seemed firm and determined in her decision to leave the theater, the next morning Kate wavered. She demanded that Laura drive her to Mount Kisco, New York, to confront the playwright, Barry.

Once at his home, she barged right into his bathroom. "I'm fired!" she shouted at him. "And you wrote the play for me. *Me. Me. Me.* Do you understand that?"

Startled, Barry sat up in the tub. "I understand it perfectly."

"Then what are you going to do about it? Howard will ruin your play. Is that what you want? They're gypping me, and gypping you, too."

Standing up in the tub stark naked, Barry confronted her. "Yes, I wrote it for you but you proved inadequate for the part. You're ruining the play. You refuse to take direction. You rewrite my lines. You've got an absolutely vicious disposition. You have no feel for light comedy. You were completely miscast, and I was totally wrong about you. I'll never work in the theater with you again."

Kate tossed him a bath towel before dashing in tears from his house, with Laura trailing her. Barry later told Howard that Kate had "sounded like a ranting fishwife, and just as vulgar."

In years to come, when Barry came to Kate with his script of *The Philadelphia Story*, he begged her to forgive him for his insensitive remarks in that Mount Kisco bathtub.

When Kate returned to New York, a call came in from producer Bill Brady, Jr. He was the best friend of young actor Humphrey Bogart. That long ago night when Kate had stormed into Tony's speakeasy, she'd seen Brady Jr. talking with Bogart and Kenneth MacKenna but had not gone over to say hello.

Brady Jr. had remembered Kate's striking entrance into the speakeasy, and he had a small part to offer her in his upcoming play, *Alice Sit-by-the-Fire*. It was going to star Laurette Taylor, one of the great actresses of the American theater. "The money doesn't matter," Kate said. "I accept."

Kate had seen Laurette on stage in *The Furies* in 1928 and was amazed at her vitality. Even though Kate had heard that Laurette had become a "confirmed alcoholic," she was still eager to appear with her. Laurette, in time, would appear as the lead in *The Glass Menagerie* by Tennessee Williams, delivering a magnificent performance, although in rehearsals, the playwright found her Southern accent was so broad as to evoke "Aunt Jemima's Pancake Hour." Surprisingly, Kate herself would star in the ABC 1973 telecast of *The Glass Menagerie,* playing the role of Amanda Wingfield herself. For many years, Kate had refused the role, claiming that Laurette had "immortalized it."

Amazingly, when actors all over Broadway were out of work, and waiting in bread lines, yet another call came in for Kate, in spite of her reputation for being fired all the time.

Luddy answered the phone and found Harry Moses, the Broadway producer, on the other end of the line. Laura and Kate were sitting on the sofa in the small apartment, listening to classical music, while Jack was in the kitchen "making one of my famous spaghetti dinners."

Picking up the phone, Kate was stunned to learn that he wanted her to co-star in the Julian Thompson play, *The Warrior's Husband*. Without asking the terms, Kate accepted the role. "You've found your warrior! I was made to play Antiope."

The next morning, she learned from Burk Symon, who was staging the play, that Moses had originally wanted Hope Williams to play Antiope. Williams had turned it down. Actually, Williams had originated the role of Antiope when it had opened at The Comedy Club, an amateur group that existed at the time on Thirty-Sixth Street. She'd been shocked to learn that Barry had written *The Animal Kingdom* for Kate and not for her. "After all," Williams later told Barry, "Hepburn was a mere understudy in your *Holiday.* I was the star."

Williams did not want to open with Kate in a competing Broadway comedy, and cited that as her reason for turning down *The Warrior's Husband.* When she rejected the role, Williams was unaware that Kate had already been fired from the part until she read in the papers that the greatly diminished role, following Barry's rewrites, had been given to Frances Fuller.

When *The Animal Kingdom* opened on Broadway, it was an instant success for Howard, who later made a film of the play, with co-stars Ann Harding, Ilka Chase, and movie vamp Myrna Loy.

After only the third day of rehearsals of *The Warrior's Husband*, Kate announced to Luddy, Laura, and Jack. "At last I've found the part to make me a star. I was destined to play the Amazon warrior."

This time Kate's prediction was right.

CHAPTER FOUR

On March 11, 1932, Depression-era audiences, at least those who could afford a ticket, flocked to *The Warrior's Husband* at New York's Morosco Theatre, unaware that a legend in the theater was about to be made that night.

Backstage, Kate, more nervous than ever, threw up twice in her dressing room. The producer, Harry Moses, had hired her, then had dismissed her in favor of a more established actress, Jean Dixon, and then had rehired her again.

The play by Julian Thompson was a Greek fable, loosely based on Aristophanes' *Lysistrata*. It told of a love story between Antiope, as portrayed by Kate, and Theseus, as depicted by Colin Keith-Johnston, a British actor known mainly for playing characters created by Shakespeare. On meeting Kate, the actor enigmatically said, "I'm better than Gielgud, but perhaps not, and definitely better than Larry Olivier, but perhaps not."

In her dressing room, when Kate had recovered from her stomach upset, she prepared her costume with the help of an overweight , black maid, Lily Beavers. Kate was drawing a salary of one-hundred fifty dollars a week, Lily seventy-five.

Facing a large jar of greasepaint, Kate readied for her role, bronzing her lean arms, legs and face. With makeup applied, Kate the warrior put on a chain mail tunic with silver leather shin guards. Spiral cones covered each breast, evoking Madonna in years to come. Beneath her tunic, she wore a green bathing suit that showcased her legs. "When word gets out about my leg show, I'll be outdrawing the burlesque houses," Kate told Lily. Lily applied the final touch to the "red mop" by curling Kate's hair out from beneath her silver helmet.

The curtain had not been up for more than ten minutes before Kate made the year's most spectacular theatrical entrance. With a "stag" (actually a stuffed deer) flung over her shoulder, and with her cape flying, Kate bounded down a treacherous forty-step stair with no railing three steps at a time. "For fame, I'd risk my life," she later told Luddy. Leaping an astonishing five feet from the stairs, Kate landed on the stage and bowed before her sister in the play, Hippolyta, queen of the Amazons, as portrayed by Irby Marshal. Throwing the carcass at the foot of the Amazon queen, Kate turned to one of the queen's attendants. "Get me a bowl of water," she commanded. "I'm in a terrific sweat." The audience went wild, bursting into thunderous applause.

Later that night, Kate tossed her leading man, Keith-Johnston, over her shoulder and at one point wrestled him to the stage.

Stage manager Phyllis Seaton years later recalled the memorable night. "Kate literally jumped at the audience, with her red hair setting off her face like a flame. Terrific grace. Transparent skin that glowed. Never before or since did her beauty shine through like it did that night."

***

The play got mixed notices, but Kate's performance was met with raves. Overnight she'd become the toast of Broadway. Richard Garland, writing in *The New York World-Telegram,* said, "It's been many a night since so glowing a performance has brightened the Broadway scene."

Later, the name of that critic was to become immortalized when a child singer named Frances Gumm, while performing at the Chicago World's Fair, renamed herself Judy Garland, and went on to become one of Kate's most intimate friends.

The review Kate liked most was Arthur Ruhl writing in *The New York Herald Tribune*. Ruhl found Kate "a somewhat tougher and more dynamic version of Maude Adams' *Peter Pan.*" As a young girl, Maude Adams had been the actress that Kate most admired on stage.

From the beginning of her early fame, Kate refused to talk to reporters or to be interviewed. Laura Harding's task each night was to fend off reporters, so that she and Kate could escape to the safety and security of Laura's long black limousine, driven by her beloved chauffeur, "Sailor."

The Warrior's Husband was to run for eighty-three performances. Facing dwindling audiences, Harry Moses demanded that the cast take a pay cut. To stay in the role, Kate was forced to agree. Her paycheck was now seventy-five dollars a week. Lily refused to take a cut. Kate told Laura, "Both my maid and I are now drawing the same salary."

Pay cut or not, Kate felt buoyed by her success and rented a townhouse at 244 East Forty-Ninth Street, between Second and Third Avenues, in Turtle Bay Gardens, for one-hundred dollars a month. Laura decorated the house, creating cozy basement rooms as a love nest for Jack and Luddy, who came and went through a private entrance.

Among the cast, Kate befriended Alan Campbell, who played the small part of Achilles in *The Warrior's Husband*. She felt that Alan "has a letch for me," as she told Lily. Kate invited him to her townhouse for an intimate dinner with Luddy, Jack, and Laura.

Once Alan met Luddy, the actor "fell under some sort of spell," as Kate told Laura. Ignoring everybody else at the dinner, Alan listened to everything Luddy had to say. "That's brilliant!" Alan would proclaim even if Luddy were asking for another hunk of French bread.

Since Luddy had found his most attentive audience, he didn't want the evening to end, even when Laura and Kate excused themselves to go to bed. In a jealous rage, Jack remained on the sofa, sitting stone-faced and refusing to budge until Alan had left the house.

The next day, Jack blamed Kate for inviting "that whorish little Jezebel" for dinner.

In time, Alan Campbell would marry Kate's nemesis, the critic and writer, Dorothy Parker.

***

As Laura accurately predicted to Kate, agents from Hollywood would be swarming to see her startling performance in *The Warrior's Husband.* Up to now, Kate had made her own deals with producers and directors, but Laura convinced her that she needed an agent "to handle all the sharpies rolling in from the West Coast."

"Hell, those bastards on the coast used to hold down jobs like selling worthless junk in Brooklyn before they started dictating American film tastes," Laura said. "Without an agent, they'll rob you blind."

As the movies learned to talk, many Hollywood agents and talent scouts were indeed seen along Broadway, signing up acting talent.

Laura claimed that she did know one of the best agents in the business—"just right for you. None other than Leland Hayward." Kate knew the name. By a coincidence, her mother's dearest friend, Mary Towle, had worked for Leland's father, Colonel William Hayward, in the U.S. attorney's office. Mary, of course, was Kate's beloved "Aunty," in whose Greenwich Village townhouse her brother Tom had committed suicide. From Laura, Kate wanted to know all about this strange man to whom she might be turning over the direction of her career.

Like Laura, Leland had been born to a life of privilege in a stone-built townhouse along Fifth Avenue not far from the Harding mansion. He'd flunked out of Princeton, and various reasons had circulated, focusing primarily on his involvement in some sort of sex scandal.

Laura had met him at various debutante parties on Park Avenue. "He was always standing at the head of the stag line, casing the joint and looking around for his sexual conquest of the evening, most often a virgin." She recalled what a fabulous dancer he was, spinning her around the ballroom of the Plaza Hotel at tea dances in the Twenties.

He was like an enameled character emerging alive from a cartoon by John Held, Jr., an artist whose drawings of Betty Co-ed and Joe College defined the age of the flapper. Laura claimed that Leland appeared to have been created by F. Scott Fitzgerald, and she suspected that Leland had read *The Great Gatsby* "more than five times." She said that he had black sealskin hair slicked down, and that he was ruggedly handsome.

Finally, Laura said she'd dated Leland for a while, and that he'd been the first man to "deflower" her in the way Kenneth MacKenna had done the honors with Kate. Laura didn't remember the seduction happily—"perhaps that's why I turned to women." Nonetheless, she assured Kate what a smooth operator Leland was. "Even the bisexual Greta Garbo has succumbed to his charms, or so I hear." Greta indeed had been added to what Leland called his "scalp bracelet," a reference to all the women he'd seduced.

Before calling Leland and going over to his office, Kate dialed Kenneth "for a second opinion," reporting everything Laura had said. Kenneth was enthusiastic about her signing with Leland, claiming he was the best agent in the business. Not only that, Leland was the partner of Myron Selznick, brother of the producer David O. Selznick.

"Watch out for Leland," Kenneth warned. "He seduces every beautiful women who comes into his office. I'd go for him myself but he's strictly a ladies' man."

***

Ushered into his office, and escorted by Laura, Kate was startled to see Leland lying under a sun lamp on top of a twenty-five foot office desk that she was to learn later had once belonged to a monastery outside Naples, Italy. He was clad in a pair of pale blue boxer shorts. Up to then, Kate thought all men wore white underwear. Like the future actor George Hamilton, Leland believed in appearing "bronzed" at all times, looking as if he'd just returned from a Caribbean cruise.

When Kate met him, he was already thirty years old. Even though he shunned sports and exercise, he had a well-toned physique. As Leland bragged to his male friends, "I get all the exercise I need in the bed of some hot woman every night."

Without getting up from his desk, Leland shook Kate's hand and asked Laura to give him a "lip lock for old times sake," which she did. Kate always remembered his china-blue eyes which seemed to be "pleading" to get what he wanted. Like a swimmer, he wore his hair closely cropped. Someone in the press had compared his hair to "the texture of a duck's down," and that phrase was eventually adopted as part of Leland's description in the media.

When he got up to put on his clothes, Kate saw his transformation from nude to one of the fanciest dressers along Broadway. His bespoke tailored suit from London fitted his body perfectly. Long before Elvis Presley popularized the pink shirt, Leland wore custom-made shirts in that color. In those days, men caught wearing pink shirts were routinely beaten up.

In front of them, Leland put on large diamond cufflinks, the diamonds also being pink. Decades before the world heard of Imelda Marcos, Leland put on a pair of beautiful green alligator shoes. "I own three-hundred and fifty pair," he told the women, "most of them made of skins from rare species like snakes known only to live in the Amazon."

Putting a bright Chinese red silk handkerchief in his lapel, he told Kate he owned more than five-hundred handkerchiefs for his breast pocket. "No white for me. I like such colors as peacock blue, emerald green, and flaming magenta—stuff like that."

Kate assured him that she liked his adventurous spirit in wearing color. "More men should follow your example."

Finally, he took in her own wardrobe. She'd worn her baggy trousers and a moth-eaten sweater. Leland had far too much breeding to comment on Kate's dress, but he was known to like his women immaculately groomed, like the screen actress Irene Dunne.

Even though Kate one day would fall madly in love with Leland, there was absolutely no spark between them at the time of their inaugural meeting, as Laura would later tell Kenneth. Besides, Leland had heard all the gossip about Kate and Laura. From his past involvement with her, he already knew that Laura was "a card-carrying lez," as he put it.

Leland told Kate that he'd begun his career by working in the publicity department of United Artists, later quitting to go over to First National, where he labored briefly in the story department. Not liking either job, he decided to become a "free-floating agent" searching for new talent to sign up. He claimed that he'd seen Kate in *The Warrior's Husband* and wanted to sign on as her agent.

"The stage is too small for you," Leland told her. "Your beauty should be captured on film."

"What about my acting talent?" Kate asked.

"That too," Leland said. He promised to talk to agents currently in New York visiting from Paramount Studios in Los Angeles. In fact, he said he'd taken the liberty of sending two agents last night to see *The Warrior's Husband.*

Right in front of Kate and Laura, Leland called one of the Paramount representatives, who had been impressed with Kate's performance and was willing to sign her to a five-year contract at one-hundred and fifty dollars a week.

"Forget it!" Kate shouted loud up enough for the agent to hear. "If that's all Hollywood has to offer Katharine Hepburn, I'll stay on the stage."

Embarrassed, Leland hung up the phone. "How much salary do you want?"

"Fifteen hundred big ones a week," Kate said. "No more, no less."

"But no untried actress gets that," Leland protested.

Kate rose to her feet and motioned for Laura to do likewise.

"I'm not really interested in films. I hear it's one minute of acting followed by two or three hours of setting up the next shot. You heard what I want. You get that for me or else there's no deal between you and me, and certainly no deal between Hollywood and me." Motioning for Laura to follow, Kate stormed out of the office.

Far from falling in love with Leland that day, Kate told Laura, and later Kenneth and Luddy, that she found the agent "hideously horrible and awesomely awful." Even though she would eventually sign with him, she claimed that Leland Hayward was the type of man she despised—"all money talk, no soul, no artistry in him."

Amazingly, instead of immediately dropping Kate because of her arrogance, Leland called her two days later, telling her that RKO had agreed to a screen test, which, if the studio liked it, would lead to salary negotiations. Kate agreed but shrewdly said she would test only if she could select the material of her choice. Leland said he thought that might be all right and would get back to her.

Kate did not tell Leland that she had made a previous and "secret" screen test for the director, John Ford, who was interested in making a film of *The Warrior's Husband* but later changed his mind. On meeting Kate for the first time, Ford found her "disappointing—not my kind of gal at all." He would later change his mind again when she became, perhaps, the most important love of his life. His professional evaluation of Kate was even worse, as he pronounced her "devastatingly bad."

Ford eventually signed up two stage actors, Spencer Tracy and Humphrey Bogart, to co-star in *Up The River.*

Fox did film *The Warrior's Husband,* casting Elissa Landi, a contract player in Kate's part. Far from being jealous of Landi, Kate wrote her a fan letter, expressing a desire to meet her one day.

***

A talent scout for RKO, Lillie Messenger, agreed to direct Kate's screen test. Kate demanded that she be allowed to perform a scene from *Holiday*, a script she knew letter perfect from having watched Hope Williams perform it nightly month after month. Messenger agreed and also allowed Kate to bring along her fellow cast member, Alan Campbell, who had become Luddy's new and secret lover.

Kate insisted that Alan's face was not to be photographed. "I've seen too many young actresses make screen tests with juveniles, only to have the boy hired and the girl ignored," she told a startled Messenger.

Over Leland's objection, Kate even demanded that for most of the test, her back would be turned to the camera. "RKO wants to see your face, not your God damn ass," Leland shouted at her. Ultimately Kate prevailed. She would not see her screen test until 1938 when she was making a film of the play, *Holiday,* co-starring Cary Grant. Grant and the rest of the crew laughed at it, but Kate was touched by her own performance. "I was horrible and looked it, but there was also something very touching about my playing of the character, Linda Seton. I was trying so desperately to be liked—so eager, so very eager. Too eager, actually."

Through his partner, Myron Selznick, Leland knew that director George Cukor and Myron's brother, David O. Selznick, were desperately searching for an actress to play the choice role of Sydney Fairchild in the film *Bill of Divorcement.* In 1931, Katharine Cornell had achieved fame on the Broadway stage in that very play.

***

Kate rushed home that night to tell her friends of the screen test. Both Jack and Laura had family plans for the evening. While she went to take a bath, she ordered Luddy to build a fire.

While in her bath, she heard Luddy frantically shouting her name. Racing wet and stark naked into the living room, she screamed when she saw him on fire. To get the fire going, he'd poured kerosene on it, and the flames had exploded, shooting out and setting his clothes on fire. She knocked him down and grabbed a throw rug, wrapping his body in it and smothering the flames.

Then she raced into the street and frantically called for help. Various men from the street poured in, mainly curiosity seekers, and they mulled about waiting for the fire department to arrive. It was only when the firemen rushed in that Kate realized she was "stark naked." She retreated to her bedroom to dress.

An ambulance took Luddy to the hospital where doctors pronounced that he had third degree burns, but nothing life-threatening.

The next day after Kate and Jack visited the suffering Luddy, she learned that Alan Campbell was slipping in for secret calls on his new lover.

In Hollywood, David O. Selznick went into a raging fit when he viewed Kate's screen test. "God damn it," he said, "that's the worst fucking scarecrow I've ever seen. Cast her in *The Witch of Endor.* She looks like a cross between a horse and a monkey."

Cukor thought Kate looked like a gargoyle—"her hair all spiked back. She seemed to bark through her nose, very nasal, and she was more mannish and mannered than Hope Williams herself." Yet maybe Kate had known what she was doing when she'd turned her back to the camera. Cukor was very impressed with a scene, shot from the rear, when she picked up a champagne glass from the floor. "It was a sad and lyric moment," he would later say. "Enigmatic yet in some way emblematic."

He wavered back and forth, being both intrigued by Kate and put off by her "jerky" movements. He told Selznick, "With these newcomers like Hepburn you go for the glints and grab the pot of gold later." "Bullshit!" Selznick had said.

When he'd gone. Cukor jotted down some opinions of Kate. "Leggy, certainly. Definitely toothy. A New England blueblood. Heiress, I hear. Very definitely a patrician WASP. An intellectual. By all means a snob. Broad Bryn Mawr vowels. Headstrong. Opinionated, I'm certain. Flashy. Strangely masculine. No doubt a lesbian!"

Irene Mayer Selznick urged her husband to sign Kate, as did Cukor when he learned that he would have use of the co-star, John Barrymore, only for a short time. "Shooting has to begin at once," Cukor told Selznick.

Kate's stock rose later that day when both Irene Dunne and Norma Shearer, after having originally expressed interest in the role, bowed out, having found "less risky" roles to play, Actress Jill Esmond also expressed interest until her husband, Laurence Olivier, persuaded her to withdraw.

Cukor told Selznick that Carole Lombard wanted the part but made an awful screen test. Desperate to fill the role, and with his wife, Irene, and Cukor urging him to take a chance on an untried actress, Selznick shouted, "Get Hepburn!"

***

Leland called Kate with glee telling her that RKO wanted her for the part, but at only five-hundred dollars a week. To his amazement, she was adamant, refusing the offer. Reluctantly, he had Myron approach his brother who finally agreed to seven hundred and fifty a week. Once again, Kate turned it down.

Although Leland thought David couldn't be pushed any more, the two men negotiated back and forth in increments of two-hundred and fifty dollars. Finally Leland came up with a compromise. Kate would throw in a week's free rehearsal and would take the part for four weeks for six-thousand dollars. David Selznick agreed to that after cursing Leland, and claiming that he hoped all his children would be born deformed.

When told that David had caved in, Kate said, "The fool must be totally insane to agree to so much money. Hollywood must be full of asses."

After Kate signed on, Cukor still had his reservations. "I think this Katharine Hepburn's going to be one bitch to work with," he predicted. "But she hasn't met a bitch until she's met George Cukor. I can outbitch any actress in Hollywood."

Still plagued with doubts about his new star, David called Leland again. "Tell Hepburn not to give up her living quarters in New York. I think her stay in Hollywood will be short. She'll soon be back on Broadway pounding the pavement and looking for work."

Although Cukor and Selznick were anxious to begin shooting at once, Kate had one final demand, which they reluctantly agreed to, even though it enraged both producer and director.

Before heading for the coast, Kate went with Laura to fulfill a previous stage commitment. Kate played Psyche Marbury in Will Cotton's *The Bride the Sun Shines On*, appearing in the stock company at Ossining, New York. Dorothy Gish had scored a hit with the play on Broadway. Her co-star was once again Henry Hull, who continued to claim erroneously that "my love-making drives her wild. Single-handedly I've converted her to men."

***

Before leaving for Hollywood, Kate was approached by backers who offered her five-hundred dollars for a supporting role in a single performance of *Electra*. It would be staged in Philadelphia, and it would star Blanche Yurka in the title role. Kate was to represent an entire Greek chorus, the actress Katherine Alexander would play the collective role of a second Greek chorus. Leopold Stokowski would conduct the music, and the venue would be the Philadelphia Academy of Music.

Lily, Kate's expensive black maid, insisted on going along for fifty dollars, and Kate agreed, although having no need for her services. "It was hard to deny Lily anything," Kate would say years later. "She was far more formidable that Hattie McDaniel in years to come scolding Scarlett in *Gone With the Wind.*"

Kate had only a speaking acquaintance with Katherine Alexander. She was the wife of Bill Brady, Jr., and Kate immediately told Alexander about turning down her husband's offer for her to co-star opposite Laurette Taylor.

On the train to Philadelphia, a distraught Alexander broke down and told Kate how unhappy she was in her marriage. She claimed that Bill was the ring-leader of the so-called "pussy posse" that prowled the speakeasies looking for beautiful women every night. Some of the other members, she said, were Humphrey Bogart and the "notorious" Kenneth MacKenna. Alexander confid-ed to Kate that "MacKenna might be bisexual."

Alexander went on to say that she feared that she had married a bisexual, claiming she'd caught her husband, Brady Jr., masturbating to some nude male sketches. "I can't handle it and I might leave him."

Kate assured her that being in the theater "one must be sophisticated about such matters." She informed Alexander that her own husband was a bisexual, and currently carrying on affairs with two men in New York. She didn't name Alan Campbell or Jack Clarke, though.

When they got to Philadelphia, Kate invited Alexander to share her room at the Bellevue-Stratford. Alexander agreed but before going to bed the first night, she went to the academy and demanded her five-hundred dollars in advance and got it. Kate "didn't smell a rat" like Alexander did, and was never paid by the producers for her one-night stand.

Later that night something happened in the bedroom of the Bellevue-

Stratford that Kate shared with Alexander. No one knows exactly what, but Alexander called the desk around two o'clock that morning and demanded to be transferred to another bedroom, leaving Kate alone.

When Alexander returned to New York, she told Bill Brady, Jr., her husband, that "Kate must have mistaken me for a bisexual like herself because she made a crude proposition to me." Brady Jr. then told Bogart and Kenneth MacKenna. Kenneth knew all about Kate's sexual life, but this was the first time Bogart was told that Kate was a lesbian or at least a bisexual.

Later when making *Up The River* in Hollywood, Bogart befriended Spencer Tracy, learning that he too was a bisexual and involved in an affair with the handsome young actor, Lew Ayres, a star in *All Quiet On The Western Front.* Bogart learned that Spencer was also carrying on with "half the women in Hollywood" as well as one of Garbo's leading men, Johnny Mack Brown.

At some point Bogart told Spencer about Kate's attempted seduction of his best friend's wife. As Bogart told Kenneth, "Tracy shrugged it off and didn't seem the least bit surprised. "We who live in glass houses can't throw stones," Tracy is alleged to have told Bogart.

***

After agreeing to go on to Hollywood, Kate cooked a dinner for Luddy, Jack, and Laura at her rented townhouse. Throughout the evening, she sat quietly listening to her friends make plans to uproot their lives and go to California with her. Even Jack was willing to abandon his job, and Luddy expected to set up a stockbroker office in Los Angeles.

At the end of the meal, Kate rose from her chair. "Luddy, would you and Jack be a dear and stay here and look after things for me in New York? I'll need only Laura to go with me to Hollywood." After saying that, she turned and without another word headed for her bedroom.

It was a hot, sweltering morning on July 1, 1932 at Grand Central. The cuckolded Jack stood loyally by Luddy on the platform, watching Laura's massive amount of luggage loaded aboard the Twentieth Century for Chicago. Kate's more modest luggage was also loaded onto the train.

Kate kissed first Jack good-bye and then turned to Luddy to kiss him. He was crying. "You're a dear to understand," she said.

As Laura remembered it, "Poor Luddy. I really felt sorry for him. With Kate gone, he could no longer even pretend to have a marriage. It was all too obvious. Kate the actress came first, then me, then her family, then Luddy."

***

As Kate settled with Laura into their private compartment, Kate held a copy of the latest issue of *Vanity Fair.* She'd made the cover. "We're embarking on a grand adventure, and if we hate the place we can always come back East in a few weeks," Kate told Laura.

Accompanying all the Hepburn/Harding Louis Vuitton luggage were two dogs. Kate's favorite was Twig, a Shelbourne terrier. A Scottie, Jamie, growled at Kate a lot, especially when she got near the dog's mistress.

As the two young women made their way to Chicago, they were leaving breadlines and soup kitchens in Depression-laden New York. An estimated fifteen million Americans were out of work. Another thirty million survived by drawing out the last of their savings, selling real estate (if the banks had not already foreclosed), and living off richer relatives or on the public dole and private charities.

It was not the ideal time to launch a film career, although Laura paid most of the bills with her inherited millions, which she'd received when the average American family would be in tears of gratitude if you handed them a five-dollar bill.

"It was on the train that I really got to know Laura," Kate wrote to Luddy. "Before we'd been running around crazily and hadn't really gotten deeply acquainted. Before reaching Chicago, we talked about our desires, our needs, our fantasies. I know that before we reach California, Laura and I will be bonded for life."

Kenneth had gone to Hollywood on an earlier train. When Luddy wrote him, the erstwhile husband lamented, "I'm afraid I've lost Kate forever. She'll probably ask me for a divorce. At least Jack is happy. He fears I was living in Kate's shadow."

***

Before the train reached Chicago, Kate learned that Billie Burke was on the same train. Burke had signed to appear as Kate's mother, Margaret Fairfield, playing the uncaring, estranged wife of John Barrymore in *A Bill of Divorcement.* Kate was eager to meet her.

Burke at the time was traveling west with a gravely ill Florenz Ziegfeld, the great impresario, who was soon to die. Their daughter, Pat, was also aboard. The Ziegfelds traveled in style in their own rail car complete with a drawing room decorated with *objets d'art.*

Burke is remembered today for her immortal role as Good Witch Glinda in *The Wizard of Oz* and for her portrayal of "bird-witted excitable eccentrics" in numerous films including *Dinner at Eight.* Born in Washington, DC, in 1885, she'd married Ziegfeld in 1914.

When Kate met her passing through a rail car, Burke was still an attractive, though aging, blonde. She was not the jabbering, fluttery lady she usually portrayed on the screen, but a poised, cultured, and highly intelligent woman. Burke invited both Kate and Laura to dine with her that night, making excuses for Ziegfeld because of his bad health.

During dinner Burke devoted all her attention to Kate, virtually ignoring Laura who took an instant dislike to the older actress. The following night Burke invited Kate—"just you, my dear"—to a private compartment she'd also rented. She confessed that she had to escape both her daughter and her dying husband in their private rail car—"or else I'll lose my mind. I can't stand it."

The two actresses sat drinking and dining in the small compartment, as Burke amused and entertained Kate with stories of the theater and all the "greats" in show business she'd known. Several times Kate got up to leave but Burke insisted that she remain a little longer.

Kate confided some of her ambitions to Burke, who from time to time placed a possessive arm around her, the way a mother might do with her daughter.

"I'm not going to Hollywood to kick around in B-movie roles," Kate said. "I'm an A-list talent planning only to make A-list movies. I might become as famous as Leatrice Joy. Of all the women in silent pictures, I most want to be like her." Kate's opinion of which movie goddess she wanted to emulate changed from week to week.

Kate flattered Burke by telling her that she looked far too young to play the role of her mother. "Does that mean you find me attractive?" Burke asked. "A very handsome woman indeed," Kate replied out of respect for the aging actress.

When Kate finally insisted that she must leave, Burke rose to kiss her goodbye. Expecting a light peck on the cheek, Kate was astonished when Burke planted several light, feathery kisses on her face, before lip-locking with her, her tongue darting out. Gently Kate escaped from her clutches, making hurried excuses that she really had to go.

Although it would become Hollywood's worst kept secret, it was not generally known at the time that Burke was a closeted lesbian. Kate carried the news back to the compartment she shared with Laura.

Unable to contain herself the next day, Laura wrote the news to Jack and Luddy, who in turn confided Burke's secret to Kenneth MacKenna, who told it to "God only knows who."

Long before *A Bill of Divorcement* was in the can, George Cukor, Burke's director, heard the news, taking delight in such a tidbit of gossip. "Sometimes hearing such scandal is better than having sex."

In Chicago Laura and Kate enjoyed a brief stopover before they changed to the Super Chief heading across country to Los Angeles. A photographer, alerted that "the new young Hollywood star" was in town, snapped a picture of Kate and Laura having afternoon tea and a slice of chocolate cake at the Blackstone Hotel. Kate chased after him to grab his camera, but the fleet-footed photographer eluded her. This marked the beginning of her sometimes violent confrontations with what for her was "the dreaded press."

As the Super Chief rolled across America's bread basket, Kate and Laura had to keep removing clothing. The nation was experiencing one of its worst heat waves, and there was no air conditioning in those days.

As the train zoomed across the American prairie, Kate after dinner pointed out what she called a "coyote moon" to Laura. "Don't look at the moon!" Laura shouted. "Bad luck comes to a person who gazes up at a new moon through window glass." That was one superstition that Kate had never heard before.

To view the moon that Kate was eager to enjoy, Laura invited her to the observation platform at the back of the fast-moving train. As the two young women were "gazing up at the moon like a hound dog," as Laura put it, a small, fast-moving object flew into Kate's left eye, stinging her retina. Kate frantically rubbed it. "Whatever it is you've got trapped there, you're only digging it in deeper," Laura cautioned her.

As it turned out, tiny steel-filing fragments floating through the air had lodged in her left eye, as if finding a permanent home there.

Back in the compartment, Kate stubbornly continued to rub and wash her eye, even though Laura cautioned her that only a doctor could remove "the invader." By morning, Kate was in great pain and her left eye had completely swollen shut. In sympathy, her right eye had turned a ghastly pink, the lid closing half way over her eyeball so she could hardly see.

When the train pulled into Albuquerque, New Mexico, Laura urged Kate to postpone their trip and to check into a hotel where she would summon a doctor to remove the foreign matter from Kate's eye. Still acting stubborn, Kate adamantly refused, claiming she would seek immediate medical attention in Los Angeles.

Still in Albuquerque, Laura and Kate were approached by an Indian who was hawking handmade souvenirs. At a tap on her shoulder, Kate turned from the Indian to confront what she later described as "a little man with the face of a fox." He introduced himself as Adolph Zukor, the chief of Paramount Studios. Kate appeared awed to be meeting one of the legendary founders of motion pictures, and was startled that he'd recognized her, a virtual unknown.

Kate told him she was taking the train to Hollywood to appear in *A Bill of Divorcement.* "You might be working for Paramount had I not turned you down," Zukor said. "I saw the test you made for *The Warrior's Husband* and decided you're not Paramount material. You're a stage actress, not a film actress, and I'm never wrong about these things. I've made more stars than any man in Hollywood. I thought you looked pretty nightmarish in the screen test. Seeing you up close and in person, I realize what a fright you really are. If we ever make *The Bride of Frankenstein*, I'll call you." With that statement, he turned and walked away to reboard the train.

As the train left New Mexico and headed for the California border, Kate's already teary eyes were made wetter and redder as she cried at Zukor's cruelty.

The train moved west as the weather got hotter when they approached the desert. Two East Coast women like Kate and Laura had never experienced such heat before, and they removed more and more clothing. Laura bribed the porter to keep bringing them a constant supply of Pullman towels soaked in ice water.

Once they crossed the California border, Kate told Laura that she'd felt she'd made a dreadful mistake in coming to California. "I will never fit in, never belong here. Besides, in their photographs, they try to make every actress who comes here look like Greta Garbo. Look at me! No one would ever mistake me for Greta Garbo. Only an idiot would attempt to photograph me to look like Garbo."

In a sardonic note, Kate, months later, would find herself in the RKO studio with a makeup woman who'd fashioned her face to look "exactly like Garbo's." In fact, some members of the press were then hailing Kate as "the new Garbo."

Leland Hayward had arranged for Kate to get off at the station in Pasadena to avoid photographers who hungrily awaited every train pulling into the center of Los Angeles. He was to be accompanied by Myron Selznick, his partner as a talent agent. Myron, of course, was the brother of David O. Selznick, who was producing *A Bill of Divorcement.*

In another one of the many apocryphal stories spread about Kate, Myron, or so it is said, exclaimed to Leland, "My God, we're sticking David *with that* for fifteen hundred dollars a week."

On seeing Kate for the first time, and not being aware of her infirmity, Myron was shocked at her "ghastly appearance."

Myron would later deny he had ever said that, "although it makes a good line." He did remember that Kate got off the train looking like a fright—"something was seriously wrong with her eyes. Her hair was pulled back in a tight knot *à la concierge*," Myron later said. "And she was wearing this strange clothing. Since I'd never met her before, I at first thought Kate was the maid and Laura the star. Laura was expensively attired in the latest Chanel from Paris, and looked gorgeous."

Kate had meant to look gorgeous and had shelled out three-hundred and fifty dollars for a new outfit, which she had purchased from a famous designer of the time, Elizabeth Hawes, who called herself "the Panther Woman of the Needle Trades." She claimed that she wanted her female customers "to look like she-wolves."

Kate wore a long navy blue skirt topped with a richly ornamented riding jacket in the style of the 19th century, something a well-bred British girl might wear on a fox hunt with The Queen. Topping her head was a blue straw "pancake hat," which Kate later likened to a beanbag when she viewed a picture snapped of her at the time. Kate also wore a dove-gray turtleneck with a ruffle at the top.

A battleship gray Rolls-Royce waited to take them and all their luggage to the dowdy Château Elysée Hotel and then to RKO. Kate demanded to see a doctor at once, but Leland told her that would have to wait because George Cukor and others had reserved time to meet with her at once.

Myron was to remember that day for the rest of his life. Everything Kate saw in California, she hated. On the way to the hotel, Myron pointed out a golf course. In trying to make conversation, he said that he heard that Kate was an avid golfer. "That course is brown—needs water," Kate said rather belligerently. "Back East, our grass is green."

"She appeared overly confident," Myron would later say. "I suspected it was but a cover-up and that deep down she was very insecure and very young. But there was a Yankee independence there, and I dreaded having to work with her, but Leland had convinced me. What I especially disliked was an air of self-righteousness about her. That alienated me. Her remarks were bitter and caustic. Not only did she look like shit, she held all of us, even Leland, in obvious contempt. It was as if she were doing us a big favor to have come to the West Coast and star in RKO's movie."

"While the girls were having their massive amounts of luggage dumped at the Château Elysée, I told Leland that I thought our new client would be a one-picture star," Myron said. "I was convinced that RKO would never pick up its option on her contract. How wrong I was! In no time at all, she was winning an Oscar and was being hailed as the new queen of RKO. Leland made me eat my words."

Even as time went by, Myron never got over his initial resentment of Kate. "I could be difficult when I wanted to be," Myron said. "But not as difficult as Kate Hepburn, though. Later, in the 1930s, I knew that she desperately wanted the role of Scarlett O'Hara in David's film. I was determined to see that she didn't get it. Call it payback time for the contempt she'd shown for me. When David was filming the burning of Atlanta scene in *Gone With The Wind,* and still had no female star, I was the guy who introduced Vivien Leigh to him. 'Brother dear,' I said, 'meet Miss Scarlett O'Hara.' Out with Kate and in with Vivien. Katharine Hepburn with her Bryn Mawr manners would have ruined *Gone With The Wind.* So would George Cukor if David hadn't fired him as director. Originally, Margaret Mitchell had wanted to call her lead character Pansy instead of Scarlett. Had Kate gotten the part, and Cukor been retained as director, David could have called the film, *Pansies.*"

***

Still complaining that she needed a doctor more than a visit to RKO, Kate nonetheless, and despite her protests, was delivered to the film studio. Laura accompanied her.

When not bedding Constance Bennett, Gloria Swanson, or Nancy Carroll, Joseph Kennedy had urged that RCA form RKO. Through its talkie patents, RCA hoped to monopolize the field of motion pictures. In that it didn't succeed, but it did learn to compete seriously with Paramount, Fox, Warners, and MGM. Two men helped RKO on its way to the top. One was the "boy wonder," David O. Selznick, and the other was his assistant, Pandro S. Berman. Both were monumental figures in the career of Katharine Hepburn.

David had been brought in to launch RKO into the big time, and he'd been given a stable of stars that included Ann Harding, Irene Dunne, Constance Bennett, and the sexy Lupe Velez with her chile-con-carne accent, along with such male leads—all but forgotten today—that included Ricardo Cortez, Richard Dix, and John Boles.

The coffers of RKO in the Thirties were to be greatly enriched by a tensely brittle young lady who arrived one day, with a type of angular beauty in spite of her bloodshot eyes and a pronounced Bryn Mawr accent. Only RKO didn't know what they had at the time. Katharine Hepburn would have to teach them.

Kate was taken to Cukor's office first, before being introduced to David Selznick. Laura tagged along. Since Cukor wasn't an important director at the time, he occupied a small, dark office on the ground floor that had recently been vacated by a fired screen writer from back East.

It was only years later that Cukor's first opinion of Kate, and her opinion of him became known. She would tell Laura that she found the director "a bit rococo." With incredibly intense eyes, he viewed her and she stared right back, red swollen eyes or not. That night she confided in Laura that she found Cukor, "ugly, fat, Jewish, homosexual —a lethal combination."

The director had little praise for Kate, telling Berman that she looked like "a boa constrictor on a fast." Years later Cukor recalled their first meeting. "She swept through RKO like a hurricane, insulting everybody in sight, including me, her director. She was a freckle-faced snotty snob, definitely eccentric, and hideously attired in expensive, but mannish dress. From the first moment, she fought senselessly with everyone in sight. Of course, she became a big star."

Kate later heard Cukor's evaluation of her, and defended herself. "I had to do what I did or else they would have cast me as floozies or else sappy housewives — maybe gun molls. From the very beginning, I had to act like a star or else I wouldn't have been treated like one."

Upon entering his office, Kate immediately asked Cukor to get her an eye doctor. He ignored her request and insisted on showing her some sketches from wardrobe. The designs were from the studio's couturier, Josette De Lima. "I'm sure these costumes are marvelous," Kate said in a condescending voice. "Perhaps you'll use them when you make a movie of the Mexican Army and need to clothe them when they go into the mountains on a rattlesnake hunt."

Cukor was furious at the insult and immediately attacked her own wardrobe as "a hideous outfit. It's obvious you know nothing about clothing."

"Have you ever heard of Schiaparelli?" Kate asked the fashion-conscious director, insulting him. "Get her to design my wardrobe. Look at Laura over there. She's wearing a Chanel. Ever heard of Chanel?"

Turning beet red at her insults, Cukor ordered her to get her hair done at once. "Maybe I can be your Svengali," he said, not disguising his despair.

He took her over to the chief hairdresser at RKO, Jo Ann St. Auger, who severely cut her long hair after washing it thoroughly. It was still frizzy and matted from the long train ride. Kate found that the stylist left "enough of my red mop to curl it slightly."

***

When Kate emerged from the hairdresser's office, she ran into John Barrymore, who graciously came up to her and kissed her hand and told her how much he was looking forward to co-starring with her. At first, she seemed awed to meet The Great Profile, and she gushed about how much she'd enjoyed some of his stage appearances.

"Well, my dear, the stage was then and this is now," Barrymore said. "Hideous factories—these movie studios. You don't need to know how to act. It's merely required that you show up."

He couldn't take his bloodshot eyes off Kate's eyes. "I see that you and I suffer from the same problem." Noting the red in her eyes, he put his hand in his breast pocket and took out a small vial of brown liquid. "I've been known to take a drink or two myself the night before. I find a few eye drops from this bottle will help make me camera ready." Barrymore handed her the bottle.

"It's not a hangover," Kate protested.

"Of course, it's not, my dear. It'll be our little secret. Remember, two drops in each eye."

He kissed her on both cheeks before departing. "Here's hoping we'll both be clear-eyed in a few days to face those cameras. God, I hate cameras!"

Before Mel Burns, RKO's chief makeup artist, Cukor lamented "all those freckles." He turned to Kate. "Did your family call you Spotty?"

Kate stoically endured his taunts. "I'll have you know that Leonardo da Vinci had freckles."

"But you're not the Mona Lisa," Cukor countered. When Kate left the room, he told Burns that he dreaded taking her in to meet Selznick.

Within an hour, Kate came face to face with Selznick. If he had a reaction, he concealed it at first, although he claimed he wanted to see his brother, Myron, and Leland later and in private.

She began by asking him if he knew an eye doctor. He called his secretary and told her to get the studio doctor, Sam Hirschfeld. Into the phone, he said, "I've got an actress from New York who looks like she's dying."

Slamming down the phone, he turned to Kate. "The ride on the Super Chief must have been rough. You look like you need some shut-eye."

"That's my problem," Kate protested. "One of my eyes has been shut for days."

Instead of Kate, Selznick turned his attention to Laura. She was more his type. "You should be in pictures."

"Oh, Mr. Selznick," Laura said, "I'll bet you say that to all the girls."

"Only the pretty ones," Selznick replied. He dismissed Kate and Laura because of urgent business but told Cukor to remain behind.

As Kate was leaving, he called out to her, "Get some of our famous California sun. It ripens oranges and will ripen you, too."

Standing outside the closed door, Kate and Laura heard Selznick shouting at Cukor. "God damn you, you Jew faggot! I shouldn't have listened to you. We could have had that beautiful *ingénue* I wanted you to cast."

"That little whore's sole qualification—and you told me this yourself—is that she gives the best head in Hollywood," Cukor said in anger.

The "little blonde whore" would not be officially signed by RKO until 1933. Although born Virginia McMath, she had taken her first name from a vaudeville act in which she'd co-starred—called "Ginger and Her Redheads."

As the dancing partner of Fred Astaire in such pictures as *The Gay Divorcée,* Ginger Rogers would one day challenge Kate for the title of Queen of RKO. She would also take home an Oscar for *Kitty Foyle,* a role Kate had turned down to make *The Philadelphia Story,* for which she too would be nominated for an Academy Award, only to lose it to her blonde nemesis.

***

Dr. Hirshfeld didn't have the right medical equipment to aid Kate, but he arranged an appointment with a woman doctor who did. After examining Kate's eyes, the woman doctor removed three steel filings with a surgical knife, giving Kate some pain-killers and placing a patch over her left eye until it healed.

And that is how, along with Laura, Kate showed up for her first day of official work at RKO.

As had been agreed, Kate arrived in Cukor's office just before lunch. Cukor was appalled that Kate had to wear an eye patch and wouldn't be camera-ready for days. "The other night I was sent a script about a notorious lady pirate in the Caribbean. Ann Bonney. You'd be perfect for the role, dear."

Ignoring his insult, Kate accepted his invitation for lunch in the commissary. David Selznick was lunching with both Leland and his brother, Myron. When he saw Kate enter the room, he is said to have swallowed a chicken wing whole.

The rival of Louella Parsons, columnist Adela Rogers St. Johns, rushed over to greet Laura and Kate, virtually demanding an interview. Kate rudely shrugged her off, but Laura remained behind. Rather cattily, St. Johns asked,

"And what is it you do for Kate?" Insulted at the demeaning tone of the question, Laura replied. "I'm her husband!"

Although the columnist could not print such a remark back then, St. Johns spread the word. Before noon the following day, half of Hollywood had heard the rumor that two "filthy rich lesbians have arrived from back East, Kate Hepburn and her concubine, Laura Harding."

***

At last filming began on *A Bill of Divorcement*. It was first-rate tearjerker material, the story of an estranged father, played by Barrymore, showing up at his former home on the day his former wife, as played by Billie Burke, is scheduled to remarry. Having escaped from a mental institution, he discovers his daughter is also planning to marry. By the end of the picture, Hepburn decides to cancel her own wedding plans, fearing her children might be born mentally defective, and devote all her energies to her stricken father.

RKO publicists had shot stills of its three major stars—Hepburn, Barrymore, and Burke. When the publicity staff asked the actors to autograph their stills for some visiting distributors from back East, Burke and Barrymore dutifully agreed. Kate flatly refused. "Autographs are silly," she told Cukor. "A waste of my valuable time and theirs." That remark angered her director. "After you've been in this business for twenty-five years, maybe your autograph will mean as much as Billie's or Jack's. Until then, do as you're told." Kate still adamantly refused to sign the stills.

Shooting began in spite of the tension on the set, much of it generated between Cukor and his new star. The first shot was a party scene hosted by Burke. The multi-millionaire Laura had been hired by Cukor as an extra, for which she was to be paid ten dollars per day.

In the scene, Kate in an organza dress, its sleeves cut like "an angel's wings," descends the staircase and breezes off with her fiancé, as played by David Manners. Laura was told to pause at the foot of the stairs and place her hand on a stage prop, a badly constructed and recently varnished newel post. As Laura's own beau in the film came over to her, she started to move toward him but for some reason the ornamental, bell-shaped finial from the sticky newel post stayed glued to her hands. Horrified and not knowing what to do, Laura handed the sticky ball to her beau. "He screamed, he actually screamed," Laura later lamented to Kate, who was well aware of what was going on, having witnessed it. A highly tense Cukor, under great pressure from Selznick to bring the picture in on time and make it a hit, barged across the sound stage and slapped Laura in the face. He fired her on the spot.

Humiliated and in dismay, Laura ran from the set. In retaliation, Kate walked over to Cukor and slapped his face. Stunned at first, Cukor slapped her back.

The whole cast waited in astonishment. It was truly a test of wills between these two highly individualistic personalities. Neither Cukor nor Kate backed down first. Finally Cukor ordered everybody back to work, the scene reshot, with another actress substituted for Laura.

From that day forth, the director seemed to have earned a begrudging respect from Kate. In time, they would work themselves into one of the smoothest functioning and most successful director/star relationships in Hollywood. He would also become her best friend.

There would be more blowups before filming ended. Seeing the rushes, Kate accused Cukor of "panting after" the handsome juvenile lead, David Manners, who was described by cast members as "hypersensitive." "I wish you'd photograph me as beautifully as you so lovingly do with Manners," Kate shouted at Cukor. "With David," he said, "I don't have to try to make him beautiful."

"*Touchée*," she said before making a hasty retreat from the studio.

With Kate's eye completely healed, Barrymore began his obligatory attempt at conquest of his leading lady. Ravished by a life of drink and debauchery, he was in his fifties and aging badly. From the beginning, he flirted with Kate and pinched her bottom a few times. Out of respect for his towering reputation in the theater, she eluded him, but in a friendly manner. She chided him, "After all, you're playing my father in the film. Such a thing between us would be incest."

Determined to get her, Barrymore invited her to his lavish dressing room for lunch one day when Laura wasn't on the set. Ostensibly, he wanted to work with her on the next scene, giving her some pointers.

Eager for lessons from the great Barrymore, Kate went alone to his dressing room. Once inside, he locked the door and immediately dropped his food-stained dressing gown which was covered with cigarette burns. An actor with a generous endowment, he stood stark naked before Kate. She later told Laura that she found him "sexually repulsive, his body caked with makeup." When she made no move toward him, he ordered her to come and lie under him on the sofa before Cukor called them back to the set.

According to Hollywood legend, Kate was "petrified" and unable to speak. Many sources quote her as saying, "No, no please. I *cahnt*. I simply *cahnt*. Really I *cahnt*. My father doesn't want me to have babies."

In later years, both Barrymore and Kate denounced these stories as apocryphal. Barrymore later claimed that he did drop his robe and attempt to seduce the young actress that day. "Kate Hepburn was no cowering little virgin," Barrymore said. "She was wise beyond her years, and was, as I quickly learned, no stranger to nudity. I heard that her father even walked around in the nude. She'd posed for a nude statue, and had a husband back East who was always taking nude pictures. With a doctor father as outspoken as hers, she certainly knew where babies came from—and also how to prevent them. The silly dialogue as reported between us never happened."

When Barrymore was asked what did happen, he said that Kate went over and picked up his robe off the floor "and helped me back into it, although I'd had a drink or two that morning. She then sat down opposite me." He quotes Kate as saying, "This picture may mean nothing to an old drunk like you, but to me it means the world. I desperately want to succeed, and you can help me. You're the greatest actor in the world, and I need all the help I can get. You brought me here claiming to help me. Now get on with it." Barrymore's version sounded much more like what Kate would have said.

From that day forth, Barrymore was touched by her sincerity. "I just acted better in the picture out of respect for her. I gave her many tips about how to project an image in front of the camera. She was overplaying, and I tried to teach her that the camera magnifies even the slightest gesture."

At one point, he told her that she reminded him of his mother, Georgianna Drew, and "dear old Mum was the greatest actress who ever lived."

Kate later claimed that Barrymore "never criticized me. He just shoved me into what I ought to do before the camera. He taught me all that he could pour into one greenhorn during that short time we were together."

Kate dismissed a second apocryphal story, repeated in many books and articles, about an alleged interchange between Barrymore and herself. According to the story, she became enraged at some stage business Barrymore was performing and allegedly shouted at him, "I'll never play another scene with you." To which Barrymore is said to have replied, "But, my dear, you never have."

Barrymore also denied the story. "I did feel she had the markings of a great star and time has proven me right. I would never have been so gratuitously cruel to a young newcomer like that. Coming from me, it might have seriously inhibited her acting."

Whether true or not, Barrymore later claimed that he eventually managed to seduce Kate toward the end of the picture. "Although I think she was initially repulsed by my crude attempts at seduction, she eventually succumbed to my charm. Instead of my attacking her, she moved toward me. I asked her about the change in her attitude." Barrymore quotes Kate as saying, "I got to thinking about it. One day I may write my memoirs, and it would be great to include a seduction scene with The Great Profile. Increased sales, you know!"

Barrymore felt that he won Kate over by taking her seriously as an actress and helping her give a better performance. He stated that he found her a "very satisfactory partner in every way and willing to do some things other actresses wouldn't." He never explained what he meant by that statement.

After their eventual "closeness" in his dressing room, Barrymore claimed that she said she found "the experience most gratifying but one I don't care to repeat." With that, Barrymore said, "she just walked away and never visited me alone again."

***

Laura and Kate hated their room at the Château Elysée, but hadn't wanted to rent a house since neither planned to stay very long in California. Hearing that a former beau, the wealthy Carlton Burke, was in Los Angeles, Laura called him and asked it he could find them a temporary house. He owned a lot of real estate in Los Angeles.

The next day, Carlton called back and said he knew just the place, and that he was the landlord. It was a little four-room cottage resting under a tile roof in Franklin Canyon, complete with a live-in maid, Johanna.

When Kate arrived with Laura, Carlton was waiting for them along with a blonde-haired, middle-aged woman whom he introduced as "Mrs. Fairbanks." She was also inspecting the house as a possible residence for her overflow guests, although she claimed she found the cottage too small. Even before Kate's appearance on the screen, Mrs. Fairbanks knew who she was and graciously invited her to dinner the following evening. Kate flatly refused, claiming other commitments. When the woman had left in her chauffeur-driven car, Kate told Carlton that "she doesn't appear very interesting."

"You have just turned down the most coveted invitation out here," Carlton said. "To dine at Pickfair with the queen and king of Hollywood, Mary Pickford and Douglas Fairbanks Sr."

"Oh, my God!" Kate quotes herself in her autobiography. The story is charming but absolutely unbelievable. At the time of their meeting, Mary Pickford, America's little sweetheart, though aging, was still appearing on the screen and had recently been voted "the most famous face in the world." It is inconceivable that a movie-goer like Kate didn't know who Pickford was, especially when she was introduced as Mrs. Fairbanks. At the time, Douglas Fairbanks, Sr. was also one of the world's most famous names with a face that was familiar to audiences from China to Australia.

Soon after their arrival, Kate and Laura rented a chauffeured car, a Hispano-Suiza, a large and very upscale touring vehicle that Pandro S. Berman had called "a cross between a drugstore fountain and the Super Chief." It had an emblem of a flying stork on its hood.

The next day, hoping to impress Cukor, Kate pulled up on the RKO lot next to his office. Cukor wasn't impressed and told her that same car had been used as a prop in several films, including the most recent, *Grand Hotel*, co-starring Garbo and John Barrymore. Even though a bit humiliated, Kate stubbornly clung to the car and was often seen driving along Hollywood Boulevard in it with Laura.

Although not getting on with the executives at RKO, Kate befriended the crew. Perhaps because of her Fabian roots, she met each one personally, learning the names of their wives and how many children each one had. She was friendly with grips, electricians, carpenters, the sound engineers, even the janitors. When she heard that a family member was sick, Kate often arrived at their blue-collar homes, with Laura carrying food that they had prepared themselves. Kate, inspired by Dr. Hepburn, "played doctor."

In time, she would inspire fierce loyalty among the crews who worked on her pictures at RKO. She developed a habit of passing around sweets to the crew at four o'clock, a time at which she demanded that shooting stop for tea.

Near the completion of the film, Pedro S. Berman invited Kate to a formal afternoon tea at his home, claiming that the occasion "will be a bit dressy." He feared what outfit she might show up in. Kate ordered Laura to dress formally and go in her place.

When the tea was underway with some thirty guests, Berman spotted "an odd figure" outside his window, wandering through his grounds in a pair of bib overalls and a fireman's shirt. "It might be a woman but possibly a man," Berman later said.

Not alerting Laura, Berman called the Los Angeles police to inform them that there was a trespasser on his grounds.

When the police came, they apprehended a struggling Kate. Seeing what was happening, Laura came to the rescue, telling Berman that the trespasser was Kate, not an intruder. After giving each of the two policemen twenty dollars and apologies, Berman invited Kate inside to join the formally dressed guests.

When Laura took Kate home in the late afternoon, Berman told his remaining guests, "I feel Kate Hepburn is in dire need of a psychiatrist!"

Seeing Kate again after the shared train ride west, Billie Burke was far too distracted with her small but difficult role in *A Bill of Divorcement* and Flo Ziegfeld's declining health to pursue Kate sexually. Burke infuriated Kate when the aging actress informed her that she was drawing one-thousand more dollars a week than Kate's salary of one-thousand and fifteen.

Midway through the film's shooting, Flo Ziegfeld died. Absent from the set for only two days, Burke bravely showed up for work. Kate's attitude toward her former pursuer gradually changed, and she told Cukor that "Billie is no cry baby. I admire her professionalism in spite of her grief."

As Kate was to learn later, Burke's marriage to Ziegfeld, although once viewed as romantic, had deteriorated into a "passive acceptance" of each other. The showman was one of the great womanizers of the Western world, and every day for most of his professional life he'd been surrounded by the most beautiful showgirls on earth. What the world didn't know was that Burke and her husband often slept with some of the same leggy showgirls.

Before the end of the film, Cukor filled Kate in on Burke's activities, claiming that the star was finding comfort at night at the home of one of Hollywood's leading female directors, Dorothy Arzner, who would loom as a figure in Kate's future, unknown to her at the time.

***

Once Kate had settled into the cottage with Laura, she called her New York actor friend, Kenneth MacKenna, who immediately invited both women to dinner. There they were promised a "mystery woman" guest who'd be joining them later.

Kenneth MacKenna was in Hollywood filming *The Man Who Came Back,* as directed by Raoul Walsh, with a patch over his blind eye. Filled with indiscreet Hollywood gossip, Kenneth told Kate that the stars of the film were two of America's reigning sweethearts, Janet Gaynor and Charles Farrell, who he cited as "Hollywood's biggest pansy," and that Gaynor "was the biggest lez in Hollywood," contrary to their public images.

Kenneth delivered his bombshell later in the evening when he said that the actress joining them was his bride-to-be.

About an hour later, Kay Francis herself, attired in mink, a black silk gown, and high heels, paraded into the Roosevelt Hotel to meet Kenneth's "New York friends."

Surely no two actresses were as different as Katharine Hepburn and Oklahoma-born Kay Francis, a brunette leading lady with sad eyes and the most lavish wardrobe in Hollywood. Kate was immediately amused that Francis could not pronounce her Rs. Kenneth had met Kay Francis when appearing in the film, *The Virtuous Sin.* The movie was directed by George Cukor, and Kenneth steadfastly maintained that the homosexual director virtually chased him—"with tongue panting"—across the set during the entire shoot, "but he just isn't my type."

Both Kate and Laura were stunned to learn that Kenneth was marrying Francis, because they'd heard stories that she was a lesbian.

By coincidence, Francis in 1946 would appear on stage in the play *State of the Union.* Two years later, Kate would appear in the 1948 MGM film of the same play with Spencer Tracy. But at the time of their first meeting, the two women had little in common. Kate was the shabby dresser, and Francis was the overdresser, claiming that "even if the script is bad, women will come to see me for my wardrobe."

When Kenneth went off to order spiked drinks, and Laura went to the ladies room, Francis took her hand and slowly began to fondle Kate's legs encased in pants. Before Laura and Kenneth returned, Francis suggested that Kate visit her some night at her place. She also invited Kate to her wedding to Kenneth.

Although Kate promised to accept both invitations, she never did.

When she was dancing with Kenneth later that evening, Kate informed him there would be no more "deflowering," as her interests had moved elsewhere. However, she told him that she wanted him as her secret confidant. "After all, I have to have someone to confide my secrets in. First, let's begin with your bride-to-be."

Her friendship, usually confined to long chats on the phone, would last his entire lifetime. In addition to calling Kenneth her "deflowerer," she also labeled him as "the keeper of my secrets."

In that, she had misjudged him. Kenneth loved secrets but thrived on gossip, and was unable to keep other people's indiscretions to himself.

Throughout her life, Kate was unaware that Kenneth was betraying her confidences. Apparently, nothing ever got back to her.

***

The weekend before final scenes were shot on *A Bill of Divorcement,* Cukor and Kate had become friends "instead of bitter enemies," as she'd first predicted. The director had even apologized to Laura for slapping her face so hard on the first day's shooting when she'd ruined a major scene.

He invited both Kate and Laura to one of his soon-to-be-famous Sunday afternoons at his house, which in time, would become a Hollywood tradition, attracting some of the biggest stars.

Kate arrived earlier than the rest of Cukor's guests because she was "desperate" to swim in Cukor's pool. Laura had to cancel because of a bad cold she'd acquired. Kate confided to Cukor her fondness for nude swimming, and Cukor told her to take off her clothes and dive in.

After Kate had splashed around alone in the pool for more than an hour, Cukor received an uncharacteristically early guest who had called the night before to cancel. Without warning and without calling again, his mystery guest of the afternoon had shown up alone at his door.

Having heard about Kate Hepburn—"the second Garbo"—she was anxious to meet her rival. Cukor ushered her out to the pool where Kate was just emerging from the pool completely naked.

"Oh, my God!" Kate said.

"Do not worry," the mystery woman said. "In Sweden we swim like that every summer."

"Kate, I'd like to introduce you to Greta Garbo."

It was the beginning of a beautiful friendship.

CHAPTER FIVE

No sooner had Cukor called a wrap on *A Bill of Divorcement* than Kate was on the Super Chief back to Chicago where she changed trains for New York. The ever-faithful Laura was at her side.

Once she headed to New York, and to Kate's acute disappointment, Cukor summoned her back to RKO to reshoot two brief scenes. Once again, Laura boarded the train West with her.

At RKO, Kate learned that preview audiences had laughed at two scenes meant to be dramatic. The reshooting went quickly, but contract negotiations were going badly.

Even before the release of the picture, Selznick had decided to sign "horse-face" to a long-term contract. "I fear with all the publicity she's gotten, some other studio like MGM will sign her."

Ironically, it was Selznick himself who was in imminent danger of being grabbed by Louis B. Mayer. Of course, in time Kate herself did end up working for Mayer as well.

At his beach house in Santa Monica, Selznick summoned his brother, Myron, and Kate's agent, Leland Hayward, to negotiate a contract for Kate. At times the negotiations became almost violent, especially when Selznick learned of Kate's demands. At one point, Selznick yelled at his brother and Leland. "Have you two faggots taken a good look at the shit you're peddling?"

One contract was drawn up and rejected by Kate. Finally, she agreed to put her signature on what Leland said was "one hell of a sweetheart deal." For a yet-to-be-tested actress, Kate was granted astonishing concessions, including star billing in future films and even approval of scripts. Not only that, she was given extended time off to return to the Broadway stage.

When Myron left his brother's house, he confided to Leland, "I fear I've conned my own brother. I've seen *A Bill of Divorcement*. It's going to be a bomb!"

***

During her first return to New York, Kate had been so preoccupied with the Hepburn family that she really avoided dealing with the reality—or lack of reality—in her failed marriage to Luddy.

Luddy, along with Jack, had waited patiently at Grand Central Station for

Kate's first return from Hollywood with Laura. On her second return, he was also waiting patiently, although Jack could not show up this time. Laura had to kiss Kate goodbye on the platform and rush to a waiting limousine to take care of business in her role as heiress to a vast fortune.

Along with Luddy, Kate rode in a taxi to their shared townhouse. En route there, he told her that Alan Campbell had tossed him aside and was dating Dorothy Parker.

Luddy confided that he was seeing a great deal of an actor-model, Stanley Haggart, a handsome, six-foot, blond-haired man from Kansas. Before leaving New York, Kenneth MacKenna had introduced Stanley to Luddy, and the two men had quickly formed an intimate relationship. Although Jack saw Stanley at social gatherings with friends, he apparently didn't know that Stanley and Luddy also met privately.

"I'm glad your love life is going swimmingly, but what about us?" she abruptly asked.

"I want to stay married to you at all costs," he said. "I can't stand the thought of your leaving me and marrying another man."

"That will never happen," she promised. "You are my first and only marriage. I've definitely decided the institution is not for me." She would repeat that sentiment many times.

Back at her townhouse, she immediately made plans to go to West Hartford to see her family. She was surprised to learn that the Hepburns had virtually "adopted" Luddy, making him one of the family. "We simply adore him," Kate's sister, Marion, later confirmed.

Luddy even had his own room, both at Fenwick and in West Hartford. It appeared to Kate that he had gradually come to replace the missing Tom in their lives.

It is not known just what the Hepburn family knew about Kate's strange marriage, as the intimate details were not discussed at Hepburn family gatherings.

"When I first met Luddy," Stanley Haggart later said, "he was absolutely obsessed with the subject of Katharine Hepburn. He enjoyed an intimate relationship with Jack, but his entire life revolved around Kate. Nearly every conversation Luddy had dealt with his wife, and he could talk for hours. I felt that he was deeply in love with her, even passionately in love. And this was hard for me to understand at the time, since that love didn't seem to be sexual."

At one point, Luddy related a dream he'd had of Kate only the night before. In his dream he lived with Kate on the coast of Maine, in a fisherman's cottage, an idyllic life there raising their three children. But the dream had a strange twist. In the fantasy, Kate was the husband, Luddy the wife.

***

Among his other friends in the theater, Stanley had become "best pal" of the actress, Nancy Hamilton, who had understudied Kate in *The Warrior's Husband.* "Here the story becomes theatrically incestuous," Stanley said. "Nancy was the number one girl of Katharine Cornell. Ironically, it was Cornell who'd first scored a success on the stage in *A Bill of Divorcement.*"

Stanley said that Kate had virtually ignored Nancy when she was her understudy for the role of Antiope.

Whenever Stanley visited Luddy during moments when Jack was present, Stanley made it a point to invite a companion, either male or female. "That way, Jack always thought I was involved with someone else," Stanley said," and that way he wasn't suspicious of Luddy and me."

One night Stanley showed up with Nancy Hamilton at Kate's townhouse for dinner. Although she had been ignored as an understudy, Nancy suddenly found herself the focus of Kate's undivided attention. Since appearing in *The Warrior's Husband,* Kate had learned that Nancy was a lover of Cornell's, and this seemed to intrigue her immensely.

"Before the evening was over, Kate asked if I would take her to the theater Tuesday night," Stanley said. She pointedly did not include Jack, Luddy, or Laura in the invitation. "But as she was telling me goodbye in the hallway, Kate asked Nancy to join us."

En route Tuesday night to the theater where they had agreed to meet Nancy, Kate apparently felt she could confide in Stanley because of their shared link with Luddy. "Since I've gotten back, all my feeling for him has died, at least in one department," Kate said. "I regard him with the love that a sister might have for her older brother. My entire life orbits around Laura these days. Luddy knows that but wants to cling to me somehow."

"Kate misstated the facts," Stanley later said. "Her whole world didn't revolve around Laura. After the theater, I invited Kate and Nancy back to an apartment I was temporarily occupying. I'd prepared a late night supper for them since Kate refused to go to a restaurant."

Stanley said that he felt that there was an immediate and strong physical attraction between Kate and the former understudy she'd once ignored. "Nancy was a charming wit, a great conversationalist, and an actress of exceptional talent," Stanley said. "Yet I felt that Kate was mainly intrigued by her because of her close link with Cornell. It was as if Kate wanted to test her charms against those of her rival, and take Nancy away from Cornell."

If that were Kate's goal, she succeeded. For the next few meetings between Nancy and Kate, Stanley gladly granted them the use of his apartment. "I hardly needed it," Stanley said. "Unknown to Luddy, I was dating Alan Campbell on the side. On the nights Luddy was with Jack, I was with Alan, and Dorothy Parker was none the wiser."

On the night that Nancy told Kate that she was deeply in love with her, and would even give up Cornell for her, Kate abruptly dropped her and refused her calls the next day.

Stanley still retained his friendship with Nancy, and watched with pleasure as she went on to become famous, not only as a performer, but as a writer and lyricist. In time, the critic, John Murray Anderson, would hail Nancy as "the wittiest and ablest revue writer in America." Years later, she'd pen her most famous work, "How High the Moon," for the 1940 Broadway musical, *Two for the Show.* The song in 1951 would become a big hit for the husband-and-wife recording team of Les Paul and Mary Ford.

Stanley recalled that the only time he ever mentioned Nancy Hamilton to Kate again, "she pretended she didn't know who I was talking about."

After her sudden departure from Nancy, Kate returned to the arms of Laura, but only for a brief few days. Stanley was at dinner at Kate's house one night when she announced that she had given in to Luddy's pleading, and that they were going on a voyage to Europe "to repair our marriage." That announcement left Jack and Laura in total shock, as Kate had been talking the exact opposite of those plans. Up to then, Laura was convinced that Kate was going to divorce Luddy before returning to Hollywood.

In anger, Laura left the townhouse and retreated back to her estate, telling Kate that, "I never plan to speak to you ever again."

"Jack finally showed some backbone," Stanley said. "He rose from the table and in his anger warned Luddy that he wouldn't be waiting here when Kate and Luddy returned from Europe."

Stanley said that unknown to either Kate or Luddy, he began dating Jack while they were in Europe—"that is, when I wasn't seeing Alan Campbell." Apparently, Luddy never found out about the affair of Stanley and Jack.

A week later, Stanley faced an elated Jack. He'd heard from Luddy. "The trip is turning out to be a disaster." First, Kate had insisted that they travel in steerage, although they could easily afford first-class tickets. Both of them got sick and vomited a lot.

From Paris, Luddy wired Jack, "It's not going to work. I want to come back to you."

Jack was willing to take Luddy back. He broke off his intimate relationship with Stanley. Jack wanted them to be friends, however, and they both dined with Laura, telling her of Luddy's "sudden change of heart."

Laura promised in the morning she was going to wire that she was willing to take Kate back "providing you never do something like this again."

Although she vowed "never again," she would continue to forgive Kate.

***

Kate and Luddy were "having a miserable time vacationing in Vienna" when Kate received a wire from David Selznick ordering her to return at once to Hollywood to begin another picture. *A Bill of Divorcement* had opened at a ten-dollar charity *première*—staged by Mrs. William Randolph Hearst—at the Mayfair Theatre in New York. The picture had been mildly received but Kate's role as Sydney Fairfield had been acclaimed.

The Hollywood Reporter proclaimed, "There is a new star on the cinema horizon, and her name is Katharine Hepburn." *The Hollywood Herald* compared her to Duse, Cornell, Garbo, and Lynn Fontanne. In New York, the *Journal-American* said she "flamed like opal, half-demon, half Madonna." *The New Yorker* called her "half-Botticelli page, half bobbed-haired bandit."

Caught unaware, the RKO publicity department swung into gear. Fortunately, Kate had condescended to pose for eight cheesecake photographs "putting on a leg show," as she called it. Not knowing the actual biographical details of Kate's life, and (perhaps deliberately) confusing her with an heiress like Laura, publicists claimed that Kate had inherited a fifteen-million dollar fortune from A. Barton Hepburn, the chairman of the board of Chase Manhattan Bank. Another story erroneously revealed that she was a direct descendant of Mary, Queen of Scots, a character she'd later portray in a John Ford film.

Even though she had been abruptly dropped by Kate, Nancy Hamilton later claimed in *Stage* magazine that her own career was advanced by merely understudying for Kate in *The Warrior's Husband.* "When various producers learned that I had understudied for The Great One, velvet carpets unrolled for me, colored boys waved fans behind me, and champagne waited to be poured into my slippers."

As a sure sign of success, reporters mobbed Kate when she returned to New York Harbor, sailing first class aboard the *S.S. Paris.* Luddy remained below the deck and out of sight, as Kate gave the worst interview of her life. "Are you married to your traveling companion, Ludlow Ogden?" one reporter from the *Journal-American* asked. "I can honestly say I don't remember," Kate replied to the astonished members of the press. A. Aubrey Walker, another journalist, asked, "Do you have any children?" Kate smiled and flippantly said, "Yes, two white and three colored!" Turning to a woman reporter nearby and uttered in a whisper, she added, "The latter came about because of my tendency to visit Harlem late at night."

The hard-working members of the press, on a serious assignment and trying to make a living in the midst of a Depression, were not amused. Kate had launched her decades-long battle with the media. *Vogue, Silver Screen, Modern Screen,* and *Photoplay*, even *The New York Times,* would become Kate's natural enemies.

One reporter, Sara Hamilton, writing for *Photoplay*, attacked Kate's eccentricities, issuing a warning that "Hollywood always laughs last. One day Miss Hepburn will painfully learn that."

In no time at all, Kate had delivered Luddy back into the arms of Jack while she boarded the train for Chicago, once again with her traveling companion, none other than Laura. On the way West, the two women temporarily repaired their relationship. But once again, it was but a momentary lull before the storm.

Through George Cukor, Kate learned that "a new beau" was waiting in Hollywood, and it was Garbo herself.

***

Waiting to welcome her back, Leland seemed to view Kate in a different light. "When I first met her, I thought she was strictly a lady for the ladies," Leland later told Myron Selznick. "But when George Cukor told me she had slept with Barrymore, I began to look at her in a different light, especially after all the newspapers started writing about how beautiful she was."

What Leland didn't say was that he liked to add big name stars to his "scalp bracelet." And it soon became clear that he had become impressed with her sudden fame.

He'd rented a bigger house, Quinta Nirvana, a Spanish-style ranch house in Coldwater Canyon, complete with a swimming pool, for Laura and Kate. In addition, he'd also secured membership for Kate in the exclusive Bel-Air Country Club so she could play golf on Saturday. Kate told Leland that she had very little money to waste, and would have to depend on Laura for any "frippery." What she didn't say was that she was sending most of her money home to Dr. Hepburn, where he would shrewdly invest it, turning her into a very rich woman in the Depression-laden Thirties.

No sooner was Kate installed in her new California home than she deserted Laura once again to slip off to accept a secret invitation, delivered through Cukor, from her favorite actress, Garbo.

***

When Laura returned home from the beauty parlor late one Saturday morning, she found a note from Kate. "Gone for the weekend. See you Monday morning. Much love."

At that very moment, Kate was at Cukor's house waiting for Garbo to show up. "She told me she likes you and *that one* doesn't talk to many people," Cukor told Kate.

Three hours late, Garbo finally showed up in Cukor's driveway behind the wheel of an old black Packard limousine she called, "the bus."

Kate later remembered being impressed with the star's outfit of dark navy blue sailor pants and a smartly tailored white jumper. A white tennis visor concealed her eyes, and her hair looked freshly washed, hanging straight.

In those days, her English was far from precise, and she spoke with a heavy Swedish accent. She made many mistakes in grammar and often invented words to describe her feelings—that is, on the rare occasions when she made her feelings known.

Garbo drove Kate to a charming cottage overlooking the ocean. Kate was amazed to find the front door unlocked. Garbo told her that the house belonged to "a very dear and close friend." She claimed that escaping to this cottage was her only refuge in this horribly bleak country. "California is a bad place where I must work and play bad women to make money. I will make lots of money and go back to Sweden. Sweden is where I go belonging."

No one knows exactly what transpired between Garbo and Kate that weekend, except from fragments that Kate later and rather tantalizingly reported to Cukor and Kenneth.

By the end of the weekend, regardless of what had transpired between them, a friendship was formed for life, even though they would go for years without seeing each other, confining their relationship at times to speaking on the telephone every two or three months.

Kenneth felt that the relationship between Garbo and Kate "was not one of equals, Kate being a worshipper at Garbo's temple."

Kate remembered being surprised when Garbo put on a phonograph record, her favorite tune, "Daisy, You're Driving Me Crazy." She invited Kate to dance. But one playing of the tune was not enough. Garbo wanted to dance to the record several times. Mercedes de Acosta, lesbian icon and muse, would later recall Garbo's ongoing fascination with this tune, and was frequently willing to indulge Garbo in this harmless fun. Kate, at the time, however, told Cukor that she found the recording "silly and boring." In front of Garbo, however, she kept her opinion to herself, not wanting to offend.

The cottage had a pool, and Kate and Garbo swam naked in it, just like Garbo would do later with Marlene Dietrich at Frank Sinatra's house in Palm Springs.

It was here that Kate learned just how "aggressively oral" Garbo could be, those words coming from her former lover, Lilyan Tashman, who spread the Swede's most intimate secrets around Hollywood.

Garbo was mainly lesbian when she first met Kate, although the great star would rapidly move toward asexuality in just a few years. In Kate, Garbo must have sensed a kindred spirit. Like Kate, Garbo detested fawning interviewers and fans and absolutely abhorred the invasive press. Garbo was delighted when she'd heard that Kate had refused to pose endlessly for publicity shots at RKO. Hearing of Kate's homosexual husband back East, Garbo claimed that for male company, she too preferred only homosexual men. "They make worship of you. They make goddess of you..." She paused. "What is the word?"

"Deify?" Kate said.

"Yes, that, and they're not demanding in bed."

Resting on a chaise longue, Garbo lit a cigarette but only after she rolled her lips around it, as if orally copulating with it. "I prefer to be with a man like John

Gilbert. In his case he's a homosexual man but not knowing of it yet. The important think is that *I* know."

Kate told Cukor that Garbo then reached over and kissed her for the first time, fondling her nude breasts. "You...and me, we be sisters under the skin. With you, freedom. With others, a prison term for me. I am very private person like you. But sex. Sex with anyone. It's like a big violation. Knocking down door on my private world."

"But you make exceptions?" Kate asked.

"What is this exception thing?" Garbo asked. "Sounds bad."

"I mean, do you have sex?"

"Sometimes..." she paused enigmatically.

"Sometimes I let privacy be invaded. But I do not like this bad thing men like. What you call this bad thing?"

"Intercourse."

"Yes, that's what you call it. But it makes me feel like cow mounted by bull in field. If a man doesn't want oral, he not man for me. Women are more friendly about that."

Around six o'clock, Garbo promised Kate she'd prepare a wonderful supper for her. "You have not eaten before you have Garbo special Swedish dishes. I will make supper for you like mama made supper for me when I was a little boy in Stockholm."

Ravenously hungry, Kate eagerly awaited dinner. She was surprised when Garbo called her into the little kitchen after having been gone for only five minutes, claiming that dinner was ready.

When she came into the kitchen, and to Kate's disappointment, she saw two pieces of old cheese on the table and a glass of milk for each of them along with a loaf of stale French bread without butter. "Years from now you can tell grandchildren that Garbo cook for you. Make nice Swedish meal."

That night Garbo consented to let Kate give her a massage. Apparently, Garbo wasn't too pleased. "You no work as a Swedish masseur." Garbo then volunteered to give Kate a massage "the Swedish way." Garbo expressed admiration for Kate's lean body, claiming that it was "the wedding of man body with woman body but in one body—not two bodies." Garbo later confided that she too considered her own body the perfect blending of the male and female physique.

"You might call us the Gemini twins," Kate said.

When Garbo drove Kate back to George Cukor's house at the end of the weekend, it marked the beginning of a sporadic love affair that would continue until 1941 when Garbo made her last picture, "a disaster" called *Two-Faced Woman* directed by Cukor himself.

Kate never lost her fascination for Garbo, both the image on the screen and the woman herself. As proof of that, Cukor cited an example where Kate tried to hire herself out for a small role as a sexy, funny maid at an inn in the film

Queen Christina, in which Garbo was co-starring with John Gilbert in an attempt to revitalize his career.

Kate approached the director, Rouben Mamoulian, who had been very supportive of her when he'd directed Nazimova in the Broadway stage play, *A Month in the Country*, with Kate playing another maid's part. Mamoulian liked the idea, thinking it would generate a lot of publicity. When he presented the offer of Kate's appearance to the producer, Walter Wanger flatly rejected it. "It would be too distracting to the picture."

Kate was bitterly disappointed because she wanted a "close encounter" to see how Garbo worked in front of the camera, "manipulating her magic."

The part eventually went to a minor actress, Barbara Barondess. In the scene, a tired Queen Christina arrives at an inn, where the maid massages her tired legs. Before the camera, Barondess ran her hands up and down Garbo's legs. When Louis B. Mayer saw the scene on film, he reacted in horror. He ordered that the scene end up on the cutting room floor.

"We're not making a lez picture," the mogul shouted at Mamoulian, although considering that the subject was Queen Christina, he was in a sense doing just that. Garbo later told Cukor that she had played the role of the "queen as lesbian."

***

Laura spent the weekend alone crying. But instead of confronting Kate with her latest indiscretion when she returned Monday morning, a remarkable transformation came over Laura. She finally came to realize that a life with Kate meant "the acceptance of abandonment from time to time," as she would tell both Kenneth and later Luddy. "It's the price that one pays for living with Kate. She's controlled completely by her desires. If she wants some adventure with either a man or a woman, she never resists her impulses. Dr. Hepburn was right when he compared his daughter to a charging bull."

The next day at RKO, Kate learned why Selznick abruptly called her back from Vienna. She'd been cast in her second RKO film, *Three Came Unarmed,* the story of an alcoholic Borneo missionary sent to live in Wales. His "jungle ways" shocked the provincial residents of the village of West Mersea, and Kate, as his daughter, saw herself "dressed in animal skins and carrying a spear throughout, a regular female Tarzan." It was based on a best-selling novel by E. Arnot Robertson. Kate was eager to meet her leading man, Joel McCrea. She told Cukor that she found McCrea one of the handsomest male beauties in Hollywood.

"So does another male beauty," Cukor said.

"What do you mean?"

"So does his lover, Gary Cooper."

That was the first time that Kate had heard that these two popular male stars were bisexual.

Two years older than Kate, the Pasadena-born McCrea was "tall and handsome in the saddle," as Kate put it. Undeniably all-American, he was not unlike Cooper himself and seemed trustworthy and decent, "though lacking fire" in Kate's judgment. "He looked too wholesome to me to be a great lover," Kate told Kenneth. His response: "Tell Joel baby he can put his shoes under my bed any night."

After contemplating and then ruling out a romance with McCrea, Kate found the actor an engaging and charming personality, and they were photographed in bathing suits at the beach at Santa Monica, where he taught her to surf.

The press at the time suggested that Kate was having an affair with McCrea. She later told Kenneth it wasn't true. "I wanted to but Joel's madly in love with Gary who is also dating Lupe Velez and maybe countless other women—or even men—for all I know."

With no possibility of a romance with Kate on the horizon, McCrea did share his dreams with her. He hoped to make a lot of money and become a rich rancher. In spite of his ongoing love affair with Cooper, the actor to whom he was most often compared physically, he said that his real goal in life was to marry a beautiful woman and take her to his ranch.

He did just that in 1933 when working on the melodrama, *The Silver Chord*. On the set, he met his co-star, Frances Dee, and married her that same year. The union would become one of the longest in Hollywood, lasting until his death in 1990.

Kate would meet Dee herself on the set of *Little Women* in 1933, when the actress played Meg to Kate's Jo.

Contrary to rumors prevalent at the time, Dee and Kate never talked of their "competition" for McCrea. Kate denied she'd had an affair with McCrea. Whether telling the truth or not, Kate said, "We did attempt it one time at a beach cabaña at Santa Monica. Somehow we started giggling when we got all jaybird naked with each other. We decided not to be lovers but good friends. Besides, that Montana Mule, Gary Cooper, is a tough act to follow."

***

Laura wanted to go out to parties, night clubs, and restaurants, but Kate adamantly refused to go with her, most often retiring to bed before nine-thirty. In the late afternoon or early evening, Kate preferred to take long walks in the hills above Hollywood with Laura and the dogs.

Perhaps out of boredom, Kate resumed her criminal activity of breaking into houses, which she'd abandoned back in Hartford when the police caught her and her friends. Dr. Hepburn had to bail them out.

How she persuaded Laura, the heiress to a banking fortune, to join her in criminal trespass is not known. Cukor, when learning of Kate's strange activity and hearing that Laura too was involved, said, "In Laura's case, it must be true love to make her join Kate in this madness. They'll end up in jail for sure."

Kate liked to boast that she could break into any home, regardless of alarms, burglar detectors, and even security guards and their ferocious dogs. She estimated that in one season alone she and Laura broke into eight Hollywood homes, leaving "friendly but unsigned notes" behind so the owners would know of their visit. Kate, and certainly not Laura, never stole any item, however.

Their most notorious break-in, which became the stuff that Hollywood legends are made of, was at the home of the fading homosexual actor, Ramon Novarro, who had scored such a big success in the silent film, *Ben-Hur*, released by MGM.

Kate had read in the papers that Novarro, who fancied himself a singer, was appearing live in a Hollywood club. The Novarro home was selected as Kate's target for the evening. From this point on, the story isn't clear. It is said that Novarro had been heckled that evening by a hostile audience, one man screaming, "Faggot!" at him. In a fit of pique, Novarro cut short his concert and returned home early.

He was flabbergasted to find Kate and Laura exploring his home. He didn't threaten to call the police, since he knew that both women "are rich heiresses" and obviously didn't have robbery in mind by breaking in. Caught red-handed, Kate confessed her "strange compulsion" to break into homes. Novarro, who had a few strange compulsions of his own, laughed and joked with the two women and invited them for a nightcap. In his foyer, as he wished them a good night, he invited both of them back "but this time you need a definite invitation."

Since the story was too good to keep to himself, Novarro called William Haines, his best friend. The next day, the gossips of Hollywood spread the hottest tidbit about Kate and Laura yet. Haines was aware that Novarro kept an ebony dildo, modeled in real life by Valentino and presented as a gift to his off-screen lover, Novarro. In Haines' story, he claimed that when Novarro returned home from his concert, he caught Kate and Laura, his trespassers, in bed together. According to the story maliciously spread by Haines, Kate was using the Valentino dildo on Laura.

When Kate heard the story the next day, she stopped breaking into houses that year, although in time she would resume the activity but with another accomplice.

***

Not always breaking and entering, Kate's mischief sometimes took less criminal ways. When the producer, Walter Wanger, whom Kate knew slightly, invited Laura and Kate for dinner, Kate declined for both Laura and herself. Later that night, Kate was curious and convinced Laura to go to the Wanger home. Slipping around to the back of the house, Kate bribed two servants, giving them fifty dollars of Laura's money to let them slip into their maid's uniforms.

Dressed as maids, both Kate and Laura emerged from the Wanger kitchen to serve each guest a helping of cherries jubilee. Invited to the party, William Haines, the former actor, now interior decorator, suspected something. "You look amazingly like that young actress, Katharine Hepburn."

Kate admitted that she was, and Wagner invited Laura to join the other guests. Kate refused. Laura and Kate then ran giggling from the dining room.

Staring in awe at Kate was a French actor, Charles Boyer, who had recently arrived from Paris to star in *The Magnificent Lie*. His first impression of Kate was one of startled confusion, finding her actions bizarre and mentally unstable. Soon he would be playing opposite Kate, and he'd quickly reverse that opinion.

The next day, the gossipy Haines spread the maid's story across Hollywood. To an increasing degree, Kate became known and gossiped about for her eccentricities.

In another act of mischief, Kate and Laura concealed themselves in the trunk of director William Welman's expensive French-made limousine. When he arrived at his home garage, Kate, followed by Laura, jumped out of the trunk and began making funny faces at Wellman.

At his studio the following day, Wellman claimed, "that Hepburn girl and her lez friend are very collegian."

Kate later explained her peculiar behavior as an attempt to make fun of *nouveau riche* directors like Wellman and his oversized car, even though Kate herself, upon her arrival in California, had used a big touring car to impress Hollywood.

One late afternoon, there was a knock on Kate's door. When she opened it, Mrs. Fairbanks stood there with another invitation to Pickfair. This time Kate made no pretense. She knew who Mary Pickford was. She accepted, especially when Pickford said, "And do bring your girl friend, Miss Harding. Doug and I understand about such things."

***

Refusing to date any of Hollywood's so-called eligible bachelors, Kate avoided Hollywood parties and *premières* along Hollywood Boulevard. She did feel, however, that it was mandatory that she and Laura attend the dinner at Pickfair.

Laura felt it might be awkward if she and Kate showed up as a couple for the dinner party of about thirty odd members of Hollywood's elite. Laura called her friend, Ford Johnson, a polo-playing playboy, who agreed to accompany them as an escort.

At Pickfair, Mary Pickford graciously received them and introduced them to her husband, Douglas Fairbanks Sr. At the time Doug Fairbanks was engaged in conversation with Gary Cooper. Kate felt that Fairbanks and Cooper had a lot in common, as they both were dating the "spitfire," Lupe Velez, Cooper rather publicly and Fairbanks very privately.

Cooper was gracious and charming to both Kate and Laura. He told Kate that, "Joel McCrea has told me wonderful things about you."

Pickford brought over the Countessa Di Frasso, and introduced her to Kate and Laura as "my dearest friend." At the time, the Countessa Di Frasso was also having a much publicized and notorious affair with Cooper, the papers hailing the so-called romance as "The Cowboy and the Countess."

Kate took an instant dislike to the fat-legged Di Frasso, who seemed to get on better with Laura. Both Laura and Di Frasso (née Dorothy Taylor) were heiresses to great fortunes and both were New Yorkers. Before she became a countess, Di Frasso had lived in New York, a state where her grandfather had once been governor. Her own father had amassed a fortune of fifty million dollars. In those days, Di Frasso told her confidantes that, "Gary is the first man who has ever satisfied me sexually."

Kate was mildly surprised, and Laura was shocked at the dinner table. Fairbanks had a habit of crawling under the large oak table at Pickfair and biting the legs of his guests, both male and female. "You'll have to excuse Doug," Pickford said to Kate. "He likes to play dog."

After dinner, Fairbanks invited all his guests for a private screening of his latest film, *Mr. Robinson Crusoe*, a modern adaptation of the classic tale in which he'd appeared with actor, William Farnum. To Laura's horror, her escort, Ford Johnson, fell asleep in the middle of the screening and started to snore. When Laura tried to wake him up, Fairbanks said, "That's okay. His reaction will probably be the same as the critics to this damn picture."

Later that night, with Johnson still sleeping it off in the screening room, Fairbanks invited Laura and Kate to "join me on my nightly rounds." A police squad car pulled up at Pickfair, and Fairbanks ushered Kate and Laura into the back seat. To amuse himself, perhaps as a real-life sequel to his acts of bravado on screen, Fairbanks had arranged for the local police to come by every night to take him on their rounds.

Before the night was over, Kate and Laura had visited several "scenes of the crime," including one tenement where a woman had stabbed her husband with a kitchen knife.

For several months, Fairbanks continued this habit of riding around with the police, preferring to travel only in squad cars that answered emergency calls in black ghetto neighborhoods. He shunned the white middle-class suburbs. Among countless others, he'd taken aspirant movie star Humphrey Bogart into the ghetto where he'd witnessed a scene of domestic violence very similar to what Kate and Laura saw. Before the advent of the drug culture, many of the scenes of crimes involved domestic violence over sexual infidelity, as a wife caught her husband with another woman or in some cases a relative, even one as close as a daughter.

Kate loved the evening, Laura absolutely loathing it.

Mary Pickford never invited them back.

***

George Cukor referred to a short pre-Code period in Hollywood at the dawn of the Talkies as *La Belle Époque* in Hollywood. He was talking about Hollywood at its more tolerant and sexually adventuresome, with an active and vibrant male homosexual and lesbian subculture. Cukor claimed it was a time of confused sexual identity when certain stars moved easily between the sexes. In that assessment, Cukor specifically included Greta Garbo, Joan Crawford, Tallulah Bankhead, Marlene Dietrich, Barbara Stanwyck, Gary Cooper, Joel McCrea, and countless others.

When Katharine Hepburn started showing up at the famous Sunday afternoon gatherings at Cukor's house, she was met with total acceptance, and "often adoration," as Cukor said. The executives at RKO might have been horrified by her masculine attire, but no one at Cukor's parties was. Her political opinions, and those of her parents, might have caused rocks to be thrown into the Hepburn household in West Hartford, but Kate found she could express the most "advanced ideas" to the clan who gathered at Cukor's, and no one would raise an eyebrow.

When Kate showed up, she never knew who would be at Cukor's. Laura generally accompanied her, but secretly confided to Kate that "these aren't really my kind of people." Likely to be attending would be Aldous Huxley, W. Somerset Maugham, Joan Crawford, and almost every big star of stage and screen, including "a trio of Barrymores." One such Sunday, Kate found herself sitting on the sofa with the British writer, Sir Hugh Walpole, with his dear friend, Rowland Leigh, the latter a lyricist and writer planning to open on Broadway with his musical *The Dubarry.*

At one party, Kenneth showed up with both Joel McCrea and Kenneth's bride-to-be, Kay Francis. Cukor had just directed McCrea and Francis in a film, *Girls About Town.* Getting third billing in the picture was Lilyan Tashman, who was known as "Hollywood's most notorious lesbian." She arrived at Cukor's with her homosexual husband, actor Edmund Lowe. (Cukor was fequently "sharing young men" with Tashman's husband at the time.) It was a lavender marriage, Cukor told Kate, the first time she'd ever heard that expression, although in time she would learn that Hollywood referred to her marriage to Luddy as lavender as well.

On the afternoon that McCrea attended with Kenneth and Francis, Kate met a young Virginian who was standing on the far side of Cukor's pool, looking with disdain at McCrea. She introduced herself to Anderson Lawler, who, she learned, was an actor who had appeared in *Girls About Town* in 1931. Although he said he was a close friend of Kay Francis, Lawler, after a few drinks, confided to Kate that he hated McCrea, calling him a "cocksucking son of a bitch." As Kate was to learn, Lawler claimed to have been having a hot affair with Cooper until McCrea took the lanky Montana man away from him.

Despite his disappointment, or maybe because of it, there was something about Lawler that appealed to Kate that afternoon. He had an obscene tongue and a mocking laugh much like his recently acquired best friend, Tallulah Bankhead. He stood tall, and like Kate, was heavily freckled with red hair. Before Kate left with Laura that afternoon, Lawler got her to promise that she would try to get McCrea to fall in love with her "so I can get Gary back." Kate rather faint-heartedly claimed she would try.

The very next morning Lawler had Kate on the phone, which marked the beginning of years of shared confidences. Although Laura didn't care much for him, Kate claimed she adored him. In time, he came to occupy a position of trust in her life equaled only by Cukor and Kenneth.

One Sunday afternoon Cukor had discreetly not invited either McCrea or Lawler to his afternoon lunch. Tallulah showed up, however, and soon after her arrival, engaged Kate in a heated dialogue, telling her of how both she and Charles Laughton had madly chased after Cooper when they were filming *The Devil and the Deep* with him. "I got him, darling, but he gave me the clap."

At that point Gary Cooper walked into Cukor's living room with the Countess Di Frasso. Jealous of Di Frasso, Tallulah, after a few more drinks, came right up to the countess and called her a "fat old whore." The entire living room heard Tallulah's booming basso voice. The countess tossed her glass of wine in Tallulah's face, only to have Tallulah repeat the insult. The second time around, the countess slapped Tallulah's face. Tallulah then lunged for the countess, threatening to tear her hair out. Kate intervened to break them up, as Cooper rushed in from the pool to escort the countess out of the room.

Kate later told Cukor that she couldn't recall having had so much fun since arriving in Hollywood.

On the way home, Laura told Kate that they were socializing with "vulgar drunks of dubious morals."

A call came in from Leland Hayward, inviting Kate to a party at the home of Zoë Akins, a screenwriter who was working on the script for Kate's next picture since the project with McCrea had been permanently shelved. Although Laura was piqued that her former beau had excluded her from the invitation, Leland assured her that his was strictly a business meeting. At the party, Kate was also going to be introduced to the new director of the picture.

En route to the home of Akins, Kate noticed a change in Leland. Up to now, he'd treated her with a cold professionalism, but when he came to pick her up, he seemed to pour on the manly charm and was quite courtly to her, even though she'd dressed in masculine attire.

He kept telling her how beautiful she'd had been in *A Bill of Divorcement*.

"You're different," she said to him. "Why the change? I'm still the same person."

He confessed that he'd had an indiscreet talk with John Barrymore. "Jack and I shared a private moment. I feel different about you."

"So," she said, "Mr. Barrymore is the kiss-and-tell type. I should have known it." She reached into her purse for a cigarette. "There are a lot of things you don't know about me," she told him.

"And what fun I'm going to have discovering them," he said.

***

At 635 Franklin Avenue in Hollywood, Leland pulled up his car at Akins's palatial pink stucco house with its liveried flunkies. As he stood on the doorstep with Kate ringing the bell, he informed her for the first time that she'd been assigned to star in a film, *A Great Desire,* based on Gilbert Franklin's best-selling British novel. It was the story of a woman pilot, Lady Cynthia Darrington, and her unhappy affair with a British politician, a role to be played by actor Colin Clive. Kate's character, according to Leland, would be based on the famed aviatrix, Amelia Earhart.

Even before she was sucked into the party, Kate was intrigued by the idea of playing an aviatrix, as she'd always greatly admired Earhart. "At least I'm not cast in some dumb Western," Kate said. "Playing some silly little girl running down the stars and asking the he-men, 'Boys, where have all the cattle gone?'"

A footman opened the door and ushered Kate and Leland into a large living room filled with at least thirty women. Kate spotted only two men, one of whom was Anderson Lawler, her newly acquired friend. Seeing her, Lawler rushed over to give her a kiss. Before doing so, he sized Leland up and down. "Why don't you come up and see me sometime?" Lawler asked Leland. The agent disappeared into the living room "to work the crowd," perhaps hoping to sign up another star client.

Surveying the party, Lawler whispered to Kate, "You and I are the only people at this party who sleep with men—well, maybe except for Tallulah."

"Oh, my God," Kate said. "Don't tell me she's here too."

Emerging almost out of nowhere, a short and rather heavy-set woman stood before Kate. Lawler introduced her as Zoë Akins, who was the scenarist for *A Great Desire.*

"I'm dying to play Amelia Earhart," Kate said.

With her very affected British accent, Akins told her that the story was actually based on the Bristish flyer, Amy Johnson, not Earhart.

"Whatever," Kate said, looking disappointed. "I'm sure it'll be just as exciting."

Before Akins could talk about the picture, Hollywood's only woman director, Dorothy Arzner, stood below Kate. With her closely cropped hair and mannish dress, she extended a firm grip. "At last I meet the star of *my* picture!" Arzner said in a rather aggressive way.

"I admire you so, and I'm really looking forward to working with you," Kate said.

"We'll have a lot of fun," Arzner promised.

Kate, like the rest of Hollywood, was very familiar with the career of Arzner, who'd been an ambulance driver on the battlefields of World War I before drifting to Hollywood and into film editing. She'd been hailed for her brilliant cutting of the bullfight scenes for Valentino's *Blood and Sand* in 1922.

By 1927, she'd become the town's only female director, turning out such films as *The Wild Party*, in which she'd managed to seduce Clara Bow, according to Hollywood legend, but only for one night.

Arzner was also said to have invented the technique of the boom microphone, when she'd ordered her soundman to attach a fishpole to the mike and follow Bow around the sound stage.

Before Kate could exchange any more words with Arzner about the picture, Jobyna Howland came up and introduced herself to Kate, kidnapping her from Akins and Arzner, and began showing off the antique-stuffed mansion with its exquisite *objets d'art*. Kate immediately suspected that Howland—not Akins—owned the house. She found that Howland was remarkably tall, more than six feet, and was strikingly fair and very Junoesque.

At one point Howland introduced Kate to the third of the only three men in the room, Lord Hugo Rumbold, the husband of Zoë Akins. Both his lordship and Howland seemed to hold each other in disdain, like two rivals circling each other.

The very effete Rumbold turned to Kate and rather contemptuously took in her mannish attire. "Miss Hepburn," he said, "you almost look like a man."

"And so do you, sir," Kate said, before turning her back to him. She managed to hook up with Lawler on the terrace. "What goes on here?"

The gossipy Lawler filled her in. "Akins is so pretentious she just had to add a title to her name. She and Howland are lovers but Akins conned Lord Rumbold into marrying her. She always wanted to be an aristocrat. Now she's called Lady Rumbold. It's a lavender marriage."

Lawler filled her in on the Howland/Akins affair. "Thanks partly to those long legs, Howland was one of the original Gibson gals. After she got over her crush on Ethel Barrymore, Akins hit Hollywood with Howland on her arm. Except for his title, our so-called Lordship is of no use to Akins."

Appearing before Lawler was a woman he introduced to Kate as Leontine Sagan. Kate had already heard about this notorious figure, who had made

Mädchen in Uniform in 1931, a film shot in Austria. It had created an international uproar because of its frank and sympathetic treatment of lesbian love.

At that point, Talullah barged onto the terrace, with Hope Williams on her arm. "Hello dah-ling," Tallulah said to Kate. "Hope here took my cherry when I was sixteen and she was nineteen. When did she take yours?"

Before Kate could respond, Arzner reappeared, taking Kate by the arm and directing her over to the far corner of the living room where Billie Burke awaited them on a flowery sofa.

Kate leaned over to kiss Burke and mutter some words of sympathy about the recent death of her husband, Flo Ziegfeld. Burke graciously thanked her and tenderly held her hand.

"No need for sympathy," Arzner said. She sat down with Burke and took her other hand before giving the blonde-haired actress a long and passionate kiss in front of Kate. "Out with Flo and in with Dorothy," Arzner said.

Kate looked on in astonishment. She'd seen a lot since coming to Hollywood, especially at Cukor's Sunday afternoon lunches, but this scene was a bit much.

"Billie is the woman I say my prayers to at night," Arzner said. "Not only that, but she plays your rival, Lady Elaine Strong, in our upcoming film."

Even before shooting began, *A Great Desire*, according to Hollywood gossip, quickly became known as "that lez movie they're shooting over at RKO."

***

After the party, Leland drove Kate to Myron Selznick's beach cottage. She'd never spent time with Leland before. Very carefully, she observed him and was absolutely charmed by his intensity. He broke the tension with an infectious grin that appeared every five minutes or so. Slim and well-built, he had a debonair style.

"You might be a sharpie, a real tough negotiator," she said. "You've certainly done well by me. I hear all the ladies call you handsome and sexy. Sexy, I don't know about. But from what I can see, you're not handsome. But, I could never fall for a real pretty boy. I think men should look a bit rugged. You must be from the Middle West."

"Nebraska, actually," he said.

"I knew it!" she said. "That's why you're quintessentially American." Rather abruptly, she asked, "And just how old are you?"

"I was born in 1902," he said.

"I was born in 1909," she claimed.

"Actually 1907," he said, correcting her. "Remember, you're my client. I've seen all the papers you have to fill out."

"Most actresses in Hollywood lie by decades," she said. "What's two years?"

Behind the wheel of the car, he told her that he suspected her appeal would transcend the decades. "But I used the wrong word—beautiful—to describe you. When it comes to you, that's such a nothing word. It's like calling a woman glamorous. You're hard to describe. You have a certain look. It's your eyes. But more. It's the way you hold yourself, but more. The way you move, but more. Your sense of mystery. You are definitely your own creation—not a copy of Crawford, Garbo, Shearer, or anybody else. You've carved out an original screen presence—independent, regal, well-bred, exciting. How can all that be encapsulated in the world beautiful? The English language needs a new word to describe you. You're unique!"

In the borrowed cottage, as they sat outside listening to the sound of the raging ocean, he kept pouring the champagne and compliments. "You not only have the makings of a star, as the press says, you are already a star. You will win millions of fans."

As they drank champagne, he amused her with stories of his life as an agent, including the time he signed up Fred Astaire and his sister, Adele, when they were appearing in *Lady, Be Good!* He got them to agree to appear at the Trocadero night club for four-thousand dollars a week. "I got my four hundred every week the Astaires were there," Leland said. "Fred's a great client but a problem. He's madly in love with me, and I don't go that route."

Leland liked to brag about his successes as a Hollywood agent, and she liked hearing of them, because she felt it meant he'd win the same high salaries and acclaim for her. He told her that with stars like Fredric March and Myrna Loy, he had increased their asking price by five times. "I'm known for doing anything for a client," he said. "When this actor client of mine was ordered by his psychiatrist to chop wood for therapy, I sent him three heavy tree trunks."

He said he could easily juggle six phones at a time. "They call me the Toscanini of the telephone." He claimed that even Ernest Hemingway wanted to sign with him. "Maybe I'll introduce the two of you. He might agree to make a woman like you the heroine of his novels. You'd be the perfect female character for Hemingway. I might even become a producer and make the films myself." Ironically, Leland would end up producing a movie based on one of Hemingway's novels, *The Old Man and the Sea,* except that it would star—not Kate—but Spencer Tracy.

She liked the sound of Leland's voice, and when he moved to make love to her, she welcomed him with open arms.

The next morning after a dreamy night, she awoke to find that Leland had risen even before she had. Their bed was covered with rose petals, Sterling Silver hybrid, her favorite.

When she went to call Laura to explain a night away from the house, he interrupted, inviting Kate (and pointedly not invited Laura) for a pre-dawn flight across the sky over Los Angeles. She gladly accepted his offer, and later adored watching the sun rise over the coast of California.

"We have some spectacular sunrises in Connecticut," she told him, "but this beats all."

He told her that he'd like to fly with her every day, "But I've got to get to the office and make a deal. Bring back the bacon."

As he was dropping her off at the Coldwater Canyon house, she asked when she could see him again.

"I'll show up tonight with about three suitcases," he said. "I'll keep my room at the Beverly Hills Hotel, but will spend most of my nights here with you."

"But Laura…"

"She'll just have to accept it," he said, before driving off.

***

Over Laura's strenuous objections, Leland moved into the Coldwater Canyon house. If she wanted to stay at Quinta Nirvana, and even though paying the rent herself, Laura was forced to handle the triangle, or else she'd lose Kate completely, and she wasn't ready for that yet.

The night Leland arrived with three suitcases of clothing, and several sets of suits on hangers, Kate chastised him. "My father claims that any man who owns more than two suits is a fop."

Leland rarely mentioned his wife, and Kate never spoke of Luddy. Kate knew that Leland had married Lola Gibbs, a legendary Texas beauty, who divorced him two years later. Leland told Kate that he had almost committed suicide when Lola had left him. Eight years later he'd remarried her.

Even though he had in a peculiar way added Lola to his fabled "scalp bracelet" once again, he didn't seem to want her once he'd reclaimed her. He preferred Kate instead. After two weeks of living with Kate, he asked her to marry him as "soon as our divorces come through." She flatly turned him down, claiming that she would never marry again.

Life at Quinta Nirvana developed into a pattern. As Kate and Laura dined early, Leland would have several cocktails with them before disappearing for the night. He claimed he had "to make the rounds," not only to tend to his "ego-manical clients" but to pick up gossip about hot properties coming up at the various studios.

Leland also kept a room at the Beverly Hills Hotel where Kate suspected he continued to have various affairs with Hollywood stars.

One night Leland returned home early to find Kate and Laura uncharacteristically staying up late and having a nude swim in the pool. He immediately pulled off his clothes and joined them.

Sometimes when he'd stumble in, he'd have to kick Laura out of Kate's bed and send her packing to her own room. Although Laura resented the dynamics

108

of their unhappy home, Kate was delighted with it, frequently sharing details with Cukor, Kenneth, and Lawler.

"I've got the best of both possible worlds."

***

Somewhere about midway through the shooting of *A Great Desire,* the film's title was scrapped in favor of *Christopher Strong.* From the beginning, Kate had lobbied to have the title changed. She didn't like Colin Clive playing the title role. She felt that the name of her character, Lady Cynthia Darrington, might be altered and the film retitled *Cynthia Daring.* RKO rejected her request, as did the film's director, Dorothy Arzner.

The good will generated at the home of Zoë Akins was largely forgotten after the first week on the set. Kate was infuriated that Arzner had originally tried to cast Ann Harding in her part, only to have the more established actress turn down the role because of another commitment. Back home, Kate told Laura that she could call her "second choice Kate—or perhaps Hand-Me-Down Rose."

From the moment she learned that Arzner had really wanted Harding, Kate became belligerent on the set by claiming that it was Arzner who was the belligerent one. As always, Kate quickly became friendly with the crew. She frequently denounced Arzner for "being completely autocratic and far too demanding of her co-workers."

At first Kate even refused to take direction from the equally strong-willed Arzner—"two feminists at odds," as associate producer Pandro S. Berman saw it. Kate claimed that Arzner's direction "is stupid and silly—you have me doing absolutely ridiculous things completely out of character." In Arzner's own defense, she said, "I had to tone down the acting of Miss Hepburn or she would have been laughed off the screen at previews. She was playing the role much too shrill."

It was an unhappy set, especially when Burke showed up for work and resumed her amorous pursuit of Kate under Arzner's jealous eyes.

Filming began before the script was completed. Zoë Akins, who was responsible for the scenario, was having domestic problems with the declining health of Lord Rumbold, who had to be put in an oxygen tent during the shoot.

As new pages of script were given to Arzner from Akins, the director ordered her key players to her elegant Greek revival home on Los Feliz Terrace. There, at night, the script would be read and choreographed before the next day's shoot.

At one such gathering, with just the three of them, when Arzner was rehearsing a scene between her live-in lover, Billie Burke, and Kate, Arzner left the room. Upon her return, she is alleged to have caught Burke in a "compromising position" with Kate. When the story later spread around the set at RKO,

Kate denied that such an event ever happened, but it quickly became part of the early Hollywood lore and legend of Katharine Hepburn.

During the filming of *Christopher Strong*, Kate tried valiantly to establish her own sense of her character in spite of Arzner's direction. She told Leland that she was not using Amelia Earhart as a role model. Complete with jodhpurs and leather helmet, Kate had taken the public image of Charles Lindbergh as her inspiration.

It was aviator Leland himself who helped her with directions about how to pilot a small craft. These mock flying lessons were abruptly terminated when Kate learned that Leland's estranged wife, Lola Gibbs, was a crack aviatrix, and it was Lola who had taught Leland to fly. Kate turned down future flying lessons from Leland. She would not learn to be a pilot until taught by a future lover, Howard Hughes.

There are only two memorable scenes in the film, one of which involved a costume ball where Kate appears in a tight-fitting moth costume in gold lamé, an outfit designed by Walter Plunkett. She is somewhat bizarrely depicted with a skull-hugging cap with moth antennae sprouting upwards.

The other memorable scene—the most dramatic scene in the film—was the most difficult for Kate to shoot. In the closing moments as Kate is setting a high-altitude record at thirty thousand feet in her plane, she rips off her oxygen mask to "die free and alone in the clouds." She'd rather do that than tell her lover that she is pregnant.

Kate's suicide on film caused tremendous mental trauma for her, evoking the suicide of her own brother, Tom, who also deliberately cut off his oxygen. Very abruptly, Kate disappeared from the set on January 26 and 27 in 1933, and Arzner never knew that she was in deep mourning for Tom.

To boost her morale, Leland released his list of the world's ten most beautiful women, citing Katharine Hepburn right up there near the top with Greta Garbo and Marlene Dietrich.

In spite of many commitments, Leland showed up on the set almost every day to provide comfort and guidance to Kate, his lover and one of his most lucrative clients at the time. In his white flannels and yachting sneakers, he cut a dashing figure. Pandro Berman recalls Leland as a "buccaneer filled with impossible demands for his clients. If I weren't heterosexual, I'd go for him myself. He could charm the pants off any woman except a lez like Arzner. He not only could charm the pants off a woman, he frequently did."

During the windswept and rain-drenched winter of 1932 and 1933 when the film was being shot, Kate came down with a bad case of influenza and had to be hospitalized, shutting down the film. While Kate was in the Good Samaritan Hospital, the highly oversexed Leland turned elsewhere for romance. He fell into the arms of actress Fay Wray, who is remembered today only for writhing in the hand of a lovesick King Kong.

To get even with Leland, Kate, from her hospital bed, called Cukor, asking him to invite the beautiful actress Elissa Landi to one of his Sunday afternoon lunches—"but not Laura or Leland." At the time Landi was shooting *The Warrior's Husband*, playing on screen the character of Antiope, the warrior amazon, that Kate had originally created on stage.

With Fay Wray already in the picture, and Landi looming in the future, Leland and Kate continued to play their sexual games with each other. Unknown to either lover, both Leland and Kate were privately but only occasionally seducing Garbo on the side. Their love affairs with Garbo were temporarily put on hold, however, when the actress called both of them, reporting that she'd come down with a severe case of gonorrhea. She pronounced the word inaccurately but charmingly. Kate rushed again to Dr. Hirschfeld, who assured her that she did not have a venereal disease.

While still in her hospital bed, recovering from influenza, Kate received a copy of the play, *The Lake*, a morbid psychological drama, from Jed Harris, "the most notorious and hated producer on Broadway." She liked it and gave it to both Laura and Leland to read. Both of her lovers loathed the play, advising her to turn Harris down.

Kate thought that her own judgment was superior, and she wired Harris that she "loved" *The Lake* but that she'd have to turn it down while RKO rushed her through three more "quickie" films that year. Harris wired back that he would delay production on *The Lake* until she was available. In response, Kate wired back her acceptance of the role, a mistake she'd regret for the rest of her life.

***

During the time that she was frantically writing in an attempt to keep up with Arzner's production schedule, Zoë Akins told Kate her husband was dying. In the middle of a shoot, Akins received a call that Lord Rumbold had died of a heart attack caused by lingering injuries sustained on the battlefields of Europe in 1916. The unhappy marriage had only lasted eight months.

Kate noticed with amazement that Akins was back on the set two days later, her official period of mourning having ended quickly. In the weeks ahead, she was seen about town with her girl friend, Jobyna Howland. Both women wouldn't duck when photographers turned their cameras on them. Instead, they posed "arm in arm."

In the years ahead, Kate would be amused when Akins wrote *O Evening Star,* a play in which Howland would star in Los Angeles in 1935. It was based on the life of the lesbian actress, Marie Dressler, who had so aggressively and hopelessly pursued the much younger Garbo when the two stars made *Anna Christie.*

For the director of *O Evening Star*, Akins chose the very butch Leontine Sagan, who had made the first lesbian film, *Mädchen in Uniform,* in Austria in

1931. It had been well received in the permissive climate of Germany's short-lived Weimar Republic. Akins also managed to write in a small part for "my good boy chum," Anderson Lawler.

When Jobyna Howland died in 1936 of a heart attack, Kate showed up at the funeral. News accounts listed Akins—the chief mourner—as "an intimate friend."

***

One day in 1933, while waiting for Pandro Berman, her associate producer, to come back to his office, Kate idly picked up a script on his desk, and was shocked to discover that it was the latest screen treatment from Zoë Akins. Before Berman arrived, she read part of it and "fell madly in love with it—the most wonderful part ever written for anyone."

Smuggling it out in a large purse, Kate read it out loud that night to Laura, who also thought it was "wonderful." Leland was out on his nightly "tomcatting" and wasn't there to voice an opinion.

The next morning, bright and early, Kate showed up in the office of Berman and demanded the part.

"I've already bought it for Constance Bennett," Berman protested.

"Has she seen it?" Kate demanded to know.

"Not yet."

"Then it's for me. I'm Eva Lovelace. *Me! Me! Me!*"

Faced with such a strong will, Berman gave Kate the role. When she met Akins, Kate learned that the star role of the actress, Eva Lovelace, was based on the real-life Tallulah Bankhead, and Akins had once, very logically, proposed to Berman that Bankhead be cast in the role.

After agreeing to give the part to Kate, and long before Arzner's reviews had come in on *Christopher Strong,* Berman sent the director the script for *Morning Glory.*

In the biggest career mistake of her life, Arzner flatly refused, telling Berman that if "you are foolish enough to cast Miss Hepburn in another film, you'll do so without me."

When *Christopher Strong* was released, the picture flopped, the chief reasons being Arzner's heavy-handed directing and Akins's dull and desultory script.

Kate generally garnered good reviews, although many of them were mixed, as best exemplified by Regina Crewe writing in the *Journal-American* in New York. "That troubled, mask-like face, that straight, broad-shouldered, boyish figure—they may grate on you, but they compel attention. Hepburn is a distinct, definite, positive personality—the first since Garbo."

At Pasadena's Union Station, Leland gave Kate a long, passionate kiss, as Laura diverted her eyes.

Later, with Laura seated across from her in a private compartment, Kate boarded the Super Chief once again to return to New York and to her family in Connecticut.

In their letters and in their calls, neither Dr. Hepburn nor Kit seemed unduly impressed with their daughter's "superficial fame," talking with more animation about activities of their own or their other children, all of which they considered "more socially significant."

Luddy, usually with Jack stashed away somewhere else, was coming to West Hartford practically every weekend to see the Hepburns.

Although eager to see her family, it was the question of Luddy and their marriage that was the primary concern of Kate as the train rolled across the great plains of America.

"For once and for all, I've got to have a showdown with Luddy," Kate told Laura.

CHAPTER SIX

When Kate, along with Laura, arrived at New York's Grand Central, a rather angry Luddy greeted them. In a taxi en route to Turtle Bay, he confronted Kate with newspaper accounts in which she'd denied her marriage. "Being married to you is my whole life," Luddy claimed.

"Don't be a silly twit," Kate said. "Jack is your life—not me."

"But when you deny my very existence, it destroys me inside," Luddy claimed. "Marriage is everything to me."

"You're certainly married to Jack," Laura said, butting in and trying to add a touch of reality to the conversation.

"What marriage?" Kate asked. "We have no marriage. Do you want me to lie to the press?"

"Don't you always?" Laura asked.

"Shut up!" Kate yelled at her.

"We are married," he protested.

"According to a slip of paper," she said. "Face up to it like a man. There is no marriage between the two of us. Besides, I'm in love with another man."

Luddy looked stunned. He turned to Laura for confirmation. Only when Kate nodded that she could speak did Laura say, "Leland Hayward. I think you know him. Or at least you shook his hand once or twice. Our darling Kate, much to my regret, is doing a hell of a lot more than shaking his hand."

"He wants to marry me," Kate said.

The cuckolded Luddy seemed devastated. He'd accepted her relationship with Laura, who was practically part of their extended family. But Kate had never mentioned the word love before.

"I've said it before, and I'll say it again, our marriage is over," Kate said. "Finished."

"It's only an affair you're having with Leland," Luddy said. "You'll get over it and come back to me."

"What does 'come back to you' mean?" Kate asked. "Sleep between you and Jack? I love Jack dearly but I can't see all three of us in bed. I want out of this marriage. I don't want to be bound to you by a contract. When the time comes, and it may be sooner than later, I'll end the marriage in spite of your protests."

Back at the townhouse, while Laura caught up on all the news with Jack, Luddy did a strange thing. He brought out his camera and began to photograph Kate. As an actress, she became so caught up in her posing that she temporarily put their argument on hold. The dissolution of her marriage would have to wait for another day.

***

That weekend Jack and Laura were asked to spend time with their families, so that Kate and Luddy could drive to Connecticut by themselves.

Although Dr. Hepburn greeted her warmly, as did her brothers and sisters, Kate met a stone wall with her mother, Kit. Right in front of Luddy, Kit accused Kate of having "gone Hollywood." As evidence, Kit produced a newspaper photograph of Kate posing provocatively behind the wheel "of some fancy car." "Are you trying to outdo Gloria Swanson?"

"It was just a joke," Kate protested.

With Luddy still there, Kit also charged that, "You're ruining poor Luddy's life."

"I'm having an affair with Leland Hayward," Kate blurted out.

"I don't want to hear it," Kit said. "I'll pretend it's not happening. As far as I'm concerned, Luddy is my devoted son-in-law, whether you stay married to him or not. Besides, isn't Hayward already married like you are?"

"Oh, mother, you know what I think about marriage contracts," Kate said.

The argument between Kit and Kate continued over dinner. "If you must be an actress, can't you at least perform in a play by Shaw?" Kit asked.

Dr. Hepburn agreed with his wife. "Shaw is, after all, a friend of mine."

"If not Shaw, then Shakespeare?" Kit said.

Before dessert was served, Kit was attacking Laura Harding. "I have an extreme distaste for her and all her society ways. Miss American Express is trying to corrupt your value system."

"There's something unnatural about that Harding woman," Dr. Hepburn said, "and I can't put my finger on it. She's a queer one, not somebody you should be spending all your time with."

Kit agreed, suggesting that Laura should "live her own life and not stand in your shadow, waiting for your next command."

"I think the relationship between you and this Miss Harding is unhealthy for both of you," Dr. Hepburn said. "It'll lead to a lot of pain." He turned to his beloved Luddy. "Here's the man who loves you. He's the one you should be taking back to Hollywood with you, if you have to go back at all."

Although she followed her father's financial advice, she didn't take his suggestion about how to lead her life once she returned to New York.

Both a hapless Luddy, along with Jack, waited on the Grand Central platform to tell them good-bye, as both Kate and Laura waved as the train to Los Angeles pulled out.

At that point, Kate didn't know that the Prince Charming of Hollywood was waiting to greet her in California.

116

***

The prince was Douglas Fairbanks, Jr., who had signed to co-star with Kate in *Morning Glory* along with Adolphe Menjou. But she didn't meet Fairbanks right away.

When Kate got back to Los Angeles, she resumed sleeping with Leland but wasn't listening to her agent's choices for her career. Leland had read the Akins treatment of *Morning Glory* and claimed he hated it, urging Kate to turn down the role. "You don't want to play some stage-struck young actress."

Kate adamantly refused to listen to Leland and drove that night to the home of Lowell Sherman, her director. He was the brother-in-law of John Barrymore, as he was married to Helene Costello. Heavyset, with a swarthy face, Sherman was hardly leading man material, although Cukor had cast him opposite Constance Bennett in *What Price Hollywood?* in 1932.

Kate later remembered him as "very plump and round, a man who had eaten too much Christmas pudding." In Sherman's case, he was fattened from all the sugar in alcohol. No longer an actor, Sherman appeared battle weary, as he'd just attempted to direct Mae West in *She Done Him Wrong.*

Drinking heavily the first night he met Kate, Sherman told her that her salary had been raised from $1,500 a week to $2,000. And now the bad news. He said they had an impossible schedule, insisting they would have only one week of rehearsal, followed by just nineteen days to shoot the picture.

Instead of fighting with Sherman, as she had with Dorothy Arzner, she felt sorry for the failed actor. The caretaker side of her character came out. He staggered drunk on the set every morning during the shoot, often as late as ten o'clock. But when Kate learned that he was dying of throat cancer, she became most sympathetic to him and despite the tight schedule, cooperated in every way she could.

The story of *Morning Glory* was a familiar one, a kind of *42nd Street* without the songs. It tells of a stage-struck young actress who comes to Broadway seeking an acting career. She becomes an overnight sensation when the temperamental star of the picture, the character of Rita Vernon, as played by Mary Duncan, storms out of the theater on opening night, and Kate goes on and emerges a star.

Morning Glory became the prototype of the starstruck-starlet-takes-Hollywood-by-storm type of movie. In a notable scene in the film, Kate, as Eva Lovelace, gets drunk on champagne at a party and starts reciting Hamlet's soliloquy.

Into the shoot, Kate told Sherman that she wasn't modeling the part of Eva Lovelace on that "foul-mouthed Tallulah," as Akins had intended, but on another actress, Ruth Gordon, who in time would become one of Kate's best friends. Kate had seen Gordon in the play, *A Church Mouse,* and she rattled off her lines in *Morning Glory* at the same breakneck speed that Gordon had used.

A memorable line in the film is delivered by veteran actor, C. Aubrey Smith, who warns Kate, playing Eva, about letting early success go to her head. It was a line that could almost have been said to the real Kate. "How many keep their heads? You've come to the fore. Now you have the chance to be a morning glory—a flower that fades before the sun is very high."

It was left to Menjou to deliver that often-repeated and immortal line: "You don't belong to any man now—you belong to Broadway."

***

Her Prince Charming, Douglas Fairbanks, Jr., playing the lovelorn playwright, Joseph Sheridan, started off despising Kate and ended up loving her. The first day he met her, he told Sherman that, "I'm jealous. Here I am the son of Douglas Fairbanks and the stepson of Mary Pickford, and Hepburn is getting all the publicity." Fairbanks also complained to Sherman about Kate's "masculine mind and her compulsion to go out of her way to insult me."

The tension between them melted on the day they were to film a dream sequence from *Romeo and Juliet.* In green tights, Fairbanks appeared looking, in his words, "like the second prize winner in a transvestite contest." He later told Kate he feared that in his costume he would evoke Barrymore's "decadent string bean." A friend of Barrymore's, Fairbanks confided in Kate that whenever The Great Profile had to appear in green tights, he stuffed a very thick sock inside them. According to Barrymore, that doubled attendance among the lady theater-goers.

Kate laughed at that and began to take a liking to young Fairbanks. In spite of his earlier words to Sherman, Fairbanks began to find her attractive, even sexy, in spite of her constant smoking while dressed in the Juliet costume. On the day of the shoot, young Fairbanks invited his father along with his stepmother, Mary Pickford. Kate claimed that the appearance of "those two made me so nervous I almost forgot my lines." Both Kate and Fairbanks Jr. later expressed their regret that their Romeo and Juliet scene had to be cut when *Morning Glory* ran too long. The actual filmed sequence has disappeared, although stills remain. "I wanted Kit to see me doing Shakespeare," Kate later lamented.

"I had been begging Kate for a date," Fairbanks said. After the Romeo and Juliet shoot, Kate agreed to go out with him. She invited him to her Coldwater Canyon home. Fairbanks learned that both Laura and Leland had returned to New York on urgent business, Leland flying Laura there in his own private plane. "By the time the dinner invitation came through, I was madly in love with Kate," Fairbanks told Sherman.

Since Kate didn't want to go out to a restaurant, she cooked supper for Fairbanks on their first date. "Healthy, not stylish food," as he remembered.

Before dinner, she invited him for the same long walk she customarily took with Laura above Mulholland Drive. Wandering in the mountains, Kate told him that she and Laura were almost killed when they challenged some hunters who, against regulations, were shooting rabbits. "The angry men turned and fired on us, and we ran for our lives."

That night, Fairbanks, contrary to what he claimed in his autobiography, *The Salad Days,* seduced Kate. "Back then, as he would tell his friend, Cary Grant, later in life, "I was right proud of myself. After all, as a teenager I'd been taught sex by an expert, my wife, Joan Crawford."

Fairbanks remembered that when he got up to go to the bathroom, he saw a black-shrouded man heading for Kate's bedroom. Thinking it was an intruder, he shouted at him and awoke Kate. "The moment she turned on the light, the figure disappeared," Fairbanks said. "Kate told me 'Don't let him bother you. The house is haunted. This fellow appears every night. We're getting used to him.'"

After Laura and Kate left the house, it was rented to Boris Karloff. Frankenstein himself must have scared the ghost off.

Fairbanks claimed that his affair with Kate lasted only "four nights in a row." He blamed the return of Leland and Laura for "breaking us up."

In his autobiography, Fairbanks writes, "halfway through dinner (on their fourth night together), she developed a sick headache." He drove her home but claimed that he only got a peck on the cheek that night. He wrote that he was so in love with her that he stayed parked waiting for her to turn on the lights in the haunted house.

"Suddenly," he writes, "the front door flew open and Kate came running out. Another car I hadn't noticed before was hidden farther up the driveway under some trees. She hopped in, and I saw a man at the wheel. I never saw his face. They drove right past me without noticing me. She was laughing happily, her hair blowing over her face!"

The strange man at the wheel was either the ghost or, more likely, Leland Hayward who had come back from New York that afternoon.

The breakup of the short affair between Kate and Fairbanks was perhaps more complicated than reported in *The Salad Days.* When Kenneth heard of her affair with young Fairbanks, he too claimed that he was having an affair with him, since "Doug is double-gaited." Not only that, but Kenneth told her that he was "also having an illicit affair with Doug's stepmother, Mary Pickford." At the time Kenneth was the leading man in the film, *Secrets*, which Pickford financed and shot in part. She later abandoned the picture before its completion because she didn't look "young enough."

To complicate matters, Anderson Lawler reported all the latest Hollywood gossip. He claimed that Fairbanks Sr. was having an illicit affair with his daughter-in-law, Joan Crawford.

"I have to get out of that scene—and be quick about it," Kate told Lawler.

Although their romance and their Romeo and Juliet ended up on the cutting room floor, Kate and her handsome and dashing young Prince Charming remained friends for decades. When not in the same city, they wrote affectionate notes, each calling the other "Pete."

With Fairbanks out of her life, and with Laura and Leland back in residence, Kate still managed to see Garbo infrequently. The Swedish star had recovered from her gonorrhea.

With all these lovers in tow, Kate was still on the verge of plunging into another wild and reckless affair, which would do more to damage her relationship with Laura than all the others.

Kate, at least for three short months in her life, was about to fall in love with a woman who was a pretender to the throne of Austria and Hungary.

***

In Hollywood, Kate showed up without Laura to meet an actress at one of Cukor's Sunday afternoon lunches. Kate had been badgering Cukor to invite who she called "the girl of my dreams." Finally, Cukor called Kate and told her this actress would be in attendance. "I tried to get her to come alone," Cukor warned Kate, "but she claims she never goes anywhere without an escort."

Kate wore rather masculine attire for her meeting with Elissa Landi, who made her appearance stunningly dressed in diamonds and furs. On her arm was a devastatingly handsome actor, Laurence Olivier.

She'd co-starred with him in a film, *The Yellow Ticket.* When Olivier went to get drinks for both of them, Kate pointedly said to Landi, "I hope Jill Esmond doesn't show up today."

"She's in New York," Landi said. "And even if she did, it wouldn't matter." Landi leaned over to whisper to Kate. "Jill's strictly for the ladies, unlike me who works both sides of the fence."

"One of those lavender marriages I keep hearing about out here," Kate said.

"Yes, a lavender marriage exactly like your own from what I hear," Landi said, staring directly into Kate's eyes.

Coming from a lesser person, Kate might have been insulted. But it was Landi's frankness that attracted Kate to her.

Kate had heard all the rumors, none of them denied by Landi. She was said to be the secret (i.e., illegitimate) granddaughter of "Sissi," the Empress Elizabeth of Austria, the beautiful but strong-willed Bavarian-born wife of Franz Josef, the monarch of the Austro-Hungarian empire who presided over its demise. After a brief affair with Humphrey Bogart, he'd nicknamed her the "Empress of Austria" and the label had stuck.

Landi preferred to be introduced simply as "Countess," having assumed the title from her mother's second marriage to an Italian nobleman, Count Carlo

Zanardi-Landi.

When Olivier returned, he found himself left out of the conversation and drifted over to join Anderson Lawler and "the boys," as Cukor called some of his more effeminate male guests.

Although Kate and Olivier didn't strike up an immediate friendship, they would become close in years to come and would in 1975 appear together in the ABC film, *Love Among the Ruins,* directed by Cukor himself.

Landi was not only beautiful but bright and quick-witted and had even written novels. Cukor had already told Kate that Landi was "double-gaited," having gone through a love affair with Myrna Loy, who was called Miss Gillette "because she shaves on both sides."

Kate and Landi immediately bonded, sharing joint experiences, talking about playing the role of Antiope in *The Warrior's Husband,* Kate on Broadway and Landi on screen. RKO had refused to purchase the screen rights for Kate.

Three hours later, Landi decided to leave the party with Kate and invited her back to her elegant home, where she threw some of the grandest "literary parties" in Hollywood, and also invited some of the more famous Hollywood notables, including William Randolph Hearst and his mistress, Marion Davies.

Anderson Lawler came over to Kate and Landi, claiming that they didn't have to worry about "Larry" Olivier, as he'd invited him out for the evening. "What Jill Esmond doesn't go for, I do," Lawler told the women before winking at them and heading back to the handsome Olivier on whom he'd developed an instant crush.

After that weekend, Kate began to see Landi as often as she could, which was almost every day. Somehow Kate still managed to fit Laura and Leland into her busy schedule as well.

Laura suspected that Kate was seeing another man, and confided her concerns in Leland. He told her that it simply wasn't so. "Kate may need another woman, but there's no way in hell she needs another man after rising from my bed."

When Kate claimed she had to make a guest appearance in San Francisco, and a Los Angeles newspaper published a photograph of Kate and Landi, both attired in mink, getting on a plane, Laura decided to call it quits. She'd had enough of Kate's philandering with other women, she told Leland.

When Landi and Kate returned from San Francisco, a note was waiting at Quinta Nirvana. Laura's secret name for Kate was "Max."

Dear Max,
I'll always love you and always be your friend, but our romance has officially ended as of today. I'm on the Super Chief back East where I belong.
Love,

121

Kate shared the contents of the note with Leland, Cukor, Kenneth, and Lawler. With Landi by her side, she adjusted quickly to Laura's departure.

"It used to be Max and Laura," Kate told Kenneth. "Now it's going to be Jimmy and Elissa."

For a few brief weeks in 1933, Kate had started calling herself Jimmy, as she'd done when she was nine years old back in Hartford. "Elissa wants me to be the man in the relationship," she told Kenneth. "What other role could I be? She claims I'm better in bed than Bogart and better than Myrna Loy but not as good as Marlene Dietrich or Basil Rathbone."

***

With Laura gone, Landi became a fixture around Kate's Quinta Nirvana. Leland later claimed that the two women could talk for hours about such subjects as, "What is Garboesque and what isn't?" Before Kate retired early at night, she read Landi's published novels, *Neilsen* from 1925 and *The Helmers* from 1930.

According to Leland, Kate helped Landi with her novel *House for Sale,* published in 1933, and gave her the idea for *The Ancestor,* released the following year.

From the beginning of their relationship, Landi flattered Kate with her remarks. "I may be European empress material, but you are definitely an American princess."

The two women were remarkably different, however. Landi liked to wear beautiful gowns and furs, often appearing at parties in stunning examples of haute couture, perhaps an emerald silk gown as one of her fans later recalled. Within a week, Landi had accomplished what no other person could do. She had Kate dressing pretty much as she did herself. The crew at RKO was stunned to see Kate showing up for work in the fashionable clothes of the era.

Landi took Kate horseback riding high in the Hollywood Hills and deliberately insisted on seducing her "at the exact same spot where Gloria Swanson seduced Valentino," an act Swanson denied in her memoirs but later admitted privately.

Referring to the former Empress of Austria, Landi told Kate that, "Sissi was a great equestrian, and I want to be like her." Landi was a devout follower of the Empress, even practicing her draconian diet of a moderate portion of raw steak daily, a glass of milk, and another glass of freshly squeezed orange juice. Landi abhorred Kate's habit of cooking bacon and eggs for breakfast in the morning. Although Kate for a very brief period in her life dressed up, she refused to follow Sissi's rigid diet.

The relationship wasn't all peaceful. One night Kate told Landi she had been miscast in the role of Antiope in the film *The Warrior's Husband,* and that Kate herself should have brought the character to screen. That critique didn't sit well with Landi, who pouted for the rest of the night.

Kate also undermined Landi's confidence in telling her what a big mistake she'd made in appearing in *The Sign of the Cross* for Cecil B. DeMille. Very accurately Kate claimed that Fredric March, Charles Laughton, and Claudette Colbert, three powerful performers, stole the picture from her.

Kate wrote Laura several letters, all of which were returned unopened. All copies of these letters are believed to have been destroyed.

Kate's relationship with Landi, at least according to Cukor's crystal ball, might have lasted longer had Kate not returned home early one afternoon, complaining at RKO that she felt ill.

To her shock, Kate found Leland and Landi, her two lovers, "getting to know each other the way David came to know Bathsheba." Those were a distraught Kate's exact words when she confided in Lawler the following day.

Kate told Lawler that she had ordered Landi from her house, claiming she could not forgive her for "this major betrayal."

"But we never promised to be faithful to each other, and you know I'm attracted to men," Landi said.

As Landi packed her suitcase, she asked, "What about Leland? He instigated it."

"With men, you expect such behavior," Kate said.

Landi did not go into mourning over the loss of Kate. The next week she began seeing Claudette Colbert very seriously.

Kate wrote Laura that she'd kicked Landi out and begged Laura to return. She also wrote Luddy and Jack, telling of her "big mistake—how could I be so foolish?"

Laura visited Luddy and Jack as well, confessing that, "I can't live without Kate. I'm asking to have my heart broken but I'm taking the next train to Los Angeles."

Back in Los Angeles, Kate made the reconciliation easy with Laura, claiming that she'd been a pig. In moments when she felt she'd behaved badly, Kate always referred to herself as a pig. Kate claimed that Laura had been noble about her indiscretions and begged to "come back and stay forever." Laura readily agreed.

However, Laura faced the upcoming shoot of *Little Women* with some trepidation, as by now she'd learned that Kate had a habit of falling in love with one or even two of the people she worked with on a film.

Laura had studied the cast and crew of *Little Women* and had concluded that Kate would not possibly have any romantic interest in any of the people either starring in or working behind the scenes on the film.

"I know you can't run off with Joan Bennett, Jean Parker, or Frances Dee because they like men," Laura said. "Paul Lukas is not your type. Your beau in the film, Douglass Montgomery, is as gay as a goose, and Cukor will probably be spending time in that pretty boy's dressing room. That leaves only dear, sweet Spring Byington. I'd bet my fortune that if there's one woman in Hollywood who's not a lesbian, it's *Miss* Spring Byington."

***

Even though Kate had kicked Landi out when she caught her having intercourse with Leland, Kate was much more tolerant of the transgressions of her agent and lover. When her gossipy friend, Lawler, came to her and told her that Leland was having a torrid affair with actress Miriam Hopkins, Kate did not confront Leland. As long as Leland guided her career in the right direction, and showed up at least on occasions in her bed, all was well.

That changed one morning as Kate and Laura enjoyed breakfast prepared by their maid, Johanna Madsen. Laura came across a story by a columnist in *The Los Angeles Times.* With only a touch of malice, Laura, still jealous of Leland's control over Kate, handed her the news story to read.

A stunned Kate read that, "Hollywood's hottest agent, Leland Hayward, believes in maintaining a close personal relationship with his clients. He works by day trying to get choice roles for his stable of mares, along with top dollars, then spends nights at their bedside catering to their personal requests. His by now famous 'scalp bracelet' is impressive. Clara Bow. Miriam Hopkins. Marlene Dietrich. Greta Garbo. Katharine Hepburn. And now his latest *protégée*—twenty-four-year old Margaret Sullavan."

Kate reacted in fury. She'd never met Sullavan but had bitterly resented comparisons between the two of them. At one point, the Broadway producer, Jed Harris, had told a columnist that the Virginia-born Margaret Sullavan was "a Southern version of Katharine Hepburn."

From what she'd heard, Laura claimed that Sullavan was "trying to out-Hepburn Hepburn."

Sullavan showed up at her studio in pants, most often blue jeans, years before it became fashionable for women to wear such attire. She did Kate one better, appearing on a motorcycle without a helmet with her hair blowing in the wind.

Like Kate, Sullavan was known for her distinctive voice. Critics called it "liquid gravel," even "liquid diamonds." Silent screen star, Louise Brooks, hailed Sullavan as "my favorite actress—that wonderful voice of hers, strange, fey, mysterious, like a voice singing in the snow." Other critics were less kind, gossip maven Louella Parsons calling Sullavan "a rude, contrary, and spiteful bitch."

Sullavan was known for flirting with any handsome man who came before

124

her, viewing herself as irresistible and a *femme fatale*. "I can't help it if men gather around me like moths to the flame."

She boasted that she could give "any man a hard-on, even a homosexual, all except Henry Fonda." The latter catty remark was a reference to her failed marriage to the then-unknown actor. As a young actress, Sullavan had a penchant for seducing future superstars, including James Stewart and Humphrey Bogart.

Sullavan would shock members of the press, whom she disdained as much as Kate herself. Many of her quotes were unprintable at the time. "There was so much prissy propriety and sexual prudery and emotional repression among the people who inhabited my early life that I suppose I went to the other extreme," she once said, following it with this final observation: "The wonder of men is that no two of them are alike, especially when making love."

Whereas Leland's other conquests, even Garbo, had not threatened Kate, the attention he was showing Sullavan, her rival, was not acceptable.

When Leland arrived in the late afternoon at the Coldwater Canyon house where Kate and Laura lived, he found his personal possessions, mostly wardrobe, packed and waiting for him. Kate had scribbled a note. "It's all over. Please leave."

He did not try to force open the locked door to her bedroom, encountering only Laura, "a Greenland icicle," as he'd later say.

He did write Kate a note in return. "Our relationship will end only when I tell you it's over—and not before. Love, Leland."

***

Although Kate broke off her sexual relationship with Leland for several months, she continued to maintain her professional role with him.

Leland had misjudged Kate's success in *Morning Glory*. But he was excited about her prospects in *Little Women*. "No more lez directors like Dorothy Arzner," Leland said, as he'd been bitterly disappointed with the box-office receipts of *Christopher Strong*. "Instead of a lez, you're safer with a queen like Cukor," Leland advised.

Kate was saddened that her mentor, Selznick, was leaving RKO for MGM and wouldn't be around for the filming of the Louisa May Alcott classic about four girls growing into womanhood in Concord, Massachusetts, while their father was away fighting the Civil War. Even though Cukor had never read the Alcott novel—and Kate suspected that he never would—he denounced the first draft screenplays as "filled with a saccharine sweet sentimentality."

A husband-and-wife writing team, Victor Heerman and Sarah Y. Mason, were hired as the scenarists, and Kate felt their final draft captured the "sternness and survival of the Alcott novel." Still resisting reading the novel, although maintaining that he had, Cukor agreed with Kate that the final screenplay was closer to Alcott's classic version.

125

An excited Kate told both Cukor and Leland that, "I was born to play Jo March. She's masculine like a boy, like I was when I demanded to be called Jimmy when I was nine years old. But she's also feminine when that's called for. She's funny. Wears her heart on her sleeve but can also be fiercely loyal and determined when need be. She's pure but not that pure." Deep into filming, Kate felt she'd captured the slangy tomboy quality of Jo March. Cukor kidded her, "Of all the *Little Women*, you're the only one playing a lesbian. The other lesbians in the film are covering their sins."

"What other lesbians?" Kate asked.

"Edna May Oliver, your Aunt March," he said. "Even your dearly beloved Marmee, Spring Byington."

Kate looked startled. "I could certainly believe that of horse-faced Oliver, but that tender, sweet, cuddly Spring Byington. There's just no way!"

Her own walking public relations machine, Kate, halfway through the shoot, proclaimed that, "I would defy any actress to be as splendid as I am playing Jo."

On the set, Cukor and Kate, though in basic agreement about the script, clashed violently at times. In a pivotal scene, Kate had to run up a flight of steps with some ice cream. Cukor warned her not to spill any of it on her dress. He said that Walter Plunkett, who had designed her famous insect costume in *Christopher Strong,* had sewn the dress together out of rare material, authentic to the Civil War era, and that wardrobe had no duplicate.

Kate ran up the steps when Cukor called for action and promptly spilled the ice cream all over herself, ruining the take and the precious dress. Infuriated, Cukor walked across the sound stage and violently slapped her face, as he had Laura's on a previous picture. "You're a God damn amateur, and you'll never amount to anything in films."

"And you're a total ass!" she shouted at him before running from the sound stage where she vomited in her dressing room. She refused to work for the rest of the day, in spite of the fact they were on a tight schedule.

She called Leland that afternoon and demanded that he contact the executive producer, Merian C. Cooper, and have Cukor fired from *Little Women.* "As long as I live, I'll never work with George Cukor again!"

***

During the filming of *Little Women,* Kate introduced the custom of bringing picnic lunches every day to the set to feed select members of the cast and crew. Her invitations were rotated, and a grip might be found sitting next to the associate producer of the picture, which was, of course, against Hollywood protocol in the commissary.

Cukor denounced the picnics as one of Kate's "affectations," but he was probably miffed that Kate did not invite him to a picnic for two whole weeks after he'd slapped her. Of course, she never carried out her threat to have Cukor fired. Once Cukor began attending the picnics, he softened his position and later came to feel that these breaks in the day, as well as Kate's fondness for stopping work for four o'clock afternoon tea, broke the tension on the set.

The heiress to a banking fortune, Laura found that her job involved arranging and setting up these daily picnics. The food was a big hit with cast and crew, especially the stews which drew rave reviews. Laura pretended that she cooked all the food, except back at their home, Johanna, the maid, was the real chef. Years after she departed from the Harding/Hepburn ménage, Johanna was still garnering raves for her old-fashioned, down-to-earth cooking.

One day Cukor invited Tallulah Bankhead to the set of *Little Women* to see "a work in progress." When Kate heard the news, she called Tallulah and asked her to the picnic and to name any favorite dishes. "Southern fried chicken, darling, and a glass of bourbon with a little branch water. And, darling, make that chicken well-done like our cook in Alabama fried it. Yankees never know how to cook fried chicken. For that, you've got to cross the Mason-Dixon line."

Although Tallulah and Kate later developed a confidential friendship, their relationship had been a bit chilled before Tallulah came to the set the next day. They did share a common bond, however, in that Anderson Lawler was their "dearest male chum." Kate suspected that Lawler told Kate Hepburn stories to Tallulah and vice versa.

At first Tallulah had found Kate "a dreary, opinionated college girl," and Kate told Cukor, "Your friend Miss Bankhead is very rude and a potty mouth." When Tallulah had made her "obligatory pass" at Kate at one of Cukor's Sunday afternoon lunches, and Kate had turned her down, Tallulah called her "the Connecticut spinster." Tallulah laughingly shared the rejection with her friends, as even then she had the gift of self-parody. "Her God damn mother back in Hartford is forever advocating birth control like that tight pussy, Margaret Sanger. What better way for her daughter to practice birth control than to have sex with me?" Tallulah would roar with laughter at her own story, whether anyone found it amusing or not.

Kate feared a hostile review the day Tallulah barged onto the set. "For God's sake, George," Kate said, "you don't invite your friend, Miss Bankhead, to see rushes from *Little Women*. *Dracula in Drag,* perhaps, but not *Little Women.*"

In addition to being outrageous, Tallulah could also pretend to be a gracious Southern lady. And that is what she was when she showed up on Cukor's set, at least for the first five minutes until Kate and Laura came over. Tallulah outrageously gave both Kate and Laura a long and passionate kiss on their lips. "That's your thrill for the day, darlings," she told the two astonished women. "The preacher at our church when I was a little girl in Alabama taught me to kiss. If you don't like it, blame him." Roaring with laughter, she went into the screening room to see the rushes. Kate didn't want to go in with her, although she was invited to do so.

Less than an hour later, Tallulah stormed onto the set. Seeing Kate, she burst into tears, as she fell at her feet. "That was a great actress I saw up there on the screen today."

Tallulah had perfected her technique of falling at the feet of great actresses, having performed this ritual with Laurette Taylor and Ethel Barrymore among others. Later at Hollywood parties she would fall at the feet of handsome actors when she met one for the first time, as was the case with Errol Flynn when she buried her face in his crotch upon introduction.

Coming up, Cukor said to her, "Get on your feet, my dear. You're not weeping for what a great actress Kate is. You're weeping for the loss of your own virginity. I'm sure that occurred at the age of six, because I hear they break in you Alabama gals early."

***

For some reason never fully explained, Kate developed an antagonism to Joan Bennett, who was playing her sister, Amy, in *Little Women.* Kate told Cukor that she found Joan "beautiful but vapid."

The feud between the actresses would continue for decades, reaching its crescendo when Kate turned down the 1950 role of Spencer Tracy's wife and Elizabeth Taylor's mother in MGM's *Father of the Bride.* Joan stepped in at the last minute to play the wife and mother.

In 1933, Kate had literally stolen the script of *Morning Glory* from Joan's sister, Constance. Partly because of that, there was a great deal of Bennett family resentment toward Kate. Compounding the feud was the fact that Kate never spoke to Joan except on camera delivering a line.

Joan, married to screenwriter Gene Markey, was pregnant and growing bigger every day, exasperating her costume designer, Walter Plunkett. After the technicians called a three-week strike, and production was delayed, Cukor screamed when Joan showed up for work. "You're a God damn balloon!" He later told Kate, "To avoid Joan's big belly, I find that I have to shoot higher and higher. Before the end of the film, I'll have to aim the camera only at her face."

"You could always change the Alcott story," Kate said in jest. "Let Amy play my sister having a child out of wedlock."

Kate and Laura never invited Joan to one of their picnics. Obviously infuriated, Joan and her husband started having picnics of their own, often inviting the same members of cast and crew. Joan bought her food at an expensive Beverly Hills delicatessen, Sam's Deli. When faced with a double invitation to Kate's picnic or Joan's spread, a member of the cast always opted to join Kate and Laura, claiming their food was so much better than the deli cuisine.

One day Joan invited her sister, Constance, to the set for one of her picnics. Along with Barbara, the three beautiful Bennett sisters were the daughters of matinee idol Richard Bennett.

Although she was soon to be given the label of "box office poison," long before that appellation was applied to Kate, Constance was the highest paid female star in Hollywood on the day she showed up, drawing a net salary of $150,000 for less than five weeks' work.

Model-slender, Constance had china-blue eyes and a marcelled blonde bob. Attired in the latest Paris fashion, she was hailed by many critics as the best dressed actress in Hollywood.

At the time, Constance, having ended her affair with Joseph Kennedy, was married to the Marquis Henri de la Falaise de la Coudraye after the gigolo had been dumped by his former wife, Gloria Swanson, who had also vied with Constance for the attention of Joseph Kennedy. Constance stood in sharp contrast to the home-spun costumes Kate wore on camera in *Little Women* or her masculine attire off camera.

The two rival picnics were conducted about two-hundred yards apart. As Kate got up and thanked Laura for bringing all the good food, the crew was stunned to see Constance striding over to Kate's camp.

At first it appeared that a major star was coming over to meet another major star. With regal grace, Constance stood in front of Kate. Suddenly, she raised her arm and gave Kate a loud slap on her left cheek. "That's for stealing *Morning Glory* from me." Constance then turned her back and walked off the set.

Nearly a decade went by before Kate returned the favor. When George Cukor was directing Salka Viertel's *Two-Faced Woman* for MGM in 1941, Kate asked her friends Garbo and the director if she could come on the set. Both readily agreed. As it turned out, Kate wasn't there to see either Cukor or Garbo. Constance Bennett was playing the third lead in the film. Kate walked up to Constance and slapped her face so hard Constance lost her balance.

"Now that's a slap," Kate said to Constance. "Not that peck on the cheek you gave to me."

Kate's appearance on the set was later viewed as a bad omen for *Two-Faced Woman*. After the failure of the picture, Garbo never appeared in another film, and Constance descended into B-movie limbo, appearing in such roles as *Wild Bill Hickok Rides*.

***

Laura claimed that horse-faced Edna Mae Oliver, playing Aunt March in *Little Women*, was definitely excited when Kate walked onto the set. Laura forbade Kate to be alone with Oliver at any point.

However, Spring Byington, playing Marmee, was according to Laura, the straightest woman who ever lived. "She's not going to make any moves on you," Laura told Kate. "She's so sweet and Hollywood's only guaranteed straight woman."

Both Laura and Kate had been amused by the screwball roles Byington played on screen. Off-camera, both women found her quite different, an intelligent and sensitive woman. As Laura and Kate viewed themselves as feminists, they were impressed that Byington's mother, Dr. Helene Byington, was one of the first women doctors in the West.

In the second week of the shoot, Byington asked Kate if, "I can bring a special and dear friend to your picnic?" Kate gladly extended an invitation, and the next day Byington turned up on the set with actress Marjorie Main. After the first two minutes of watching the two women together, Kate concluded that Laura had been wrong about Byington. She indeed was a lesbian, and made it rather clear that she and Main were locked into a torrid affair. In closeted Hollywood, Kate somewhat admired Byington's obvious adoration of Main.

Those who remember Main from her hard-bitten Ma Kettle roles and her "sack-of-taters" figure might find it hard to imagine the actress in any sexual liaison. But in her day, Main had a rather pretty face and a decent figure, enough to get her offered a job as a chorine dancing in New York and appearing in the show *Burlesque* with her co-star and lover at the time, Barbara Stanwyck. Main would immortalize herself in the 1947 *The Egg and I*, in which she appeared with another lesbian actress, Claudette Colbert.

Both Kate and Laura were enchanted with Main and her voice, which was often described as evoking a crow. She was a candid and down-to-earth mother figure, with square shoulders and a wicked sense of humor that appealed to Kate.

When Byington and Main invited Kate and Laura over to their house to "meet two fellows I think you'll like," Kate at first hesitated. "You're not trying to fix us up with anybody, are you?"

"I'm too smart for that," Main said. "These two guys are already fixed up with each other."

***

Always on time, Kate arrived, with Laura in tow, thirty minutes before the other two male guests, the names of which had not been revealed to her. Byington and Main were warm and cordial hosts and seemed to want to get together for more dinners and some lesbian bonding. Kate, although initially intrigued with the two character actresses, was fond of them but did not pursue the friendship once the filming on *Little Women* ended.

Late or not, the two male guests of the evening finally strolled in, wearing matching clothing of white flannels and navy blue shirts. Main and Byington introduced Kate and Laura to Cary Grant and his "roommate," Randolph Scott. Other than Spencer Tracy, no other actor would appear opposite Kate as often as Grant.

Main told Kate that she'd met the two actors when she'd made a film with them, *Hot Saturday* in 1932, directed by William A. Seiter. Main had played a gossip, and both Scott and Grant had taken second billing to baby-faced Nancy

Carroll, then in the throes of a big romance with Joseph Kennedy after he'd left the arms of Gloria Swanson and Constance Bennett.

A native Virginian, Scott was an impressive sight, standing six feet, four inches. A well-built man, he was lean and well-muscled, cutting an impressive, athletic figure. His square-cut jaw gave him a slightly horsey face. He was well-tanned and seemed to tower over Kate who quickly dubbed him "The Giant." Weighing just under two-hundred pounds, he had a slow but swinging walk.

Kate was more attracted to Grant, another six-footer. This brunette British-born actor was even better looking and was far more outgoing than Scott. Grant had a smooth manner and a gentlemanly air. When he interrupted Scott in mid-sentence and received an icy reprimand, Grant quickly shut up. Kate easily determined who was the "boss man" in the relationship.

At the time of their meeting, Laura and Kate had the dubious honor of being the most gossiped- about lesbian couple in Hollywood, although they rarely made the columns. Not so with Grant and Scott. Almost daily there was an item inserted about them in some gossip column. The current issue of *Modern Screen*, in writing about the two actors living together, called Grant "the gay, impetuous one," and accurately claimed that Scott was more "serious and cautious." When the acid-tongued and homophobic Hollywood columnist, Jimmie Fiddler, saw photographs of Grant and Scott, clad in aprons doing the dishes in their kitchen, he wrote that these two actors were "carrying the buddy business a bit far."

Over drinks at Main's house, Grant asked Kate how she and Laura managed to keep their names out of the columns. Laura answered for her. "We eat dinner at six o'clock and Kate's in bed by nine-thirty. She never wants to go out."

"That's not because I'm afraid of the press," Kate said. "That's the way I like to live."

Byington kept running back and forth between the kitchen and the dining room, Main chimed in occasionally, but most of the dinner conversation was between Kate and Grant. Scott sat rather stoically throughout the evening observing the other players.

At one point Main suggested that Laura should serve as a beard for Scott and Kate as beard for Grant. "You guys would make a handsome foursome out on a double date. You'd get your pictures in the papers, riding in Randy's shiny new Cadillac one night and Grant's Packard roadster the next night."

"That might work," Scott said.

Main uttered a word of caution. "If you gals go out with my boys, take along a fat purse. Cary here is a penny-pincher, and Randy has the calculating eyes of a crooked horse-trader and the heart of a cash register." Main had accurately assessed the character of Scott. He went on to become one of Hollywood's richest investors, stashing away twenty-million dollars.

"I save my money," Grant protested, "because I grew up 'po'," he said. "Bristol, England. Not a pot to piss in." He amused the dinner guests with stories about his early life as Archibald Leach and his career as an acrobat, including a gig as a stilt walker on Coney Island.

"I'm a great acrobat," Grant said. He got up from the table and asked Kate or Laura if one would agree to balance herself on his shoulders. The more athletic Kate agreed, and he easily held her up in the air, her bare feet resting on his broad shoulders.

"You folks can take that act on the road if they ever bring back vaudeville," Byington said.

Kate and Grant shared director stories, as Lowell Sherman had directed Grant in *She Done Him Wrong* and Kate in *Morning Glory.*

"What's it like to work with Mae West?" Laura asked.

In *She Done Him Wrong*, the sultry West delivered one of the most famous but one of the most misquoted lines in film history, when she'd invited him to "Come up some time and see me."

"You don't act with West," Grant told the dinner party. "You just stand there looking real pretty waiting for her to deliver her next zinger."

"When you're appearing with the diamond-studded Lady Lou, that siren of the Bowery, you don't step on her line," Main said. She revealed that she'd worked with West on the stage in New York in a play called *The Wicked Age* in 1927. She said that she still visited West frequently at her apartment in the Los Angeles suburb of Ravenswood. Kate said that of all the actresses in Hollywood, she would most want to meet Mae West. Main promised to call her friend the next day and arrange it.

As the evening progressed, more and more talk centered around Howard Hughes, who had originally "discovered" Scott, a male model. Scott had introduced Grant to the tycoon, and Hughes had seemed to fall even more for the younger and more fascinating Grant. Even though very much in love, either actor appeared ready to drop each other to rush to Hughes's bed if summoned. Laura and Kate would later speculate that Hughes was involved in a three-way with Grant and Scott.

Even though they were told with a certain fondness, the stories Kate heard about the reclusive Hughes seemed to turn her off the man, as she told the trio of women when Scott and Grant excused themselves and drove to Santa Monica after the dinner party.

"He doesn't sound like my kind of man at all," Kate claimed to Byington and Main.

Later Kate told Cukor, "Hughes sounds a little too perverted for my tastes. Perhaps he's your kind of man."

"He's my kind of man," Cukor said. "The trouble is, he doesn't like fat, ugly guys like me."

Unaware of the important role Hughes would play later in her life, Kate didn't press Scott or Grant for an introduction to the tycoon. Instead, she was looking forward to meeting Mae West.

Early the next morning, a call came in from Main. Kate picked up the receiver.

"At first Mae pretended she didn't know who you were," Main said. "Finally, a bulb went on in her head. 'Oh, that Hepburn dame,'" Main said, doing a perfect impression of Mae West better than any female impersonator. "'I'm not much into the schoolteacher type,'" Main said, imitating Mae again. "I told her you would like to meet up with her. Mae flatly turned us down. Mae

132

says that Dietrich is stalking her night and day. Mae said…," Main paused and did a perfect impersonation. "'With one lez after me, I don't think I could handle the Hepburn gal too. My gorgeous body belongs to the fellows.'" Main roared with laughter into Kate's ear. "What's your reaction to this, Kate old gal?"

"I have a message to deliver to your friend, Miss West," Kate said, "To quote Queen Victoria, 'We are not amused.'" Kate put down the phone.

***

Even before *Little Women* became a big hit, Kate was being proclaimed by some writers as the new queen of RKO. Big projects were being developed for her. She told Laura, "I'm almost giddy with excitement."

At various times it was announced that she was going to portray Nell Gwyn, one of the most famous of all the mistresses of the Kings of England. Not only that, but Hollywood learned that Kate had "virtually signed" to portray the great actress, Sarah Bernhardt. Kate was also given a screen treatment for a projected film, *The Tudor Wench*, to be based on the life of Queen Elizabeth I. According to the trade papers, "It's almost certain" that Katharine Hepburn was going to appear in a film based on an original screenplay, *Without Sin*, written by Jack Kirkland and Melville Baker.

As promising as most of them were, all these film projects bit the dust. On Leland Hayward's misguided advice, Kate signed to star in *Spitfire,* playing a young, uneducated faith healer in the Ozark Mountains. It was based on *Trigger*, a play by Lula Vollmer. Even before filming began, word on the RKO lot was that Kate was horribly miscast. Even members of the crew, including the grips, told Kate not to go ahead and play a hillbilly yokel. "You've got too much class, gal," Billy Brady, a sound engineer, told Kate. She didn't listen.

Little Women opened at Radio City Music Hall in November of 1933. A reporter for *Vanity Fair* claimed that the film "brought out from their lairs elderly ladies who all but drove up in fringed surreys to see their first film since *Birth of a Nation.*"

However, the same magazine ran a review that said, "I have yet to be convinced that Katharine Hepburn is a great actress. She brings the same mannerisms to all her work. I feel when I see her that she is simply being Miss Hepburn."

In spite of Kate's own mixed reviews, *Little Women* became one of the top ten money makers that year.

Kate did not get an Oscar nod, although the scenarists, Sarah Y. Mason and Victor Heerman, did win, and Cukor received an Oscar nomination as director. Nonetheless, Kate was delighted in her first "above-the-title" billing. For her performance, one of the greatest she was ever to deliver in film, Kate won the Best Actress Award at the Film Festival in Cannes in 1934.

When she was playing the role of Eva Lovelace in *Morning Glory,* Kate's character was warned of the danger of being a morning glory. Like the flower itself, which bursts into stunning bloom in the early dawn, Kate's career began to slide in 1933 and would continue its downward spiral until 1938.

Everything had come too much and too soon, with a hit play on Broadway, four movies—one an Academy Award winner—and the other (*Little Women*) hailed almost before its release as a film classic.

Although anxious to return to New York to do a play for "bad boy" producer, Jed Harris, Kate had to delay her trip east to appear in *Spitfire*.

The sophisticated Bryn Mawr graduate, a cultured, educated young New England woman, reported to the set at RKO to deliver herself into the hands of John Cromwell. Although a "director with credentials," she found his reputation as a member of the Broadway "pussy posse," a bit dubious, its members also including Kenneth MacKenna and Humphrey Bogart.

Even before the first week of filming, Kate told Laura. "I want to be on the next train to New York. But if I walk out now, RKO will sue me for every penny I have."

***

The director, Cromwell, ordered his cast to move to the San Jacinto mountains in southern California near the Mexican border. He felt the setting evoked the Ozarks, although he'd never seen those American mountains.

Once shooting began, Kate found herself having to deliver impossible lines. When a lout tries to kiss her, she called him a "consarned son of Satan." The normally sophisticated Cromwell actually had her say that line, written on a bad hair day by Lula Vollmer.

Kate was even more disappointed when she met her two leading men, Robert Young and Ralph Bellamy. Kate went to Cromwell to talk candidly about Young and Bellamy. "There is about as much spark between Young and me as there is between Marie Dressler and Ramon Novarro." The Chicago-born Young, who was Kate's same age, had a bright speaking voice, and Cromwell felt that he was "trustworthy, dependable, and inoffensive."

"Then I'll have to be the offensive one in this picture," Kate promised and kept her word.

If Kate thought Young was weak lemonade, she was even more horrified by another Chicago-born actor, Ralph Bellamy. "I can see why he always loses the girl in a film," Kate told Cromwell.

In the future, Kate would have a few discreet and quickly forgotten romances with some of her leading men. But trapped in the Ozarks with Bellamy and Young, her only "stud choices for the night," she preferred to honor her marriage vows to Laura.

As shooting progressed, the placid Young particularly infuriated Kate. During one tense afternoon, she slapped his face and told him, "Go back to being a bank teller." Complaining to Cromwell, she said, "I don't thing Young could raise a boner even if you cast Jean Harlow in the part."

Completely frustrated, Kate called the executive producer, Merian C. Cooper. He'd also been her executive producer on both *Morning Glory* and *Little Women*. During her talk with Cooper, he did not give her any sympathy at all. Even worse, he shocked Kate by telling her that he'd advised the actress, Dorothy Jordan, to turn down the role.

134

From that day forth, Kate no longer trusted Cooper. "In other words, the script isn't suitable for your whore but it's okay for me to go out there and make an ass of myself."

Cooper, it was true, did show favoritism to Dorothy Jordan, because he was in love with her and planned to marry her.

To play Trigger Hicks, the rustic lead in *Spitfire*, Kate demanded that Leland get her a guarantee of fifty-thousand dollars for four weeks of work. Then Kate made yet another demand. Eager to get to Broadway, she demanded and received a contractual agreement for another ten-thousand dollars per day beyond that figure if the film wasn't completed in four weeks. At the time, that was the highest per diem figure ever contracted in the film world.

The cutoff date for filming *Spitfire* was November 15, 1933. Working desperately against a rapidly ticking time clock, Cromwell failed to bring in the picture that afternoon at 3:45pm, the cutoff date. Kate defiantly told him that "my time is up. I'm leaving the set."

At 6:15pm, production chief Pandro Berman called from RKO, telling Kate that two scenes, including the ending, remained to be completed and ordered her to return to work. Berman claimed that, by agreement, he had use of her services until midnight that day. A compromise was reached. Kate agreed to show up the following morning and work five hours and forty-minutes to meet the midnight agreement requirement.

When Cromwell still hadn't finished the last scene at 3:45pm that afternoon, Kate again walked off the set, even though Cromwell desperately needed another hour of her time. Kate demanded and got the $10,000 payment previously agreed upon.

Although she hauled off a fat paycheck and an additional "bonus" of $10,000, she created a lot of ill will at RKO—"and that studio, like the elephant, has a long memory," Berman later said.

Berman also called Leland and denounced him as a "dirty, whore-chasing blackmailer," and he blasted "lesbian actresses and their demands" to Cooper. "If I had my say, Hepburn will never work another day for RKO."

Spitfire opened to empty movie theaters across the country. According to Hollywood legend, Kate received the most disastrous reviews of her screen career. Actually, that wasn't true. Many of the reviews, while not exactly raves, were respectful of her performance as Trigger, although usually noting that she was miscast.

Richard Watts Jr., writing in the *New York Herald Tribune*, found that Kate made the girl, Trigger, "a surprisingly real creation." The critics for the *London Times* wrote, "After the story of *Spitfire* is forgotten, memories of Miss Hepburn's performance will remain." The public wasn't influenced by Kate's good reviews, and stayed away in droves, in direct contrast to the hordes that turned out for *Little Women.*

Cromwell would survive the disaster and go on to make still-remembered films, including *Of Human Bondage* with Bette Davis and *Since You Went Away* with Claudette Colbert. Cromwell would praise the talents of many actresses. But when asked about Kate, he claimed, "She is the most spectacularly untalented actress in Hollywood. In fact, she doesn't know how to act, Oscar winner or not."

***

When a "wrap" was called on *Spitfire*, Kate, along with Laura, boarded the first available airplane back East.

As Cukor said with a sigh at the time, "Poor Kate was about to go from the frying pan of *Spitfire* into Jed Harris's *Lake*."

CHAPTER SEVEN

When Kate arrived by train at New York's Grand Central Station with Laura, she was mobbed by fans and reporters. "It's proof that you've finally made it as a movie star," Laura told her. But instead of being gratified by the reception, Kate was seriously annoyed, as she had only twenty days of rehearsal before the scheduled opening of *The Lake* in Washington, D.C. Originally, Harris had demanded at least four weeks of rehearsal, but the scheduling of her work on *Spitfire* in Hollywood had made that impossible.

Escaping in a taxi from the mob of reporters, Kate was shaking with fury. She was so nervous about her upcoming debut that a rash had broken out on the left side of her face. "I feel like I'm here to take a long walk to the gallows," she told Laura and others, including Hepburn family members.

As a harbinger of what was to come, Kate and Harris had already conflicted on several key issues, including a bitter dispute over which play she'd appear in. Harris had, indeed, offered her star billing in *The Lake.* But more immediately, and more urgently, he wanted her to return to the Broadway stage playing the third lead in a play called *The Green Bay Tree.* Defined at the time as "a shocking drama about homosexual life," it had been a success, albeit a notorious one, when it had opened in London. Noël Coward had encouraged Harris to acquire the American rights to the play, and also to cast "that divine boy," Laurence Olivier, as the lead. Harris responded favorably. "Why not? A homosexual playing a homosexual—perfect casting."

But whereas Coward had encouraged Harris' involvement with *The Green Bay Tree,* he strongly advised Harris not to produce *The Lake.* According to Coward, "It's a very British play—and not suitable for American audiences."

Supremely intolerant of other people's opinions, Harris nonetheless decided to buy the American rights to both plays, even though he told Coward that he found *The Lake* "common, stupid, and sentimental." Harris went on to say that his decision was based not upon the play's art, or lack thereof, but because "I can hear the rustle of money."

Faced with the decision of which actors to cast within his new pair of plays, Harris continued to urge Kate to return to Broadway with an appearance in *The Green Bay Tree.* He argued that if she opened in a minor role, it would be interpreted by audiences as a testimonial to her humility, thereby attracting praise from the critics instead of provoking their ire. Otherwise, he reasoned, if she opened in a blockbuster role, with strong references to her status as a major

Hollywood star, that "the butcher of Broadway will be waiting for you." His reference was to Brooks Atkinson, theater critic for *The New York Times,* and no fan of Katharine Hepburn's.

But from the beginning, Kate suspected Harris' motives. She had been warned that he wanted to maneuver her into a third-ranked role in *The Green Bay Tree* by dangling the prospect of an eventual starring role in *The Lake.* Referring to Laurence Olivier, and the Oscar she had recently won for *Morning Glory,* she told him, "You want me to save the day for what you refer to as 'your classy British fairy.'"

Harris, incidentally, had been one of the first producers on Broadway to learn about Olivier's homosexuality, long before it became public knowledge. Harris also was personally acquainted with Jill Esmond, Olivier's wife, and was well aware of her attraction to young women. Contemptuous and characteristically indiscreet, he told anyone who was interested that the Olivier/Esmond marriage was a sham that existed "in name only."

As the Hepburn and Harris exchanges became more venomous, Kate accused Harris of planning to betray her, claiming that he would leave her "rotting away" in a minor role in *The Green Bay Tree,"* and then cast another actress for the bigger role in *The Lake.*

During dialogues Kate had with Olivier at the time, the actor told her that he had made a big mistake by appearing in New York in a Harris play. Olivier claimed that Harris was "the most hurtful, arrogant, venomous little fiend known to exist." Years later, Olivier would assert that he used Harris as the role model for his terrifying and leering stage portrait of *Richard III.* Olivier went on to cite Noël Coward, who had compared Harris to "a praying mantis, that strangely ruthless insect."

Although many biographers have placed Kate's ill-fated first meeting with Harris during the weeks of rehearsals that preceded the opening of *The Lake,* Harris and Hepburn had actually met several years before. And at the time of their doomed collaboration, she already had first-hand knowledge of why he was hailed as "The Vampire of Broadway" and one of the most hated theatrical figures of his day.

In the late 1930s, when she was a struggling actress trying to make a name for herself on Broadway, Katharine Hepburn had waited for an interview, like thousands of other actors before and since, in Harris' offices above the Moresco Theatre. For three days, the producer had not been able (or had not wanted) to see her. During those long and tedious delays, Kate became friendly with Jimmy Schure, who worked as Harris' secretary, and who Kate suspected was a homosexual. She liked him, and he liked her, and they sometimes went out together for lunch. She enjoyed his "insider's point of view" about Broadway and its thousands of intrigues. He promised that he would be on the lookout for a role that might be suited to her particular talents.

When Harris, partly because of Jimmy's urging, finally agreed to interview

Kate, Harris was not impressed by her physical stature or bearing. He particularly didn't like her freckles, and immediately dismissed her without letting her read any lines.

But as she was leaving the outer office and saying her goodbyes to Jimmy, Harris overheard Kate telling her new friend that she was planning to drive to Connecticut that afternoon. Harris immediately perked up, showing an intense interest in her after learning that she not only knew how to drive, but that she owned her own car. Harris loathed taxis, finding them inelegant, preferring to be chauffered about town by a cooperative personal driver instead. He struck a deal with Kate. "If you'll drive me around to my appointments, I'll cast you in an upcoming role within one of my productions—and that's a promise."

Taken aback, Kate reluctantly agreed. "If this is what it takes to become a Broadway star, you've got yourself a driver."

"C'mon, kid," Harris said, exiting his office and heading for the street. Once he got there, he immediately fired his chauffer, who was waiting on the street, and got into Kate's car, where he demanded to be driven to a townhouse in Greenwich Village. There, he told her to wait in her car at the curb since, "I'll only be a minute." He remained inside the building for two hours. When he finally came out, he was adjusting his clothing. It was years later before Kate learned that he was paying "a conjugal visit" to the actress Ruth Gordon, who would eventually become one of Kate's most intimate friends.

For hour after hour, at great personal inconvenience, Kate drove Harris on his errands and appointments around town, although no offer of any role—not even an audition—was ever made by him. But she was a fiercely determined aspirant actor, and she continued to do his bidding.

On one occasion, she was terribly disappointed to learn that one of his appointments involved lunch with Noël Coward, who was visiting New York as part of one of his periodic visits from London. Kate begged Harris to let her park her car and go in to meet the famous playwright. Harris refused, and made her wait in her car at the curb throughout the entire duration of the lunch.

When he eventually emerged from Sardi's, he shared some of the tidbits of his conversation with Coward. Harris told her, "I just out and out asked Coward, 'What is it about women that so offends you fairy boys?' And he shot back with that old cliché, 'Some of my best friends are women. Take Gertie Lawrence or Meg Anderson, dear pals. I adore women.' 'If that's true,' I told him, 'why don't you like them in bed like a regular man does.'" Harris at this point burst into laughter. "'All that open plumbing absolutely revolts me,' he said. 'I can only imagine that being in bed with a woman would be like feeling the skin of a snake.'"

During the period that Kate served as Harris' driver, he was seeing a lot of a blonde and actually quite beautiful theatrical agent, Jean Dalrymple, who later provided the author with much of the information noted here about the interaction between Hepburn and Harris. Dalrymple would later become one of a handful of formidable female film producers, exhibiting an artistic and business acumen that was sometimes compared to that of Kate's dear friend, Irene Mayer Selznick. A writer for *The Cleveland Plain Dealer* described Dalrymple as "fragile as a Fragonard painting, but hep and with a sense of timing like a Garand rifle."

During the period that Kate Hepburn was chauffering Harris around Manhattan, Dalrymple worked as an actress and theatrical agent, representing, among others, the budding careers of both Archibald Leach (who was later renamed Cary Grant) and James Cagney, for whom Dalrymple arranged work on the Keith-Orpheum vaudeville circuit, with bookings across the East Coast.

Ever the braggart, Harris later boasted about how he handled Dalrymple's clients, even Dalrymple herself. "I fucked both of her boys, and plugged Dalrymple nightly until I got tired of the bitch—and I didn't give any of them a contract."

Here's how Dalrymple related the tale: As part of her ongoing promotion of James Cagney and Cary Grant, Dalrymple took Harris to see Cagney, who was at the time dancing in a review where Cagney played the role of a sailor on shore leave. According to Dalrymple, Harris related to both her and to Kate that he was impressed with the "feisty young hoofer" and promised to take him to London for a role in a show he was producing there.

With malicious glee, Harris told how Cagney had packed his bags, sending them ahead of time to an ocean-going liner that was to depart for England early the next morning. As Harris related to Dalrymple, "At the last minute, just before Cagney sailed, I changed my mind and gave the part to an English actor instead. Cagney and I were, just prior to his scheduled departure, at a late hours club. It was about three o'clock in the morning, and we'd been drinking heavily. For some reason, I kept postponing telling him that he was fired. Finally, I caught up with him in the men's room. He was standing at the sink, drunk, and washing his hands. While taking a piss, I gave him the bad news. At first he thought I was joking, but I convinced him that he'd lost the part. Know what that pansy did? He broke into hysterical sobbing, even fell on the floor. Somehow, I got turned on by seeing a man do that. I pulled down his pants and stuck it to him up the ass. The pansy didn't resist, but just lay there sobbing all during my fuck. After I shot my load, I pulled up my pants and left. The poor little fairy was still there sobbing when I left him."

As related by Dalrymple, Harris then continued a tale that, by the standards of most listeners, would have been interpreted as sociopathic, or even demonic. "As for that other pansy actor you represent, Archie Leach, I made him come to my office at three o'clock every afternoon for five days in a row, promising him a showcase. Once he got there, I whipped it out and told him to suck it real nice. Even though I did it to humiliate the fairy, I think he really liked doing it. By the end of the week, on Friday afternoon, after I shot off, I kicked him away from me. He landed on his butt. Towering over him, I told him he had no talent and to get the hell out of my office." Dalrymple went on to relate how, in between acting jobs, Grant walked on stilts through the throngs of Times Square, carrying advertising boards on his shoulders. Sometimes he wore a stiffly starched shirt studded with light bulbs that flashed on and off.

As related years later by Jimmy Schure, Kate Hepburn was also told by Harris about his cruel and abusive treatment of Cagney and Grant. Jimmy related a tale about how Kate had approached him, wondering if the above-mentioned claims were true or not. According to Jimmy, he told Kate, "They're true, all right. Harris pulls the same shit with me once or twice a week, but he's doing it less now that he's getting tired of me. He's made Larry Olivier go down on him too."

The last time Kate ever chauffered for Harris involved an incident with the police. He had gone into Sardi's, leaving her illegally parked beside the curb in front. A mounted policeman had taken notice of how long she had been waiting and rode over to confront her. He dismounted and was writing out a ticket, in spite of her protests, when Harris emerged from the restaurant. Seeing what was happening, he tore up the ticket the policeman had written. "Do you know who I am?" Harris demanded of the policeman. "I'm Jed Harris. Mr. Broadway himself. No one in this town gives Jed Harris a ticket."

"Oh yeah, what about a ride to the pokey instead?" the cop asked.

In fury, Harris struck the policeman and they struggled. At one point Kate watched in astonishment as the producer bit the policeman. Two other policemen were called over to break them up. Kate feared that Harris would be charged for assaulting an officer, and jailed, but no charges were ever filed. Harris later bragged that the policeman who gave Kate the ticket ended up on a lonely beat up in the Bronx. "I taught him not to fool around with Jed Harris."

***

In 1933, several years after her stint as Harris' driver, and many roles in Hollywood later, a more confident and perhaps more confrontational Kate arrived, fresh from California, at Harris' offices above the Moresco Theatre to talk about her upcoming role in *The Lake.*

Only recently, she had heard an upsetting story about Harris' conflicts with the grand diva, Ina Claire, who had appeared on Broadway in a Jed Harris production of a play written by Edwin Justus Mayer, *The Gaoler's Wench.* Kate learned that during rehearsals, Ina Claire had become so upset over Harris' attacks on her acting that she had assaulted him with an unexpected right hook. He fell to the floor, whereupon Claire plowed the toe of her stiletto heel into his much-used testicles. She then called him a "sadistic son-of-a-bitch" and stormed out of the theater.

Even now, despite Kate's status as a Hollywood star, Harris—as was his custom—kept her waiting outside his office door. Kate used the time to renew her friendship with Jimmy Schure. She confided in her friend that she had recently received an unsolicited letter that had been hand-delivered to her townhouse in Turtle Bay, Manhattan. It was from Helen Hayes, who had once appeared in Harris' production of *Coquette.* In her letter, Hayes had warned Kate, "Don't let Jed direct you. He will completely destroy your confidence."

In addition to the many disturbing alarm signals that she had been receiving about Jed Harris, Jimmy informed Kate about one of Harris' bizarre new habits. "He's receiving people these days, male or female, stark naked."

In response, flippantly, she had quipped, "Why spend money on electric fans when you can keep yourself cool for less money by standing nude in front of an open window?"

"You think I'm joking, but I'm perfectly serious," Jimmy said. "The other day, George S. Kaufman had an appointment to see Harris. Kaufman got to see him, all right. Harris was nude the whole time, and when Kaufman concluded his business and stood at the door, he called back, 'Oh Jed, by the way, your fly's open.'"

Kate thanked Jimmy for warning her, and decided to handle Harris' nudity with the same sophistication that Kaufman had. After all, she had been reared in a family where nudity was commonplace, and she had grown used to seeing Dr. Hepburn walk around nude and, in some cases, with a full erection.

When she was eventually ushered into his office to discuss her role in *The Lake,* Harris was just as naked as the day he was born. He got up from his desk to greet her. She suspected that he had been playing with himself before her arrival, because she noticed that by the end of their meeting, he had shrunk quite a bit.

Throughout their session, she made not the slightest reference to his lack of clothing, seemingly taking it gracefully in her stride. She suspected, however, that he was deliberately trying to upset and provoke her, perhaps as a prelude to the other important negotiations at hand. But as nervous as she was, and became, she managed to conceal her anxieties before him, at least during this particular encounter.

Sitting across from her, the thirty-two-year-old, and almost universally disliked Harris was known at the time as "the boy wonder of the American theater." Thin and dark, he stared at her through hooded eyes so fearsomely intense that they would "freeze the hottest summer lake." Saturninely handsome, he almost always appeared with a five o'clock shadow, even if it were only eleven in the morning. There was an almost Svengali-like malevolence about him, and many actresses found this oddly seductive. His "scalp bracelet" contained more trophies than that of Leland Hayward. Even actress Ruth Gordon had given birth to a boy born out of wedlock, citing Harris as the father. She named him Jones Harris. Gordon later said of her former lover, "If Jed thought his mother was wrong for a part, and her life depended on it, he'd still fire her."

142

When he wasn't naked, Jed cut a striking figure around Broadway. During the winter months, he often wore a camel's hair overcoat that he slung like a cape over his shoulders, with a snap-brim fedora resting at a rakish angle on his head.

Kate had heard some of the theater gossip about Harris, and almost expected him to make a pass at her that day, although he didn't. She finally concluded that she was not his physical type, although Lee Shubert, at the Shubert Theatre, was widely quoted as saying, "Jed Harris would fuck anything, even a snake if he could get hold of one." The famous writer, Ben Hecht, had said, "Harris possesses a Dracula-like hunger for the blood of any actress, especially beautiful ones."

He spoke to Kate in a whispery voice that evoked the hiss of a rattler. Every few minutes, he flashed the grin of a sorcerer, especially when he told her he was prepared to pay her only five-hundred dollars a week, in sharp contrast to her last paycheck in Hollywood for an hour's work on *Spitfire* for ten-thousand dollars.

Eager to return to Broadway, Kate was ready to take the role at any price. A surprise in their meeting came when Harris invited himself to Fenwick for the weekend. Kate said she'd check with her parents, but feared that Kit and Dr. Hepburn would not be amused by Jed Harris, whom she suspected would represent the worst of American theater to them, boy genius or not.

After calling the Hepburn residence, Kate was told by her father that it would be all right to bring Harris "but only for the weekend." He also warned Kate of a possible conflict of interest. "Luddy will be here, of course—know that in advance."

***

Both Kate and Luddy were waiting for Harris when he arrived at Fenwick. The other family members were not in attendance that day. Kate introduced Luddy to Harris "as a devoted family friend." She immediately invited Harris for a long walk along the shoreline. In Manhattan, Harris didn't even like to walk one city block, but he agreed to go anyway. Luddy tagged along too, with his camera in hand.

As was his custom, he always took endless pictures of everybody who showed up at Fenwick, and Harris was no exception. What Luddy didn't know was that Harris strenuously objected to photographs being taken of him. At one point he turned angrily on Luddy. "No more pictures!" Harris shouted at him. Although Luddy was a sweet and considerate man most of the time, he had what Kate called "a deaf ear" about a person's request not to be photographed.

Luddy continued to take pictures of Harris. Infuriated, Harris grabbed Luddy's camera and smashed it on the ground, stomping on it. "As I said, no pictures, you God damn idiot!"

The action reduced Luddy to tears, and he retreated back to Fenwick. An hour later, Kate persuaded Harris to make up with Luddy. "He's a dear man and meant no harm," she pleaded. "He's just some kind of nut about taking pictures."

At first Harris threatened Luddy with bodily harm if he ever approached him with a camera again. But at some point Kate prevailed. To make up for the hurt Harris had caused Luddy, she suggested that the two of them might go for a swim together on a remote beach. "You can swim in the nude," she told him, "and I know you'd like to do that."

At first, Harris wanted Kate to go with him but she insisted that he take Luddy instead. She held out a promise to Harris that he would be vastly rewarded if he'd do this favor for her. Reluctantly, Harris agreed, although reminding Kate that she would owe him for this favor. He went inside the house and asked Luddy to go to the beach with him. Somewhat stunned at Harris' abrupt change of attitude, Luddy agreed to accompany him.

Kate stood on the grounds of Fenwick, watching as her producer and her husband faded into the distance. She noticed that Luddy was taking his spare camera with him, possibly for more pictures in spite of the warning by Harris.

They were gone for hours. When Harris and Luddy returned, they seemed to be most compatible. Luddy excused himself to go and shower. Alone with Harris, Kate asked, "How did it go?"

"First, I found out—and I was shocked—that Luddy is not just a family friend, but your God damn husband. You didn't tell me. I thought you were a lez or else I would have been fucking you myself. I also found out that your husband is a homosexual."

"Oh, that's just a rumor," she said, covering up for Luddy.

"It's no God damn rumor, baby," he said. "Can you believe it? This Luddy has never seen a cut cock before, and he was fascinated by mine. He obviously doesn't screw around with Jewish men. He begged me to let him take a picture of my cock. I made him go down on it instead." Before her startled face, he turned and headed upstairs to shower and get dressed for dinner.

Kate would later speculate with Laura and Cukor about whether Harris had actually told her the truth.

Dr. Hepburn and Kit were away in Hartford on the first night of Kate's visit with Harris. But they returned on Sunday and invited him to dinner. As Kate had predicted, the meal was a disaster. The Hepburn family was horrified at Harris' aggressive, rude behavior.

After Harris had gone, Dr. Hepburn told Kate, "It's because of producers like Jed Harris that I didn't want my daughter to go into the theater in the first place."

Kit also reviled Harris, telling Kate that, "You've brought a monster into our Fenwick. If you'd rather be with men like Jed Harris instead of dear Luddy, then it's your choice. And what a wrong choice it is!"

144

Harris had not been invited to stay overnight at the Hepburn home. Kate had secured accommodations for him at a nearby hotel. But because the hotel was overbooked, Harris was assigned a makeshift accommodation within a curtained-off section of the dining room.

Monday morning, Harris was awakened from his slumber by the singing of a choir of Rotarians, whose convention was dominating most of the hotel. Because of this, and because of his inferior accommodation, Harris became furious at the hotel's owner, who insisted on charging him sixty dollars for the bed, even though he claimed it wasn't worth ten dollars. She was adamant that Harris pay up or else she threatened to call the police.

Before packing his suitcase to drive back to New York, Harris found a large black crayon. On the white dining room wall in front of the breakfasting Rotarians, he scrawled: "MRS. PERKINS IS A CUNT!"

***

Rehearsals on *The Lake* started at the Martin Beck Theatre on Forty-Fifth Street, just west of Broadway. The short, plump Tony Miner had been hired to direct Kate who was to appear opposite such established stars as Blanche Bates, born in 1873, and Frances Starr, born in 1881, both well-respected and extremely talented Broadway veterans. The male lead was to be played by Colin Clive, who had starred opposite Kate in the ill-fated film, *Christopher Strong.* Clive lives today in film memory for playing the title role in the 1931 version of *Frankenstein,* with Boris Karloff as the monster.

Although intimidated by working with such veterans, Kate established her warmest relationship with Jo Mielziner, brother of Kenneth MacKenna. (MacKenna had changed his name several years previously for theatrical billing.) Jo would go on to become one of the century's greatest set designers.

After the first day of rehearsals, Bates told Harris, "The critics are wrong in hailing Hepburn as the new Eleanora Duse or Sarah Bernhardt. She'd going to be dreadful in the part. I have a sixth sense about such things. Miner can't save the play with Kate in it. My advice is to cut your losses immediately. Fire both of them!"

On the second day of rehearsals, Harris showed up to watch Miner direct Kate. Miner practically gushed over the star. "You were great!" he kept telling Kate after every scene. "Better than you were in *Morning Glory.*"

Harris walked onto the stage and confronted Miner. "You're nothing but a faggoty worshipper of film stars." The next day Harris, in front of an astonished cast, fired Miner and took over direction himself.

Almost in defiance of that crude denunciation, Worthington (Tony) Miner eventually became a much lauded theatrical director. He would work again with Kate in 1937 during a Theatre Guild production of *Jane Eyre* when Kate was deep into her chaotic romance with Howard Hughes.

Years later, Miner said, "During my brief stint as Kate's director, I treated her like the sensitive artist I knew her to be, recognizing how frightened and uncertain she felt playing the lead in a Broadway play. Like Helen Hayes and others claimed, Harris set out to destroy every actress he meets, with the exception of Margaret Sullavan. Many of his female stars faced their opening night in tears and completely demoralized. He's a prick! I hate him!"

Yet despite the huge animosity that seemed to radiate out from him, Jed Harris, the most anti-actor producer on Broadway, became Kate's director on *The Lake*. Fueling Harris' normally abusive behavior was an additional factor that compounded his autocratic demands: The play was almost entirely funded with his own money. But whereas he might, with impunity, fire Miner, he couldn't fire Kate, since he was depending on her name and reputation for advance ticket sales.

Unbeknownst to Kate, Harris at the time was already envisioning another play that would, at least in theory, be funded with the success of *The Lake*. Based on a script written by Harris' sister, Mildred Harris, it was entitled *Correspondent Unknown*. Harris had already offered the lead in his sister's play to Margaret Sullavan.

First produced by Tyrone Guthrie in London, and written by Dorothy Massingham and Murray MacDonald, *The Lake* had been a huge success in London. Years later, Kate claimed that she had not been impressed with the play itself, but had wanted to "help" Harris rise again as the biggest producer on Broadway, as his career had waned. Kate never explained why she wanted to help a man who had used her as an unpaid, unrewarded driver and had often ridiculed and mocked her requests for him to give her a job in the theater.

In the play, Kate plays Stella Surrege, who marries a man she doesn't love, her heart already belonging to a married suitor. After the wedding ceremony, the bridegroom has an accident on a road near a lake. His car skids and overturns into the water, fatally pinning him under. Kate's character is left with her guilt.

The warning from Helen Hayes had been apt. From the very first hour of rehearsals, Harris attacked Kate's every movement on stage. "Miss Movie Star from Hollywood thinks she's a stage actress," was his first comment on her performance in rehearsal. If Kate moved in one direction, Harris yelled at her to take another route. He didn't like any gesture or line she delivered. Before the first day of rehearsals ended, Kate had been reduced to tears several times.

On the second day with Harris, Kate was asked to play a piano on stage, with the keyboard visible to the audience. Recorded music would be piped in from off-stage. Harris insisted that she repeat the scene over and over. Finally, she broke down. "I can't do it!" she screamed at Harris. "I can't say my lines and concentrate on my hands at the same time."

He walked over to her. "A real actress like Helen Hayes learned to play the piano on stage for me." Suddenly, Harris slammed down the keyboard cover on her hands. Kate screamed in pain and ran from the stage.

After this brutal assault, Kate showed up for rehearsals the next day with her right hand bandaged. Harris had no sympathy for her, nor did he apologize. It seemed that he resumed his abuse of her with more ferocity that before. Before lunch, he'd denounced her as a "God damn fool, an imbecile married to a cocksucking nonentity. I've worked with great actresses like Ruth Gordon— even fucked them—and you're not worthy of being her handmaiden on stage." Letting the cast break for lunch that day—often he didn't—Harris shouted at Kate, "Get off the stage. I need a stiff drink. I can't stand the sight of you!"

That afternoon, as rehearsals resumed, Harris became even more bellicose. The time came for Kate to deliver her immortal lines, which for decades would be standard material used by female impersonators of her. Kate strode out on stage and, in front of Harris, but in a shrill voice, said, "The calla lilies are in bloom again. Such a strange flower. I carried them on my wedding day. And now I place them here, in memory of someone who is dead."

"Stop! Stop!" Harris screamed at Kate. In front of the entire cast, Harris became a mincing homosexual, mocking Kate and doing a devastating impression of her. After his ridicule of her, he said, "You don't come to a dramatic stop. You merely pose and strike a false attitude. You're constantly leaning against a door with leg akimbo. You put a limp hand to your forehead. You pause in mid-sentence for no dramatic reason. You're a hysterical babbler. You raise a hand to your throat like some dying Victorian heroine. What are you playing? Camille? Your voice is not a voice. It's a rasp. I sold myself to the Devil by casting you. All for money. Where is Margaret Sullavan now that I need her?"

Already infuriated with Leland's romantic attachment to Sullavan, Kate could take no more. She lunged toward Harris, pounding her fists into his face. Colin Clive, her co-star, later claimed that Harris "virtually dragged her into his office, and they were gone for more than two hours."

"When Katharine came out," Clive said, "she had a shiny face and almost looked gloriously content. That began what I think was an affair with Harris that lasted for about ten days. Even though Katharine was known as a strong and independent woman, she apparently could be overpowered by a Satanic devil like Harris, a true bastard and shithead. Let's say that she succumbed to his overpowering masculinity."

The next day at rehearsals, Clive, along with co-stars, Frances Starr and Blanche Bates, assumed that the producer would curb his attacks on Kate's acting. He didn't at all. He continued his outbursts, at one point claiming, "You weep tears at every moment. You look full of self-pity. You're totally inept. The complexity of this character is just too daunting a task for you."

To the shock of the cast, Kate ran to Harris and virtually fell into his arms.

"Oh, I love you so," she said.

Until the end of his life, Harris seemed to continue his attack on Kate, usually breaking into a sarcastic smile before launching into another denunciation of Kate's acting. In 1973, when Kate assumed the role of Amanda Wingfield in Tennessee Williams's *The Glass Menagerie* for an ABC telecast, Harris said he watched her performance in horror. "She was babbling like a fool and calling it acting. Before we opened in New York, I knew that I had tried the impossible: to make an artificial showcase for an artificial star. It wasn't in this untalented stage fraud, Katharine Hepburn, to handle it. We cheated the audience. They should have demanded a refund on their tickets."

Years later Kate was still wondering why she'd ever been attracted to Jed Harris. "At least our affair was mercifully brief," she told Kenneth MacKenna upon her return to Hollywood.

***

Harris ordered his cast to Washington for the opening of *The Lake* at the National Theatre. He housed Kate and Laura and the Hay-Adams Hotel, booking lesser cast members in cheaper accommodations. After checking in, Kate and Laura renewed their acquaintance with Leopold Stokowski, riding up to their rooms in the elevator with him.

Kate thought that dinner with Stokowski the following evening would be the highlight of her trip to Washington. Kate and Laura dined with him at a private reception aboard the John Hays Hammon yacht anchored in the Potomac.

The next day an even greater invitation came in for Kate, but this one didn't include Laura. In spite of his almost hysterically busy schedule, trying to bring the nation out of The Great Depression, President Franklin D. Roosevelt invited Kate for tea at the White House. An ardent Democrat, Kate was thrilled at the chance to meet the president and immediately called her parents. Both Kit and Dr. Hepburn presented Kate with a lengthy list of demands for social reform, and urged her to present them to FDR. Kate responded indulgently to her parents, but had no intention of embarrassing the president with these calls for action.

The only good thing that came out of Kate's experience with *The Lake* involved the hiring of a driver, Charles Newhill, for her Lincoln Town Car. He would become not only her chauffeur, but a lifelong friend, staying in her employment for the next forty-three years. He drove her around only on the East Coast, as Kate preferred to do her own driving in California. When Kate was in Hollywood, Newhill took care of what Kate called her "glorified boarding house" at Turtle Bay in New York City.

Newhill drove Kate to the White House, waiting until the exact moment printed on the invitation before pulling up at the gate. While her driver waited for her, Kate was ushered into the White House. Roosevelt kept her waiting only 15 minutes before he entered the room in a wheelchair.

The debonair president struck an immediate rapport with Kate. Both liberal American patricians, they shared a common political bond. The president claimed that he'd seen her both in *Morning Glory* and *A Bill of Divorcement* and that his wife, Eleanor, had seen *Little Women* twice. He expressed Eleanor's disappointment at not being in Washington that afternoon, but promised that his wife would make contact with her some time in the future.

Roosevelt amused Kate with stories, at one point telling her that when he was selling Liberty Bonds during World War I, he fell off the chair he was standing on and landed in the lap of Marie Dressler. "She handled it well," Roosevelt said to Kate. "She's more of a man than I am."

The president apologized that neither he nor Eleanor could attend the opening night performance of *The Lake,* as each of them had previous commitments. The Washington Bryn Mawr Club had purchased the entire theater, and tickets were being hawked for the alma mater. Kate's parent's showed up for the event, even Margaret Sanger.

Kate made her entrance in Laura's castoff jodhpurs, as Harris refused to finance her wardrobe, although he'd spent a lot of money to dress the other actors in the cast.

"Hepburn was acting for the choir," Harris later said. "The rabidly pro-Hepburn audience adored her. Frankly, I wanted to close the play on opening night out of sheer embarrassment. But on that same night, I got word that the New York box office had counted up forty-thousand dollars in advance bookings on the strength of Katharine Hepburn's name. Obviously the fools hadn't seen *Spitfire* yet."

After the performance, Kate was eager to hear Harris' appraisal of her performance. He pronounced it "perfection itself," but the sarcastic leer on his face indicated otherwise. She knew she had not yet conquered the part and begged him for more time on the road. He refused, informing her instead that *The Lake* would open on Broadway the day after Christmas, 1933.

***

On opening night at the Martin Beck Theatre on Broadway, Kate was plunged into a disaster, both professional and personal. Not only did she have to face an extremely critical, even hostile, audience, but Jed Harris chose that inopportune moment to introduce her backstage to Margaret Sullavan, who was to become her nemesis. Sadistically, Harris chose the moment ten minutes before curtain time when a performer is the most nervous and anxiety-ridden.

Leland Hayward's romantic involvement with Sullavan had already led to a temporary split between Kate and the man she called her "beau."

When Harris introduced Kate to Sullavan, he told her, "This is the actress I had wanted to star in *The Lake*—not you."

Kate, in spite of her nervousness, extended her hand to Sullavan, who refused to shake it. "Now that I'm in town, Jed will have no more need of your services."

"You mean..." Kate was flabbergasted. "You're going on instead of me?" She turned to Harris as if ready to pounce, before looking back at Sullavan. "But I don't understand. You're not even dressed for the part."

"What a silly girl you are," Sullavan told her. "I'm not appearing in this stupid play. I mean, now that I'm back from Virginia, Jed can spend his nights in my bed—not yours!"

"Oh, I see..." Kate was floundering, as Harris' assistant Geoffrey Kerr, warned her of the imminently approaching curtain.

"Maggie—not you—was meant to play the role," Harris told Kate. "She would have brought the accurate sense of pathos that the part needs. Perhaps captured the play's moody, brooding sense of tragedy which you have failed to do. I've made a grievous error casting you instead of Maggie. Maggie has that piquant personality to win over an audience. With her wit, charm and personal magnetism, she should have gone on as Stella Surrege instead of the gawky Bryn Mawr school gal I'm sending out there on stage tonight."

Kate burst into tears, as Harris was called away by Kerr to answer an urgent call.

That left Kate standing awkwardly in the wings with her rival. "I assumed you've dumped Leland," Kate asked.

"No," Sullavan said. "One week Leland was spending time in my bed in Virginia. As soon as I'd packed him off, Jed would arrive. My bed didn't even have time to cool off. Speaking woman to woman, I've got to ask you a question. Which one do you find better in bed? Jed or Leland? I find that both of them are tigers, but somehow Leland gets in there and digs dirtier and deeper."

"Miss Hepburn," Kerr said, "the curtain is going up."

In tears and a blinding rage, Kate turned from Sullavan's mocking face and went out to face the most critical theater audience of her career.

***

Before Kate was three minutes into her performance, she knew that her love affair with Jed Harris was over. Like the heroine she was playing in *The Lake*, Kate had a broken heart.

She'd wanted to strike Sullavan in the face. As Kate proceeded with uncertainty through the play, she was more overcome with her own problems than the ones of the fictional character she played. Like an albatross, Sullavan had entered her life to stay.

Margaret Sullavan was called "the other Hollywood rebel," Kate being the first one. Two years younger than Kate, Sullavan, the daughter of a prominent Virginia stockbroker, had been stage-struck since the age of six. She had made her Broadway debut in a play called *A Modern Virgin*, a play that had been attacked by critics as a "dank mess." She was singled out for rave reviews, however, and went on to survive four more Broadway flops, each time receiving personal critical praise. She finally found the right play, *Dinner at Eight*, which won her a movie contract with Universal.

At the time Kate met her, Sullavan had no intention of being "a modern virgin." Prior to Leland and Jed Harris, she'd already had countless affairs, preferring handsome actors, the lot having included the likes of Kenneth MacKenna, Humphrey Bogart, and James Stewart.

She'd entered into a brief marriage with aspirant actor Henry Fonda, but had divorced him in 1933. Harris broke up the Fonda/Sullavan marriage.

In his memoirs, *My Life*, Fonda wrote of waiting on the street down below and looking up at his apartment, knowing that "that son of a bitch [a reference to Harris] was in bed with my wife." Fonda claimed that the situation "just destroyed me, completely destroyed me. Never in my life have I felt so betrayed, so rejected, so alone."

***

Kate remembered walking through her opening night "like an automaton," her unreliable voice going higher and higher, as it always did when she was tense and nervous. "Big stars came out to see me make a fool of myself," Kate said, referring to such luminaries as Nancy Carroll, Kay Francis, Gertrude Lawrence, George S. Kaufman, Judith Anderson, and even Amelia Earhart, who still believed that Kate had based her character in *Christopher Strong* on her.

When the curtain mercifully fell, Kate waited backstage to receive her fans, foes, and friends. Noël Coward once again came backstage to greet her. "You mucked it up, my dear," he said. "But haven't all of us? The critics will roast you. Don't give up. Keep at it and you'll find your way."

It was an awkward moment when Leland came backstage to congratulate her. He'd already heard about the Sullavan confrontation, and he knew that Kate's romance with Harris was over. "We both lost to the psycho," Leland told her. When he went to kiss her good-bye, she avoided his lips, leaving him kissing the air. Her reconciliation with him was yet to come.

Unknown to Kate, Dorothy Parker was standing in the lobby about to deliver an immortal *bon mot*. When asked what she thought of Kate's performance, Parker said that Kate "ran the gamut of emotions from A to B." Parker's flippant remark became the most quoted "nonreview" in the history of Broadway, remembered long after *The Lake* closed. Parker's barb the following day was published in nearly every newspaper between New York and Los Angeles.

Over the years there has been much speculation among theater gossips. Some critics claimed that Parker wanted revenge on Kate, suspecting that she'd had an affair with her husband, Alan Campbell. In truth, it was Luddy who had seduced Campbell, not Kate.

Parker's friend, Robert Benchley, stated his views in the *New Yorker*. He wrote that Kate was "not a great actress, by any manner or means, but one with a certain distinction which, with training, might possibly take the place of great acting in an emergency."

The reviews were so bad that Kate began to attract "theatrical voyeurs," an audience desperately wanting to see her fall on her face. In spite of the critical blasts, the play still held strong because of the heavy advance bookings by Hollywood fans who had been lured to see Kate. Even she admitted, "No one with any sense is buying tickets—maybe people wanting to see a movie star with egg on her face."

Early in the run of the play, a concert performer came backstage to greet Kate. She'd virtually appeared out of nowhere and had bribed Geoffrey Kerr to take her to Kate's dressing room.

"Who are you?" Kate asked, always suspicious of strangers.

"I'm Suzanne Steele, and I can save this play for you."

Those were the opening lines in what became an intense personal friendship.

***

The night she met Steele, Kate claimed she'd given the worst performance of her career. Steele felt she could give Kate emergency help, "so you could sound less like a character on the Amos and Andy comedy hour."

The sudden appearance of Steele in Kate's life remains one of the enigmas of all her romantic involvements. "It was so unexpected," Laura told Luddy and Jack. "I mean, just who is this mystery woman?"

Very little is known today about Steele. Some biographies call her a "plump opera singer," although she had a rather shapely figure, and had performed, somewhat unsuccessfully and without much critical attention, as a concert singer.

Even though Robinson-Duff was still giving Kate voice lessons, Steele prevailed. Although Laura objected, Kate invited Steele to stay over in a guest room at her Turtle Bay residence. The two women began voice lessons the next day, Steele going over every line of *The Lake* with Kate. And for a while, Steele attended every performance, both matinee and evening.

From all reports, Steele had a melodious voice and delivered every single line from the play "as it should have been." Before meeting Kate, Steele had translated the Molière classic, *The School for Wives*, from French into English, and had presented several dramatic readings from that work, assuming both the male and female roles. Her presentation, although generally acclaimed, found a dissent from the critic for the *New York Sun*, who suggested that she confine her future work "to women's clubs and to other audiences in which she will not

152

be judged by too high a standard."

Amazingly, Steele lived up to her promise. Colin Clive, and even the highly critical Frances Starr and Blanche Bates, claimed that Kate's performance, under Steele's tutelage, improved remarkably. As her performance picked up, Kate begged Harris "to return to the scene of the crime." He refused, sending word to her that "I can't endure seeing you massacre my play one more time."

As the weeks quickly passed, Kate grew in confidence as an actress. She later said, "I began to find myself in the part. I was learning to act. I was learning to be a *star.*"

On the domestic front, the relationship between Laura and Kate deteriorated rapidly. "It was all I could endure to think of Kate with Jed Harris," Laura told Luddy and Jack. "Now there's this Steele creature."

When Laura arrived unexpectedly one afternoon at Turtle Bay, she found Kate and Steele in bed. Kate protested that they were merely rehearsing and were in bed because it was a cold day and the bed was more comfortable.

Laura was having none of that. She packed her possessions and called for her chauffeur. She walked out of Turtle Bay without a good-bye to Kate, but left a loving note to Jack and Luddy. "This time it's forever," she told the men. "Kate and I are through!"

***

Kate chose Laura's departure as the time to move Luddy and Jack out of her Turtle Bay house. But they didn't go far, renting a townhouse in back of her house, both residences linked by a communal garden. When Kate was in her sitting room or rear bedroom, her view overlooked the living room of Jack and Luddy.

Even though he had been evicted, Luddy still walked across the garden and entered through Kate's back door any time he chose, coming through the dining room. Ever devoted to Kate, he remained at her beck and call. If a radio broke down or a pipe burst in winter, she summoned him on a moment's notice, since "Luddy could repair almost anything." One day Kate returned home from the theater to find that Jack and Luddy had repaired the crumbling ceiling in her bedroom and were repainting it "but not in a color I would have chosen."

Even though the new living arrangement between Kate and Luddy remained cozy, the Hepburn family was greatly saddened to learn of it. Kit and Dr. Hepburn had always maintained that "Kate and Luddy will be married until death separates them." But for the first time, the family members began to realize that that might not be true. In her diary, Katharine's sister, Marion, expressed her fear that Kate might divorce Luddy. "I thought it would never happen," Marion wrote. "Now I fear the inevitable."

Marion wrote that the family had been gladdened by the news that Laura had departed, blaming the heiress for any difficulties between Luddy and Kate.

Dr. Hepburn felt that with Laura out of the picture, Kate could "now be a proper wife to Luddy, who loves her more than any man she'll ever find in her life."

Dr. Hepburn's assessment of Luddy's love may indeed have been accurate.

***

Kate's appearance in *The Lake* had gained her a lot of newspaper notoriety. More was to come when Kit went to Washington in front of flashing cameras. As the mother of a major star, Kit generated more headlines than the occasion called for.

Attracting press coverage across the country, Kit was the keynote speaker at the American Conference on Birth Control, an event organized by Margaret Sanger herself.

In Washington, Kit was joined by old friends and supporters, including Amelia Earhart and Charlotte Perkins Gilman. Later, arm in arm with Sanger, Kit marched with other angry women over to Capitol Hill for hearings to muster support for the Pierce Bill, legislation that would permit the dissemination of birth control data by doctors.

Kit's chief opponent that day was Father Charles E. Kaufman, who equated birth control with "the advancement of Communism." Kit called him a "ridiculous idiot." She also battled another cleric, Charles Coughlin, a popular radio evangelist, who claimed that "birth control will lead to the collapse of American society." That battling duo made a headline in a Washington paper the following day—RADIO FATHER VS. MOVIE MA.

To charges that birth control would lead to the "suicide of the species," Kit faced her opponents and cried, "NONSENSE!" More headlines were on the way. *The New York Times* in a banner proclaimed, STAR'S MOTHER IN FIRM STAND.

In Hollywood, RKO executives were horrified at Kit's national exposure on such a controversial issue as birth control. Pandro Berman feared it would lead to a boycott among Catholics and audiences in Bible Belt America. But in reality, even without the potentially negative influence of Kit's position on birth control, Kate's movies had never fared particularly well in the Bible Belt.

After performances of *The Lake,* many reporters waited for Kate outside the stage door. The most typical question was, "What do you think of your firebrand mother?"

Only when cornered, would Kate answer, "I stand by her one-hundred percent. But stop referring to her as Katharine Hepburn's mother. She's far more important than I am. She's trying to bring about social change. I'm a mere actress offering a momentary diversion on the stage or screen—nothing more."

***

When the company manager, Joe Glick, informed Kate that Harris planned to take *The Lake* to Chicago after its New York closing, she was horrified. Having embarrassed herself in New York, and in spite of her performance having improved, she wasn't eager to endure a sea of fresh new critics. She also wanted to either return to RKO, or to appear in some new Broadway plays.

Matters worsened when *The Chicago Tribune* on its front page ran a box that read, "Chicago audiences are going to have the misfortune of having to look at Katharine Hepburn in *The Lake.*"

Ten days later, Kate called Harris at four o'clock in the morning, the first voice contact they'd had since the disastrous opening night. She demanded to know why he was taking the play to Chicago.

"Money, and for no other reason," Harris told her.

Kate knew the only way out was for her to pay him off. "How much?" she said.

"How much have you got in the bank?" he asked her.

"I have thirteen thousand, six hundred, and seventy dollars and fifty-five cents," she said.

"You've got yourself a deal, sweetheart," he said. "Have the check hand-delivered to my office before nine o'clock this morning. Now, let me get some sleep."

Years later Kate learned that when she'd called Harris that early morning, he was in bed with her rival, Margaret Sullavan.

The Lake closed on Broadway on February 10, 1934.

Two days later, Kate sailed for Europe with Suzanne Steele, leaving a jilted Laura and a cuckolded husband behind.

***

The Hepburn/Harris affair was over. She would never speak to Harris again, but would have a chance encounter with him in the lobby of a theater years after the closing of *The Lake.* By then, Harris was a bitter and broken figure, a theater has-been. Kate walked right by him without speaking.

Around the same time, and down on his luck, Harris arrived in Hollywood and went to call on Myron Selznick, who was still Kate's co-agent along with Leland. In his office, Selznick chastised Harris for taking all of Kate's cash to buy her way out of the play at the time of that long-ago disaster. Harris claimed that he didn't realize Kate was upset over the transaction and immediately wrote out a check for Selznick to give to Kate.

The next day, Selznick presented Kate with Harris's check. She tore it up in front of him. "Blood money," she told Selznick. "I'm sure the check would bounce anyway."

Leland would also run into Harris later in life, meeting him in the lobby of a theater in Philadelphia. Still confrontational, Harris came up to his former rival and shook his hand. "I only fucked Sullavan. You married the bitch."

"I'd rather not talk about Maggie." Leland said. "Why did you try to ruin Kate?"

"For reasons known only to myself," Harris said enigmatically.

"You didn't do a very good job of it, did you?"

***

Before departing for France, Charles Newhill, Kate's chauffeur, drove her to Hartford where her family provided much support and encouragement "as I licked my wounds," Kate later recalled. Her siblings were becoming young adults, both Marion and Margaret ("Peg") having gone to Bennington College, in Vermont, not Bryn Mawr. Marion had shown an interest in literature, Peggy in science. Richard had chosen Harvard and wanted to spend a future "writing great plays for Kate." Robert ("Bob"), too, had graduated from Harvard and wanted to follow in his father's footsteps and become a doctor. Like Kate, Bob had had a brief fling in the theater, appearing in drag as a "glamorous chorine" in a Harvard Hasty Pudding revue.

Both Jack and Luddy asked to sail to Europe to be a part of Kate's vacation. She flatly turned them down, warning Luddy that "we must have a serious talk about our marriage when I get back." With Laura out of the picture, Kate was enraptured with Suzanne Steele, inviting her to share her stateroom on the ship sailing to France. Luddy, in a fit of generosity, or perhaps guilt, agreed to pay for the first-class tickets for Kate and her new-found playmate.

***

Kate knew that the Academy Awards ceremonies were coming up in Hollywood, but she didn't think she'd win for *Morning Glory*. That year Kate faced stiff competition from such veterans as May Robson in *Lady for a Day* and Diana Wynward in *Cavalcade.*

Kate showed her contempt for the ceremony by embarking on her ocean voyage on the very night of the awards. She would not show up to receive any of her future Oscars either.

Suzanne Steele and Kate entered the vessel through steerage, hoping to escape reporters, although two women in mannish attire always stood out in the crowd. One clever photographer figured out that Kate would do just that and was waiting for her as she and Steele headed up the third-class gangway. As a photograph of Kate and Steele was taken, Kate yelled back at him, "It'll be a lousy picture." In tomorrow's newspapers, a headline ran: "KATE WAS RIGHT!"

A reporter on board asked Kate why she hadn't stayed in Hollywood to await the decision of the Oscar committee. She told him that she was afraid to show up for the ceremony because she felt it might "give me dyspepsia."

Later she would facetiously remark, "In private life I always try to avoid shiny gold men. Besides, these Academy Award ceremonies are just country club dinners and filled with backslapping." In those days, Oscar presentations were "glorified buffets" in Kate's words.

The ceremony wasn't the media lavish event it is today. When Kate won her Oscar, *The New York Times* reported it on page 10 on March 16, 1934, along with the obituary of a Long Island newspaper editor.

In the 1930s reporters were allowed to remain aboard a departing vessel until attendants called ALL ASHORE. It was easy to bribe a member of the ship's staff to learn the number of Kate's stateroom. Many reporters pounded on her door and refused to heed the shouts from inside urging them to, "Go away." Finally Suzanne was forced to step outside the private cabin to confront the press with a brief announcement. "Miss Hepburn and I, her publicity representative, will be abroad for four or five weeks, visiting Paris and the Riviera, where she will accept an award in Cannes."

Before she sailed for Le Havre, rumors were rampant in the press that Kate was sailing to France to divorce her husband. Steele's last "official" action as Kate's spokesperson was to deny these stories. "There will be no divorce," Steele told reporters. "Mr. and Mrs. Ludlow are happily married, a devoted couple, and plan to stay together until we get our blue cheese from the moon."

As her ship, S.S. *Paris*, was en route to France, Kate received a telegram from Leland that she'd won her first Oscar for *Morning Glory*. Impulsively, she went to the ship's communication headquarters and dictated an ill-conceived response. "I do not believe in acting contests, finding them silly, and therefore must refuse your offer of an award."

The telegram was sent to Leland, with instructions to deliver it to the Academy and also to hold a press conference, announcing her action to the world.

Leland read the telegram and locked it in a bank vault. In Kate's name, he sent a hand-delivered letter to the Academy, thanking them most graciously for the honor. Later, when Kate learned of Leland's action, she said she regretted her rash decision—"I was childish"—and thanked him for saving her career.

***

By the second day of the crossing, Kate, "trapped in a cage" with Steele, realized how incompatible she was with her voice coach. Apparently, Steele had been looking forward to a glamorous ocean voyage. But she quickly discovered that Kate wanted to remain in her stateroom at all times.

Instead of lavish meals in the ballroom-like dining room, Kate preferred food delivered to her stateroom by room service. Detesting the drinking and partying at night, Kate wanted to go to bed right after dinner and read until nine-thirty when it was "lights out."

In her frustration, Steele took to drinking heavily in front of the temperate Kate. Reacting to the deteriorating friendship, Kate booked Steele into a cabin in steerage.

Before the ship docked in France, Kate told Steele that she wouldn't be able to accompany her to Paris, but gave her the money for a safe return to New York. From all reports, both Kate and Steele departed company with great animosity.

On the train taking Kate to Paris, she wrote an urgent cable to Laura, begging her to take her back and admitting she had made "a big mistake" in sailing to France with Steele. Laura showed the cable to Jack and Luddy and told her friends that she hoped that "once again, Kate has come to her senses."

To Jack's amazement, both Luddy and Laura were prepared to welcome Kate back into their open arms the moment she returned to New York.

As for Suzanne Steele, she'd experienced what in years to come Andy Warhol would call her "fifteen minutes of fame."

***

Bored with France, Kate booked an immediate return on the S.S. *Paris,* and then secured passage for Steele on a vessel that was sailing back to New York the following week. Kate had spent only four days in France before cabling her parents, Luddy, Laura, and Leland—the "three Ls" as she called them—about her imminent return.

Leland cabled her back at once, urging her to dine aboard ship with "my clients," Marlene Dietrich and Ernest Hemingway. He warned her that the author was traveling in second class and would have to be smuggled into the first-class dining room, providing someone could find a tuxedo for him.

Kate had long known of Leland's attempts "to take over Papa's career and direct all his publishing contracts and movie deals." She was also intrigued by the prospect of meeting Dietrich, as all of Hollywood had heard of her romance with Mercedes de Acosta and countless others, male and female.

Kate speculated about what romance Dietrich would be pursuing on the return voyage to New York, only to learn later that the glamorous German diva was accompanied by her eight-year-old daughter, Maria.

Having judged Hemingway only by his photographs, Kate had found the macho writer very sexy and appealing—"my kind of man." She preferred delicate beautiful women but liked her men big and strong, with a sense of adventure. Hemingway fit her criterion.

Before Kate boarded the *Paris*, Leland sent her another of his many cables. "Perhaps you and Ernest will come up with some big literary triumph, one I can sell to the studios. I can be the agent on the deal for him as the writer and you as the star of the picture. A blockbuster novel will be followed by a film which will lead to your second Oscar." Leland added a footnote. "When Ernesto comes on strong like the wolf he is, remember that your heart belongs to Daddy, slaving away all alone back here in Hollywood for his divine *Morning Glory.*"

Because Kate loved Leland, in spite of his affair with Sullavan, she was beginning "to find it in my heart to forgive him." Perhaps some of her softening toward Leland was because he too was being cheated on by Margaret Sullavan, and Kate claimed that she felt sorry for her agent/lover because of the abusive treatment he was receiving at the hands of her nemesis.

When Kate heard that Leland was about to make one of his frequent trips to New York, she invited him to Hartford to meet her family. She had also been relieved to hear that Leland's divorce was coming through.

Even before arriving in New York, Kate received one final and urgent cable from Leland. "Divorce Luddy. Marry me. I can't live without you. I know that now."

She didn't respond, and the cable threw her into a state of confusion. Although Laura had seen Kate live out her love affair with Leland in front of Laura's very eyes, Kate could only wonder what effect a marriage to Leland would have on Laura.

Before dealing with Leland's proposal, she knew that she had to "make things right with Laura." Complicating matters was the fact that "the most blood-sniffing of press hound dogs" awaited her arrival.

***

Meeting Hemingway for the first time aboard the *S.S. Paris* sailing for New York, Kate discovered that the writer was very unlike his publicity. She hadn't expected him to be so petty. Most of their first meeting, as Kate would later reveal to her most trusted friends, consisted of listening to his attack on Gertrude Stein. Kate never learned exactly why Hemingway was so disenchanted with the famous American author, living an expatriate life in Paris with her longtime lover Alice B. Toklas.

From what Kate could gather, the rather masculine Stein had told Hemingway "to look at yourself in the mirror of reality."

Apparently, and Kate was only guessing, Stein had urged the author to "confront some bitter truths about yourself." There may have been a suggestion on Stein's part that Hemingway's early affection for "the very pretty" F. Scott Fitzgerald was "not just platonic."

Hemingway was fuming that Stein's amusingly titled *Autobiography of Alice B. Toklas,* as serialized in the *Atlantic,* was damaging his literary stature in its claim that she had helped mold him and influence him as a writer. Considering the way Hemingway's writing was going, Stein suggested that she might be both "a little proud" and "a little ashamed" of what she'd created.

Stein and Toklas were planning an extended tour of the United States in late 1934. Hemingway was being urged by the magazine, *Esquire*, to which he was already writing informal "letters," to pen a rebuttal to Stein. The editor of *Esquire* claimed that it would be "a sure-fire piece." Hemingway showed Kate the letter from the editor and asked her advice.

As Kate would later claim to Leland, she urged the author to show restraint. She feared that an attack on an institution like Stein would make Hemingway "look catty, like a gossipy woman."

Hemingway boasted to her that it would be easy to kill Stein with a sharp sword, like a matador facing the most ferocious bull in the ring. "Somehow I feel superior in the knowledge that I could kill her off at the moment of truth," Hemingway is said to have told Kate, or at least that was the way she remembered it. Hemingway claimed that he found it difficult not to cave in to his temptation to "slam the old lez bitch around."

Of course, Hemingway, being a "bitch" himself, didn't follow through on his honorable intentions, as expressed to Kate. At least in print, he slammed Stein repeatedly. In his introduction to James Charterer's memoirs of Montparnasse, Hemingway subtly attacked Stein, and in a passage from *Green Hills of Africa*, he wrote that Stein had once been talented but was all "malice and nonsense and self-praise…Women of letters…salon women. What a lousy stinking life."

He even claimed that instead of Stein "forming" him as a writer, she had learned to write dialogue by studying his own fiction, notably *The Sun Also Rises.* For his *coup de grâce*, Hemingway, in his memoirs, *A Moveable Feast,* lifted that sharp sword and plunged it deep into Stein's heart, even though she was resting in her tomb at Père-Lachaise cemetery in Paris at the time.

It took the whole first day of Kate's meeting with Hemingway for him to "put alcohol in my blood and get rid of the poison left there from the last time I saw Stein."

When he'd accomplished that, he began to pay some attention to Kate, although he was initially put off by her lack of glamour, especially her "male drag." Lacking a certain chivalry, Hemingway told Kate that in a man-to-woman meeting, he preferred that the man wear the pants. "It's better that way," he lectured her.

She wasn't offended but shot back, "Women can do anything a man can except father babies. God only knows, men have done that job too well. Surely, there are enough babies to go around. Just listen to my mother."

"But women are forced to turn to men for sexual pleasure, if nothing else," he told her.

"No, they aren't!" she adamantly said.

It was the second night of the crossing, and both Kate and Hemingway sat at a table in first class. Kate had smuggled him into the dining room, and the writer wore "a tux borrowed from a pal in first class."

Both of their eyes were diverted to the top of the staircase. A hush fell over the dining room. Every man and woman put down their knives and forks for the grand entrance of Marlene Dietrich in a tight-fitting, white-beaded dress.

Her descent into the dining room would become part of her Hollywood legend.

***

In the apocryphal tale, Dietrich makes her descent into the dining room to join a table of twelve. Since she is superstitious and fears the number 13, she declines joining the table. At a table nearby, Hemingway sees her dilemma and graciously offers his services as the fourteenth diner.

Since Leland had already arranged for his clients to dine privately with each other, that tale didn't reflect the way Dietrich actually met Hemingway and Kate. In fact, Kate usually gets left out of the narrative completely.

Three American legends came together at table, and Hemingway, it seemed, had eyes only for Dietrich. From the very first moment of their meeting, Dietrich and Hemingway became soul mates, a friendship that would endure for their lifetimes. He called themselves "victims of unsynchronized passion."

Soon she was calling him "Papa," and he was referring to her as "The Kraut," or more affectionately, "Daughter." Kate, meanwhile, was left out of most of the conversation. Before Kate's very eyes, Dietrich began to emerge as a Hemingway heroine. She was never to appear in a film based on his fiction, although in time she wanted to play Catharine Barkley in *A Farewell to Arms,* eventually losing the role to Spencer Tracy's lover, Ingrid Bergman. In a disguised fictional form, Dietrich did appear as "The Good General," the wife of Thomas Hudson, the hero of Hemingway's *Islands in the Stream.*

From the beginning, Hemingway kidded Dietrich about "your lady friends," as he'd no doubt heard of her lesbian love affairs. 'We'll never be lovers," he said. "I don't have the right equipment."

Since she moved in international circles in Paris, she had heard rumors of his own sexual confusion, even rumors about his own homosexuality. But whereas he could blithely challenge and even mockingly kid her, Dietrich graciously didn't do that to him, perhaps realizing that although she could take the ribbing, he couldn't handle "castrating jibes," even affectionate ones from her.

It was as if both of them had made a pact that night whereby she would never demand sex from him. Speaking years later, Dietrich confirmed Kate's earliest impression of the unusual friendship. "Sex with Papa was not on the table," Dietrich said. "It would have destroyed a beautiful relationship."

On the first night of their dining trio aboard ship, Dietrich rose to her feet early to excuse herself to get back to her stateroom to look after her daughter.

That left Kate and Hemingway alone again. Once again he concentrated his full attention on her, and she seemed to blossom under his intense scrutiny. He invited her for a midnight walk on the windswept deck, and she gladly accepted.

Soon he was holding her hand and speaking of grand adventures. He told her that as soon as the ship docked in New York, he was heading for Key West "for the most intense season of hard writing in my life, and always on my feet at the typewriter, as I don't want to sit in a chair and get a writer's fat ass."

He told her that he not only wanted to produce a great novel, one that would dazzle Fitzgerald and especially Stein, but one that would make so much money that it would finance his return to Africa, "perhaps with Pauline [his wife at the time] at my side," or perhaps not. "Perhaps even with you," he said to Kate.

The thought of a safari with Hemingway thrilled her, and impulsively she offered to finance the trip herself since he didn't have enough money. "You need not wait," she said. "I have no pictures lined up. I want to go at once. It'll be the grandest adventure of my life."

For the rest of the night and for most of the trip, they talked about the upcoming safari. At one o'clock that morning, Hemingway invited her down to the bar to sample his taste in a "good French brandy." By two-thirty on that same morning, she invited him into her stateroom. After thinking about it for a minute, he accepted.

***

Aware of the affair that was blossoming before her eyes, Dietrich showed not the slightest sign of jealousy. The following morning, she invited Kate to drop into her stateroom. When Kate knocked on Dietrich's door, "The Kraut" opened it herself. If Kate were astonished to see Dietrich in the nude, she showed no sign of it, as accustomed to nudity as she was.

Dietrich was an exhibitionist, as would be shown time and time again in her life. Even when entertaining the troops during World War II, she would barge unannounced into the men's shower room, often with thirty naked men soaping themselves. Perhaps she viewed that as another means of entertaining "the boys." Private William Phillips once said, "Giving thirty men who hadn't been with a woman in months instant hard-ons might, in looking back, be viewed as cruel and inhumane punishment."

Actually, Dietrich wasn't completely nude in front of Kate. She wore an elegant hat. Still naked, she tried on several hats before Kate, seeking her advice. Kate declined comment, claiming she wasn't "too receptive to women's hats."

When Dietrich put on her robe, she invited Kate to have a whiskey with her. Kate preferred that she ring room service instead for some hot tea.

No one knows exactly what transpired that afternoon between Dietrich and Hepburn. It is highly doubtful if sex took place between them. Back in Hollywood, Kate insisted to her gay pals that it did not, although she felt, per-

162

haps justifiably, that Dietrich was making a pass at her by showing up at the door in the nude.

Even though Dietrich epitomized an alluring bisexual sensuality, and was well on her way to becoming an international symbol of unattainable glamour, she was too exotic for Kate's more wholesome tastes in women.

Despite their differences, the women did have much in common. Kate had had a brief affair with Dietrich's longtime companion, Mercedes de Acosta, and both women were having a lesbian relationship with Greta Garbo. Although Kate was not interested in Dietrich's latest hat acquisitions, the two women over the years did enjoy many a bonding session over their wearing of masculine attire, Kate's apparel being more butch and thrown together haphazardly and Dietrich appearing in only the most elegant of clothing inspired by male attire.

Before Kate left that afternoon, Dietrich told her that she had no intention of arranging "the seduction of Ernest Hemingway." Over lunch that day, as Kate was striding the decks, Hemingway had told Dietrich that she was a "woman meant only for the loveliest of a man's dreams. I can't picture you lying under some sweaty male pounding into you for quick relief. You are someone to be idolized. You're not a woman a man approaches for sex."

"Papa fears I'm too much woman for him—too experienced, too capable of judging his performance," Dietrich said to Kate. "With you, he'll be safer."

Over a final toast, Dietrich told Kate that in spite of her reputation as an international vamp, she was not a sex maniac. "Women are the best lovers, but I adore the company of men. Of course, because they're men, my companions often want sex. I try to satisfy them with my lips. If that fails, I give in, but it's not my favorite thing. It's what I do to keep the relationship, as in the case of Josef von Sternberg."

"What about love?" Kate asked.

"We will be friends," Dietrich said, "but you and I will never love anybody but ourselves. Call us self-enchanted."

Although somewhat put off, Kate launched a lifetime friendship with Dietrich. But it was always a "hands-off" relationship, something akin to the one she maintained with Tallulah. She would see both actresses on occasions throughout their lives, and many of those times brought meaning and even joy to Kate's life. But she backed away from intimacy, even thought she could easily have seduced either woman.

Perhaps Tallulah was far too flamboyant for Kate, and perhaps Dietrich was too glamorous. As she was to confide to George Cukor and others, "Tallulah or Marlene would be like eating a plate of black orchids grown in a poisonous jungle—and maybe not quite of this earth. Not for me!"

Hemingway spent every night in Kate's stateroom for the duration of the voyage, although they continued to see Dietrich during the day and to dine with her.

Before the ship docked in New York, Kate was proclaiming to Dietrich that she was "madly in love" with the author. The more sophisticated Dietrich urged Kate to view the short affair "as a mere shipboard romance."

***

Seventeen days after she'd first departed with Suzanne Steele, Kate arrived in New York's port on April 4 and encountered an avalanche of press. With freckles showing, she wore only a scarlet slash of lipstick. Her hair had not been fashionably stylized like Dietrich's blonde tresses.

Hemingway knew that Dietrich was capable of charming an army of press corps members and probably could even "give me a lesson or two." On the other hand, he feared that Kate was more vulnerable, and gallantly agreed to stand by her side when she faced the reporters at the pier.

Hemingway warned her not to face the press cameras looking like she was posing for a mug shot for the police. Talking his advice, she learned from the steward that twelve reporters were waiting to interview her. She ordered them sent into her stateroom and the steward to bring champagne for all.

She answered their questions one by one, claiming that she wore men's trousers for greater comfort. She completely denounced news stories that she'd sailed to France to seek a divorce. "If I plan a divorce, you'll be the first to know," Kate claimed, lying to the press. She said that she planned to return to the stage in spite of the disaster of *The Lake*. "It's like learning to ride a horse. If you fall off, pick yourself up and get back on." She announced that her next stage appearance was most likely to be a dramatization of Jane Austen's *Pride and Prejudice*. Without having anything in writing, she also claimed that she planned to return to Hollywood to star in another costume picture, *Joan of Arc*, by Thornton Wilder. The script, she said, had been based on the play, *Saint Joan*, written by her father's pen pal, George Bernard Shaw.

After she was back in Hollywood, Kate confirmed to Cukor, Kenneth MacKenna, and Anderson Lawler that she indeed had had an affair with Hemingway. She even claimed that she could restore "the manhood that Stein had stolen from him," although it would be hard to imagine the author falling for a line like that.

Years after the Hemingway-Hepburn affair, the author's son, Gregory Hemingway, claimed that Papa had confided in him, citing Kate's "schoolgirl crush on me." Hemingway boasted that Kate had probably "never been fucked by a real man," and he even went so far as to say that he suspected he'd "cured her of her lesbianism in just one sea crossing."

On shore, much like the charging bull cited by her father, Kate aggressively pursued Hemingway, although in spite of their brief involvement, she did not appear to be his kind of woman.

Gregory also maintained that after his father arrived in Key West, Kate actively "bombarded" him with phone calls, cables, and letters, begging him to allow her "to come and be at your side."

According to Gregory, his father flatly rejected "the lovesick fool." Hemingway finally cabled her that he was "far too busy writing" and could not see her. He also asked her to stop trying to communicate with him.

Humiliated and in despair, Kate stopped writing to him. She wasn't to meet him until years later when she showed up in Cuba.

Spencer Tracy was at her side, and he'd signed to star in Hemingway's *The Old Man and the Sea,* to be produced by Leland Hayward.

Kate's reunion with Hemingway was to turn into a disaster.

***

It was an emotional reunion when Kate arrived back at Turtle Bay in Manhattan. Jack and Luddy waited for her with hugs and kisses. Laura fell into her arms crying.

Kate told Luddy that their "marriage was as solid as a rock." Taking Laura to her bedroom, she embraced her recently alienated friend, insisting that her romances "with other women" would end on that very day.

She beseeched Laura to go with her to Mexico, where she planned to obtain a divorce from Luddy in spite of what she'd just told him. "I couldn't tell him the truth—not right now," Kate said. "But I'll tell him before we go to Mexico."

Laura was stunned that Kate would not spend the first night with her. Kate claimed she had urgent family business in Hartford and wanted to go there with her chauffeur. Luddy also protested when she told him of her plans, claiming he wanted to accompany her. Kate held him off, saying she needed time alone with the Hepburns to talk over "a personal family matter."

After kissing Luddy, Jack, and Laura good-bye, Kate got into the car driven by Newhill. Blowing kisses at "my beloved creatures," Kate ordered Newhill to drive five blocks and "pick up a man on the corner."

After five blocks, Newhill spotted a familiar face waiting on the corner. Throwing open the rear door for him, Kate urged him into the backseat. She quickly embraced him, as the handsome, virile man madly kissed her face and her mouth. Long, passionate kisses.

"I've missed you so," he said. "My divorce has come through." Leland Hayward looked deeply into her eyes. "Will you marry me, my Morning Glory?"

"Yes, yes, dear one."

CHAPTER EIGHT

Within a movie star's boudoir, or in a sophisticated urban environment, Leland Hayward was usually a virile and capable man, but in the "wilds" of New England, Dr. Hepburn pronounced him a "sissy." Leland didn't dress right for the Hepburns, who were known for their casual apparel. He appeared for dinner in Savile Row black suits and pink diamonds. Kit suggested that he wear regular cufflinks and donate the diamonds to Margaret Sanger's birth-control movement.

Fifteen-year-old Marion suggested that Leland doused himself with so much cologne that he "smelled like a French whore," not that she knew what a French whore smelled like. A bit hypochondriacal, Leland arrived at the Hepburn residence with a Louis Vuitton valise filled with salves, ointments, and various lotions for the soothing of mosquito bites. Invited to join the Hepburns for a vigorous hike in the surrounding woodlands, he contracted a bad case of hives, which Dr. Hepburn subsequently treated.

Over dinner, instead of talking about the New York theater scene or the latest Hollywood gossip, the two subjects Leland knew best, the Hepburns preferred to discuss Roosevelt and the New Deal. Later, Leland proclaimed that he "absolutely adored" Kit. For her part, Kit informed Kate that she wouldn't "trade one Luddy for one-hundred Lelands."

Marion, Luddy's chief admirer, told Leland, "If you marry my sister and expect her to be a good little wife sitting home darning your socks while you're out gallivanting, you've picked the wrong woman."

Marion even expressed her fears about Kate's upcoming divorce in her diary. "I don't know why she [Kate] does it because Lud is so much nicer than Leland."

Although Kate was aware that no one in her family approved of Leland, she announced her plans to her family when the weekend came to an end. She said she was returning to New York with Leland. Once there, she said her intention was to break the news to Luddy that, with Laura, she was going to Mexico to file for divorce. "And when my divorce is finalized, I plan to marry Leland," Kate said.

Her family reacted with great disappointment as its members stood on the grounds watching Kate's car pull out of the driveway and head for New York with Leland at the wheel.

***

After midnight at her Turtle Bay house, Dr. Hepburn called his daughter. A sleepy Kate answered the phone. Her father had been reviewing her finances and had discovered that she'd spent more than one-hundred and twenty-five thousand dollars of Luddy's funds. After an angry fight with Kate, he informed her that he was transferring that much from her fund back into Luddy's account in Manhattan. "It's only fair," Dr. Hepburn told her, "the way you've treated Luddy."

Even before officially informing Luddy of her intentions, Kate was besieged by reporters outside her Turtle Bay home. Enjoying the cat-and-mouse game with reporters, Kate the following afternoon ushered Laura out her back door, walked through the communal garden, and entered Luddy's house through their back door, Then, exiting their dwelling through Luddy's front door, she maneuvered her way through the neighboring streets to a nearby *bon voyage* party that was being thrown for George Cukor, David Selznik, and David's wife, and Irene Mayer Selznick. The Selznicks were about to sail with Cukor to London aboard the *Majestic*, a White Star vessel. The producer had asked Cukor to accompany him to England for a pre-production holiday before shooting began on his film, *David Copperfield.*

Kate, in a voice that everyone in the living room could hear, told Cukor and the Selznicks that she planned to divorce Luddy in Mexico and marry Leland. Laura, who still wasn't aware of the pending divorce and anticipated re-marriage, had gone to the toilet and didn't hear the announcement.

Irene had actually been among Kate's first admirers, urging her husband to sign her when he was still at RKO before moving to MGM. The two women bonded at the party but didn't pursue a friendship until years later. Irene urged Kate to rush through her divorce and then join David and her in Paris where she could honeymoon with Leland. With great enthusiasm and promises, Kate agreed.

Upon first meeting her, Irene told Kate how excited she'd been by her screen test. "They thought you were gawky, but I saw grace there. You moved on the screen like a young colt. The camera caught a sense of panic in you but you were also sure-footed. At times you looked a bit like an amateur, but there was something totally original about your look, and you have one of the most arresting personalities on the screen. Believe me, as the daughter of Louis B., I've judged screen tests in my day. When I saw the final version of that *Divorcement* thing, I told David, 'You've given birth to a star!'"

Kate liked Irene at once. "Is it true that you were with your father when he discovered Garbo in Berlin, and that you influenced his decision?" Kate asked.

"That's a rumor," Irene said, laughing, "but I'm not doing anything to dispel it."

She also claimed that she adored Leland and urged Kate to marry him. "In our Jewish tradition, the older sister marries first," Irene said. "Then the younger sister."

"But I'm already married," Kate protested. "That's why I'm getting a divorce."

"But that marriage didn't count," Irene said. In her answer, she revealed that she knew more about Kate than she would pretend in later journalistic interviews. Irene spent hours talking with both Laura and Kate, sharing intimacies with them, and she was well aware of Kate's lesbian relationship with Laura. Even though her father, Louis B. Mayer, had severe reservations about homosexuals, especially male (he could barely accept the fact that lesbianism even existed), Irene was gay-friendly before the term was invented. Throughout her entire life in the movie colony, she'd been surrounded by gays and lesbians, some of them household names.

Irene later said, "I've spent my entire life keeping my eyes wide open and my lips sealed about what I saw and what I knew."

Although urged by some editors at the publishing house of Alfred A. Knopf in 1983 to "spill the beans" in her memoir, *A Private View*, Irene Mayer Selznick chose to be discreet and protect old friends like Kate, even though their friendship by that time had grown stale.

***

A short time before, Kate had assured Luddy that their marriage was still valid, but at midnight she summoned him to their communal garden and told him she was leaving in the morning for Mexico. Once there, she would arrange a quick divorce from him. Jack, Laura, and others would later learn fragments of that meeting in the garden.

Some biographers have claimed that Luddy remained stoic at the time. But intimates of both Kate and Luddy said that he fell down and cried in the garden. At one point he was on his knees, begging her not to leave him. He said that marriage to her was so tied into who he was that he'd be nothing without her presence. Luddy claimed that he found it enthralling to be married to a movie star even when people called him "Mr. Hepburn."

He related to her that when he'd married her, he'd been dropped from the *Philadelphia Social Register*, but that it hadn't mattered to him.

When Kate adamantly refused to give in to his pleas, he delivered his bombshell, promising to leave Jack if she would stay married to him, even though he knew that it would be a celibate marriage. She urged him to stay with Jack. "You'll never find anyone to love you like that, certainly not me," she said.

At last, when all of his entreaties failed, he capitulated to her wishes, taking her in his arms and promising that he wouldn't block her marriage to Leland. He told her that beginning in the morning he would instruct his attorneys to cooperate with her in every way.

"Good, dear Luddy," she is reported to have told him. "You'll be my friend for life. It's better this way. Things go wrong between a man and a wife. As friends, we'll be there for each other until the grave."

He told her that if she ever needed him, if she were ever sick or even dying, he would "drop my life" and tend to her needs until she was well again or else had expired. She promised to return such a commitment.

Years later, in a rare interview with Barbara Walters, Kate reflected on her marriage. "I was self-interested. He was a nice man. I felt sorry for him. I say, I broke his heart, spent his money—and my sister took his blood, when she was very ill and he was the right type. We have remained friends all our lives."

***

Leaving New York en route to Mexico, Kate journeyed to Miami with Laura. Once in Miami, she made a rather desperate call to Hemingway in Key West, begging the author to see her. He flatly rejected her request. Laura, it seemed, was unaware of Kate's romantic obsession with Hemingway.

The next day, Kate sailed with Laura on the S.S. *Morro Castle*, one of the few cruise ships leaving from the Florida coastline in those days. The ship sailed first to Havana and then went on to the Panama Canal before going up the coast of Mexico to their final destination in Mérida.

In the history of maritime disasters, the *Morro Castle* lives on in legend. Months after Laura and Kate sailed on it, it exploded on the night of September 8, 1934, off the Atlantic seaboard, killing some one-hundred and twenty-five passengers and crew members. Evoking the advertising for the *Titanic, Morro Castle* had been touted as the "safest ship on the sea."

In Mérida, Laura and Kate checked into the Hotel Itza, Kate registering as Laura's maid, Katharine Smith, a name she had, at the beginning of her marriage to Luddy, once rejected. Ostensibly they were in the Yucatán to see the Mayan ruins.

Two days later in the Second Civil Court, Kate's lawyer filed for divorce from Luddy, with Laura functioning as her sole witness. Luddy had hired a local lawyer to represent him, but had given him instructions not to challenge any of Kate's charges.

Although the desertion was of her own doing, Kate charged Luddy with being separated from her for more than three-hundred days at a time. She also cited "incompatibility of character." Actually, except for their sexual preferences, the pair seemed like virtual soul mates. Kate also made the somewhat irresponsible accusation that her view of life, as opposed to Luddy's, was at such variance as to constitute severe mental cruelty. At the last moment, Kate may have instructed her lawyers to drop this reckless and rather meaningless charge.

Luddy's attorney introduced a petition "begging" the court not to impose a waiting period before either of them could remarry. The divorce and the remarriage petition were granted by the rather lenient judge, who accepted a bribe of two-hundred and fifty dollars to keep the notice out of the local papers.

Even so, within forty-eight hours, news of the Hepburn/Ogden divorce was leaked to the press. By that time, Laura and Kate were on a seaplane to Miami where they could make a rail connection back to New York.

From Miami, Kate made one final call to the Hemingway house in Key West. Papa didn't take her call but had left word with his maid that he'd speak to "The Kraut" at any time, even in the midst of a big writing session.

Throughout the entire divorce proceedings, Leland had kept in constant touch with Kate. He claimed to be "saving my heart just for you." Even so, when newspapers were brought aboard the train on the final day of their north-bound transit, the eagle-eyed Laura discovered a picture of Leland and Margaret Sullavan snapped at a local night club in New York City.

As Laura later confided to Jack, Luddy, and some of her friends, she'd received a "blood commitment" from Kate in the Yucatán that she'd never remarry. "For once, I really believe her," Laura said.

***

When Kate arrived back in New York, Leland was in Hollywood, planning to fly East at the first available moment. In the meantime, the press virtually camped out on the doorstep of Kate's home in Turtle Bay.

Kate set up housekeeping with Laura as before, with Jack and Luddy "only a holler away," as she put it. That remark hardly sounded like a Bryn Mawr graduate and must have been left over from her *Spitfire* script.

Caught at his business office by the press, Luddy said, "I don't plan to remarry. Mrs. Ogden has assured me that she doesn't either. I'm sure we'll get back together again and will remarry. We're both more mature now. She was quite young when she married me."

Kate was trapped into speaking to a member of the press only after he rescued her cat, which had escaped onto the street. "If you want to sacrifice the admiration of many for the criticism of one, get married," she said. Actually, unknown to the reporter, she was quoting directly from Dorothy Dix. As the forerunner of today's popular advice columnists, Elizabeth Meriwhether Gilmer wrote under the pen name of "Dorothy Dix" and was the most highly paid and most widely read female journalist of her time.

Even after the divorce, Kate and Laura and Luddy and Jack remained an amicable quartet and frequent companions, with their respective households communicating across the communal garden. On weekends, Luddy and Kate sometimes opted to drive by themselves to either Fenwick or Hartford to see the Hepburns. Once, when Luddy was spotted with Kate, walking hand in hand with her along the beach, newspapers erroneously printed that they were once again living together as man and wife.

Leland returned to New York for a reunion with Kate, urging their immediate marriage. When Kate invited him to Fenwick, Luddy also turned up, snapping frequent photographs. Leland begged Kate to remove Luddy from the house, but she refused, although she did reproach Luddy once or twice, asking him to go.

Firmly entrenched within the Hepburn family, and rather adamant on the issue, he claimed that "an ex-husband has certain rights that must be respected, especially if he doesn't demand conjugal visits." In the face of such overwhelming logic, she retreated and told Leland that he'd have to put up with Luddy's presence—or else there would be no marriage.

Back in New York, Kate did not see Leland every night. Sullavan had returned to the West Coast, but he was still being photographed at various nightclubs with glamorous women, most often actresses. If Kate asked him to explain that, he continued to maintain that the "woman in the picture" was either a client or else an actress he was pursuing as a client.

Tallulah Bankhead claimed that she'd gone to bed with Leland during Kate's post-divorce period. "I wanted to find out what all the excitement was about," Tallulah said. "Frankly, I've had better. And believe me, darling, I've also had worse."

In spite of any "blood commitment" Kate might have had with Laura, she continued to dangle the possibility of marriage in front of Leland.

He said that since both of them were divorced, "There is nothing to stop us from getting married right away."

Actually, there was.

Kate herself.

***

Luddy begged Kate to turn down all offers from Hollywood and "return to your roots," in live theater. He wanted her to take over the role of Judith Traherne in George Brewer's melodramatic tragedy, *Dark Victory*. He convinced her to go with him and Laura to the Ivoryton Playhouse in rural Connecticut, and open the play in June.

The directors of the playhouse, Milton Steifel and Julian Anhalt, were delighted to have Kate—"now a big-time movie star"—back at their playhouse, where she'd appeared in summer stock in 1931.

The role of the hard-drinking, hard-riding Judith Traherne, a society girl with a brain tumor, had gone through almost countless revisions but in many aspects seemed ideal for Kate. Steifel called it, "A rip-off of *Camille* without the consumptive cough."

From the first day of rehearsal, trouble developed between Kate and her co-star, Stanley Ridges, the British character actor. Just as Jed Harris had criticized Kate's every stage movement in *The Lake*, so did Kate attack every single line

172

and step Ridges made on stage. Eventually, Ridges collapsed, claiming that he was ill, and resigned from the play. Although any number of actors could have filled this lackluster role, the producers decided to abandon the play and offered Kate *Holiday* instead, the play that had brought acclaim to Hope Williams on the stage. Kate liked the play but refused their offer, much to the chagrin of Steifel and Anhalt, who simply didn't understand why she'd done that.

Unknown to her producers, Kate had received what she (mistakenly) believed was a firm offer from Theresa Helburn, of the Theatre Guild, to return to Hollywood to appear in a screen adaptation of Eugene O'Neill's *Mourning Becomes Electra*, a work in which she had desperately wanted to perform ever since she'd seen Alla Nazimova and Alice Brady perform it on stage.

Helburn had totally misled Kate, claiming that Louis B. Mayer had agreed to release Greta Garbo from MGM to go to RKO to play the mother. Leland could have immediately put a stop to such ridiculous fantasies, but he was not consulted, Kate conducting the negotiations with Helburn in secret.

Kate was mislead by Helburn about the degree to which Mayer was enthusiastic about the project. Helburn did, however, receive a letter from O'Neill, stating that Kate "would make a great Lavinia," but that he feared that the Code's "idiotic" censorship would destroy his play. Savvy about the high-maintenance ego of the reclusive Swede, O'Neill, as it turned out, had never recommended Garbo as a candidate for the role of the aging mother.

When Helburn eventually pitched the idea to Mayer, the film mogul went into a screaming rage, claiming he'd never release Garbo to RKO, especially to play anyone's mother. "Isn't this play about incest?" Mayer asked. "That's what someone told me." The screenplay was also sent to Garbo, who never responded.

Eventually *Mourning Becomes Electra* was made into a film in 1947, with Rosalind Russell playing Lavinia. Fans of O'Neill compared the film version of his famous play to "corned beef hash."

***

In 1938, Kate became a player in the intrigue that surrounded the production and casting of a film version of the play which had previously been abandoned in Ivoryton, Connecticut, *Dark Victory*. RKO had begun a dialogue about securing the role as a film vehicle for Kate. Clouding the issue was the fact that Tallulah Bankhead had already flopped in the role on Broadway. Tallulah claimed that from the beginning, "I detested the role." Its secret backer, John (Jock) Whitney talked her into playing the role. "He fucked me into the part, darling," Tallulah said.

Despite the play's failure with Tallulah on Broadway, at MGM, Louis B Mayer made a bid for *Dark Victory*, envisioning the role of Judith Trahearne as a vehicle for Greta Garbo. As it turned out, Warner Brothers outbid MGM, eventually acquiring the rights in 1939, giving the lead to Bette Davis, Kate's rival. In the film, now a screen classic, Davis co-starred with her real life lover, George Brent, along with supporting players who included a miscast Humphrey Bogart appearing as a stable hand and Ronald Reagan playing a closeted, alcoholic homosexual. Off-screen, Reagan kept busy fleeing from the groping hands of the director, Edmund Goulding, who had developed a powerful crush on Reagan.

But during the brief time that Pandro Berman thought that RKO would get the rights to the script, he offered the male lead to Spencer Tracy. That actor turned it down, claiming it was a "tearjerker strictly for the ladies." Nostalgia buffs note that had Berman succeeded with his "dream cast," he would have launched Katharine Hepburn and Spencer Tracy into movie history books long before they actually worked together.

Where Bankhead failed, Davis triumphed, even winning an Academy Award nomination in 1939 for *Dark Victory*, which she lost to another actress, Vivien Leigh, playing Scarlett O'Hara in *Gone With the Wind*, a role that both Hepburn and Davis desperately wanted.

***

A starring role of O'Neill's *Mourning Becomes Electra* never materialized, much to Kate's disappointment. But soon, Leland came through with a hard-cash offer from RKO that made its allure look pale in comparison. It involved a six-picture deal that would pay Kate fifty-thousand dollars per film, an astronomical figure back then. In contrast, Bette Davis, when she was Queen of Warner Brothers, earned only thirty-five thousand dollars for her role in *Dark Victory*.

Entrenching the importance of his role in her life, Leland once again asked Kate to marry him, and she held out a promise that she would. As for the recently divorced Luddy, he got a good-bye kiss from Kate at New York's Grand Central Station as she boarded a California-bound train, once again accompanied by Laura.

On the way West, Laura was bubbling with enthusiasm at Leland's latest cable, claiming he would secure six of Hollywood's hottest properties for Kate's comeback to films. But functioning to some degree, as was her habit, as her own theatrical agent, in spite of hiring Leland, Kate was reading a screen condensation of *The Forsythe Saga*, which she turned down.

Despite the fame and money it had brought her, Kate still did not take the film world seriously. "Movies are the same lark to me that summer stock is," she told Laura. "The Broadway theater is all that matters. I won that Oscar for *Morning Glory*, and audiences lined up around the block to see me in *Little Women*. But film acting is a mere backdrop—a means to make one famous—nothing more."

Laura never knew if Kate actually meant that or whether she was merely protecting herself with an "affected disdain" in case she failed, as she had in *Spitfire*— in her upcoming RKO appearances..

When the train got to Chicago, Kate received the script, which Pandro Berman rushed to her through one of RKO's sales representatives, for *The Little Minister*, a screen adaptation of the novel and play by Sir James M. Barrie, the original author of *Peter Pan*. Kate was initially impressed when she saw that Sarah Y. Mason and Victor Heerman were the scenarists. Heerman and Mason were the husband-and-wife team who'd written the screenplay for *Little Women*, and Berman wanted to pull off another costume picture blockbuster to match Kate's success in that film.

Before the train had reached Pasadena, Kate told Laura that she hated the script and planned to reject it. Even before kissing Leland, who appeared at the station to welcome her back to California, Kate told him that she wouldn't appear in *The Little Minister.*,

However, her plans changed drastically that night when Kate spoke on the phone to Walter Plunkett, her costumer at RKO. He told her that Berman had already pitched *The Little Minister* to Margaret Sullavan and that, with Leland as her agent, this Southern belle had agreed to play the role, and was delighted at the opportunity.

Leland didn't arrive at the newly rented house of Laura and Kate until nine that night. The moment he walked in the door, Kate told him she'd changed her mind and was already memorizing dialogue for the role of Lady Babbie. Completely aware of the havoc this would wreak with whatever agreements had been reached between Sullavan and Leland, Kate claimed that she'd be "delighted" to play the role.

Leland slipped out of the house later that night, and Kate must have known that he was heading to Sullavan's home to take back the script from her.

The next morning, Kate called both Kenneth MacKenna and Anderson Lawler to tell them she was back in town and what had transpired over the script of *The Little Minister*. "Sometimes it's not the greatest victories that make life worth living but the little triumphs," she told her friends.

***

Kate told Cukor that she and Laura had settled into Hollywood "like an old married couple." Laura was still claiming to friends that she was Kate's "husband."

Kate, with Laura, eventually leased a big residence on Angelo Drive above Benedict Canyon. The view of Los Angeles was panoramic, and there were two tennis courts and a swimming pool. The house had belonged to the director Fred Niblo, who had piloted Ramon Novarro and a cast of thousands through the shooting of *Ben-Hur*, the silent screen film, shot in Rome.

"The only problem was," Kenneth MacKenna later said, "you took your life in your hands to reach it. The road was winding and filled with dangerous curves. No drunk should ever have attempted to visit Kate and Laura."

In 1934, with Laura lugging a picnic basket, Kate reported to RKO to begin work on *The Little Minister,* playing Lady Babbie, an insufferably quaint Scottish blueblood—the "daughter of a summer night, where all the birds are free"—as described by Sir James M. Barrie, her creator. The great stage actress, Maude Adams, whom Kate admired, had successfully created the role on Broadway back in 1897. The story had been made into three silent-screen versions, the most recent from Paramount in 1921, starring Betty Compson.

The saga was set in Scotland in the 1840s in Barrie's home town of Thrums. Kate, as Lady Barrie, impishly dresses up like a gypsy wench, strolling through the countryside, eventually falling in love with a priggish "man of the cloth," as played by the handsome but vapid actor, John Beal, one of the weakest of all of Kate's male co-stars.

Almost from the first day she met him, Kate seemed to realize that Beal was assigned to the second rung of stardom. During the initial casting of the part, the handsome actor, Franchot Tone, had found the role of the minister weak and had turned it over to Beal. "Let Beal make an ass of himself—not me," Tone said.

Kate had attacked Leslie Howard's shortness. But at her first meeting with Beal, she said, "You're too tall. The role calls for a little minister." At Kate's request, Beal was forced to shave down his heels. "But then Hepburn towered over me!" he said when viewing the rushes.

Kate met her director, Richard Wallace, and later told Laura and others that she found Wallace "hopelessly incompetent." Wallace's claim to fame was that previously, in 1929, he had directed Gary Cooper and baby-faced Nancy Carroll in *The Shopworn Angel.* In time it appeared that *The Little Minister* may have derailed Wallace's promising career as a director.

Almost from the beginning, Wallace complained about Kate to Pandro Berman, claiming she was miscast. He had a point. Kate played Lady Babbie with Bryn Mawr vowels and a fake Scottish burr. Wallace insisted that the part called for a "Maude Adams-like actress"—one of the "adored and elusive personality, who had the piquant charm to interpret a Barrie character." Berman dismissed his complaints and ordered him to forge ahead with the film.

Even though he had been cast in the role of Gavin Dishart, a weak-willed "mama's boy," Beal was judged as too weak for the part by Kate. In one of the silliest scenes ever recorded in a Hepburn film, Kate describes to Beal the kind of man she must have—"dominant, defiant, brave, upholder of the weak, master of women. He must rule me. He must be my master."

Beal responds, "Your Lord and Master. Babbie, I am that man!" But far from looking like her master, the limp-wristed and pretty boy Beal could have easily passed as her slave. Instead of loving Kate, it appears he still loves his mommie, to whom he has already expressed undying devotion.

In fact, in one of her lines, Kate says, "Oh, if I were a man!" Costumer Walter Plunkett privately suggested that the actors' roles be reversed. "Let Beal play Lady Babbie and give Kate the minister's role."

Always friendly to her crew, Kate had a favorite cameraman, Henry Gerrard. She insisted that Laura bring a picnic lunch every day, and that Gerrard sit next to her.

One day he didn't show up, and Kate threatened to walk off the set, refusing to allow Gerrard's assistant to photograph her. Then news reached her that Gerrard had been stricken by an attack of appendicitis.

Instead of going to a reputable surgeon or a hospital, he went to an unlicensed chiropractor, who performed the surgery. The cameraman did not survive the operation, and Kate burst into tears, comforted by Laura. "If only my father had operated on him!" Kate shouted loudly so that all the crew could hear.

By the second week of shooting, Kate was feuding with Wallace, who always retreated at the sound of violence in her voice. The louder she became, the softer he became. By the end of the picture, as Beal later claimed, "The film was completely out of focus and so was Wallace, who didn't seem to know what he wanted. Forgive me, but he was pussy-whipped by Hepburn. He wouldn't stand up to her. She had balls, and you could hear them clanking. He must have had balls the size of peanuts. The film suffered because of that."

Faced with Kate's second flop in a row, Pandro Berman told director Wallace, "She's just not a movie star. I should not have brought her back to Hollywood and let that cocksucking Leland talk me into a six-picture deal. She's not a Norma Shearer, Garbo, or even a Mae West or Joan Crawford, who can carry a weak picture with the force of their personality. Hepburn lacks that special magic a star needs to attract an audience. *Little Women* was a box office hit in spite of Hepburn. She's a hit in hit pictures and a flop in flops."

Ginger Rogers did not endear herself to Kate when she penned a vindictive note and asked makeup artist, Mel Burns, to deliver it personally to Kate. "I've seen *The Little Minister.* These are troubled times. Audiences want to see Fred and me dance, not some period piece from that *Peter Pan* writer, a silly goose if there ever was one. Better luck next time, providing you don't try to step on my toes like you did those of poor Maggie."

Ginger was referring, of course, to Margaret Sullavan, who, it is said, danced a jig on learning of Kate's failure in the role.

Along with Margaret Sullavan, Ginger Rogers moved rapidly toward the top of what Kate called her "shit list." Their famed rivalry, although not as lethal as the one that raged between Joan Crawford and Bette Davis, began the day that Ginger had makeup artist, Mel Burns, deliver her ill-conceived note to Kate.

The Little Minister opened at New York's Radio City Music Hall, drawing the largest single audience in the history of that theater. That was the film's only moment of glory. After that, it played to only small and in some cases, nonexistent Depression-era audiences. Even so, because it was not a high-budget film, it lost only ten-thousand dollars.

Some critics lambasted Kate, others damned her with faint press. Richard Watts, Jr., in the *New York Herald Tribune*, recognized the lavender-and-old-lace quality of Barrie's dated story but felt Kate had turned the role "into something possessing dramatic vitality and conviction."

Eileen Creelman in the *New York Sun* cattily suggested that Kate should have left the role to Maude Adams. On the other hand, Regina Crew, in the *New York American*, claimed that Kate "made the character leap alive from the pages of Barrie's book."

George Cukor, saw *The Little Minister* and called Kate. "The next time you must walk on terra firma. More *firma*, less *terra*."

***

There is a disagreement to this day about what happened during a night when Kate was three weeks into shooting *The Little Minister*. But as a result of the incident, the police were summoned up the mountain to the Angelo Drive house shared by Laura and Kate.

Kate, apparently, had called the police over a serious domestic dispute that had ended in violence. The usually self-composed Laura Harding had attacked Leland. She is alleged at one point to have picked up a poker from the fireplace and struck him severely over the head, causing him to black out. Using all her so-called medical skill, Kate tried to revive him. At one point it was feared that Laura might have killed Leland, or else caused permanent brain damage.

Before the police had summoned an ambulance to take Leland to an emergency ward, Pandro Berman, with RKO lawyers, was driving frantically up the hill for damage control. It was feared that if news of the Leland and Laura fight, with its jealous lesbian overtones, leaked to the press, Kate's career in films would be over.

From that point, the screen goes black. No one knows what Pandro Berman and his lawyers worked out with Kate and Laura, much less the police, but Leland never filed charges against Laura. No case was ever presented to any judge. Taking his cue from Louis B. Mayer, who knew how to cover up scandal, Berman no doubt bribed the police.

Berman's efforts with Leland, when he recovered, proved heroic. In blunt terms, Berman is alleged to have warned Leland that if he ever filed any charges, the agent would never sell another picture, star, or project to RKO. Leland was also threatened with blacklisting at other studios, including Metro-Goldwyn-Mayer, since studios banded together in those days when they felt mutually threatened.

178

Not wanting to jeopardize his own career, Leland met with Kate when he was released from the hospital. His instructions to her were perfectly clear. "Keep Laura and lose everything," Leland warned her. "Let Laura go. If you do so, you keep me and the career."

Kate was said to be rather discreet in talking to such friends as Kenneth, Cukor and Lawler, although they pressed her for details. She was vague in her response. But it appears that Leland had told Laura that she was no longer needed in Kate's life. When both Kate and Leland had been married to others, Laura had served as an effective "beard," concealing the romances between the agent and his star. But now that both Kate and Leland were divorced, Laura had no such role to play.

Actually, this active, vital, and intelligent woman had little to do in Hollywood, except bring picnic lunches to the crew at RKO and sit quietly at home with Kate at night before she had dinner and turned in early. Whenever Leland came over, Laura retreated to her bedroom to listen to the radio or read.

From what pieces of evidence that remain, Laura had become violently incensed when Leland had shouted at her, "Get a life of your own! Stop living in Kate's shadow. Get out of here. You're not needed anymore."

Those were obviously painful words for Laura to hear. She'd built her entire life around Kate, and in spite of their many break-ups, Laura had told Cukor that "this time we're back together for good."

Before the blow-up, Laura had complained for weeks of boredom. "Just how many picnics can I oversee? Just how many shopping expeditions with Cukor can I go on looking for art and antiques?"

Laura also hated Hollywood, preferring the monied environments of Fifth and Park Avenues in New York. "So many of the big names out there were prostitutes, card sharks, girlie dancers, hustlers, car thieves, or kosher meat peddlers—not my kind."

Laura, perhaps, never learned what would have been the cruelest insult of all. It came not from Leland, but from Kate, who spread the word to several of her friends, including Kenneth. "She's a dear, sweet person but I've simply outgrown her. I'll always be her friend. But she's not someone who challenges me. I don't need for her to be in my life every day."

The ambition-crazed crowd who traveled frequently between New York and Hollywood had definite views about Laura. Tallulah Bankhead called her "Hepburn's dull little wren," evoking an appellation once applied to Bette Davis. Makeup artist Mel Burns found Laura "so dull and unappetizing" that he suggested to her that he could perform a cosmetic overhaul, completely revising her appearance, for a "huge sum of money." She turned him down, saying she knew more about style and taste that he did, which was true. At best, he could have only made Laura fakely glamorous, but he had little to teach her about style and taste, two elements she possessed to a massive degree.

Leland failed in his attempt to drive Laura from Hollywood.

That would require a woman who was about to appear in Kate's life.

***

Faced with the dilemma that he had Kate under contract for five additional pictures, for which he'd have to pay fifty-thousand dollars each, Pandro Berman searched desperately for a proper vehicle for his star, hoping to break the spell of her string of flops.

Perhaps forgetting the failure of the script of *The Little Minister*, Berman once again hired the husband-and-wife scenarists, Sarah Y. Mason and Victor Heerman, to come up with a shooting script.

Mason and Heerman turned up with an inadequate script from a story by Lester Cohen called *The Music Man*. Enraged by the script, Berman fired the Heermans and called in another writer, Anthony Veiller, the same way he'd been forced to hire Jane Murfin for rewrites on *The Little Minister*. The firing angered Kate, who liked the husband-and-wife team, even though they had not done well by her since *Little Women*.

Initially Kate was enchanted with the idea of playing the role of Constance Dane, who was married to a brilliant but struggling and temperamental composer, Franz Roberti. Originally, Berman wanted John Barrymore (who was under contract to MGM at the time) for the male lead, hoping to repeat the success he'd had with Kate and The Great Profile in her first movie.

Louis B. Mayer sent word that Barrymore was occupied with another project. Leland had a different point of view: "Jack must have read the script." From the very beginning, Leland found the story weak, pronouncing it "a marathon talk with cigarettes."

In the film, Constance discovers that Roberti is seeing another woman and abandons him, only to be pursued by a clean-cut suitor. Roberti becomes an alcoholic. When she learns of this, she deserts her handsome young beau and goes back to Roberti. She "rescues" him by sitting down at the piano and playing "our song," which miraculously seems to cure him of his heavy dipsomania. It was real soapy tearjerker material, with some of the most nonsensical lines Kate ever delivered. "I've loved you for such a long time—since late this afternoon."

At first Kate was relieved to hear that Philip Moeller had been hired as her director. Born in 1880, Moeller had little film experience, although he'd directed Irene Dunne in *The Age of Innocence*. His efforts in that film had been called "lifeless and static." Kate respected Moeller for directing some of the most prestigious productions of the Theatre Guild, including *Strange Interlude* and *Mourning Becomes Electra*, in which she had so desperately wanted to star.

On the third day of production, Leland showed up on the set and privately told Kate that Moeller was trying to turn *The Music Man* into "another one of this six-hour Eugene O'Neill tearjerkers—what an ass!"

180

Kate soon realized that Leland was right. She quickly lost confidence in Moeller as a director and began to direct herself, not even listening to his advice. He seemed too weak to oppose her. She reverted to many of the same theatrical mannerisms that had brought on the ire of Jed Harris—clenching and unclenching of fists to show emotion, exaggerated speech patterns, a trembling chin, a grave smile, a flood of tears.

On her first day of work, Kate encountered John Beal. Both actors commiserated with each other for their failures in *The Little Minister.* Beal was saddened to learn that Berman had cast him as the third lead. "I was just getting started as a leading man, and already I've been demoted to a supporting part."

She assured him that he'd do just fine, and she promised to help him, the way she had when she'd tried to "electrically charge" him in *The Little Minister.*

Behind his back, Kate told Moeller that she had no respect for Beal as an actor. "All the directing in the world will not give *this one* star presence," she said. "Not if it doesn't exist in the first place. It's like drawing water from a well. Totally impossible if the damn thing's dry."

On the fourth day of production, Kate met her leading man for the first time. Francis Lederer walked onto the set.

***

When the Czech actor arrived on the set of *The Music Man,* he'd had the greatest Hollywood build-up since Samuel Goldwyn had launched his folly, Anna Sten, as "the greatest actress since Garbo." Born in Prague at the dawn of the 20th century, Lederer would eventually play characters during his career that included German and Austrian barons, and stiff-necked Teutonics during the 1960s on both *Ben Casey* and *Mission Impossible.* He died in Palm Springs in 2000.

He'd been a matinee idol in Germany and had scored a success on the Berlin stage in *Romeo and Juliet.* Playing a musician in London in the 1931 production of *Autumn Crocus,* Lederer scored an even greater hit when the show moved to Broadway. That success brought him to the attention of RKO, who signed him up to play an Eskimo in the dismal flop, *A Man of Two Worlds.*

He'd followed that in 1934 by co-starring with Joan Bennett in *The Pursuit of Happiness.* At first, Lederer had wanted to ingratiate himself with Kate, although she noticed that all his conversation centered around himself.

Although a bisexual, Lederer was having a torrid affair with Joan Bennett at the time he met Kate. Unknown to the actor, Kate had no love for Joan Bennett after having appeared with her in *Little Women*, especially after Kate had been slapped by her sister, Constance, during one of her long-ago picnics on the set. Lederer admitted that he was not the only "man on the sidelines" in hot pursuit of Joan, who, incidentally, had a husband, the screen writer Gene Markey.

181

His main competition for Joan's attentions, according to Lederer, was Spencer Tracy, who had appeared with her in *She Wanted A Millionaire* in 1932. Lederer claimed that both he and Tracy, had almost simultaneously fallen madly in love with this beauty from New Jersey.

Extremely embittered, he called Tracy an old drunk and claimed that he might even be crazy. He told Kate that a bedraggled-looking Tracy had once showed up on the set in evening dress after a night of carousing. "He wrecked the set and shouted obscenities at everybody," Lederer said. "He even came up to the fluttery actress, Una Merkel, and asked her if he could play with her pussy."

Lederer claimed that Tracy "tries to seduce every woman he meets—the star of the picture, the script girl, the woman who carries a tray of hot dogs onto the set. I also hear from very reliable sources that he likes very handsome young men on the side—take Lew Ayres for instance."

Although she listened politely, Kate had nothing but disdain for Lederer. Later, she told Laura, "He's such a gossip he'll soon take over from Louella."

Over tea that afternoon, Lederer continued his tirade against Tracy. "I don't know what Joan sees in the fool. At one point on the set, he took out his penis and pissed on an elegant sofa where Joan was supposed to sit. He also can't act. Just plays himself. He's not the classical actor I am. Could you possibly picture Tracy playing Shakespeare?"

Since Kate didn't know Tracy, she could listen to these attacks on the actor with relative calm. But what really incensed her was when Lederer looked up at her freckled face with no makeup, silently appraised her masculine apparel, and then proceeded to praise Joan. "Other than her sister, Constance, a real fashion plate, Joan is the most perfectly groomed woman in Hollywood—not a hair out of place. She's also the most beautiful woman I've ever loved. Not only that, she's a great actress. I hate to say it, but she stole that picture, *Little Women.*"

That final remark sent Kate into a state of rage, although she managed to control any outburst until the following day. As actual work between the two of them began, Kate soon learned that Lederer was even more temperamental than she was. At one point, she heard the Czech actor tell Moeller, "This is not a Katharine Hepburn film. It's a Francis Lederer film."

"Like hell it is!" Kate yelled from the sidelines.

After that, relations between the two stars moved quickly to the breaking point.

Without a mishap, Kate got through her first scene with Lederer. Moeller told her that it was "your most brilliant scene on film to date."

When Lederer saw the rushes the next day, he shouted at Moeller. "You did not show my good profile. I won't be photographed from the wrong side."

Kate held out, demanding that Moeller keep the scene, since it was her best. Lederer was persistent, and finally Moeller gave in, ordering the scene reshot with Lederer's best profile. Kate told Laura, "I lost my fire in the second shoot and was nowhere near as good."

Her fury against Lederer mounted. Behind his back, Kate launched an attack, motivated in part by his arrogance, but also by his romantic link with Joan Bennett, another nemesis, though not one that incensed her as much as Margaret Sullavan.

In front of both Berman and Moeller, Kate maintained, "There is no chemistry between us. We're supposed to be lovers. Impossible. Even I am not that great an actress."

Kate criticized Lederer for having no concept of the character he was playing. "He can't even remember his lines, assuming he can pronounce them in English if he knew them. He ruins take after take. On screen we appear more like a mongoose with a snake than lovers. Our speech patterns are not harmonious. I speak at a certain pace, and he talks like a German first-grader learning English." At one point, she charged that as an actor Lederer was "fussily mannered," although the same charge had often been leveled against her. "There's more," Kate said. "I take eight showers a day. But in a close-up with this swine, I nearly faint—not for romantic reasons. As a European, he takes one bath a month. When he puts his arms around me, I feel the smell will make me topple over."

Berman refused to give in to Kate's demands that Lederer be fired. "Then I'm going home," Kate said, rising to her feet. "Don't call me. I'll call you."

Berman desperately phoned Leland, who still had great powers of persuasion with Kate, in spite of the disastrous blow-up with Laura. After spending three hours with Kate, Leland got her to agree to finish the picture. For her to return, Kate insisted that Lederer be fired. Not only that, she wanted the name of the picture changed.

In spite of her flops, Berman was still intimidated by Kate. After screaming at Leland for an hour, Berman gave in to Kate's demands. He called Lederer to his office and in front of Leland, fired him on the spot. The actor stormed out of the studio.

Before the week was out, Berman announced that the picture was to be retitled *Break of Hearts*.

Kate's new co-star was to be the handsome and debonair French actor, Charles Boyer.

***

"You are the greatest and most beautiful movie star in the world." In front of the cast and crew, those were the opening words of Jane Loring, the film's associate editor, to Kate Hepburn. Like Dorothy Arzner, Loring had competed successfully against men to gain a foothold in production. Loring would never become a director, but she'd come to guide Kate through her next few films.

Always hidden behind sunglasses, even on the cloudiest day, the brunette was not an especially attractive woman. Dressing in mannish attire, she was usually seen in black pants, perhaps a white blouse. She had a strong, determined face, and had worked in silent films. Her origins remain uncertain, even today.

Her boss, film editor, William Hamilton, said he thought she came from Nebraska. The associate art director, Carroll Clark, claimed she was from Texas, and the makeup artist, Mel Burns, said "Loring was definitely from California."

Loring remains somewhat a mystery. She was not given to supplying rich biographical details, believing in concentrating only on the project at hand instead of reminiscences.

She was to capture Kate's attention and to hold it for many years. Before leaving the studio that afternoon, Kate invited Loring to join Laura and her for a picnic the following day.

Loring showed up the next day, talking a language that was foreign to Laura. "Women get so few breaks in films," Loring told Kate. "I can't turn down an A-picture, even though I detest the script on this turkey. Everybody but Mae West and Mickey Mouse has appeared in this hackneyed old plot."

Kate especially liked Loring's candid appraisals, and was especially relieved to hear that, "RKO doesn't know how to handle you." That seemed to rationalize Kate's string of recent flops.

Kate seemed mesmerized by Loring's vision for her future. Loring claimed that had she directed *Christopher Strong*, instead of Dorothy Arzner, it could have been made into one of Kate's greatest successes. Loring boasted of the scripts they could concoct together, and claimed that Kate could go on to become the greatest female star of the 20th century.

The only person left out of the conversation was Laura. Usually she stayed around until afternoon tea and the end of the shoot. But after the picnic with Loring, Laura told Kate she wasn't feeling well and asked to be excused.

Kate generally came home early for dinner. That day she didn't get in until shortly before midnight. Laura had gone to her separate bedroom. Over breakfast the next morning, she did not ask Kate where she'd been. Kate suggested that Laura go to a museum or to the beach that day, explaining that a picnic on the set wasn't necessary. Instead of the beach, Laura retreated to George Cukor's house since he was at home, and not shooting that day. She revealed to Cukor what she called "Kate's new love. I fear I've lost her. I can't compete."

At RKO, Kate invited Loring to her dressing room for lunch that day "for more film talk." Loring was the first to recognize that Kate was both a screen personality and a great screen actress, "but you can't have one without the other, or else a film won't work."

Both Kate and Loring agreed that Philip Moeller was too weak a director. The assistant director, Edward Killy, claimed that on that very day of "the dressing room conference," Kate and Loring conspired to take the picture away from

Moeller. Supplementing her natural intuition and extensive experience with advice and guidance from Loring, Kate began directing herself.

Throughout their long relationship, Laura had offered wide-eyed, loving, and unconditional support, usually "caving in" to Hepburn's points of view, especially about film. But Loring challenged Kate at every turn. Instead of being offended, Kate enjoyed their dialogues, probably because it reminded her of the animated "sparring sessions" that had been the norm over the dinner table at the Hepburns.

As Moeller put it, Loring and Kate enjoyed a conversational exchange among equals. Kate maintained that she could "play any role, including any part from Shakespeare." Loring differed, claiming that roles had to be carefully written, photographed, directed and edited to bring out Kate's unique screen personality.

Near the end of the shoot, Kate announced that she was determined to play the part of Lola Pratt, the baby-talking heroine of a film adaptation of Booth Tarkington's *Seventeen*.

"Are you out of your mind?" Loring challenged her. "The role is that of a baby vamp, like those that that tough little slut Shirley Temple did in her burlesque numbers as a kid. The character is bird-brained, dangling a pink parasol and walking around with a fluffy dog named Floppit."

"I'm in love with the plot, and I know I could do it," Kate protested.

"Do you want to pretend to awaken lust in teenage boys?" Loring asked. "Say *ess* for yes? My God, woman, you're meeting Charles Boyer tomorrow. A great lover of the screen. Wouldn't you rather play love scenes with him than with Freddie Bartholomew or Mickey Rooney?" It took two hours, but Loring finally convinced Kate to abandon her dream of starring in *Seventeen*.

Ironically, it was the script for another Booth Tarkington creation, *Alice Adams*, that was sent over to Kate's dressing room by Berman that afternoon.

Even though Leland was still hovering in the background, Garbo a "sometime thing," Laura waiting at home; and Jane Loring on the actual set, it was love at first sight for Kate when Charles Boyer walked up to her and introduced himself.

***

That night after meeting Boyer, Kate called Anderson Lawler for a long talk "about the new love in my life." A cockroach didn't cross Hollywood Boulevard but what her gossipy friend knew about it.

In years to come, Kate would express her disdain for gossip. But at this period of her life, she tolerated it, especially if she wanted information, which she equated with power. Her first question was, "He's married, isn't he? Not that that would stop me, because I don't give a damn for marriage contracts."

Lawler assured Kate that Boyer had married a beautiful aspirant actress, Pat

Paterson, after knowing her for only twenty-two days. Paterson had been born in the Yorkshire textile city of Bradford in 1910, the daughter of a wool merchant.

"She's all blonde cuteness," Lawler said. "I was at a party with her the other night, and I danced with the bitch. God, can that pussy shake it. She told me she studied tap at the age of five and ballet by the time she was eight."

"What's my competition like?" Kate demanded to know.

"She's like a mischievous pixie with dancing green eyes," Lawler said. "Rather pretty face with very limited talent. She's in a picture with Spencer Tracy. *Bottoms Up.* It seems like a very gay title, even though I hear Tracy is a top."

"She sounds like so many hundreds of other hopefuls arriving daily at Union Station," Kate said.

"You've nailed it. But she has her admirers. I'm sure you know that Leland has launched a torrid affair with Boyer's new wife."

There was a long silence on the other end of the phone. "I didn't know that at all."

"But of course, you're the only woman Leland loves," Lawler assured her.

"Yes, right," she said. "Me and that Virginia magnolia, Miss Margaret Sullavan, nymphomaniac from hell."

"Leland has signed this Paterson creature to a contract, and he's told her he's going to make her bigger than Jean Harlow."

"How cute!" Kate said. "Tell me everything you know. I'm all ears."

Lawler knew plenty. He claimed that even though Paterson and Boyer were madly in love, they still shared their sexual charms with other partners.

"I've heard enough about this so-called wife," Kate said. "Tell me what you know about Boyer. I'm immensely attracted to him."

Lawler called Boyer "the last of the *boulevardiers*." He was always seen in Paris in perfectly tailored clothes strolling around town with a pretty woman draped on his arm like a clothing accessory. "He's a bit stuffy. But I hear all his leading ladies have fallen for him. He generally adopts an air of take-them-or-leave them—most often he takes them."

As an aggressively open homosexual, Lawler also wanted to fill Kate in on the gay gossip about Boyer. "His friend, Maurice Chevalier, has the hots for him. I heard that from the mouth of Kay Francis herself. She claims that Chevalier is lousy in bed, and always attacks homosexuals so as to throw suspicion from himself."

Lawler provided Kate with another tantalizing bit of information. When Francis Lederer, so recently "fired" by Kate, worked briefly in Paris for Boyer's good friend, director Julien Duvivier, Lederer fell madly in love with Boyer as well. "From all reports, Boyer did not return Lederer's affection. From what I hear, the last time Boyer had a homosexual liaison, he was fifteen years old and it was with his English tutor."

186

At the time of her meeting with him, Kate had never seen Boyer on screen. He'd played a chauffeur in 1932 in *Red-Headed Woman*, a vehicle originally intended for Joan Crawford, but eventually starring Jean Harlow. "Boyer and Harlow had an affair," Lawler assured Kate. "Jean has to get it from somebody. And she's not getting it from Paul Bern, that impotent little-dicked bastard."

Boyer's first major picture had been *Caravan* for Fox in which he'd co-starred with Loretta Young, with whom he'd temporarily fallen in love. But he'd found Spencer Tracy formidable competition for the affections of that pristine beauty. When Young, who preferred Tracy, dropped Boyer, he appeared in *Private Worlds* with Claudette Colbert, in 1935. "No problem on that front," Lawler said. "Colbert and Boyer are great friends but the French dwarf prefers women. She's a true lez in spite of all she does to conceal it. Boyer then launched an affair with Joan Bennett, although once again he found himself competing with Spencer Tracy."

"How does that bitch Bennett find time to have babies with her husband and conduct all these affairs?" Kate asked. "I just found out that Bennett's had an affair with Francis Lederer, although God knows why she wanted to. Poor Gene Markey."

Lawler told her that before Kate had approved Boyer for *Break of Hearts*, he was planning to return to his native France. "He's giving his American career one last chance," Lawler said. "He wants to work with you. He said he was utterly fascinated with you when he saw you and Laura at that director's house, the time you disguised yourself as maids. He said that French audiences appreciate you more than Americans."

Before hanging up, Lawler assured Kate that "you've got it made with Boyer."

"Sex on a movie set between a star and her leading man is taken for granted," Kate said. "I think my love scenes with Charles will be more believable if we rehearse in my dressing room. When I was a struggling actor, John Barrymore seduced me, as the big movie star he was. Now I'm a big movie star and Charles is the struggling actor. My role is reversed. I'm going after him, although he seems somewhat the reluctant lover. But he's a real gentleman, and you don't meet many like that among the usual bastards of Hollywood."

***

Kate did nothing to conceal her obvious adoration of Boyer during the entire filming of *Break of Hearts*. She could often be seen kneeling at his feet between takes, listening to his stories of his native France and his misadventures since arriving in Hollywood.

"I simply adore his accent," she told Laura. She insulted her best friend by asking her not to bring any more picnics to the set. During the filming of *Break of Hearts*, Kate preferred to have lunch alone with Boyer in her dressing room.

Although cultured and debonair, Boyer had an arrogance about him that matched Kate's own. He was given to saying such lines as, "Who would have thought that I, of all people, would actually marry an uncultured English chorine?"

Ignoring his own affair with Kate, Boyer attacked his wife, Pat Paterson, for her "boy-craziness—anything in pants. She'll go after any chorus boy who is not homosexual, or even one who is."

Kate at first had been surprised at how candidly Boyer talked about his recent but "ill-fated" marriage to Paterson. "I was at a party standing side by side with Spencer Tracy," he told both Moeller and Kate. "We met her at the same time. She later left the party with Tracy for a little midnight fun. When I got home, I found that she had slipped her phone number into my pocket. After three nights, Tracy dumped Pat and went back to the arms of Loretta Young, Joan Bennett, or any of the very handsome young men he secretly seduces on the side. Even though I'm considered handsome myself, I'm too old for Tracy, so he never made a proposition to me. But I did notice him observing me very closely when he stood next to me at the urinal."

In 1934, Tracy, appearing on screen with Pat Paterson in the film, *Bottoms Up*, was also seen offscreen with her as well. *Bottoms Up* also costarred John Boles and the ill-fated Thelma Todd, who would die the following year at the age of thirty. Murder? Suicide? Or an accident?

Boyer told Kate that Paterson had advised him to take voice lessons to get rid of his French accent.

Currying favor with him, Kate said, "Your accent is bedroom romantic. I feel it will make—not break—your career. It's more than your voice, it's your eyes. A woman could lose herself in your eyes. No wonder they call this picture *Break of Hearts*. It should be named after you: Heartbreaker." Remarks such as these could be heard on the set in front of cast and crew. No one knows what Kate told Boyer in her dressing room.

Their romance soon became the number one gossip item in Hollywood. Boyer may have had Paterson waiting for him at his house—often he didn't— and Kate had ever-faithful Laura, but that didn't matter. After work, he could be seen opening the door to his Duesenberg for long romantic drives in the Hollywood Hills. Other lovers were put on hold while Boyer and Kate enjoyed the sunsets over California. In his opinion, these beautiful and panoramic sunsets were the only "miracle" that made life on the West Coast bearable.

On the set, Kate's voice sometimes became distinctly strident as she attacked Philip Moeller's direction. With his soft-spoken accent, Boyer could usually soothe her temper. He would flash her a sly little smile, and she would come to him, in the words of film photographer Robert De Grasse, "like a bear to honey."

Boyer told Moeller and Kate that he thought in French before delivering his lines in English. She persuaded him to begin to think in English, claiming it would give his delivery more meaning. Later, film editor William Hamilton joked with the cast that Kate also taught him to think in English while having intercourse with her "to make the fuck more meaningful."

At one point, Boyer broke down in tears on the set, and Kate rushed to comfort him. "He was the most unhappy actor in Hollywood," Moeller later said. "I don't think I've ever known anyone who hated Hollywood more, with the possible exception of Greta Garbo."

At the time, Boyer was "heartbroken" over the failure of his horrendous flop, *Caravan*, in which he'd costarred with Loretta Young. Even today, the film is considered one of the great movie disasters of the 1930s. When Kate first met Boyer, he was fresh from making *Private Worlds* over at Paramount for Walter Wanger. All of its stars—Claudette Colbert, Joan Bennett, and Joel McCrea—would eventually play some role in Kate's life, as would the picture's director, Gregory La Cava, who would direct her in the 1937 film, *Stage Door.*

Moeller claimed that both Kate and Boyer often attacked California as an uncultured place, with Kate longing to return East and Boyer wanting to go back to Paris. "It's all a game out here," Boyer said, "and I don't know how to play it."

Kate chimed in, "Even if I knew how to play the game, I wouldn't. I don't want to give them that much satisfaction."

On the set, Kate began to care for Boyer as if in a dress rehearsal for her eventual caretaker relationship with Tracy. Boyer was very sensitive about his receding hairline and feared encroaching baldness. She countered that a man with a receding hairline "most often has a very high intellect." He confided that when he'd appeared in the French film, *Liliom*, the director Fritz Lang had insisted that he wear a toupée.

Kate was very sympathetic to Boyer's vanity and his concern for his looks. Future co-stars wouldn't be so kind. When Bette Davis co-starred with Boyer in the 1940 *All This and Heaven Too*, she claimed that he was, "Terribly serious about his looks. Christ! A wig. A corset. Lifts in his shoes. A padded crotch for all I know. I didn't investigate that. At night when he takes off all his accessories, he must look like the Pillsbury Doughboy."

When Boyer wasn't talking about his personal appearance, he enthralled Kate with stories of how Paris was constantly accommodating filmmakers from the East, fleeing from the Nazis and Hitler. He predicted to both Kate and Moeller that war in Europe was inevitable, and that literally hundreds of refugee filmmakers—"some highly talented"—would show up in Hollywood seeking work in the film industry.

The Boyer/Hepburn romance heated up until it became fiery hot. Boyer was considering filing for divorce from Paterson. "I didn't know her when I married her. It was an impulsive kind of thing. If this picture is a success, I will stay in Hollywood and make another film. If it fails, I will leave both my wife and Hollywood. In Paris, I'm much more appreciated as an actor."

At one particularly intense stage in their relationship, Kate told Cukor that she too was going to Paris with Boyer, where she would marry him as soon as his divorce came through. She would learn to speak French perfectly and would become his co-star in French-language films. "And I'll dub my own voice in English for the American release."

The director told her that she was "out of your mind" and predicted that she'd drop Boyer the moment shooting ended on *Break of Hearts.*

That is exactly what happened. Once the picture was wrapped, so was the hot romance.

After the affair ended, gossipy Anderson Lawler demanded that Kate tell him how Boyer was in bed. "Sometimes these so-called great lovers don't live up to their reputations. Gary Cooper always did, at least with me, but there are many others who don't."

"Boyer was surgically precise," was Kate's enigmatic response.

Kate was forced to have one more reunion with her erstwhile French lover and that was when she co-starred with him in *The Madwoman of Chaillot* in 1969. By then, their former passion for each other had long dimmed.

Although Boyer's marriage to Pat Paterson appeared doomed in 1935, it went on to become one of the most enduring marriages in Hollywood, lasting until her death in 1978. Before that, their son, Michael, had committed suicide.

Just two days before his seventy-ninth birthday and only two days after his wife's funeral, Boyer took a fatal overdose of barbiturates.

Kate's former rival at RKO, actress Irene Dunne, called and asked Kate to go with her to the Holy Cross Cemetery in Los Angeles for the funeral. Kate flatly turned her down. "I prefer to remember Charles as he was."

***

RKO went all out to hype *Break of Hearts*, promoting Kate and Boyer as on-screen lovers. Throughout the country, billboards appeared, advertising, "The star of a million moods *together* with the new idol of the screen."

In spite of this, *Break of Hearts,* like *Spitfire,* turned out to be another misfire for Kate. None of the reviewers liked the script, but many critics had praise for both Kate and Boyer in their "valiant attempt to save the picture."

Sydney W. Carroll of *The London Times* praised Kate's genius, noting that she got "absolutely no help from the story or part." In judging the film, Eileen Creelman of the *New York Sun* wrote, "The audience's heart never quite breaks."

Some film critics noted that *Break of Hearts* is "basically a smoking contest between Hepburn and Boyer." Boyer clearly won that contest, as he smoked, either on or off the screen, six packages of cigarettes a day.

In spite of critics and in spite of RKO's aggressive promotion, *Break of Hearts* is viewed by some of Kate's most loyal fans as "her worst picture."

With Kate's film career in serious jeopardy, she was rescued by a script sent over by Pandro Berman. It was called *Alice Adams*. Its delivery to Kate became fodder for Hollywood legend.

For reasons known only to themselves and still unexplained, Kate and Boyer had chosen the venue of the back seat of her roomy car for their final act of love-making instead of either of their dressing rooms. It was the final day of shooting for *Break of Hearts.*

George Stevens, the newly appointed director of *Alice Adams*, had arrived on the set of *Break of Hearts* for a script meeting that had been set up between himself, Berman, and Kate. When she couldn't be found, Stevens went looking for her.

Fresh from his own shooting on another film, the director was covered in mud and black dust he'd gotten by "down-and-dirty" directing of his rollicking stunt men.

As if by radar, Stevens seemed to know where Kate was. Stalking the lot, he spotted movement in her car. There had been a long drought in Southern California, and Kate had not washed her windows, which were caked with dirt and streaky.

Rubbing a small viewing box for himself, the long-jawed director put his flat nose up against the car's window and looked into the back seat.

It was a case of *coitus interruptus*.

"I'm George Stevens," he told Kate. "You're late for an appointment with Berman."

Ever the director, Stevens ordered Boyer to "finish your business and turn the star over to me." He tightened the lips of his sensitive mouth and stalked away toward Berman's office.

As the coolly intractable thirty-year-old George Stevens faded away, Kate demanded that Boyer "carry on," as she'd later confide to Lawler. "But he seemed to have lost his ardor. It was our last time."

As Kate pulled up her pants and kissed Boyer good-bye, she rushed to her meeting with Stevens and Berman.

Once again, she was going to meet "the love of my life."

Kate remembered her first meeting more discreetly in her memoirs, *Me.* "One night after work I was sitting in the front seat of my car flirting unsuccessfully with Charles Boyer when I looked up and there was a face looking in through the window."

So much for self-serving Hollywood biographies.

CHAPTER NINE

During the filming of *Alice Adams*, there was as much drama behind the cameras as in front of them. Originally Pandro Berman had wanted William Wyler to direct the picture, even though expressing doubts that this Alsatian, who'd studied business in Switzerland and music in Paris, could accurately capture Booth Tarkington's vision of small-town America.

An apocryphal story that spread throughout Hollywood claimed that Berman and Kate tossed a coin to see if the director would be Wyler or George Stevens. The first coin, according to the story, came up Wyler. Kate and Berman were reported to have then agreed to toss the coin a second time. On the second go-round, the coin awarded the directorship to Stevens.

Berman later denied that this ever happened. What really took place was that Kate had learned that Margaret Sullavan, her nemesis, had carried on a torrid affair with Wyler that had led quickly to an ill-fated marriage. Without justification, Kate attacked Wyler to Berman, claiming that "he will deliberately direct me badly, photograph me horribly, and will sabotage the film just to ruin my career—all because of his love for that magnolia-scented nymphomaniac."

Gruff, slow-talking, and enormously talented, George Stevens came to the RKO set as an untried director. During the actual production of the film, Kate regretted several times that she didn't go with Wyler. When she later saw what a lover and mentor Wyler became to Bette Davis, she "doubly regretted" not working with him. At the time he lost the director's job for *Alice Adams*, Wyler had already made *Dodsworth* from the novel by Sinclair Lewis. In contrast, Stevens was green, with a previously undistinguished career.

Born in Oakland, California in 1904, and three years older than Kate, Stevens began his career as a cinematographer at the age of seventeen. Actually he'd made his professional acting debut at age five in the company of his actor parents. From 1927 to 1930, he'd been the principal cameraman at Hal Roach Studios, where he'd shot classic two-reelers that included Laurel and Hardy's *Two Tars* in 1928. He'd also directed such Bert Wheeler and Robert Woolsey features as *Kentucky Kernels* and *The Nitwits,* on the set of which he'd begun an affair with blonde starlet Betty Grable.

Having recovered from being caught in her car with Charles Boyer, Kate had arrived at the meeting in Berman's office slightly flustered. Since Stevens had said virtually nothing at the time of their first meeting, she later called Cukor to report her impressions, and perhaps to extract gossip. "He's an odd duck in the flock," she said. "He's big and attractive like a bear should be, and has this weathered look far beyond his years. He's very distant, striking me as if he's above the fray. For a director, and completely unlike you, my catty, talkative darling, Stevens hardly says anything. He could be very stupid for all I know. Or else that silence is the mask for a film genius."

The second script conference found Kate ill with the flu. She demanded that both Berman and Stevens drive up to her Angelo Drive home. Laura made tea with honey and cinnamon for Kate while serving Stevens and Berman stiff drinks. With no makeup, and her head completely clogged, Kate admitted that she must have looked a fright, as she lay on the sofa in while silk pajamas with a satin dressing gown borrowed from Laura.

Once again, Berman and Kate did all the talking. Stevens had absolutely nothing to say about Jane Murfin's adaptation of the Tarkington novel. After that night, Kate nicknamed him "the watcher," and privately expressed grave doubts about Stevens to Berman. "He literally has not one insight into this script." Within a week, Stevens admitted to her that he had not read either the novel or the shooting script, so he had had no understanding of either the plot or the characters during their first two meetings.

Alice Adams had been filmed once before as a 1923 silent movie starring Florence Vidor. It's about a poor small town girl putting on airs above her station in life. The main character is an intelligent, sensitive, lovely but lonely young woman with hopeless affectations. She meets a handsome visiting engineer, Arthur Russell, played by Fred MacMurray, and desperately tries to impress him with her fictionalized position in life. Actually her father, played by Fred Stone, works in a glue factory.

In the film, Ann Shoemaker plays Kate's nagging mother, and Frank Albertson is her brother. A snobbish Hedda Hopper appears in a minor role. In time Hopper, of course, would go on to rival Louella Parsons as a Hollywood gossip columnist. Kate snubbed Hopper during their first encounter on the set, launching a bitter feud that would span decades.

Berman had warned Stevens that Kate would try to direct the picture if he allowed it. "Stand your ground—be firm," Berman said. Stevens assured his boss that, "I know a hell of a lot more about the Adams family and the Midwest than some hotsy-totsy gal from Bryn Mawr."

On the first day of the shoot, Kate approached Stevens in front of the cast and crew. Very arrogantly, she told him, "I'm the star of this picture. You're nothing but an untried director known for custard pies in the face. It was because of me that you got hired in the first place. Remember, this is my picture—not yours."

Stevens stood looking at her for a long moment, then said, "We'll see about that." He did an about-face and walked away.

Throughout the shoot, Jane Loring was at Kate's side, hawkeying every move. The tension between Loring and Stevens became almost unbearable.

The photographer, Robert De Grasse, claimed that Loring was, in fact, secretly trying to direct the picture behind Stevens' back.

"Loring was constantly seen in a huddle with Hepburn, bolstering her ego and second-guessing every move Stevens made on the set," De Grasse said. "At one point, Stevens was tempted to fire Loring or else walk off the picture himself. The two truly despised each other."

Loring was spending all her time with Kate, as Laura Harding seemed virtually to have disappeared from the scene. Rumors at RKO were rampant. Kate was said to be breaking up with both Leland Hayward and Laura Harding. "It was obvious that the new woman in her life was Loring," De Grasse said. "But since Hepburn had an almost equal attraction to men, the crew was wondering who her next male victim would be, since apparently no woman alone could satisfy Kate's double-gaited tastes in sexual partners."

Kate found that her new leading man was actually her tall, wavy-haired, and virile co-star, Fred MacMurray. At first he struck her as being very dull. One day she spotted him lounging shirtless outside his dressing room. "My God," Kate later told Lawler. "Fred looked as if his chest had been sculpted by Michelangelo. I just have to have him."

She quickly became enamored of this onetime saxophone player, who'd toured the country with various bands in the 1920s and early 30s until he'd attracted the attention of Paramount talent scouts.

Kate embarked upon what became known as her "ten-day affair." Her sexual involvement with MacMurray triggered interest in her by Stevens. Apparently, the director had assumed that Kate was giving all her loving to Loring. In the opinion of De Grasse, when he saw MacMurray disappearing into Kate's dressing room at lunchtime, he became jealous.

Many members of the cast and crew, notably the future gossip maven, Hedda Hopper, felt that Kate and Stevens had been attracted to each other right from the beginning. "There was so much sexual tension in the air you could cut it with a knife," Hopper later claimed.

During her ten-day affair with MacMurray, and apparently in an attempt to make Kate jealous, Stevens started inviting Betty Grable to the set every day at lunch. As MacMurray disappeared with Kate, much to the fury and consternation of Jane Loring, Stevens would sometimes be gone for nearly two hours with Grable.

Grable's affair with Stevens would not last long. Actually it had gotten off to a poor start when he demanded that she dye her "Quicksilver Blonde Tresses" back to their original color.

Kate was introduced to Grable on the set but chose to ignore her. As if to punish MacMurray for his sexual romp with Kate, Stevens demanded that take after take with the actor be reshot. Nothing the hapless MacMurray did on camera seemed to please Stevens. At one particularly low point, Stevens demanded that MacMurray shoot a front porch scene eighty times. Both MacMurray and Kate were furious at their director.

During one love scene between MacMurray and Kate, Steven's reshooting exhausted both his actors. When Kate demanded to know why he was asking for another take, Stevens told her, "I've got to get rid of your flared nostrils. Who do you think you are? Rudolph Valentino?"

At first glance, *Alice Adams* had all the earmarks of a program filler, although Tarkington had won the Pulitzer Prize for his novel about small town nostalgia. During the first weeks of shooting, Stevens had not been impressed with Kate. He told Berman, "She has no technique and seems to want none."

He opted for simplicity from his star and struggled with Kate's exaggerated mannerisms on camera. She yelled at him, calling him a "son-of-a-bitch" in front of the crew and claiming that he was "destroying the naturalness of my performance." He shot back, "You don't know what naturalism is. You're relying on mechanical tricks."

"I hate you!" she shouted, storming off the set, trailed by Loring.

An hour later, the devoted Loring emerged from Kate's dressing room. She informed Stevens that Kate was going home for the day, as she'd developed a splitting headache and could no longer act.

"Act?" Stevens shouted at Loring. "Is that what Miss Hepburn has been doing? You could have fooled me."

He stormed off the set and headed for Berman's office. It was years later before the details of that meeting with the RKO production chief was revealed.

Unknown to Kate at the time, Stevens demanded, unsuccessfully, that she be taken off the picture and replaced with Ginger Rogers.

***

Kate quickly ended her affair with MacMurray, citing "total boredom" to Cukor. "He's got the body and everything's in the right place. But he just doesn't have magic." Caught up in another of her many affairs, Betty Grable no longer showed up on the set. Even so, tension between the star and her director mounted daily.

In spite of their battles, Berman had seen the rushes and felt that Stevens was extracting a touching performance from Kate. He told Stevens that Kate as *Alice Adams* would be an equal match for her performance as Jo March in *Little Women*.

Berman went on to say even more: "In spite of MacMurray's wooden acting, this could well be a masterpiece of American cinema. It might revive Kate's sagging career."

Stevens and Kate continued to indulge in squabbles until their first major stand-off, which involved a crying scene. Stevens insisted that Kate, in full view of the camera, stand at a window where the rain outside would be matched by her own tears. "I'll cry only on the bed with my face buried in a pillow,"

Kate shouted back at him, refusing to take direction.

"You'll cry at that fucking window or else I'll walk off this God damn set and go back to ordering stunt men to toss custard pies."

"You son-of-a-bitch," she shouted back at him from the top of her lungs. "You're yellow! A quitter!" Kate called Stevens "a silly fool" and "an idiot," claiming that she should have gone with Wyler as the director.

"Okay, bitch," he yelled at her. "I'll photograph your stand-in from the rear and have the sound of crying dubbed in. A real actress like Margaret Sullavan could have pulled off this scene. Maybe I'll bring in Barbara Stanwyck—I'm directing her next picture. Unlike you, that lez can really act."

Kate stood looking dumbfounded at Stevens, as if he could hardly believe the words she was hearing. Stevens got his tears all right. Sobbing hysterically, she rushed to her dressing room. She wouldn't even let Jane Loring come in, although the film editor stood pounding on her door.

Surprisingly, an hour later, Hattie McDaniel, playing the role of the slatternly maid, Malena, knocked on Kate's door and was ushered in.

Another hour passed before Kate emerged from her dressing room arm-in-arm with Hattie McDaniel. Kate told an angry Jane Loring that she could not see her that night and that she was going on a tour of the black night clubs in Los Angeles with Hattie. She also informed Loring that she was not going to show up for work the next day.

***

Deep into an affair with Tallulah Bankhead, Hattie McDaniel, Hollywood's most memorable black mammy, was just the right person to take Kate "on a tour of Harlem West," as the fat performer later described her one night with Kate.

Although Hattie was yet to appear in her defining role in *Gone With the Wind,* she was already a well-known performer at the time of her meeting with Kate. She'd been the first black woman to sing on radio, and before playing maids on camera she'd actually been a real-life maid. When criticized for creating black stereotypes on the screen, Hattie countered, "Honeychild, it's better to play a maid than be one."

Kate was enchanted with the naturalism of this larger-than-life creature. No one knows for sure what transpired that night between them. Hattie, with Kate sitting on the sidelines, appeared at The Blue Note and belted out "St. Louis Blues" to shattering applause.

At another club, The Black Widow, and by request, Hattie got up from the audience and sang spirituals to the enthralled black audience. In real-life, she'd been born in Wichita, Kansas, in 1898, the thirteenth child of a Baptist preacher. Her own mammy had been a singer of spirituals.

Somehow beyond the caricature that Kate had seen on the screen lurked a marvelous human being. It was easy to understand why Tallulah had been intrigued with this woman, who became the original Beulah on both radio and television.

Kate saw beyond her broad, black, shining face to discover a woman of real ambition, hopes, and desires. "I would prize more than anything a chance to appear in a singing film," Hattie told Kate. "To show what I can do. I can belt out a blues number with the best of them."

After their tour of the clubs, Kate was invited to Hattie's home. Once there, Hattie prepared her a late-night supper of pork chops and collards, her all time favorite foods. At that hour of the morning, Kate might have preferred breakfast.

The night that Kate and Hattie spent together sparked a series of rumors that swept across Hollywood. Speculation of a Hepburn/McDaniel romance was fueled mainly by Hedda Hopper and Tallulah Bankhead. "Wait till I catch up with that Bryn Mawr heifer," Tallulah said to Cukor. "I'm the only white woman who's allowed to nestle into my black mammy's breasts."

In spite of the wagging tongues of Hopper and Tallulah, there is no evidence that Kate had a one-night stand with Hattie McDaniel.

When Kate learned that Hattie McDaniel had been cast as the black mammy in *Gone With the Wind*, she wrote the actress a personal note, claiming how much she was looking forward to appearing on the screen with her. "With me as Scarlett O'Hara, and you as Mammy, we'll both take home Oscars. " Kate was partially right. Although Vivien Leigh was eventually cast as Scarlett, and Kate lost the role, Hattie McDaniel became the first black person to win an Oscar.

After smacking her lips on the last of Hattie's greasy pork chops and collards, Kate drove herself home. It was perhaps four o'clock in the morning.

Waiting on her front doorstep was a shadowy figure. Frightening her, Leland Hayward seemed to emerge out of the dark.

Leland had been waiting outside because Laura, still angry at him in the aftermath of their fight, had refused to let him inside the house.

He drove Kate back to his hotel to spend the night, since he could no longer stay under one roof with Laura. Although Kate had not been enchanted with Leland as of late, he won her over that night.

After making love to her, Kate did agree to attend a peacemaking dinner the following night with Leland and Stevens. However, she still adamantly refused to show up for work that day, insisting that she was going to call in and claim she was ill. Nonetheless, she promised to have recovered from this imaginary illness in time for the dinner with Stevens. Even her agreement to go out to a restaurant was a big concession on Kate's part. Leland was well aware that his client/lover hated dining in public.

At a secluded table in the rear of the Ivy & Vine Restaurant, Kate that night had a close-up view of the difference between Stevens and Leland. Stevens wanted to share his dream of life in small town America, as was being so poignantly depicted by Kate in *Alice Adams* under his direction and in spite of their mutual squabbles.

Although his world view would in time grow more bitter, Stevens in 1935 seemed to be an optimist, believing in a better life and at least the possibility of a fine world.

He was almost a romantic in his assumption that there was something innately good about people. "Virtue remains in mankind," Stevens told Kate and a somewhat bored Leland. "Call me an idealist, but I believe in the intrinsic good of people. It's not the people who are bad. It is the imperfect world that corrupts them."

Leland seemed so impatient with Stevens he couldn't wait for him to stop pontificating. The agent was far more interested in talking about money and deals than he was in any romantic visions of people or small-town America. Unlike Stevens, Leland viewed most people as "sharks waiting to take a bite out of you."

Almost for the first time, Kate became aware of Leland's sexism. "For Kate here, I demand and get top dollar," Leland confided. "But I don't go that far out to get the big bucks for the rest of my female clients. Ginger Rogers knows that, and she's furious at me right now. But it's the game out here. My males get the better deals and the most money. I think it's the male actor drawing both men and women to the box office—not a woman. A woman is secondary to most pictures." He turned and smiled at Kate, toasting her with his drink. "Of course, Miss Katharine Hepburn is the exception to all the rules. She can carry any picture by herself. In Kate's pictures, the males are secondary." He looked over at Stevens. "Kate can even survive a bad director." Neither the director nor his star were enraptured by Leland and gave him a cold shoulder.

Before departing, Leland turned to Kate and said," As independent as you are, my pet, remember it's a man's world and only a man can best represent your interest."

When Leland had gone, George Stevens moved closer on the banquette. He took Kate in his arms and gave her a long, passionate kiss. "You're going home with me tonight."

***

As Kate would giddily relate to her friends, "George is a real man—not somebody I can push around. I think this is my first thinking woman's romance. He is the first director to take me seriously as an artist—even the other George (George Cukor) never did that."

When *Alice Adams* opened at Radio City in New York, the theater billed Kate as "America's greatest actress." Berman was delighted with the opening grosses, and it appeared that Kate had broken the jinx on her series of box-office flops.

Not all the reviews were favorable, however. The most widely quoted critique appeared in *Time*. "Though Katharine Hepburn is possibly the least versatile of all of Hollywood's leading stars, it is precisely this limitation which makes her ideal for Alice. The woebegone grimaces, the expressions of half-childish and half-addleheaded so startlingly misplaced in her portrayals of women of the world, are precisely those which make her portrayal of a girl she really understands her masterpiece to date."

Kate won her second Academy Award nomination, and the film itself was also nominated.

Before the night of the Oscars, Bette Davis, also nominated for her role in *Dangerous*, placed a phone call to Kate. "I know you're going to win the Oscar for *Alice Adams*, and I also know you won't show up to accept it."

"Are you sure I have a chance?" Kate asked.

"Christ!" Davis responded. "Of course you do, my dear, or else I wouldn't be wasting my time to call you. I deserved the Oscar for *Of Human Bondage*. I wasn't that good in *Dangerous*. I don't have a chance. Will you let me take home the Oscar for you?"

Overwhelmed by such rare generosity from this rival screen diva, Kate embarrassingly granted Davis permission to accept the Oscar on her behalf, although she had already designated others.

As it turned out, Bette Davis did win the Oscar for 1935, beating out not only Hepburn but Claudette Colbert in *Private Worlds*. *Alice Adams* lost to *Mutiny on the Bounty*, with Charles Laughton and Clark Gable.

As grosses across the country continued to mount for *Alice Adams*, Berman in a reckless moment granted Kate the rare opportunity to select not only her director for her next picture but the script as well.

Kate that night called George Cukor, who was reading Compton MacKenzie's novel, *The Early Adventures of Sylvia Scarlett*. In spite of its bisexual overtones, Cukor thought it would make "one hell of a film—and, Kate, you'll get to play that boy you always wanted to be."

As Cukor remembered it, Kate was wildly enthusiastic about the idea.

The next day Berman met with both Cukor and Kate in his office, as they pitched the idea of this transgendered role for Kate. Although Berman at first had serious doubts about Kate masquerading as a boy in the film, he finally gave in to their pressure and succumbed to their joint enthusiasm.

It was a decision, as he later confessed, "I have lived to regret."

***

With Garbo still in the background, but only rarely; with Jane Loring now the number one girl in Kate's life; with Leland still hanging about for occasional stud services; and now with a new affair with George Stevens launched, Kate had less and less time for Laura.

One night she returned home late to find that Laura had packed her bags and left. "This time it will be forever," Laura wrote in a note. "We'll always be friends and I love you dearly. But I will no longer live with you. Laura."

Laura, whom fan magazines had hailed as "The Power behind Katharine Hepburn" had decided to return to her roots in the East and stop "living Kate's life for her."

Laura later commented publicly on her departure. "After a few years, it was apparent to everybody that I had no real role to play in Hollywood. I was not needed by Kate, and I certainly had no place in the picture business. When Kate became a big movie star, she no longer needed me. Increasingly, I found life as lived in Southern California to be meaningless and sterile. My social milieu back East was completely different from Kate's, and day-and-night different from Hollywood. Our family was in the railroad business and in American Express. Our friends were the moneyed class who never approved of Kate's bohemian ways and many of her friends. I have the greatest admiration for Kate, but I wisely decided to remove myself from the bull's eye of her existence."

***

Kate and Leland were driving toward Malibu for a swim. Her agent was claiming that he didn't like Kate's new film editor, Jane Loring, "but she has the most instinctive understanding of your peculiar qualities on film, and she knows how to bring out your beauty and charm better than anyone to date." Even so, Leland advised that Kate drop her relationship with Loring and see that she didn't work on any more of her films.

Kate adamantly refused, even though warned by Leland that with Laura out of the picture, gossip about a possible lesbian link with Loring was rampant throughout Hollywood—and not just around the lot of RKO.

"So what if there's something going on between Jane and me?" she asked defiantly. "That's our own God damn business, and I prefer that you stay out of it. I don't demand to know the details of your affair with that bitch, Miriam Hopkins."

"There's nothing romantic between Miriam and me," Leland protested.

"Oh, Leland," she said. "You're such a liar."

Suddenly, he let out a low moan and slumped over the wheel. She quickly urged him to pull off the highway. With great difficulty, he managed to do that. Helping him slide over to the passenger's seat, she got behind the wheel and broke speed records on the way to the nearest hospital. A motorcycle policeman pulled her over.

"I'm Katharine Hepburn," she shouted at him. "This is Leland Hayward. He's dying. Help us!"

With no further urging, the policeman, with sirens blasting, led the way, as he sped to the hospital with the stricken Leland in the car—piloted by Kate—behind him.

After he was rushed into the emergency ward, Kate never left his side, not even to go home and sleep. Because she was Katharine Hepburn, the movie star, she was allowed to sleep on a cot by his bed. The caretaker side of her personality took over, and she administered to him better than any nurse on duty would. Somehow the crisis brought them closer together again.

During his confinement for a battery of tests, Leland and Kate reached several agreements. In spite of their personal conflicts in the past, he agreed to hire Laura in his New York office—not that she needed the money, but to give her something to do.

He promised Kate that he would continue only as Sullavan's agent—not as her lover. At the time, Sullavan at parties on both coasts was doing "the most devastating and on-target impressions ever of Krazy Kate and her Giddy Girlfriends." Sullavan, a brilliant mimic, could turn parties into riotous laugh fests with her deadly accurate imitations of Kate's more exaggerated screen mannerisms and her love affairs with such women as Elissa Landi, Laura Harding, Suzanne Steele, and Jane Loring.

In return for these concessions, among others from Leland, Kate said she would seriously consider his offer of marriage. Although she didn't agree to give up Loring, she did say that she'd stop sleeping with George Stevens if Leland would quit bedding Miriam Hopkins.

After running a battery of tests on Leland, doctors concluded that he might possibly have cancer of the prostate. An immediate operation was recommended. "It could be a matter of your life and death," Dr. Philip Burns told Leland.

Since Kate didn't trust West Coast doctors, she persuaded Leland to fly with her across America where Dr. Hepburn would operate on him in Hartford. Leland reluctantly agreed.

Evoking future flights with aviator Howard Hughes, Leland—a skilled pilot—flew Kate in his two-seater craft cross country. Experiencing difficulty with his plane, Leland made a forced landing in St. Louis for emergency repairs.

Jeb Burnhill, a mechanic, recalled that Leland was very tense that day. "Hepburn retreated to the ladies' toilet while Hayward supervised the repairs to his plane. We asked him when he was getting married to Hepburn. He practically snapped our heads off. 'Quit asking me questions about my private life,' he said. 'I'm no God damn film star. I'm only the husband of a movie star.' Just as his plane took off, I called in the tip to a local newspaper. Before the rumor was squelched, some papers had already run stories about the secret marriage of Hayward to Hepburn."

As the news was picked up by the wire services, reporters and photographers were waiting en masse for the couple as Leland's small plane landed at the airport at Pittsburgh. Perhaps concentrating on the unruly crowd waiting for them, he landed badly, nearly crashing into another small air craft.

After refueling, Leland took off again, heading for the airport at Newark. During the Pittsburgh stopover, Kate never got off the plane.

At Newark, more reporters and photographers were waiting for them. Getting off the craft, Kate in a russet-colored sweater and elephant-brown pants, started to flee. Not looking where she was going, she ducked under the forward fuselage of a small plane and was nearly decapitated by propellers in motion.

A car was waiting for her. Escaping death, she jumped into the back seat of the car as her driver pulled off. Left behind to deal with the press, Leland was quizzed about the reports coming out of the Middle West about a secret marriage. He looked angry and belligerent that morning, although he usually handled the press with great skill and smoothness. "Fuck you!" he shouted. "No, we're not married, you bums. I'd be a total fool if I married Kate Hepburn."

The next morning, some papers carried the headline, "Hepburn Dares Death to Elude the Press." Others headlined Leland's violent denials of any secret marriage.

In a separate car, Leland was driven to Hartford Hospital, where Kate and Dr. Hepburn were waiting for him. Dr. Hepburn examined him that afternoon and told Leland that it was imperative that he operate within forty-eight hours.

Through an unknown tipster at the Hartford Hospital, the press learned of the operation. The next day, headlines screamed, "Movie Star's Doctor Father Operates on Daughter's Fiancé." Reporters descended by the car loads onto West Hartford.

In an effort to get a picture of Kate, photographers hid behind the garage of her family home. When Kate emerged from her parents' house, they jumped out and photographed her.

The flashbulbs exploding in her face incensed her. She kicked one photographer and tossed his camera on the ground, stomping it. Then she turned and stormed back into the house looking for the family shotgun. Peggy later recalled that Kate was in such a rage that she feared that her sister was going to kill one or more of the photographers. Fortunately, before that could happen, Kit chased them away with a pitchfork she was using for yard work.

The publicity department at RKO was horrified at Kate's impulsive actions. She was going beyond the evasive actions of Greta Garbo, not only almost killing herself at the airport, but threatening to kill others. At that point, her career needed all the help from the press it could get. But Kate refused to cooperate in any way. "She was a walking public relations nightmare for RKO," said Henry Cable at the studio. "We hated her. If she wanted to be so God damn secretive, why in hell did she become a movie star in the first place? On the other hand, her rival, Ginger Rogers, was a living doll."

After Leland recovered from his surgery for a week or so at the Hepburn family home, Kate drove him to New York where they checked into a hotel. Wanting to avoid Luddy, she did not go to her Turtle Bay town house. Through

Kit, she had specifically requested that Luddy not drive up to Hartford while Leland was recovering. Although terribly hurt, Luddy had agreed to that.

Leland visited his New York office and chatted briefly with Laura. Kate did not see her former lover but spoke on the phone with her. Although Kate and Laura would repair their friendship within a few months, and would eventually resume their love affair on a sporadic basis, their relationship had considerably chilled. It would never be the same again.

Before Leland sailed to Europe without Kate, he allowed his client, the lesbian author, Edna Ferber, to throw a private engagement party for Kate, himself, and a few select friends who happened to be in New York, Noël Coward among them.

Hosting the party, Ferber wore a dark blue double-breasted suit. Coward showed up in almost the same outfit. On seeing his host, Coward said, "You almost look like a man."

"So do you," Ferber parried.

Ferber, in an attempt to curry favor with the Algonquin crowd, invited the likes of Alexander Woollcott, Heywood Broun, Ruth Hale, George and Beatrice Kaufman, Robert Benchley, and even Dorothy Parker. Kate still had not forgiven Parker her quip about *The Lake,* and studiously avoided her throughout the evening.

As a surprise for Leland, Kaufman and Ferber revealed that they had a "terrific idea" for a play. It would be called *Stage Door* and would be about life in a theatrical boarding house. Kate would be asked to spearhead an all-star cast of women.

Although she feared that *Stage Door* was a bit too evocative of *Morning Glory,* Kate agreed to star in their play.

Ironically, in patterns that imitate many other theater castings, Kate was never offered the role when *Stage Door* was eventually cast on Broadway. To offend her even more, her nemesis, Margaret Sullavan, opened in the play. To compound matters, "a woman I hate," in Kate's words, Joan Bennett, took the play on a highly successful road show. Kate, however, managed to snare the lead in the picturization of the Ferber-Kaufman play.

When Leland sailed to Europe, Kate returned alone to California. She promised her agent/lover that she would set a definite date for their marriage upon his return.

***

When Kate returned to Hollywood, Cukor presented her with "a sensitive and challenging" script from the acclaimed British novelist, John Collier. Kate eagerly read the first draft of the script of *Sylvia Scarlett* and initially loved the project, although demanding changes. Eventually Gladys Unger and Mortimer Offner were called in as "script nurses."

Kate wanted the role so badly she had to wire her old friend, Arthur Hopkins, that she would be unable to appear on Broadway in Helen Jerome's stage adaptation of *Pride and Prejudice.*

Cukor told Kate that for three-quarters of the picture, she'd have to have her head shaved as she'd be appearing in the transgendered role as a boy. The director said that he hoped to bring out Kate's piquant quality, calling her *une garçonne.*

Of all the A-List films released by major studios in the 1930s, *Sylvia Scarlett* was labeled as the most bizarre. Kate, as Sylvia, was cast as the daughter of an English embezzler, Henry Scarlett, as played by the Pickwickian and apple-cheeked Edmund Gwenn. To elude the police, who were hot on her father's trail, she disguises herself as a boy and becomes Sylvester, fleeing with him to France.

En route, they team up with Cary Grant's character of Jimmy Monkley. With the perfectly cast Cary Grant, playing a Cockney ne'er-do-well, they work their way back to England traveling as Punch-and-Judy players. Kate was delighted to be acting with Grant, calling him "slightly plump and full of beans." Sylvia, dressed as a boy, falls in love with an artist, a character named Michael Fane.

Although Kate and Cary Grant had both been awarded roles as two of the picture's principal characters, there were still doubts about who would play the role of Michael Fane. Pandro Berman recommended a very handsome and dashing Australian, Errol Flynn, for an audition, and even arranged for him to take a screen test. But after only five minutes, Cukor dismissed Flynn brusquely from his office.

Cukor later told Kate that Flynn had exposed his rather generous endowment during the interview, promising Cukor that he could avail himself of "my big lollipop" throughout the shoot. Cukor admitted that he found Flynn one of the sexiest actors he'd ever interviewed, but opted not to haul out the casting couch. Kate applauded his integrity.

When Berman persuaded Kate to look at the screen test Flynn had made, she said, "I can't see him for dust," adding her veto to that of Cukor.

Subsequently, Berman became very bitter at both Cukor and Kate when Flynn escaped from his contract with RKO to sign with Warner Brothers, where he became one of Hollywood's biggest male stars. "Look at all the money I lost because of you two," Berman chastised Cukor and Kate two years later. "I don't know which one of you is the bigger and more demented diva."

***

The part of Michael Fane in MacKenzie's picaresque novel went to Brian Aherne, the British romantic leading man. Fresh from his affairs with tobacco heiress, Doris Duke, and his "Moon Goddess" Marlene Dietrich, with whom he'd made *Song of Songs* in 1933, Aherne shook Kate's hand. "I generally take a dim view of American women," he told her. "But I understand you're an exception."

"What's wrong with American women?" she asked.

"I have found them to be spoiled and unhappy in spite of their lively charm and beauty," he said.

"I'm neither spoiled nor unhappy," she said, "and we'll get along just fine." From the very beginning, she realized she detested Aherne.

In the film, Kate *en travestie*, says, "I won't be a girl, weak and silly! I'll be a boy, rough and hard!" Sexual ambiguities abound, and the film never quite resolves the plot it launched.

At one point, Bunny Beatty, playing a maid, kisses the pants-clad Kate passionately on the lips, presumably thinking she was a boy. Grant is shown fondling Kate while she's dressed as a boy, and there are many risqué references to bisexuality, most of which were pitched over the heads of the film's intended audience. Playing an artist, Aherne says to Kate, "I don't know what it is that gives me a queer feeling when I look at you."

At one point during the filming, Grant relaxed off-camera with Kate. "I think I like you better as a boy than as a girl. As a girl, you're far too skinny, and I don't like skinny women."

"Do you like women at all?" she provocatively asked him.

"Occasionally, but only on that very odd night," he said. "But usually, Randy and Howard have a lot more to play around with." He got up and wandered off as if distracted by something.

The next day Kate confided to Grant. "Cukor has lost it with this film, and we'll sink along with it. He doesn't even know what the film is about and neither do I. Cross-dressing? Androgyny? Gender confusion?" Grant responded that only a small segment of the movie-going people, and among them, homosexuals, would understand the film.

Kate made an entry in her diary which later became public. In it, she wrote: "This picture makes no sense at all, and I wonder whether George Cukor is aware of that fact. I certainly don't know what in hell I'm doing."

Cukor later destroyed the integrity of the film by tacking on a beginning and an ending that made a mess of the plot and that tried to soften the transgendered aspect of Kate's portrayal. "I thought I was playing it safe," Cukor said, "by focusing on Kate's womanhood. It was a mistake. I shouldn't have."

Kate refused to talk to the press during the filming, but Grant was far more obliging and relayed many compliments to them about his co-star. "She is the most magnetic person I've ever met. I will probably not meet up with the likes of her again. You had to look at her, you had to listen to her, there was no escaping her. But it isn't just beauty. It's her style. She's an incredibly realistic and natural person, tolerating no nonsense. She cares deeply and isn't the insensitive monster some people have found. It's just that she cares about what really matters in life."

Before shooting had begun, Elsa Maxwell had intervened and gotten Cukor to cast Natasha Paley in the role of Lily, Aherne's primary love interest in the film.

Paley, who had fallen on hard times, was the daughter of the Russian Grand Duke Paul, the uncle of the Czar (Nicholas II) who had been deposed during the Russian Revolution. In spite of her shaky English, Cukor granted her the part.

The elegant and beautiful Paley arrived on the set fresh from affairs with both Maurice Chevalier and Charles Boyer. Cukor seemed enchanted with her, and Kate developed a harmless crush on this Russian aristocrat, in spite of the jealous eyes of Jane Loring.

Perhaps because of their mutual love interest in Boyer, Kate and Paley had much to talk about. Cukor was always impressed with European royalty, so much so that in making *The Women* in 1939, he cast Paley again as the gossipy manicurist, Olga.

In the middle of shooting, the cast was stunned by the arrival of an unexpected guest.

Howard Hughes literally flew in.

***

George Cukor was directing a scene, and Kate was sitting off-camera chatting with Frank Horn, Cary Grant's longtime personal secretary. This former fellow vaudevillian of Grant's looked like Humpty-Dumpty. He was telling her that because of his size and personal appearance, it was impossible for him to romance the handsome, young, and Adonis-like men he so desired. To compensate, he claimed that he hired only the cream of male hustlers in Hollywood, most of them aspirant actors. He told her that he had accumulated what might be America's greatest collection of male pornography, which he shared with Grant and Randolph Scott.

Horn even invited Kate over to view his collection, including shots of some movie stars who had posed in the nude before becoming famous. Kate told him that "as fascinating an invitation as that is, I must decline. The excitement would be too much for my poor heart."

Hearing a noise, she looked up at the sky where she saw a Boeing Scout circling over the set. Cukor had discovered one of the most photogenic strips of beachfront along the Southern California coastline. Much of the action in *Sylvia Scarlett* was shot above the rolling dunes of Trancas Beach.

Cukor immediately called for his cinematographer, Joseph August, to stop filming. Hands on his hips in exasperation, Cukor also rubber-necked along with the rest of his crew. "Don't that beat all!" his sound recorder, George D. Ellis, said.

Kate later described the landing of Howard Hughes in a windswept meadow nearby, overlooking the roaring surf below. "His plane just seemed to emerge from the offshore fog. It was about noon. I can still picture the late morning sun glinting off the silver nose of his craft. It was as if Cukor were directing an aerial scene, not the action on the ground. The wings dipped, and the pilot came to a beautiful landing, the small craft gliding gracefully down. At that point, I decided I wanted to be an aviator myself. From the cockpit the pilot emerged. He was one of the tallest and boyishly handsome men I'd ever seen—a wondrous sight, really. He wore a brown leather flight jacket, with the sign of an eagle sewn on the left pocket. He also wore elephant-colored jodhpurs and jet-black Cordovan boots with some sort of silver ornamentation on them. The rangy figure came toward us."

Kate told her maid, Johanna Madsen, "That landing was a bit too close—too God damn close."

In contrast to the dashing aviator, Kate looked rather plain that day. Her red hair had been closely cropped, and she looked very much like a boy, wearing a nut-brown polo coat she'd borrowed from her makeup artist, Mel Burns. She'd splashed alcohol on her face, which had streaked her screen mask.

On seeing "the fastest man alive," the fabulously wealthy Hughes coming toward her, she retreated to the safety of her dressing room before Grant could make an introduction.

There she remained for about thirty minutes before emerging again. This time she'd slashed a scarlet mouth on herself and had slipped into a pair of olive green gabardine slacks with a tailored man's white shirt she'd purchased at Brooks Brothers. "With her short hair, she looked like a sodomite's dream," Cukor later said. "Those slacks accentuated her slim hips." Under one arm, she carried a basket of freshly made scones baked by Johanna.

Kate walked over to a blanket that Johanna had spread across a patch of scrub grass. Hughes was sitting between Cukor and Grant, who was his friend. Hughes rose to greet Kate.

What Hughes thought of her appearance is not known. He'd dated some of the world's loveliest women, including actress Billie Dove, who'd been called the single most beautiful woman on earth. He'd also had affairs with such bombshells as Jean Harlow, although both Hughes and Harlow denied such reports.

Other than shaking his hand, Kate didn't seem impressed with the man who had been dubbed by the press as the playboy of the Western world. He was also a record-breaking aviator and a film mogul who'd produced such classics as *Hell's Angels.*

She seemed put off by the high-pitched sound of his voice. "Such a manly looking man should have a deeper, richer voice," she later confided to Cukor.

Ignoring him throughout her picnic lunch, she acted rather arrogantly in Hughes' presence. Obviously she didn't want him to think she was impressed with either his wealth or fame.

Hughes had so little to say to her that she later told Grant that "he acted like a deaf mute" during the whole picnic, not even complimenting Johanna on her famous fried chicken. As it turned out, Hughes was not overly fond of fried foods.

After Hughes had left, Grant told her that his friend was really a fascinating fellow but was partially deaf and could not hear much of their conversation.

Not only that, but Hughes was working on one of his secret airplane projects at the time and found small talk boring. Grant did admit that Hughes didn't need to jabber all the time and would often invite him over to sit for hours at a time with him, not saying a word.

When Kate later complained that she didn't like the way Hughes had barged in, interrupting the filming of the picture, Grant confessed that he'd actually invited the aviator. Each day the stars of the picture, along with Cukor, had been asked to invite the most interesting person in their acquaintance to one of their picnic lunches. Grant had selected Hughes.

Only because of his great love for Grant did Hughes tear himself away from his work and answer Grant's pleadings. At that stage in their relationship, Hughes gave in to Grant's every wish. Hughes told Grant that he'd fly in but could only stay a short time. He was intrigued, however, at the idea of meeting Kate, because he admired "this magnificent Yankee's free spirit."

Throughout the picnic, Kate never made eye contact with Hughes. "I never looked at him—not even once after I shook his hand," she told Jane Loring. "He had some nerve flying over us like that. The British would call it cheeky."

The following day, and in spite of Kate's wall of coldness to him, Hughes was intrigued. He'd even come up with a nickname for Kate, calling her "Country Mouse." It was a nickname he would use for her during their long relationship, in spite of its unflattering overtones.

Although cold-shouldered by Kate at the time of their introduction, Hughes was interested enough to accept another invitation from Grant to fly in the next week for yet another picnic, this one prepared by Cukor's own personal chef. Kate and Brian Aherne were invited as the guests of honor.

It was only later that Kate was to learn that this complicated charade was part of Grant's elaborate plan to bring Kate and the aviator/lover together.

This is how Aherne remembered the second visit: "Without warning, Hughes came back. A biplane roared up and set down on the makeshift landing strip above the dunes. Out stepped Howard Hughes looking like Charles Lindbergh. The crew erroneously thought at the time he was already having an affair with Kate. Later we found out that wasn't true. If he was in love with anyone, it was with Cary. Hughes was fascinated by Cary. As I recall, Cary was a bit of a prick-teaser at that picnic. Hughes came over and spoke to Kate and me. He had a high-pitched voice that struck me odd. Kate had told me that he was almost deaf. She seemed to mock his handicap during the picnic. She was playing up to Grant as if he were her lover. She'd lean over to Grant and whisper to him, 'Please, pass me another chicken leg.' It was all innocent enough, but the look on her face was making it seem that she was coming on to Grant. Hughes couldn't understand a word they were saying. He sat there getting angrier by the minute. When he could take Kate's cuddling of Grant no more, he got up and stormed away, heading to his plane. 'I've had enough of this shit!' he shouted back at Kate and Grant. The two doubled over in laughter. Grant promised to explain everything to Hughes later that night. Frankly, I thought it was rather sadistic of Kate to taunt Hughes like that."

Aherne said that after Hughes flew off, Cukor ordered everyone back to the set. The actor overheard Grant tell Kate, "You know what? Howard Hughes would make a perfect new beau for you."

"You must be kidding," she said. "Me and that rich playboy? Could you see me taking that womanizer and 'manizer' home to meet Kit and my father? They'd take a shotgun and run him off the grounds. A romance between Katharine Hepburn and Howard Hughes? Hell will freeze over before that day ever comes."

***

The preview of *Sylvia Scarlett* at Pasadena became another part of the Hollywood legend and lore about Katharine Hepburn. Although Jane Loring pleaded with Kate to take her to the preview, she chose to invite Natasha Paley, the Russian princess, instead.

The preview turned out to be "absolute agony" for Kate. "I thought the audience was going to lynch me," she later told Cukor and Paley. In another post-mortem, she confided to Grant, "The film is about as funny as a baby's open grave."

As Kate on screen was reciting a poem by Edna St. Vincent Millay, half of the audience walked out. The other half remained to boo and hiss at the screen. Some of the audience stood up and shouted at the screen, calling Kate a lesbian and Grant a fairy. Only Aherne escaped with his heterosexual credentials intact.

After the screening, Kate drove with Paley and Cukor to his home where a furious Pandro Berman waited for them. Both Cukor and Kate promised Berman that they would make the next picture for him for free.

"There's no way in hell I'll ever work with the two of you clowns on another picture," Berman shouted at them. "Not after this disaster."

Berman ordered Loring to re-edit the film, taking out some of the more glaring homosexual scenes. Although Loring didn't want to do that, she had little choice.

Even after more work on the film, Berman was still ashamed of it and held up its release for six months. He finally "unleashed it on an unsuspecting public" in January of 1936.

The reviews were poor, the box office receipts a disaster. *Time* magazine found "Katharine Hepburn better looking as a boy than as a woman." Richard Watts, Jr., in the *New York Herald Tribune*, found that "Miss Hepburn is the handsomest boy of the season," but Eileen Creelman of the *New York Sun* thought that "she makes an unconvincing boy."

Upon seeing the picture, comedienne Fanny Brice asked Kate and Cukor, "What the hell were you two thinking when you made that picture?"

Viewed as a cult classic today, the film, when it was released, was condemned by the Legion of Decency. Only Cary Grant emerged unscathed. Until cast in *Sylvia Scarlett*, he'd played conventional leading man roles. After *Scarlett*, his stock skyrocketed. "George Cukor taught me how to be funny," Grant later said. "He brought out the Archie Leach in me." Grant stole the picture not only from Aherne and the secondary actors, but from Kate as well.

Sylvia Scarlett went on to lose more than a quarter of a million dollars. Some modern-day film critics have suggested that Kate's character of Sylvia appealed to some heterosexual men through a deep-seated Freudian wish for an incestuous sexual link with a "son/daughter" figure. It has also been suggested that Kate stirred up feelings of bisexuality in men by her presence on the screen as a beautiful boy.

After the disaster of *Sylvia Scarlett*, Kate told Cukor that if she didn't succeed in her next three films, she would be washed up in Hollywood, a prediction that almost came true.

Berman had two scripts for Kate, either of which he claimed would rescue her. RKO ordered Anthony Veiller to adapt *Marie Bashkirtseff*, a Hungarian play, for Kate. Louis B. Mayer at MGM sought her services for a historical romance, *The Gorgeous Hussy*, which was finally filmed in 1936 with Joan Crawford.

Kate didn't do either of these pictures but rushed immediately into a different film and a love affair that would rank among the most memorable of her life.

Pandro Berman, in spite of his threats never to work with Kate again, informed her that he'd cast her as the lead in *Mary of Scotland*, opposite Fredric March. The picture was to be directed by John Ford.

***

Kate sat talking with Cary Grant at Cukor's lavish Cordell Drive home above Doheny Drive and Sunset Boulevard. This was where the elite of Hollywood's gay male colony gathered on Sunday, with the occasional lesbian celebrity such as Hope Williams showing up. Tallulah Bankhead could always be counted on to be here when she was in town, although her film career was going nowhere. She always insisted that the silver screen "is just too small to capture this gal's abundant charms, darling. Movies are for the little people."

On one lazy Sunday afternoon, Kate was sitting beside the pool talking with Grant, as they reviewed their work on *Sylvia Scarlett*. Grant predicted that it would be Cukor's last film for RKO. "Before I was offered *Mary of Scotland,*" Kate said, "I thought it would be my last film for RKO or any other studio."

A radio was softly playing in the background, as Grant bitched to her that he resented being paid only fifteen-thousand dollars for a six-week stint. He envied her pulling in fifty-thousand dollars for the picture. He spoke of his great ambition and plans and claimed that he would soon be making anywhere from one-hundred fifty-thousand dollars to two-hundred thousand dollars per picture, although she viewed such amounts as mere fantasy figures.

On that day, Grant was deeply troubled about the columns of the homopho-bic writer Edith Gwynn, who consistently tried to expose him (or "out" him, to use a term of today) as a homosexual. Her references were veiled. She called Hollywood "a long-haired town for males," and suggested that there was "something queer" about the lives of Cary Grant, Randolph Scott, Gary Cooper, and James Cagney. She was fond of pointing out that Cagney had launched his acting career appearing in drag.

At first Grant told Kate that he'd defied Gwynn. One night in the wake of a particularly vicious column by her, he had deliberately showed up, arm in arm with Scott, at the Trocadero night club. But since his studio had raised so many objections, he'd been forced to be seen around town with women, notably Betty Furness, with whom he enjoyed a platonic relationship.

Since the pressure was building on Grant, and gossip about Kate and Jane Loring wasn't going away, he proposed a solution for her. "Randy and I may have to marry women a few times in our lives, although we'll always see each other. Things are going to get rough on you too if you don't give in to the sys-tem."

"Just what are you trying to tell me?" she asked.

"Start dating Howard Hughes," he abruptly said. "The fan magazines and the newspapers will promote it so much it'll knock Hitler out of the news. You and Howard will be the perfect beard for each other. He'll shield you from exposure, and reporters will be so busy writing about what a hot couple the two of you are, they won't have time to search out what each of you is actually up to."

"The idea is absurd," she said, "and I'd like to dismiss it without the slight-est consideration. What are your real motives?"

"You know what they are," he said. "With all the talk about Randy and me, I don't want more speculation about Howard and me. Besides, I think the two of you have a lot more in common than you think. Of all the potential 'beaus,' as you call them, Howard in many ways is the ideal choice. You crave privacy more than any other actress that I know, and he's got the power and money to give you that."

"I'll think about it," she promised. "My first reaction is negative, though."

A bulletin coming over the radio caught their attention. An announcer said that Hollywood's most famous agent, Leland Hayward, had married the screen actress, Margaret Sullavan.

Kate was so stunned she burst into tears, and Grant took her in his arms to comfort her. Cukor came over to offer his condolences as well, although he wasn't as sympathetic as Grant.

"How many times did he propose marriage to you, and how many times did you turn him down?" Cukor asked. "You knew he was seeing Maggie. It was in all the newspapers. Besides, Leland told me he wanted to have six children. *At least.* I can't imagine you having even one child."

"I know, I know," she said, standing up on wobby legs. "But still, I feel betrayed. I could have forgiven him a marriage to any other woman. Even Ginger Rogers. But not that southern belle tramp!"

As Grant reported the conversation he'd just had with Kate about Howard Hughes, she went to call her mother, Kit, in Hartford. Later, Kate told Cukor and Grant that Kit had uttered somewhat the same words that Cukor had. "Kit put it bluntly," Kate said. "You didn't really want Leland but you didn't want any other woman to have him either, especially that Sullavan creature of all women."

Kate decided to be noble about Leland's marriage and sent a wire that afternoon congratulating both Sullavan and her agent. The telegram was received at a party for the newlyweds. Kate later learned that Sullavan mockingly read it aloud, imitating Kate's voice. In front of the party and Leland, she tore it up and tossed it on the floor. "That dykey bitch!" she said, grinding the telegram into the carpet with the spike on her heel.

Back at poolside, Kate demanded that one of Cukor's hired bartenders for the afternoon, one of the most strikingly handsome men she'd ever seen, serve her a stiff drink. Although known to take a drink from time to time, she was rather temperate on most occasions. Not this afternoon. She told the bartender to keep the drinks flowing.

Grant would later claim that she propositioned the boy, although the bartender had been booked to spend the night with Cukor. Grant excused himself to make a call before joining Kate with Cukor at poolside. She was debating if she should fire Leland as her agent or continue with him. Both Cukor and Grant urged her to keep him on, as they felt he'd handled her career brilliantly and had brought in top dollar for her.

The handsome bartender came out and whispered something to Grant, who excused himself and went out the front door. When he returned, he smiled at Kate. "Surprise of surprise on this dark day of Leland's marriage. Howard is waiting outside in a battered car, and he wants to take you for a joy ride."

***

Howard Hughes was a tall, lanky, mustachioed, and smart man, and he knew that Katharine Hepburn would never become an addition to his harem of beautiful young women and handsome young men. He sensed that none of the labels placed on him by the press would impress her: moviemaker, matinee-idol handsome playboy, ace pilot, genius inventor, or even billionaire.

When she agreed to get into his car outside Cukor's house that late Sunday afternoon, he immediately used a line on her he'd never employed on a glamorous woman before.

"I've decided that you would make my ideal mate," he told her. "In you I could find the perfect woman. You're the only woman I've ever met who could equal the beauty and sensuality of my own mother."

Kate went for the bait. As he drove her to Santa Monica, she wanted to ask questions about his mother. But first, she complimented him on his car. Since everyone knew that Hughes could purchase a whole fleet of cars, even the automobile-manufacturing company itself, she was impressed with the vehicle he'd arrived in to pick her up.

Hughes said that he'd borrowed the car from his cook. It wasn't really so much an automobile as a wreck that would travel down the road only with a little coaching from Hughes, an expert on engines. It was so beat-up that it looked as if it should long ago have been sent to the junk heap.

Not only battered, but filthy. The cook apparently didn't like to eat his own food but preferred hamburgers-to-go, along with bottles of orange juice, all the empty containers thrown haphazardly into the back seat. She was particularly amused that there was no hood to conceal the ferocious-looking and rusty engine, which looked as if it were going to expire before ever reaching the sands of Santa Monica.

"A jalopy without a hood—perfect for me," she exclaimed. "I don't know about you, but personally, I believe that no car should be retired until it gives off its last gasp."

She leaned back and let the breezes blow through her hair. Here she was, riding with the richest man in the world in a God-awful car that looked like he had rescued it from a wrecker's junkyard. She couldn't have been happier, as she was later to report, and she began to like this man. Sometimes if there was noise on the road, as from a passing truck, he couldn't hear her exact words, but he always nodded and smiled in agreement.

When she learned that his plan for the evening was to take her to a public restaurant, she absolutely refused, claiming she never dined out. "I can't stand to have people watch me eat," she claimed. "It literally makes me faint."

When he pulled the car to a stop at The Rusty Pelican, he turned and faced her squarely. He looked thin and bronzed, with dark, searching eyes that seemed to take in every detail of her own slim frame. "Don't you think I know that already?" he asked. "Cary has told me everything. The restaurant is reserved for just the two of us tonight. I don't like people either. We'll be all alone."

Persuaded to go in, she was happily surprised to see that The Rusty Pelican

214

lived up to his promise. An all-male band had been hired for the night, and the eight-man waitstaff existed only for the two of them.

In the light of the restaurant, she appraised his clothes more carefully. He was a six-foot-three beanpole in a pair of khaki trousers she knew all too well, as she herself had purchased a pair at a local department store for one dollar and ninety-eight cents. What made his pants intriguing was that they came within six inches of reaching his ankles, and his "time-capsule" old jacket had sleeves that also came within six inches of reaching his wrists. His two-toned shoes in brown and white were scruffed up. What amused her was that instead of a belt, he held up his pants with an old tie with a ragged edge.

If the elaborate kitchen staff thought it was going to be an evening of lobster, caviar, and champagne, they were disappointed. Hughes, as she was to learn, always ate the same meal every night: a ten-ounce and very lean steak, a small helping of canned—never fresh—peas, and a dessert of one scoop of vanilla ice cream with a caramel topping.

She was appropriately modest in her demands, ordering only a grilled chicken breast and three side vegetables followed by instructions not to overcook the vegetables. Unlike Hughes's canned peas, she insisted that all her food be fresh.

Hughes figured that since he was paying for the band, he might as well avail himself of its music. He asked her to dance. At RKO she'd never competed with Ginger Rogers to get dancing roles with Fred Astaire. If called upon, Kate could dance a little. Hughes also offered Astaire no competition. On the dance floor, he held her so tightly that her feet were hardly touching the floor. She called him "the Bear-Hugger," and was greatly relieved when they could return to the table.

Instead of champagne, both of them ordered plain tap water, although a wine steward was standing impatiently by with nothing to do. The bartender hired for the night waited in vain for drink orders that never came. Kate had had enough to drink that afternoon at Cukor's party.

After dinner, Hughes pushed back his plate. She seemed to think that the time had come for him to tell her about his mother. Instead, he leaned over and in a very confidential tone whispered to her that he'd killed a man.

Since Hughes was not a kidder, she believed him at once and demanded to know all the details. "I'm interested in many things," she told him, "especially cold-blooded murder."

He revealed the whole story to her. While spending time in Santa Barbara with some of his aviation buddies, he'd met Nancy Bell Bayly. She was a strikingly beautiful local debutante who slightly resembled his former wife, Ella Rice.

He claimed he dated Bayly several times, including one muggy summer night as he was driving through the clouds and fog in Los Angeles, heading for the *faux* Polynesian restaurant of Trader Vic's.

215

After leaving the amusement park at Santa Monica pier, where Hughes had taken her for a ride on the roller coaster, they came to the badly lit junction of Lorraine Avenue and Third Street. An oncoming car appeared to be heading for a frontal crash with their vehicle. Swerving to avoid it, he struck something. "All I knew was we heard this loud thump," Hughes said.

That "something" turned out to be a tailor, Gabriel Meyer, aged fifty-nine. Struck by Hughes's vehicle, he had died on impact. Hughes told Kate that he quickly put Bayly on the next streetcar as a crowd gathered, claiming that he didn't want her to be implicated or questioned by the police.

"What happened?" Kate demanded to know.

"I was taken to Central Jail and booked on suspicion of negligent homicide," he said. "I was given a sobriety test but passed it even though we'd been drinking."

"Is the case pending?" she asked. "Are you going to jail?"

"Nothing like that," he said. "If you run over someone in this town, I'll get Neil McCarthy to represent you. He could get you off a murder rap if you plunged a butcher knife into an innocent man's heart in front of ten witnesses."

"Sounds like a good man to know when I eventually kill Margaret Sullavan, as I know I will," she said.

"I got off, but the poor victim's family protested and threatened to make more trouble for me. I sent a personal messenger over with twenty-thousand dollars in one-hundred dollar bills, and I haven't heard one word out of them since."

She sat back on the banquette, her face a mask of contradictions and confused emotions. As she later told her friends, when she gleefully reported the details of this evening, "I just didn't know what to make of this man who could buy himself out of anything. I was both impressed and appalled at the same time, if that's possible."

Not wanting to comment on his actions, as she sat with Hughes in the restaurant, she abruptly asked him, "What about this mother I remind you of?"

***

Cary Grant had coached Hughes carefully, accurately suspecting that Kate "will be all ears" on hearing about Hughes's bizarre childhood. Grant had told Hughes that he'd absolutely held Kate in rapture when he'd related his own nightmarish childhood as Archie Leach growing up in England.

Hughes told Kate that his mother, Allene Gano, had been "the most desirable woman" in Dallas, Texas, when she'd met his father. A steady parade of gentleman callers, he claimed, showed up at the doorstep of this beautiful woman, with golden brown hair, who was attired in the latest fashions. A Social Register debutante, she was the granddaughter of a legend-making Confederate general, and had been descended from French Huguenots. She could have her

216

pick of some of the richest swains in the Dallas Blue Book, but she had chosen the womanizing, heavy-drinking Howard Hughes, Sr., a man with no money and no prospects.

Before coming to Dallas, he'd been a Mississippi riverboat gambler, a newspaper reporter in Denver, and a zinc miner in Oklahoma, among other professions. Howard Sr. didn't even have a steady job when he'd met Allene.

Actually he did have $49,100, all of which he blew on a 1904 honeymoon in Europe where he managed to spend two-thousand dollars a day. Even the biggest spenders of the time, robber baron families such as the Astors and the Rockefellers, found five-hundred dollars a day for two extraordinarily lavish for enjoying the finest the Continent had to offer.

Born just eighteen months after the honeymoon, Hughes, Jr. claimed that his birth had been the most difficult ever witnessed by the attending doctor in Dallas, Oscar Norsworthy. "I literally ripped my mother's insides open causing massive hemorrhaging," Hughes told Kate. "It took nine hours of incredible pain. Every day of my life, my mother reminded me of that excruciating horror she'd suffered at the Dallas Baptist Hospital."

A team of three surgeons managed to stem the flow of blood, and Allene was saved at the last minute.

Hughes claimed that as he was growing up, his mother never wanted to let him out of her sight. His father was always off on road trips, hawking a drill bit that was making a vast fortune for him and consequently changing the nature of oil exploration all over the globe. His nights were spent in the arms of showgirls.

"From the day I was born, I always slept in my mother's arms," Hughes told Kate. "Always naked. Even as I grew older and started to get erections when she touched me intimately, she held me so tightly I could hardly breathe on some nights."

Allene seemed obsessed with germs and with obsessional fears about her son's health. Hughes claimed that she would wake him an hour earlier than needed every morning and "go over my nude body like a fine-tooth comb." He said that she would examine the most intimate parts of him in her feverish search for the slightest sign of a pimple or rash. If she discovered something, however minor, she would immediately call a doctor or else rush him to a hospital.

His mother would even inspect his anus by inserting her finger in it as if she might discover hemorroids. "She even laboriously inspected kneecaps and elbows looking for something," Hughes said. "Every night she'd repeat the same inspection, having me stand nude in front of her as she examined my ears and even my teeth." He confessed as he grew older, he'd felt embarrassed as his mother in minute detail inspected his genitals, skinning back the foreskin on his developing penis and looking for any skin irritation.

He told Kate that when he went to the toilet, Allene insisted on going with him and often held his hand firmly during bowel movements, afraid that with a hard stool he might rip his flesh the way her own flesh had been torn apart giving birth to him. "She never let me flush until she'd inspected my stool."

In painful detail, Hughes confided that he had been forced to take cod liver oil and some Russian mineral oil every morning at six o'clock. "At night it was Epson salts."

Even as Hughes grew into adolescence, his mother continued to bathe him, paying special attention to his genitals and his anus.

She used a milder soap for his ears and face, but for his private areas she insisted on using a powerful lye soap because she claimed that it was in the "nether regions" that germs and infections were most likely to occur.

"When I had to go to the potty during the middle of the day, my mother insisted on thoroughly washing me back there. She was horrified that most men and women walked around with feces clinging to their butts all day."

Hughes claimed that Allene turned him into a Little Lord Fauntleroy. Boys at school called him a "sissy." When Hughes was beaten up by a pack of hell-raising boys his own age, Allene hired a burly bodyguard to protect her son. From the very beginning, she infused his brain with the idea that he was superior to all other boys.

By donating one-thousand dollars to the Christ Church Cathedral, she managed to have Hughes crowned King of the May Day Spring Carnival.

"When I was fourteen I started to get erections when my mother bathed me," Hughes said. "She began to masturbate me to provide relief. Sometimes I'd go to her three or four times a day for her to masturbate me. It did bring me some relief and cut down on my nervousness."

He told Kate that he'd once heard one of the boys at school talk about what he'd gotten a girl to do with his penis, claiming she'd taken it into her mouth and "swallowed my seed." That night Hughes begged Allene to do that to him, but she adamantly refused.

"Instead she would take this pink porcelain bowl and approach me," Hughes said. "I always knew I had to spill my seed into that bowl." Hughes also claimed that sometimes his mother would approach him with the porcelain bowl even when he didn't want to be masturbated. "But I always came through for her, so to speak."

As Hughes grew older, he began to complain of all sorts of ailments. These included various chills and headaches, even "strange pains." When doctors examined Hughes in minute detail, they could find nothing wrong with him. "They told Allene that I was just imagining these ailments," Hughes said. "They even suggested hypochondria but Allene knew my pain was real in spite of what the doctors said."

"Sometimes I'd get a cold, and Allene would bring in three different doctors for consultation," he told Kate. "Once when I broke out with hives, she went into a screaming fit and had to be sedated."

218

Because Hughes did not gain weight like a normal child, Allene began to view her son as "delicate." Night after night she began to tell him that he was a girl trapped in a boy's body. At first he resisted, but in time he allowed his mother to dress him in beautiful dresses that she'd expensively purchased. This was always done in the privacy of her suite, and she never let even a servant witness her son dressed as a girl. "It was a very private thing between the two of us."

On the rare occasion that Hughes Sr. came home, Allene sent him to sleep in his upstairs study where she had installed a most comfortable bed for her husband.

Hughes told Kate that one day he woke up and couldn't move his legs. "At first Allene thought I had polio. She brought in every specialist in the country but they couldn't find the reason for my mysterious illness."

"The doctors could find no physiological cause but Allene knew something was wrong," he said. "Eventually with therapy I learned to walk again."

"Is that when you became deaf?" Kate asked.

"No, that was caused by a diving accident."

Hughes said that in a foolish move his parents decided to have another child in 1921, perhaps to compensate for the absence of her son when he was sent away to school.

Her body had been too ravaged by giving birth once before. But, ignoring the advice of her doctors, Allene wanted another son and demanded that her husband resume sexual intercourse with her. To make matters worse, in February of 1922, doctors discovered that Allene had a tubular pregnancy, where the fetus develops outside the uterus. Doctors pronounced her pregnancy life-threatening.

On March 29, 1922, Dr. Gavin Hamilton gave Allene a gas anesthetic before proceeding with the operation. But her heart stopped. She was thirty-nine years old at the time.

"I've never recovered from her death," Hughes confided to Kate.

The brief story of Hughes's childhood appealed to the caretaker side of Kate and she immediately decided, "I can help this man."

At first she'd planned to resist him and ask him not to fly into her life again, the way he'd done on the set of *Sylvia Scarlett*.

Now she was irresistibly drawn to him. When she related the events of the evening to Cukor and other friends, including Anderson Lawler, Kate said that Hughes was "like a little boy, so different from his playboy image. He doesn't need a woman in the sense that a regular man needs a mate. He needs a mother figure in his life. Since I'll never have a son, I might as well adopt him."

When Hughes in his private plane flew over Kate's house on the morning of the next day, he dipped his wings as if to acknowledge that they had embarked on what might be called a love affair.

It was to be the strangest relationship of Kate's life.

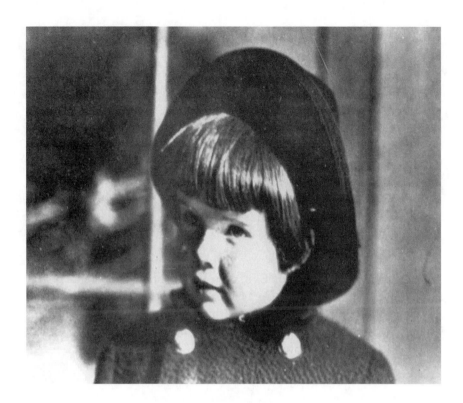

A SCANDALOUS FAMILY Kate at age four was born to maverick New England parents, Dr. and Mrs. Thomas Hepburn. "Neighbors considered my mother, Kit, a dangerous and wicked woman because of her unpopular political stands such as birth control," Kate said. Her doctor father could talk for hours about venereal disease, even when the ladies at tea called for their smelling salts.

THE TRAGEDY OF HER LIFE In their fetching antiseptic bonnets, Kate at age two is escorted through the Connecticut woods by her loving brother, Tom (left). He was her greatest friend and confidant, and grew into a handsome, athletic, and intelligent boy. His suicide by hanging during the Easter season of 1920 cast a long, dark shadow over her young life.

THE LIONESS IN WINTER AT 18 An intrepid tomboy who demanded to be called "Jimmy," Kate became withdrawn and morose after Tom's death. She developed and relished her eccentricities such as a lifelong passion of breaking into other people's homes to invade their privacy. Yet, if someone, especially the press, invaded her own privacy, she would often assault them.

GROUNDED Marion (center) and Peggy (right)-Kate's virtual double-were captured on film on the grounds of the Hepburn family home in 1940 as Kate was making a comeback with *The Philadelphia Story*. Kate always overshadowed her sisters and got them to wear pants when "respectable" young ladies did not. Rumors that the sisters were "insanely jealous" of their fabled sibling were just that--rumors.

MY DEFLOWERER That was Kate's pet name for the handsome young actor, Kenneth MacKenna, who took her virginity in 1928. On looking back years later, Kate said, "Someone had to do the dirty deed. Why not Kenneth?" They became lifelong confidants, each sharing the secrets of a bisexual life with each other. On one occasion they ended up seducing the same man--Douglas Fairbanks Jr.

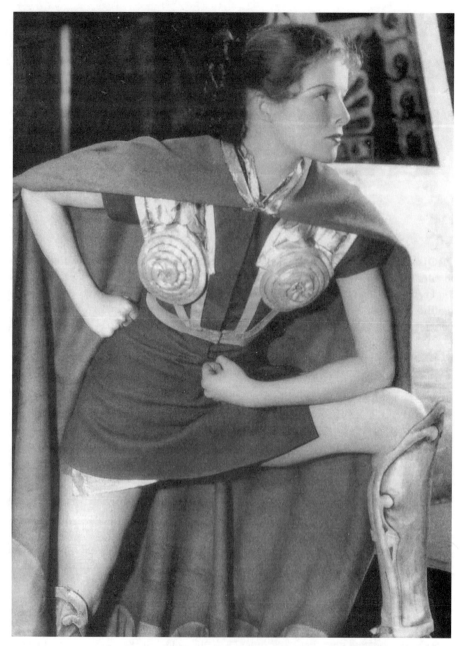

MOVE OVER MADONNA With athletic prowess and a masculine demeanor, Kate viewed her 1932 sex-role reversal comedy on Broadway, *The Warrior's Husband*, as "putting on a leg show." She was perfect as an Amazon who keeps her husband in place. She brought down the house in one scene where, to show her physical agility and strength, she lifted one actor over her head. The breast-plated heroine initially told Hollywood talent scouts, in rather impolite terms, where they could stash their Hollywood contracts

THE RELUCTANT CELEBRITY Snapped on the streets of New York near her rented townhouse (which she later bought) in 1934, Kate hated having her picture taken at random. Often she'd grab the camera of the photographer and smash it. Here her determined face endures what she viewed as an assault on her privacy. At this point in her life she was living with her homosexual husband and his lover.

MILITANT CRUSADER Kit Hepburn, Kate's mother, was one of America's leading advocates of women's suffrage. Waving a placard, young Kate often paraded in protest marches with her mother, including one to shut down the brothels of Hartford--not because of moral reasons, but as a means of preventing the spread of venereal disease. Kit was also a disciple of Margaret Sanger in the advocacy of birth control.

BUTCH NUMBER

"My role model," was the way Kate later described lesbian actress Hope Williams when she appeared in the leading role of *Holiday,* the comedy by Philip Barry that opened in 1929 at Brodway's Plymouth Theatre. As Williams' understudy for the role of Linda Seton, Kate waited in the wings every night, studying her every move, hoping for the actress to break a leg or at least an ankle. To defy Kate, Williams went on even when sick.

ONE NIGHT STAND

After her aborted romp in the hay with actor Leslie Howard, Kate could never understand why Scarlett O'Hara in *Gone With the Wind* pined for his character of Ashley Wilkes. "Thank God," Kate told George Cukor after seeing the movie, "that Miss Scarlett never actually went to bed with Ashley. She would have been so disappointed." After he seduced Kate, the London-born actor was so disappointed with her that he fired her from the 1931 play, *The Animal Kingdom.*

"I NEVER GOT INTO HIS BATHING TRUNKS" That was Kate's sad lament when she arrived in Hollywood and briefly dated handsome leading man Joel McCrea. The two stars were to appear in a film together, *Three Came Unarmed*, but script problems arose and the movie was never made. Kate later recalled, "I think he was in love with Gary Cooper at the time--who wasn't?--but Frances Dee was waiting in the wings."

NAUGHTY BUT NICE In 1933, one of Kate's alltime most successful films, *Little Women* teamed her with Joan Bennett (on the left) whom she hated; Jean Parker (whom she ignored, second from left), and Frances Dee (far right), who did succeed in getting those bathing trunks off McCrae. That's Kate, of course, with the leering grin (second from the right). Playing the hoydenish Jo March, Kate won favorable reviews--except one. Critic Philip Barnes claimed that "Louisa May Alcott is turning over in her grave."

THE TOSCANINI OF THE TELEPHONE Deal maker, super agent, and super stud, Leland Hayward, was Hollywood's hottest agent in the Thirties. Clients ranged from Ernest Hemingway to Judy Garland, including Kate herself. When Hayward was not seducing Garbo, or Kate was not seducing Garbo, Hayward became Kate's magnetic lover until "that dreaded fiend" [Kate's words] Margaret Sullavan, stole him away from her.

"THAT GOD DAMN MOTH COSTUME" Kate's assessment of her alltime most famous costume, worn in the 1933 RKO picture, *Christopher Strong*, was negative, but it turned out to be the best thing in the picture. Around the RKO lot, the movie about a female aviatrix, as played by Kate, was nicknamed *Sapphos on Parade*. The reference was to the lesbianism of Kate herself, her director (Dorothy Arzner), her co-star (Billie Burke), and the scenarist, the notorious Zoë Akins.

THE VAMPIRE OF BROADWAY Broadway producer Jed Harris, in a characteristic pose with a cigarette, liked to receive business clients-male or female-in his offices stark naked. He often seduced his leading ladies, including Ruth Gordon (with whom he had a son), and he sometimes forced actors to perform fellatio on him, especially if they were straight. Kate's best friends claimed that Jed Harris was Kate's only S&M love affair--"that is, if you could call anything with Harris love," in the words of Helen Hayes.

CALL IT INCEST Kate made her film debut in the 1932 film, *A Bill of Divorcement*, with John Barrymore playing her mentally unbalanced father. According to Hollywood legend, The Great Profile invited Kate to his dressing room, pulled off his clothes, and suggested that the two of them "get on with it." Legend has it that Kate ran shrieking in to the afternoon, claiming her father didn't want her to have any babies. The truth? Both Barrymore and Kate later admitted that he succeeded with his seduction plans, "but only on the second attempt."

TO SHOW OR NOT TO SHOW BASKET That was the question for Douglas Fairbanks Jr. when he appeared in the balcony scene of Romeo and Juliet with Kate in the 1933 *Morning Glory*. Fairbanks told Kate that John Barrymore, his pal, always claimed that whenever he stuffed a sock into his green tights, theater attendance rose. Kate advised the young actor to "wear a jock strap so as not to distract from my performance as Juliet." Despite her precautions, the scene ended up on the cutting room floor.

THE TRUE LOVE OF KATE'S LIFE American Express heiress, Laura Harding, began her romance with Kate in 1928 and the love affair, even after passion's fire died, lasted until Harding's death in 1994. Kate took Harding with her on her honeymoon with her husband, Ludlow Ogden Smith, as well as his male lover. Kate told friends that Laura might as well go along on her divorce trip, too. They are pictured at the New York airport waiting for their flight to Miami where they would sail to Mexico for the divorce.

"DON'T BE A MUG" That was the advice from Ernest Hemingway when he heard that Kate planned to elude the press as the ocean liner, *S.S.Paris*, sailed into New York harbor. Fresh from her ocean-going affair with him, she agreed to put on a "crimson slash of lipstick" and to "face those beastly cameramen." For Don Ernesto, it was only a shipboard romance that Kate took too seriously. When he dumped her, Kate told friends, "At least he went for me-and not Marlene." The woman Hemingway called "The Kraut" (Marlene Dietrich) also sailed on the homebound journey.

SPITFIRE--BAD ACTING, BAD PICTURE After seeing the final cut of the 1934 box office bomb, *Spitfire,* associate producer Pandro S. Berman asked director John Cromwell, "What idiot thought to cast Hepburn, with her Bryn Mawr accent, as Trigger Hicks?" A good question. Pictured above with Sara Haden (left), Kate played a hillbilly yokel of hopeless ignorance---hot tempered, uncouth, a warmhearted hoyden and a rustic. She was given such lines as "consarned Son of Satan." This Ozark Lizzie should probably have been played by Judy Canova.

A CONTINENTAL NOSE JOB *Break of Hearts*, the 1935 RKO release, was another disaster for Kate, although it launched her into a brief affair with her co-star, Charles Boyer. Kate was momentarily intrigued with the seductive sound of this Frenchman's Gallic voice, that and his heavy-lidded look with dark eyebrows. Today, he's mimicked and ridiculed for a line he never said in *Algiers* ("Come wiz me to ze Cashbah"). Kate didn't find him a joke at all, but the audience didn't buy this modern-day romantic piffle.

SHARING JUICY HOLLYWOOD TIDBITS Tossed aside after his long affair with Gary Cooper, actor Anderson Lawler met Kate around George Cukor's pool. They became "confidants for life." If Kate needed to know something, Lawler was the first man she called. Usually he'd already called her first. Kate once expressed a desire to find a person in whom she could speak frankly about her sexual affairs. In Lawler, she found that man. Tallulah Bankhead also used Lawler-"and everybody else"-as her confidant as well.

"THAT DYKEY BITCH" That was rival Margaret Sullavan's opinion of Kate when she saw this RKO released photograph of Kate. When Pandro S. Berman spotted the photograph, he asked that it be recalled. "We're not filming The *Well of Loneliness*," he told the publicity department, referring to the best known lesbian novel of its day. Berman ordered the department to take some "cheesecake pictures" of Kate to counter this hard-bitten Sapphic image of his star.

SEX KITTEN! RKO at first didn't know what to make of its new $1,500-a-week contract player. So they decided to pose her like a sultry siren with plunging *décolletage*. On viewing the studio glossies, Kate said, "There's nowhere to plunge."

"ONE OF THE BEST MALE BODIES" That was Kate's assessment of Fred MacMurray, the first day she encountered her co-star resting in the sun without his shirt on the set of the 1935 *Alice Adams*. Of course, she was speaking of the physique standards of her date. MacMurray filled out and developed his chest even more in the years ahead. Kate found him a "real catch," but they soon drifted apart.

THE POSEUSE (HEPBURN) & THE VIRILE ROCK (MacMURRAY) In her famous frontporch scene with Fred MacMurray, Kate gave one of her most memorable performances playing *Alice Adams*, a young, ambitious woman striving for social recognition. Her interpretation of the Booth Tarkington heroine, who was actually a klutz, won Kate her second Academy Award nomination. Even though initially attracted to MacMurray, Kate eventually gravitated to her director, George Stevens, finding that in spite of his rather bland façade "he was all fire and brimstone when you peeled off his layers."

SEXUAL AMBIGUITY Thinking Kate is a boy, actor Brian Aherne, in the gender-bending film, *Sylvia Scarlett*, seems enchanted. The picture bombed, but Kate was hailed as the handsomest boy of the year. The homosexual overtones of George Cukor's direction was largely lost on the Thirties audience. Cary Grant, a study in sexual ambiguity himself, stole the picture with his bitingly humorous role of a Cockney ne'er-do-well.

THE NYMPHOMANIACAL SOUTHERN MAGNOLIA Kate's nemesis, Margaret Sullavan, was called a "rude, contrary, spiteful bitch" by columnist Louella Parsons.

She stole Leland Hayward from Kate. He later confided in Kate that he regretted the marriage. "She castrates a guy," Hayward says. "Makes him feel like two cents-and two inches." Maggie was said to have invented highway pickups before they became fashionable. She waited in her car and blinked her lights whenever she saw a virile, handsome guy walking by.

"ALL ACTORS ARE CRAP." Director John Ford had harsh words for his performers, but fell big for Kate in spite of his initial judgement. A heavy-drinking Irishman of few words and a political reactionary, John Ford became the "third most important love" of young Kate's life, after Laura Harding and ultimately Spencer Tracy. Kate failed in her attempts to pay off Mary Ford, offering her $150,000 if she'd give John his freedom. Mary booted Kate out the door.

THE RUDE SURPRISE UP KATE'S DRESS Handsome Fredric March was cast by John Ford as Kate's co-star in the badly received 1936 film, *Mary of Scotland.* March viewed it as "obligatory" to make passes at his leading ladies. His reputation had preceded him when he entered Kate's dressing room to seduce her. As he later told producer Pandro S. Berman, "My God, I reached up her dress and felt nine hard inches-maybe ten. Kate Hepburn is a man after all!" What March felt was actually an unripened banana Kate had placed there waiting for his roving hand.

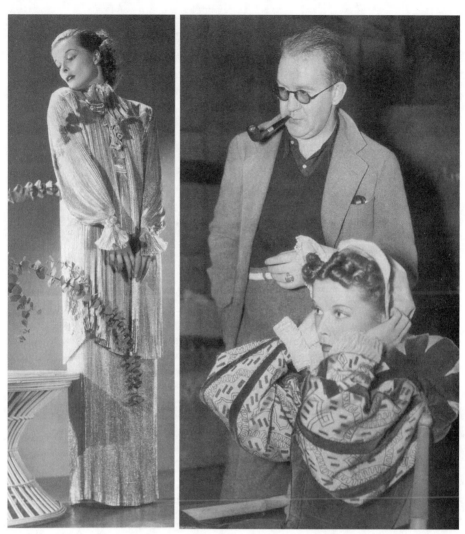

"A DRIED UP BOOT" Acid-tongued Cecil Beaton, known for his glamorous portraits, had nothing but praise for Kate's beauty when he photographed her in the mid-Thirties. Seeing her in later years, he changed his opinion. "Her appearance is appalling, a raddled, rash-ridden, freckled, burnt, mottled, bleached and wizened piece of decaying matter. It is unbelievable, incredible that she can still be exhibited in public."

"HALF-TYRANT, HALF-SAINT, HALF SATAN, HALF-GENIUS" Trying on her *Mary of Scotland* bonnet, Kate sits as her lover, pipe-smoking John Ford stands. He had discovered Spencer Tracy on Broadway in the early Thirties, and thought Tracy could make it as a film star, even though not particularly good looking. But when he tested Kate, then appearing in *The Warrior's Husband*, he later concluded that she had no sex appeal at all. By the time he'd cast her in *Mary of Scotland*, Ford had changed his mind. She found him "wayward and odd." He responded with flattery, letting John Wayne know that "Kate Hepburn is the kind of woman a man could *almost* leave his wife for."

"SEEMINGLY SLEEPY BUT INTENSELY WATCHFUL" That's how Kate found her director George Stevens when they teamed together to make an ill-fated costume drama, *Quality Street*, in 1937. Kate later told her confidants that "George is a perfect example of the adage that still waters run deep." She never quite explained exactly what she meant by that. The director not only propelled her through the picture but skillfully lured her to his bed where she would remain--on and off--for years until she met Spencer Tracy. Of course, there was the matter of "the invading praying mantis," as Kate said of her rival, Ginger Rogers.

JAWBREAKER Her male co-star in *Quality Street* was the suave, sophisticated Franchot Tone, married at the time to Joan Crawford. With his looks, education, and breeding, Kate found Tone appealing, but she didn't fall in love with him as Bette Davis did when they filmed *Dangerous* in 1935. After a one-night stand with this super-endowed Hollywood stud, Kate pronounced him "too much man for me," sending him back home to Crawford.

CHEEK-TO-CHEEK Ginger Rogers and Kate Hepburn hardly manage to conceal their loathing for each other when they made *Stage Door* in 1937. Kate had utter contempt for "Miss Ginger Snap," and often told friends, "If you have anything good to say about Ginger Rogers, don't say it in my presence." Kate found herself competing with Rogers for some of the same men--Howard Hughes, George Stevens, Jimmy Stewart. Kate went after Ginger's husband Lew Ayres, but Howard Hughes got to him first.

GARBO? NO, HEPBURN Shielding her face from photographers (they weren't called *paparazzi* back then), Kate was consistently voted the most uncooperative actress in Hollywood by the members of the women's press corps. Columnist Hedda Hopper once said, "The damn dyke always claimed that she wanted nothing more than to be famous. Once famous, she went psychotic whenever someone tried to take her photograph. You figure! Dames. I'm glad I'm not one!"

DON'T ASK, DON'T TELL Kate and Cary Grant, the two most closeted bisexuals in the history of Hollywood, appeared together again in the 1938 Columbia film, *Holiday,* for which Kate had once understudied Hope Williams on Broadway. Both Kate and Cary spent their lifetime denying who they were for career reasons. When Kate was living at the Muirfield estate of Howard Hughes, Cary was his bedtime partner--not Kate.

"THE GRANDE DAME OF ALL WEST-ERN DYKES" Noël Coward was talking about veteran actress, Constance Collier (right), more than he was referring to Kate. When the two actresses came together to make *Stage Door* in 1937, they embarked on a lifelong love affair. Nonsexual, that is. Kate was constantly attacked for her voice and her Bryn Mawr diction, and Constance struggled valiantly to help her overcome some of her worst problems. The skilled thespian even taught Kate how to play Rosalind in Shakespeare's *As You Like It.*

"HOLLYWOOD'S MOST HAPPILY MARRIED COUPLE" This was Joan Crawford's assessment of Cary Grant and Randolph Scott photographed in a cozy scene when they lived together. Crawford had also made the same assessment of the "marriage" of actor William Haines and his lover, Jimmie Shields. Kate and Laura Harding were often guests of Grant and Scott when they were live-in lovers, until studio pressure forced them to live separately and even get married to women. It was suggested that Kate, Laura, Randy, and Cary go out on double dates to confuse snoopy columnists, who'd accurately hinted at the time that all four of them might be homosexuals, or at least bisexuals.

CRAZIEST! WACKIEST! SCREWIEST! *Bringing Up Baby,* which co-starred Kate once again with Cary Grant, flopped upon its release in 1938 but later built up a cult audience. Before Kate had ever appeared in a film with Cary Grant, much less a leopard, Marlene Dietrich warned her about how foolish it was to fall in love with a homosexual. Kate became Cary's friend instead, although George Cukor felt the relationship was more "like two sisters."

THE SUPER AGENT & THE ÜBER BITCH Fans loved Ginger Rogers, who top-
pled Kate as Queen of RKO. To retaliate, Kate taught Rogers the real meaning of a high
kick. After Kate's boot, the blonde-haired beauty ended up in the hospital. The
dancer/actress was always stealing Kate's men--most notably, deal broker Leland
Heyward who proposed marriage to both women on the same day!

A BATHING SUIT FOR A CHANGE   Emerging in a bathing suit from George Cukor's pool, the elusive Swede, Greta Garbo, preferred swimming in the nude the way they often did in her native Stockholm.   When Kate first met Garbo, it was Kate who was nude emerging from the same pool.   George Cukor provided the introductions. Garbo and Kate became sometime lovers and forever friends.   "Both women carried their privacy to psychotic limits," said Anderson Lawler.

"A MARRIED MAN WHO IMPREGNATES HER"   Van Heflin did not have the conventional good looks of the "usual" leading man, but he captured Kate's fancy when she saw him in a play on Broadway.   She recommended that RKO cast him as the married man who impregnates her in her 1936 film, *A Woman Rebels*.   She launched an affair with Heflin that did not survive beyond the bed.   Remembering him, she later lobbied to get him cast in the role of the reporter in the stage version of *The Philadelphia Story*.   When she did not insist to its producers that he be cast in the screen version as well, Heflin broke off relations with her.

AN ENIGMA WITH MANY FACES Kate's "romance of the century," as hailed in the press, with Howard Hughes was a sham. The bizarre aviator and tycoon had far more emotionally incestuous ties to his once beautiful but dead mother than he ever did with Kate. Hughes hated to pose for pictures unless he was standing in front of an airplane. The picture (center, bottom of the page) is one of the few ever taken of Hughes with a smile on his face. "Stinking like rotting horseshit," his own words, Hughes is seen in the back seat of a limousine with New York's Mayor Fiorella LaGuardia after his grueling but record-breaking flight around the world.

SEXY, SHOCKING, SCANDALOUS Both Howard Hughes and Katharine Hepburn led complex, mysterious, action-packed lives. But, contrary to thousands of published reports, their so-called love affair was one of the most misunderstood of the century, ranking right up there with the Duke and Duchess of Windsor. Hughes did ask Kate to marry him, but at the same time he had proposals out to Joan Fontaine, her sister Olivia de Havilland, and Ginger Rogers. Kate told her friends that she thought Cary Grant would be a more suitable bride for Hughes. Pulp fan magazines, such as *Modern Screen,* gushed over this non-romance.

EMPTY WITHOUT YOU   In later years, the notorious lesbian letters between Eleanor Roosevelt and Associated Press reporter Lorena Hickok have been published. Although many of those letters were destroyed, enough have remained to reveal the passion between those two remarkable women. Beginning in the early 1940s, the First Lady also wrote equally passionate letters to Katharine Hepburn. It was an unrequited love affair, the outpouring of affection coming mainly from the White House. When there was talk of Mrs. Roosevelt seeking the presidential nomination in 1948, Kate burned the letters "lest they fall into the wrong hands."

LOVE AT FIRST SIGHT One of Kate's longest and most enduring lesbian affairs was with Cecil B. DeMille's "alluring siren," the chic and totally feminine French actress, Claudette Colbert. Kate found her "incandescent." Colbert, winner of the 1934 Oscar for *It Happened One Night* opposite Clark Gable, is pictured here in costume for the film, *Zaza*, that big flop. Even famed Fanny Brice couldn't help Colbert in this role as a music hall trouper. Kate's affair with Colbert, with lots of other men and women in between, lasted for eight years. Then one night in 1948, the relationship came to an abrupt end. The scandal was hushed up.

BOYISHLY HANDSOME AND ON THE MAKE. He managed to elude the clutches of Marlene Dietrich, only to fall into Kate's arms where he "polluted myself" [his words]. Kate wasn't his only love. Jimmy believed in sharing the wealth with her two most dreaded female enemies--Ginger Rogers and Margaret Sullavan. Actor Wendell Corey once said of Jimmy: "There was a whopping big ego underneath that allegedly shy, stuttering, bumbling persona." Kate set out to discover what made him tick when the lights went out.

LOVE TRIANGLE In the 1940 *The Philadelphia Story,* Cary Grant, playing Kate's former husband, was supposed to be jealous of her new romantic fixation on handsome Jimmy Stewart. In real life, the scenario was different behind the scenes. The picture's director, George Cukor, desired Jimmy but knew he didn't have a chance. Cary Grant made his romantic intentions very clear to Jimmy, but was rebuffed. Kate, like the "charging bull" her father claimed that she was, went after Jimmy and got her man. Kate had competitors, of course. Even Noël Coward came onto the set and volunteered to help Jimmy get into his bathing trunks.

SEAFOOD CHOWDER FOR THREE Elliott Roosevelt (center), son of Franklin D. Roosevelt, served cups of New England style seafood chowder when the President invited Kate and other stars to his home at Hyde Park, north of New York City, in 1940. Freckles showing, with just a slash of lipstick, Kate shunned the specially commissioned train the president had arranged for his other guests, and arrived alone in a seaplane. Roosevelt discovered her, covered with mud, arguing with one of his security guards and gave her a lift in his limousine. Kate later learned that Eleanor became terribly jealous whenever one of her trusted friends paid too much attention to the President and not to her. If they did, Eleanor gave that friend the boot.

THE OBJECT OF THEIR AFFECTION On the set of the 1940 *The Philadelphia Story,* both Kate and George Cukor (right) wanted to "de-pants" Jimmy Stewart to learn what all the excitement was about. With her beauty and charm, Kate beat out the ugly director. But Kate's nemesis, Ginger Rogers, made off with the prize. The shy, lanky actor's reaction to both Kate and Ginger: "I polluted myself with both of them."

THE CURE FOR IMPOTENCE In spite of what the fan magazines proclaimed, the romance of Howard Hughes and Kate was going nowhere. Bette Davis, meeting the lanky, uncommunicative filmmaker and aviator at the Tailwaggers Ball in Beverly Hills in 1938, felt that she knew a secret way to get a rise out of this reluctant swain.

THE ODD COUPLE Spencer Tracy, who demanded top billing, was teamed for the first time with Katharine Hepburn in the highly successful 1942 *Woman of the Year.* This film would mark a string of Tracy/Hepburn movies [he always demanded top billing]-some good, some bad. It would also mark the beginning of Hollywood's most notorious pairing of lovers. Highly touted as one of the great romances of Hollywood, the coupling was anything but, and was marked by turbulence, infidelity, heavy boozing (on his part), and many a violent fight.

ANOTHER HOLLYWOOD ODD COUPLE Irene Mayer was the daughter of Louis B. Mayer, when she wed David O. Selznick, who is today primarily remembered as the producer of *Gone With the Wind.* Although she pretended to, Kate never forgave Selznick for his failure to cast her as Scarlett O'Hara in *Gone With the Wind.* The producer had been responsible for bringing Kate to Hollywood in 1932 to appear opposite John Barrymore in *A Bill of Divorcement.* Years from the date this picture was taken, Kate would begin an affair with Selznick's wife, Irene, Irene's only known lesbian relationship.

THOSE SMILES ARE MISLEADING Spencer Tracy's long-suffering wife was Louise Treadwell, an actress who met and married Tracy when they were both struggling in the theater. When a drunken Tracy was being particularly cruel to Kate, he claimed that Louise had been a much "better actress than you'll ever be." Louise and Tracy had two children, John and Susie. John was born deaf, and Tracy used his son's affliction to justify his heavy boozing on many an occasion. Contrary to hundreds of published reports, Louise knew of the Hepburn/Tracy affair from the beginning. Her reaction? "I'm going to be Mrs. Spencer Tracy until the day I die." And so she was.

THE UNHOLY TRIO George Stevens (center), with a pipe, directed Spencer Tracy and Katharine Hepburn in their first picture together, the 1942 *Woman of the Year* for Metro-Goldwyn-Mayer. In this rare photograph of the three of them, taken off-camera during the shooting of the film, Stevens seems to be carefully eyeing his male competition, Tracy. At some point, Stevens decided that Kate was falling in love with Tracy and bowed out. Up to then, he'd been dating her on and off. But before kissing her goodbye, he warned her that life with Tracy would be "living hell." She responded, "no more so than coming in unexpectedly and catching you buck naked in a bathtub with Ginger Rogers."

THE CANDLE DIDN'T BURN TOO BRIGHTLY In *Keeper of the Flame*, the second pairing of Spencer Tracy and Katharine Hepburn for Metro-Goldwyn-Mayer in 1942, the odd couple fizzled in this unlikely casting. Both Kate and Tracy, inspired by George Cukor, had set out to make another *Citizen Kane*, but Cukor was no Orson Welles. Cukor also lacked Alfred Hitchcock's talent for making a psychological thriller. The film was shot at the height of Kate's love affair with Tracy, before the onset of "the bad years."

"A WASTE OF FINE ACTORS' TIME" Spencer Tracy and Katharine Hepburn must have desperately needed a film role when they agreed to make *Without Love* in 1945. Kate knew Philip Barry's play well, having flopped with it on the stage. Nonetheless, her friend, writer Donald Ogden Stewart convinced both Tracy and Kate that he could rewrite the script and make a hit out of it. It was a promise made in vain. At the end of the war, the flower was off the bloom of the Tracy/Hepburn romance. They had begun to redefine their romance as something akin to an obsessive co-dependency.

"TWO CHINESE COOLIES"

In the decade's biggest case of miscasting, the exotic Turhan Bey--known among the ladies as "The Turkish Delight"--appeared with Kate in Pearl S. Buck's *Dragon Seed. The Good Earth* it wasn't. Bey once admitted to having what he called "the kind of crush on Katharine Hepburn that only a teenage boy can have for a movie star." Upon meeting, no sparks were ever generated either on or off camera. With Lana Turner, it was a different story--"Ecstacy, my dear! But not for every day."

BOX OFFICE POISON-- "If I can act, I want the world to know it. If I can't, *I* want to know it." After a string of failures at the box office in the mid- to late 1930s, the Independent Theatre Owners Association published a list of actors they considered "box office poison." Kate's name led the list. She was in distinguished company: Greta Garbo, Marlene Dietrich, Joan Crawford, *et. al.* In this photo, Kate parodies herself for having been tossed away in the garbage dump.

KATE'S "DATE RAPE"

When Kate met Robert Mitchum on the set of *Undercurrent* in 1946, she began by claiming she hated him and accused him of getting by on his good looks--not talent. The more she attacked him verbally, the more Hollywood's "most outrageous maverick" began to view her assault as a disguised form of physical attraction for him. One day in his dressing room, he proved to her how right he was. Going from hobo to star, Robert Mitchum turned out to be a "devil with women." Katharine Hepburn marked the beginning of his almost systematic seductions of movie queens.

BEHIND THE MOON AND OVER THE RAINBOW

When Judy Garland made a major revelation to Kate about what was really going on in her marriage to Vincente Minnelli, Kate befriended her and was touched by her beauty, poignancy, and pain. Kate fell in love with "Dorothy," and it became an enduring affair. The first person by Garland's side after her suicide attempt in 1950 was caretaker Kate herself. Kate's relationship with Garland went from the white heat of passion of 1946 to loving support by 1961 when an ailing Garland appeared with the ailing Spencer Tracy in *Judgment at Nuremburg.*

THE LAWN NEEDED MOWING Directed by young Elia Kazan, *The Sea of Grass* was the fourth Tracy/Hepburn film, this one also released by Metro-Goldwyn-Mayer. Kazan faced a lame script; footage of the grass already shot in Nebraska; a male star "with a ton of lard around his waist," and a female star who more or less directed herself. Kate overacted, and Tracy's underacting resembled boredom. He was also increasingly bored with their own relationship, and was patronizing male hustlers and seen dating an occasional woman on the side during the filming.

STATE OF THE DISUNION During the filming of the 1948 MGM film, Frank Capra's *State of the Union*, Tracy told his friend, George Cukor, that he'd rather be spending nights with his co-star, handsome Van Johnson, than with Kate herself. Right-wing critics found the movie "part of the Communist conspiracy." But when President Harry Truman, victim of several jabs in the film, claimed he liked it, the movie sailed by without any more protests. Claudette Colbert had been slated to play Kate's role, Mary Matthews, until "It" Happened One Night, and the two actresses never spoke to one another again.

TWO SUITORS ON AND OFF THE SCREEN In one of the worst career decisions of her turbulent career, Kate in 1947 signed to make the box office failure, *Song of Love,* co-starring two handsome leading men, Robert Walker (far left) and Paul Henreid (center). Kate was cast as the pianist, Clara Wieck Schumann, married to Robert Schumann (Paul Henreid) in the film but loved by Robert Walker, miscast as Johannes Brahms. Kate, Henreid, and Walker didn't even light a match on celluloid. But the sparks dazzled off screen.

"THE DUMB BLONDE" WITH THE IQ OF 172 Kate saw Judy Holliday as Billie Dawn on stage in Garson Kanin's play, *Born Yesterday*, and predicted to Spencer Tracy that she'd be a big star. Kate lobbied to get Holliday cast in the 1949 film, *Adam's Rib*, with Spencer Tracy and herself. Kate cajoled director George Cukor into "throwing the picture" to Holliday, which became film history's most elaborate screen test to win for her the Oscar-winning role in the screen version of *Born Yesterday*. Off-screen, Kate found the bisexual actress "mesmerizing" and invited the doomed comedienne for several "sleepovers" at her Turtle Bay townhouse in Manhattan.

THE BATTLE OF THE SEXES The movie-going public at the time of the 1949 film, *Adam's Rib,* had thoroughly confused the characters that the romantic pair played on screen with Tracy and Hepburn in real life. When the camera wasn't rolling, Tracy and Hepburn were going through the most painful and difficult time in their long-term relationship. His excessive drinking and violence made her want to flee from him. By the end of the Forties, both of them were dating other partners-- both male and female.

THE DECEIVING SMOOCH On screen this is a loving moment between Spencer Tracy and Katharine Hepburn as they appeared as battling attorneys in *Adam's Rib,* directed by their friend George Cukor. Their co-stars were stage actors Judy Holliday and Tom Ewell, playing an even more battling husband-and-wife team before the camera. The off-screen antics of the stars were also the stuff of high drama. Kate was falling madly in love with the bright, witty, and charming Judy Holliday. George Cukor, Tracy, and Tom Ewell were devoting their off-screen nights to the patronage of some of the most high-priced male hustlers in Hollywood.

THE WOMAN WHO GOT AWAY After the making of *Adam's Rib*, Judy Holliday virtually dumped Kate as a lover but wanted--even demanded--her lifetime friendship. At first, Kate was bitter, confiding to trusted friend Patricia Peardon that she'd been used by Holliday. Later, Kate forgave Holliday for her desertion and did indeed form a to-the-grave-friendship, Kate offering support and professional advice. Holliday often didn't listen to Kate and turned down her professional opinion that she should take the dumb blonde role in *Gentlemen Prefer Blondes*, which went to Marilyn Monroe instead.

THE TWO "MEN" IN HEPBURN'S LIFE A brief courtroom scene in *Adam's Rib* called for Judy Holliday to wear drag. Kate, playing an attorney, had asked the jury how they would judge Holliday's character of Doris Attinger, accused of shooting her husband, if she were a man. This rare photograph was taken off the set during the filming of this courtroom scene. Tracy suspected at the time that Kate's interest in Holliday was more than professional and had gone personal. But considering that he was secretly having an affair with Nancy Davis (later known as Nancy Reagan), and renting male hustlers on the side, he could hardly protest.

WHEN TITANS CLASH In the only known photograph ever taken of Katharine Hepburn dining at a public restaurant, Kate (far right) was snapped against her wishes, talking to Tracy (left), and her friend, the author and actress, Ruth Gordon (second from left), and her husband, playwright Garson Kanin. Their subject of conversation was the upcoming screenplay of *Adam's Rib*, co-authored by Gordon and Kanin. Kanin seems to have eyes only for Kate. He once confided to friends that his original intent was to marry Kate instead of his much older wife, Ruth. The Tracy/Hepburn household and the Gordon/Kanin household often clashed with each other--a deep but troubled friendship where they'd sometimes go for months without speaking.

TWO FALLEN KINGS With their jowls drooping, their drinking heavy, and their midriffs expanding, Spencer Tracy (left) and Clark Gable were by the late Forties no longer the box office champions of MGM. In this candid photograph, Tracy is telling Clark Gable that he is turning down the role of the mayor in the 1950 film, *A Key to the City.* Gable accepted the role instead. The female star of the picture was to be Loretta Young. Years before that, during the filming in 1934 and 1935 of *The Call of the Wild*, Gable had impregnated Young. She gave birth to a daughter out of wedlock and then pretended that she was the adoptive, rather than the biological, mother. Tracy had had an even more intense affair with Young in 1933 and briefly considered divorcing his long-standing wife, Louise, to marry her. He once told Gable, "I love Loretta more than I've ever loved Kate."

CHAPTER TEN

Howard Hughes had flown without warning into her life. After their bizarre dinner together, he had flown out just as mysteriously. She had no idea where he'd gone or when he'd be back.

Much more predictable was her steadfast friend, Jane Loring. She would always be a Kate's beck and call on any night she was needed, abandoning anything she was doing to rush to Kate's side.

After Hughes entered the picture, Kate felt that she'd neglected George Stevens. With great hesitation, on their most recent night together, he had told her that he was in love with her. She hadn't shared those same sentiments with him, but her lovemaking, at least according to what she told Cukor, "should be enough to convince any man that I care for him."

Stevens had given her the key to his home. When Hughes left with no good-bye note, Kate decided to drive over to the director's house and surprise him with a midnight love visit.

When she slipped in through his garden door, there was the thrill of adventure for her, like breaking into an unknown house. The lovely California night held out an erotic promise of adventure for her. In the living room, only a dimly lit night lamp was turned on. Straining her eyes, she tried to make out the contents of the room. George's car was parked in his driveway, so she assumed he was home, perhaps sleeping in his upstairs bedroom.

At the end of the hallway she saw another light, also dim. Since she'd been here before, she knew that light was coming from a large downstairs bathroom where she'd once showered with him.

With her heart beating with both fear and desire, she tiptoed down the hallway. The sound of splashing water signaled her that he was in his bathtub.

Before opening the door, she slowly removed all her clothing. When she'd spent the last night in his house, he'd surprised her in her shower when he stepped in stark naked. She'd do the same for him, gliding like a graceful white swan into the bubble bath waters with him.

To surprise him, she opened the door suddenly, discovering that the shimmering light came from a trio of candles resting in a wrought-iron holder placed on a marble table near the tub.

It was George Stevens all right, and he was in the tub naked. But the candles also revealed the soft features of a beautiful young woman sitting in the tub opposite him.

"Oh, dear," Kate said. "Please forgive the intrusion." She turned quickly and fled from the room, picking up her male clothing that she'd discarded in the hallway.

As she headed quickly to the living room, trying to dress herself as she did, he chased after her, clad only in a large terrycloth bath towel. "Kate, wait up! I can explain everything. It was a rehearsal—strictly business. There's a shampoo scene in the upcoming film, *Swing Time.*"

"Oh, George," she said, slipping into her pants. "Thank God you're a director and not an actor. You'd be so unconvincing on the screen."

"No, I'm perfectly serious," he said.

"What on earth are you talking about?" she asked.

"Pandro Berman is going to sign a contract with me to direct the next Astaire and Rogers picture. For the shampoo scene, we were testing which shampoo would hold up under the intense lights on the set."

"Those lights weren't intense," she said with tears in her eyes. "If memory serves, they were gently flickering candlelight."

Suddenly, a female voice chimed in. It was the mystery woman from the bathtub, her question sounding like an accusation. "Surely you have no objection to my keeping Georgie company while you're flying around with Howard Hughes?" George went over and turned on the living room lights. By that time, Kate had haphazardly slipped on her clothes.

Standing before her in a pink *négligée*, with lots of shampoo in her hair, was Ginger Rogers.

* * *

The following morning, after a sleepless night wherein even Jane Loring could not offer Kate comfort, she was summoned to the second-floor offices of Pandro S. Berman.

Driving to the studio, Kate could not make up her mind. Did she hate Margaret Sullavan more than she hated Ginger Rogers? On this particularly dreary morning in Los Angeles, Rogers had moved to the top of her shit list.

Ushered into Berman's office, Kate received some stunning casting news.

"Bette Davis wants to play Elizabeth, although John Ford laughed at the idea," Berman said.

"The part is much too small for her."

"But it's a great role, and Bette wants to appear in a cameo," he said. "When a star as big as Davis wants to be in a film at little old RKO, who am I to say no?"

Kate had been summoned to the office to wait for a call from Jack Warner. He was to make the final decision about whether he'd let Davis appear as Elizabeth.

Right on time, at ten o'clock, the call came in from Warner. With Kate standing by, Berman took the call from his rival studio chief. After talking for a few minutes, Berman put down the phone and turned to Kate. "'No way in hell' is Jack's final word. Davis is off the picture."

"Great!" she said. "That means that scene-stealer won't steal a scene from me, and God knows the cow would try."

"You're not off the hook yet," he warned her. "Guess who's arriving this morning demanding a screen test with you? Ginger Rogers wants to play Elizabeth."

With memories of her last encounter with Rogers raging through her head, Kate burst into laughter. "You've got to be kidding. A chorus gal?"

"That's exactly the point," he said. "Ginger has great ambitions as an actress. She's tired of always being taken for a dancing fool, whirling around with Astaire. She wants to prove that she can carry a strong dramatic role."

"Surely you're not casting this dyed blonde floozie as Queen Elizabeth?" she asked. "I'm astonished at your judgment."

"Ford would never go for it," he said, "but I've got to at least seem to comply with her wishes. I hate to say this, old gal, but it's those Astaire and Rogers films like *Top Hat* that are keeping this studio afloat. Not Katharine Hepburn pictures. Should I mention *Spitfire*? What about *Sylvia Scarlett*?"

"I guess I deserved that," she said.

"I want you to cooperate with me and Ford in every way on this picture and make it a hit," he said. "You're not a bankable star. I know I threatened never to work with you again. Consider yourself lucky that I bought *Mary of Scotland* for you. On this film, you've got to listen to Ford's direction. He's a great director. Your first assignment is to make a screen test with Ginger Rogers."

"I appreciate your support of me," she said. "All right, I'll be Mary meeting her Majesty, Queenie Rogers. I'm surprised, though, because I heard that George Stevens is directing Ginger in her next picture with Astaire."

"You heard right," he said, "but that's not happening right now. First, I've assigned Stevens to do *Annie Oakley* with Babs Stanwyck."

"At least that lady won't be trying to get into George's pants like Rogers," she said.

"Be careful about defining Stanwyck as a lez," Berman said. "No one really knows for sure."

"Hell, Marjorie Main told me she's slept with Stanwyck."

"Marjorie Main! Now you've got to be kidding."

"Main didn't always look like a broken down old washerwoman. She was once a chorine on Broadway."

"You could have fooled me," he said. "Now that you brought it up, what's the truth about you and my film editor, Jane Loring? I've heard talk. And what about you and Laura Harding?"

"You know how Hollywood gossip is," she said.

"I've got a lot of RKO's money riding on you," he said. "If there's a lesbian scandal about you, it could sink our ship."

"Trust me, Pandro," she said. "I am not a lesbian."

He thought for a minute, studying her carefully. "You're a very bright woman, and I think you might have worded that very cleverly. Perhaps you're not a lesbian. But you didn't deny that you're bisexual."

At that moment, as if on cue, Rogers herself called up through the open windows of Berman's office. "Pandro, I'm here. I'm going to my dressing room to get ready for my test. Is the Hepburn creature here as well?"

Kate appeared at the open window to Berman's office. She was startled to see that Rogers was attired in a stunningly beautiful mink coat.

"Lovely, isn't it?" Rogers asked Kate.

Kate made no comment but turned and walked away, as Rogers chatted with Berman. (In her memoirs, *Ginger My Story*, Rogers wrote that is was George Stevens' office, not Berman's.)

In about two minutes, Kate returned with a pitcher of ice water. She held it out the window and poured its chilly contents onto Roger's coat.

Screaming in horror, Rogers stepped back from the building and began brushing away this totally unanticipated shower.

"If it's real mink," Kate said, "it won't shrink! See you on the set!"

***

Before Berman had acquired *Mary of Scotland* for Kate, she'd patched things up with Laura Harding in New York and had gone to see the Maxwell Anderson play on Broadway. The play was the success of the 1933-34 season. Both Laura and Kate had been impressed with Helen Hayes playing Mary Stuart and another Helen, Helen Menken, the ex-wife of Humphrey Bogart, appearing as Elizabeth.

Kate and Laura had gone backstage to congratulate Hayes after the show. Unexpectedly the two women had encountered Tallulah Bankhead. Tallulah was there to meet Menken, not Hayes. "Helen Menken and I are having a hot affair," Tallulah confided to Kate and Laura. "Humpy Bogart could never satisfy her the way I can. Both of you darling girls will have to call me up one night. We'll have a wicked three-way that will be truly delicious."

Laura was horrified at Tallulah's suggestion, but Kate merely shrugged it off, as she had long ago grown used to Tallulah's outrageous behavior.

After Tallulah left to round up Menken, the stage manager introduced Kate and Laura to Fredric March, who was co-starring with Helen Hayes, playing the Earl of Bothwell, a role he would eventually portray in the film version as well.

Helen Hayes had seemed reluctant that night to allow Kate into her dressing room, but finally, she agreed to at least open the door. "Oh, my dear," Hayes said to Kate, ignoring Laura. "I know why you're seeing the play. You want to do the screen version for Pandro Berman, I'm sure. You're too late. Louis B. Mayer has already acquired the rights, and he called me yesterday to tell me

I've been cast. Perhaps you'll play Helen Menken's role of Elizabeth. Although after seeing you in *The Lake*—I noticed you didn't take my warning about Jed Harris—I think Mr. Mayer had better stick with Menken." The First Lady of Broadway abruptly shut the door in their faces.

***

Since Mayer did not follow through with his tentative offer to acquire the rights to *Mary of Scotland*, Berman moved in quickly and grabbed the property.

Because of that, Kate, dressed as Mary Stuart, found herself seated on an RKO sound stage at a long, draped refectory table with Ginger Rogers, lavishly dressed as a fully aged and made-up Elizabeth Tudor.

Although Kate, Berman, and John Ford were aware of a ruse Rogers played, the star had insisted on fooling the crew of *Mary of Scotland*. She showed up on the set using a pseudonym, Lady Ainsley, claiming she was a British actress. She wore a plastic skull cap which stretched to her eyebrows, creating an arched and very high forehead like the real Elizabeth. In ghostly white makeup, she appeared with a slit-like mouth and narrow, beady eyes. With a mammoth, stiff and very starched white ruffle around her neck, Rogers sat quietly under Kate's stern glare.

"You don't look like any God damn Queen of England to me," Kate said to Ginger. "And why all this pretense that you're some British aristocrat who likes to act on the side? And that phony British accent sounds like pure Missouri to me."

"I am from Missouri and you know that already," Rogers said.

Ford had chosen to remove himself from the set that day, not wanting to get involved in what he called a potential "cat fight" between two rival stars. He assigned the nonspeaking test to his photographer and cameraman, Joseph H. August, who, although he usually remained diplomatic and detached on the set, was later to report on the dialogue he'd heard between Kate and Rogers.

Since there was no sound recording, August encouraged the two stars to talk about anything they wanted.

"I enjoyed your performance in *Morning Glory*," Rogers said, "and I'm looking forward to working with you on *Mary of Scotland*."

"I don't think that day will ever come," Kate said. "Thank you for liking one of my performances. Sorry I can't say the same about one of yours. But I haven't seen any of your films. I don't go to chorus gal films. You may not know this, but I turned down William Seiter when he offered me *In Person*. Dreadful script."

"That role called for me to wear false teeth in some scenes," Rogers said. "You would have looked idiotic with false teeth, but I pulled it off because I have talent as a comic. I'm very versatile. Dancer, dramatic actress, and comedienne. *Some* big names in Hollywood can hardly get through a dramatic role, much less do anything else."

Without warning, Kate kicked Rogers in her shins with her booted foot. Rogers screamed in pain.

"Who do you think you're fooling with your stupid disguise and that dreadful accent?" Kate asked. "You're just a two-bit whore. No style. No class. Your kind is a dime-a-dozen in Hollywood. You're not a serious actress. I hear you're a good cock-sucker though. I also hear your husband sucks cock even better."

Kate was referring to actor Lew Ayres.

Rogers later said that she'd never heard such an outburst from a fellow star. "Her look was that of a cat ready to pounce on the canary, and I was the canary. History was reversing itself, 'Mary' was going to behead 'Elizabeth!'"

August called a halt to the screen test. "Ford wanted to see how you two interacted together. We've seen that."

Kate abruptly left the set. Rogers remained behind, complaining of pain. Hearing the news, Berman rushed to the set to personally examine Rogers' damaged leg. He viewed her legs as "RKO's biggest money maker."

Fearing any damage, Berman ordered his associates to call an ambulance and have Rogers sent to the hospital for a thorough examination.

"You make her pay for this," Rogers warned Berman.

"I'll settle with Kate," he promised, although he never mentioned the incident to his other star.

Two weeks later, at the urging of Fredric March, Berman and Ford agreed to cast Florence Eldridge, March's wife, as Queen Elizabeth.

Fast forward to the Cocoanut Grove nightclub in 1982, where Bette Davis chatted with Ginger Rogers after Davis was honored with the American Movie Award as a token of her fifty-four years in show business. Both women laughed when they recalled they'd vied for the same role in Ford's *Mary of Scotland* back in 1936.

Although wearing her seventy-one years gracefully, Rogers told Davis, "You and I are two old broads now, either of whom could play the role without makeup. Back in 1936 Mel Burns at RKO would have had to age our faces."

In a rare moment of kindness to a fellow actress, Davis replied, "I could play Elizabeth as I look today. You're still far too young. They'd have to paint wrinkles on your face like they did with Gloria Swanson in *Sunset Boulevard.*"

***

Before shooting began on *Mary of Scotland,* Kate encountered John Ford coming out of a sound stage.

She was clearly bored hearing that he was one of the greatest, if not the greatest, American film director since D.W. Griffith. Unlike George Stevens,

226

who was inexperienced when he'd directed Kate, "Pappy" Ford, as he was called, had already scored successes with the 1931 *Arrowsmith*, starring Ronald Colman and Helen Hayes, and the 1934 *The Lost Patrol*, with Victor McLaglen and Boris Karloff. He'd directed Humphrey Bogart and Spencer Tracy in *Up the River* in 1930, and had even directed Kate's dearest friend, Kenneth MacKenna, in the 1930 film, *Men Without Women*, in which John Wayne had appeared in a smaller part. Ford's biggest success had come with the 1935 *The Informer*, which had brought an Oscar to Victor McLaglen as best actor of 1935.

Later in her life, Kate felt that Ford bore a striking resemblance to her father, although no one else shared that opinion. At the age of thirty-four, Ford did not resemble Dr. Hepburn in the slightest.

The director always smoked a small Irish clay pipe. He looked at the world through round spectacles with smoky lenses, his face almost hidden by a battered old felt hat dyed a palomino brown.

Every day he wore the same sweat-soaked blue shirt and the same pair of yellow trousers, which were piss-stained at the crotch. Like Howard Hughes, he held up these pants with an old necktie that should have been long retired. He always smelled of pipe tobacco and body odor.

She shook his hand and recalled her ill-fated but long-ago screen test with him in New York, in which she'd appeared as Antiope in *The Warrior's Husband*.

"You weren't any good in that test," Ford chastised her. "Maybe you'll do better in *Mary of Scotland*."

Her pride wounded, Kate thrust a copy of the magazine, *Liberty*, into Ford's hands. "Read what Adela Rogers St. Johns said about me only this morning."

Ford quietly and slowly read the remarks of St. Johns: "As vital as Mussolini, as natural as a small boy sitting on a fence, as honest as her own freckles, Katharine Hepburn is not only a great actress, and potentially the greatest we have ever had in this country, she is the finest type of girlhood and womanhood America possesses."

Taking the magazine from him, Kate turned and walked away, without saying another word.

Before filming began, Ford had seen every one of Kate's pictures. "I've studied that face from every angle," he told Berman. "That long neck. That defiant mouth. That sharply angular profile set off by a nose that looks like it was chiseled in stone. Those eyes...those eyes looking at you and judging you ferociously. As for the voice, God help us. How we're going to turn those broad Bryn Mawr vowels into something British, I honestly don't know."

"You're a man's director and she's a woman's woman," Berman told Ford. "I'll referee this one."

Berman had a point. Ford was known for his outdoor epics, and he'd never been cited for his direction of women, preferring to concentrate on his male actors and using his women as mere decoration. The hard-drinking, uncouth

227

Irishman was more at home with a Western than a picture about an event in Scottish history whose chief action pivoted around a woman.

Originally, Kate had demanded George Cukor for her director, but in this case Berman stuck to his vow to never make another picture with Cukor again. "I'll never re-team you two."

The first day of the shoot hadn't gone well at all. When Ford showed up, he was having what in time would be called "a bad hair day." He had just revisited his doctor, Harley Gunderson, who had originally diagnosed an enlarged liver and various symptoms attributed to his excessive drinking. "Every time you take a drink, you commit a slow suicide," Gunderson had warned him. Ford had promised Dr. Gunderson and also his wife, Mary, that he would never take another drop, but neither believed him.

Kate didn't help matters that day by arriving early on the set and sitting in the director's chair. Provocatively, she mimicked Ford by wearing a beaten-up old hat pulled down over her head to shield her eyes. Like Ford, she was smoking an Irish clay pipe.

Kate had even gotten four female members of the crew, including Jane Loring, to smoke a clay pipe too.

Ford went about his business of setting up the first scene. He pretended to take no notice of the women smoking.

During the first week of the shoot on *Mary of Scotland*, Kate and Ford circled each other like Indians surrounding a stagecoach in one of his westerns.

When she saw that it would be difficult to get him flustered, she warmed to him, and in a few days was calling him Sean, his actual name.

She was amazed at his directing or lack of directing. The scenarist, Dudley Nichols, had eliminated most of Maxwell Anderson's blank verse from the shooting script. Even so, Ford would rip up three pages of dialogue from Nichols and substitute some sparse lines that he'd make up right on the spot.

Kate was impressed with that. She was less awed when she had to deliver such silly lines as, "The gods set us tasks, my lord, what we must do."

Ford was not the most articulate of directors—in fact, at times he said nothing at all or used a pantomime and a grunt. The actor, Ward Bond, claimed that Ford had some silent way of conveying his message to an actor. "One time he came up to me and tied a red handkerchief around my neck, and I sort of instinctively knew what he wanted from me." Other actors, including John Wayne, called Ford's directing style "some sort of thought transference."

Ford with his stiletto tongue did attempt verbally to direct Kate, whom he called "half New England Puritan, half South Seas pagan." Several times he warned her "to stop it with those flaring nostrils." Once again, in a criticism she'd heard before, her style was compared unfavorably to the screen acting— "with nostrils flaring"—of Rudolph Valentino.

At one point, Ford told Kate, "When playing a queen, it's okay to be regal. Regal posturing, however, is quite a different matter."

228

She responded in anger, accusing him of being interested only "in glittering daggers, clanking swords, and galloping horses."

She echoed somewhat the same sentiment to Berman, claiming that Ford was paying too much attention to the spectacle of the film, especially its historical pageantry, and not devoting enough time to the development of her character, Mary. Berman sighed in despair. 'What can I, a mere studio boss, do at this point?"

Kate constantly complained to Ford that she didn't like the character she was playing. "Mary of Scotland was a silly ass," she said. "I think Elizabeth was justified in wanting her killed."

From afar, she sensed that Ford was a deeply troubled individual. She detested his stinking clothes but noticed that he always arrived on the set every day with a clean, linen handkerchief, no doubt inserted there every morning by Mary, his wife. "His nerves were so bad," Kate later recalled, "that he literally ate that handkerchief. By the time I invited him to tea at four o'clock, that piece of cloth looked moth-eaten."

Victor McLaglen, one of Ford's favorite actors, visited the set on the third week of shooting. Ford was still proud of his fellow Irishman for having won the Oscar for his appearance in *The Informer*, playing the dull-witted turncoat, Gypo Nolan.

McLaglen was very impressed with Kate, especially when she told him of her skills as a horseback rider. Kate though McLaglen was "a hell of a man," standing six feet, three inches, with jet-black hair and a twinkle in his blue-gray eyes. She later described him as a "British-born Wallace Beery" although she may have read that somewhere.

McLaglen warned her that on every film, Ford singled out a scapegoat. "He needs to test people. Be careful—you could become his scapegoat on this Mary picture."

Ford tried to amuse Kate with stories of how he'd encouraged McLaglen to drink heavily before filming scenes on *The Informer*. "As a result we got a real mental fog from Victor here—perfect for the movie."

Kate objected to the principle of that. "If you used alcohol to help him act the fool, then he shouldn't have won the Oscar." She got up and, in anger, walked away.

At one point, Ford grew tired of hearing Kate complain about what a skilled horsewoman she was—"not like those sissy cowboys you cast in your movies."

He had planned to use a stuntwoman, or perhaps a man disguised in a dress, but decided to take Kate at her word in one difficult scene.

The action called for Kate, in high-heeled pumps and a heavy, bulky gown, to bound down a flight of stone steps at breakneck speed and jump on the back of a stallion side-saddle and dart away.

"It was pure sadism on Ford's part that he demanded eleven takes from Kate," Jane Loring said. "He might have killed her. It was as if Ford was trying to destroy her spirit, sort of break her in."

At the end of the eleventh take, Ford came up to an exhausted Kate and said, "You're one hell of a woman. You'd probably make some man a fine wife if he could teach you who wears the pants in the family."

On yet another occasion, Ford no longer risked Kate's life but saved it. In one scene she was riding side-saddle at an incredible speed, seemingly unaware that she was approaching the large branch of a tree. At the very last minute, Ford shouted, "Kate, duck!" It was just in time to keep her from a possible decapitation. She later said that she was "eternally grateful" to Ford.

***

During the filming of *Mary of Scotland*, Kate—accompanied by Jane Loring—walked around the RKO lot with a little brown-colored monkey perched on her shoulder. The adorable primate was attached with a leash to the shoulder strap of her dungarees.

Ford was too sophisticated to ask Kate why she carried the monkey on her shoulder, pretending that he didn't find anything unusual about that. Finally, when he continued to pay no attention to the monkey, she told him that she rented it for three dollars a day, and that the monkey was highly trained.

"I hope so," Ford shot back, "Otherwise the star of my picture is going to have a shitty shoulder."

The director did give her some advice. "You'll attract even more attention if you strap the monkey to a high chair in the back seat of your car and ride around Hollywood."

Kate followed that advice, shocking local motorists, especially when she and Loring stopped for a red light. Astonishingly, the monkey had been trained to give friendly waves to motorists and to blow them a kiss.

As if the monkey didn't garner enough attention, Kate came up with another device to catch the eye. She insisted that Loring wear the same matching men's clothing that she did, and the film editor willingly complied.

To compound her reputation for eccentricities, Kate resumed breaking into Hollywood homes, especially if she spotted an open window. It seemed strange that a woman who valued her privacy—or at least said she did—would so willingly invade the privacy of others. With Laura Harding out of the housebreaking business, Kate found a willing new accomplice in Loring.

Loring later confessed that she was terrified at breaking into someone's home, fearing that they would be shot. She claimed she did it "just to humor Kate who became very ill tempered when I turned down her slightest request and threatened to cut off her love from me."

From the first moment they met, Ford and Loring virtually declared themselves "natural enemies." Ford complained to Berman that Kate had "forced the lez down my throat." He severely resented the closeness of the two women.

230

"Whenever I look for Kate," Ford said, "she's in a huddle with that mannish-looking bitch."

Ford was even more horrified when he saw how Loring was editing the film, and he paid several raging visits to Berman's office. When Berman agreed with Ford and threatened to fire Loring, Kate claimed she'd walk off the picture, shut down the whole production, and retreat back to Connecticut.

Ford's assessment of Loring as a film editor was that she had a certain brilliance about close-ups of Kate, but didn't have the slightest sense of the movie's dramatic flow. "She was interested only in saving scenes where Kate photographed beautifully, and she did this better than anybody else in the business. But she destroyed the finished product. After fighting many a losing battle, I threw in the towel. At one point, I became so exasperated with Kate that I asked her to direct a scene with March and went for a drink."

***

Kate and her extraordinarily handsome co-star, Fredric March, had no real chemistry between them, either on or off the screen. Although widely hailed as one of the finest stage and screen actors of his time, Kate was not impressed with March.

When learning that March had been cast opposite her, she bitterly complained, claiming she detested his Oscar-winning performance in *Dr. Jekyll and Mr. Hyde* in 1931. "I thought he was grotesque. All that slobbering all over his make-up. As Hyde, he seemed to devour all the scenery not nailed down."

Kate was later to praise the performance of Spencer Tracy when he tackled the same role in the 1941 version of *Dr. Jekyll and Mr. Hyde*, with his lover of the time, Ingrid Bergman. Kate loved Tracy's acting, and wrote to him praising his performance, in spite of the roasting he took from the critics that year. On the other hand, she despised Bergman's portrayal, as she did the actress herself.

On the set when forced to talk with March, Kate indulged in idle chit-chat. He told her that his favorite actor was Spencer Tracy. "He's the only actor who can match me on the screen. I'd like to be cast opposite him. It would be the greatest acting competition ever among men in Hollywood." March got his wish but had to wait until 1960 when the director, Stanley Kramer, cast both of them in *Inherit the Wind.*

Carole Lombard, who would make the highly successful *Nothing Sacred* with March in 1937, had met Kate at one of Cukor's parties. "March is known for making the obligatory pass at any pretty actress he meets, especially his leading lady," Lombard claimed. "Just like John Barrymore, and I don't need to enlighten you on The Great Profile. We've all been down that road."

Lombard said that March had once invited himself into her dressing room during a visit to her studio. "I was ready for the lothario. I wore a very sexy *negligée* and opened the door with my come-hither look. March wasted no time getting down to business. Within minutes I felt that smooth hand of his gliding up my thigh. A shocked look came on his face, and he suddenly withdrew his hand when he reached my honeypot. Without saying a word, he quickly got up and left my dressing room."

"I don't understand," Kate said. "Did he feel something he didn't like?"

"Instead of getting to feel my juicy pussy, he felt a big black dildo I'd artfully placed there," Lombard confessed.

Since his wife, Florence Eldridge, was rarely on the set, because her scenes with Kate were so small, March felt free on the third week of the shoot to invite himself into Kate's dressing room. Once he asked for an invitation, she deliberately appeared eager to see him in private.

Just as Lombard had described her own encounter with March, the actor within minutes was gliding his hand up the sixteenth-century costume worn by Kate. When he encountered not a vagina but a phallic object, he quickly withdrew his hand. With Lombard, he'd retreated from her dressing room. With Kate, he pretended that nothing happened and launched into a rather pedantic discussion of the roles they were playing.

When Kate next encountered Lombard, she told the actress that, "I was fresh out of dildos but I always keep a bowl of fresh fruit in the dressing room. I picked the largest banana I had and stuffed it inside my bloomers and held it in place with tape."

March never mentioned his fiasco in Lombard's dressing room, but he did spread the word around Hollywood that Kate was actually a young man. "When she played a boy in *Sylvia Scarlett*, that was no act."

Some people actually believed March, who claimed that he'd discovered Kate had a penis when she'd invited him to her dressing room to seduce him.

"I don't go that route," March said. "I may be the only heterosexual actor in Hollywood."

Although dismissed as ridiculous by most Hollywood insiders, the rumor about Kate being an actual man persisted for years until wiped away by fresher scandals.

***

Kate endured it for as long as she could, but at some point she felt compelled to confront Ford about his dirty clothes and body odor. "I'm known for taking six to eight cold showers a day," she said to him one day on the set in front of others, including the photographer, Joseph H. August, whom Ford had nicknamed Quasimodo. "May I ask you a personal question?"

"You can get as personal as you want," Ford said, "but you might not like what you hear."

"Perhaps it's the heat from all these lights," she said, "but when I get a downwind from you, I'm almost intoxicated by the aroma."

232

"That's the smell of pure testosterone," he chided her. "It's so strong an aroma that it makes weak women buckle at the knees. Do you know that even in the animal kingdom, bitches grow wild at the smell of a male crotch?"

"I've heard of such things," she said, "but I must request that if you're going to continue as the director of this picture, you've got to bathe at least once a day. It's more than a request, actually, a demand, really."

"If it's so God damn important to you that I take a bath, why don't you give me one yourself?"

As the cast looked on in astonishment to see if Kate would back down, she said. "That's fine with me. You won't be the first man I've bathed. I used to bathe my brothers, and I've assisted my own father in his bath. As soon as you shut down shooting for the day, I'm taking you home and giving you a serious rub down, perhaps with some lye soap."

"That's an offer I'm going to hold you to." Seeing that all the cast and crew were staring at them, Ford ordered everyone back to work.

True to his word, Ford left the set that afternoon with Kate, the scene witnessed by the jealous eyes of Jane Loring.

***

No one knows what took place that Friday night at Kate's home, but Ford emerged squeaky clean the following Saturday morning.

Shortly thereafter, he invited Kate to go sailing with him aboard the *Araner*, a double-masted sailboat stretching one-hundred and thirty feet. He'd bought it in 1934 for thirty-thousand dollars, naming it after the Aran islands of western Ireland, birthplace of his mother.

Even before she boarded, Kate had heard about it. Ford had taken members of his posse, including John Wayne, for sails up and down the coastline of Southern California and Mexico. Arriving at a port in Mexico, Ford would hire a mariachi band to trail his posse as they made their drunken rounds from whorehouse to whorehouse. Although Los Angeles had whorehouses, posse members preferred their counterparts in Mexico instead, partly because they could get very young teenage girls, sometimes no more that twelve or fourteen years old, at bordellos south of the border.

For the sake of appearances, Ford told Kate that she should invite a friend—"anybody but that Loring bitch," as a kind of chaperone. When Kate learned that the generally tolerant Ford had invited his longtime friend, George O'Brien, and not one of the more homophobic members of his entourage, she selected George Cukor.

With Cukor on her arm, Kate arrived at the pier wearing a white turtleneck and striped shorts. Her only makeup was a slash of scarlet-colored lipstick. For a present, she'd purchased Ford's favorite brand of pipe, having noticed that he'd gnawed through the stem of his old one.

On board, Kate and Cukor were introduced to the handsome George O'Brien, who was one of the leading players in Ford's casual stock company. He often cast the same actors again and again in his pictures.

Famous for his beefcake photographs, and known to have posed for frontal nudes, O'Brien was called "The Chest." He was fond of telling prospective dates, either male or female, "As you'll soon see tonight, there's a lot more to me than just a chest."

Sexy and exhibitionistic, the screen actor was involved in a torrid affair at the time with his best friend, Spencer Tracy, whom he'd invited to go sailing with him. "Spence was too drunk to make it today," O'Brien told Kate.

"What a shame," she said. "I was so looking forward to meeting him, I admire him so."

"Back off, bitch," O'Brien said, smiling to soften his words. "That Irishman belongs to me." He looked over at Ford, who was issuing orders to cast off. "You can have *that* Irishman instead."

Going below, Kate was disappointed that Ford had assigned a small and terribly cramped cabin to themselves, whereas Cukor and O'Brien got to share the master bedroom with its elaborate four-poster bed.

Before entering the cabin with Cukor, O'Brien said, "Since I'm likely to be drunk, hot and horny tonight, you can have me later on but only from the waist down." He winked at Kate.

"Usually handsome young men like you tell me I can have them from the neck down," Cukor said.

"In your case, we'll confine it to the waist down. If you were prettier, I'd give you wider range."

After lunch, Cukor was startled to see Kate on deck gently massaging Ford's feet.

He told O'Brien, "I never thought I'd see that happen. Finally a man with balls enough to tame Katharine Hepburn. Something to tell my grandchildren."

"At the rate you're going, you'll never have grandchildren," O'Brien chided him. "Unless me and you make a baby tonight."

O'Brien later said that he liked Kate at once, because she immediately became one of the boys. "She didn't keep reminding you that she was a lady, like some of the women Ford had aboard. Many of those floozies were no ladies, but wanted to be treated like one."

That afternoon Ford shared his disappointment that neither John Wayne nor Spencer Tracy were free to sail with them. "They're great guys. You'll probably end up making movies with them one day."

"That I doubt," she said, predicting that Berman would cast her opposite the dull Herbert Marshall in her next film. Unknown to Kate at the time, Marshall would indeed be assigned to her next film for RKO.

Kate asked about Tracy, and Ford freely shared his memories, claiming he was the first Hollywood director to have discovered Tracy when he was appearing in the John Wexley death row drama, *The Last Mile*, on Broadway, playing Killer Mears.

Ford said that he and Tracy had visited every whorehouse on the East and West coasts, Ford ranking New York City's Lu Lu's as his all-time favorite. "Tracy's been barred from Lu Lu's. He's a real mean drunk and likes to beat up on the whores. Sometimes we stay in these houses until ten o'clock in the morning. I used to drive Tracy back to his apartment in New York, where his wife, a very angry Louise, would be waiting for him, along with his son. A real sweet boy named Johnny. He's deaf."

"I'm sorry to hear that," she said. "Anything that one can do for the boy?"

"Believe me, Louise has had him to every specialist in America. She's devoted to him. I think she's become Johnny's ears."

"Actually, I wasn't aware that Tracy is married," she said. "He sure keeps his wife in the background."

"You look disappointed," he said. "I don't know why. I'm a better man than Tracy and can hold my Irish whiskey better."

She smiled at him and kissed him. "After last night, I need no convincing."

Like voyeurs, Cukor and O'Brien sat nearby, monitoring the talk between Ford and Hepburn as their romance blossomed.

"Tracy is the most insecure actor I've ever worked with," Ford said. "I've become his mentor, really his father figure."

Knowing something about Ford's own insecurities, she asked, "Isn't that like the blind leading the blind?"

"You are a very provocative She-Devil," he said. "As captain of this ship, I have the right to make you walk the gangplank."

"No, not that!" she said in mock protest.

"I guess we'll have to settle for a paddling. Have you ever had a man paddle you before he does other things to you?"

"Never!" she protested. "I don't think I'll allow that."

"You can let me paddle you alone," he said, "in the privacy of our little room, or else I'll strip you and have Cukor and O'Brien hold you down while I do the dirty deed."

"Faced with only those two choices, I'll vote to be paddled alone with you."

***

When not sailing on the *Araner*, Kate and Ford could often be seen on the golf course at the California Country Club, where the director would drive her in his battered old two-seater Ford Roadster. Kate often beat him at golf, which would seriously infuriate him.

When Ford one day didn't show up on the set by eleven o'clock in the morning, his assistant, Cliff Reid, knocked on Kate's dressing room door. She ushered him in, where she learned that the director was so drunk at his

Hollywood Hills home that he couldn't come to the set to finish the picture.

"Where's Mary Ford?" Kate asked.

"She's not there," Reid said. "She and the kids are gone. I've been unable to sober him up. He's calling for you."

She quickly dressed and was driven by Reid to Ford's home. Entering his bedroom, she found Ford stripped naked with a sheet barely wrapped around his body. There were three empty Irish whiskey bottles on the floor, with another half-filled jug on the bed beside him.

Reid explained that this was the first time Ford had ever gone on a drunk before the completion of a picture. "He usually waits until it's all over, then gets Mary to buy him about a thousand dollars worth of Irish whiskey. For days or even weeks at a time, he drinks himself into a stupor. Since her husband is going to be zonked out for days at a time, Mary also uses the occasion to down an ocean or two of hooch too."

As if in a dress rehearsal for her twenty-seven years as a caretaker to Spencer Tracy, Kate believed that she knew what to do. Only she didn't.

Incredibly, she seemed to think that if she made him drink a large glass of whiskey and a big helping of Castor Oil, it would sober him up. It had the opposite effect. After drinking the witches' brew, Ford completely passed out. Reid and Kate could barely hear his breathing. At one point, she thought she'd killed him.

Fearing that she'd attract attention from the press, Kate unwisely didn't allow Reid to call a doctor. She also refused to let him to haul Ford to a hospital.

The director rallied a bit after a deep sleep of three hours. Kate later told Kenneth MacKenna that, "It was a process of elimination as he slept. Reid and I had to serve as hospital orderlies. Thank God my father is a doctor, and I'm not squeamish about such matters. No sooner would we place John on clean sheets than he'd dirty them again."

When Ford came to, Reid drove his boss and Kate to the Hollywood Athletic Club where the staff was used to him. She waited patiently as they gave Ford massages and steam baths, along with some solid food and lots of mineral water.

Finally Kate thought it was safe to return Ford to the RKO lot. She didn't want Berman to find out, fearing the studio chief might fire Ford and hire another director to finish *Mary of Scotland.*

Like Tracy looming in her future, Kate felt that Ford was driven to self-flagellation which meant a drunk lasting a minimum of two weeks and often six weeks. "Kate never figured out what drove me to this despair," Ford later told John Wayne. "I'm driven by my demons, which are very different from those demons chasing after Spence."

The night after she sobered him up, Kate berated Ford for risking his career and her picture. "You're the most brilliant director in the business and have the ability to make one masterpiece after another. I can't understand why a man with such creativity and with such promise wants to slowly kill himself."

In spite of his drinking, Kate launched herself into her most torrid affair to date with Ford. On the surface they seemed at the far extremities of each other—and not just on the issue of personal hygiene.

Ford had a strong masculine ego, believing that women such as his wife, Mary, should knuckle under to a man.

A leggy, toothy, New England patrician like Kate was fiercely independent. She lived in a world of self-enchantment and was used to having her own way, dominating instead of being dominated.

If she were flashy and feminine, although at times aggressively masculine, he was subdued, shunning ostentation. Yet Kate and Ford shared much in common, as John Wayne later claimed. "They were quick tempered. They developed grudges very quickly over the smallest slight. They both were creative as hell and as strong-willed as a bull. Downright pigheaded if you ask me."

Yet for all Kate's differences and bickerings with Ford, the director once told Wayne, "With her, I found the happiest and most contented moments of my entire life. She never understood me but had respect for this Devil that lived inside me, inhabiting my very soul. Old Spence and I used to have many boozy talks about our inner Devils. Kate, on the other hand, had too much self-discipline to ever let an inner Devil take over her soul. Maybe it was all those cold showers she took. Water like that can drive demons away. As we got older, Spence and I once talked about how much Kate loved both of us broken down old drunks. But, if I remember it right, Spence told me, 'As much as she loves both of us, I still don't think Kate has even a clue as to what either of us is about.'"

***

At the end of filming, Jane Loring stayed in Hollywood to edit the ill-fated *Mary of Scotland,* and Kate invited John Ford to spend a few weeks with her at Fenwick so they could play golf every day and go sailing on Long Island Sound. "Tell George O'Brien and John Wayne that those Mexican whorehouses can wait until you get back to the Coast," she said.

Completely smitten with Kate at the time, Ford accepted her invitation to go East. When he was packing to go, Ford and his wife, Mary, had a bitter fight over Kate. At one point, he struck Mary in the mouth with the back of his broad hand, causing her to bleed.

As he was going out the door, she screamed after him that she wouldn't be there waiting for him when he returned to Los Angeles. "You'll be here, you God damn bitch, much to my regret. I wish you would pack up and get out, but I know that when I open the door when I come back, there you'll be nagging and hounding me until I want to kill you."

As Ford headed East with his new love, he related to Kate all that had happened between Mary and him.

"There must be a way that Mary will give you a divorce," Kate said. She'd already discussed this with all of her friends, except Loring. Cukor, Leland, and her entire gang were firmly convinced that Mary would not divorce her husband. Leland had encountered John Wayne and the Western star had confirmed that, "Jack and Mary fight like cats and dogs, but they'll live together until the Grim Reaper comes for one of them."

Arriving in New York, Kate invited Ford to stay with her at her Turtle Bay townhouse. He'd gladly accepted but was none too thrilled during their first evening.

Jack and Luddy were in Kate's living room waiting to welcome her home. Ford found Luddy's cuddling affection toward Kate "a bit peculiar," as he later confided to her. "I haven't read any books on etiquette about how an ex-husband is supposed to behave around his former wife, but I don't think this Luddy character has read one either."

"Luddy adores me and I adore him," she said. "We are very open in our affection for one another, but it's not sexual—oh, no, never that. It was never sexual."

"That's pretty obvious to me," he told her. "He seems quite taken with this Jack boy."

"They love each other very much," she told him.

"I can see that, and it's their own business," he said. "But holding hands and even kissing each other in front of others is a bit much for me. As a Hollywood director, I've worked with lots of homosexuals in my day. If they must love each other, and I know they must—it's in their nature, and you don't mess with Mother Nature—but they at least should do it in the privacy of their bedroom."

"I'll concede your point," she said, "and I'll speak to Luddy. But it's hard to put a damper on his affections. He's like a big shaggy dog that likes to jump up on your lap and lick you on the mouth."

"Enough of that," he said. "I'm going to take a long bath since you like me smelling good."

As he undressed in front of her, she told him that she'd invited an old friend for dinner that night. "Laura Harding, she's an absolute dear."

"Who in hell is Laura Harding?" he asked.

"You don't know? She's the banking heiress. A dear, dear friend."

Standing in his underwear, he said, "You sounded just one too many dears for me. I hope this is not another Jane Loring situation. I think you're one swell gal, but I really don't like these intimate relationships you seem to have with women. I know my best friend, George O'Brien, takes it up the ass but I don't want to think about that. As far as I'm concerned, I judge George by what I see, and that body beautiful can take on six of the wildest Mexican spitfires in one night. By the time Wayne and I have gone through three of those little *putas,* we're exhausted."

"Or, perhaps too drunk," she suggested.

"Speaking of alcohol, I suspected you didn't have a supply of my favorite Irish whiskey in the house, so I've called and ordered a case sent over. I hope you don't mind."

"I mind, of course, but there's nothing I can do about it. I wish you wouldn't drink so much."

"It's the only remedy for killing pain."

As Ford bathed, she was eager to report her conversation with Ford to both Jack and Luddy. As they were later to tell friends, Kate seemed amused, but they were not.

Luddy told her that although Ford was a vast improvement over Jed Harris, he went on to confess that he simply didn't like the man.

"I think he belongs out West with all those cowboys," Jack said. "Before you hauled him back East, you should have housebroken him."

Luddy dreaded the oncoming evening with Laura Harding.

"I don't think Ford will cast Laura as the female lead in his next picture," Luddy said, "and that's my understatement of the year."

***

Kate had never seen Laura look more stunning than when she arrived suntanned and wearing a chicly tailored gown designed personally for her by Chanel. She'd had both her hair and makeup done by Maxwell Gadder, one of the leading specialists who'd flown in from London for six weeks "to work over New York's society women—and make ladies of them."

Laura didn't need to be taught how to be a lady, since she already was one, but Gadder had vastly improved her appearance. With lots of hugs and kisses, she was warmly welcomed not only by Kate but by Jack and Luddy, who seemed to adore her.

When Laura extended her hand to Ford, it was a different matter. He'd already been drinking heavily when she arrived, and he took her hand and squeezed it so hard she winced in pain before retrieving her mauled fingers.

To Luddy, it appeared that Ford was deliberately trying to injure her. "I grew up in an era where ladies did not extend their hand to men," Ford said. "That was a good custom back then. Maybe you'd better think twice before offering your delicate little paw to a tough man. You might get your fingers broken."

Laura did not endear herself to Ford when she told him that she'd never seen any of his pictures. "Luddy and Jack wanted to take me to see *The Informer,* but it sounded much too dreary for me. I like pictures with more gaiety, and can't wait to see Kate in *Mary of Scotland.* I hear Kate's terrific."

239

"It's not terrific," Ford said. "There are a lot of things wrong with the picture, and the critics, I hear, are sharpening their teeth, just waiting to dig into my leathery old flesh."

"Sorry to hear that," Laura said. There was a long, awkward pause before Kate ushered everybody into her living room, trying to break the tension. By then, it must have been obvious that bringing her two lovers together, Ford and Laura, had not been a brilliant casting call. She was sure that Laura was viewing Ford as just some old roustabout that Kate had picked up in the West and was foisting on East Coast society.

As Ford continued to drink heavily throughout the evening, he found nothing at the dinner table to his liking. He became incensed when Jack got a dab of whipped cream stuck on his lip and Luddy leaned over and licked it off. "C'mon boys," Ford said, "we'll have no more of that. Kate gave you a napkin."

At one point, Ford, drinking even more heavily, began to feel left out of the conversation. The focus of attention had shifted to Laura and Kate, who had many memories to share. The two women held the undivided attention of Luddy and Jack. Ford found all of this "East Coast prissy talk ridiculous," as he later was to tell his cronies back in Hollywood. He also revealed to his friends that he did the one thing he knew "that would piss Kate off." He began to talk glowingly of his wife, Mary McBride Smith.

To hear Ford tell it, Mary was a regular Annie Oakley and had been a stunt rider in the rodeo. "That woman used to make her own bootleg gin in the bathtub. She was famous for her gin torpedoes. She got some of her naval buddies to bring her the kind of alcohol used as the propellant for torpedoes. Mixed with a little ginger ale, it made a helluva cocktail."

He sat back in his chair and told his uninterested listeners that "Mary got real jealous of Ollie—that's Harry Carey's wife—when she was seen driving around Hollywood in her Lincoln town car with a Navajo Indian wrapped in a blanket sitting in the back seat. Just to get even, Mary hired herself a real tribal chief complete with squaw."

Pouring himself another drink, Ford then seemed to reverse his description of Mary. No longer portraying her as a rough-and-tumble pioneer from the Old West, he seemed to want to convince Kate and Laura that he'd married an American blueblood. A rival to their own heritages.

"I met her on St. Patrick's Day back in 1920," he said. "It was a party given by the director, Rex Ingram, who'd cast that WOP Valentino in *The Four Horsemen of the Apocalypse*. Mary later became a friend of his. He used to stop off at our house and cook spaghetti."

Looking over at Kate, Ford said that he'd never known "a woman with such a delicate bone structure and such fine classical features as my Mary. She has more elegance and style than any woman I've met before or known since."

Ford told of his whirlwind romance with Mary. "We had a real, wild, hot-blooded time. It was the best time to be an American. Women locked up their corsets and smoked cigarettes. Mary and I danced the Hesitation Waltz at speakeasies and shared tables with Al Capone and Bugs Moran. We drank from our hip flasks and made love in the back of a Tin Lizzy."

"Of course, don't get me wrong," he said. "Mary knows all about East Coast high society and fancy boarding schools just like you gals. In one school, she even shared a room with Dorothy Parker. She's a real North Carolina Presbyterian with blueblood roots. A number of her uncles or nephews attended West Point or Annapolis. Did you know that the surgeon general of the United States, Rupert Blue, was Mary's uncle? Her father was a wealthy Wall Street investor. Mary came from real money. My God, she is a direct descendant of Sir Thomas More, and her family can even trace their ancestors back to the seventeenth century. When I wed my Mary, I certainly married far beyond my station in life."

After yet another whiskey, Ford was addressing a tableful of listeners who showed him the respect of silence but didn't ask any questions, fearing that would only goad him into more revelations.

"The thing I like most about my Mary is that she understands male behavior," he claimed. "She often gets together with Tom Mix's wife. Once she told her that if a man doesn't have a mistress on the side, it means he can't afford it."

That was it for Kate. She stood up, announcing that her dinner party was over and it was time to go to bed.

Ford wasn't surprised when she informed him that he'd be sleeping in the guest room. She claimed that Laura was sleeping over and would be sharing her bed in the master bedroom.

***

The next morning, after Ford's drunken tirade, he and Kate made up. She kissed Laura good-bye and sent her back to New Jersey. Ford went with her to the Theatre Guild where Kate agreed to appear on stage in *Jane Eyre* as her next project. Ford was enthusiastic, claiming that he wanted to film the play after its "almost guaranteed successful run."

Kate had already talked to Dr. Hepburn. He was none too enthusiastic about receiving Ford at Fenwick. "As far as I'm concerned, he's just another one of those hypocritical Irish Catholics—and a married man to boot—chasing after my daughter who should know better."

Kit was already in New York "on birth-control business," and Kate agreed to drive her and Ford back to Fenwick, since Ford objected to being chauffeur-driven by Charles. "I don't do that sort of thing. When I can no longer drive myself, I'll give up riding in a car and take to horses, which will surely break my neck."

Kit was also leery of Kate's involvement with a member of the Roman Catholic Church, as she was under attack from Cardinal Patrick Hayes. Hayes had only recently accused her of being "in conspiracy with the Devil," claiming that the Sanger birth-control movement was merely a shield to conceal its ultimate motive, which was to keep lower-class Italian and Irish immigrants from having more children and thereby influencing WASP-controlled voting patterns in America.

But by the time Kate reached Fenwick, Ford, "a Socialist Democrat," had impressed Kit with his individualism and nonconformity.

He also told Kit that he wasn't going to be "pussy-whipped" by Kate. She didn't like his choice of words, but she appreciated his ability to stand up to her daughter, who Kit claimed was so strong-willed that she usually got exactly what she wanted.

"Before filming on *Mary of Scotland* began, I told Kate, 'if you don't give your best performance, I'll break you across my knee,'" Ford said.

At Fenwick, both Dr. Hepburn and Ford got off to a rough start, but Ford also won the respect of Kate's father after several heated arguments. Thinking that Ford could talk only about show business, Dr. Hepburn was surprised to find the director well-versed in history and politics.

Ford was known for making provocative remarks. "I have a soft spot in my hearts for Negroes and Indians, and so I want to live to see their liberty. Even though some of my best friends are Jews, I take a jibe at them on occasion. There's one man who works for me—his name's not important—but I always call him the Christ -Killer."

"You know that some people don't like Roman Catholics," Dr. Hepburn reminded him.

"I didn't reach this point of my adult life without finding that out a long time ago," Ford said. "The stories I could tell you. I came from a family of thirteen." He looked over at Kit. "My mother obviously didn't believe in birth control."

***

During the long, lovely month that Kate and Ford spent sailing on Long Island Sound, they fell in love. Watching sunsets became a ritual with them. At first Kate used to exclaim how beautiful the sunsets were. But Ford taught her how to rest in his arms and take in the visual. He didn't like wordy scripts, and he didn't like Kate proclaiming everything she saw as "fascinating." "Let's just use our eyes to enjoy, not our mouths to exclaim."

Between their respective job commitments, they found time to contemplate, read scripts, and to make plans for the future. Even when word reached Ford that Jane Loring had been ordered to drastically recut *Mary of Scotland*, Ford tried to take it in stride, although in despair, he resumed his heavy drinking.

242

Before that, Kate had managed to taper him off. "I'll never work another day for RKO," he threatened.

Every night Ford telephoned his wife back in the Hollywood Hills. He told Kate, "When you signed to play *Mary of Scotland*, my wife was very enthusiastic about you. She said that you were a woman of class and breeding, and some of your aristocratic qualities would wear off on me and make me less shanty Irish."

"What does she think of me now?" Kate asked.

"She calls you a husband-stealing whore!" he said, before looking for his pipe and heading for his favorite chair, placed on the sandy front yard overlooking the Sound.

Kate realized that Mary Ford viewed her as the most dangerous adversary to ever come into her husband's life. Mary could cope, barely, with her husband's infatuation with the classically cool, blonde, and beautiful British actress, Madeleine Carroll, but in Kate, Mary faced her stiffest competition to date.

Ford dazzled Kate with stories of his many sexual conquests, claiming he'd bedded "the most beautiful woman in the world," Billie Dove, when they were shooting *The Flying Heart* back in 1925. "Even though she's a lez, Janet Gaynor couldn't get enough of me when we were shooting *The Shamrock Handicap* and later, in 1926, *The Blue Eagle*."

According to Ford, Leatrice Joy, one of Kate's all-time favorite actresses, had fallen in his arms during the shoot of the 1929 *Strong Boy*. "Myrna Loy, even though she's mainly a lez, went for me when we made *The Black Watch* in 1929," he said. He also claimed that in 1929, during the shooting of *Salute*, Joyce Compton had rejected John Wayne in favor of him. Claire Luce, according to Ford, came under his spell during the 1930 filming of *Up the River* with Spencer Tracy. "At least she was attracted to me when she wasn't in Spence's dressing room," he said. He also boasted that Mona Maris, hailed at the time as the fellatio queen of Hollywood, practiced her specialty on him during the filming of the 1931 *Seas Beneath*. Both Sally O'Neil and Virginia Cherrill, later Mrs. Cary Grant, "had the hots for me," he claimed, during the shooting, in 1931, of *The Brat*. Perhaps to make his stories more believable, he claimed he struck out with Helen Hayes, who refused his advances, when they shot *Arrowsmith* in 1931.

"All this comes as news to me," she said jokingly. "I'd heard rumors that the only affair you ever had with one of your actors was with Stepin Fetchit, sometimes with you, Fetchit, and Wayne in a three-way."

Later, Kate told her father that even though Ford brags a lot about his many conquests, "I truly believe he's never been unfaithful to Mary until I came along."

"My suggestion is you run along and find yourself some unmarried man," Dr. Hepburn advised, "and let the poor lovesick Irish fool go back to his wife."

Only in financial matters did Kate tend to follow her father's advice. As each day went by, she plotted to get Ford to divorce his wife and marry her. The two of them even began to plan their honeymoon, which Ford said he wanted to spend "in the isles of my ancestors," the Aran Islands off the western coast of Ireland.

Long before Spencer Tracy overwhelmed her with the problem, she became aware of something called "Catholic guilt." Ford had severe emotional problems with the mere idea of divorcing Mary and marrying Kate.

Although Kate felt Ford was a brilliant director and complimented him so frequently that he often had to ask her to shut up, she soon became aware of how little respect he had both for his own talent and for himself as a man. "I'm just not adequate," he said. "Mary points out my failures all the time and she's right."

"How can you be drawn to a woman who castigates you all the time?" she asked. "That is, if I've judged her correctly."

"You've nailed the bitch," he said.

Even though he denounced Mary, Kate noted that he returned time and time again to her arms and her biting criticism. Kate began to feel that there was some dark bond between them that all her love and support could not separate.

Nonetheless, she pressed on with her demands that he divorce Mary and wed her as soon as possible. She wasn't comforted by the fact that her friends in Hollywood were writing her, claiming that Mary was going around town, vowing, "I'll be Mrs. John Ford forever."

The break in Kate's relationship with Ford came when he traveled to Portland, Maine, to visit his father, John Feeney. Ford had long ago dropped the use of his family name of Feeney. In Maine he discovered that his father, already eighty-six years old, was wasting away, his health declining almost daily.

After hearing from his dying father about how disappointed he was in him for not having become a priest, Ford departed immediately for Hollywood, without paying a final visit to Fenwick.

Back on the West Coast, Ford received word that his father had died. Ford knew at once that he had to leave Hollywood immediately and see that his father received a proper burial according to his wishes.

He placed a call to Kate at Fenwick but she was in New Jersey with Laura. Kate always regretted not being there to receive that call.

Ford later told his assistant, Cliff Reid, that he'd summoned the courage, in the immediate aftermath of his father's death, to ask for Kate's hand in marriage.

When she returned to Fenwick and learned about his telephone call, she phoned him back, but he'd gone. Bewildered, she knew she couldn't write him at his Odin Street address in Los Angeles because Mary might read her letter first. Instead, she sent her letter of love and condolences to his office at

Twentieth-Century Fox, labeling it *personal*.

Ford was not to read her letter until after he returned to California from his father's funeral.

By then it was too late. Ford told Reid that he'd withdrawn his "impulsive offer of marriage" to Kate.

He would never extend such an offer to her again.

CHAPTER ELEVEN

Although several days had passed since Kate's return to Hollywood, she had had no word from John Ford. She did, however, receive in the mails the opinion of Dr. Hepburn, Protestant teetotaler. "You were only a teenager when I discovered that you were dating a Catholic boy. If you recall, I once spotted the two of you together, and you hid your head in shame. And he wasn't married, unlike your heavy drinker, Mr. Ford. Charming as he is, remember this, and Kit concurs: Catholics are political reactionaries. They are against birth control and they oppose votes for women. Need I repeat myself? Even though Mr. and Mrs. John Ford were not married in the Roman Catholic Church—and that would make divorce easier, as you endlessly pointed out—don't go through with it! Leave him and find someone of your own faith, preferably someone who's unmarried. Your loving Father."

For comfort and understanding, Kate turned to someone who, indeed, wasn't either Catholic or married: Jane Loring, who talked again and again about the careers that loomed before them, insisting that she would direct Kate in pictures that would win several Oscars for both of them.

Days in Hollywood passed, and she still hadn't heard from Ford. Impulsively, and in defiance of her father's wishes, Kate drove herself to the Odin Street home of Mr. and Mrs. John Ford. She demanded to see Ford but the maid told her that he wasn't home. Then, Mary Ford came to the door and asked Kate to come in. When Kate tried to shake her hand, Mary declined.

Seated in her living room, Mary took glee in telling her that her husband had sailed in his ketch, *Araner*, to Hawaii. "From what I was told, he took along some of his salty maties and a lot of easy virtue young women. Naturally, they loaded themselves down with plenty of good Irish whiskey. Speaking of the devil, I think I'll have a drink myself. How about you?"

Kate could not remember when she'd had a drink in the morning, but her hands were trembling, and she accepted the whiskey from her hostess to steady her nerves.

"You might think you're tough," Mary said, seated facing Kate, "but you're not woman enough to handle John Ford. You've got to be tough as nails to deal with a man like that, and, frankly, I don't think Miss Katharine Hepburn, Miss *Mary of Scotland*, has the balls to do it."

"You're wrong about that," Kate protested, "You see, I've fallen in love with your husband and I'm going to take him away from you. Face facts. I bring out the artist in him. You destroy his creativity."

"Why don't you go fuck yourself?" Mary said, standing up and towering over Kate. "First off, if you knew Jack, you'd know he hates the word *artist*. Artistry? He tells guys to round up the cattle and turn on the cameras. Have you seen *Mary of Scotland*? It's a piece of shit. That's what happens when the two of you get together to make art."

"Yes, I admit we failed," Kate said. "But we'll try again and again until we get it right."

"Not on your life, bitch," Mary said. "You and Jack Ford will never make another movie together. Get a hold on reality. My husband is not the man for you. Do you want to spend the rest of your life being some God damn nurse-maid to some broken-down old Irish drunk?"

Eerily, Mary Ford was presenting Kate with a preview of her oncoming life with another Irish drunk, Spencer Tracy.

"I've given Jack no grounds to divorce me," Mary said. "He'll never leave me. You see, and this may be too hard for a little Bryn Mawr stuck-up like you—a woman everyone calls Katharine of Arrogance—to understand. You try to build Jack up. Big mistake! In the dark of night of his blasted soul, he does-n't need a woman to build him up. He needs a woman to tear him down, to remind him every rotten day of his stinking rotten life what a no-count bum he really is."

Kate slowly rose from the sofa and confronted Mary. Trembling in spite of the whiskey fortifier, she faced her adversary with all the courage she could muster.

"I can have one-hundred and fifty thousand dollars in cash delivered to this house tomorrow morning," Kate said. "That's the amount I'm getting for my next three pictures. It'll all be yours if you agree to give him a divorce."

"You brazen little hussy," Mary screamed at Kate. "Do you think you could buy me? You fool. How dare you!" Quick-tempered and dangerous when riled, Mary lunged at Kate, grabbing her by her hair and yanking her as she slapped her face, knocking her to the floor.

From her spread-eagled position on the floor, Kate kicked Mary even hard-er than she'd kicked Ginger Rogers, knocking the woman down. She was sent sprawling, falling over her coffee table and the liquor glasses.

Seeing her route clear, Kate jumped up from the floor and darted to the door. Blinded by tears, she drove recklessly to Cukor's house where she report-ed every word of her confrontation with Mary Ford.

Her favorite director offered what comfort he could, but deliberately didn't invite her to his next Sunday afternoon *soirée*. The story she'd told him was just too good to keep to himself. In fact, it was a story that he would dine out on for another month.

***

Leland Hayward came back into Kate's life after her return to Hollywood, and shortly after his marriage to Margaret Sullavan. She restored him to her good graces, but not to the bed that she now shared, on an alternating basis, with both Jane Loring and John Ford. George Stevens phoned, but she didn't return his calls. Keeping the home fires burning, Luddy and Laura wrote frequently, urging her to hurry back to New York.

During Kate's reunion with Leland, he presented the fruits of his recent successes as her agent. At RKO, Pandro Berman, despite her many box-office flops, had offered her two-hundred thousand dollars for an agreement that she would make four new movies. Although that figure didn't represent a monetary increase (she was already drawing fifty-thousand dollars per picture), it guaranteed Kate four additional spotlighted roles. Leland urged her to take it. "And I think that a film version of that play they're about to produce in New York, *Stage Door,* would be right for you."

What Leland didn't dare tell Kate was that he was simultaneously lobbying to have his wife cast as the lead in the Broadway version of that same work.

"So, how's your marriage going with The Steel Magnolia?" Kate asked.

"She castrates me," Leland said. "I don't know how Fonda and Wyler put up with it. She makes me feel like I have a two-inch dick—even when it's hard."

Several times that night, Leland predicted that the aggressively re-edited version of *Mary of Scotland* would be the biggest hit of Kate's young life.

Only it wasn't.

***

Despite the ballyhoo, with RKO publicists claiming that Kate was a direct descendant of the Scottish queen, *Mary of Scotland* was Kate's most dismal flop, and did nothing to boost the reputation of John Ford as a director. Likewise, it did nothing to help the career of Pandro Berman. He had invested eight-hundred thousand dollars of RKO's money, more than he had on any of the Fred Astaire/Ginger Rogers movies, and RKO would manage to recoup only a small percentage of it.

Typically, many critics gave Kate good reviews, while damning the picture as a whole. William Boehnel, a writer for the *New York World-Telegram,* stated that Kate brought the Queen "vividly, glowingly to life." Sidney W. Carroll of *The London Times* found that Kate had scored a new triumph, even though her accent "was not of the Highlands, the Lowlands, but pure Hepburn." *Time* magazine disagreed, stating that "Katharine Hepburn often acts like a Bryn Mawr senior at a May Day pageant."

Howard Broyer, writing in a newspaper in Atlanta, articulated the public's increasing dissatisfaction with Kate. "This New England blueblood gets lost somewhere in the Scottish Moors as she wanders aimlessly around, perhaps waiting for her head to be chopped off. Actually, she plays the role as if her head has already been chopped off. She and March make a handsome couple, but the picture is only for suckers. Hepburn has disappointed her fans once again. If RKO keeps casting her in such dribble, this former Oscar winner will soon have no fans left. We doubt if the picture will run in Atlanta for more than two nights."

***

During her extended dalliance in Connecticut with John Ford, RKO had assigned Kate to *A Woman Rebels,* playing the role of Pamela Thistlewaite opposite the lackluster Herbert Marshall with his "secret" wooden leg. Mark Sandrich had been hired as director, although Kate had aggressively lobbied for Loring. Berman wasn't happy with the way that Loring had cut *Mary of Scotland*, but, at Kate's insistence, he agreed to name her editor for *A Woman Rebels,* finding the suggestion that Loring could actually direct the picture "laughable." Scenarist Anthony Veiller, who'd written some of the most disastrous dialogue on Kate's flop, *Break of Hearts*, had foolishly been hired, along with scriptwriter Ernest Vajda, to concoct a screenplay of Netta Syrett's novel, *Portrait of a Rebel.*

It was another elaborate period drama, with Kate playing a Victorian woman struggling for emancipation. Herbert Marshall was cast as her faithful suitor, and young Van Heflin as an amorous young man who leaves her with a child born out of wedlock, "the kiss of death" for a woman in the Victorian era and "stroke-inducing" to Pamela's father, as played by Donald Crisp.

With Jane Loring at her side, Kate was welcomed back to the set by a familiar old crew: photographer Robert De Grasse, art director Van Nest Polgase, and makeup artist Mel Burns. Kate sent a copy of the script to Kit back in Hartford, knowing that her mother would approve of the pro-feminist slant of the story. Pandro Berman personally came to the set to give his blessings to Kate. He predicted that, "*A Woman Rebels* will bring us another great success like *Little Women*. Like the character of Jo, Pamela Thistlewaite will also fly against Victorian morality. It's a natural for you. You might as well tell your *Morning Glory* Oscar that he's soon going to have a twin to stand beside, bare-assed and beautiful."

Kate detested her director, Mark Sandrich, partly because he had been selected instead of her first choice, Jane Loring, and partly because he'd directed many of the most successful Fred Astaire and Ginger Rogers films, including *The Gay Divorcee* in 1934, *Top Hat* in 1935, and *Follow the Fleet* in 1936. Kate ignored him throughout the first week of shooting, looking away if he gave her directions. She told Loring that she had forgotten more about movie-making than Sandrich would ever know. "Before the end of this picture, he'll probably ask Herbert Marshall and me to dance 'Cheek to Cheek,'" Kate told Loring.

At one point Kate objected so violently to a scene she was playing with actress Elizabeth Allan, portraying Flora Thistlewaite, that Kate screamed at Sandrich. "Why don't you cut the whole fucking scene and throw in a Ginger Rogers number? Surely you could rescue something from that clunker, *Roberta*. What a piece of shit!"

When Kate was really mad, "she could curse like a sailor," Loring claimed, "and she didn't care how many people were listening."

"Don't think I'm a Ginger Rogers fan," Sandrich once told her. "I hate being assigned to one of her pictures. Astaire can't stand her either. To me, Rogers is just a model to drape clothes over and whirl around the floor. There's no talent there, whatsoever. But Astaire is a genius. I always rush to congratulate him at the end of every number....But I try to avoid the blonde bubble-head whenever I can."

Kate enjoyed Sandrich's appraisal of Rogers, and almost kissed the man with glee. But their truce didn't last long. When he complimented Marshall or Heflin on every scene, and didn't bat an eye at her, she felt he was appraising her talent to be as thin as Rogers', and this infuriated her.

Evocative of Laura and Kate when they were a couple, Jane Loring presided over daily picnics on the set, but at no time was Sandrich invited. Relations between Kate and Sandrich became so poisonous at one point that she burst into tears and claimed that, "You're destroying my career. Berman has deliberately forced me into this picture to finish me off at RKO. You want that dyed whore, *Miss Rogers*, to become the undisputed Queen of RKO...box-office champ, or should I say, 'tramp.' You're both trying to sabotage me." Sandrich listened politely but didn't respond to her.

Her director infuriated her even more when Loring overheard him telling Berman, "You should have listened to me and cast Irene Dunne in the picture. I'm trying my best to direct her, but she's a complete mediocrity. Despite our hopes and hard work, I think the public will stay away from this turkey in droves." Sandrich turned out to be a prophet.

Relations between the director and his star came to the boiling point when Kate and Sandrich conflicted bitterly over a lace gown he wanted her to wear. It was accessorized with a lace hat, ringed with a garland of flowers, and a lace parasol to protect her head from the sun.

Although Walter Plunkett, the costumer, had designed the costumes for many of Kate's previous pictures, she refused to wear "this frilly thing that makes me look like some virginal maiden aunt."

Sandrich knew that her refusal to wear the dress had devolved into a con-tract-breaking test of wills. He shut down the picture and stormed over to Berman's office. After hearing the news, Berman went directly to Kate's dress-ing room, and remained with her there for nearly three hours. Finally, after an acrimonious exchange and threats of lawsuits, Kate emerged from her dressing room, put on the costume, and shot the scene. In the process, she developed such a loathing for Sandrich that years later, when she was asked about the shooting of *A Woman Rebels*, she claimed, with apparent sincerity, she could not recall one single event during production.

Throughout the rest of the shooting, Sandrich was stiff, formal, and businesslike with Kate, who remained cool and aloof. She called him "Mr. Sandrich," and he referred deferentially to her as "Miss Hepburn."

During the rest of the fifty-four days it took to shoot *A Woman Rebels*, and during the twenty-two costume changes ordered by Walter Plunkett, incorporating the range of styles that were in vogue between 1869 and 1890, Kate listened to Sandrich's direction and said nothing, trying to get through the picture as fast as she could and be off to her next project. And when the picture was finished, she never spoke to him ever again.

"I will never make another God damn period piece as long as I live," Kate loudly proclaimed, not only to Jane Loring, but to all the cast and crew.

Yet only ten days after that widely quoted proclamation, Kate signed to appear in the film *Quality Street,* which was set during the time of the Napoleonic Wars. And she also agreed to appear in *Jane Eyre*, a theatrical adaptation of Charlotte Brontë's novel that would go on tour with the Theatre Guild.

***

Since Kate wasn't talking to Sandrich, she chose to invite her leading man to her daily picnics, although confessing to Loring that, "As God as my witness, he is the dullest actor ever cast as a leading man in Hollywood. How can a beast like that Gloria Swanson be entranced with him?"

The urbane British actor, Marshall, was seventeen years older than Kate. He was known for his elegant and refined characterizations, but "he doesn't have any magic," in Kate's view. She did admire, however, how he carried on with a prosthetic leg, having lost his original limb in the British Army during World War I.

He had a round face under slicked-back hair, stood tall, and walked perfectly in spite of his handicap.

Once or twice Kate insulted him with what had by this time become one of her favorite digs. She would learn an actor's former profession and suggested that instead of films, he or she should return to his or her old job. In Marshall's case, she insulted him by saying, "I hear you were a very good accountant. That's a good business to be in. You can always find work, since the world needs accountants. With actors, roles grow slim as one grows older."

At the first picnic, she provocatively asked him, "What would a cyclone like Gloria Swanson see in you?"

He didn't appear to be flustered, but, in his refined voice, said, "She thought

I was the most cultivated man she'd ever met, that I had a devastating smile, and that my voice is so perfect it is music to her ears."

"I just don't get it," she said, trying to break through his debonair façade.

"I think Norma Shearer gave me the best endorsement I've ever heard," he said. "Once she saw me play a love scene, and she told Irving Thalberg, 'I thought I have never seen a lady so thoroughly and convincingly loved. Marshall is both manly and wistful. Women go for him because his face expresses tenderness and silent suffering.' I think that instead of hearing what famous ladies of the screen have said about me, you should sample the treasures for yourself."

"I'm not opposed to that, and I must admit that I'm interested, but what do you do with your wooden leg when you're making love?"

The actor slowly got up off the picnic quilt and walked away, although the next day he was as friendly as ever to Kate, ignoring her insult.

During the second week of the shoot, Marshall came to her and pressed his case for seduction. "If you'd like to know what drives Kay Francis and Miriam Hopkins wild, I suggest you give me a try."

"These ladies seem to be keeping you well-occupied," Kate said. She could smell liquor on his breath, and had heard from Loring that he was a heavy drinker.

"You've heard of men having what they call a third leg," he said. "In my case, I've got two legs."

"A few years ago I might not have known what you meant, but being around George Cukor, I actually get that. You aren't exaggerating, are you?"

"I can prove it to you," he said. Unknown to her, he somehow had unzipped his pants. He took her hand and placed it inside his fly. Since she thought it was expected, she felt him professionally before withdrawing her hand.

"Very impressive endowment," she said. "The most impressive I've ever felt up."

"It can all be yours," he promised. "I hear only Franchot Tone has got me beat."

"Actually, you're a little late," she said. "Even though he's much smaller than you, I have just given my heart to my amorous swain in this movie. The boyishly handsome Van Heflin, who doesn't stretch my nether regions like a bull mounting a cow."

Kate later told Cukor all the details of her encounter with Herbert Marshall, calling it "another romance that never was."

***

Making his screen debut, the Oklahoma-born Heflin was three years younger than Kate. Heflin was not a pretty boy, but was most often referred to as "ruggedly handsome." Years later, in 1942, he would appear with Robert Taylor, for which Heflin would win the Oscar as best supporting actor in *Johnny Eager*.

There was something about Heflin's square-cut features that appealed to Kate. She told a jealous Loring, "I feel like I want to mother him." In contrast to Marshall's Savile Row tailoring, Heflin usually appeared on the set with his clothing rumpled, as if he'd slept in them the night before.

He immediately expressed his dissatisfaction with the "effete role" he was playing. He claimed that as a graduate of the Yale School of Drama, he wanted meatier parts and that his heart really belonged to the theater.

She so agreed with that sentiment for herself that she reached out and embraced him. Although it was meant only as a friendly gesture, he grabbed her and kissed her, hard and erotically.

"Why did you do that?" she asked. "It was merely an affectionate hug."

"There are no affectionate hugs between hot men and sexy women," he claimed. "When a beautiful woman like you reaches out for my body, I respond. I'm merely a man."

After that kiss, Kate, once again her father's "charging bull," began to carefully appraise this six-footer.

She'd been born the daughter of a doctor, and he was the son of a dentist, and together they discovered that they had much in common. She understood perfectly what he meant when he said he wanted to be "an actor's actor."

Between takes, he enthralled her with his adventures, claiming he'd been drawn to the sea. He told her about when he'd sailed aboard a tramp steamer and stopped off for wild nights in remote, sin-filled ports "where every form of human depravity is practiced with relish."

He said he'd sailed the Pacific for three years and had visited "at least half the whorehouses of the world "where I've seen every form of sex known—and some unknown—to man." He had tales of Hawaii, South America, and Mexico.

He claimed that he'd once attended a slave auction where handsome blond boys kidnapped in Europe were sold to perverted Arab sheiks. "Those boys with the softest, roundest bottoms brought the best prices. My buddies and I knew what fate awaited those poor kids."

She shared in his wanderlust and confided in him that instead of being an actress, she too secretly wanted to sail the Seven Seas. "You might say I have a seaman's heart."

Like Kate, he shunned the Hollywood spotlight and hated "phony parties, phony people, and all the pretense." And even though she was already a star, he helped her with her acting technique, toning down some of her showy flourishes and histrionics in her scenes with him, and getting her to play her role in a more convincingly subdued fashion.

He said that if he ever developed a film career, "it will be a fluke." As each day went by, and in spite of Loring's attempt to intervene, Kate was drawn more and more to this manly actor of French-Irish descent.

Both Heflin and Kate, during the long waits between takes, talked prophetically of appearing on Broadway together, although remaining realistic about the theater as well. "Broadway is like Hawaii," he told her. "You dream you can reach up and pick mangoes or beautiful babes out of the trees. But once you get there, you find that it's just another place. I've always been torn between the sea and the theater," he said. "One of my first jobs on Broadway was in a play that was, ironically, named *Sailor Beware.* I wish you could see me on the stage instead of in some silly film."

"But I've already seen you on the stage. I was impressed when I went with a friend of mine, Laura Harding, to see you in a play called *End of Summer.* I saw an incredible acting talent on stage that night. In fact, I was the one who urged Pandro Berman to cast you as my suitor in this film."

"I wondered who was behind all this," he said. He pulled her close and kissed her passionately. "What did you see on that stage that attracted you to me?"

"A very manly man," she said. "Just the type I so desperately need from time to time."

"If you'd like to know me better and get acquainted with all my body parts, and I yours, all you have to do is invite me over tonight," he said. "I take loving a woman as seriously as I do sailing the high seas, and I view love-making as an art form."

"You sound just like you do when you're performing on stage," she said, "with that rich, deep speaking voice that sends shivers through me."

"When I get up out of a woman's bed," he said, "I like to make her feel as if she's been loved from the tip of her brow to her big toe."

"Please," she said. "You're giving me goose bumps."

The next morning, after a night with Heflin, Kate called Anderson Lawler and reported on the course of the affair, including what she claimed was the mating game leading up to his actual performance in bed.

"He's a medium-built man, if you know what I mean," she said to Lawler. "But a most satisfactory one. I love those sleepy eyes and his wavy hair, a kind of sand color. There's one thing I didn't like though."

"I hope it wasn't the vital part," Lawler said.

"No, he's okay in that department, perhaps even more than okay. He views lovemaking as a performance, with me as the director. Every minute or so, he stops and asks me how he'd doing and if he's hitting all the right spots."

Kate and Heflin continued their on-again, off-again affair for years. Although she'd meant to do him a favor by getting him cast in *A Woman Rebels*, she had actually derailed a promising film career, or at least seriously delayed the launch of it.

Because *A Woman Rebels* flopped so miserably at the box office, Heflin was assigned to what actors in those days called a "purgatory of B movies." That exact term was used by another struggling actor of the time, Humphrey Bogart.

Before the end of the 1930s, Kate, with her own film career in shambles, would remember her earnest, hard-driving lover, and would urge playwright, Philip Barry, to cast him as the cynical, left-wing reporter in *The Philadelphia Story*

.

***

Toward the end of the 1930s, as her box-office receipts slipped and Kate needed good press more than ever, she seemed to do everything she could to further alienate film magazine and newspaper reporters. When rumors surfaced that she was the mother of children, she admitted to having "ten in my brood, the product of three different marriages." She stated that family pictures would never become available since she wanted to keep her children out of the lime-light. Not realizing that her offspring were purely imaginary, some Hollywood writers actually reported as fact the sardonic claims that she had made. Whenever this happened, Kate found it "all too amusing," although she never attempted to pull such a stunt with the more savvy reporters of Hollywood or New York.

In complete contradiction to what she'd said to more gullible reporters, she told an interviewer in Hollywood, "I made the decision not to have children many years ago. And I don't regret it."

In other remarks that same day, she lamented that she was "paying too high a price for fame and fortune...It's been virtually impossible to enjoy my life since I achieved success in motion pictures." Those remarks did not set well with millions of Americans standing in long breadlines in front of watery soup kitchens through the bleak vastness of The Depression.

Back in West Hartford, Kate hid in the back seat of her car under a blanket as her chauffeur, Charles Newhill, drove her for a visit to her father's hospital. Anticipating her arrival, Kate was "ambushed," as she later claimed, by two cameramen and a newspaper reporter from Hartford.

When she got out of the car, the flashbulbs went off. Grabbing a tennis racket from her back seat, she slammed it into the foreheads of the cameramen, beating them furiously. The reporter, Philip Davis, was hit so hard he bled. Later, he threatened to sue her for assault and battery, until Dr. Hepburn talked him out of it, claiming he would give him free medical care, and extend the benefits to his wife and three children, for ten years if he'd drop all charges against his daughter.

When Kate returned to Hollywood, Pandro S. Berman bluntly told her, "You really need psychiatric help." He'd voiced his concern before. "Both you and that Hughes should be put in straitjackets. Avoiding the press is one thing. Actually committing assault and battery on them is a very serious matter. If all the bad movies you make for us won't destroy your career, beating up on the press will surely deliver the death blow."

Her physical assault on the press was viewed as aberrational in those pre-Frank Sinatra days. Actually, Kate was a pioneer. By the 1980s, celebrities attacking the paparazzi and reporters was not only commonplace, but the subject of repeated television shows.

Since Kate battered the press, they fought back, not with tennis rackets but with words. One magazine writer stated that, "Instead of striving for sincerity in a tender moment in a scene in *A Woman Rebels,* Katharine Hepburn delivers the line as if she were asking the milkman not to call next week."

Another critic suggested that "at the age of twenty-eight, it is time for Katharine Hepburn to retire from the screen. Give her a rest and certainly give her public a rest—that is, if she still has a public after the release of *A Woman Rebels.*"

Kate was still compared to Garbo as a screen star of mystery, who went to great pains to shroud the actual details of her private life. One reporter wrote, "the chief mystery about Katharine Hepburn is why she remains a screen star, or, why she ever became one in the first place." Noting her temperament, the fan magazine writer asked, "Why has her fire not caused her to be fired?"

In yet another so-called "fan" magazine, Kate read, "Hollywood is fed up with the gaucheries of this red-headed New Englander, who has no beauty, no figure at least in the conventional Hollywood sense, no facial bone structure, and is decidedly unglamorisable."

Of all the things written about her, those remarks seemed to provoke the most anger in her. She started carrying around a copy of *Liberty* magazine, showing it to anyone who seemed to show the slightest interest. The article stated, "You don't have to have taken drawing lessons to see that Katharine Hepburn has a lovely skull and that's one thing the studio can't change."

"At least I have something left that the world appreciates," she exclaimed. "If only my skull. But I have a brain, too. The stupid magazine didn't even mention that."

The most devastating attack was yet to come. Berman himself showed her a news feature story by the writer, Phyllis Sheldon, in which she provocatively wrote: "Considering the personal rumors circulating about Katharine Hepburn, why hasn't the office of Mr. Will Hays, charged with overseeing the morals of the stars, stepped in and acted on behalf of a decent community? Didn't Pandro S. Berman get the unmarried Miss Hepburn to sign the standard morals clause before hiring her? Or is this strong-willed star, flitting from one affair to another, beyond traditional morality, as practiced in our country of God-fearing Christians. This sole black sheep of the Hollywood flock should have been *baa-arred.*"

Her former beau, Douglas Fairbanks Jr., tried to apologize for her to the press, claiming she just didn't want to be a part of the media circus surrounding the stars—"and that is her right. She does say if you don't like my attitude, you can lump it, or even better, go to hell! Kate has the courage to say and do what a lot of us feel but we fear we'll lose our jobs if we don't cooperate. In contrast, she says, 'If I lose my job, I'll just go back East to daddy. I don't need the money, and I don't need fans.'"

When cornered and asked to explain her hostile actions to the press, she responded, "What the hell are they going to do about it if they don't like it? Even the tone of my voice rings with a certain violence. So, I'm violent? So what? I feel good about it. I come by it naturally. I loved one Hollywood producer who said if I were cast as Little Red Riding Hood, I'd end up eating the wolf. After all, I never pretended to be as saccharine as Ginger Rogers. Oh, God, anything but that!"

***

In an action that some of the financiers of RKO judged as "insane," Pandro S. Berman once again cast Kate in a period drama, *Quality Street*. Because George Stevens had momentarily rescued Kate's career when he'd directed her in *Alice Adams*, Berman secured his services again, hoping he could pull off the same stunt.

Although leading man, Franchot Tone, who was married at the time to Joan Crawford, had turned down working with Kate before, he accepted the role of Dr. Valentine Brown opposite Kate's character of Phoebe Throssel.

Later, George Cukor would tell Kate, "The name of Phoebe Thrassel alone should have tipped you off that you were making a box-office bomb like we did with *Sylvia Scarlett*."

As if doomed to repeat her mistakes, Kate found herself signed to do another film based on a play by Sir James M. Barrie, although she'd flopped with an adaptation of another one of his works, *The Little Minister*, in 1934.

In this new script, Kate's suitor, as played by Tone, goes off to one of the Napoleonic Wars and is gone for a decade. When he returns, Kate's character has turned into a dowdy old maid. Back home, her warrior suitor doesn't even recognize his former flame.

Coquettishly, Kate disguises herself by dressing up as Phoebe's glamorous, fictitious niece. Tone, along with other handsome suitors, falls hopelessly in love with this niece in disguise, actually Phoebe herself, no longer looking plain.

Before the end of the film, Tone proposes marriage to his long-suffering bride-to-be. As Anderson Lawler later remarked, "You kept your virginity for ten years waiting for your lover to come back. The concept is unique in the annals of Hollywood."

A decade earlier, Marion Davies had scored a modest success with the same Barrie story, but fans had changed a lot since then. Even before shooting began, Berman began to have doubts, wondering if the world, about to go to war, really cared about a "rich girl in crinolines carrying a lace parasol and tossing up between several handsome young men." He later told Kate, "Maybe we thought it escapist fare or some God damn thing like that. Well, the only thing that escaped was our money. All of it. Down the drain."

Early one Monday morning, Berman summoned Kate to his office to tell her that Stevens had nixed the idea of Jane Loring as editor. "'No way!' he told me. He's hired Henry Berman—no relation to me—instead."

"We'll see about that," she said. "Stevens needs to be taught once again who's the star of this picture."

"Well, if you want to have it out with him, he's reshooting a final scene on *Swing Time* with Ginger Rogers right now. I don't want to get involved."

With her face contorted into a grimace, Kate marched toward the set of *Swing Time*. She hadn't seen her former lover since she'd caught him in the bathtub with Ginger Rogers.

***

When Kate arrived on the set of *Swing Time*, she was first introduced to the film's chief photographer, David Abel. Before taking her over to Stevens, she also met Henry Berman, who had been selected instead of Jane Loring as film editor for *Quality Street*. Berman was also the film editor on *Swing Time.*

After shaking his hand, she was very blunt to Berman. "I'm here to meet with Stevens," she told him. "If that meeting is successful, you won't be working as editor of *Quality Street*. Jane Loring will. I insist that all my films be edited by Loring. Why don't you stick to this silly fluff with the blonde chorine?"

Not knowing how to answer her, Berman directed her over to Stevens who sat in the director's chair, going over his script one final time. On seeing Kate, he got up to shake her hand but his reception was a bit chilly.

"So!" he said. "We're going to be working together again. I've read the script from Mortimer Offner and Allan Scott. I don't like it. Needs a lot of work. Think we can pull this one off?"

"Of course, we can," she said, voicing an optimism she didn't really feel. "It'll be a grand costume epic. Better than *Little Women*."

"Don't you repeat that sentiment with every period turkey you make?" he asked rather provocatively.

Her face stinging with his insult about her box-office failures, she smiled with all the self-assurance she could muster. "I've seen Walter Plunkett's costumes, and they look gorgeous, though not my sort of thing. But the role calls for it. Mel Burns will be on hand making me look gorgeous. Of course with my genes I gave him a lot to work with."

"If you're searching for a compliment that you're holding up well, you've got it," he said. "Could you excuse me? Ginger's coming on the set, and this has proven to be one of our most difficult scenes to shoot."

"I'm surprised," she said sarcastically. "Surely you and Ginger have had plenty of practice learning how to shampoo. Besides, isn't shooting any scene with Ginger difficult?"

Kate plunked down in the director's chair so recently abandoned by Stevens. When Rogers spotted Kate on the set, she pointedly ignored her.

Kate later claimed that she deliberately jinxed the shampoo scene with Rogers. In the scene, Rogers becomes angry with Astaire and goes into the bathroom to shampoo her hair, leaving him alone in the living room. There he sits down at a piano and breaks into song. Hearing its sound, Rogers comes out to make up with her beau, with her hair full of bubbling soap. They kiss and reconcile their differences, and the feel-good film eventually ségués into a happy ending.

The photographer, David Abel, explained to Kate that Stevens and Rogers had tried at least two dozen brands of soap and shampoo. Each time the product got hot under the intense lights, it ran down her face and onto her neck. Even shaving cream didn't work. Stevens finally suggested egg whites.

Somewhat nervous at being hawkeyed by Kate, Rogers tried the scene with egg whites but the fierce overhead lights cooked the egg in her hair.

Seeing that the scene wasn't working, Kate called out, "What kind of shit are you cooking up here, George? The Ginger omelette?" She deliberately laughed raucously, interrupting the scene, which was no good anyway.

A determined Rogers headed for her dressing room and came back once again, this time informing her director/lover that she had decided on her own to try whipped cream for a change. It was piled on her head like a soda jerk might top off a delectable banana split. Amazingly, after all those tries, the take worked. Rogers walked triumphantly by Kate without speaking and headed once again for her dressing room.

Stevens came over to greet Kate.

"If only I could direct Ginger Rogers," she said to him. "It would be the ditzy blonde's last motion picture, and the world would be a better place."

***

In spite of her trying to disrupt the final takes on *Swing Time*, Stevens accepted her invitation to dinner at her five-acre Laurel Canyon house. With all her "live-ins" gone, Kate resided there alone except for her cook and housekeeper, Johanna Madsen, and a pair of cocker spaniels, "Mike and Pete." Months before, Ford had persuaded her to return the "waving shoulder monkey" to its keeper. The primate had developed a case of chronic diarrhea.

Freed from Laura, Kate liked being alone. Jane Loring was at her side whenever she was needed, but she didn't live on the premises. That left Kate free to entertain as she wished. As was his habit, she had come to expect Howard Hughes to arrive without advance notice at virtually any time. .

Laura, along with Jack and Luddy, had recently come to California for a reunion and a week-long holiday, and Kate had thoroughly enjoyed their company. She promised that after *Quality Street* was shot, she'd be back East to see all of them.

On one occasion, at six o'clock in the morning a short while after her trio of friends had departed, a neighbor spotted Leland Hayward, or "Margaret Sullavan's husband," as he was known to some, driving down the hill from Kate's Laurel Canyon home. This led to speculation that the two erstwhile lovers "were back at it again."

On the evening of George Steven's appearance at Kate's home, she prepared their dinner herself. Only that afternoon, she had told Kenneth MacKenna that she fully expected to get Loring back on the film as editor of *Quality Street.*

What exactly transpired that night between Kate and her director isn't known. "Stevens managed to pull a fast one," Pandro S. Berman later confided to his art director, Robert De Grasse. "He not only got Kate to agree to let Henry become the editor, but that devil Stevens became her on-again, off-again lover once again."

***

As shooting began on *Quality Street,* Stevens remained bitter that Alfred Santell had been assigned to direct *Winterset.* He told Kate that, "I had my heart set on directing that picture." At times Stevens seemed more interested in hearing news of *Winterset* than he was in directing Kate in *Quality Street.*

Later interpreted as one of the most avant-garde of the *film noire* genre, *Winterset* was a stark and abbreviated 77-minute adaptation of a Maxwell Anderson play, a dark and brooding drama, made in 1936, about an immigrant, Bartolomeo Romagna, who was falsely accused, condemned, and then executed for a payroll robbery. Cast members included Burgess Meredith in one of his first major roles and the actress billed only as "Margo." Trivia buffs take note: Long before her later fame as a TV comedienne, Lucille Ball had a minor and uncredited role in the film as a walk-on.

Because of his disappointment at losing the directorship of *Winterset,* Stevens seemed to rather recklessly try to sabotage his own director's efforts on the set of *Quality Street.* Later, he admitted, "I don't think I did Kate or her career any good by directing this bomb. She became more and more precious as the film progressed—I doubt if progress is the right word—and preciousness was always her weakness. I should have stepped in and helped but I didn't. All I could think about was *Winterset.* I allowed *Quality Street* to become a disaster, and it was all my fault."

Stevens became infuriated when Kate insisted on bringing Jane Loring to the set every day, even though she had not been hired by RKO in any official capacity. The two women went into their usual huddles, and he suspected that once again Loring was trying to become a frustrated director, taking over his own job. Often Loring gave Kate advice that completely contradicted his own direction. Kate and Loring were joined by a coterie of two other female advisers, Kate's stand-in, Eve March, and Emily Perkins, Kate's secretary. She referred to her cohorts as "my gang of girls."

In a fit of fury one day, Stevens got angry at all of them. He kicked Perkins, March and Loring off the set, forbidding their return.

"I don't want your God damn stooges advising you," Stevens shouted at Kate in front of the cast members Fay Bainter and Bonita Granville. "I'm the fucking director on this picture—not a pack of lesbians!"

Kate was furious and walked off the picture herself, threatening never to return. Pandro Berman drove up to Laurel Canyon later that afternoon and prevailed upon Kate to return to work the following morning. Reluctantly, she agreed.

After Pandro Berman's departure from Kate's house, Loring drove up the mountain. She was furious. Not only had she been demoted from film editor to the role of an unpaid advisor, she'd even been kicked off the lot. She demanded that Kate stand up to Stevens and fight him. No longer did Loring want to be editor of the film, but its assistant director.

When Kate told her that Berman would never go for that, she and Loring had a bitter fight. Accusations whirled, the exact nature of which are not known. However, when Kate called Cukor in the morning, she claimed she never wanted to speak to Loring again. "We're through!" she told Cukor. "The bitch said I merely claim to be an independent woman, but when it comes to standing up to a real man, I always give in like I'm doing with Stevens."

Loring had a point. When Stevens drove up later that night and spent the night making love to her, Kate the next day appeared rather docile on the set, the camera picking up on an unusual passivity.

Her truce with Stevens didn't last long. She was soon battling him again during the day, although making love to him at night. "It was amazing," Berman recalled, "having something to do with opposites attracting. It was as if their battles on the set during the day only goaded them into more intense lovemaking at night. I think George felt he couldn't control Kate on screen but took pride in subduing her off-screen. Perhaps that made him feel more like a man. When you're around Kate, you always have to grab your nuts to make sure they're still there."

***

In 1936 and 1937, during the filming of *Quality Street,* Kate befriended a young actress, Joan Fontaine, who had been cast in the film as the minor character of Charlotte Parratt. Initially, Kate was impressed with the delicate, though insipid, *ingénue*. More than impressed, really. Kate suggested to Cukor that she'd been tempted to try to seduce Fontaine. Cukor told her, "Don't even try. Joan's heterosexual credentials are solid as a rock."

Though deciding that an attempted seduction would be hopeless, Kate admired Fontaine to the point that she scheduled a meeting about her with Pandro Berman. She urged the studio boss to "Put that girl in leads in 'B' pictures."

Of course, that request could be interpreted as either a compliment or as an insult, but years later, Fontaine expressed her gratitude to Hepburn for the many valuable lessons that those mostly unworthy early films had taught her.

Fast forward to 1940: Bette Davis in *The Letter* and Kate in *The Philadelphia Story* are the odds-on favorites to triumph over Joan Fontaine's performance in *Rebecca*. However, in the last few weeks before the Academy voted, there was speculation that Fontaine might win. And although Kate had pretended to the press that she didn't care about the Oscar race, she jealously told Cukor. "I shouldn't have pushed Fontaine's career. I should have let her sink into the oblivion she so richly deserved."

Ironically, Fontaine, Bette Davis, and Kate all lost to Kate's least favorite star, Ginger Rogers, who won for the role that Kate had rejected, the lead in *Kitty Foyle.*

***

Unlike some of her other leading men, the suave, New York-born Franchot Tone impressed Kate with his breeding, sophistication, and background. As she told Stevens, "He can't help it if he had the bad taste to marry Joan Crawford. Poor man!"

Only two years older than Kate, Tone was struggling to break through as an A-list star. Regrettably, he would never achieve the prominence he so desired. He had won an Oscar nomination as the midshipman Byam in MGM's *Mutiny on the Bounty*, supporting lead actors Charles Laughton and Clark Gable. Mostly he was cast as rich playboys, often in a tuxedo, performing such ridiculous stunts as wanting to run barefoot through Jean Harlow's hair in *Bombshell.*

Although married to Crawford, Tone was a notorious womanizer. Bette Davis was said to have fallen madly in love with Tone when they starred in her Oscar-winning melodrama, *Dangerous.* It's not clear if Davis was really in love or whether she merely wanted to piss off Crawford by seducing her husband.

During their first week of working together, Kate was attracted to Tone, but she felt he was not getting the sexual signals she was sending out. She confided his lack of interest to her make-up artist, Mel Burns.

"Have no fear," Burns assured her. "Tone will come around. He heard what happened to poor Fred MacMurray when Stevens directed you guys in *Alice*

Adams—take after take under those intense lights to punish Fred for seducing you. Tone thinks you belong to Stevens, and he's staying clear. Only Spencer Tracy is foolish enough to go after the director's mistress on some of his films."

Abandoning plans to seduce Tone, Kate concentrated on finishing the film. At her luncheon picnics, he amused her with stories, especially about his having just made another tedious period drama, *The Gorgeous Hussy* with Joan Crawford. Kate was extremely interested because the lead in that film had originally been intended for her.

"Usually it's the leading lady who goes for me," Tone confided. "But in *Hussy*, I had three pansy boys—Robert Taylor, Lionel Barrymore, and James Stewart—lusting after me. Melvyn Douglas and I were the only straight actors in that turkey."

A highly competent stage actor, Tone had appeared with Katharine Cornell on Broadway in *The Age of Innocence*. Both Tone and Kate agreed that films were not for them, the actor claiming, "The theater is in my blood."

He confided to Kate that he hated his contract with MGM, viewing it as a form of bondage. "Louis B. Mayer simply doesn't know I'm a serious actor. To ease the pain of being trapped in Hollywood, I take to the bottle or run after women. Sometimes when I get really frustrated, I beat hell out of Joan. She escapes over the wall to our next-door neighbor, Barbara Stanwyck. That lez loves seducing my wife. Joan reciprocates. And whenever Frank Fay beats the shit out of Babs, she climbs that same wall for love and comfort from Joan."

Having written him off as a possible beau, Kate became enchanted with Tone once again when she saw how he liked the plays of Shakespeare, the poetry of Keats, and classical music. As she later told Cukor, "I think I fell in love with him the day he came into my dressing room all distraught. At first I thought he was trying to seduce me. But after he closed the door and came inside, he broke down and sobbed in my arms. 'I can't tell you what happened last night,' he said. 'But Joan has taken away my pride as a man.'"

After that day, she grew closer to him, as he filled her with his dreams of returning to New York. "It's the only civilized place to live," he said. "Late night suppers. Champagne. Opening nights. Museums, concerts. And you and I, Kate, would appear on stage together. Just as the orchestra is tuning up for the overture, I'd kiss you without spoiling your makeup. Then we'd appear before the bright lights and deafening applause. The two of us. The toast of Broadway!"

One day on the set she served him afternoon tea, and as he got up to leave, he said, "Gee, you're a nice dame."

She looked startled. "No one's ever called me a dame before."

"I only said that because those were the first words I ever uttered to Joan Crawford. I met her on the set when we were making *Today We Live*. In her case, I was wrong. But in your case, I think I got it right."

"Makes me sound like a horse up for sale. I don't think of myself as a dame."

He smiled winningly. "Dame is the nicest compliment a man can pay a woman."

Soon Kate quit inviting cast and crew to her picnics, narrowing her guest list down to just Tone and Stevens. She seemed to revel in the homage paid to her by both her macho director and her handsome leading man, as photographer Robert De Grasse would later recall.

One afternoon when Kate was having tea alone with Tone, she pointedly asked him. "My curiosity is just too strong—it's a bad trait I have. I've got to know what Joan Crawford did to reduce you to sobs."

"I guess I can tell," he said, "since I've had to get used to it. One night she invited Clark Gable over and told me that he had been her lover for a very long time, and that he was going to continue to be her lover. She said that Gable planned to visit our house at least two nights a week. During those nights, I could either go to a hotel or else shack up with any other woman I was attracted to."

That night, a Thursday, Kate looked forward to returning alone to her Laurel Canyon home. On Thursday night she dismissed her entire staff, preferring one night of the week for herself. Invariably, she worked in her garden, "letting the dirt pile up under my fingernails," as she would say. All her life, even deep into old age, she preferred to do her own gardening.

Seeing that it was eight o'clock and that the twilight had long ago faded, she went inside the house. Not wanting to track dirt into her bedroom, she shucked her dirty clothing downstairs and headed for the shower. She'd had so many sandwiches at afternoon tea that day that she didn't want any dinner, not even a light supper. She did drink a glass of milk, however.

After her shower, and with only a large towel draped around her body, she headed for her bedroom. As she turned on the light, she screamed.

Lying stark naked in the center of her bed was Franchot Tone.

"How did you get in?" she asked.

"Through the back door," he said calmly. "I came through the garden. I heard you in the shower."

"You'll have to go," she said nervously, although she wasn't afraid of this intruder.

"C'mon, Kate," he implored her. "I have signed affidavits from some of the most famous actresses in Hollywood about what a great lover I am. First, my wife, Joan Crawford. Need I go on? Marlene Dietrich. Bette Davis. Garbo, of course, has eluded me."

"Get out!" she shouted at him.

He looked down to his genitals. "You can obviously see what the attraction is."

"I can see that your endowment would be more appropriate on a horse that on a mere mortal," she said.

"My chief asset is beginning to rise at the sight of your beauty," he said. "Please drop that God damn towel so I'll have something to write in my memoirs about the night I seduced the great screen actress and Oscar winner, Miss Katharine Hepburn."

Kate must have been intrigued because the towel eventually came off, and she headed over to the bed to join him. "What the hell!" she said. With great care, he reached for her and took her in his arms, pressing his body against hers.

The next morning, after preparing breakfast for Tone, she kissed him goodbye, and he drove off in his own car. Neither one of them wanted to be seen arriving on the set together, lest word about the situation reach George Stevens.

Immediately after Tone had left, Kate called her friend, Anderson Lawler, to review the events of the evening with him. She loved to do that.

"I hear Tone is fantastic," Lawler said. "All the queens—and I don't mean just the female ones—in Hollywood want him. But he seems strictly off-limits to us boys."

"After last night, I'm seriously considering flying home and having my father sew me up down there. I don't know how Joan takes it."

"Darling, if you'd only called me beforehand," Lawler said. "I could have warned you. Among the fellators of Hollywood, Franchot Tone is known as 'jawbreaker!'"

***

Before the final shooting had ended on *Quality Street,* insiders at RKO were privately voicing their concerns that this Stevens-directed picture would be Kate's last film for the studio. Both Stevens and Kate were talking daily, near the end of shooting, about their fears that "We have a failure on our hands."

Maybe it was because he was making love to Kate most nights, but Stevens feared he had lost his objectivity about his star. In a rare candid admission, he told Berman, "I'm not some Jane Loring, hopelessly swooning over Kate. I can't control her mannerisms. They're worse in this film than ever before."

Ominously, word leaked out to the press that Kate had another turkey on her hands. Many columnists predicted the end of her film career. *Variety* wrote, "A succession of unfortunate selections of material has marooned a competent girl in a bog of box-office frustration. There is probably no one in pictures who needs a real money film as much as this actress, yet we hear *Quality Street* will continue her string of disasters."

Quality Street finally opened, playing to practically empty theaters and losing one quarter of a million dollars. Most reviewers were horrified by Kate's "clawing, scratching, and back-arching impersonation of Phoebe Throssel."

The New York Times delivered the *coup de grâce:* "Katharine Hepburn's Phoebe Throssel needs a neurologist far more than a husband. Such flutterings and jitterings and twitchings, such handwringings and mouth-quiverings, such

266

runnings about and eye-brow raising have not been seen on the screen in many a moon."

Long before she read the reviews, Kate had fled from Hollywood. "I've made four skunks in a row," she told Kenneth MacKenna. "It's time to get out of Dodge and head for the border, as John Ford might say."

To save face and with no other offers of movie roles on the horizon, Kate announced that she was giving up her film career and returning to her first love, the stage.

She put her romance with George Stevens "straight from the oven and into the pantry to cool down."

Her unrequited former "beau," Howard Hughes, was about to fly back into her life.

***

In California, Kate was rootless, always renting—never buying—a house there. Home was Connecticut, and it was there she went to lick her wounds after her (perceived) failure in films.

There, she turned to Dr. Hepburn for solace. His trim, six-foot body was still in great shape because of constant exercise, and although streaks of gray had appeared at his temples, he was youthful looking as he approached his fifty-eighth birthday. He told her to quit making "silly period pictures" and to accept the role of *Jane Eyre* as a means of reinforcing her reputation as a serious dramatic actress. (Apparently he was ignoring the fact that *Jane Eyre* was also a period piece.) And as if foreseeing what lay in her future, he also suggested that Kate should consider light comedies.

Upon her arrival in Hartford, Kate found one-hundred roses—"the most perfect ever grown"—waiting for her along with a diamond bracelet from Howard Hughes. She kept the flowers, but returned the diamonds with a note. "Dear Howard," she wrote. "I've been accused of many things. But a Las Vegas prostitute I'm not. Your bracelet is beautiful, but not my style. Of men, I've never demanded—no ice, no dice. Love, Your Country Mouse."

In spite of the bitter cold that winter, she went swimming every weekend at Fenwick, jumping into the icy waters of Long Island Sound until "I turned into an icicle." Before the rest of the family got up, she rose every morning at four-thirty, cooking her favorite breakfast of chicken livers with eggs.

She still called men her beaus but didn't really have one. Hughes was a mere flirtation. Leland Hayward, though still her agent, had gone into "cold storage in my heart." She'd temporarily abandoned George Stevens, and soon heard reports that he was once again dating Ginger Rogers. Laura remained her steadfast friend and occasional romantic liaison. Since the Hepburns were not enamored of Laura, Kate preferred to see her at Turtle Bay in Manhattan or else at Laura's house in New Jersey.

Luddy continued to visit on the weekend and he and Kate had become "old comrades like a comfortable pair of well-worn bedroom slippers," as she liked to say. Luddy was still in love with Jack, but he confided privately to her that he could not go on forever leading the life of a homosexual. "One day I'll marry," he told her, "if only for the sake of appearances."

"I have a friend like that in Hollywood," she said. "Archie Leach. You know him as Cary Grant."

"For him, I would become a permanent homosexual," he told her.

The Theatre Guild wired her an offer of one-thousand dollars a week to star in Charlotte Brontë's *Jane Eyre* on the road before taking it to Broadway. Calling it "blood money," she demanded and was reluctantly granted another five-hundred dollars a week before agreeing to the contract. "That's for not giving me the five dollars a week pay raise I demanded when I appeared as a maid in *A Month in the Country*," Kate wrote to Theresa Helburn, the Guild's producer.

The original version of the stage play had opened on October 13, 1936, to mixed reviews in London. In various reincarnations, *Jane Eyre* had already been seen in America, as it was a favorite show to take on the road. Leland viewed *Jane Eyre* as dubious comeback material for Kate's reappearance on the stage, although both Luddy and Laura thought it would be a suitable vehicle for her.

The latest version of *Jane Eyre* had been written by Helen Jerome, with whom Kate would tangle later. "Victorian melodrama or not," Kate threatened, "I'm going to punch up the role." Although Hughes might have nicknamed her "Country Mouse," Katharine Hepburn was no mouse. Instead of a shy, retiring heroine as modestly conceived by Jerome, Kate planned to bring a little "fire and brimstone" to the character of Jane Eyre. "I want her to be outrageous, provocative, and a fiercely independent woman," she told Leland.

To fortify her to go ahead with the play, John Ford wrote, not with a proposal of marriage, but with a "firm commitment" to bring the classic to the screen. He was never to carry through on that promise, however.

When *Jane Eyre* finally reached the screen in 1944, it starred not Kate, but the fast-rising Joan Fontaine. Cukor took Kate to see the movie, which co-starred Orson Welles and "such children" as Margaret O'Brien and Elizabeth Taylor.

After the film ended, Cukor asked for Kate's opinion about Fontaine's acting. "I liked her better in *Blond Cheat* and *Maid's Night Out*," she said sarcastically, referring to the potboilers Fontaine had made for RKO in the late 1930s.

Kate was doubly delighted to learn that Tony Miner would be her director for *Jane Eyre*. Unlike Jed Harris, Miner had always been her supporter and had always praised her performances, good or bad.

Jane Eyre was to begin rehearsals and open in preview in New Haven. Kate wanted to commute to rehearsals from West Hartford. The Guild arranged a sleek black limousine for her. It turned out that it had been rented from Weinstein and Sons Funeral Home. On the door was the sign, REST IN PEACE. The owner of the funeral parlor, Harry Weinstein, insisted on personally chauffeuring Kate back and forth between West Hartford and New Haven, "because I loved her in *Little Women*."

Working once again for the Theatre Guild, Kate felt that she was among friends, and she was. All three of the Guild's producers were admirers of hers, including lavender-haired Theresa Helburn. The co-founder of the Guild, the volatile, hawk-faced Lawrence Langner, remained one of Kate's dearest friends for years, as did his wife, the shrewd but soft-hearted Armina Marshall.

Kate had veto power over the casting of her leading man. When she signed for *Jane Eyre*, she was told that the role of Edward Rochester, her co-star, would be played by Laurence Olivier. When it turned out that he wasn't available, George Cukor suggested John Barrymore, claiming that he had sobered up. "That will be the day," Kate said, turning down the suggestion. Finally, a "non-star," British actor Dennis Hoey was signed for the role.

Hoey was no Barrymore or Olivier. He was an actor with very little talent and no presence on the stage, and was practically "devoured" by Kate. After the first day of watching the actor in rehearsals, Kate poured out her disappointment to Helburn. "Hoey's adequate, but, oh, so unexciting." Even though they could easily have dismissed him, the Guild, amazingly, kept Hoey on.

Although she was technically a failed actress, both in Hollywood and on the stage, Kate still demanded the treatment that was due to a great theatrical diva. The blonde-haired actress Patricia Peardon, playing a minor role, said she was "just amazed when Hepburn demanded that screens be placed around her on the stage so that she could not be seen at work by prying eyes. Imagine any other actress making such an outrageous demand."

George S. Kaufman seemed to agree with Peardon's appraisal when he dropped in to see how rehearsals were going. He told Theresa Helburn, "Kate is doing this just so that she won't catch 'Acting.' Good luck with this turkey. There are many people allergic to the peculiar charms of your star, including a huge segment of the movie-going public."

Although she'd been signed because of the star power of her name, Kate told a shocked Lawrence Langner that she wanted her name under the title and in the same print as the other actors in the play. Although he wanted to feature her with star billing to increase ticket sales, Langner said, "That's very generous of you." "Like hell it is!" she countered, "I don't want to be blamed if this play fails. I've drowned in *The Lake*. By the way, when this play reaches New York, Dorothy Parker is to be banned from the theater or else I won't go on, even if it's opening night."

Jane Eyre opened on December 26, 1936 in New Haven. One-thousand long-stemmed roses arrived backstage for Kate. She read the note: "Dear Country Mouse. Become the mouse that roared. Love Howard."

That night when Kate went on, she felt that the audience wasn't responding to *Jane Eyre,* and she voiced her concern later that night to the theater directors. "That bastard, Jed Harris, forced me to go on stage in New York in *The Lake* to face those critics when I wasn't prepared, and I'm not going to let this happen with *Jane Eyre.*" She reminded them that her contract called for extended pre-views if she felt the play needed doctoring. She claimed that the problem lay within Helen Jerome's script, and she demanded extensive rewriting, especially of the third act.

Earlier, Kate had confided to Patricia Peardon. "If I don't make it big on Broadway in *Jane Eyre*, I might as well say good-bye to the theater too. My film career is already in shambles."

Filled with dread and anxiety, and even beginning to regret her decision to appear in *Jane Eyre* in the first place, Kate, along with the cast, headed for a shaky run in Boston, not knowing the surprise that would await her there.

***

Since Laura was involved with family business in New York, Kate, feeling rather lonely, checked into The Ritz Hotel in Boston. Her only companion was the stout-hearted, no-nonsense Yorkshire woman, Emily Perkins, her secretary. Rather mannish and speaking in a brogue, she had met Kate when she'd served as a wardrobe mistress, having been hired by Walter Plunkett, the costumer on *Mary of Scotland.* John Ford had become immensely fond of her, and she called him "Pappy," preferring "Baby" as Kate's nickname. They called her "Em."

As Em slept in a nearby small maid's room, Kate had gone to bed in a master four-poster around nine-thirty. About midnight, she heard a door opening. Jumping up, she reached for her gown and looked to see who the intruder was.

When she flipped on the lights, she was stunned to see Howard Hughes standing in the living room of her suite. He'd booked the suite next door and had bribed a hotel clerk to open the locked door to Kate's connecting suite.

"He looked so helpless and so lovesick, I couldn't object," Kate later told friends. "I likened him to John the Baptist about to lose his head."

Hughes stayed up talking to Kate until three o'clock that morning. He even ordered champagne sent to their room. She joined him for two glasses but that was her limit, although he managed to down three bottles: normally he wasn't such a heavy drinker. He told her that he was filled with excitement and wanted to share a secret with her.

As she'd later tell her confidants, she thought that after all those roses and the offer of the diamond bracelet that he was going to declare his undying love for her.

His secret turned out to be quite different, although infinitely more exciting in terms of the world. He revealed to her that in January, when the westerly winds would be howling in from the Pacific Ocean, he was going to attempt to

270

set a coast-to-coast aerial speed record. "With that wind billowing at my back, I'll fly faster than any man before me."

"How thrilling!" she said. "A lot different from crossing the country by stagecoach and fighting off the Indians."

Impulsively, she asked if she could fly with him.

He looked amazed at the suggestion. "There's room for only one pilot in the cockpit." Seeing her disappointment, he offered to teach her to fly. Leland had once made the same offer, but she'd turned him down. Enthusiastic about Hughes' dream, she accepted his offer and got his reassurance that it was "no idle promise."

As she would later tell Anderson Lawler when she returned to Hollywood, Hughes "didn't kiss me—not even on the cheek. I was beginning to think he was more homosexual than bisexual. He shared his great dream with me, and the telling of it seemed to sap all his energy. He fell asleep on my sofa. I went and got a blanket for him. Don't believe all those stories from maids who were each given a hundred dollars to report that they caught us both naked in bed together, going at it like animals in heat. We became great friends on that night he 'broke' into my suite like a rapist. Poor Howard. I don't know if he really knows how to rape a woman. In his heart, he remains mommie's little boy. He's so unlike George Stevens and John Ford. Perhaps with some of the same problems of Ernest Hemingway."

***

After opening in Boston, Hughes had to disappear "wherever he disappeared to," she said. She was left alone to face the ire of the Boston theater critics, one of whom found that "Hepburn's famous voice is the least prepossessing quality she has as an actress." Another critic praised only her smile. She dismissed that review with scorn. "It sounds like an ad for my dentist," she told Theresa Helburn. What made Kate genuinely furious about the reviews involved the discovery that any praise heaped on *Jane Eyre* was because of the acting of Dennis Hoey.

The following afternoon Kate demanded a rehearsal. When the playwright Helen Jerome appeared, she denounced the script. "The script is still weak—too old-fashioned. You've reduced Brontë's subtlety and tangled webs to genteel Victorian parlor drama. You've turned it into a soap opera. The production is completely unfocused."

Refusing to give in to her demands, Jerome stormed out of the theater, but not before shouting, "The only God damn thing unfocused in this play is one Katharine Hepburn."

Before flying to Chicago, Kate was shown the kindest review, which found *Jane Eyre* "healthily alive but in a very unfinished state," her own sentiments exactly.

On her opening night in Chicago, Hughes flew in again. When he was spotted in the theater, the Chicago press went on red alert. "We handled the story with the same excitement we'd handle any other, even, say, the assassination of President Roosevelt," claimed Johanton Elder, a reporter at the time. "In other words, Second Coming headlines."

On the second night, crowds formed around the theater—not just playgoers, but thousands of local fans wanting to catch a glimpse of the famous couple. Hughes and Kate seemed to enjoy the various ruses they used to escape their fans and the rubber-neckers. Once Kate arrived at the theater in a garbage truck, entering through the back alley.

Almost overnight she and Hughes became the most famous couple in America. There was endless speculation about their possible marriage.

Actually, Hughes had already proposed to her, in the interconnecting suites they shared on the Ambassador East Hotel's ninth floor.

Their relationship still hadn't been consummated. "He hadn't even kissed me yet," Kate later told Cukor. However, Hughes did give her the largest diamond ring she'd ever seen as an engagement ring, perhaps forgetting that she'd rejected his "ice" before. Not just a ring, he also presented her with the diamond bracelet she'd returned to him and a new diamond tiara.

The actress Patricia Peardon found the gift of the tiara ludicrous. "Hughes should have given it to me. I'd have been glad to get it. Imagine Kate Hepburn wearing a diamond tiara!"

In essence, Hughes had given her a fortune in diamonds in Depression America. Perhaps to show her disdain, she did not wear the ring, which she left, along with the bracelet and her tiara, unguarded in her dressing room. When she returned after the third night's performance, she found the jewelry stolen.

She was afraid to report the theft to the police, fearing it would make headlines. In despair, she called Dr. Hepburn for advice. "Thank God, those gems are gone," he told her. "You have no need for stuff like that anyway."

Amazingly, when she'd reunited with Hughes, he never inquired about why she wasn't wearing the engagement ring, and he never again mentioned the valuable diamond bracelet and the colossal diamond tiara.

To her dismay, Kate learned that Brooks Atkinson, "the butcher of Broadway," had arrived in the audience to see the play before its opening in New York. This was against all so-called ethics of theater critics. Atkinson didn't seem to mind being caught reviewing a play in its out-of-town tryouts. As always, he was no admirer of Kate's performance.

He wrote, "It is to be feared that the current play is only a pedestrian adaptation, and Miss Hepburn is not yet the sort of trouping actress who can mold a full-length performance out of scrappy materials. When the play is finished you have, accordingly, no feeling that anything vital has happened."

Armed with Atkinson's review, Kate once again confronted Helen Jerome, demanding that she completely rewrite the third act, which Kate viewed as the most disastrous. Jerome adamantly refused, and even the Guild's directors, siding with Kate, could not get this determined woman to change her mind.

Kate demanded and got more time on the road, claiming that she would be slaughtered by "the pit vipers of New York" including yet another attack from Atkinson, if they dared take *Jane Eyre* to Broadway. "It would be *The Lake* all over again," Kate said. "God knows what that alcoholic cow, Dorothy Parker, would think to say this time."

***

Just as mysteriously as he'd arrived, Hughes just as mysteriously disappeared. Only Kate knew that he was headed for the Hughes Aircraft hangar in California to prepare for his historic flight across America. He called her every night to keep her abreast, as she was most anxious to hear of the slightest detail, regardless of how technical.

Wanting the inside story, Kate's friends at the Guild—Helburn, Marshall, and Langner—pressed her for insiderish details about the national question: Would Katharine Hepburn marry Howard Hughes?

Instead of answering the question directly, she preferred to tell them amusing stories of about how Hughes had begun dating her, beginning with how he'd landed his plane on the bluffs where *Sylvia Scarlett* was being shot.

She claimed she learned that they shared a mutual interest in golf when she was playing on the wide greens of the Bel Air Country Club. "Howard landed a Scout on a very narrow expanse of the greens," she said. "He had to maneuver between two towering pine trees. He had only three feet on either side for his wings to clear. The manager of the club ran out and started to denounce the pilot until he saw that it was Howard Hughes. He didn't want to anger Hughes too much, fearing he might buy the golf course and fire the manager."

Kate said that after Hughes emerged from the Scout, he played nine holes with her and then she drove him home. Since it couldn't take off on the greens, the Scout had to be disassembled and towed back to the hangar, all at a cost of ten-thousand dollars.

As amusing as that story was, it wasn't really what the directors wanted to hear. Of course, they were interested in Kate's personal welfare, but the trio also had their radar on the box office. Every night *Jane Eyre* was performed, it was standing room only. There was the usual thrill at seeing a real-live movie star, but there was also the added excitement of the possibility that Howard Hughes himself might show up in the audience on any given night.

Back in Hollywood, Cary Grant told friends, "When they speak of each other, they are a mutual admiration society, and they have more in common than bad dressing, of which each is the worst in his or her category." In her phone call to Grant and Cukor, Kate claimed that she admired Hughes's "verve and stamina," although the latter had never been demonstrated in her bed. "He's the top of the available men in the world, and I of women. And both of us have a wild desire to be famous."

She had already succeeded in making the world aware of herself and in a few days, Hughes was about to become even more celebrated than she was.

Hughes told Grant and his associates that Kate was "a brilliant woman—totally without pretense, without sham of any kind. She is, in fact, the most totally magnetic woman on the planet that I plan to fly around sooner than later."

Actually, it was Hughes who was keeping Kate in the headlines, as she was almost on the verge of joining the long list of stars who soared brilliantly in the Thirties, only to see the twilight of their careers on the eve of World War II, as new stars such as Lana Turner and Betty Grable rose to take their places.

As she faced the possible end of her career, Kate was just twenty-eight years old. But Hughes, at the age of thirty, was just on the dawn of his greatest acclaim. As a man, he was viewed as the single most desirable catch in the world.

Only such close friends as Cary Grant and Kate herself knew that Hughes was not the dashing stud aviator and the serial seducer of women that he pretended to be to the world.

***

Although the Empire of Japan was plotting to devour China, and Hitler was involved with "the final solution to the Jewish problem" and threatening to conquer Europe, much of America seemed fixated on the exploits of Howard Hughes as he flew across the country. And of almost equal importance was the possibility of his marriage to Katharine Hepburn.

It was a windy, foggy morning at 2:14am on January 19, 1937, that Hughes in his *Flying Bullet*, which had cost him one-hundred and twenty-five thousand dollars, taxied down the tarmac of the Union Air Terminal in Burbank, California.

Leaving behind a cheering crew, he was about to fly into history, as he piloted the well-built craft to an astonishing and record-breaking altitude of twenty-thousand feet. He'd banked the plane to the right, as he piloted the craft toward the San Bernadino Pass. Nothing, perhaps, could have seemed as distant at that time and place as the East Coast of America.

In Chicago, an anxious Kate joined the rest of America in waiting for the news. Sitting by her radio, Kate learned to her horror that the *Silver Bullet* had lost radio contact with the world somewhere over the skies of northern Arizona. She screamed in panic. Radio announcers speculated that his plane had crashed.

She was standing by as an official bulletin came in from the National Aeronautical Association. The world was informed that no word had been

274

received from the "millionaire playboy hero of the air"—those were the official words of the NAA—for five hours. It was presumed that the plane was lost, and search parties were being rapidly organized in the Southwest to look for Hughes's body and the wreckage.

Kate was teetering on the verge of a nervous breakdown when Theresa Helburn brought her an extra edition of the *Chicago Daily Tribune*. Upon seeing the headlines, she tossed the paper aside and burst into tears. AVIATION HERO LOST!

It seemed that all of America, including Kate, was listening to their radios, when the first bulletin came across the Associated Press wires. A pilot coming in for a landing at Army Field in Middleton, Pennsylvania, had spotted Hughes's *Silver Bullet.* Kate screamed in joy and hugged her friends at the Guild. Tears were running down her cheeks.

She never left the sound of the radio, as bulletins continued to pour out of East Coast America until a headline-blazing announcement was made.

Hughes's silver racer "just seemed to shoot out of the clouds," in the words of one announcer. "It was going at the astonishing rate of three-hundred and eighty miles an hour. It plunged toward the earth in less than a minute, a distance of twelve-thousand feet. Observers thought the plane was in a tailspin and heading for a crash."

Finally, the news Kate had been waiting for came on the radio. She heard these words: "Ladies and gentlemen, we interrupt our regular programming to bring you this late-breaking bulletin from Newark, New Jersey."

"Howard Hughes, millionaire aviator and playboy, has landed in Newark at 12:45pm Eastern Standard Time. He left Burbank, California, seven and a half hours ago and has slashed his own speed record for flying across the continent by one hundred and seventeen minutes. Feared lost for five hours, he has emerged as an aviation hero, his fame and achievement topped only by Charles Lindbergh. Even before Hughes was on the ground, commercial aviation experts are predicting coast-to-coast flights for everybody at these record-breaking speeds."

Hundreds of people began to descend on the Newark Airfield, hoping for a glimpse of Hughes. After disembarking from the plane, he brushed off the press and immediately went to send a telegram to Kate. "Am down and safe at Newark. Love, Howard."

Waiting to go on for her matinee, Kate received another extra, this time from the *Chicago Daily News.* In two-inch headlines, it proclaimed, HUGHES SPANS THE U.S. BY AIR IN 7 ½ HOURS.

Kate went on for her matinee, and Theresa Helburn claimed she gave her most brilliant performance ever in *Jane Eyre*

***

With Hughes safely on the ground, speculation renewed again over the possibility of an imminent marriage to Kate. "In America at least," Theresa Helburn said, "interest was greater than King Edward VIII's giving up his throne to marry 'the woman I love.'"

Back in Chicago together, and in adjoining hotel suites, Hepburn and Hughes resumed their "hot but chaste romance," as she put it, he putting off telling her the actual details of his flight "because right now I can't stand reliving one moment of it."

Kate was so overjoyed at his safe return and his incredible accomplishment that after her performance in *Jane Eyre* that night, "I got smashed, along with Howard," she told Patricia Peardon. "We toasted and toasted, then toasted some more. I told Howard, 'for two people addicted to fame, we have gone beyond our wildest fantasies.'"

He pressed her for an answer to his marriage proposal but she still put him off. That night newspapers broke a story from the Cook County clerk's office. The clerk, Michael J. Flynn, claimed that a "man said to be an agent for Mr. Hughes" had called to inquire about what requirements were necessary to obtain a marriage license. The clerk also reported that the manager of the Ambassador Hotel, where Kate and Hughes were staying, had also placed a similar call that day.

The next morning, Kate and Hughes awoke in separate beds to read the latest headline proclamations: HUGHES AND HEPBURN TO MARRY TODAY.

A mass exodus of people descended on the theater. Kate wondered if she'd be able to reach the stage door in safety. She later told her beloved "Em": "I feel like a fox cornered by a pack of snarling hound dogs."

She couldn't be seen anywhere in public without having to face the question, "When's the wedding?" Or "How's Howie?"

The following afternoon, a crowd of screaming teenage girls, whose numbers were estimated at three thousand, ignored the recent snowfall and virtually staged a riot as Kate arrived at the theater to rehearse some script changes for *Jane Eyre*.

By the time the curtain went up that night, radio announcers were claiming that some ten-thousand spectators—"and not just teenagers"—would be descending on the theater where *Jane Eyre* was playing.

By four o'clock that afternoon, Mr. Flynn, the Cook County clerk, held a press conference. He claimed that he would hold his office open late that night for the arrival of "America's most celebrated lovebirds." Reporters noted that Flynn was wearing a new navy blue pin-striped suit with a maroon-colored carnation with a matching tie.

Flynn's gesture was in vain. At 5:15pm that same afternoon, the concierge at the Ambassador Hotel released a message to the press. "Miss Hepburn wishes to announce that she and Mr. Howard Hughes will not marry today."

Enigmatically, headlines in the *Chicago Daily Tribune* the next morning

276

proclaimed: LA HEPBURN'S WEDDING DAY IS REALLY SOMETHING!

Hughes told Kate that he had to have an answer to his marriage proposal before curtain time that night. Even as late as fifteen minutes before she was called to the stage, she still hadn't decided what to do.

Because of the thousands of people waiting outside his hotel, Hughes dared not risk coming to the actual theater but remained in his suite.

She delayed her answer until just five minutes before curtain time, as Hughes waited patiently on the phone.

Just was she was heading out of her dressing room, she picked up the receiver, "It's your Country Mouse," she said to him in the presence of "Em." "Yes, God damn it, let's stop all this fuss once and for all. I'm going to become the second Mrs. Howard Hughes, and a hell of a lot better wife to you than Ella Rice."

Before flying out of Chicago, Hughes telegrammed his staff "to get ready for the arrival of one Miss Katharine Hepburn, about to undergo a name change."

Muirfield was going to have a new mistress.

CHAPTER TWELVE

Both Kate and Theresa Helburn, along with other Theatre Guild backers, agreed that *Jane Eyre* was not ready to face the harsh critics of New York. To save face, Helburn announced that *Jane Eyre's* Broadway opening had been postponed because of film commitments by Kate. That was a lie. No producer in Hollywood, including the usually loyal Pandro S. Berman, was offering Kate a film role during that period of her career.

In the meanwhile, however, the play continued slogging through previews in cities that included St. Louis, Toledo, Columbus, and Pittsburgh. But despite the continued rehearsals, and ongoing tinkerings with its structure, the play never really found its "voice" or managed to satisfy either its backers or its leading actress.

Kate's relief from the tension and tedium of the out-of-town previews revolved around the unexpected arrivals of Hughes, who would fly in and out of a city where she was appearing any time he could. Hughes was with Kate when the play "mercifully" shut down in Washington, D.C., after a run of only fourteen weeks.

The fallout from *Jane Eyre* didn't do anyone any good. Lukewarm discussions continued halfheartedly about bringing it to Broadway. But when the Guild allowed its rights to the play expire, they reverted back to Helen Jerome. And when that happened, the playwright announced that she'd give her approval for a Broadway production, but only if the Guild agreed not to cast Katharine Hepburn in the lead. "Who does this bitch think she is?" Jerome asked Theresa Helburn. "Sarah Bernhardt? Miss Arrogance—and she alone—ruined my play."

Years later, like she did with *The Lake*, Kate obliterated the memory of *Jane Eyre* forever from her life.

***

In 1937, a surprise offer came in from Broadway producer Max Gordon. Kate shuddered when she read it: The projected script was based on another work by Sir James M. Barrie, a writer she'd come to loathe after her film failures based on his works, *The Little Minister* and *Quality Street.*

Gordon assured her that, "No actress from Maude Adams on down has ever failed with *Peter Pan.*" Laura and Luddy both endorsed the project. But Leland Hayward, speaking as her agent, cautioned against it, and so did Hughes. Kate was still wavering when a letter came in from John Ford, who was—of all things—at Fox directing the box office champion, Shirley Temple, in *Wee Willie Winkie.* "I think Little Miss Temple would be better in the role of *Peter Pan* than you, my dear Kate. Love, John." That was all she needed to hear. The next day, Kate wired Gordon her rejection: "I won't be flying in your *Peter Pan.* Sorry. I'm going sailing instead." She signed it, "Kate Hepburn, ex-actress."

***

She'd accepted an invitation from her groom-to-be to sail the Caribbean aboard Hughes' spectacular yacht, the *Southern Cross,* which stretched luxuriously for three-hundred and twenty feet.

On the first day of their sail, Kate was "burning up alive with my ambition to fly instead of sail." She told him that the only thing she had waiting for her in Hollywood was the flying lessons he'd promised her.

Eager to install her at Muirfield mansion in the exclusive Hancock Park section of Los Angeles, Hughes agreed to take time out from his many business affairs and aviation interests to give her the lessons that any of his many trained pilots could have done for him.

Since her plans as an actress had been frustrated, Kate began to pursue her dreams of carving out a career in aviation. She wrote John Ford, "Soon the world will forget that Charles Lindbergh and Amelia Earhart ever existed. When aviation history is written in the future, it will have chapters devoted to the exploits of Katharine Hepburn and Howard Hughes."

Aboard the *Southern Cross,* sailing first to Nassau, then on to Jamaica, Hughes finally told her about his ordeal within the *Silver Bullet.* Kate's so-called lover had almost died while flying thousands of feet up in the air. He had a theory, and in essence it proved true but dangerous. His belief was that his speed would increase and he'd use less fuel if he flew at higher altitudes, where there was less oxygen.

But no more than an hour and a half into his flight, while over Arizona, he was overcome by the dizzying effect of hypoxia. It was true that he was flying faster than any man before him in the thin air, but his breathing was growing more difficult by the minute.

As Kate would later relate, Hughes told her, "I couldn't breathe. I was gasping for air, but my oxygen mask wasn't working properly. I moved my fingers but couldn't feel my right hand on the throttle. I felt my brain swelling like it was going to bust. I was hurtling through space. It was a pit of darkness out there. At the time I was going three-hundred and fifty miles an hour. I desperately pulled on my oxygen mask. No luck! My oxygen had been trapped by an air bubble. I didn't think I could drop altitude in time to save myself. I actually cried out in desperation. Don't tell anyone, but I was sobbing hysterically. Finally in a fit of desperation, I actually bit through the rubber hose feeding into the mask. My left arm was numb, and I sucked the air into my lungs just at the moment I felt I was going to pass out. As I sucked the air, my paralysis receded. As I flew across the country, the throbbing pain in my head was unbearable. All I could do for relief was to scream for periods of about five minutes at a time. Only then could I focus on the dials. I flew on but feared, especially when I went over Ohio, that my air was going to give out. Just as I thought I was about to land in Newark, the fucking imbeciles gave permission for another plane to take off. If I'd landed, I would have crashed into it. I was out of radio contact at the time, but surely they knew I was coming in. I flew into what's called a *chandelle* maneuver—something I learned from a pilot when we shot *Hell's Angels.* That way, I was able to circle the airport for another God damn fucking, hair-raising eighteen minutes until that shit of a flight cleared my airspace. After that, it was gravy. I came in and landed. A perfect three-point pisser."

After relating this harrowing, near-death experience, he told her of his most ambitious plan to date. She was enthralled as she listened.

As she would later say, "Right then and there, I knew that I didn't want John Ford, but this great man of vision and dreams, Howard Hughes. John and I were merely making entertainment for the masses—in my case, not even doing that. Howard was writing history with all the daring of a Columbus. I found him absolutely fascinating. In spite of my earlier indecision, I more and more wanted to be less Miss Katharine Hepburn and more Mrs. Howard Hughes, a name I would wear with pride, unlike what I did with my first husband. Of course, even with Howard, a lady is entitled to change her mind."

After returning from her cruise and spending a night with Laura, Luddy, and Jack, Kate made a decision that would forever be a part of her life. In 1937, perhaps unconsciously deciding that there was little future as Mrs. Howard Hughes at Muirfield Mansion, she purchased her Turtle Bay townhouse in Manhattan for thirty-three thousand dollars. At her death in 2003, it was worth four and a half million dollars.

Even as she acquired the deed to her new home and set out with Hughes to create a new life, she told Laura, "I'll be back. I have no intention of ever settling down in Los Angeles. It's not my kind of town."

Leland Hayward once again had come back into Kate's good graces, when he "pulled a miracle rabbit from my hat." After a series of deadly failures that had nearly bankrupted RKO, Leland once again persuaded Pandro S. Berman to sign an amazing four-picture contract in the summer of 1937. According to statements Berman made at the time, RKO awarded Kate the then astounding figure of one-hundred and fifty thousand dollars per film in a day when top stars were making only twenty-five to thirty-five thousand per picture. Even more astounding, only two of the four films would ever be made.

To this day, no one knows why Berman agreed to such an extravagant deal.

"But he did," Kate gleefully said, sharing news about the seemingly inflated offer with Hughes, her family, and her friends in Hollywood.

Years later, trying to justify his generous offer to Kate, Berman said, "At the time—except for perhaps Ginger Rogers, who hadn't yet won her Oscar for *Kitty Foyle* and who was identified primarily as a dancing partner for Fred Astaire—we simply had no one who matched the caliber of Kate Hepburn. Leland convinced me to get her out of period dramas and into light comedies. Our greatest leading ladies, including Irene Dunne and to a lesser extent, Ann Harding and Constance Bennett, had already left RKO, and Kate was still a very big name, inspiring great loyalty among movie-goers. Of course, we had Joan Fontaine, but at that point, she was still a B picture star with a knack for pot-boilers. After Kate showed that she could be successful in light comedy, time proved that I was right to have signed her up for more contracts. But by that time, unfortunately, she was working for Louis B. Mayer—not RKO."

The exact terms of Kate's controversial contract remain a mystery even today. Many reliable sources at RKO claimed that Berman never really told the truth about the numbers behind Kate's sweetheart deal. A draft of one contract that was seen at the time assigned Kate only seventy-five thousand dollars per picture—not twice that amount.

It now appears that RKO only guaranteed Kate seventy-five thousand dollars per picture. The remaining seventy-five thousand had been guaranteed by a "sugar daddy" behind the scenes. It wouldn't take Basil Rathbone, playing Sherlock Holmes, to figure out that Kate's mysterious benefactor, hoping to revive her career, was none other than the lovesick Howard Hughes.

Even though she hadn't been offered a film script in months, Kate turned down Berman's first script, which she later learned was a second offer. *The Mad Miss Manton* had originally been offered to Irene Dunne before her departure from RKO.

It was the story of a madcap debutante who discovers a dead body during a treasure hunt. Kate accurately predicted that the film would be a disaster. Spared from filming it, she let the "bomb" explode in the face of its eventual star, Barbara Stanwyck.

***

Back in Hollywood, Kate moved into Muirfield mansion, chasing away the ghosts of Howard Hughes' former wife, Ella Rice, and the only woman he'd ever really loved, Billie Dove. It was a beautiful spring day in 1937. Only that morning, Kate had read in a Hollywood column that she and Hughes had been named "the world's most romantic couple."

She didn't arrive at Muirfield alone. Kate brought some baggage that included, naturally, her personal maid, Johanna Madsen. Although she used to drive herself around Hollywood, Kate had acquired her personal chauffeur, Louis Prysing. Johanna no longer did all the cooking, that assignment going to Ranghild Prysing, Louis' wife. None of this new staff of permanent guests set well with Richard Dreher, Hughes' personal valet and *major-domo*. He also wasn't impressed when "Button," Kate's French poodle, immediately bit his ankle. She also brought along two cocker spaniels—one gray, Mica, another black, who answered to the name of Pete.

The *major-domo* assigned Kate "to the bedroom of the first wife," as he put it. He proudly proclaimed it "the master bedroom."

"Where is Mr. Hughes going to sleep?" Kate asked.

She was told that he preferred to sleep in a makeshift bed in his private study, directly above her master bedroom.

"I guess that way I can hear him walking around during his sleepless nights," she said.

Hughes' staff also had to make way for a collection of Kate's New England antiques that arrived in a truck the next day, along with her wardrobe—mostly slacks—and a virtual library of books and plays.

To her astonishment, Kate found that many of the rooms at Muirfield were locked. Even some of the rooms that were open were darkened by black velvet draperies. She set out immediately to order some spring cleaning, demanding that the curtains be pulled back and the windows opened to let in the fresh California air. She was truly establishing herself as the *châtelaine* of Muirfield—and not just in name only.

Cary Grant later said that Kate's time with Hughes was the most peaceful and stabilizing of his life, even though they were definitely an odd couple. He constantly urged them toward matrimony, although she couldn't help but notice that while she slept alone, it was Cary Grant himself who arrived at least two nights a week to share Hughes' bed.

Even so, for a few weeks she genuinely liked her life with Hughes. Their two shared passions were not for each other, but for playing golf and flying. Day after day, regardless of how busy he was, he was teaching her to become an aviator. She seemed to like flying a hell of a lot more than appearing before a movie camera.

On the mantelpiece in his parlor, Hughes had placed his most beloved possession, only recently acquired. It was the Harmon International Trophy, and it had been awarded to him by none other than President Franklin D. Roosevelt himself. Somehow the president's blessings seemed to be the final endorsement Hughes needed to qualify him as a genuine aviation hero.

Nonetheless, he assured Kate every night that his greatest achievements were yet to come. He also had something else to be elated about. As the world moved toward war, the American economy was slowly coming out of the Great Depression. That brought a resurgence to the Hughes Tool Company. More and more orders were pouring in every day, and Hughes was getting richer and richer.

Muirfield mansion adjoined the Wilshire Country Club. All Kate and Hughes had to do was climb over a rather modest fence to play golf, sometimes thirty-six holes a day.

On the nights Hughes went out with Grant or wasn't at home, Kate continued to see John Ford on the side, but always secretly. She had long ago become convinced that he had no intention of divorcing Mary and marrying her.

On her secret dates with Ford, she listened to him talk, as she was eager for conversation. Hughes preferred to be mute for hours at a time. He and Grant would often sit together for hours, just enjoying each other's company, neither of them saying a word.

"Even if I talk, which as you know I do all the time," Kate told Ford, "Howard can't hear half of what I'm saying. His deafness seems to grow worse by the day. I think one day he's going to live alone in darkness and silence—a sad life, really."

In *Collier's* magazine, a popular periodical of the day, Ford had become enchanted with a short story, *Stage to Lordsburg,* that he'd read. He wanted Kate to star in the screenplay that he planned to commission. Without even reading the story, she agreed to appear in the film. Like so many other film projects, the movie was never made.

Pursued by reporters and photographers, Kate had entered the most dramatic phase of her life as the so-called mistress of Howard Hughes. It was a world of vast amounts of money, of flying in airplanes he piloted, or sailing yachts down to Mexico or over to Catalina Island. Occasionally they went out to formal affairs, Hughes having to rent a tuxedo or Kate having to borrow a gown, but mostly they avoided such gatherings, preferring to be by themselves or to entertain at home.

"They certainly believed in staying clean," their servant, Richard Dreher, would later say. "Miss Hepburn always took six to eight cold showers a day, and the poor laundress, Florence Foster, was kept busy pressing their table linen and the five or six clean shirts Mr. Hughes insisted on wearing in one day. He was obsessed with germs and would change his underwear eight times a day. He always insisted that his shorts be carefully pressed. He felt that the heat from the iron destroyed germs."

"Even if he only had to urinate," Dreher claimed, "he always carefully washed his genitals after he was through. If he had a bowel movement, he would insist on a complete bath followed by a shower to rinse off any residual uncleanliness. It was truly amazing. The table would always be set with the best of crystal goblets and Haviland china. Even though sparkling clean, Mr. Hughes would often return to the kitchen to wash his plate, glass, and utensils before he would eat."

Johanna Madsen was always amused when she'd bring Kate some tea in the parlor, Dreher related. Even on the hottest of days, a fire would be roaring in the large colonial-style fireplace. Hughes never dressed around the house, but was seen wearing his favorite but tattered old maroon-colored robe and a pair of frayed house slippers. Kate insisted that the windows stay open, and she and

Hughes always fought over her demand, as he claimed she was letting germs into his house. They had other battles, too, mainly over her smoking. Hughes could not abide tobacco smoke.

Sometimes, Kate could be persuaded to go out on the town accompanied by both Hughes and Cary Grant. During one of these events, Kate made one of her infrequent appearances at a restaurant, the Cock 'n Bull, and lit up. After she'd taken one puff, Hughes leaned over and took the cigarette from her mouth, violently crushing it out in an ashtray. Grant thought that she might put up a fight, but he claimed she said nothing and immediately changed the subject and appeared light and gay for the rest of the evening.

Hughes finally won the tobacco war. In time, Kate gave up cigarettes.

One night Hughes came home early. He never told her where he was going or where he'd been. "Tonight I'm going to reveal my greatest dream to you," he claimed. "It's going to make us married before we actually wed."
She misinterpreted what he'd said, thinking that at long last he was going to come to her bed to consummate their relationship.

Instead of coming to her bedroom, Hughes invited her to go for a ride with him. "You're going to see a part of me I've shown to no other woman," he told her. "Only Cary Grant has seen it before you."

"I assume you're talking about your cock," she said sarcastically.

Impulsively, he slapped her face.

***

Before they reached the airfield, Hughes apologized and won her forgiveness for slapping her. To make up, he promised to take her on a glorious trip to San Francisco. In the meantime, he wanted to share his special treasure with her.

Hughes had hired Ralph Langer, a pilot he paid in cash off the books, to work at his hangar a few weeks. The young blond pilot was so startlingly handsome that Kate wondered if Hughes wanted him for something other than piloting. Langer's face lit up when he saw Hughes drive up, although he showed disappointment—"perhaps jealousy" as she later told Cukor—when he was introduced to Kate.

Langer opened the hangar, and Hughes ushered Kate in to see his sparkling Sikorsky S-43. This was a twin-engine amphibian with seating for a crew of six. It could hold enough fuel to fly across the Atlantic Ocean.

Hughes was like a little boy with a treasured toy, showing off his new aircraft to Kate. He invited her aboard, smelling the scent of the new red leather upholstery with her. He pointed out all the features of the plane, even the camel-colored carpeting. "It cost half-a-million dollars," he said proudly. "But I can afford it."

He informed her that in this little plane, he was going to encircle the globe.

"I won't be some hotshot aviator in some fucking air race. I'll make history. My flight will show the world that the future of commercial aviation is unlimited. Passengers will regularly fly from New York to London or Paris. Commercial aviation will mark the end of the great transatlantic ocean liners."

He filled her with his enthusiasm, and she begged him to let her go on the flight, but he refused.

"It was that very night, in spite of the jealous eyes of Langer boring in on me, that I knew I was truly in love with Howard Hughes," she later told Kenneth MacKenna. "Maybe my love only lasted one week, but it was love for as long as it lasted. I was overwhelmed with his raw courage, his sense of adventure. Actors I had known such as John Barrymore and Van Heflin didn't seem to matter any more. When compared to Howard Hughes, not even directors like George Stevens mattered. Even great writers such as Ernest Hemingway were diminished when compared to Hughes. And, yes, my white heat passion for John Ford was mellowing into a friendship. As I became more and more involved with Howard, John seemed less and less real for me. Here I was standing with a man about to circumnavigate the globe and make history, and John didn't even have the balls to leave that shrewish wife of his!"

Kate claimed that the next few weeks were like bliss for her. Sometimes with her piloting their small craft, they flew to Catalina and swam nude in the tranquil waters of the lagoon. Although she normally liked to go to bed early, he would keep her up all night with plans for his global flight. She constantly pleaded with him to take her on the flight, but he had many reasons why that would not be possible.

He did fly her to San Francisco and surprised her with the purchase of an astonishing one-million dollars worth of jewelry that night. He pressed his desire to marry her. She delayed the marriage proposal and even returned the jewelry. Years later, she told Laura and Luddy, "What a fool I was. Do you know what that jewelry would be worth today? I could have retired on that cache."

Like movie actor George Raft and Frank Sinatra in years to come, Hughes hobnobbed with gangsters who included the violent mobster Lucky Luciano. Kate was astonished one night to learn that she'd be hosting a dinner for the notorious gangster, Bugsy Siegel.

She was also surprised to learn from the housekeeper, Beatrice Dowler, that Hughes used "special dishes" for entertaining his mobster friends. Gone were the Haviland china and the crystal goblets. Out came the cheaper ware. "When the mobsters leave, Mr. Hughes orders me to destroy all the dishes they ate on. He feels their germs won't wash away even if the plates are sterilized."

Viewing it as a challenge and an adventure, Kate gallantly presided over the dinner for Bugsy. As she later told Anderson Lawler, "Each one of the rough-and-tumble cohorts he brought with him looked like they could slit your throat at the slightest provocation. In fact, I'd hazard a guess that they had slit many

286

a throat in their day."

To her surprise, Kate found the so-called "Casanova of the Mafia" intriguing. She even admitted to Lawler that —"on some other day"—she might have entertained a sexual proposition from him. "I know why women like Jean Harlow are attracted to him." Long before he became a bullet-riddled body in a Mafia slaying, Bugsy was good looking, well-groomed, and wearing smartly tailored clothes when he met Kate. "He was far better dressed than I was," she later said.

He might have started out small, stealing cars in Brooklyn, but he was at the height of his power when he was entertained by Hughes and Kate. She was startled to learn that the Countess, Dorothy di Frasso, the millionaire divorcée, had taken up with Bugsy. Kate had met the Countess when she was the lover of Gary Cooper, much to the annoyance of the jealous Anderson Lawler. The Countess had even taken Bugsy to Italy with her, where she'd introduced him to, among others, Mussolini.

Bugsy utterly fascinated Kate with his stories of adventure, including a tale about an expedition with the Countess to the Cocos Islands. They'd purchased a rare map said to guide their way to a vast treasure trove buried by the captain of a Spanish galleon in the eighteenth century. "We used enough dynamite to blow up New York City blasting for that damn treasure, but came up empty-handed."

A friend of such stars as close pal George Raft, along with Clark Gable and Gary Cooper, Bugsy lived the life of a high-rolling movie star, evocative of Rudolph Valentino in his heyday. He went on gambling sprees to the French Riviera with Raft, seduced one starlet after another, and even invited Kate to spend a weekend on one of the illegal gambling houses he operated aboard an offshore casino ship.

Before leaving for the evening, Bugsy shared his greatest dream with Hughes and Kate. He claimed that "in no time at all," he was going to turn the little desert town of Las Vegas into a gambling mecca.

"I'm going to build a resort hotel out there that all of Hollywood's big shots will flock to," he predicted. He leaned over to Kate. "In fact, pretty lady, I'm going to give you the honor of naming the joint. What's it gonna be called?"

Looking over at a large photograph Hughes had taken of bird life in the Florida Everglades, she said, "Oh, I don't know. Flamingo, I suppose. Something as inappropriate to a desert setting as that."

"Okay, pretty lady, you're on," Bugsy said. "Flamingo it will be."

***

Kate was with Hughes the night he learned that another Sikorsky amphibian had crashed. He was subsequently denied approval "by the Feds," as he called them, to fly his own similar plane. At first enraged, Hughes was then galvanized into renewed action.

In the days and weeks ahead, he ordered his workers to begin adapting a new Lockheed 14. Unlike the six-seater Sikorsky, the new craft was a twelve-passenger plane. Glen Odekirk, the chief of Hughes' crew, worked for two months getting the Lockheed ready to circumnavigate the globe.

The craft had to be fitted with new engines and its fuel capacity beefed up. Hughes had purchased and installed the very latest technology and electronic equipment.

Remembering his near-death experience over northern Arizona and his loss of air and radio contact, Hughes ordered a trio of completely independent radio systems in the event one or even two of them shut down. He also arranged for the installation of a self-contained oxygen supply system.

Kate was almost vicariously living Hughes' life until the offer of a lead in a film arrived from the offices of Pandro S. Berman.

It was *Stage Door.*

Although she desperately wanted to star in the film, her only regret was that Leland had once promised her the lead in the stage play but the role had gone to his wife, Margaret Sullavan, instead.

"Oh, well," Kate said as she called Cukor and asked for his advice. "Should I reprise that bitch's sloppy seconds?"

"Do it!" he urged her. "You desperately need a good film. The role won't be sloppy seconds if you're better than Sullavan. Besides, her performance will be but a distant memory one day when no one's ever heard of Margaret Sullavan. Your portrait on the screen will live forever."

***

Based on the stage play by Edna Ferber and George S. Kaufman, *Stage Door* had been adapted for the screen by scenarists Morrie Ryskind and Anthony Veiller. Berman had paid one-hundred and thirty thousand dollars for the film rights to *Stage Door.* He assured Kate that she'd be surrounded by familiar faces "for your comeback," and these included photographer Robert De Grasse and art director Van Nest Polglase. Mel Burns would still do her make-up, but Muriel King, not Walter Plunkett, would be her costumer.

Of course, the crucially important question for Kate was the name of the director. Berman told her that it would be Gregory La Cava. Kate had met him before when he had been temporarily assigned to direct her in *Three Came Unarmed*, co-starring Joel McCrea. Shortly into its production, that film had been permanently shelved.

W.C. Fields had called La Cava "the best comedy mind in the business—except for yours truly, of course. Both of us are known to take a tipple or two from time to time."

Born in 1892, La Cava had made numerous silent films. Before directing

Kate, he had scored two successes with *She Married Her Boss* in 1935, co-starring Claudette Colbert and Melvyn Douglas, and *My Man Godfrey* in 1936, co-starring William Powell and Carole Lombard.

Surely there was no more oddball director in Hollywood of the Thirties than Gregory La Cava. He never watched anybody else's films—only his own—and was almost unbelievably unfamiliar with even the names of the major Hollywood stars.

Kate was shocked when Berman told her that La Cava didn't even know who she was when he informed the director that she'd been cast as his star.

"How could the fool not know me?" she protested. "I'm the queen of RKO. World famous. I'm even known in Tibet."

"He doesn't know Ginger Rogers from Lucille Ball," Berman said. "I don't dare ask him if he knows who Clark Gable and Greta Garbo are. He doesn't read *Variety*. No newspapers, no fan magazines. He only reads the cartoons. He really wants to create cartoon characters, and that's how he spends all his time when he isn't directing a picture."

"Sounds like I'll get along great with this Mickey Mouse," Kate predicted, sarcastically.

It was only after signing to do the film that Kate learned that Berman had cast Ginger Rogers as her co-star. Not only that, but Rogers, Kate learned, was to get star billing over her.

Filled with fury, she stormed Berman's office to protest this "outrage." He told her the truth. "You were lucky that RKO even signed a new contract with you after that dismal flop, *Quality Street*. You were awful in it. I can't invest any more of the studio's money in your name alone. I need more box office assurance, which Ginger can bring. You might say that I'm hedging my bet. We have absolutely no assurance that your name can carry any picture, even a good one if you ever got around to making one. But people will buy tickets if Ginger's name is on the marquee. She's the new queen of RKO. Your reign is over. But in the event that you and Ginger aren't enough for the marquee, I've also lined up some brilliant gals to be the support team: Gail Patrick, Eve Arden, Andrea Leeds, Constance Collier. A great team. Even that little whore, Lucille Ball. Mostly we've been calling on her up till now to fuck any out-of-town dignitaries that we have to entertain. But I think that Ball has more talent than shaking her moneymaker at a lot of fat, married bankrollers from the East."

In spite of all the previous disappointments, Berman had been her champion. But that afternoon she left his office reduced to tears by his bluntly realistic talk.

The next week Kate learned more bad news. She would no longer be billed second to Rogers. Berman had reduced her to third billing. Playing the role of *Stage Door's* producer, Anthony Powell, Adolphe Menjou would share second billing with Rogers.

To compound her pain, Kate realized that Menjou "at his oiliest," in her words, would be playing a character based on the dreaded Jed Harris. Kate not only detested Harris, but also loathed Menjou ever since they'd co-starred in *Morning Glory* back in 1933. She called him a "right-wing fascist."

When Kate once again stormed Berman's office to protest the Menjou billing, he was uncharacteristically rude to her. "Listen, you'd be lucky to get sixth billing in a successful film after your track record." She was devastated.

In contrast, La Cava did not turn out to be the disappointment Kate had feared. Evoking a polar bear, he was a compelling personality under his battle-ship gray hair, with his dark, almost black eyes, and a face showing "all the emotion he ever felt, both good and bad," as she told photographer Robert De Grasse.

In spite of his drinking, La Cava was a director of almost boundless ener-gy, and Kate found herself attracted to him. However, she nixed the idea of any romantic involvement, as she'd had enough trouble with George Stevens and John Ford, both of whom she continued to see in secret trysts far removed from the eyes of Hughes.

She realized on the first day of shooting that La Cava, like Ford, had a seri-ous drinking problem. Except for a relapse now and then, Ford usually waited until the film was in the can to get drunk. Not La Cava. Kate claimed that he showed up drunk every day, yet somehow managed to direct the cast with a cer-tain brilliance. "If he is that brilliant drunk," Kate said, "I could only imagine what a genius he'd be without the gin-soaked haze that surrounds his head." Berman agreed with her but was strangely tolerant of his boozy director.

Kate found that the young stage actress she was playing on screen in *Stage Door* eerily evoked her own beginnings on the stage and most definitely the personality of Eva Lovelace for which she'd won the Oscar for *Morning Glory.* One reviewer later suggested that had he gone to see *Morning Glory*, fallen asleep in his seat, and awakened four years later, he would think he was still seeing the same movie.

The play centers around the Footlights Club, which houses a coterie of poor but beautiful young women intent on a career in show business. Each girl is waiting for her big break.

As Terry, Kate, a rich, smug, and self-confidant debutante, moves into the boarding house merely "to soak up atmosphere."

La Cava carefully showcased Kate's entrance on the screen, just as meticu-lously as Cukor had introduced her to the world in *A Bill of Divorcement.* In *Stage Door*, she makes a dramatic entrance dressed in black with a hat, stand-ing out immediately in the midst of the rapid-fire barrage of dialogue that char-acterized the other struggling actresses living at the Footlights Club.

Unlike her rivals in the play, Kate, as Terry, wins an important Broadway role because her wealthy father has been a "secret angel," putting up the money for the producer, as sleazily played by Menjou.

Up for the same role, Andrea Leeds, playing Kaye Hamilton, really deserves the part. Wasted by malnutrition, she is crushed to see the dilettante Kate win her part instead. On opening night, she commits suicide.

Although playing a bad actress, Kate is so moved by the suicide that she rises to emotional heights of greatness on opening night and is brutally shaken out of her arrogance.

Kate's roommate in the film is Ginger Rogers, playing Jean Maitland as a flippant, cynical dancer. In the view of Kate/Terry, Rogers is a chorine of inferior breeding as opposed to Kate's own more cultured background.

Kate found the male actors, other than Menjou, amusingly cast. The rising young star, Jack Carson, put the make on her but she politely turned him down. Franklin Bangborn was his usual fussy, effete, effeminate self, in an era when the only way to depict homosexuals on the screen was to make them "sissies."

Drunk or not, La Cava worked patiently with each player in the film. Playing the tragic, defeated actress, Andrea Leeds claimed that the director treated her "like a lifelong friend, bringing out the best in me." That he did. Leeds almost stole the picture from Kate and Rogers.

Informally, La Cava asked each actress to reveal to him some of her struggles on the way to stardom. Ignoring the script's actual dialogue, he often incorporated some of their own experiences into the screenplay.

He called it "cuff shooting," a term he'd learned from his days in silent pictures when directors made up the story and dialogue as they went along. Kate was horrified at the idea, as she preferred working with a carefully controlled script and detested improvisation. "What the hell?" she asked La Cava. "Make up my lines as I go along? What nonsense!"

During the second week of shooting, George S. Kaufman, the play's co-author, was in town. Through a contact at RKO, he had secretly obtained a copy of the screenplay and was furious. "La Cava and Berman have only used the title Edna Ferber and I came up with. The screenplay is just a skeletal framework of our hit play. Not only that, but behind your back, La Cava is in a conspiracy to build up Ginger's part at the detriment to your own. The God damn film should be called *Screen Door* instead of *Stage Door*."

***

The set bristled with latent hostility, the photographer, Robert De Grasse, later claimed. "Although they had a surface politeness with each other," he said, "most of the tension was generated between Rogers and Hepburn who were photographed chatting together as Kate knitted to relieve her tension. There was definitely no love lost between those two felines. Over at MGM, the feud was comparable to the hostility between Joan Crawford and Norma Shearer, which would boil over when they shot *The Women* for George Cukor in 1939."

Perhaps because she wasn't invited, Rogers objected violently to the cast breaking to attend one of Kate's four o'clock teas every afternoon. "I don't know why Pan Berman allows this," Rogers told La Cava. "I'm the fucking star of this picture, not that burnt out stack of bones from some New England bog."

In moments of spite, Rogers, when forced to talk to Kate, brought up provocative subjects, especially their mutual agent, Leland Hayward.

Waiting to be called to the set for a scene, Rogers chose that moment, with Robert De Grasse and Van Nest Polglase listening in the background, to tell her about her wedding to Lew Ayres.

"I finally got Lew away from the clutches of that old Irish drunk, Spencer Tracy," Rogers said, seemingly not caring if she were being overheard. "Leland arrived in a limo to drive me to the chapel. I must admit I looked absolutely gorgeous in my Chantilly lace dress and my Lilly Daché hat. He embraced me like a long lost lover. Mother caught us. She told him that, 'Ginger is marrying Lew today—not you.' On the way to the Little Church of the Flowers in Glendale, Leland took me in his arms and practically crushed my dress he was so amorous. He told me that I was making a big mistake in marrying Lew, that he was in love with me and I should be marrying him. He even said he'd make one whale of a husband. For the killing blow, he told me that he'd heard that Lew had reverted to homosexuality again and was privately seeing Tracy. For a while, Lew, because of strong religious beliefs, had given up that slimy stuff. Leland begged me to turn the car around and run away with him to Santa Barbara."

At that moment, La Cava, through an assistant, ordered Kate and Rogers onto the set. Putting down her knitting, Kate looked down at her still-seated rival. "What a quaint little story," she said sarcastically. "If only a word of it was true."

Bristling at the insult, Rogers was furious and wouldn't speak to Kate for the rest of the week.

Although she pretended indifference, Kate called Anderson Lawler that night. Her friend knew all the gossip. "The marriage of Miss Ginger Rogers and her fellow pansy boy—Ayres and I have a lot in common—is all but finished. The blonde bitch is getting it regularly from Leland. He still has two or three hot pieces on the side, but he's really pumping it to Ginger baby." He chuckled with that wicked laugh he had, which more and more was reminding her of the mischievous cackle of his best buddy, Tallulah Bankhead.

"I don't believe the bitch is actually in love with Leland," Kate said. "She's just doing this to spite me. Well, two can play this wicked little game. I'm going to get even with her, although right now I don't know how, other than to take *Stage Door* away from the cow. But one day, sooner than later, I'm going to pounce on Miss Ginger Snaps like a great big calico cat ready to have a dyed-blonde mouse for lunch."

***

With one exception, Kate remained aloof from the rest of the female cast. Lucille Ball, years later, said, "The way Hepburn talked was terrifying to me. They called it Bryn Mawr diction. I didn't even know how to pronounce Bryn Mawr, much less know where in the fuck the place was. Hepburn never looked into my eyes or spoke to me directly. Sometimes, though, she'd talk in my presence if other people were around. I guess I wasn't worthy of such a *grande dame*. Somehow she managed to ignore me throughout the whole God damn filming." Ball broke into a chuckle, eerily evocative of Tallulah's. "What must Hepburn have thought when little hooker me ended up buying the whole fucking studio?"

Also years later, when asked about Ball, Kate replied, "She wasn't beautiful—no, not that. No one thought she was beautiful, most of all Ball herself. She had a certain talent to amuse even back then. I guess you'd call it funny. At least some people like that kind of broad humor—not me, of course. I think Ball had spunk more than anything else."

Kate "just didn't get" the Alabama-born Gail Patrick, who'd made her screen debut at Paramount in 1933. Kate, knowing that she'd married Robert Cobb, owner of the famous Brown Derby restaurant, immediately informed Patrick that, "I don't go out to restaurants—they make me feel faint. I also heard that Gloria Swanson was nearly poisoned at your husband's greasy spoon." None of these sentiments exactly endeared Kate to Patrick.

As Kate stood on a stage ladder in the background, she was like an overseer when La Cava ordered his lead actresses to gather on the set. His writers had come up with a list of clever lines for the women to say on camera. He was actually parceling out the lines to the various actresses. They were told they were going to hear a line, then one of the actresses was to speak up if she thought she could deliver it. "La Cava read one very clever line and no one grabbed it, and I spoke up," Eve Arden later recalled. "A second good line was read and I went for that one too. All of a sudden we heard Hepburn's piercing voice, echoing across the set. 'She's the one to watch out for, gals.'"

"When Kate wasn't on the set, the tart-tongued supporting actresses engaged in a bitchfest about her," Arden said. "After I told a particularly bitchy story about the affairs that Hepburn was having with various women in Hollywood, Ball interceded on Hepburn's behalf. She cautioned me, 'Don't bitch the broad too much. She's a bigger star than any of us might ever be. A star, plain and simple. Something you and I aren't. She knows the combination to the safe—to everybody's safe, including that of Miss Ginger.'"

Arden claimed that after that, she shut up and quit mocking Kate for the rest of the production. "Actually, to tell the truth, I held her with a certain awe. Not envy, but I had a special kind of respect for her. In those days I wasn't as tolerant of lesbians as I am today. Hepburn did have one annoying habit that pissed me off, though. She constantly gave all of us unwanted advice."

Kate bestowed her greatest kindness on the teenage Ann Miller, who came to her one day, sobbing. "They claim in wardrobe I'm flat-chested," Miller said. "I'm only fourteen. Mine haven't grown yet."

Kate felt sorry for the youngster but was horrified to learn her true age. Miller had falsified a birth certificate which she'd given Berman, claiming she was eighteen years old. "For God's sake," Kate warned her, "if RKO finds out your age, or worse, some authorities, they might shut down production on us. We might get arrested for employing child labor."

"I need the money," Miller pleaded. "Please help me."

"Help yourself by not blurting out your true age anymore."

Miller kept her mouth shut and went on to play "String Bean" to best pal Rogers in the film. Miller told Kate that she'd almost lost the part when Rogers felt she was too tall for her. Miller said that in front of Rogers, she burst into tears, begging her to let her keep the role. Miller told Rogers that in school she was her idol and that she was always willing to trade twenty pictures of other movie stars for one of Rogers.

Rogers was impressed with that story and let Miller stay in the picture. The problem of height was solved when Rogers wore higher heels and a higher top hat, and Miller's heels were shaved.

"I even plucked out my eyebrows," Miller told Kate, "to look more like Ginger. Look! They've never grown back."

Miller also recalled that when they were working on the set, word reached the sound stage that Jean Harlow had died of uremic poisoning. "My father— he's a urologist you know—could have saved her," Kate announced to the crew.

"Oh, my God, poor Jean Harlow," Miller said, smacking her gum.

It is not known if La Cava knew who Jean Harlow was. But he did notice Miller's casual gum-smacking and later improvised a similar scene in *Stage Door.*

"Thank God he hasn't walked in and caught me taking a crap," Eve Arden said. "The way he is, La Cava would have me dumping the big one in front of his damn cameras."

***

The aging Constance Collier was cast as the superannuated drama coach in the film. The moment Kate met this heavyset woman with black hair—often called "gypsyish" in print—Collier became her lifelong friend. Collier had just finished shooting *Wee Willie Winkie*, directed by John Ford and starring little Miss Shirley Temple.

In some ways, the British actress reminded Kate of her former voice teacher, Frances Robinson-Duff. Collier had a wicked sense of humor and "more talent than any actress deserves," Kate later said. From the beginning, Kate became "bonded at the hip" with Collier.

Although there were rumors of a romantic link between the two, the rumors were just that. Kate was well aware that Noël Coward had branded Collier "the great dyke of the Western world." The playwright had been in the vanguard of using that word, which would not gain universal popularity until 1942.

Although she was not a great beauty, Collier personified theatrical glamour to Kate. A witty and brilliant conversationalist, Collier mesmerized the younger actress. Coward had yet another appraisal of Collier, which he would one day share with Kate. "She comes toward you like a runaway antique armoire, her mouth oddly evoking a galosh. But once that mouth opens, pure poetry flows out."

Kate was impressed with Collier's Shakespearean background and would later call upon the woman's talents to help her when she "tackled the Bard," as she put it.

Born in 1878 at Windsor, outside London, Collier had made her film debut back in 1916 when D.W. Griffith had cast her in *Intolerance*. Before meeting Kate, she'd been in some twenty films, mainly typecast in *grande dame* parts.

The theatrical diva had also appeared with the Barrymores in *Peter Ibbetson* and as Gertrude to John Barrymore's *Hamlet*. She'd also appeared on stage as Charlotte Vance (the Marie Dressler screen role) in *Dinner at Eight*. She referred to Eva Le Gallienne, Ivor Novello, and Katharine Cornell her "dearest, dearest friends."

Collier was a charter member of the famous and so-called lesbian "sewing circle," some of whose cast members included Cornell, Alla Nazimova, Laurette Taylor, Diana Wynward, and Mercedes de Acosta.

"Almost immediately, Constance became everything to me," Kate confided to Kenneth MacKenna. "My mother, my mentor. My drama coach. But mainly a shoulder I could lean on with my many woes."

Kate became her pupil, joining an alumni that over the decades would range from Mae West to Marilyn Monroe.

***

In *Stage Door,* there is a play—*Enchanted April*—within the play. La Cava had a caricaturist's eye for the absurd detail. He conceived a situation whereby Kate would deliver a devastating parody of her now notorious Broadway fiasco, *The Lake*. The point was to show what a bad actress she was.

At first Kate resisted, but finally gave in to La Cava's demand. In one of the takes for the scene, Kate glided across the stage in a filmy white dress with a bouquet of oversized flowers. In a flat, toneless voice, she delivered once again her infamous line, "The calla lilies are in bloom again." At the end of the scene, Kate burst into tears, as if recalling Jed Harris and that horrible opening night on Broadway. She turned pleadingly to La Cava, and asked him, "Will I, like the calla lilies, bloom again one day?"

The next day, La Cava, while directing his play within a play, was so drunk that he fell off the stage of the Biltmore Theatre in Los Angeles where part of *Stage Door* was being shot.

Ever the caretaker, Kate rushed to his side. With the aid of Robert De Grasse, she got La Cava on his feet again. "I learned that hot coffee was better than the Castor Oil and Irish Whiskey I forced down the gut of poor John Ford, nearly killing him."

When RKO officials in New York learned of La Cava's drinking, they demanded that Pandro Berman fire him at once.

At that point, Kate threatened to walk off the picture. Having seen the rushes and pronouncing them brilliant, Berman stood with Kate and propped up La Cava until the final day of shooting.

Kate's curtain speech, which she makes at the end of the play within a play, upon hearing of the suicide of the Andrea Leeds character, originally ran four pages. La Cava shortened it to ten lines. Standing before her mythical audience, Kate says, "The person you should be applauding died a few hours ago. I hope that wherever she is, she knows and understands and forgives."

A closeup of Rogers listening to the speech was needed, although she hadn't actually been on the set to hear it. To get her to cry on cue, La Cava told her that her house had burned down. "She bawled all right and we got a perfect take. That's acting for you."

***

Even at previews, Kate knew she had broken her box-office jinx and had a good movie on her hands. Film critics have claimed that *Stage Door* was the best backstage drama until the release of *All About Eve* in 1950 with Bette Davis. Audiences had never seen anything quite like *Stage Door*, with a host of female players talking richly and idiomatically, their voices interrupting each other as if to drown each other out.

As the film previewed in Pasadena, Menjou and Rogers shared star billing. But many review cards came back proclaiming *Stage Door* the best of all Hepburn films. Before going into general release, Berman finally gave in to Kate's urgings and restored her to star billing.

Opening at Radio City Music Hall in October of 1937, *Stage Door* took in nearly two-million dollars, a respectable profit but not enough to put Kate into the big league of box office winners. However, RKO officials viewed the film not as a triumph for Kate but as a group effort, with the added dynamite of a new big name like Ginger Rogers helping to carry the picture. Kate's most intransigent critics suggested that had Irene Dunne been cast in her part, the film would have grossed even more.

Both Rogers and Kate lost out when the Academy Awards were announced. Andrea Leeds was nominated as best supporting actress, losing to Alice Brady for *In Old Chicago*. La Cava was nominated for best director but lost, and *Stage Door* was nominated for best picture of the year but it too lost.

Kate learned from Berman that *Stage Door* had launched Ginger Rogers as a serious dramatic actress. "As for you, my dear," he said, "we're planning a screwball comedy."

The script was *Bringing Up Baby,* a zany screwball comedy in which Kate once again would be appearing with Cary Grant. Playing a stuffy paleontologist, Grant was cast as a daffy professor in owlish, horn-rimmed glasses. Grant's professor character was preoccupied with discovering the missing bones of a Brontosaurian dinosaur. Complaining to Howard Hawks, the director, that he didn't know how to play the role, Grant was instructed to borrow heavily from Harold Lloyd, the silent-screen comedian.

His character of David Huxley was to play opposite Kate's Susan Vance, a madcap-devil-may-care heiress from Connecticut. "Is this type casting or what?" Kate asked upon reading the script.

Two weeks into shooting, Kate learned that her own role had tentatively been offered to Carole Lombard, who had a lot more experience than Kate in playing in screwball comedies.

Before Grant was cast, Berman told Kate that she'd be appearing opposite Ronald Colman. He turned it down, followed by a similar rejection from Robert Montgomery. Then Berman offered the script to Fredric March, Kate's co-star in *Mary of Scotland*, and he too passed on it, as did Ray Milland. Finally, an acceptance came in from Leslie Howard. But Kate turned him down, as she still had bitter memories of having worked with him before. Everybody, including Kate, seemed to have agreed on the casting of Cary Grant, although Berman had still not recovered from pairing the actor with Kate in *Sylvia Scarlett.*

Kate immediately called Kenneth MacKenna to report the news. "Can you believe it? I'm with Cary again, the man I share Hughes with, with Cary—not me—getting all the action."

She was a bit alarmed at her third co-star, an eight-year-old Brazilian leopard named "Nissa," who practically had third billing.

"God damn it," Kate later told Cukor. "I have to compete not only with that scene-stealer, our own Cary Grant, but with a man-eating leopard—and Asta to boot."

"Who's Asta?" he asked.

"You know," she said. "The mutt who stole *The Thin Man* from William Powell and Myrna Loy."

Fortunately, Nissa, the "Baby" of the film's title, would be constantly accompanied by her trainer, Madame Olga Celeste. Grant was afraid of the beast, but Kate got along with the animal until one day she swirled around in her long, white gown, frightening Nissa. The beast lunged for her back but Mme. Celeste was there with her whip to save Kate from attack. She cautioned

Kate that if she wore heavy perfume, she would make Nissa more playful and not so dangerous. The trainer's final judgment of Kate was that if her film career collapsed, she could always make a living as an animal trainer.

Veteran actress May Robson was brilliantly cast as Kate's rich aunt, from whom Grant is trying to get a million-dollar grant for his museum. Superbly funny was Charles Ruggles, playing a big-game hunter. Kate felt surrounded by John Ford's loyal posse. Not only was one of his best friends, Ward Bond, cast as a motor cop, but his beloved Barry Fitzgerald was playing the gardener, Gogarty.

Ford's right-hand man, Cliff Reid, was associate producer. Ford's favorite screenwriter was Dudley Nichols, who had written most of the screen play from a story that Hagar Wilde had published in *Collier's*.

Cast as a roustabout, the actor Jack Carson was among the players. As he had in *Stage Door*, the Canadian actor—known for playing dull-witted lunkheads—once again tried unsuccessfully to seduce Kate. In a drunken interview years later, Carson indiscreetly said, "I always wanted to fuck a big name star. Hepburn and countless others turned me down. I only hit pay dirt when I played opposite Joan Crawford in 1945 in *Mildred Pierce*. She tossed me off a mercy fuck."

To see "how my boys are treating Kate," Ford came onto the set one day. Kate eagerly embraced the big shambling man with his corrugated face and thinning red hair. The writer, Dudley Nichols, spotting Ford, also came up for an embrace. "Don't trust him," Ford cautioned Kate. "He's only partially Irish. I always tell him to spare the dialogue so as not to spoil the film."

Although Kate still had a deep and abiding affection for Ford and would occasionally sleep with him before he went away for five years during World War II, she knew on the set that day that their once-passionate love affair had cooled considerably. "But it's not over yet," she later told Lawler. "John and I still have a few more rounds to go."

Grant's snooty fiancée in the film, the dark-haired, dark-eyed Virginia Walker, was cast in the role of Alice Swallow. Walker was only twenty years old and very beautiful. Much to Kate's annoyance, her producer and director, the hatchet-faced Howard Hawks, seemed to be spending more time with Walker than with Kate. She feared that he was beefing up Walker's part at the expense of her own. Later she learned the reason for Hawk's avid attention. He was actually wooing the Boston society girl, and she'd become wife number two when they eloped to Mexico.

Before working with her director, Howard Hawks, Hughes himself assured her that she could trust his judgment. Hughes had once hired Hawks to direct his 1932 film, *Scarface*, that had starred Paul Muni, George Raft, and Ann Dvorak.

At first distrustful of Hawks, Kate responded eagerly to his direction. She was impressed with his manliness and admired how he wanted to produce his own movies and to declare his independence from the major studios.

His direction of her got off to a shaky start. "Kate took awhile to get the hang of comedy," Hawks later said. "At first she seemed to laugh at her own antics. I told her that great comedy comes only when the actors are deadly serious, like Charles Chaplin playing The Little Tramp."

Hawks went so far as to hire Walter Catlett, the veteran comedian from the Ziegfield Follies, to teach Kate how to act in comedy. Catlett began by demonstrating one scene with her opposite Grant. "He had me down pat," Kate said. "My mannerisms and everything." Catlett ended his scene by kissing Grant passionately on the lips. The moon-faced comic said, "I've always dreamed of doing that, and Hawks is paying me to boot."

Hawks directed Kate through one of the most memorable scenes from Thirties' screwball comedies. In the film, Grant steps on Kate's dress, ripping it. At first he tries to cover her exposed back and lingerie with his top hat but then is forced to walk "in tandem" through the restaurant with her, causing pandemonium. Grant tops that scene with May Robson when she spots him wearing Kate's marabou-trimmed *négligée*. His own clothes have been sent to the cleaners. She demands to know why he's dressed in such a manner. His immortal response is, "Because I just went gay all of a sudden."

***

As Kate remembered it to her friends, she and Cary Grant spent much of their time between takes talking to each other about Howard Hughes, the man they shared, "with dear Cary getting the bigger slice," as she claimed.

Grant was still urging an immediate marriage on Kate, and she kept stalling. "I told Cary that one day in a more enlightened society, people would be able to marry whatever sex they chose," Kate quoted herself one day to Anderson Lawler. "With at least an ounce of sincerity, I suggested to him that the perfect married couple might not be Katharine Hepburn and Howard Hughes, but Cary Grant and Howard Hughes. Cary did not find that amusing and got up and walked away, refusing to speak to me for the rest of the day."

The next day Grant was much friendlier as he introduced Kate to a minor actress, Phyllis Brooks, whom he seemed to be dating more for the sake of appearances than any torrid love affair. She was a five-foot five-inch blonde from Boise, Idaho, with a slightly waiflike look.

When Grant had gone to his dressing room, Brooks immediately became confidential with Kate, which was not at all unusual, since many people she'd just met did that with her. As Kate explained it, "people immediately assumed I was either their doctor or their psychiatrist."

"I don't understand men," Brooks told her. "Since you've dated such complicated men as Howard Hughes or John Ford, perhaps you can explain my own complicated fellow, one Mr. Cary Grant."

"I don't think I'd even attempt to look too deeply into that dark soul," Kate told her.

"I'm desperately in love with him and want to marry him," Brooks said. "But I can't understand his actions. One day he showers me with flowers and even presents—not expensive ones, of course, because Cary is a bit of a tight-wad. The next day I try to call him, and Randolph Scott won't even let him come to the phone."

"Do you think Scott is the trouble?" Kate asked provocatively.

Brooks laughed nervously. "Oh, that! Cary assured me that those are just rumors. You won't believe this, but only the other day I heard a rumor about Cary Grant and your Mr. Hughes."

"That's ridiculous," Kate said defensively. "In the case of Mr. Hughes, I can assure you there is no truth to those rumors. They're just good buddies, like Spencer Tracy and Clark Gable or James Stewart and Henry Fonda."

Brooks leaned over to Kate and spoke confidentially. "There is something that isn't a rumor. The other night I was invited over to see Marion Davies at her place. She was told by her keeper, Mr. William Randolph Hearst, to get a message to me. It seems that Mr. Press Tycoon, for reasons not clear to me, had Cary investigated. The detectives learned that Cary is a Jew on his mother's side. Marion warned me about the problems involved with a Gentile marrying a Jew. But I'm no racist like Hitler. I'd marry Cary regardless of his racial pro-file."

"Good for you," Kate said. "To hell with Hearst. He's nothing but a pro-Nazi pig anyway."

Changing the subject quickly, Brooks spoke in lighter tones, telling Kate that she would soon be appearing with the box-office champion of the world, Miss Shirley Temple, in *Little Miss Broadway*. "Darryl Zanuck has already for-bidden Cary to come on the set to see me. You see, Shirley has this mad crush on Cary. Zanuck is afraid she'll be too distracted if Cary appears."

Shirley Temple and Cary Grant would come together in 1947 when they made *The Bachelor and the Bobby-Soxer*, which one cynical film reviewer would one day term "a precursor of the child molestation films."

Before Brooks departed for lunch that day with Grant, Kate warned her, "Don't let Howard Hawks hear that Cary is part Jewish. Dear Mr. Hawks, I've learned, is a vicious anti-Semite."

The next day the newspapers ran a picture of Cary Grant and Randolph Scott leading the dancing conga line at the appropriately named La Conga nightclub. For some reason, Grant had not invited Brooks to serve as his beard and had defiantly dated Scott in public and in front of cameras.

Pointing out the candid snapshot to Kate, Hawks said, "Those two fairies must really have balls to think they can get away with shit like that."

His remark infuriated Kate, who became very defensive of them. "Don't be homophobic," she cautioned him. "Otherwise, you'll alienate half your cast and crew on *Bringing Up Baby.*" She stood up from her chair placed on the set. "Better to be a homosexual than a Hollywood director who likes to fuck under-age girls."

She turned and walked away, leaving him to only imagine what she knew about one of his darkest secrets. In his future lay the teenage Lauren Bacall, a discovery with whom he would become enamored, apparently overlooking the fact that she was Jewish.

Of course, Humphrey Bogart was waiting in the wings to grab that prize as well.

***

In the closing days of shooting *Bringing Up Baby,* Kate woke up on the morning of May 30, 1937, to receive one of the biggest and most rage-producing shocks of her life. Harry Brandt, president of the Independent Theatre Owners of America, had taken out a full-page advertisement naming major stars who were, in his words, "box office poison." Kate led an impressive list that also included Greta Garbo, Marlene Dietrich, Mae West, Joan Crawford and Fred Astaire. On a more minor note, Edward Arnold and Kay Francis were also on the list.

Kate wept uncontrollably, especially when she learned that newspapers all over America were carrying the story, adding to her humiliation. Her eyes teary, she told Hawks later that morning, "So, I'm a has-been. If I weren't laughing so much, I might cry."

"You're already crying," her director said. "Your eyes are so red I can't shoot you this morning. Go to your dressing room and try to do something to them."

Her associate producer, Cliff Reid, delivered a hand-written note of condo-lence to her from John Ford. "On that box office poison list, with you headlin-ing, were some of the greatest talents Lotus Land has ever known. If it makes you feel any better, read the list of box office champions." In his note, he had written out the names of Shirley Temple, Deanna Durbin, and Ginger Rogers, drawing little caricatures of each of these big money makers.

As the day progressed, Kate grew more and more despondent. Her eyes got only redder, Hawks noted. He ordered his photographer to shoot around Kate for the rest of the day.

Anderson Lawler came by the set at noon to comfort her, but he made mat-ters worse by telling her of the latest exploits of Howard Hughes in London, one of the cities where he'd gone to arrange flight plans for his around-the-world trip.

As always, Lawler was up on all the latest gossipy details. While staying at the Savoy Hotel, Hughes had encountered the still attractive Woolworth heiress, blonde-haired Barbara Hutton. "They had an affair," Lawler told her.

"Rather torrid, and Babs is dining out on it. She's revealing all the most intimate details, as the very rich have a way of doing. We now know what went on between Hughes and this poor little rich girl in her round bed covered in Valentine red satin with its dyed pink ostrich feather canopy."

"Must you tell me?" Kate asked.

"As you may have heard, Hutton has great difficulty reaching orgasm," Lawler related, seemingly oblivious of Kate's hurt feelings that day. "It seems that Howard easily reached orgasm but couldn't bring one to Miss Rich Bitch. She tried to bring herself off but he brushed her hand away. He wanted to be in charge. He told her that the only way he was going to let her get off was if he did it with his own equipment—not her fingers."

"Oh, Andy," Kate pleaded with him. "Don't tell me anymore. I can't stand it on this rotten day of rotten days. I feel so despondent. What was begun so brilliantly only six years ago—my movie career—now seems to be over."

Before leaving that day, Lawler predicted, "You'll rise again. *Bringing Up Baby* will put you right back on top."

***

What happened on the morning of the following day is still shrouded in mystery. All the main principals covered up the incident. Only in later years did makeup artist Mel Burns supply sketchy details.

After a sleepless night, Kate arrived for her early morning appointment with Mel Burns, who was ready to "paint a face on her," as he had on so many mornings of her previous movies. But he found that her face looked worse that it had yesterday. "Her eyes were still red as Santa's suit—not only that, but her face was swollen. She was not normally a heavy drinker but her breath smelled foul like she'd downed a whole quart of rotgut bourbon."

He later claimed that he began to work on her face but felt that he had to go tell Hawks that "there is no way I can repair the damages to the point where she'll be camera-ready."

Burns was gone for about twenty minutes. When he returned, he found Kate standing on the ledge of the building. To his horror, she was threatening to jump. He pleaded with her to come inside but she threatened that if he so much as touched her, she'd jump to her death.

"Even though the building was only two floors, it was pretty high up because the ceilings were tall," Burns later said. "The jump might not have killed her but then again it might have. It would have broken her into pieces, perhaps paralyzed her for life. I was crying myself by that time, since I didn't know what to do."

He later related that Kate told him that her dearest friend and companion in all the world, her brother, Tom, had committed suicide years before. "I never knew that." She also claimed that many members of her family had committed suicide before that. Burns remembered that Kate told him, "suicide runs in my family. I won't be the first to kill himself—no, nor the last."

Burns said he felt trapped. "I was afraid if I left her to summon help, she'd surely jump. I also feared that if I stayed, all I could do was to stand helplessly by watching her about to either end her life or ruin herself by making herself a hopeless cripple."

Someone walking by must have spotted Kate and summoned help. "When Hawks and Cliff Reid—God knows how many others—tried to storm in, Kate threatened that if I let one of them in, she'd jump for sure," Burns said.

After about an hour of pleading with her, Burns got her to agree to see Cary Grant, "since he's the only one I trust," Kate told Burns.

As Burns later revealed, Grant must have spent more than an hour and a half cajoling and pleading with Kate to come in off that ledge. "I was ordered out of the room," Burns said, "so I don't know what they actually talked about. I did listen at the door. From the very best I could gather, I thought Cary was revealing to her the details about his own attempted suicide—and what a wrong decision that would have been for him."

Grant was no doubt referring to an incident that occurred on October 6, 1934, when he placed an emergency call at two o'clock in the morning to the police. Later the actor was seen being wheeled into an emergency room by Police Surgeon C. E. Cornwell and ambulance driver Burt L. Tinker. Grant had been discovered lying naked on his bed in his apartment. At the Los Angeles Receiving Hospital, he had his stomach pumped. He had consumed more than two quarts of Scotch and had taken some kind of pills.

At first there were rumors that Grant had taken a slow-acting poison pill. Cornwell ordered a search of Grant's apartment, which led to the discovery of a full, unopened bottle of bichloride of mercury tablets in the medicine closet.

Grant was placed under psychiatric observation for ten days before he was released.

Whatever the actor told Kate, he was obviously convincing. He got her to come in off the ledge. Downstairs, Berman had an ambulance waiting to take her to the hospital for a thorough check-up and a psychiatric examination. The studio chief was desperate to get her in shape to finish the last few days of shooting on *Bringing Up Baby.*

The ambulance pulled away with Grant in the rear holding Kate's hand. Watching the ambulance go, Berman bitterly confided to Reid, "We still have a contract with that sick bitch, but I think I know a way out of it," he said enigmatically. "She'll end up paying us money instead of us shelling out lost dollars on her box office poison."

***

303

On the Eastbound train, Kate was filled with despair and planned to remain alone in her cabin for the duration of the trip, ordering food brought to her by her attendant.

Four hours into the trip, there was a knock on the door. Thinking it was the conductor, she discovered, to her surprise, Marlene Dietrich standing in the corridor, looking more glamorous than ever. She was attired completely in white from her hat to her high heels—even a white ermine coat.

Kate kissed her on both cheeks, took her hand, and invited her in. "The press, as you know, are calling us the *poisonalities*."

"We are now charter members of the Box Office Poison Club," Dietrich said, sitting down and offering Kate one of her long-tipped cigarettes.

"That theater association guy sure has a poison pen," Kate said. "I'm devastated. But at least I was at the top of the list—at least the list I read."

"I should be at the top myself," Dietrich said, revealing what had just happened to her in Hollywood. "Paramount made film history by deciding that the film, *French Without Tears*, would be less dreary without me. But I was compensated."

"How, pray tell?" Kate asked.

"They paid me two-hundred and fifty-thousand dollars *not* to make their damn picture. They told me to get lost."

"I guess that makes you the most highly salaried member of the unemployed in the world," Kate said.

"What a dubious honor," Dietrich said. "I don't know what to do. From New York I'm sailing on the *SS Normandie*. Back to Europe. Back to my roots."

"Both of us have had far greater success with our pictures in the European market," Kate said. "It takes more sophisticated audiences to appreciate us. We can't do baby burlesque like that child vamp, Shirley Temple."

"Yes, but even the European market may dry up for us," Dietrich predicted. "That dirty little man, Hitler, will have his great big war."

Kate burst into tears, and Dietrich tried to comfort her. "I can't believe we're being paraded out in public for humiliation like this," Kate sobbed. "Why don't they shave our heads and march us down Hollywood Boulevard while our former fans throw rotten tomatoes at us?"

"The people behind those ads—idiots, total assholes, all of them," Dietrich said, as her own fury bubbled up. "We are not to blame. What about the damn studios that forced us into their disasters with their rotten scripts? Each screenplay, weak lemonade. Even Garbo made their stupid list. Also, the pop-eyed one. Now that at least I can understand. Who wants to pay good money to look at that disaster?"

Dietrich was referring to Bette Davis, perhaps assuming that she, too, was on the list.

Between puffs on her cigarette, Dietrich leaned over and gently placed a kiss on Kate's lips. "But you, my darling. You, of all stars. It's not to be believed." She settled back on the cushioned seat, crossing her stunning, white-stockinged legs. "So who have the sick bastards back there got left who can play roles we might have handled? I can think of only one. Irene Dunne. But she's dull. No mystery. No magic." She looked out the window at the American landscape she was leaving behind her. "This is madness."

Over dinner that night, Dietrich told Kate what had recently happened to her. "In spite of my pictures losing money, I thought it would be all right. Frank Capra over at Columbia likes the looks of me in slacks. He wanted to cast me as George Sand in a picture. Spencer Tracy was set to play Chopin, my lover. We would have been a natural together. Spence in real life has been one of my lovers. Don't you think he would be brilliant playing my lover/composer?"

"I think Tracy could play anything," Kate said. "Ax murderer. Child molester. Gangster. A woman in drag in *The Mae West Story.*"

"My affair with him lasted for ten days—maybe two weeks, give or take a day as you Americans say. Like so many men I've bedded, Spence is basically a homosexual."

"He looks so manly," Kate protested.

"My dear heart, you must trust an older and more experienced woman. Some of the most manly men in the world are homosexuals. Including one we know in common. *Papa.* My dear Ernest Hemingway. But there are so many others. Cary Grant. Gary Cooper. James Stewart. Henry Fonda. Even your Mr. Hughes is suspect. I have an incredible instinct for detecting homosexuals."

"Whatever," Kate said, as if the subject, especially as it concerned Hughes, made her feel distinctly uncomfortable.

Dietrich also claimed that Tay Garrett, the director, wanted her for a remake of *One Way Passage.*

"That old shipboard tearjerker," Kate said. At the sight of Dietrich's archly raised eyebrow, she quickly backed down. "Of course, you'd be terrific in it. Far better than the original."

"When that box office poison ad came out, both Jack Warner and Harry Cohn caved in to the fallout and pulled the plug, as you Americans say, on both films."

"I'm so sorry," Kate said. "But in my case, there are no offers on the table. No plugs to pull."

When Dietrich ordered champagne, Kate joined her, still despondent over making that list.

As they sat talking and sipping champagne in the darkness of her cabin, Kate pondered why they were on the list. "If you've noticed, all of the actresses—the poisonous ones—portray mature and independent, even rebellious, women on the screen. It seems that American filmgoers don't want to see that. They want to see us tamed, giving in to some man. They definitely want to see us in aprons." Ironically, Kate was predicting the ending of a film she'd make

305

in the future with Spencer Tracy.

"What are you going to do when you reach New York?" Dietrich asked.

"What I always do when I'm broken-hearted. Head home to Daddy. He is my refuge. RKO has thrown me to the wolves."

"Come to my arms," Dietrich said in her softest and most alluring of voices. "It will be just to hold you to get through the night. No sex—just the kind of love a mother might bestow on a daughter who is experiencing that special kind of pain that comes only in the middle of the night. Always before the dawn. It is a pain I know so well."

CHAPTER THIRTEEN

Back in New York, Kate freely shared her experiences on the train with Laura, Luddy, and Jack and spoke of how comforting Dietrich had been to her during her troubled Eastbound trip.

"She's one hell of a survivor," Kate said. "I have renewed respect for her. I know why Hemingway likes her so. The question is, why doesn't *Ernesto* like Katharine Hepburn?"

Back on familiar turf at Fenwick, Kate spent lonely days sailing Long Island Sound, pondering her future career, and contemplating marriage to Hughes. She could sit for hours watching the Atlantic breakers.

To her, Old Saybrook had never looked more beautiful, as the fruit trees burst into bloom with their snow-white or cherry-pink blossoms. Her favorite were the magnolias, which had also burst into bloom, making Old Saybrook look like the Deep South. The oaks standing proudly along the coast, along with the salt marshes and the sand dunes once roamed by Indians, inspired her to go in search for clams.

She eagerly awaited the arrival of Hughes, who had at last agreed to be presented to her family. One of her regrets involved Luddy, who had insisted on joining them for the weekend. She feared that her former husband had nurtured a romantic fixation on Hughes, because he had collected dozens of photographs of the aviator, which he proudly displayed in his town house, much to the chagrin of a jealous Jack. Luddy told her that he was not only anxious to take his own pictures of Hughes, but had brought along some of his cameras so he could "catch him in action."

She warned him that Hughes didn't like to be photographed, but Luddy turned what she called "his deaf ear to me."

Before arriving at Fenwick, Hughes had told Cary Grant about his three grand plans: To marry Katharine Hepburn "before the frost comes on the pumpkin;" to circumnavigate the globe in record-breaking time; and to make Hughes Aircraft "the giant of the aviation industry."

Only that morning, Kate had told her family, having previously informed her friends, that "Regardless of what happens, my career must come before love. I must prove myself as an actress before becoming some famous man's playtoy."

What she didn't realize that beautiful May morning was that her aviator had plans so big that they would eventually dwarf her own "silly ambitions," as she was later to refer to them.

***

Before meeting the Hepburn clan, Hughes had good news for Kate. Back in California, Hughes had negotiated a deal with Pandro Berman after he learned about the studio's reluctance to invest more money in the release and distribution of *Bringing Up Baby*. Hughes told an overjoyed Kate that he had purchased the film from RKO and would soon be distributing it through the Loew's chain. He had seen the film and told Kate that "my two favorite stars in all the world, Cary and Kate, have a hit on their hands."

Actually, Hughes was right, but it would take decades for the film to become a classic. Despite rave reviews, moviegoers stayed away from *Bringing Up Baby*, preferring instead the likes of Spencer Tracy as Father Flanagan in *Boys Town*.

Both Kate and Grant would live to see the film achieve its audience decades later. In fact, years later, Cary invited her to see the 1971 remake, *What's Up Doc*, starring those improbable lovers, Barbra Streisand and Ryan O'Neal, who turned out to be no Hepburn and Grant.

While at Fenwick, Kate received what she felt was the ultimate insult from Berman, making her realize that "my star has been shot from the sky." She was offered the starring role in a short, low-budget "programmer," *Mother Carey's Chickens*. "That's a deliberate insult!" she shouted at the creaky walls of Fenwick. Amazingly Hughes recommended that she take it.

She turned it down anyway, soon after reading in Louella Parson's column that the role would star Ginger Rogers instead. With Leland's help, Rogers too managed to avoid the role which was eventually awarded to a minor actress, Anne Shirley, "who truly deserved it," as Kate would cattily claim later on.

Once again, Leland Hayward, fickle lover or not, proved what a strong and powerful agent he was. He flew to New York with an offer from Harry Cohn of Columbia. The studio chief wanted her to star in *Holiday*, where once again she'd be paired with Cary Grant, with George Cukor directing. Having previously understudied for Hope Williams in this Philip Barry play, she readily accepted. Leland told her, however, that because she was still under contract to RKO, she'd have to give Berman half of her salary of one-hundred and fifty-thousand dollars.

That night a gleeful Kate announced to both Hughes and her family, "Box office poison or not, I managed to beat out Irene Dunne for the role. At long last after all these years, I'll get to play the role of Linda Seton. No more waiting in the wings watching that cursed Hope Williams go on instead of me."

Only eight years before, *Holiday* had been filmed at RKO with its then reigning queen, Ann Harding, playing Linda Seton opposite Robert Ames as

308

Johnny Case (the Cary Grant role in the new version).

Almost lost amid the good news was a minor casting note that would affect her future. The third lead, that of her brother, Ned Seton, would be played by the boyishly handsome Lew Ayres.

"My God," she said, "the husband of Ginger Rogers. We'll have to see about that."

***

Following patterns previously established by both John Ford and especially Jed Harris, Hughes did not win over the Hepburn family, whose communal heart still belonged to their beloved Luddy.

Kit found Hughes a rather sullen figure, as he sat at their dining table, not actually sharing either their dinner or their conversation. Hughes would later eat alone in his room, late at night after the family had gone to bed.

Dr. Hepburn complained that Hughes never joined in any of the lively family debates. "He can't hear a word we're saying," Kate told her father.

With his camera, Luddy relentlessly chased after Hughes on the golf course, sometimes disrupting his game. Hughes complained bitterly to Dr. Hepburn. "Luddy has been taking pictures of us every day since he first arrived at Fenwick," Dr. Hepburn said. "He'll no doubt be taking them long after you're gone. Now let's get on with the game. Drive. Incidentally, you need a seven iron."

Hughes followed Dr. Hepburn's advice. He sunk the shot in two. As Kate remarked, "Cool in a pinch."

It didn't help matters that night when Kit, in the presence of Hughes, referred to Luddy as "our dear sweet ex."

In spite of her family's disapproval, Hughes continued to plead with Kate to marry him. She finally agreed, vaguely remembering that she had already agreed to marry him. She was completely confused at this point about the exact status of their engagement. Somehow word via Louella Parsons leaked out to the *Los Angeles Herald*. On May 28, newspapers carried the headline, HEPBURN TO WED HUGHES. Already Hughes had ordered his chief honcho, Noah Dietrich, to redesign the master bedroom aboard the *Southern Cross* for their honeymoon.

With Kate's final reassurance that she'd marry him that summer, Hughes departed for New York where he was going to fly back to Los Angeles to continue making plans for his flight around the world. Hughes seemed as eager to depart from Fenwick as the Hepburns were to see him go.

She was disheartened when Anderson Lawler called her with the latest gossip. Although engaged to her, Hughes had taken up with actress Luise Rainer.

Rainer had virtually broken the world's heart with her Oscar-winning performance as the Chinese peasant in the film adaptation of the Pearl Buck novel, *The Good Earth*.

Kate called Constance Collier and chastised her for teaching the Viennese-born actress English for her screen debut in the 1935 *Escapade*.

Kate told Kit, "It doesn't seem to matter to Howard that Rainer is already married to Clifford Odets."

"Hughes is somewhat like my daughter," Kit admonished her. "Since when did you let a wedding band come between you and a man you wanted?"

After dinner on the night before Kate's departure to New York, her brother, Dick, called all the family in to hear his new play, *Sea-Air*. For weeks he'd been typing madly in the bedroom.

As he read deeper and deeper into the play, Kate was shocked that its premise was based on "a handsome, good-looking millionaire aviator who comes to visit the New England family of a young woman who is a Hollywood actress."

Even before Dick had finished the play, Kate was on her feet denouncing it, claiming he had "maliciously and wickedly invaded my privacy—Howard's privacy too."

Both Dr. Hepburn and Kit agreed, joining Kate in her wishes that Dick burn the play in the fireplace page by page.

Dick held his ground and adamantly refused to destroy his work. He claimed that he'd shop it from Broadway producer to producer and, using a phrase that genuinely infuriated Kate, said he might even "show a copy of it to Jed Harris."

From this point on, the history of the play is shaky, and it is not known if a copy still exists. Garson Kanin, about to become a dear friend of Kate's, later claimed that he had read the play and found it "amusing, insightful, and entertaining—somewhat evocative of Coward's *Hay Fever*."

Kanin said that the character evoked by Hughes serves as a catalyst as he enters the home of a New England family and proceeds to tear away their pretenses.

On Broadway, rumors abounded that Kate had bought up the play to keep it from being produced. Others claimed that Hughes himself had purchased the rights to the play and then destroyed it.

Since Dick believed that this play was his finest creation, and because his lifetime goal involved becoming a playwright, it was heartbreaking to have the work go unproduced. Nonetheless, Dick put on a brave smile as he went with Kate to West Hartford, where she was maid of honor for their sister Marion's garden wedding.

Before leaving Fenwick, Kate had a long meeting with her father, Dr. Hepburn, part of which was conducted during a three-hour walk along Long Island Sound. It was a time for contemplation and renewal. She sought his advice about what to do with her RKO contract, viewing it to an increasing degree as a form of bondage, a potential for humiliation, and a disincentive for making better movies at other studios.

"Pandro Berman is about to cast me in some truly horrible movies," she predicted. "Any one of them would get me laughed off the screen."

Dr. Hepburn agreed with her, fearing that RKO would completely wreck whatever chances she might have for a future screen career. He told her that he'd invested her money wisely, and that she—if she wanted to—could afford to buy out her contract. The painful news was that a buy-out of her contract would cost two-hundred and twenty-thousand dollars. He warned her that it would be "a crushing blow to your investments." Caught in a numbers crunch, but fearing that she had no other reasonable course of action, she asked Leland Hayward to negotiate a buy-out deal with RKO, thereby ending her contractual obligations.

From Hollywood a week later, Leland called Kate, informing her that Berman "was only too eager to take the money and let you go." With bitterness, Kate vowed never to work for RKO ever again.

Columbia's offer of a leading role in *Holiday* renewed Kate's hope in her own greatly diminished career. After all, Joan Crawford, even though labeled box-office poison along with Kate, had been offered a new five-year contact from Metro-Goldwyn-Mayer, granting her an annual one and a half million dollars for three pictures a year.

Kate's favorite male star, Spencer Tracy, had filmed *Mannequin* with Joan Crawford. In New York to see theater, Franchot Tone telephoned Kate at her Turtle Bay residence. Claiming that Crawford had broken his heart once again, he wanted a repeat bedtime performance with Kate. "I want you to tuck me into my bed," he told her. "That's tuck, my pet."

"I know what tuck means," she said.

"Joan's not satisfied with Gable," Tone said. "Considering the size of his equipment, what woman would be? Now she's gone after the town's second biggest star. She's deep into an affair with Spencer Tracy."

Kate had a reaction to that. "Is there any beautiful woman or handsome man in Hollywood not having an affair with Tracy?"

In spite of Tone's urging, she turned him down, citing the presence of Hughes in her life.

Tone had a reaction to that. "Don't tell me you're being faithful to Howie baby. Only the other night he called Joan up for a date. Even though my wife dates about every man in Hollywood, and a lot of the women, too, she turned him down."

"Why?" Kate asked.

"Joan prefers homosexuals only to pal around with," Tone claimed. "For bed partners, she seeks out straighter arrows."

"Oh, I see," Kate said before putting down the phone.

***

Dethroned as queen of RKO by "that cheap blonde floozie and truck-stop cocksucker" [Kate's own words], Kate arrived at the studio gates of Columbia Pictures for inaugural discussions about her work in *Holiday*. A relatively minor company at the time, it had enjoyed a big success in 1934 with *It Happened One Night*, starring Claudette Colbert and Clark Gable. The head of the studio, "the gruff mad bulldog," Harry Cohn, was said to have invented the casting couch. Upon meeting him, Kate bluntly pointed out, "Don't try to pull that casting couch routine with me. I'm not one of your little chorus girls."

Looking at Kate in no makeup and pants, Cohn said, "Baby, you'll have nothing to fear from me. You can keep those bloomers fastened tight!"

The day before, Kate had driven to RKO to pack up the personal possessions in her dressing room. She called Pandro Berman, asking him to escort her to the front gate. Instead he sent Garson Kanin. Kanin had made his debut as an actor on Broadway in 1933, and at the time of his meeting with Kate, he wanted to be a screen writer and director for RKO. Although she liked Kanin and found him pleasant, she could not imagine at the time that he would become one of the key figures in her life, on the level of George Cukor.

On the subject of their first meeting, Kanin later said, "I fell madly in love with this skinny stunner. In those days, my hormones were working overtime. I even asked her out to a restaurant—not knowing how she loathed restaurants—and could not believe my good fortune when this bigtime star accepted. Perhaps she was touched by the fact that I was the only person there to say good-bye to RKO's fallen queen."

Kanin later recalled that he lured her to Chasen's, the deluxe landmark restaurant in Los Angeles. "When we came in, the dining room was almost empty, since Kate insisted on eating early. We started talking and became absorbed in each other. Slowly the restaurant began to fill up, and Kate didn't even seem aware of it. When she finally looked around and saw all these faces staring at one of her rare public appearances, she went into a sense of panic and fled from the restaurant."

The incident was observed by the drunken novelist, John O'Hara, who needed to fill up some space for his column in *Vanity Fair*. He maliciously wrote that Kate was merely "leading on the lovesick fool, Garson Kanin, as she did most men, her interest obviously lying with another sex." The horrified editors at *Vanity Fair* quickly removed O'Hara's suggestion of lesbianism from the copy. In private, throughout the rest of his life, O'Hara after a few drinks would forever after refer to Kate as a "prick-teaser."

The same novelist once told Ernest Hemingway, "Hepburn wouldn't know what to do with a stiff dick if she collided with one."

"That observation, John, my good man," Hemingway replied, "is just about as truthful and insightful as one of your novels."

312

***

Even before filming began on *Holiday,* Leland arrived with an offer from Paramount. The studio wanted Kate to sign a contract for a one-picture deal for ten-thousand dollars. Refusing to even look at the script, "which I know must be horrid," she angrily turned it down. "How the mighty have fallen," she told Leland. She later shared her humiliation with Hughes, who, to her shock, actually urged her to take the offer. "Stay in there," he advised her. "Otherwise, after *Holiday*, you may be forgotten."

As her dear friend, George Cukor gave Kate a warm welcome on the set of *Holiday*, reminding her that when Ann Harding, then queen of RKO, had made the first film version of *Holiday*, she'd been nominated for an Academy Award. "I think you'll not only be nominated like Ann, but that you'll actually win that marvelously phallic creature."

Her enthusiasm for the role was slightly diminished later in the day, however, when Cukor informed her that she had been Harry Cohn's second choice for the role. The director claimed that Cohn had wanted to reunite Cary Grant and Irene Dunne in the wake of their big success with *The Awful Truth* in 1937. "I was the one who prevailed on Harry to cast you," Cukor told her.

On her first day on the set, Kate had a tense meeting with Donald Ogden Stewart, who along with Sidney Buchman, the most erudite of the Columbia scenarists, was adapting the Philip Barry play for the screen.

Kate bitterly recalled that Stewart had been her enemy during the time she'd understudied for Hope Williams in *Holiday* on the stage. In the stage play, Stewart, also an actor, had played Nick Potter, best friend of the male star, the character of Johnny Case. Along with a coterie of other cast members, Stewart had conspired to keep "that little Bryn Mawr bitch" from going on during Williams' absence even when the star fell ill.

Upon meeting him again after all these years, Kate found Stewart alcoholic, dissolute, and in dire need of money to pay off creditors in active pursuit of him. She had more sympathy with him this time, forgiving him his past sins. He was bitterly disappointed that he hadn't been recast in his original role. The character of Potter had gone to Edward Everett Horton, the "high strung and easily excitable fussbudget" (code word at the time for homosexual).

Horton and Kate were a bad cocktail mix, as she seemed to view him "tainted" from having appeared with Ginger Rogers in such films as *The Gay Divorcée* in 1934 and *Top Hat* in 1935. Horton got off on the wrong foot with Kate when he told her how much he personally liked Rogers and what "incredible talent she has."

Having heard the plot night after night onstage, Kate was only too familiar with her role of the rich heiress from Park Avenue, Linda Seton. She was to play the black sheep daughter of a New York banker. Her snobbish sister, as

313

played by Doris Nolan, brings home Cary Grant in the role of a dashing non-conformist, Johnny Case. They plan to be married. But Grant is dreaming of taking a holiday to find out "who I am," a sort of voyage of self-exploration evocative of the hippie movement of the late 1960s.

Barry originally wrote the script before the Wall Street crash of 1929. Unfortunately, it would eventually play to a radically different audience in the late Thirties. When Kate falls for her sister's beau, she vows to follow him in his pursuit of a European holiday. Upon his return, she claims that he can sell peanuts for all she cares—"Lord, how I'll believe in those peanuts!"

Selling peanuts, or at least apples, on the street was hardly a joke to audiences at that time. It was all too real for many of them. Audiences would show little interest in the woes of a "poor little rich girl," as played by Kate, and were shocked when Grant turned down an offer from his screen father, as played by Harry Kolker, of a well-paying job as a banker. At that time, millions of Americans were still out of work and would have taken any job.

When not writing such an implausible scenario, Stewart was mouthing "Marxist gospel," or at least that was the view of Grant. When Kate's former co-star, the right-wing Adolphe Menjou, saw *Holiday*, he claimed it was part of "a communist conspiracy to ridicule capitalism."

Cukor was going through a tense, nervous period during the shooting of *Holiday*, as he was more concerned with directing the upcoming *Gone With The Wind*, with Kate as a possible Scarlett O'Hara. He often clashed with the tyrannical Harry Cohn, who was disappointed at the rushes of *Holiday*. Cohn found Kate "strident and shrill," and urged and screamed at Cukor "to tone down the bitch—make her more realistic." Later, Cukor and Kate also clashed bitterly over this command from Cohn. In the end, Kate prevailed.

As Grant later said, "Cukor was never known to be of even temperament. On the set of *Holiday*, he often threw tantrums. Only Kate seemed to soothe his nerves."

Kate was actually giving one of her most memorable performances in *Holiday*, playing the tough yet vulnerable Linda. But she would have to wait decades before future audiences were to appreciate *Holiday* and re-define it as one of the classic comedies of the 1930s.

Harry Cohn in time would be disappointed with the box office returns of *Holiday* and would never offer Kate another picture. His daring campaign to promote *Holiday* had backfired. He had arranged for billboards to appear around Los Angeles asking, "Is it true what they say about Hepburn? That she is *Box Office Poison*?" To Cohn's chagrin, the public answered with a resounding YES.

During the filming of *Holiday*, Grant continued to spend one or two nights a week with Hughes when the aviator was in town. Sometimes he drove to the studio the following morning with Kate. On other nights he was most often with Randolph Scott, though still dating the actress Phyllis Brooks, whom he affectionately called "Brooksie."

The world at the time didn't know about Grant's homosexuality, and dozens of fan clubs—composed mostly of female admirers—sprouted up across the United States and England, deluging the studio with letters. Some of the writers declared their undying love for him.

In spite of studio pressure, he continued to act indiscreetly and even in some cases rather flamboyantly with Scott in public. As if she'd caught both actors with a smoking gun, the actress, Margot Grahame, reported to Louella Parsons that she'd spotted Grant passionately kissing Scott in the parking lot of the Mocambo night club. Other spectators confirmed Grahame's sighting. The item was too hot for Parsons or her column to handle.

One evening, in an attempt to throw off the press bloodhounds, Grant was photographed at a night club with the "sex siren of the sarong," Dorothy Lamour. However, in her memoirs, *My Side of the Road*, Lamour reported that Grant was a perfect gentleman and never made a pass at her.

Ever curious, Kate grilled Grant about his intent with Brooks. "Of course, I'm going to marry her," Grant said with absolutely no conviction in his voice. "We'll have a house full of kids—that's what life is all about, isn't it? It's what everybody agrees on, isn't it? Are you and me the only people in the world who know *The Awful Truth*?" he asked, citing the name of his recent movie.

When Grant wasn't talking about Hughes, Scott, or Brooks, his mind was more occupied with his upcoming film, *Gunga Din*. He told her that Howard Hawks would have been designated as the film's director, but that he was passed over because of having gone way over budget on *Bringing Up Baby*. "The new director—and you know him as David knew Bathsheba—is none other than our very own George Stevens."

Grant was thrilled at the prospect of working with Stevens, and he was also excited that Spencer Tracy "has virtually signed in blood that he will play second lead to me." But despite his promises, Tracy later bowed out, and Grant ended up making the film with Douglas Fairbanks, Jr. and Victor McLaglen.

"What about the female role?" Kate asked. "I need a job. Maybe I can get Stevens to build up the part for me. Sounds to me that with all those men in the cast you'll need a strong female to balance things out."

Kate might have been right, but Stevens eventually awarded the part to Joan Fontaine, who Kate was learning to admire less and less.

Somewhere during the shoot, Grant revealed to Kate that he was not going to marry Phyllis Brooks. He'd insisted on a prenuptial agreement, whereby they would relinquish all rights to each other's property. She'd refused and also turned down the second condition, which was that her mother, Mrs. Steiller, would not be allowed into their marital home.

***

In *Holiday*, the actor sometimes known as "the beautiful Lew Ayres" was cast as Kate's spoiled younger brother, Ned Seton. The role called for him to be sweet-tempered but alcoholic. This former college dropout from San Diego and Hollywood bit player had skyrocketed to stardom as Pierre Lassalle, Garbo's leading man in *The Kiss* in 1929. But mainly, his fame rested on his role of Paul Baumer in *All Quiet on the Western Front* in 1930.

Kate wasn't interested in his film credits—only that he was the husband of Ginger Rogers. "And he's gorgeous," Cukor interjected. "But I saw him first, bitch. I was Lew's dialogue coach on *All Quiet on the Western Front*."

"I bet you taught him a lot," she said sarcastically.

At the time of his meeting with Kate, Ayres had already made the one film and appeared as the one character with whom he'd always be most identified. *Young Dr. Kildare* was shot in 1938, leading to a series of spin-offs which Ayres continued to make until he was drafted into the Army in World War II. He outraged the movie-going public by declaring himself a conscientious objector, which many patriots at the time viewed as tantamount to treason. Theater owners throughout the country vowed never to show a Lew Ayres film again.

After the war, with memories fading, Ayres relaunched himself as Jane Wyman's co-star in her Oscar-winning portrayal in *Johnny Belinda* in 1948. Ayres at the time befriended Jane Wyman both on and off the screen as her marriage to Ronald Reagan was coming to an end.

But all that lay in his future. On the set of *Holiday*, Ayres was introduced to Kate by Cukor. She was surprised to find him as boyishly handsome and soft-spoken off the screen as on. In her meetings with so many actors, including Bette Davis, they didn't look in real life like they did on the screen.

Once again, she lived up to her father's description of herself as a "charging bull." She swept into Ayres' life and was frequently seen in social situations with him away from the set. During the making of *Holiday*, he was often the only guest at her on-set picnics.

Grant very seriously complained to her that, "I, too, have the hots for Lew, and you're completely monopolizing him, leaving nothing for Cukor and me."

"You can have him when I'm through with him," she promised.

Since Hughes was rarely at Muirfield, Kate had plenty of time on her hands. She booked Ayres for every night he was available, as he was spending almost no time with his wife, Ginger. Ayres confided in her that the two famous "lovebirds, Ginger and myself," were on the verge of flying away from each other.

Not since Luddy had Kate met a man as interested in classical music. Ayres had once been a dance-band musician when, still in his teens, he was discovered by a Hollywood talent scout attracted to his exceptional male beauty. Ayres could play the banjo, the organ, and the piano, and was also an arranger and composer.

Kate and Ayres would slip away many an evening to a secluded apartment owned by a friend of his. There, they made not love but spent the night listening to such composers as Bach and Brahms for hours at a time.

When not with Kate or his wife, Ayres spent all his time studying and writing about religion. He shared with her his greatest dream, which was to be a Renaissance man, with the ability to compose a symphony like Beethoven, to create a sculpture like Michelangelo, and to write a play like Eugene O'Neill.

Although still not going to bed with Ayres, her relationship was growing closer and closer and much more confidential. He claimed that he felt he could open up to her and share his darkest secrets, "With Ginger, I live in fear that she'll find out about me."

"What, pray tell, is there to find out? I want to know."

He put off any revelations that night. "In time, I will tell you everything because I feel I can trust you."

The following night he took her to the home he shared with Rogers, because she had to go on a trip to San Francisco. Once there, he showed her a home movie which he'd shot in 1934. It was called *Little Red Riding Hood*, and its star was Ginger Rogers. Kate was not impressed with the performance.

He amused her with stories of his married life, including the time he brought home two wild coots (sluggish, slow-flying blackbirds) that he'd shot. Not knowing that these birds weren't edible, Rogers baked them and "smelled up the house like a convention of skunks," Ayres told her.

He took Kate to the Santa Monica pier on weekends, renting a boat with himself as the captain and heading out on deep-sea fishing expeditions.

In the closing weeks of filming of *Holiday*, Kate was getting desperate. So far, she'd been unable to seduce Ginger Rogers' husband. She admitted to Cukor that she'd originally wanted revenge for Rogers' seduction of Leland Hayward—"and countless other horrors." But over a short period of time, she claimed to have fallen in love "with this dear sensitive man who has many of the qualities of Luddy but with more manliness and virility."

One night Kate thought her luck had changed. It was after eleven o'clock when Ayres called her at Muirfield mansion. Fortunately, Hughes, as per usual, was not a home, and she was eager to accept Ayres' invitation to visit the secluded apartment retreat they often shared.

When she drove there, she found him visibly upset. She immediately got to the source of his deep anxiety. It seemed that Hughes had pressed Ginger Rogers to speed through a divorce and marry him. "Your beau has proposed to my wife."

"At this point I can believe anything that Howard does," Kate said. "I think he proposes to a different woman every month—God knows how many men he asks to marry him as well."

Ayres said that that very afternoon he'd been called over to the office of Hughes' attorney, Neil McCarthy.

"I've heard of him," she said. "He's the best in Hollywood. He even got Howard off one night when he killed a pedestrian."

Ayres broke down and told Kate of the evidence that Hughes' detectives had collected on him in case he opposed Rogers in any way when she went to get a quick divorce from him.

"The son of a bitch has amassed this whole dossier on my deepest, darkest shame," Ayres said. "He told me that my career in Hollywood would be ruined if word of this got out."

"What are those skeletons?" she asked.

"That I carry on a secret life as a homosexual," he said.

"I knew that already," she assured him. "At least I've heard about you and Spencer Tracy."

He seemed shocked that she knew that much, but told her that "there are others, notably my flesh-and-blood dream man, Joel McCrea."

"You did better than me with that one," she said. "I almost had Joel when I first arrived in Hollywood but he got away—no doubt into your arms."

He told her that McCrea, while dating his future wife, Frances Dee, often went on hunting trips with him where they made passionate love far from the eyes of Hollywood. "Hughes knows all about it," Ayres told her, his hysteria mounting.

In her take-charge way, Kate promised, "I'll intervene with Howard and get him to call off his mad dogs. I can even set up a meeting between the two of you boys and get him to give back all that blackmail evidence. I'll confront him with what I know about Ginger and him, and that will do the trick. After that little embarrassment, Howard will agree to anything."

But when Kate faced Hughes with the Ayres/Rogers scandal, he didn't admit to anything. In fact, he denied it all, but agreed to meet with Ayres.

The next week Hughes flew to Texas, and Kate called Ayres to come over for dinner at Muirfield. With a little help from her cook, Johanna Madsen, she prepared all his favorite foods. Remembering how Rogers had botched the wild fowl dinner, she cooked the most delicate of pheasant.

Dinner was ready at seven o'clock but no Ayres. By nine-thirty a call came in for her. "Sorry, Kate, something came up at the last minute and I was literally whisked off my feet."

"I know you're calling long distance," she said. "Dare I ask where you are tonight?"

There was a long hesitation on the other end of the phone. "Texas," he said shyly.

"I don't think I'll ask the next most obvious question. Or perhaps I shall. Let me guess. Did someone we both know fly you to Texas today?"

"Kate, I can explain. I went to meet him like you'd arranged. I don't know what happened. He knew my weaknesses. One thing led to another. He overpowered me."

"Sure he did," she said, slamming down the phone.

She was never to see Lew Ayres again.

***

Even before *Holiday* was wrapped, Cukor began making preparations to direct *Gone with the Wind.* Kate had already read Margaret Mitchell's novel and had literally begged Pandro Berman to buy it as a vehicle for her. He turned her down, claiming that fifty-thousand dollars was too much to pay for a novel.

In addition to Kate, it seemed that every other actress in Hollywood also wanted to star as Scarlett O'Hara, and many were tested. Among the contenders were Claudette Colbert, a Frenchwoman who presumably wasn't entirely familiar with the morays and intricacies of the Deep South before the Civil War, as well as Irene Dunne, Miriam Hopkins, Carole Lombard, and Ann Sheridan. Kate was furious to learn that Margaret Sullavan had a good chance at the role, possibly to be teamed with her former husband, Henry Fonda.

Under *Believe It Or Not*, Kate heard that Lana Turner and Lucille Ball were also being considered.

David Selznick eventually bought the property for fifty-thousand dollars, and Cukor urged him to cast Kate as Scarlett. Selznick had his doubts, claiming, "I can't imagine Errol Flynn, if we go with him, chasing after Kate all those years."

Cukor told Kate that Errol Flynn had once again made a casting-couch visit to his office, "plea-bargaining" to be cast as Rhett Butler.

"Even though it's against your usual practice," Kate said, "did you once again manage to resist his sexual overtures?"

"I'm a man of mere flesh, and he overcame my resistance," Cukor said. "After we'd done the dirty deed, I had to warn him that there still wasn't any guarantee that he would play Rhett."

"When Flynn comes to New York, give him my number at Fenwick," Kate said. "I want to convince Selznick that Flynn is very attracted to me."

"Okay," Cukor warned her, "but in Flynn's case you'll be getting sloppy seconds following your director's conquest of this handsome Aussie devil."

Cukor in the next few days showed her one of Selznick's infamous in-house memos. "Regarding the casting of Katharine Hepburn as Scarlett O'Hara. She has two strikes against her—first, the unquestionable and very widespread public dislike of her at the moment, and second, the fact that she has yet to demonstrate that she possesses the sex qualities which are probably the most important of all the many requisites of Scarlett. At the moment, I am seriously considering Paulette Goddard. However, she may not be legally married to Chaplin. This could raise a moral issue with all those fanatical religious groups, especially in the Bible Belt South."

When Kate learned from Cukor that another nemesis, Joan Bennett, was testing for the part, she responded angrily: "Why doesn't Selznick cast Ginger Rogers as Scarlett and let her dance through the part?"

As every week went by, Cukor told her of yet another actress who had moved to the top of the list, Jean Arthur, whom Selznick once had developed a crush on. He said that Bette Davis was still angling for the part too.

When Cukor told her that Selznick had decided on Loretta Young, Kate hoped to sabotage the deal by giving him some information that she'd learned from Anderson Lawler.

"If Selznick is worried about a morals problem with Goddard, wait until he hears what's about to blow up with Young." Kate had heard that Louise Tracy was about to divorce Spencer after all these years, because of his ongoing and torrid affair with Young. "It'll be on the front page of all the papers," Kate predicted.

"At least Young is willing to test," Cukor admonished her. "Something you refuse to do."

Kate angrily shot back. "Both you and Selznick are completely aware of my capabilities as an actress. My God, it was the two of you who brought me to Hollywood in the first place."

Cukor told Kate that even Tallulah Bankhead was flying to the West Coast, claiming that because of her Alabama birth she was the only one of the actresses in the lineup who could convincingly play a Southern belle. "'After all,'" Cukor quoted Tallulah saying, "'Bette Davis and Katharine Hepburn are Yankified New Englanders.'"

Kate's response was that Tallulah was "too long in the tooth to be Scarlett."

While vacationing in Fenwick, awaiting the arrival of Howard Hughes, Kate read an erroneous report that Margaret Mitchell wanted Kate to play the role of Scarlett. The Atlanta novelist later denied the story.

The public, it seemed, was casting the roles themselves. As Selznick considered such unlikely actors as Humphrey Bogart, Ronald Colman, and even Cary Grant, the public overwhelmingly voted in opinion polls that only Clark Gable could be Rhett Butler. Gable nixed the idea. "I'd cast my vote for Gary Cooper. Let him—not me—mess up a big picture like this."

Before departing for the East, Kate cabled Selznick. "You know what I look like on the screen. You know I can act. And you know the part was practically written for me. *I am Scarlett O'Hara.* So, what's the matter?"

Selznick did not respond directly but Cukor informed Kate that she had moved to the top of the list. Just at the same time, Leland Hayward, in contrast, told her that he'd spoken to Selznick who said "Kate will only play Scarlett O'Hara as a last resort if I don't find some more suitable actress. If it's any comfort, know that I'd cast Kate over Bette Davis any day."

On the train back home to New York, Kate optimistically wired Luddy,

Laura, and Jack with the news. "The part of Scarlett O'Hara is all but mine."

***

In New York, just before beginning his epic around-the-world voyage, Hughes stayed with Kate at Laura Harding's apartment to avoid reporters camped out at her Turtle Bay residence. Not seeing Hughes at night, reporters thought he was staying over at one of the residence halls being readied for the New York World's Fair of 1939.

At night he and Kate talked not of love but of the minute details and challenges of his upcoming flight. He was frank in relating to her the dangers involved. "Other pilots have lost their lives doing exactly what I'm trying to do," he warned her. Both of them were aware that he'd lost his friend, Amelia Earhart, only the year before in a mysterious disappearance over the South Pacific.

Kate bravely expressed confidence in his new Lockheed Lodestar, claiming that she was certain that he would beat pilot Wiley Post's existing record for two trans-global flights in the 1930s. On July 10, Hughes climbed into the back of Kate's Lincoln, chauffeured by Charlie Newhill, and was driven to Floyd Bennett Field, the only airport in New York at the time, as La Guardia and Idlewild were yet to be constructed.

Hughes held her in his arms, hugging and kissing her all the way, even though their relationship had not been consummated. He vowed his eternal love for her and dedicated his flight to her, promising that he'd dip the wings of his plane as he flew over Fenwick en route to Paris. He promised to cable her at every stop en route, as well as when he made radio contact with ships over the Atlantic.

Stopped by a traffic cop, she cautioned her hot-tempered driver to accept a ticket for speeding and not get into an altercation with policemen in a squad car. For once, Charlie held his tongue and took the ticket with a smile. At no point did the ticketing officer look into the Lincoln's back seat at the two world-fabled passengers.

At the airfield, Charlie unloaded the roast beef and Swiss cheese sandwiches that Kate had prepared herself for Hughes and his crew, wrapping them in butcher paper. Before that, Hughes had spent weeks of preparation studying the nutritional value of more than a dozen different breads until he found the one he believed was the most vitamin enriched.

With one final and passionate kiss for Kate, Hughes emerged from the back seat of her Lincoln. He tipped his brown snap-brim felt hat to her. His last words to her, and she feared they might indeed be the last words she'd ever hear from him, were, "You'll hear from me, kiddo."

Not wanting to join him and face a mob of reporters and well-wishers, Kate remained seated, concealed behind large sunglasses in the back seat of her Lincoln until take-off. Shortly before takeoff, Grover Whalen, head of the city's upcoming World's Fair, christened Hughes' aircraft, *New York World's Fair of 1939.*

Kate watched, as did most of the world (or at least heard about over the radio), as Hughes' aircraft took off. It was dangerously loaded with 1,500 gallons of fuel and 150 gallons of oil. At first appearing as if it would never become airborne, the plane and its contents weighed thirteen tons.

Kate ordered Charlie to drive her back to Fenwick where she'd sit by the radio listening for news of Hughes.

By the time she reached Fenwick, Kit handed her a cable. "See you in three days. Love, Howard." What he'd told her only a short time before was that his dream involved successfully circumnavigating the globe "so that I will be worthy of you when we get married by the end of summer."

He had slipped her a note that she was not to read until he'd gone so far from America's shores as to lose radio contact. At Fenwick, she tore open the hand-written note. "On this flight you are my silent partner, my spiritual co-pilot. Love, Howard."

"Who couldn't love a man who'd write a note like that?" Kate asked her mother.

Before going to bed, Kate listened to radio broadcasts, only to learn that gambling ships off the coast of Atlantic City, outside U.S. territorial waters, were giving her aviator a fifty-fifty chance of survival.

***

Kate eagerly read her first cable from Hughes dispatched somewhere over the Atlantic from an Italian ocean liner that Hughes had made radio contact with. "All is fine. Love, Howard."

Through another liner, *Île de France*, he cabled Kate once again. "The Irish coast is breathtaking in all its beauty. Will contact you from Paris. Love, Howard."

Three-thousand Parisians, braving the rain, waited to greet the Hughes plane upon its landing at Le Bourget. This was the same airfield where cheering crowds greeted Charles Lindbergh eleven years earlier when he'd flown in on his *Spirit of St. Louis*. In spite of turbulent weather over the Atlantic, Hughes had made landfall in Paris in sixteen hours and thirty-eight minutes, cutting Lindbergh's historic flight in half.

On hearing the news from Paris, Kate at Fenwick stood up and gave a raucous cheer. In Paris Hughes cursed the delay when he learned that a crucial piece of his landing gear had blown off during the storms over the Atlantic. He claimed that precious hours—actually a total of eight—"would be wasted" while his Lodestar was repaired.

It was raining when he flew out of Paris "hideously late." By that time, it wasn't the weather he most feared, but getting shot down by enemy aircraft. In London, the BBC reported that, "Luftwaffe pilots were itching to get the famous American aviator, Howard Hughes, in their sights." The *International Herald Tribune* trumpeted this bulletin: *STERN WARNINGS FROM HITLER TO HUGHES.*

The Nazi dictator had sent word to Hughes that his plane would be shot down if it flew over German territory. Apparently, Hitler feared that Hughes' aircraft was actually a spy plane gathering valuable reconnaissance on the dictator's upcoming preparations for war. Hughes countered that he would be flying at twelve-thousand feet over Germany, thereby making any aerial reconnaissance impossible with the instruments of that era.

Nonetheless, the moment Hughes entered German air space, five fighter planes were ordered into the sky. The leader of the squadron, in making radio contact with Hughes, screamed *VERBOTEN! VERBOTEN!* into Hughes' nearly deaf ear. Ignoring the warning, Hughes continued his eastbound flight.

The moment he cleared German air space, Hughes told his co-pilot, Harry P.M. Connor, "Now we can breathe again."

Kate was sitting by her radio when word came that Hughes had landed safely at Moscow the following morning at 11:15am.

"Hello America," came the greeting. "This is Radio Moscow." The announcer said that thousands of well-wishers were storming Hughes' *New York World's Fair of 1939.*

In Moscow the Russians greeted Hughes with bowls of corn flakes and fresh milk. Josef Stalin even sent a container of his rarest caviar, but Hughes turned down the gift, claiming, "It's much too heavy and on this flight every pound counts."

By 1:13pm, Hughes was airborne over Moscow, flying toward the desolation of Siberia. Kate was not a religious woman, but she prayed for her aviator's safety as he flew across one of the most uncharted territories in the world.

Word reached Kate by radio that Hughes' plane had landed in Omsk, an industrial city in western Siberia. She was also informed that half the male babies being born in America were being named Howard by their mothers.

"If Howard and I ever marry, he won't become Mr. Katharine Hepburn but I will definitely become Mrs. Howard Hughes," Kate told her family.

Modern Screen asked the question on everyone's lips. *WILL AMERICA'S HERO, MR. HOWARD HUGHES, MARRY KATHARINE HEPBURN?* On the cover of the fan magazine was a glamorous picture of the handsome aviator with a stunningly beautiful Kate, fortunately not dressed as a man this time.

After refueling, Hughes took off once again before eventually landing in the

323

port city of Yakutsk in northern Siberia. He would later tell Kate that "this God-forsaken place was a town on the edge of the world suspended somewhere between the sun and the moon."

His airplane almost never made it, as he was using inaccurate maps supplied by the United States Hydrographic Survey. Mountains that he thought rose to a height of six-thousand five-hundred feet were nearly ten-thousand feet. His craft, its wings loaded with ice, had to rise to ten-thousand feet and even beyond. Even so, Hughes narrowly missed the ninety-seven-foot crest of a mountain range.

At Yakutsk he had trouble making the natives understand his need for fuel. Some locals feared that his aircraft had miraculously flown backwards from some mysterious era in the future. They didn't understand why his craft contained "1939" as part of its name, when it was only 1938.

"Still safe, HH," was the terse cable Kate received from Yakutsk.

Reaching Fairbanks, Alaska, at 3:01pm on July 13, Hughes was greeted by the widow of Wiley Post who kissed him and wished him a safe return. Her own husband had died in a plane crash with Will Rogers on August 15, 1935.

A violent storm prevented Hughes from flying into Manitoba, so instead, he piloted his craft to an unexpected landing in Minneapolis. Only one reporter was there to record the event for a world audience. On ground for only thirty-four minutes for refueling, Hughes headed for Floyd Bennett Field in Brooklyn.

The moment Kate heard of the landing in Minneapolis, she ordered Charlie Newhill to drive her to her Turtle Bay townhouse to await the return of her aviator.

***

"You're the toast of New York," a control operator via radio alerted pilot Hughes as he was about to land in New York. "Get ready to get mobbed."

From his pilot's seat, Hughes could see masses of people—an estimated thirty-thousand—converging on the airfield. Breaking through police barricades, they were surging toward the runway on which he was scheduled to land. To avoid the crowds, Hughes diverted his Lodestar to a more isolated airstrip.

Sporting a four-day growth of black beard, Hughes stepped from his airplane to thunderous applause. He had set a world's record and, like Charles Lindbergh, was a true American hero.

His "voyage into history" had taken three days, nineteen hours, and seventeen minutes.

Pandemonium broke out on the ground as both fans and reporters rushed toward Hughes and his crew. As reported in *The New York Times*, "Microphones were pushed in his face, flashbulbs blinded him throughout the episode, and the crowd became a mob."

The sleepless Hughes uttered a few incoherent words. A Western Union man tried to push through the crowd to get a message to Hughes but could not break into the inner circle surrounding the aviator. It was a telegram of congratulations from Kate, the first of thousands that would pour in from all over the globe.

At the time of the landing and mass hysteria, Kate at her Turtle Bay residence was receiving a phone call from Cary Grant. He urged her to announce her upcoming marriage tomorrow morning—"and for God's sake set a date and stick to it." The actor told her that her announcement of her upcoming marriage would be a marvelous way to cash in on all the worldwide publicity enveloping Hughes. "It will revitalize your career," Grant assured her. Before ringing off, he also claimed that if she'd make an announcement to the press, "it will push Selznick over the edge in granting you the role of Scarlett."

Waved on by the cheering masses, Hughes was driven to the Greenwich Village mews house of Grover Whalen, head of the 1939 World's Fair. Waiting to toast him in Whalen's parlor was Mayor Fiorella LaGuardia and at least a dozen other dignitaries.

Pleading that "I smell like dead skunk," Hughes quickly excused himself and headed upstairs toward the bathroom. Instead of taking a bath, he escaped through the rear door, hailed a taxi and headed for Kate's townhouse at Turtle Bay.

As the Yellow Cab approached Turtle Bay, Hughes spotted the unruly mob that had formed around Kate's townhouse—reporters, photographers, and rubberneckers—hoping to catch a glimpse of the aviator on the way to see his lady love.

He ordered the cabbie to turn back and take him to the Drake Hotel on Park Avenue instead. Once in his suite, Hughes reached Kate on the phone and talked to her for nearly thirty minutes, filling her in on the more harrowing details of his historic flight.

Telling her that he loved her and still wanted to marry her, he put down the phone and fell "into the sleep of the dead," as he was to later recall.

The next morning Hughes was the man of the hour as he was driven in an open car through the "Canyon of Heroes" of New York for the traditional ticker-tape welcome reserved for only the most notable of visiting heroes. Looking up at the towering buildings, he faced a paper snowstorm. *The New York Times* estimated that a million well-wishers lined the streets. Another eight-hundred thousand jammed in the area between Lower Broadway from the Battery to City Hall.

Hughes faced the inevitable speeches. As he waited to be introduced, he kept biting and licking his chapped lips. He took off his hat, only to put it back on again, and repeated this action endlessly.

Whalen mistakenly introduced "the star of the hour" as Edward Hughes.

Hat in hand, Hughes told the throng that his flight had placed the United States as the number one force in world aviation.

Even more sensational was the "photographer's dream night" when Kate, her arm linked with Hughes, showed up at an official reception Whelan had staged for the aviator along the Jersey shore.

Around midnight the same evening, the manager of the Drake Hotel placed a DO NOT DISTURB sign on the door to the Honeymoon Suite, housing Kate and Hughes.

Shortly before two that morning, the tall, lanky frame of Hughes appeared at the door to Kate's bedroom. As she would recall later, he was completely naked except for the felt hat he'd worn on his flight around the world.

In his hand he held the pink porcelain bowl his mother back in Texas so long ago had repeatedly held up before his genitals.

As he moved toward Kate's bed, she instinctively knew what act he wanted her to perform on him.

***

Hughes left early the next morning for Washington, D.C., and another parade. Before checking out of the Drake Hotel, he delivered an ultimatum to Kate. She had just three days to answer his proposal of marriage. After that, he was "withdrawing the offer forever."

She immediately called Cary Grant and burst into tears. "He doesn't want a real woman. He wants me to be his mother. I can't do it. It won't work." Even when he learned more details, Grant still pressed marriage onto Kate. "His demands on you will be few, and you can pursue other affairs."

"Sounds like the perfect marriage," she said before ringing off.

She called Cukor and told him what had happened. "I think I love Howard. I think he feels the same way about me. But in the end both of us desire fame more than each other. I feel ambition has won out over love." She paused. "Or should I say *like?*"

She spent the rest of the day contemplating whether to call Hughes and discuss his offer of marriage or whether she should let the three-day ultimatum pass with no response.

That afternoon a call came in for her. "Miss Scarlett, this is your Rhett Butler speaking."

It was Errol Flynn.

The handsome Aussie actor had gotten her message that she wanted to speak with him, and he was eager to meet with her. She invited him to come at once to Turtle Bay.

Within the hour, he was knocking on the door to her townhouse. Dressed in a dark blue suit, red tie, and starched white shirt, with two-tone shoes, he looked even sexier and more dashing than he did in his films.

Taking his hand, she ushered him in, thrilled at his virile presence. "David Selznick thinks you wouldn't find me sexy enough to chase after for ten years."

"David is wrong," he told her, reaching over and gently kissing her nose. "If I had a chance at you, I'd give up all other women. Of course, I wouldn't wait ten years."

As Flynn enjoyed a few drinks, and while Kate ordered afternoon tea, he told her that he very much wanted to be Rhett Butler. He also believed that her agent, Leland Hayward, could sell both of them as a package. He revealed, with some degree of mockery, that Bette Davis was willing to take herself out of the running to play Scarlett because of her adamant refusal to appear opposite him as Rhett.

Despite his sarcasm, he seemed deeply disappointed about Davis' position, and threatened that he'd get even with her at some future date. Yet he seemed buoyed at the idea that an actress (Kate) who was "far better than Miss Davis" thought he would make the ideal Rhett.

Kate had a plan, and she wanted to share it with him since she needed his complete cooperation.

But before the evening ended, "the inevitable happened," as Kate later confided to Anderson Lawler. "Errol's charms are legendary, and I'm but a woman. He spent the night, and what a glorious night it was. So unlike being with Howard in a suite."

She would also tell Kenneth MacKenna that, "I could have fallen in love with him. Now if *he* had asked me to marry him, I would have said yes. But I had already heard that Errol is incapable of genuinely loving anyone—even himself."

The following morning, as Kate prepared a full breakfast for herself, Flynn preferring only coffee, she introduced him to Luddy. Her "adorable ex," as she called him, seemed to be totally mesmerized by Flynn, even more so than he'd been by Hughes.

Kate's chauffeur, Charlie, hauled all three of them to an old studio near Columbus Circle where silent films used to be shot. Once there, she introduced Flynn to Richard Moseley, a makeup artist, and Robert Ridley, a costumer.

At her expense, she'd hired Ridley to secure Scarlett and Rhett costumes for them. Errol, with Luddy's avid assistance, enjoyed getting in and out of his various Rhett costumes, and Kate appeared as Scarlett in seven different antebellum outfits. Luddy madly photographed Kate and Errol in provocative, sexy poses. Although she wouldn't submit to a screen test, she was eager for Selznick to see these photographs of Flynn and her.

"How dare Selznick say I'm not sexy enough," Kate said. "He's a total idiot."

When Luddy developed his pictures, he sent the best of them to Selznick.

Selznick never responded. It is not known whether any of Luddy's photographs still exist today.

She was eager to pursue a romance with Flynn and asked him to call her again. She also offered to take him to Fenwick for a month of swimming and boating. He declined the invitation but promised to telephone her in three days.

As Kate would tell Cukor in 1946, "Thank God I'm not still sitting by the phone waiting for the call that never came. I guess Selznick was right. I'm not that sexy after all."

***

That summer, Kate stood nude in front of a mirror at her Turtle Bay residence. Both Luddy and Laura were eager spectators. As she approached her thirty-first birthday, she admired what she saw in the mirror. Radiantly tanned, she looked more glorious than she'd appeared in years.

That weekend she was going to Fenwick for a meeting with playwright Philip Barry, who had been critical of her acting in the past. Immaculately attired in the latest Brooks Brothers fashion, he walked with her that Saturday afternoon on the shores bordering Fenwick. He had brought to her the idea of a "play in the works" that would eventually be called *The Philadelphia Story.*

The play focused on an aloof and arrogant Philadelphia Main Line society girl named Tracy Lord, and the plot centered on her impending marriage to a boring blueblood in the character of George Kittredge.

On the eve of Tracy's impending marriage, her fatally charming former husband, C.K. Dexter Haven, shows up. The wedding of this spoiled heiress is disrupted by an unwelcome team of tabloid journalists, a reporter, Mike Connor, arriving with his photographer, Liz Imbrie, who is secretly in love with him.

Tracy finds herself falling in love again with her former spouse, as well as being attracted to the handsome reporter, with whom she takes a nude swim.

In Barry's view, Kate's character had to evolve from an "ice goddess" to a compassionate, loving woman before the end of the play.

Kate was immediately thrilled with the character, and couldn't help but see the similarities between herself and Tracy Lord. A distrust of the press. A craving for privacy. A love of swimming. She agreed to work with Barry, tailoring the role to her own mannerisms and voice patterns.

In a private plane lent to her by Hughes, she flew often to Barry's retreat on the coast of Maine to supervise the writing of the play, which she hoped would bring renewed interest in her flagging career.

Writing madly, Barry later said that he painstakingly studied Kate's every movement, "even the quirk of her head, the dart of her eyes, and I incorporated all of her characteristics into the role of Tracy Lord. It was tailormade for her."

Even in its unfinished state Kate was eager to take Barry's play to the Theatre Guild. She did just that, meeting with its directors, Theresa Helburn

328

and Lawrence Langner.

Sadly, she learned that they had serious financial woes and could not back the play, having recently lost sixty-thousand dollars on *Jeremiah*, a Biblical extravaganza.

Langner bluntly told Kate. "Let's face it. There will be no investors for this one. You are box office poison, and Barry has had four flops in six years."

Kate rushed to the rescue and began to act as producer herself. Barry, in addition to being a playwright, was also wealthy. He agreed to go in with Kate and together they would underwrite one-fourth of the production costs. Somehow the Guild managed to scrape up another one-quarter.

For the rest of the money, Kate called Hughes in California. It was not with an answer to his proposal of marriage, as his three-day ultimatum had expired. He would not bring up the subject again. Sight unseen, Hughes agreed to provide the rest of the money. He also advised Kate to accept ten percent of the Broadway gross in lieu of a salary, plus another twelve and a half percent of the road show take. He also told her to put up twenty-five thousand dollars of her own money and secure the screen rights before it opened on Broadway.

Kate warned the Guild that she would have to abandon the play at any moment should David O. Selznick call her to Hollywood to star in *Gone With the Wind*.

In the meantime, a September day broke ominously under black clouds and a turbulent surf. Kate was so excited with all this frothy action in the sea that she went for a swim.

Only an hour later she was involved as a real life star in her own drama of *Gone With the Wind*. Except this one was boiling up not in the Deep South, but on Long Island Sound.

***

The famous hurricane of September of 1938 came without warning. In those days, the U.S. Weather Bureau had no hurricane-warning service in Connecticut.

The morning broke calm. After her ritual dip and a hearty breakfast, Kate went with a family friend, Jack (Red) Hammond, for a game of golf.

At first she found the winds refreshing but as they neared the end of their game, the gusts were growing stronger.

Amazingly, after returning home, she dared to go into the surf again. At that time, the wind was howling and the waves rising like sheets in the wind. She told Hammond that "the winds are so powerful they can hold me up." Ignoring the danger, she continued to ride the waves.

But as she and Hammon were returning to the house, a sudden gust practically blew her away. The sands started blowing wildly, stinging her eyes. Fearing it would damage the paint job on her Lincoln, she went inside and ordered Charlie Newhill, her chauffeur, to drive her car to Saybrook and put it into a garage.

Kit, her brother Dick, Hammond, and Fanny the cook waited inside the house as the winds howled around Fenwick. Looking out the window, Kate saw a Ford literally picked up and flown through the air, landing in the waters of Long Island Sound.

Next to go was the laundry wing at the back of the house. The grounds of their home were now under flood waters, as the high tides had risen up over the bulkhead.

It was Kate who gave the orders to flee this rickety old Gothic-styled cottage with its paper-thin walls. The old house that had stood up against all assaults of Nature was shaking, rattling, and rolling, just coming to pieces bit by bit. A chimney here. Windows flying through the air. A second chimney.

At first Kit stubbornly refused to leave her home, claiming that her husband only last week had checked the brick pilings under the house and had found them secure.

Dick had to drag her out through a dining room window, with Kate providing a push from the rear. Suddenly, Kate turned back, tempted to save some prized possession. She later said, "I remembered this beautiful gold clock that Howard Hughes had given me, and I rushed upstairs to get it. But halfway up, I thought 'What the hell am I worrying about a gold clock when my mother might drown?' So, I tore back downstairs again without it, and no one else ever found it. At least no one said they did."

With Kate leading the way, the Hepburn household battled the roaring winds and escaped across a field to higher ground. Dick had brought along a rope, and each member of the household clung to that rope so they would not be blown away.

Finally, reaching the top of a hill, Kate, along with Dick and Kit, stood looking at the winds blow Fenwick away. "It went flying into the winds," Kate later said. "Like one of Howard's planes."

Finding refuge at the appropriately named Riversea Inn, Kate, along with some strong, sturdy men, formed a brigade and charged out again into the winds. They went from door to door, ordering cooks to put out all fires in the kitchen, fearing that one wooden home going up in flames would touch off fires in the colony of other wooden homes. Later, the mayor of Saybrook commended Kate for her heroic action.

That night as Kate and her brood huddled at the inn, two-hundred-mile per hour winds roared across southern Connecticut, taking six-hundred and eighty-two lives. As reported the next day in the Hartford press, "The winds were demoniacal, a whining shriek from Hell—Nature's horrible vengeance on all of us."

330

The next morning, because phone lines were down in Fenwick, Kate made her way to the Saybrook Telephone Company. There she placed a call to Dr. Hepburn in Hartford after experiencing considerable difficulty getting through. After he received assurance that everybody, especially Kit, was all right, he said, "I suppose you didn't have the brains to throw in a match before the house blew away. It's insured for fire."

Under a bright morning sun, Kate and Dick, along with Kit and the rest of the brood, made their way back to the grounds of Fenwick. They managed to dig through the ruins and excavate eighty-five pieces of silver and Kit's prized tea service, which she had frequently used to serve tea and refreshments to some of America's leading feminists, including Margaret Sanger.

That afternoon, one of Hughes' pilots flew in with fresh water and food. Kate held up one of the bottles of water in front of Kit and her household. "Water—not wine," she said. "Somehow symbolic of what my relationship with Howard has become."

The next day Luddy somehow managed to get through the roads of southern Connecticut, even though much of the state was in ruins, its roads littered with storm-tossed debris. Instead of helping the Hepburns dig out, he spent all his time taking photographs, including one candid snapshot of Kate in the lone bathtub in the ruins that the winds hadn't swept away.

That afternoon Kate and Dick followed a trail to their old house, following a trail of debris that littered the edge of the strangely tranquil Sound. They discovered Fenwick lodged against a stone bridge about a half-mile from its original site.

Kate carefully scaled the precariously perched building. Amazingly, she found the top floor completely dry when she entered through a window into her brother Dick's bedroom.

In his typewriter she discovered a new play he was working on. It was about a stage actress who goes to Hollywood and rises like a meteor, only to fall to earth again, her radiance giving off an incandescent glow before its inevitable crash. The play was called *The Fallen Star*.

***

In New York to meet with the Theatre Guild, Kate and Laura Harding stopped off first at FAO Schwarz. There she purchased a set of child's blocks. She told Laura that she was taking these blocks back to West Hartford where she and her family would design a new home.

Construction began a few weeks later, and the house still stands today. It was there, in fact, in her bedroom, that she was to die in 2003 after a long life.

Kate lent her father the money for reconstruction, demanding that her bedroom be an annex to her parents' master chamber. That way she could walk directly into their room without having to go through the hallway. This new arrangement of Fenwick aroused jealousy in the siblings, indicating that Kate had a special relationship with their parents not enjoyed by the rest of the brood.

Even as the casting of *The Philadelphia Story* got underway, Kate was assured by Leland Hayward that she was still in the final running for the role of Scarlett and that the list of candidates had been narrowed to eight. Selznick was still demanding that she take a screen test, and she still stubbornly refused. Apparently, those pictures taken in costume with Errol Flynn had not convinced him that she was his Scarlett.

Nonetheless, through Leland, Selznick sent word to Kate that she had the role, but she remained suspicious, not trusting him. She noticed that there was no announcement in the press and no contract forthcoming.

On December 10th, Selznick sent a "for-your-eyes-only" memo to his wife, Irene Mayer Selznick. The list for Scarlett had narrowed down to Paulette Goddard, Jean Arthur, and Joan Bennett.

"Vivien Leigh had been suggested by Myron (a reference to his brother, the agent, Myron Selznick, who also happened to be the business partner of Leland Hayward) "but she's strictly a dark horse," David revealed to Irene.

Unknown to Kate at the time, she had just been eliminated from the race.

On December 10, while filming the burning of Atlanta, Selznick met Vivien Leigh. The long nation-wide search for his Scarlett had finally ended. Kate would burst into tears on learning the news over the radio that David O. Selznick had finally cast Scarlett O'Hara.

Later, through her close friend Irene, Hepburn encountered David Selznick. Among her first words to him were, "Frankly, I think you should have cast Doris Jordan as Scarlett." Her remarks were obviously sarcastic, although Selznick interpreted them literally. (Doris Jordan—a hardworking actress who is remembered today mostly by Hollywood trivia enthusiasts—almost made it to Selznick's final list of the "five gals" being considered to play Scarlett. Using the revised name of Doris Davenport, she built a film career that fluttered briefly, notably in 1940 in a role played opposite Gary Cooper in *The Westerner*.)

Remarkably and to everyone's surprise, Kate eventually become a close friend of the emotionally troubled Leigh. But she later admitted to Cukor, who had been fired as director of *Gone With the Wind*, that she felt "a lot of jealousy and a little bit of hostility," in 1939 as Spencer Tracy presented Vivien Leigh with her Oscar for her portrayal of Scarlett. To Kate's delight, Hattie McDaniel, who had befriended Kate on the set of *Alice Adams*, also won an Oscar for *Gone With the Wind* as supporting actress. "Frankly, I think Hattie deserved the Oscar more than Vivien," Kate later claimed.

Recovering as quickly as she could from her disappointment at having lost the role of Scarlett, Kate signed for *The Philadelphia Story* on December 29,

1938, with rehearsals to begin on January 16, 1939.

Philip Barry was still struggling with the third act, which Kate had come to regard "as hopeless." She met with her new director, Robert B. Sinclair, who had stylishly directed Clare Boothe's *The Women* on Broadway to brilliant acclaim. In time he would also lobby to direct the film version with Joan Crawford and Norma Shearer, but would lose the job to Kate's dear friend Cukor.

All thoughts of Scarlett O'Hara faded as Kate opened the door to her Turtle Bay townhouse to greet a handsome and charming actor who'd signed as her co-star in *The Philadelphia Story.*

His name was Joseph Cotten.

***

"Who wouldn't fall in love with Joseph Cotten?" Kate later told Anderson Lawler. "What is there about him not to love? He's handsome. Talented. And, oh, so charming. His voice is so melodious and sexy he could talk a gal out of her pants in five minutes."

"Send him over to share my bed," Lawler said, almost serious. "Mama, buy me that Southern boy for Christmas."

Before his work with Orson Welles in the Mercury Theatre, Cotten had risen from the swampy bogs of Tidewater, Virginia, to Miami, where he became both an ad salesman for *The Miami Herald* and the city's "potato salad king." His hawking of potato salad in Dixie cups to lunchtime workers had allowed him to save up enough money to go to New York for his fateful meeting with Orson Welles, who would help launch his theatrical career.

At the time of his meeting with Kate, Welles was already planning to star Cotten in *Citizen Kane*, arguably the greatest film ever made.

Over tea, Kate became so enchanted with Cotten, she excused herself. When she returned, she'd made up her face better, covering up some of her more glaring freckles. She began by complimenting him, claiming that she and a friend, Laura Harding, had gone to see him in the Orson Welles' farce, *Horse Eats Hat.*

Cotten laughed at that. "I remember opening night. I was disappointed at my performance and finally told Orson that I was afraid that I would never make it as an actor. Orson agreed with me, but then he said 'That's true, but as a star, I think you'll hit the jackpot.'"

"You don't know this, but it was the 'boy genius' himself who called me to come and catch your performance with the idea of casting you as the male lead in *The Philadelphia Story*," she said.

"For that and for other reasons, I'll always be grateful to Orson," Cotten said. "I really owe him something for introducing me to the country's greatest actress."

She smiled at that, but she rarely succumbed to flattery, just as she tried to avoid most criticism unless she was specifically taking voice lessons.

Two hours later, when she'd switched from tea to serving him alcohol, he became mischievously charming but with such an amusing kind of grace one could never tell if he were serious or not. "I've always wanted to ask you something—that is, if I ever met up with you. Rumor has it that you go to bed with all your leading men. Not exactly Darryl Zanuck's casting couch. A more subtle approach, really. Is that true?"

She smiled. "I see that my reputation has indeed preceded me. It's absolutely true! As one of the backers of this play—not to mention its star—I absolutely insist on the casting couch. Tallulah does too. Even if her co-star is a woman."

"Well," Cotten said getting up and reaching for her hand. "There's nothing wrong with an actor being asked to audition. It's expected in the theater actually."

She gripped his hand. "I guess that means you're spending the night."

"By all means," he said, "that and many more nights. I have a feeling this audition is going to go very well."

***

Cotten's audition went so well that Kate faced a major dilemma the next day. In the play, Cotten had been cast as C.K. Dexter Haven, her ex-husband. Van Heflin was cast as his rival, Macauley Connor, a reporter, appearing at the Lord household with Shirley Booth, who played the wisecracking photographer Liz Imbrie.

The trouble was that Van Heflin was scheduled to show up the following day for rehearsals, and had more or less expected to move into Turtle Bay with Kate. She was eager to resume her relationship with the actor with whom she'd had an affair during the filming of *A Woman Rebels*.

But she faced the dilemma of how to balance Heflin and Cotten, keeping both actors in her life during the long road show when they would be staying in the same hotel. She had little doubt that both Cotten and Heflin would want to share her bedroom.

"Tomorrow's problem," she said.

In the meantime, she came up with a convincing lie. She told Cotten that she'd have to slip away and see him in his quarters, because her ex-husband, Luddy, was always dropping in on her unexpectedly. Even though they were divorced, Kate claimed that he was still jealous of the other beaus in her life.

Cotten took this at face value and said he understood. Their affair would be conducted in secret, he promised her. "No one," he said, "not even my future wives will know about my love affair with the great Miss Hepburn, although I'm sure it'll make a sizzling chapter in the autobiography that all stars write one day."

That night, after spending an afternoon with Cotten at a hotel, she was home, freshly showered, and about to be taken into the arms of Van Heflin. "I've missed you so," he said, hugging her close and kissing her so long and hard she had to plead to break away for air.

As she later told Lawler, who was visiting New York at the time, "One night with Van and I forgot all about Joseph. The next afternoon with Joseph, and I forgot all about Van. That is, until I rushed back to Turtle Bay and into his arms."

Lawler responded, "How do you guys find time to rehearse?"

On the road to New Haven, where the show was to open in previews, Kate maintained this "double-gaited" (her words) relationship. If either Cotten or Heflin were aware of her charade, neither actor made his protests known. Fortunately, Kate had long ago established a reputation for privacy and a desire to be left alone for long periods of time. Citing Garbo's line, "I want to be alone," Kate somehow managed to slip one actor out of her suite to make way for another, and did so "smoothly and graciously, as befits milady," as her faithful "Em" (Em Perkins, her dresser and secretary) would later say.

On weekends in New Haven, she would desert both Heflin and Cotten and spend time with her family. Sometimes she'd drive down to Laura Harding's estate in New Jersey or else would go to Fenwick to oversee reconstruction.

Abandoning behavior patterns she had established in earlier plays, she started hanging out with some of the cast members of The Philadelphia Story, including, as noted, Cotten and Heflin, as well as fellow actors Dan Tobin and Frank Fenton. She called them "my four cavaliers."

During this period, she also started drinking rather heavily, preferring champagne to the whiskey favored by her cavaliers. Instead of rising at four-thirty or five o'clock in the morning, Kate started getting up at eleven in the morning or even noon. She'd have to look carefully to see which of her leading men was in the bed with her—either Heflin or Cotten, never Tobin or Fenton.

Before the play's opening in New Haven, there were tensions backstage. Cotten complained bitterly to Kate about his role. "I just seem to come out of nowhere and have nothing to do. For God's sake, get that fucking Barry to put some meat on my bones."

Barry showed up the next day to watch the run-through rehearsals. He came backstage to face demands, mainly from Kate, that he completely rewrite the third act.

"You're the most congealed bunch of hams I've ever seen," was Barry's blunt response.

When truly angered, Kate could become a crusty old foul-mouthed sailor who'd been too long sailing the oceans. "You God damn conceited prick," she shouted in her own defense and that of her fellow cast members. "You're nothing but a little rich boy with a feather up his much sodomized ass. You're nothing but a human swine who should never be allowed to talk to actors."

Barry threatened to shut down the play that night, but by the next morning he and Kate made up, blaming "opening night jitters."

In spite of its problems, the unfinished play opened to good notices in New Haven and went on the road, playing to audiences in Boston, Washington, D.C., Baltimore, and naturally, Philadelphia, the play's alleged setting.

Until the very final decision was made, Kate continued to fight with Guild directors, pressing her claim that the play wasn't ready to face the most critical of all audiences: Broadway. She was voted down although she warned Theresa Helburn that, "I fear I'm going to drown in another lake." She was referring, of course, to her ill-fated Broadway production with Jed Harris, *The Lake.*

***

In New York, Kate didn't want conflicts arising romantically between her two leading men. To solve the problem, she booked herself into a suite at The Waldorf Towers. Her stated reason was, "If I stay in a hotel, I can still pretend I'm on the road, and not back home."

She chose to see Cotten only at the Waldorf, preferring to entertain Heflin on overnight visits to her Turtle Bay residence. Luddy was quite taken with Heflin, and the actor responded warmly to "Kate's ex." However, Heflin turned down Luddy's request to pose for nude pictures.

A nervous wreck before opening night, Kate kept going around telling the cast to imagine that they were in Indianapolis, not New York. Even flowers sent by Hughes didn't soothe her nerves. Nor a big Valentine-like box of candy from Cukor, or even a telegram from John Ford.

She greeted Kit and Dr. Hepburn, along with Laura, Luddy, and Jack, all of whom showed up for her opening night. However, she issued a warning to Theresa Helburn. "If that God damn bitch, Dorothy Parker, shows up tonight, trip her on the stairwell and send her sprawling. Then rush her off to the hospital until the curtain falls. Perhaps a vaginal probe would be in order as well."

When the curtain went down on the first act, Kate feared the play was doomed. No one had laughed at the jokes. By the time they took bows, however, the audience had warmed up and applauded wildly.

Even the butcher of Broadway and her leading theater critic, Brooks Atkinson, wrote in *The New York Times* that at last Kate had "found the joy she has always been seeking in the theater."

Except for a barb here and there, most of the reviews for both Kate and the play were raves. They had a smash hit on their hands. In spite of the heavy competition on Broadway that season, every seat was sold out. The play would run for four-hundred and fifteen performances, grossing nearly a million dollars. When Dr. Hepburn tallied up Kate's take from Broadway and from road shows, it would come to nearly half a million dollars.

***

Midway through the run of the play, another surprise invitation came in from President Roosevelt, inviting her not to the White House, but to his home at Hyde Park, near the Hudson River. She didn't want Charles Newhill to drive her up in her Lincoln, and she opted not to get there in the special train that Roosevelt had arranged for his honored guests. Instead, she hired an independent pilot, George Briggs, to fly her up the Hudson River in his seaplane.

In the Thirties, following her first introduction to the President at the White House, Kate, an ardent Democrat and Roosevelt New Deal supporter, had been invited to a number of grand functions at the White House. She had met the President and Eleanor Roosevelt on several occasions, but it was mainly "reception line chitchat," as she later told her friends and her parents. When invited to the White House, she always responded eagerly and showed up on time, unlike her attendance at the Academy Award presentations. Kate also wore elegant female attire—never pants—and the proper makeup to conceal her freckles.

After a take-off from New York's East River, near the Fifty-Ninth Street Bridge, in weather that was punctuated with heavy gusts of wind, Briggs piloted the plane to safety on a small tributary of the Hudson River near the Roosevelt estate.

Kate had worn pants this time. She rolled them up to her knees and took off her shoes, wading ashore, after dismissing Briggs. She told him she'd find someone with whom she could ride back to Manhattan.

As she approached the frontier of the Roosevelt compound, two blue-suited members of the President's Secret Service accosted her angrily, warning her that it was private property.

Only that week J. Edgar Hoover had warned the President's staff that "foreign agents" might attempt to assassinate the President on the eve of the U.S. entry into World War II, which was already raging as England stood alone against the Nazi *blitzkrieg.*

Facing down the Secret Service, she protested, "I'm Katharine Hepburn, and I've been asked to have lunch with the President."

Recognizing her familiar face at once, and most definitely "that voice," the men let her wander on.

As she moved toward the main estate, she spotted a rushing stream where she proceeded to sit on its banks and take off her muddy shoes and wash her feet.

After an emergency clean-up, she continued walking along the road leading to the main house. Suddenly, the President's chauffeured limousine appeared, slowing down upon seeing her. "Katharine," the President called out to her. "What are you doing wandering about looking like a ragamuffin?"

She quickly explained about the landing of the seaplane and all the mud. He laughed heartily at her dilemma. "Please get in," he ordered. "You're our honored guest. We'll have you arrive at the front door in style. Even my mother will be impressed."

Long before Bo Derek endorsed the candidacy of George W. Bush in 1998, FDR was in the vanguard of presidential candidates who recognized the power of movie stars to influence voting patterns. At his 1940 gathering at Hyde Park, he had invited a "whole gaggle of stars" to discuss possible contributions they might make to help him with his candidacy against the Republican challenger, Wendell Willkie.

News of the gathering would be flashed around the world, as pictures were taken of the President of the United State hob-nobbing with film stars. "It made him look more human," Willkie later said. "I should have done more movie-star hob-nobbing myself."

The most famous picture taken was the President sitting with Kate on his left, being served tea by his son, Elliott.

Before the luncheon, Kate was struck by Roosevelt's remark to her, as a member of the Secret Service opened the limousine door after it stopped in front of the Hyde Park manse. She instinctively knew that he didn't want her to see him being lifted from the car by members of the Secret Service because of his paralyzed legs, so she agreed to go ahead.

As she got out of the car, he called back to her and extended a withered hand. "You cannot imagine how flattered I am that someone as important as you would go through all this muck just to see a broken- down old man like me."

***

Searching for a ride back to Manhattan, Kate unexpectedly ran into Eleanor Roosevelt in an unbecoming black hat and a matronly navy-blue dress with white polka dots. She was preparing to have her own driver take her back to the city for a speaking engagement that night. Grateful for Kate's agreement "to work vigorously for Franklin" in the campaign, Mrs. Roosevelt graciously offered Kate a ride with her in the back seat.

"We've never had a chance to say more than hello," Mrs. Roosevelt said. "Or in my case, how much I liked you in *Little Women*. Jo has always been one of my favorite characters in literature."

In the back of her limousine, Kate found the First Lady "warm, compassionate, and vitally attuned to everything around her, but strangely distant when the conversation veered to her husband or to her children," as Kate later reported to her family and friends, both in New York and Hollywood.

Mrs. Roosevelt spoke sadly of the war raging in Europe and privately told Kate that her husband thought it was only a matter of time before the United States would be drawn into the conflict, as it had been during World War I.

She enlisted Kate's support in case of war, claiming that movie stars could assist in the effort by selling war bonds, by appearing on patriotic broadcasts, and in general helping the people face "our grave crisis by keeping us entertained." Kate promised to offer what help she could, and indeed, when the United State actually entered the war following the attack on Pearl Harbor, she would carry out the commitment she made that day to Mrs. Roosevelt

At one point, Mrs. Roosevelt quit talking about war and politics, and tenderly reached for Kate's hand, caressing and holding it for the duration of the trip until they reached Manhattan.

The First Lady turned the conversation to personal matters, claiming that her husband had complained about the White House menus. "I must admit I approved them. Perhaps I wasn't paying attention, but Franklin shouldn't have been served sweetbreads six nights in a row."

"Franklin even wrote me a memo," she continued. "He said, 'My stomach positively rebels at sweetbreads, and this does not help my relations with foreign powers. I bit two of them today!'"

Kate laughed at that, realizing for the first time that Mrs. Roosevelt had a sense of humor. Kate promised that when the war came, she would personally volunteer to come to the White House and cook for the first family. "I'm a pretty fair chef even if I do say so myself."

Mrs. Roosevelt admitted that she had little interest in food. "It's a means of survival—nothing more." Noticing Kate's bedraggled look, she commented, "Like you, I don't spend too much time worrying about what I'm going to put on, as you can tell by what I'm wearing."

She recalled that whenever movie stars posed for pictures with her, "they always dress up in their best finery." She remembered such a meeting with Jean Harlow in particular. "I was positively embarrassed to pose with Miss Harlow. I'm afraid the contrast between the two of us gave my critics added ammunition to poke fun at me."

"I think you are a beautiful person," Kate assured her. "Beauty comes from within."

Mrs. Roosevelt chuckled and clasped Kate's hand a little tighter. "Oh, I hope you truly mean that."

Kate looked Mrs. Roosevelt squarely but tenderly in the eye. "I do indeed. Even more so, I think you have one of the most beautiful faces in America."

Mrs. Roosevelt chuckled again and seemed embarrassed. "Don't tell news photographers that. I'm famous for my catnaps. They're always trying to snap me unaware with me snoring and my mouth open. I run around so much, get so little sleep, I have to catch up whenever I have a little break. Most often I'm commuting from one place to another."

Curiously enough, Kate found herself talking about hair styles with the First Lady, the last subject she expected to be discussing with her. She could never tell Kit or Dr. Hepburn that they had talked about hair styles, fearing that she would be severely chastised for wasting precious moments with Mrs. Roosevelt when more important topics, such as birth control, might be broached.

"I have to be extremely careful what I say," Mrs. Roosevelt said. "Otherwise, I might eliminate entire industries."

"I don't understand," Kate said.

"I once attacked fripperies—time-wasting things like women spending valuable time at the hairdressers," Mrs. Roosevelt said. "Hairdressers all over America rose up against me, and I had to apologize and back down so as not to add more woes to the nation's economy."

"I get it," Kate said. "It's like when Clark Gable took off his shirt in *It Happened One Night*, revealing he wore no undershirt. Undershirt sales all over America dropped. How did you back-pedal?"

"I issued some lame excuse, saying that it was perhaps necessary for all women to spend time at the milliner's, the dressmaker's, or the hairdresser."

As the First Lady's limousine neared the outskirts of Manhattan, Mrs. Roosevelt spoke more confidentially, as if desperately trying to take Kate into her confidence and win her friendship.

In a soft voice, she confessed that she was perhaps a Puritan. "Franklin is more hedonistic than I am. He can actually have a good time. I've been known to take a glass of champagne now and then but no one has ever called me a drunkard. They've said everything else about me. But not that." She confessed that a member of her family—she didn't want to name him—was currently drinking himself into an early grave.

Mrs. Roosevelt ordered her driver to take Kate to the entrance to her Turtle Bay townhouse. Proud to be seen with her, Kate invited her in. "Please, not now. But I'll slip by and dart in on my next visit to New York," Mrs. Roosevelt promised her. "I've known you for so very little time, but I feel close to you. Somehow I think we've established a bond."

"You don't know what that means to me," Kate said. "Coming from the greatest lady the world has ever known—that means a lot."

Then, as Kate admitted later, "I got carried away and said, 'Do you realize that one day you'll go down in the history books as more famous than Cleopatra or Catherine the Great?'"

Mrs. Roosevelt smiled modestly. "I'm afraid you overstate the case," she said. "It is Franklin who is the charming one. He overpowers a room. I'm the ugly ducking in the corner. When I do have to venture forth, it frightens me and adds another gray hair."

"I know stage fright too," Kate assured her.

"Until we meet again," Mrs. Roosevelt said, "and I hope it will be sooner than later in these uncertain times." Impulsively she leaned over and planted a tender yet firm kiss on Kate's lips.

Startled, Kate stood on the sidewalk, feeling bewildered and confused. As Mrs. Roosevelt's limousine faded from view down the street, Kate rushed into her house. First, she'd tell Luddy what had just occurred. Then Laura. Definitely her parents, although she'd alter the story for their consumption. By all means, Cary Grant, George Cukor, Kenneth MacKenna, and Anderson Lawler. She also thought she'd phone Patricia Peardon, the actress whom she hadn't seen since Chicago when they performed together in *Jane Eyre*. "Yes, definitely," Kate said to herself. "Patricia must know about this."

In fact, it was Patricia Peardon she called first to report every single detail of the trip back to the city with Mrs. Roosevelt.

It was the right decision to call her, Kate later told Laura. "That Patricia knows what's going on."

At the time, Peardon was dating a member of the White House inner circle who, as it turned out, already had a wife.

"I've learned from my beau that if you want a friendship with Eleanor, you must not be too chummy with the President," Peardon claimed. "The moment Eleanor feels that one of her friends is merely using her to get close to the President, or else has fallen for the President's facile charm, she will freeze you out like a pan of water left out in zero weather."

"I'll remember that," Kate said. "In the future, I will show loyalty to the President, but devotion to Eleanor."

***

Before *The Philadelphia Story* ended its Broadway run, it seemed in Kate's view that half of Hollywood had come to see the play, notably Louis B. Mayer with Norma Shearer on his arm. They came backstage to congratulate Kate, but she was initially suspicious of Shearer. She knew from his reaction that Mayer liked the play and might one day acquire the rights to it from her. But she feared that Shearer saw it as a film vehicle to revive her own sagging career, following the death of her husband, producer Irving Thalberg.

Leland told Kate that when Mayer originally heard of *The Philadelphia Story*, his plan was to purchase it and turn it into a vehicle for Joan Crawford's increasingly stalled career.

Kate's most delightful backstage visit came from George Cukor, who had flown in from California to see the play with the hope that he might one day direct its film version. On his arm was the radiantly glamorous Claudette Colbert, whom Kate had admired ever since her Oscar-winning performance in *It Happened One Night* with Clark Gable. Cukor had just finished directing Colbert in the unsuccessful film, *Zaza*, the story of a music hall performer who falls in love with a handsome chance acquaintance as played by Herbert Marshall. Both Colbert and Kate exchanged gossipy stories about having appeared with Marshall.

Kate was excited—"even thrilled," as she later put it—to meet Colbert in the flesh. The two women seemed to want to extend their visit to each other, but both Cotten and Heflin showed up, along with her two other chevaliers, to escort her to a cast party.

Colbert gave Kate a gentle kiss on the lips and promised to call her when she returned to Hollywood.

"If I ever return," Kate corrected her before kissing Cukor with promises to meet again on the West Coast.

At the cast party at a New York nightclub named Passy, Tallulah came back into Kate's life. The actress congratulated her on *The Philadelphia Story*. "I guess those people who can't get a ticket to see me in *The Little Foxes* go over to your play."

Suddenly, Tallulah seemed to become aware of Cotten for the first time. "Who is this divine creature?" she said, blinking her eyes. She heaped lavish praise on his performance, using words like "the most skillful I've ever seen." She was "overwhelmed" by his charm. She found his comedic timing "impeccable—not even Chaplin could have done better." She said he was so "sexily handsome as to be hypnotic." As if realizing she'd gone overboard, she abruptly said, "And now, go fuck yourself!" She barged away seeking another victim.

Before the Broadway run ended, Theresa Helburn and Lawrence Langner were urging Kate to appear as Rosalind in Shakespeare's *As You Like It*. "Don't get carried away with our success in a Barry play," Kate cautioned them. "I will never perform in anything by William Shakespeare. I'm just not a good enough actress."

Even before *The Philadelphia Story's* Broadway run ended, movie studios expressed interest in acquiring the screen rights. William Wyler came backstage with a pitch to her from Samuel Goldwyn. He wanted to star Kate in the screenplay and promised to cast Gary Cooper for "extra box-office insurance." When Wyler returned to Hollywood and presented the idea to Cooper himself, the lanky actor turned him down. "I won't play opposite Hepburn," he said. "No way."

342

Jack Warner contacted Kate with an intriguing idea. He wanted to buy the rights and cast her opposite Errol Flynn, his leading star. Actually, as it was later revealed, he really wanted Ann Sheridan to play Tracy Lord. Just as Kate was mulling over the possibility of another sexy encounter with the dashing Errol Flynn, a call came in from Louis B. Mayer.

No longer thinking of Norma Shearer, he wanted Kate to star in the role. Going against promises she'd made to Cotten and Heflin, Hepburn ditched them both and demanded Clark Gable and Spencer Tracy as her co-stars. Mayer said he'd try but that he didn't think he could get either of his biggest stars.

Kate called Leland Hayward. "Mayer's got a deal. But he'll have to come up with my asking price of one-hundred and seventy-five thousand dollars for the screen rights, plus another seventy-five thousand dollars for me to star in it. That's my once-and-final offer."

Mayer met her demands, and Louella Parsons broke the news in Hollywood. True to Mayer's prediction, Tracy and Gable turned down the roles. Instead Mayer assigned the co-starring roles to Cary Grant and James Stewart.

The casting deeply embittered both Cotten and Heflin. Kate had more or less promised them the roles. Heflin was so angry that he later deserted the road show production "while I'm still in my salad days" to go to Hollywood to film *The Santa Fe Trail*. Their affair was over.

Cotten, too, drifted to Hollywood where Kate, as compensation to him for losing the star part, pleaded with Leland to take him on as a client.

Even as Kate rode the rails back to Hollywood, her legend was growing. Writing in *The New York Times,* Jack Gould said, "The legend of Hepburn today ranks close to that of the bigness of Garbo's feet."

Before leaving New York, she'd called Leland and told him that, "it's almost a certainty that I'm going to win an Oscar for playing Tracy Lord."

Leaving Laura behind, she claimed that she was "hysterically happy" facing Hollywood again.

Claudette Colbert had placed four calls to Kate in New York, extending an "open invitation" to get together as soon as Kate hit town.

Kate was eagerly looking forward to entertaining the glamorous star.

***

No longer the *châtelaine* of Muirfield mansion, Kate had asked Hughes to let her stay in his guest cottage until she found more permanent lodgings. He readily agreed that marriage was no longer an issue between them.

She was just settling in and unpacking her things, when Hughes' *major-domo*, Richard Dreher, knocked on her door and informed her that an Army car had just delivered her a letter. It was on White House stationery.

"Oh, my God, it's from the President," she said, eagerly open the envelope.

To her surprise, it was from Eleanor Roosevelt. On reading the first two sentences, she decided to sit down and study the letter in total privacy. She excused herself and shut the door, retreating to the sanctity of her bedroom.

As she read deeper into the letter, she was shocked and almost near tears.

In a call to Cukor later that night, she said, "The letter is from a very lonely woman. I can describe it only as a love letter."

CHAPTER FOURTEEN

Values in Hollywood had changed drastically by the time Kate returned there in 1940. The Thirties, with its sweeping sense of glamour, had come to an end, and its epic sense of grandeur as symbolized by the filming of *Gone with the Wind* had been scaled back to something grimmer and grittier. England had declared war on Germany in 1939, and America began, consciously or not, to brace itself for its eventual immersion in the conflagration as well.

In the guest cottage of Hughes' Muirfield estate, Kate settled in as best as she could, although the staff no longer treated her with the deference it did when she was estate's ruling *duenna*. Within its kitchen, even before calling Claudette Colbert, she cooked one-on-one dinners for some of her closest pals—George Cukor, then Kenneth MacKenna, and, finally, Anderson Lawler.

She found her friends as devoted to her as ever as she adjusted to the artistry and demands of her new studio, MGM, and its executive producer, Joseph Mankiewicz. During her dinner with Cukor, who had been designated by MGM as director of her newest project, she learned that Philip Barry would not be writing the screen version of *The Philadelphia Story*, because Mayer and Mankiewicz thought that he had asked for too much money. Cukor had several good suggestions for changes in the script of the Broadway play, and had already communicated them to the film's new scenarist, the left-wing Donald Ogden Stewart.

Kate liked virtually everything she heard about the new arrangements until Cukor told her that in the screen version of *The Philadelphia Story* she'd have to accept second billing to Cary Grant. Having headlined whatever cast she'd been part of for the previous eight years, she was reluctant to agree to that condition, but when she realized that she had no choice, she gracefully acquiesced.

"What the hell!" she finally said. "No one reads credits anyway. I'll steal the picture from Cary."

The following evening, Kate learned from Kenneth MacKenna that McKenna's acting career was completely stalled and going nowhere. Having adapted to this sad reality, he had accepted a job as story editor in the acquisitions department of MGM. Aware of the job's potential for creativity and influence, he promised he'd rush her all the hottest scripts.

On the third night after her return to Hollywood, when Anderson (affectionately known as "Andy") Lawler dropped in, Kate realized that he, too, had experienced the collapse of his acting career. Partly as a means of staying in touch with the Hollywood community, and partly because he found the role

345

diverting, he had become a "walker" (before the term was invented) for some of the *grande dames* of Hollywood, especially those whose husbands were too busy to attend gala events with their spouses. "Even though, when under duress, I used to fuck Kay Francis, most husbands consider me a harmless date for their wives." Since he loved to gossip, and because he knew more about Hollywood after dark than either Louella Parsons or Hedda Hopper, he filled her in on some of the seamier news, at least some of it centering around Howard Hughes.

Early one morning, Kate went to answer the ring of her doorbell and discovered Greta Garbo standing there with a bouquet of flowers. Kate eagerly embraced her and invited her in for breakfast. She was later to tell Cukor that she'd spent one of the most blissful days of her life with a relaxed Garbo, part of it enjoyed while swimming nude in Hughes' pool, as they had done many months before in Cukor's.

Garbo told her a startling bit of information. "I'm going to retire from the screen and return Sweden."

Kate was stunned at the news and urged her to reconsider, claiming that "your greatest roles lie in front of you."

Garbo seemed to have the determination of steel. She said that in the next few months, she was going to make *Two-Faced Woman* for MGM, and that Cukor was going to direct her. "But even if the picture is good and removes me from the *poison box* list, I'm still going to leave the screen and be alone."

Later, Kate told Laura, "Greta has carried her reclusiveness almost to the point of obsession."

***

Very late at night during one of her first nights back in Hollywood, Howard Hughes showed up unexpectedly, ringing the doorbell to her cottage. In bed at the time, she sleepily got up, put on her nightgown, and hurried to greet him. Even before throwing open the door, she knew who it was.

He appeared to have been drinking heavily and rewarded her with a light kiss on the cheek. His beard looked like it had grown for several days without a shave. Like Hollywood and the rest of America, he too seemed to have changed. The little lost boy quality that had initially attracted her to him had vanished. His new-found status as a hero had made him more self-assured, and he no longer seemed as shy as he used to be. If anything, he was more assertive and more demanding, and his increasing deafness had made his own voice more strident.

But instead of talking about himself, he wanted to discuss their investment in *The Philadelphia Story*. He reminded her of something she already knew. If

346

this picture couldn't rekindle her stalled career, she might no longer be a player in Hollywood. "You'll find yourself with the same has-been status as Garbo, or, worse, like Norma Shearer or even Mae West."

"Yes, just like Mae West," she said as she chuckled with a kind of gallows humor.

Hughes' dress still appeared haphazard and sloppy. That night he wore a white shirt with cigarette burns on the front, soiled white dungarees, a snap-on black tie, and tennis shoes covered with caked-on red clay. Knowing how obsessively secretive he was, she asked no questions about his personal life, but thanks to Anderson Lawler, she knew that he had proposed marriage to Olivia de Havilland and that at a surprise party he threw for Olivia at the Trocadero, her sister, Joan Fontaine, had showed up. Hughes had slipped Joan his phone number and later, he had also proposed marriage to her. In the meantime, Hughes still dated Ginger Rogers, also urging her to marry him.

Hughes, or so Kate had been told, had ended his brief, stormy, and deceitful relationship with Bette Davis. "She's telling everybody, all over town, that she cured Hughes of his recurring impotence with women by performing oral sex on him in a room she'd filled with glossy photographs of Hollywood's handsomest men—all shirtless," Lawler said.

Hughes, according to Davis and the tales she was spreading, also had problems with premature ejaculations. "And then, if you can believe Bette," Lawler told Kate, "She acquiesced to his request that she use scatological language with him. And then, she said she ordered Hughes to close his eyes and imagine it was a man performing fellatio on him. Bette said that after the deed was over, she made him some warm milk and that he fell asleep while suckling on her big tits."

"Naughty Bette!" Kate said. "Kiss-and-tell Bette. Remind me never to go to bed with *that one.*"

Lawler also told Kate that the current love of Hughes' life was none other than Errol Flynn. Hughes had flown a plane to the set where Flynn was filming *Dodge City* with Hughes' "fiancée-of-the-hour," Olivia de Havilland. "Then he flew away, not with de Havilland, but with Flynn, to a private all-male party in Los Angeles," Lawler gossiped. "And in Flynn, Hughes found someone far better at fellatio than Bette."

Lawler revealed that when Hughes "isn't with Ginger or Olivia or Errol or Cary, he dates Robert Taylor and Tyrone Power."

"That doesn't surprise me," Kate said. "Howard wants only the best. Only the other day I saw a fan magazine in my doctor's office. It called Power and Taylor the two handsomest men on earth—not bad."

Lawler said that recently Hughes had openly patronized homosexual clubs in Hollywood, especially BBB's Cellar, a gay hangout which Tallulah Bankhead and Marlene Dietrich sometimes visited, Bankhead showing up with actor William Haines and his lover, Jimmie Shields.

Lawler went on to say that although Hughes' name had recently appeared in gossip columns—including the one within *The Hollywood Reporter*—as the great womanizer of the Western world, Hollywood was actually buzzing with news that the aviator hero also liked guys.

At three o'clock that morning, after a few more perfunctory discussions about their shared investment in *The Philadelphia Story,* Hughes got up to leave the cottage. None of his after-dark diversions mattered to Kate. She had had her chance with him, and she had retreated, knowing in her heart that marriage to him would not work. After she showed him to the exit, he kissed her cheek once again. She kissed him on the lips. "For old time's sake," she said before gently closing the door.

***

Kate didn't call Claudette Colbert. Instead, one of the screen's brightest ornaments and one of its most skilled *comediennes* called Kate. "At last I tracked you down to where you're staying," Colbert said. "I think it's easier getting the mysterious Garbo on the phone than Miss Kate."

Kate poured out her profuse apologies, claiming she had a "lot of unfinished business to get out of her way—notably some members of the male sex."

"I long ago learned to handle the men in my life," Colbert said, "even husbands. During my seven-year marriage to Norman Foster, we deliberately lived in separate houses. I told Louella that was how we kept our love alive, and the bitch believed me."

Kate chuckled at that. "During my marriage, I think I spent only a few weeks a year with my husband and always in separate bedrooms."

Colbert paused. "When it comes to men, I always believe in separate bedrooms, unless, of course, there's someone you really *want* to sleep with. But for God's sake, never a husband!"

"No, never that!" Kate said, laughing.

The next night Colbert showed up for dinner, bringing as a gift for Kate a bottle of French perfume she'd brought back from a recent trip to Paris. Unlike Kate in pants, the French-born actress wore a well-tailored red suit from the House of Chanel with delicate pink accessories, including her shoes.

Relaxing after dinner by the fireplace, Kate pointedly said, "I read in Louella's column that you're married to a Dr. Joel Pressman."

"Since 1935," Colbert responded. "You must go to him if you have a problem with your ears, eyes, or nose. He's a specialist. I have this severe sinus problem. The California climate aggravates it. That's how I met him. He's a real man's man. A no-nonsense type and always unflappable. He's ten years younger than me but most people think he's much older."

"Sounds like a good man to have around the house," Kate said. "Like my Luddy. A real handyman."

348

Colbert held up her glass of brandy and tantalizingly said, "Sometimes a man—even a good man—can't give a woman what she really wants."

The next morning Kate complained to Lawler. "I thought after a remark like that, that we were practically in the sack. Not so! In a few minutes, she got up, adjusted her red dress, and that was it."

"She'll come around," Lawler said. "From what my lez friends tell me, women don't rush into bed as quickly as men."

"And I don't see why not. I believe in equality between the sexes."

"By the way, has it ever occurred to you that only a bisexual could possibly be attracted to both Claudette Colbert *and* George Stevens?"

"That's why we have twice the fun," she said before ringing off.

In the days ahead, Colbert visited Kate almost every evening, forgetting about her husband. Kate was still reluctant to make the first move. Each day she called Lawler in her frustration. "I keep waiting for her, and she seems to be waiting for me. One of us will have to move in fast or else we'll be too old to get excited any more."

Kate found that she could sit and talk for hours with Colbert, and they never ran out of subject matters or interest in each other, regardless of how minute the detail. Sometimes the topic was merely about where to buy the best fresh vegetables.

On some nights Kate drove Colbert out to Malibu where they would sit, look at the starry night over California, and listen to the surf.

Finally, Kate decided that they had known each other long enough. The next time Colbert arrived for dinner, Kate had planned the perfect evening. The food was better than she'd ever prepared, as she admitted later to Cukor. The brandy by the fireplace was just as romantic.

"With the brandy sweet on her breath, I took her and kissed her," Kate confessed to Lawler the next day.

She'd heard how Hughes had wooed Bette Davis, and she decided to imitate the master. She'd gone to the florist that day and had ordered dozens of gardenias. Removing her stuffed animals from their usual position astride her mattress, she'd carpeted her bed with gardenias. Their sweet, heady fragrance filled the air, as she led Colbert into her bedroom.

The next morning, as Kate would relate to Lawler, "for the first time with a woman, I felt I was making love to an equal. Up to now, the women in my life were often subservient to me."

"Aren't you forgetting about Garbo?" Lawler chastised her.

"Oh, my God," Kate said. "How can one forget Garbo? She's not my equal. She's my superior."

"What's in store for Colbert and you? Will you forsake all others?"

"Nothing like that," she said, "we're going to carry on a secret affair that no one in Hollywood will ever find out about unless you tell them. She's got her beard—her husband. I haven't gotten a beard yet but I'll find one one day.

349

During the time that remains for Claudette and me, I'll enjoy things more by knowing I'm pulling off one of the great romances of history right in the center of the most gossipy town in the world."

For decades, Kate managed to pull off this coup. But eventually, savvier Hollywood locals would discover her long-suppressed secret. Along with Laura Harding and Spencer Tracy, Colbert would rank as one of the most important love affairs of her life until their world together came crashing down in 1948.

***

On the set of *The Philadelphia Story*, as Kate eagerly awaited her introduction to James Stewart, she was fitted for costumes by Adrian. He'd designed for Garbo, and Kate felt that he'd dressed her appropriately for the role of Tracy Lord. She was also delighted at the perfect sets created by Cedric Gibbons, pronouncing them "an abode for the rich but with nothing ostentatious. Old money."

As for her interactions with the press, Kate hadn't mellowed at all. She retained the same spiky, saucy, tempestuous interviewing style she had from the beginning. Hedda Hopper, hoping for some juicy tidbits for her column, showed up on the set, asking Kate how *The Philadelphia Story* had changed her. "For a start, I've grown three inches," Kate said.

Kate also told an astonished Hopper, who at the time was wearing an absurdly large picture hat in the shape of an ocean liner, that she felt making films was humiliating. "It's like being a common prostitute having to sell your body."

On the first day of shooting, she enacted what eventually became one of the movie's most famous scenes—a scene which was not within the original Phillip Barry play. Kate appears at the door to the Lord family mansion carrying a set of Grant's golf clubs. Pulling a club from the bag, she breaks it over her knee and flings it at him. Fed up with her arrogance, and standing outside the house, Grant stalks toward the door. Placing his hand over her face, he flattens her with a firm shove backward, sending her into a pratfall. Kate interpreted this piece of carefully rehearsed stagecraft as marvelous fun.

During the eight weeks it took to shoot what became a film classic, Kate breezed through the scenes with Cukor with only an occasional blow-up. And at first she got along well with her producer, Mankiewicz, having admired his previous work. She complimented him for having produced *Fury* which was directed by Fritz Lang and had starred Spencer Tracy and Sylvia Sidney. Kate told him how eager she'd been to have Tracy cast in the Grant role in *The Philadelphia Story.* "You would have miscast the film," he said. "Tracy should have been cast in the Jimmy Stewart role." Kate thought about that for a minute. "By God, you're right."

But since Mankiewicz was always around, he began to get on her nerves. On one tense day of shooting, she even accused him of having "Svengali-like powers" which she claimed he was trying to use on her. "You're not my type of man," she angrily told him. "And believe you me, you're not my type of woman," he shot back.

The next day they made up, going on to make two more films together, eventually becoming great friends.

Sometime during the initial stages of shooting, the real man of her dreams walked onto the set. As he approached her, his body reminded her of Howard Hughes in that it was tall, underweight, and gangly. He was cheerful and most engaging, with a slightly adolescent air about him.

'Kate," he said immediately, calling her not only by her first name but a nickname at that. "It's wonderful to meet you at last. I'm Jimmy Stewart."

***

If there was one thing she was determined to do, it was to make Jimmy Stewart forget the charms of Ginger Rogers and Olivia de Havilland.

In spite of his body, Kate thought that he was one of the most handsome men she'd ever met. There was a soft-spoken quality to Indiana-born Jimmy that endeared him to her. She felt an innate kindness in him. She told Cukor that it was an "appealing diffidence, a certain boyish earnestness that I find most fascinating."

"God, I wish I was gorgeous like you," Cukor said, "and not fat and ugly. I want Jimmy for myself. But I don't have a chance with him. Besides, he's fully booked up."

"You mean with *Little Miss Tap Shoes* and with *Little Miss Melanie* whenever Scarlett's not being her midwife?"

"Oh, darling, where have you been?" Cukor asked. "He's one of the most sought after studs in Hollywood, now that his long fling with Henry Fonda is over and he's back to women again."

"*Fonda*?" she said in astonishment. Surely Hollywood could hold no more surprises, yet she managed to find something surprising every day. "I'll have to get Anderson Lawler to fill me in on Jimmy boy," Kate said.

True to form, Lawler did just that the next day. "He's being pursued by, among others, Marlene Dietrich, Joan Crawford, and Norma Shearer."

"Bigtime pussies," Kate said mockingly.

He paused. "You're going to hate this. But he's also bedded your favorite gal and mine, the Venus's flytrap from Virginia, Miss Margaret Sullavan. Miss

Magnolia tells everybody that Jimmy can go all night, unlike her former husband, Hank Fonda, whom she calls 'the one-minute man.' Jimmy, according to reports, lost his virginity to that sexual predator, Miss Sullavan, when he was still a junior in college."

Kate sighed. "Do you think I'll ever meet a man who hasn't bedded Ginger Rogers and Margaret Sullavan? Is Hank Fonda still in Jimmy's picture?"

"Apparently, except for a fling with Joshua Logan, Jimmy's only real homosexual love affair has been Hank," Lawler said. "That's mellowed into a deep friendship at this point, but who knows? Joan Crawford told me that Jimmy, by his own estimate, has dated two-hundred and sixty-five of the most glamorous women in Hollywood. So, given those statistics, we must assume he is ninety-nine percent straight and only one percent gay."

"Who would think it to look at him," she said. "Perhaps in his case, still waters run deep."

"He doesn't like women to chase after him," Lawler said. "He found Crawford and Dietrich too aggressive. Marlene herself told me that she met Jimmy during wardrobe fittings for *Destry Rides Again*. She said she became pregnant after their first sexual encounter and had to have an abortion. Even when he was closely involved with Hank, Jimmy also had numerous affairs with women. Take that nympho, Wendy Barrie, when they made *Speed* together, and let's not forget Jean Harlow when they made *Wife vs. Secretary*."

Kate was further dismayed that night when Colbert arrived for an intimate dinner. This time she brought long-stemmed roses instead of French perfume. When Kate steered the talk to Stewart later in the evening, Colbert confessed that she, too, had had a brief but most exciting fling with Stewart when she'd made *It's a Wonderful World* with him for MGM in 1939.

She also told Kate that she didn't like the director, Woody Van Dyke. "I always insist on being photographed left profile shots only," Colbert said. "That idiot Van Dyke insisted on my right side, which I find defective."

Kate assured her that the right side of her face "was perfectly adorable. Now let's hit the sack."

***

Since Kate learned that Stewart didn't like women to pursue him, the next day she was puzzled as how to seduce him. Lawler showed up on the set for one of her picnic lunches. "I was at a party last night where Carole Lombard was the guest of honor. She too has had an affair with our studly Jimmy when they made—what an appropriate title—*Made for Each Other* for MGM in '39. Carole assured me that Jimmy's penis is twice the size of Clark Gable's."

"Oh, Andy, do you always have to go around measuring men?" Kate asked

352

in despair.

"Gary Cooper has spoiled me for all other men," he said.

Both Kate and Lawler were startled to see Loretta Young suddenly appear on the set. The actress looked over in their direction but did not come over to greet them. She headed instead for Stewart's dressing room.

"What goes here?" Kate asked Lawler.

"Hollywood's nymphomaniacal Loretta isn't satisfied with Spencer Tracy and Gable—she had a kid with 'The King'—she's hot for Jimmy too. Apparently, this super-manizer can't break up Tracy's marriage to Louise, and Gable these days has the hots for Lombard. So Young's obsessive passion spins around Jimmy. She's trying to get him to marry her, but apparently Jimmy is giving off the wrong signals."

Kate and Lawler heard angry words coming from Jimmy's dressing room. Soon Young barged out, only to run into Joseph Mankiewicz. The producer put his arm around the actress and walked off the set with her.

"While Loretta is trying to get a wedding ring from Jimmy," Lawler claimed, "she's also carrying on this torrid affair with Mankiewicz."

"A busy girl," Kate said dismissively.

"You don't know the half of it. Would you also believe George Brent—she took him away from Bette Davis—Gilbert Roland, and Ricardo Cortez. Dare we mention Herbert Somborn, Gloria Swanson's second groom? There are those socialite playboys, Jock Whitney and Willis Buckner, not to mention directors Eddie Sutherland and Gregory Ratoff. Don't forget writers John McClain and Robert Riskin. Oh, there's the tennis star, Fred Perry. Beautiful Tyrone Power when he's not with your Howard. Yes, and David Niven and Wayne Morris. I'd go for Morris myself. Even the gayest goose in Hollywood, Cesar Romero, has screwed Loretta when he's not fooling around with his true love, Desi Arnaz."

"I don't know who is more amazing," she said. "Loretta, for carrying on like that—I'm a bit envious, really—or you for knowing every midnight rendezvous in Hollywood."

At that point, another columnist, Adela Rogers St. Johns, arrived on the set. Kate pretended to be nice to her.

Louella's rival had already heard of Young's entrance. "Loretta is carrying around this monstrous torch for Jimmy boy," St. Johns said. 'She's without shame the way she chases after him. Frankly, I think she's making a God damn idiot out of herself. Jimmy's not going to marry her." She looked at Kate. "Speaking of love affairs, who do you currently have a crush on?"

"George Cukor," Kate said before turning and walking away.

Over a picnic lunch at noon, Stewart told Kate that he'd just learned from Mankiewicz that she had wanted Spencer Tracy to play his role. He assured her that he was enjoying the part and was glad that "old Spence didn't get it."

She told him that he'd been misinformed, claiming that she had actually wanted Tracy to play Grant's role. That seemed to make Stewart feel better. He told her how much he'd admired Tracy when he first worked with him.

"I didn't realize you'd made a film with Tracy," she said in astonishment. "I've seen every film he's ever made."

"I was introduced in a Tracy film," he said. "*The Murder Man* in 1935 for MGM. I was an eager news reporter named—of all things—Shorty."

"I saw the film but don't remember you," she said.

"Just what every actor wants to hear!" he said, getting up from the picnic table.

She confided to Cukor her gaffe later in the day. "I've lost him with my stupid remark."

"Just as well," Cukor said. "I've just talked to Cary. He, too, has got the hots for our Jimmy boy. He told me that he's going to make Jimmy before the shoot ends. Right now, he's practically throwing himself at Jimmy but is waiting for him to make the first move."

"Hell will freeze over before that happens," she predicted.

***

During the filming of *The Philadelphia Story*, Kate was entertained frequently by Cary Grant and Randolph Scott. Grant informed her that his contract called for a salary of one-hundred and seventy-five thousand dollars for *The Philadelphia Story*, all of which he planned to donate to the British War Relief.

Once, at a big, mostly male dinner party at Grant's, Kate renewed her friendship with model and struggling actor, Stanley Haggart, who had remained a close pal of both Luddy and Jack back in New York. Haggart told her that Randolph Scott arranged occasional jobs for him as an extra at RKO, where he sometimes appeared as a good-looking face in a crowd. Haggart at the time was also supplementing his income by catering dinner parties, usually charging $35 for a night's work, and that he had prepared the food for several of Scott and Grant's private dinner parties. He said that Howard Hughes was a frequent visitor to their home.

At this party, Noël Coward was the guest of honor, Kate the only female. Haggart raced about, making drinks for the celebrated guests. He'd been cooking all day. Later, Haggart's recollections, his journals, and his role within Hollywood as a source of gossip for Hedda Hopper added enormously to the store of information used in the compilation of this biography.

According to Haggart, that night after dinner, all the guests, including Kate and himself, now that he was relieved of his servant's duties, gathered around the piano. Haggart was mildly surprised at how effeminate Grant behaved when in the company of trusted friends, all of whom were homosexual.

Haggart related that Grant announced to the crowd how important it was for him "to be able to let my hair down from time to time." He claimed that he hated Hollywood and his own image "because I'm always pretending to be something I'm not."

Haggart later said that Grant told him and several other witnesses at the time that he was still deeply in love with Randolph Scott—and "always will be"—but predicted that both of them, during the course of time, would be in and out of several different marriages.

Haggart's recollections later in life included having witnessed many aspects of Cary Grant's hot affair with Clifford Odets, the reigning playwright of the American stage. Odets had emerged from a protracted divorce from the Oscar-winning actress, Luise Rainer, and had gone through a disastrous relationship with the mentally ill but talented actress, Frances Farmer. Haggart also testified to yet another secret derived from the presence of Noël Coward at the party that night: The witty and clever Coward had arranged for a series of night club appearances in South America. He planned to use these gigs as a "beard" for his real role, which was that of a secret agent, reporting on pro-Nazi activities in the southern Hemisphere, especially Argentina.

On the night of that party, Kate excused herself early and kissed everybody good-bye. She had to race back to the cottage for a late night bottle of champagne, and other events, with Claudette Colbert.

The actress had managed to put her husband to bed early that night.

Before leaving the party that night, Kate invited Coward to visit her for a picnic lunch on the set tomorrow. "To meet Jimmy Stewart, I'd travel across America on a camel," Coward said. "I'm simply mad about the boy."

As Kate headed out the door, Coward was telling the other guests about a dinner party. George Cukor had invited him to. "I found myself placed next to Joan Crawford at table. She reminds me of an unnamed Du Pont product." As Kate quietly shut the front door, not fully understanding Coward's joke, she heard the party burst into hysterical laughter.

As she would later tell Colbert, "Although I'm flattered to be invited as one of the boys, I decided it was best to leave them alone and let them have their fun. We ladies can always find other diversions for ourselves."

***

Unknown to her, Noël Coward had come onto the set while Kate was filming a scene with Jimmy Stewart. When the actors had performed to Cukor's satisfaction, Coward came up to greet them. Giving Kate a quick kiss, he turned his entire attention to Stewart, claiming that the actor had given one of the best performances he'd ever seen on film. He even went so far as to predict that

Stewart would win the Oscar. As incredible a long shot as it seemed at the time, Coward's prediction turned out to be accurate.

Cukor approached Coward, seeking his advice, and fretting about how the script called for a nude swim scene between Kate and Stewart. Because it was a film, and consequently subject to censorship, Cukor said that unfortunately, he'd have to have them emote in their bathing suits.

On hearing that, Stewart protested loudly. "If I appear in a bathing suit, I know it's the end of my career. Perhaps the end of motion pictures."

Feeling very impish, Coward said, "But, dear boy, I hear you're one of the best hung men in Hollywood."

At first Stewart looked embarrassed. "Oh, I bulge in all the right places in a bathing suit. But that's not my problem. I'll look like a God damn skeleton."

Finally, Coward helped broker a settlement. The nude swimming scene would only be suggested. Coward felt it might be more subtle if both Kate and Stewart appeared in robes after their swim.

Kate invited Stewart and Coward to her picnic lunch, where the conversation seemed to revolve around the two of them, leaving Kate to fear that Coward had rekindled Stewart's homosexual tendencies. "I could never have delivered the line to Kate—'You've got hearth fires banked down in you'—if I'd known the great Noël Coward had come onto the set," Stewart said.

"You did it brilliantly," Coward assured him. "I'm seeing another dear boy, Larry Olivier, tonight. When I tell him how brilliant you are, he'll be jealous."

"I'm not in his category," Stewart said modestly.

"As long as Larry was married to Jill Esmond, he was always available to me," Coward said. "Now he seems so romantically involved with Vivien that he doesn't seem to have much time for me."

"Please!" Kate protested. "Can we change the subject? Both George and I are still furious at getting kicked off *Gone With the Wind*."

"Of course, precious one," Coward said. 'I'm sure you would have made the greater Scarlett O'Hara."

"Why not me for Rhett Butler?" Stewart asked jokingly.

Impulsively Coward leaned over and kissed him on the lips. "Sorry, old boy," he said, backing away from his action. "I couldn't help myself. You are, after all, the sexiest man in Hollywood. And the best lay, I hear."

Suddenly, Cukor called Coward away. Excusing himself, he blew kisses at both Kate and Stewart.

After he'd gone, Kate said, "Oh what the hell! I'm tired of waiting." She leaned over and gave Stewart a passionate kiss on his lips. "I know you don't like women like Loretta and Joan Crawford chasing after you, but like Noël, I simply could not resist."

At first surprised, he must have decided he liked the kiss. He reached for her and took her into his arms, kissing her far more passionately than she had him. After he'd done that, he invited her out for a date that night.

She called Lawler an hour later. "It's happened," she virtually screamed into the phone. "I feel tonight's the night. Will I have a story to tell you in the morning. The problem is, I've got to bow out of my engagement with Claudette for the night. I'll make up some story. After all, she's already had Jimmy. Why can't I, like the little blue birds, fly over the rainbow, too?"

***

As Kate was later to say, "Jimmy stood six-foot-three and weighed—oh, I don't know—one-hundred and twenty five pounds, give or take. Although he mumbled and stammered, he was actually quite smart. All that 'Aw, shucks, ma'am,' act was, I think, just an act. Looking at him, he was everything that Lotus Land disdained in its male stars. Ironically, he went on to become the best loved star in Hollywood."

In his recently purchased LeSalle convertible, Stewart drove up to her cottage at Hughes' Muirfield estate. Enjoying a cocktail before dinner, she asked him if he had a cigarette. He reached into his pocket and removed a solid gold cigarette case studded with dozens of tiny diamonds. She took the cigarette, but also examined the case. "Don't tell me you're a gigolo accepting expensive gifts from women."

"How do you know I didn't buy that for myself?"

"No way Jimmy Stewart is going to buy that."

"You've nailed me. It was a gift from Norma Shearer. When she asks me for a cigarette, she likes me to pull the case out and show it off. It's her way of showing that I'm a possession of hers."

"But you're not! No man—not even a husband—should ever be the possession of a rich woman."

"As you'll find out soon enough, I belong to no one," he said.

She knew about his friendship with Leland Hayward, who was also his agent. "How do you feel he's handling your career?"

"He told me the other night, 'The movie business is fickle—get yourself a rich broad and settle down to a life of ease.'"

"Don't take Leland's advice," she cautioned. "All of us should be independent, especially women. Leland didn't take his own advice. I mean, he married that girl friend of yours, Margaret Sullavan, with whom you made all those movies."

"Maggie and I are just friends now," he said, eager to change the subject. "We had a big fight a few weeks ago. The romance is all over between Maggie and me."

"You mean you were carrying on with her even though she's married to Leland?" she asked.

"Yeah, if you must know, we've been carrying on and off ever since she got my cherry when I was in college. Maggie and Leland have an understanding. He takes out two or three stars—or would-be stars—every week. That gives Maggie time to sample what's in some other trousers."

Remembering her dinner, she suddenly excused herself and went to the kitchen. Later, over her candlelit table, he complimented her on what a good cook she was. "Marlene is a great cook," he said. "Crawford's lousy in the kitchen. Doesn't even know how to make my favorite—chocolate milkshakes with marshmallows."

As the evening wore on, she sensed that he was unhappy on the set and decided to ask him why. "You seem alienated from the rest of us. Why so?"

"It's Cukor," he said. "Also Grant. That Cukor is a little much. He insists on substituting himself for you in rehearsals for our love scenes. He says it's to get his points across as a director."

"As is obvious, he has a crush on you," she said.

"I find that very embarrassing," he said. "Rehearsing love scenes with me is as close as Cukor is going to get to what's in my drawers."

Oh, George is harmless," she said. "He's a dear friend of mine. My advice is to just go along with it. He's coaching you into a great performance. Cary and I are insanely jealous that he's spending twice as much time with you as he is with us, the real stars of the picture."

"It got out of hand the other day," he said. "Although I practically insisted that I wouldn't be filmed in a bathing suit, Cukor demanded to see me in one. And then he adjusted my prominent bulge to make it more discreet for the camera."

"I agree," she said. "That was a bit much. You should be flattered, though. In most cases, Cukor has a strictly hands-off policy when it comes to actors he's directing."

"The other problem is Grant," he said. "He's coming on strong, like the homosexuals I faced daily as a struggling, starving actor in New York when I used to pal around with Bogie, Broderick Crawford, Hank Fonda, and Joshua Logan. Grant hasn't exactly made a pass at me—that's not his style—but he's getting so chummy it's out of hand. Whenever he can, he shows up at my dressing room. Yesterday he made his intentions so obvious, I rebuffed him. Now he's not speaking to me off-camera."

"Big stars have big egos," she said. "You've probably hurt his vanity. Why don't you give him a roll in the hay, satisfy his curiosity, and be done with it."

"He's not my type," he said. "Actually, I'm not going to have any time for Grant. Louis B. Mayer has cast me in an upcoming film with 'the most beautiful gal in the world.'"

"I thought that title belonged to me," she said jokingly.

"You are a beautiful gal," he said. "The most beautiful American gal. This is the most beautiful foreign gal. I'm doing *Come Live With Me* opposite Hedy

Lamarr. Racy title, don't you think? I hear Lamarr devours men. Looks like I'm not gonna have any time for Ginger, Olivia, or Norma—and I'm especially not gonna have any time for Grant."

"Not even me?" she asked provocatively.

"Present company is always excluded," he said, "as my daddy used to say in Indiana."

Over brandy by her fireplace, which was becoming part of her seduction ritual, he moved toward her on the sofa and gave her a long, deep, kiss. But suddenly, he withdrew, although to judge by his trousers, he was ready for action.

"Enough of that for now!" he said, getting up and adjusting his clothing. "You've got me hot and bothered. I've got to go home and pollute myself."

With that enigmatic remark, he was out the door.

***

Although Cukor had been fired as the director of *Gone With the Wind* and replaced by Victor Fleming, "a man's director," Cukor still met privately with Vivien Leigh throughout the course of the filming and coached her in how to play Scarlett. In the process, a friendship was forged between Leigh and the ousted director.

Many months later, long after the dramas associated with the production of *Gone with the Wind* ended, Leigh as Lady Hamilton and Olivier as Lord Nelson were in Hollywood filming *That Hamilton Woman*. When Cukor subsequently invited Leigh to one of his Sunday afternoon gatherings, Kate threatened not to make an appearance. "I still haven't forgiven her for taking the role of Scarlett O'Hara from me."

Cukor protested that "you should blame David O. Selznick for that. Come on over and meet Vivien. She'll be there with Larry. You'll love her."

Kate only reluctantly agreed. She'd met Olivier before, when they'd both worked on Broadway for the dreaded Jed Harris.

"At first Kate, when she got to my party, circled Vivien like Indians around an armed camp of early settlers, waiting to move in for the kill," Cukor said. "But when the women started talking, they found they had much in common. It was the beginning of a lifelong friendship, even though they would be up for some of the same roles in the future."

For the first fifteen minutes, however, that friendship got off to a rough start. When Olivier excused himself to talk to Cukor and Anderson Lawler, Kate found an opening. She was well aware that Leigh and Olivier had been secretly living together, waiting for the divorce courts to end their marriages to their respective spouses.

"You know, of course, that you're marrying a homosexual," Kate said, hoping to slice into Miss Scarlett's heart. Normally, Kate wasn't that vicious but the loss of the Scarlett role was still too painful.

"Oh, darling," Leigh said, seemingly not at all alarmed by Kate's words. "You Americans are so silly about such things. In Britain, we know that all our actors are homosexuals, some more so than others. That's why we have such great theater."

As Kate later related to Cukor, "that remark coming from one so young made me enthralled by Vivien right away. It just won my heart. I decided to never be bitchy with her again. It was not her fault that she made such a bad Scarlett, and I would have been a great Scarlett."

Leigh told Kate that to keep expenses down, she and Olivier were sharing a rented house in Beverly Hills with Garson Kanin.

"How fascinating," Kate said. "That man knows how to keep a secret. He's never told me he was living under one roof with the world's most romantic couple."

"Oh, it's not a three-way," Leigh countered.

"I only indulge in those every month or so myself," Kate said. "The last time was with Louis B. Mayer and Ann Miller." She walked away from Leigh to answer Lawler's summons. He'd heard that Spencer Tracy, also a friend of Cukor's, had arrived in the driveway, and he wanted to introduce the actor to Kate, knowing how much she admired him.

Kate stood in the hallway waiting for him, but Tracy didn't come in. Lawler went to investigate and returned shortly thereafter.

"No Spence?" she asked. "Did he hear that I was here and ran away?"

"Don't flatter yourself," Lawler said. "When Cukor saw what condition Tracy was in, he had his driver take him home so he can sleep it off. That Irishman sure likes his whiskey."

"Without Spencer at this party, that means I'll have to make a play for Olivier," Kate said.

En route to the toilet, Leigh heard that. "Oh, Kate," she said, "dear one, don't bother, really. Larry wouldn't know what to do." With that enigmatic pronouncement, she disappeared into the toilet.

Lawler and Kate stood looking at each other, not knowing what to say.

Years from that late summer day in 1940, Kate told Cukor, "Even though on three different occasions, I was presented with the opportunity to go to bed with the world's second greatest actor—Spence is still number one in my book—I turned Larry down each time. I must have heeded Vivien's long-ago warning."

***

On the night Garson Kanin arrived at Kate's house for dinner, he pitched to her the idea of a new picture based on the life of Julia Dent Grant, the wife of

360

general and later president Ulysses S. Grant. Kanin had tentatively entitled his screenplay simply *Mrs. Grant*.

To Kate's astonishment, she found that General Grant didn't even appear in the script. She protested vigorously about that, claiming that the general had to appear, even if only once, to give the film balance.

In the heat of their argument, an urgent call came in from Olivier, who would not explain or provide details, but told Kanin that he had to return to their shared house in Beverly Hills at once. It was all very hush-hush.

With profound apologies to Kate for his hasty departure, Kanin left, but got a ticket for speeding because he drove so fast in response to the phone call. Once he reached the house, he found Olivier and Leigh dressed for a wedding. Their own. It seemed that Ronald Colman and his wife, Benita Hume, had arranged for them to get married at their ranch at San Ysidro, an eighty-mile drive north toward Santa Barbara.

"Couldn't you have waited a little longer after your divorce?" an exasperated Kanin asked Olivier. "I was just pitching a film to Kate Hepburn that would have won her an Oscar—that is, if she is still speaking to me. I also have other plans for Kate. In other words, if you guys had waited, it might have been a double wedding."

"Oh, fiddle-faddle," Leigh said in her Miss Scarlett voice. "We want you to be best man. Let's get going."

"Who's going to be your maid of honor?" Kanin asked. "Dame Sybil Thorndyke?"

"We haven't thought about that," Leigh said.

In a flash, Kanin proposed Kate for matron of honor, and the couple agreed.

Olivier and his bride-to-be, dressed formally in their wedding finery, piled into the back seat of Kanin's car, as he drove back to Kate's house. She had gone to bed, and she sleepily opened the door attired in a night gown. He quickly explained the situation and asked her to be matron of honor, telling her that Leigh and Olivier were already waiting, fully dressed, in his car. "All right," she agreed, but she demanded to take a shower first. "C'mon, Kate," he implored. "Time for baths later. Besides, haven't you already had eight showers today?"

Kate took that final shower after all, but was fully dressed and in Kanin's car in just ten minutes. The first part of the trip went reasonably well, as Kate assured them that they would soon dethrone the Lunts and the Barrymores and become the new king and queen of the theater, both on Broadway and in London. The couple, soon to be universally known as the Oliviers, liked that a lot. What they didn't like was when Kate said, "I adore how the two of you have been lovers for years while married to other people."

After that, the atmosphere in the car soured. Kanin got lost, and both Olivier and Leigh began to fight bitterly over directions, even though neither of them had ever been to Santa Barbara before.

"Before Garson and I knew it, Lord Nelson and his Lady Hamilton (aka Miss Scarlett O'Hara) were fighting bitterly," Kate later said. "Neither one of them would give in. I didn't give this marriage much of a chance."

Olivier became so upset with Leigh at one point that he demanded that Kanin stop the car. He got out and told Kanin to drive on. "I'm not marrying that bitch. Have the wedding without me."

Kate got out of the car and after about thirty minutes managed to persuade Olivier to get back into the rear seat with Leigh and to continue north for their upcoming nuptials.

They arrived an hour and a half late at the Colmans. To keep the minister, Judge Fresh Harsh, there, Ronald had been plying him with whiskey. Harsh faced the wedding party completely sloshed.

Olivier wanted to be married in the living room, but Leigh demanded the rose-covered terrace.

Kanin later said, "there was something in the night air I was allergic to. I had history's worst case of hay fever and coughed all through the ceremony."

The judge pronounced her name "Lay" and called him "Oliver." Although he asked Olivier if he'd take Leigh as his lawful wedded wife, he forgot to propose a similar question to Leigh. Benita had purchased the wedding ring for Olivier so as to maintain secrecy, but Kanin as best man forgot to produce it. It seemed that everybody forgot about the ring, until razor-sharp Kate called for it.

After Judge Harsh drunkenly pronounced the Oliviers man and wife, he shouted "Bingo!"

After the wedding, Kanin and Kate drove the newlyweds to San Pedro, where Colman's schooner, *Dragoon*, was waiting to take them on a brief honeymoon to Catalina Island.

Kate and Kanin came aboard, where they enjoyed two bottles of champagne and caviar arranged by the Colmans. After kissing the Oliviers good-bye, Kate stood on the pier with Kanin watching them disappear into the dawn. It could have been a scene from *That Hamilton Woman*.

Delivering Kate back to her doorstep, Kanin in the early morning sun grabbed her and kissed her passionately. "How about you running off with me and getting married next week?"

"We'll be too busy getting *Mrs. Grant* ready to show Mr. Mayer," she said before gently closing the door in his face.

When the Oliviers returned from Catalina Island, they visited and thanked her for serving as their matron of honor. Olivier said that "Vivien and I spent the first day of our honeymoon listening to the radio broadcasting news about our marriage. Apparently, we were so secretive that nobody, not even the newspapers, found out. The next day I had to disguise my voice and call the city desk and alert the sluggards to this big news development."

"You wanted them to find out and tail us, didn't you?" Kate asked, a bit perplexed.

The next night when Kanin showed up to pitch his script again for *Mrs. Grant*, Kate was very dismissive of him. She was preparing a dinner for Claudette Colbert. "I've decided that I don't want to play *Mrs. Grant*. Perhaps her husband one day. Pitch me your next best idea, and I'll go for that."

She turned out to be a woman of her word.

***

As Kate was to relate to Anderson Lawler, and as he was to tell virtually everybody else, Jimmy Stewart finally got around to explaining his "pollution" to Kate. It came during a pillow talk moment, when Margaret Sullavan's name was brought up once again.

Sullavan had seriously damaged the sexual reputations of both Fonda and Stewart, denouncing them as "faggots" to the Hollywood community whenever she wasn't attacking Kate for her lesbianism.

Kate learned that "pollute" meant to masturbate. The actor, Burgess Meredith, Stewart's roommate for a number of months beginning in 1940, revealed later that the actor would come home "hot and bothered" from a date and announce that he had to go and "pollute myself."

Apparently, not all of Stewart's many romances with Hollywood stars led to seductions. He confessed to Kate he'd been polluting himself since he was six years old—sometimes as often as five times a day.

He said that when he turned fourteen, his mother had urged him to "save your clean and godly body until the right woman comes along. Bring to your marriage bed an undefiled, uncorrupted, and unpolluted temple of manhood."

"For years I took my mom's advice," he told Kate, "but she didn't say anything about using my fingers. I'm a bit excessive with them."

Kate found all this intriguing, especially when he told her that he could go "the stretch" with a woman but always had to pull out at the last minute and let his fingers do the rest of the work. He said that Sullavan had accused both her former husband, Henry Fonda, and himself of being "adolescent boys." He said that Henry was "quick on the draw, but I take forever. At least I don't suffer from premature ejaculation like Hank does. In fact, it's Hank's marriage bed horror stories that have kept me from committing to one woman. Still trying to stay virginal until marriage to please dear old mom."

"Let me understand this," Kate said. "You penetrate but pull out and call your right hand into duty to finish off the night. Absolutely fascinating!"

"I wanted you to understand that before giving me a try," he said. "That way you won't be disappointed. I once went the full run with Marlene, but she ended up getting pregnant."

"Let's give it a go," she said. "If it's really bad, I can take you home to father. He's a doctor and knows about such things."

Kate skipped a description of the final details of that night when relating her evening to Anderson Lawler.

Lawler later told Cukor, "Kate must have liked it, because she's been alternating seeing Jimmy one night and Colbert the next, with George Stevens thrown in on that odd evening."

What happened to make this romance a quickie, lasting no more than two weeks? Stewart was never certain, and Kate never explained.

The end came the morning she asked if she could accompany Stewart in his small one-engine plane for a flight over Los Angeles. She told him that she was an expert pilot herself.

Even before his craft got off the ground, she reminded him that she'd piloted Howard Hughes—one of "the world's greatest aviators"—and that he had complete confidence in her abilities in the air. Stewart was already an ace pilot and would later serve twenty years in the U.S. Air Force Reserves.

As Stewart was taxiing down the runway, Kate began checking his instruments finding "cause for alarm." "She shouted that my oil pressure was too low," Stewart later recalled. "It wasn't."

"During the entire flight, Kate was screaming that we were going to crash," Stewart said. "If anything could go wrong on a plane, she conjured it up. When the needle on one of the instruments wavered a bit, she began shouting that we were heading into a tailspin."

He claimed that even as they were flying over the beautiful land and seascapes of the coast of Southern California, she found nothing to distract her attention from the instruments. "Look!" she'd shout, discovering another alleged malfunction. She said nothing like this had ever happened when she was flying with Hughes.

"When I could take it no longer, I headed back," Stewart said. "Kate grumbled all the way. As I approached the landing strip, she shouted in a rage at me that I was coming in too high and would land halfway down the runway. She predicted that we were going to crash into the hanger."

To his amazement, Stewart was shocked when the landing didn't come off well at all. "We didn't collapse the hanger and kill ten men. But sudden wind gusts knocked my plane off course. My landing was like a controlled crash."

"When we were finally on the ground," Stewart said, "Kate got out of the cockpit without looking at me or even saying a word. Her chauffeur was waiting. She bolted over to her car, got into the back seat, and drove off. Even when I won the Oscar for *The Philadelphia Story*, she never had a word to say to me."

Their romance was over.

Like so many other affairs with Kate's male co-stars, this relationship ended as abruptly as it had begun.

Kate went back to spending many of her evenings with Claudette Colbert, with George Stevens breaking the routine with the occasional stud duty. A variation on this theme involved an occasional overnight stopover by Leland Hayward.

***

Her idyll within Muirfield cottage was cut short when Kate impulsively moved out one day without even bothering to tell Hughes. She had rented the old John Barrymore house that crowned a hill, Tower Grove, opening onto a panoramic view and the twinkling lights of Beverly Hills.

"It was one of the best residences she'd ever occupied," Kenneth MacKenna said. "She had more privacy here than at any of her rented homes up to then."

To celebrate her new abode, Kate extended an invitation to Laura Harding to spend two weeks with her. Since Colbert had announced her intention to be out of town with her husband, Dr. Pressman, at the time, that didn't present any inconvenience to their relationship.

At the end of her visit, just after Laura packed her luggage and headed back East, Kate invited "my old beau," the sculptor, Bob McKnight, to come and visit her.

McKnight took advantage of the situation and once again asked Kate to pose for a nude sculpture in her garden. She complied but later complained that while she was posing for it, she got severely burned in the hot noon-day sun of California.

When her new friend, Garson Kanin, arrived one night, Kate proudly displayed "my latest nude. I've posed in the buff before—and I will again," she told him.

She never did, however. The whereabouts today of the final McKnight sculpture of Kate are not known. For as long as the statue was in her possession, however, Kate always referred to it as "The Naked Truth."

Leland assured her that Louis B. Mayer—surrounded by "more stars than there are in heaven"—was terribly pleased with her work in *The Philadelphia Story*. He told Leland that he was trying to decide if he should make Kate the new reigning star of Metro-Goldwyn-Mayer, though "at the moment, I'm considering giving the throne to Greer Garson."

In New York, *The Philadelphia Story* opened on Christmas Day at Radio City Music Hall. When the sum of box office receipts became available on January 21, 1941, figures revealed that the film had broken the all-time attendance record, which till then had been set by Walt Disney's *Snow White* in 1937.

The Philadelphia Story marked the end of an era, the twilight of the so-called screwball comedies that had dominated the screens of the Thirties, especially when Carole Lombard starred in them. Although Kate and Cary Grant would remain friends, the film would be her last screen appearance with him. A new leading man loomed in her immediate future.

Grant wasn't nominated for an Academy Award. The honor went to James Stewart as best actor—not supporting actor—even though the role was minor. Another Stewart, Donald Ogden Stewart, won for best screenplay. *The Philadelphia Story* was nominated for best picture but lost to *Rebecca*.

Cukor, as director, lost to Kate's friend, John Ford, for *The Grapes of Wrath* which starred Jimmy Stewart's friend, Henry Fonda. Ruth Hussey, the wise-cracking photographer in *The Philadelphia Story*, lost to Jane Darwell in *The Grapes of Wrath*.

The most painful loss as best actress was suffered by Kate herself.

Bette Davis, nominated for best actress for *The Letter*, tried to console Kate with a phone call. "Miss Ginger Snaps in *Kitty Foyle*!" Davis said sarcastically between puffs on her cigarette. "Christ, that's what Hollywood called acting."

"Hell, yes," Kate said, "Ginger's little soap opera for which I was offered ten-thousand dollars in which to appear. It's the revenge of the little people on me. All those members knew I was the best. Voting for that blonde whore was a way to get even with me. To take Katharine of Arrogance down a peg or two."

"I think you and I should put on our dancing shoes in our next pictures," Davis said mockingly. Her comments remain ambiguous because *Kitty Foyle* was a dramatic role, not a musical.

"You and me, kid," Kate said with a kind of false bravado, "Both of us will go on to win many more Oscars, long after the world has forgotten who the hell Ginger Rogers ever was."

***

Eleanor Roosevelt was known for writing effusive letters to both women and men. Hundreds of them began with "Dearest" and ended with "Devotedly," with a lot of excessive gush in between.

None of these letters were more notorious than her love letters to Lorena Hickok, the Associated Press reporter. Some of these letters were published in 1998 in a book, *Empty Without You*. Hickok had already burned the more sensational of the letters.

Those that remain reveal a lesbian relationship between the two, one of such emotional intensity that the First Lady speaks of lying down with Hickok, a confirmed lesbian, and kissing her on the mouth.

In the early Forties, Mrs. Roosevelt also wrote Kate a series of love letters of such emotional intensity that Kate found them deeply disturbing. She shared them with her Hollywood pals, including Cukor and Kenneth MacKenna, but chose for reasons known only to herself not to show them to Anderson Lawler or even to Kit and Dr. Hepburn.

The First Lady was seeking a deeper relationship with Kate than Kate wanted. Cukor advised her to answer each letter very carefully, so as not to insult the First Lady. He doubted very seriously if the august Mrs. Roosevelt would actually pursue a sexual relationship with Kate. "It seems to me she'd like nothing better than to hold you in her arms and maybe plant kisses on your beautiful face. She's certainly not getting anything from FDR."

Kate started calling actress Patricia Peardon in New York, reading both Mrs. Roosevelt's letters and her own responses.

Beginning with one serious affair with a member of Roosevelt's inner circle at the White House, Peardon had graduated to three different affairs with some of the President's closest advisers. All of these men were married. Partly as a result of these links, Peardon got invited to all major White House functions. Later, Ms. Peardon would appear on the cover of *Life* magazine for her starring role in *Junior Miss.*

Peardon was not at all surprised to learn that Mrs. Roosevelt was a lesbian. "It's a well-known fact within the White House," Peardon said. "The President even cattily remarks about Eleanor running off from time to time to what he calls her Honeymoon Cottage which she shares with Hickok." Often, Peardon dictated part of Kate's response. The two women agreed that Kate should compose letters showing great affection and respect for the First Lady, although without the emotional intensity of Mrs. Roosevelt's letters.

By the time the third letter arrived, Mrs. Roosevelt was writing: "Kate, darling." She signed off with a "Good night and many kisses to you."

In the fourth letter, Mrs. Roosevelt said that, "I want to wrap my arms around you and give you many kisses."

The sixth letter Kate found the most astonishing. In it, Mrs. Roosevelt was openly considering a break from her husband, whom she referred to as "F.D.R." She stated her fury at his "lies to me," although she never said exactly what those lies were.

Kate quickly wrote back, urging great caution and advising against any impulsive move. "All of a sudden," she confided to Peardon, "the roles are reversed. Instead of her being the mother and me the daughter, now I'm being the mother and she the rash daughter."

Two weeks later, another "Kate, darling," letter arrived from the White House. Mrs. Roosevelt's fury against the President had subsided a bit, and she apologized profusely for having unduly concerned Kate and involved her in her own personal struggles.

The First Lady claimed that she would "never break openly with F.D.R." and that she "just shuts up" and pretends to believe his lies to her.

She wrote: "My dearest darling one, I must take a chance at happiness wherever I can find it, but only in small ways. Sometimes I go for weeks at a time before I grab a little bit of joy here and there. I classify receiving letters from you as one of those joys. Do not feel sorry for me. I made my life and, as heaven knows, must live it as I sail over life's rough seas. The other night I became so angry, however, that I used profanity for the first time in my public life. I don't think the newspapers will report on it, however, since I was too shocking. Regardless of how I am provoked, I vowed to myself I will never do that again in public or private."

Mrs. Roosevelt did not explain to Kate the circumstances where she used profanity. In one letter, Mrs. Roosevelt had a request to make to Kate, wanting her to narrate *Women in Defense,* a documentary she'd written herself for the Office of War Information. Kate eagerly volunteered her services, as she was excited by the offer. She called Cukor. "This is the first time in my life some-one wanted me for my voice."

The film was released shortly before the Japanese attack on Pearl Harbor. The First Lady wrote Kate another one of her overly affectionate letters, claim-ing she'd seen the film—"and so has F.D.R."—and both of them thought it was a great success and "will be of immense value for the war effort."

The First Lady, as Kate noted, felt that it was "very likely that we will be involved in the war at any minute."

By 1943, and for no apparent reason, the letters from Mrs. Roosevelt abruptly stopped. Nonetheless, although the First Lady would maintain casual contact with Kate throughout the rest of her life, she would become much clos-er to Laura Harding. Mrs. Roosevelt urged Laura to devote her life to charity work, which she did.

In 1948, when there was serious talk of running Mrs. Roosevelt as the first woman presidential candidate, Kate feared that the letters she'd saved from the former First Lady might fall into the wrong hands and damage the woman's rep-utation.

One early morning at Fenwick, she got up at four-thirty and slowly—page by page—burned each of the letters.

She later told Peardon, "I felt I was destroying historical documents, but some things the world shouldn't know."

Peardon told Kate that she'd made a "grave mistake."

During her own lifetime, Peardon saved the five indiscreet letters she'd received from Prince Philip when they were having an affair in London during the early stages of his marriage to Princess Elizabeth.

***

After filming *The Philadelphia Story,* Kate took the play version on the road again, although by now, she'd tired of the vehicle. She gave her last performance on February 15, 1941, in the play's namesake city of Philadelphia.

Although it was true that MGM had no immediate properties for her, it is not true that she was without offers after the end of filming for *The Philadelphia Story*. Even George Bernard Shaw, who had turned her down as a candidate for the role of Saint Joan, suggested that she might star in his play, *The Millionairess*. And her friends in the Theatre Guild kept muttering about her doing Shakespeare's *As You Like It*.

Philip Barry was in Florida working on a new play with her in mind. Kate invited Laura Harding to go with her on a vacation to Hobe Sound, Florida, next to Philip Barry's rented property.

After hearing of Barry's concept for a work in progress, Kate later confided to Laura that she felt that the playwright's depiction of the foibles of the very rich dated from the early Thirties and had little reality to a world already at war, a critique about Barry that had been expressed by others many times before.

Yet another rescue to her film career came when Garson Kanin sent her a synopsis of a film script co-authored by Ring Lardner, Jr. and Michael Kanin, his brother. The idea for the film script had evolved after a dinner Garson had with Dorothy Thompson in Washington, D.C. Thompson, personally expelled by Hitler from Nazi Germany in 1934, had been chosen woman of the year in 1935 and was the most influential political columnist of her day. She was married to Pulitzer Prize winning novelist, Sinclair Lewis, who said of her, "She thinks and works like a man but remains very much of a woman."

Garson had been drafted into the U.S. Army, so he'd turned the germ of his idea over to Lardner Jr. and his brother, Michael, a musician and a very minor screenwriter who had already authored a B film, *They Made Her a Spy*. Lardner Jr., of course, was the son of the celebrated humorist, Ring Lardner Sr. But at the time Kate began working with these writers, however, neither man had ever made more than three-thousand dollars for a script.

Originally entitled *The Thing About Women*, the script deals with the romantic conflicts between a sportswriter, the character of Sam Craig, and his pundit columnist, the character of Tess Harding. Garson had named the role after Laura Harding.

Kate eagerly read the first draft and notified Garson that she was heading back to New York where she would personally "husband" the project through with Lardner Jr. and his brother, Michael. She cautioned, however, that the writers were not to announce to anyone that they were preparing the script. Already a plan was ticking in Kate's head, as she and Laura took a train back north from Florida.

Returning to Hollywood, Kate worked with the two writers around the clock at the Garden of Allah until she thought the script was ready to present to Joseph Mankiewicz, who she wanted to produce the film as he had *The Philadelphia Story*. Mankiewicz liked the treatment and sent it immediately to

Kenneth MacKenna in the story department of MGM for his opinion, with instructions to prepare a synopsis for "Louis B. himself."

Kenneth liked the script and called Kate to find out the name of the writers. Normally, she confided all of her secrets to her "deflowerer." This time she was strangely mysterious, which caused Kenneth to explode in anger, the first breach that had ever come in their relationship. He quickly repaired it the next day, however.

In a secret memo to Mayer, Kenneth claimed that he knew the identity of the two anonymous writers. "It's got Ben Hecht and Charles MacArthur written in ink on every page." These playwrights had teamed together to create "the ultimate play about a newspaper," *The Front Page.*

Other than the salary she would eventually ask for the struggling writers, Kate had another reason to keep Lardner Junior's name a secret. William Fadiman, Kenneth's boss in the story department at MGM, had called Lardner Jr. a "trouble maker," because of his struggle in the Screenwriter's Guild to gain recognition for that union. Fadiman had issued an order that MGM was not to purchase any property written by Lardner Jr.

Finally, Kate felt that the screen treatment was in satisfactory shape to present in a preliminary meeting with Mayer. She stormed his office and was happily surprised to learn that he liked the material.

Impulsively she demanded Spencer Tracy as her co-star. "Without Tracy, I won't make the film." To her disappointment she learned that Mayer had sent Tracy to the Florida Everglades to film *The Yearling*, to be directed by King Vidor.

Instead of Tracy, Mayer suggested Clark Gable. "Perhaps Walter Pidgeon," the mogul told her.

"Tracy or nothing." Kate appeared adamant in her negotiation position.

Mayer warned her that if Tracy accepted the role of Sam Craig, Kate would have to take second billing, as she had with Cary Grant in *The Philadelphia Story.* She agreed to that.

Kate also demanded that her lover, George Stevens, direct the film. Mayer had no objection to that—"providing Harry Cohn over at Columbia doesn't."

Mayer promised Kate he'd send the script to Tracy in the Everglades. "We'll see what the old drunk has to say," he told her. He warned her that Tracy went on alcoholic binges that might even shut down production. He also told her that he had forced Tracy to sign a contract, agreeing not to have even one beer while shooting a film.

"I've dealt with John Ford," Kate reminded Mayer. "I'm sure I'm woman enough to straighten out your Mr. Tracy."

***

The rumblings about a possible Tracy/Hepburn movie began to shake the ground in Hollywood. When Hedda Hopper caught up with Kate, she demanded to know, "Why haven't you met Spencer before?"

Eager to get rid of the columnist, Kate claimed, "Because I'm years younger than he is and move in a much higher social class. In other words, I'm not a member of the Irishmen's Whiskey Drinking Association like Pat O'Brien and Jimmy Cagney. Don't print that!"

Even in the Florida Everglades, Tracy was hearing of Kate's demands that he co-star with her in a picture. Garson Kanin, a friend, had already sent him a warm-up letter in preparation for the arrival of the script. He reported that Kate had told him that she'd seen his Oscar-winning performance in *Captains Courageous* an astonishing fifty-two times—"and I wept every time."

Tracy wasn't impressed, claiming he'd never seen one Katharine Hepburn picture. "I avoid RKO pictures," he boasted.

Grunting with disinterest, Tracy told Victor Fleming that, "I don't think that woman and I would make a good team." After Mayer kicked King Vidor off the directorship of *The Yearling*, Fleming had stepped in the way he had when Cukor was fired as director of *Gone With the Wind*.

Before Kate's actual meeting with Tracy, Colbert had warned her about him. "He's nothing but a letch, really." The actress had appeared in *Boom Town* with Tracy, Clark Gable, and Hedy Lamarr. "Both Tracy and Gable kept making passes at me during the entire filming. I turned them down. I think both boys got lucky with Hedy Lamarr, however."

"A married man's roving eye is just fine with me," Kate told Colbert. "I'm probably a better seducer of women than Tracy is—or men, for that matter. Tracy will have met his match when he meets up with me."

"It's amazing what Tracy gets away with," Colbert said. "Dating a fifteen-year-old Judy Garland. There should be laws against that. Poor little Judy shouldn't even be allowed in the same room with Tracy without a chaperone."

***

Faced with the possibility of working with Tracy, Kate called Anderson Lawler for an update on the actor's private life, since she knew, as did all of Hollywood, that he was no longer living with his wife, Louise, although still married to her.

"Would you believe that he's bedding dear, sweet, virginal Ingrid Bergman?" Lawler asked.

Kate knew that Tracy had made *Dr. Jekyll and Mr. Hyde* with Bergman and Lana Turner. In fact, she had written him a fan letter praising his acting in the film. "That woman," as Tracy always called Kate, "was the only person in Hollywood who liked me in the part," Tracy told his director Victor Fleming on the set of *The Yearling.* Fleming had also directed Tracy in *Dr. Jekyll and Mr. Hyde*, when both of them, although normally friends, had fallen for Bergman.

"I don't know what Tracy sees in that Swedish peasant," Kate told Lawler. "I hear she's got fat ankles. What man would want a woman with fat ankles?"

"You didn't let Garbo's big feet turn you off," Lawler said jokingly to her.

"He shacked up with Hedy Lamarr for a while," Lawler continued, "until Mayer assigned both of them to *I Take This Woman.* Tracy likes to play practical jokes. In one scene it called for Hedy to sit on Tracy's lap. He went and got the biggest banana he could find. Unripened, of course. When Hedy sat down on his lap, she screamed and jumped ten feet in the air."

"I used that old banana trick before Tracy ever did," Kate boasted. "I used it on that lothario, Fredric March, in fact. He never put his hand up my pants again."

Tracy wrote Garson Kanin that instead of co-starring with "that woman," meaning Kate, he would prefer to appear in a series of films with Myrna Loy, the way she'd starred in Thin Man films with William Powell. "I liked her a lot when I made *Test Pilot* with Gable and her. I think, in fact, I may have cured Myrna of her lesbianism. Thank God I got to her before *that woman* did."

Deplorable working conditions in the Florida Everglades led to the closing down of *The Yearling*, which would not be made until 1946, this time starring Gregory Peck in the Tracy role.

Hordes of insects swarmed the set, causing monstrous welts on Tracy and sticking to the camera lens, ruining the shoot. After six weeks of fruitless struggle, Mayer pulled the plug.

Tracy, after a stopover in New York, was heading back to Hollywood for his long overdue meeting with "that woman."

Even before encountering her, Tracy had troubling doubts about co-starring with Hepburn. In a secret memo to Mayer, he wrote: "Do you think two odd birds like us could fly together? We're so God damn different. I know you don't like me to curse. If you don't mind an abrupt shift in my fowl and fauna reference, I fear that if Hepburn appears on the screen with me, she would look like a graceful, fleet-footed gazelle about to be devoured by a hungry old lion— namely me."

***

With her producer, Joseph Mankiewicz, on her arm, Kate stormed Mayer's office one final time now that Tracy had been set to do the picture with her. Mayer had tentatively offered her one-hundred and seventy-five thousand dollars. She wanted more, and she planned to present the demands herself and not use Leland Hayward.

She wore whipcord pants and a jacket tailored by Eddie Schmidt ("by appointment only") the leading tailor of Hollywood, who designed for such stars as Clark Gable, Errol Flynn, and Tyrone Power.

To meet Mayer, Kate wore what she called her "trick shoes," a set of high heels that added four inches to her height, and wore her hair piled high. Appearing in these platform shoes, she used height as a weapon around such MGM executives as Mayer, who was only five feet, six and a half inches tall.

"With my trick shoes," Kate often said, "I can put any executive in Hollywood in his place." She added, "When a woman looks down at a man, it does something to his frail ego. Quite extraordinary, really. They become so threatened they immediately give you what you want."

On confronting Mayer, Kate demanded two hundred and eleven thousand dollars.

"Why the odd amount?" Mayer asked.

"The ten thousand will be divided between my two agents, and the final thousand is for phone bills and things."

Although initially shocked by Kate's asking price, Mayer, after shedding a few tears, finally granted her request before going to take a call from Greer Garson.

Outside his office, Kate jumped up and down in glee. Mankiewicz kissed her on the nose and backed away. "I've just kissed the Blarney Stone," he said.

On the way to tea in the commissary, Mankiewicz hailed his friend, Spencer Tracy, who was just coming out of the Irving Thalberg building where *The Philadelphia Story* had been screened especially for him.

What happened next is the Hollywood equivalent of Henry Morton Stanley meeting up with David Livingston in the African jungle.

Kate towered over the five-foot nine-inch Tracy by two inches. She grasped his hand when Mankiewicz introduced them. "Where did you learn to shake hands like that?" Tracy asked, rubbing his paw. "A stevedore taught you?"

What happened next became one of the most apocryphal stories in the history of Hollywood.

"I fear I may be too tall for you, Mr. Tracy," Kate said.

His alleged reply to her was, "Don't worry! I'll cut you down to *my* size."

A cute line, except it was never said.

Even if the details weren't accurately reported, the most celebrated Hollywood love story of the century was born that afternoon.

CHAPTER FIFTEEN

Nearing the end of his life, Joseph Mankiewicz, at a party hosted by the "queen of off-Broadway," Lucille Lortel, at her apartment at the Sherry Netherland Hotel in Manhattan, finally revealed what words were actually exchanged between Tracy and Kate when he originally introduced them.

"There was no mention of her being too tall for him, or his putdown that he'd cut her down to his size," Mankiewicz claimed. "Sometimes biographers have attributed that putdown to me. I think these lines actually appeared in an early film script by Garson Kanin, but they were never used."

Breaking his long silence, Mankiewicz re-created the dialogue as he remembered it.

KATE: Well, Mr. Tracy, we meet at last.

TRACY: It was bound to happen if we're going to make a picture together.

KATE: I hear you drink a bit.

TRACY: On one or two occasions. My birthday. Christmas Eve.

KATE: I told your friend, Mr. Mayer, that I desperately want to co-star with you. "Even drunk, Tracy would be great," I said to him.

TRACY: You've got that right, kiddo. So, you've heard stories about my drinking. I've heard a few stories about you too.

KATE: I guess you've heard that I'm a card-carrying lesbian.

TRACY: That's okay with me. I like the girls too.

According to Mankiewicz, Kate once again shook Tracy's hand and departed.

"After she'd gone, Tracy told me that he'd appear with her on the screen but could be counted out for any off-screen shenanigans," Mankiewicz said. "'I wear the pants in any relationship. I don't like women in pants.' Tracy told me. Then he added, 'except maybe on Dietrich.'"

"You're not being asked to fuck her," Mankiewicz told Tracy. "Just appear in a movie with her."

The producer denied widely published reports that have even made it into biographies that Tracy criticized Kate's "dirty fingernails."

"That's ridiculous," Mankiewicz said. "Katharine Hepburn is the cleanest woman in the history of Hollywood, past and present. Any woman who takes six to eight showers a day doesn't have dirty fingernails."

"The next day, Mayer asked me what I thought about casting these two temperamental stars in the same film," Mankiewicz said. "I told him that Kate has met her Petruchio. Stick around and watch *The Taming of the Shrew.* Curtain going up!"

***

Before he shot his first scene with Kate, Tracy told her that the script was "okay but doesn't give me much to do as it stands now. Even so, Shorty, you'd better watch yourself in the clinches."

A showdown between the two actors came almost immediately, on a set designed to simulate Bleeck's, the old Herald Tribune bar in Manhattan.

Nervous at appearing with Tracy for the first time, Kate turned over a glass of water. Stevens kept the camera running. Improvising, Tracy handed her a handkerchief to mop up the water. She frantically mopped. When the water ran off the table, she crawled under it and continued mopping, which, of course, placed her in a subservient position to Tracy, who kept a tight-lipped grin of amusement at her antics.

"From the very beginning, Spence showed that he'd have the upper hand in any scene," Stevens later said. "I found Kate's act better than Laurel and Hardy."

When Stevens finally called cut, Kate stood up and denounced Tracy. "You son of a bitch!" she said to him before heading back to her dressing room.

Stevens later said that Kate and Tracy were like "fire and ice in the first days of the shoot," which began on August 29. Fay Bainter, who played Kate's crusading aunt in the film, also noticed the tension between Tracy and Kate during the first days of shooting.

Making his debut in the film as a bartender, William Bendix, said, "I could tell that Tracy wasn't going to get this gal. I hoped I might have a chance with her but decided she was out of my league."

In the film, Tracy calls Kate the "Calamity Jane of the fast International Set, and she refers to him as "an ostrich with amnesia." "Kate truly relished that line," Bainter said.

During the first week of shooting, Tracy sucked loudly on a piece of peppermint candy, which he claimed kept him from the bottle. On his most recent films, he had been kowtowed to as the star. As he complained to Stevens later in the day, "*That woman* is running the show. She thinks she's the producer, ordering everybody around. I'll be God damn if I'm going to take my marching orders from her."

Stevens reminded Tracy that it was Kate who had put the film package together.

"Don't remind me," Tracy said. "I think I might even walk off this picture. I don't want any part of it. Mayer wanted to give it to 'The King' anyway." It was Tracy himself who had nicknamed Clark Gable "The King."

During the filming, Kate turned to Stevens for advice about her acting. To him, she expressed her fear that she was playing it "too sweet" for a Dorothy

376

Thompson-like character. "Katie, my dear, you get out there and be as sweet as you can be. You'll still be plenty nasty."

When Kate finally forgave Tracy for making her mop up the water on camera, she came to him for advice about her acting. "Just learn your lines," he told her in his standard response to that question, "and don't bump into the furniture." She'd heard him quoted as having said that many times, and was annoyed at him for not giving her more of an individualized response than that.

He later asked her if she had any problem with him taking star billing, claiming that "Garson Kanin had suggested that for the sake of chivalry I take second place. I told him, 'this is a movie, chowerhead—not a lifeboat!'"

A mysterious event occurred on the night of September 3, just five days before shooting. John Ford and Spencer Tracy had once been best friends. But Ford came to feel that Tracy betrayed him by turning down the starring role in *The Plough and the Stars* despite Ford's fervent and repeated requests. Even before an affair between Tracy and Hepburn actually began, Ford had heard from his associate, Cliff Reid, that Kate was in love with Tracy. This second "betrayal" turned out to be too much for Ford.

Even though he was sleeping with Kate very rarely at the time, he felt he "didn't want to turn her over to Tracy."

Ford came by the set and drove Kate home for one final night with her. She never revealed to any of her confidential pals, such as Cukor, exactly what happened that night. Ford until the day he died never commented on that night even to a close pal like John Wayne.

Mary Ford later told Wayne that her husband came home the following morning and announced to her that he was leaving town, traveling aboard the Union Pacific Streamliner, for a short business trip to Washington. "He didn't even pack a suitcase," Mary told Wayne. "Only a battered old briefcase."

Ford later called Mary from Washington, informing her that he was now wearing a military uniform.

Except for a brief visit here and there, Ford would not return to his Odin Street home in Los Angeles for another five years.

He was never to know Kate's intimate embrace ever again.

***

On the sidelines, as director, Stevens claimed he saw the love affair between Kate and Tracy developing right before his lens. Tracy no longer called her "that woman" but Kate or Kath. Later he would have other nicknames for her.

She called him Spen*suh*. The first time he heard her say that, he scolded her. "Christ, woman. Why do you always have to sound like you have a broomstick up your ass?"

"A new aura came over Kate," Stevens said. "She seemed more like a woman fulfilled. She still wore pants to work, but off-screen she appeared with more makeup. Her clothes weren't as sloppy. They became more tailored like the kind of pants Dietrich wore. I decided to back away and give Spence a clear playing field."

Stevens said that soon after filming began, he accepted an invitation to Kate's house for one final romantic dinner. "That's what I liked about her. She had style. I told her I was bowing out because of Spence. She also knew I was going off to war. She gave me one final round of bedding 'for the road,' as she so gallantly put it."

Tracy and Kate began to spend all their time together both on the set and after five o'clock. She abandoned her customary picnics. During her lunch hour, he was seen entering her dressing room.

Stevens often had a hard time getting his two stars to return to the set for the afternoon shoot.

His assistant director, Robert Golden, later said, "It would take a fool not to see that Hepburn had fallen in love with Spence. As for Spence, I think he was intrigued by this Yankee phenomenon. To this day, though, I have never believed that Spencer Tracy was in love with Katharine Hepburn. Spence had two loves in life—himself and the bottle."

Even so, before the end of the shoot, Golden said he heard Tracy call Kate by various nicknames that included Flora Fench, Laura La Plante, Madame Curie, Olive Oyle, Molly Malone, Coo-Coo, the Bird Girl, Carrie Nation, Miss America, Madame Defarge, Mrs. Thomas Whiffen, Dr. Kronkheit, ZaSu Pitts, and sometimes just "the Madam."

From the beginning, Tracy told Kate that marriage was out of the question. "I actually proposed to Loretta Young. What a public relations mess that was. I was prepared to divorce Louise. Somehow the studio put out some cover-up statement claiming that I could never marry because Louise and I are both Catholics. I'm Catholic. She's Episcopalian."

"Don't worry about marriage around me," Kate said. "I'm not the marrying kind."

***

Halfway through the shooting of *Woman of the Year*, Tracy disappeared, off on another one of his famous binges. Kate feared that he would wreck his career at MGM, not to mention violate the no-drinking clause of his contract that Mayer had forced the actor to sign.

It was Thursday. Kate called George Stevens and explained the situation. She begged him to shoot around Tracy on Friday, and she said that she would also call in tomorrow and claim that she'd caught a virus.

Desperately she drove to see Jimmy Cagney to get his help in locating Tracy because he knew the whereabouts of Tracy's drinking haunts. Cagney refused to help her, and, in fact, slammed the door in her face, for which she would never forgive him.

Tracy's former roommate, the actor Pat O'Brien, volunteered his services. Together they drove around Los Angeles until they finally located Tracy in an Irish bar called The Shamrock. The owner of the bar, Sean MacArthur, had locked Tracy in the back room.

He'd been forced to close his bar when Tracy had gone on a rampage. He'd picked up bottles of liquor and started hurling them at the other patrons before tossing the bottles against MacArthur's cut-glass mirror over the bar, which he'd imported at great expense from Dublin.

Taking charge of the situation, Kate called Leland Hayward to come to the scene to help Pat O'Brien and her. She negotiated with the bar owner who demanded fifteen-thousand dollars in damages, claiming that he was going to call MGM. He'd heard that studios often paid big money to get their major stars out of trouble. "One of my customers knows for a fact that Mayer got Gable off when he ran over a man and killed him," MacArthur told Kate. "Gable was drunk."

Even before Leland arrived with two of his male assistants, Kate had negotiated the bartender's "blood money" down to six-thousand dollars. She agreed to pay the money herself and would never present a bill to Tracy.

With the help of Kate's all-male posse, she ordered that Tracy be brought to her home for the weekend. He'd long ago passed out and didn't know what was happening to him.

At her house, Kate ordered Leland and O'Brien to strap the actor to her bed.

Years later, O'Brien recalled, "I couldn't believe I was actually strapping my best friend into the bed of this woman. But Hepburn prevailed, and I carried out her wishes. I knew she was working for Spence's best interests. Mayer might have fired him. She claimed that she would have him sobered up by Monday morning and ready to resume shooting."

O'Brien, as he was being shown the door, along with Leland and his assistants, asked Kate, "How is Spence going to potty?" The actor claimed that she told him that her father was a doctor, and she knew perfectly well how to handle bodily functions in a hospital.

Amazingly, Kate showed up with a sobered-up Spence on Monday morning. "We'll never know exactly what happened during that three-day weekend," O'Brien later said. "But it was the beginning of a love affair that would span the years."

"Unlike what she played on the screen, unlike the way she deferred to Spence when people were around, Katharine Hepburn that weekend determined who truly wore the pants in that family," O'Brien claimed.

For the rest of the shoot, Kate kept Tracy from drinking by brewing one fresh pot of black coffee after another for him.

***

At the beginning of their relationship, Kate was put to the test one night when she arrived at Tracy's rented quarters. He always insisted that she call before coming over, but apparently she'd forgotten.

As she was coming up the hedge-lined pathway, she spotted Ingrid Bergman leaving. The two future screen legends glared at each other but never exchanged a word.

"Didn't you even slug her?" Kenneth MacKenna asked the next day. "Have a real cat fight?"

"I was pissed off at the bitch," Kate said. "I thought it was over between the two of them. But I was wrong. On the other hand, since I have a woman in *my* life, I guess I'll have to accept the fact that he's entitled to one too. Isn't that what this equality of the sexes is all about? It's going to take some mental adjustment on my part, however. Right now, I'm mad as hell. I think I'll get even with Spencer by going on the road and leaving him to his own devices for a while. That way, I'll know if he misses me or not."

Joseph Mankiewicz said that Ingrid Bergman, even when she learned about Tracy's involvement with Hepburn, "was still crazy about Spencer. Don't forget. She was there before Kate came onto the scene. Bergman was a stunningly beautiful creature. I hear she was also the greatest lay in Hollywood this side of Joan Crawford. Bergman was also smart. Kate hated her like a natural enemy."

"Kate bore a lifetime grudge against Ingrid," Humphrey Bogart later said after he'd become friends with Kate. "Kate never forgave Ingrid for trying to come between Spence and herself. One day in the jungle when we were making *The African Queen,* Kate told me, '*Casablanca* instead of *Citizen Kane* might have become the greatest movie of all time if it weren't so miscast with Bergman as your co-star. You saved the picture but she almost ruined it. She played it like a Swedish cow. Very bovine.'"

"Who should have been cast?" Bogie asked, baiting her. "Hedy Lamarr? She was a gal friend of Spence's too."

"Ann Sheridan could have pulled it off," was Kate's dismissive reply.

In her own memoir, *Me,* Kate was rather dismissive of Ingrid Bergman, a three-time Oscar winner. In mentioning the film *Dr. Jekyll and Mr. Hyde* that Tracy made with her, Kate wrote: "Ingrid Bergman played the whore; she won an award, I think."

Kate was referring to an Academy Award. In that, she was mistaken. Bergman would not win her first Oscar until 1944, and it was for *Gaslight.*

* * *

It seemed that all of inside Hollywood learned about the so-called "illicit love affair" of the already-married Tracy and Katharine Hepburn. But, amazing-

380

ly, except for some suggestive items inserted into columns over the years, the affair would not become public knowledge until the Sixties. The columnist, Sheilah Graham, called it "the greatest love story *never* told."

Every friend of Kate's had definite opinions, some of which they expressed to her face.

Colbert continued to be dismissive of Tracy, still viewing him as "the old letch" or the "soggy Irish drunk." But Kate defended Tracy to her female lover, repeating what had now become a rehearsed speech which she delivered to many of her friends and associates. "He's made me a better actress—and, yes, a better woman. I was too self-centered before I met him. He's taught me to see something else other than my mirrored reflection. By caring for him, I've learned to care for myself—-not for vanity's sake, but as a real woman capable of acting better both on and off the screen. Before I met Spence, I was a total pig, the way I was with my first husband, Luddy. Today, I often put his interests before my own."

Colbert, even so, remained disdainful of Kate's relationship with Tracy, telling her friends, including her husband, "that it won't last. It would take a masochist to put up with Tracy. Kate is no masochist."

Cukor, who had only recently directed Colbert in *Zaza*, also thought the relationship would last as long as Kate's other affairs.

Cukor had known Tracy only casually at the time the actor began his affair with Kate. But the director and Tracy soon became the closest of friends.

At first Cukor told Tracy that he'd been bitterly disappointed that Kate had asked George Stevens to direct *Woman of the Year* and not him. "Well, it's not as bad as losing *Gone With the Wind*," Tracy told him.

He admitted to Cukor that he and Kate were having an affair. "I mean she anchored herself in my living room almost every night. What's a man to do? I don't know for sure yet, but I think she's not for me, boy. You can have her. I'm sick enough without getting mixed up with someone who might be sicker than me. You know she sometimes wanders around Hollywood at night with some companion or other breaking into homes."

"Yes," Cukor said, smiling smugly, "I'm privy to all of Kate's secrets."

Cukor, in later life, remembered that after a few days, Tracy softened his position on Kate. "I recall her telling me she loved him, but in all the years I knew him, I never once heard Spence say that he loved her in return. Instead, he came to have great respect for her."

On his Sunday afternoon gatherings, or at private dinners to which he'd invite Kate and Tracy, Cukor expressed shock at how he treated her. "Right from the beginning, he called her a bag of bones. If she was talking, as she always did, he'd interrupt rudely if he wanted to make a point himself. He'd just tell her to shut up. She'd smile demurely and take it. But only in public. What was going on behind the scenes was a very different matter. When they were not on exhibit, Kate was clearly in the driver's seat."

Both of Kate's confidants, Kenneth MacKenna and Anderson Lawler, agreed with Cukor.

At Cukor's house, sometimes in the presence of others, Tracy would humiliate Kate by bragging on the accomplishments of his wife, Louise Treadwell. He claimed that when she was a popular leading lady in stock, she was a better actor than either Kate or him. He spoke often of how Louise had worked valiantly with their first born child, John, who suffered from deafness at birth.

It was true that Louise had founded the John Tracy Clinic to aid deaf children. For nearly half a century, she won many awards as a world famous expert in the field, even serving on Presidential Commissions.

Once, when in reference to Tracy's son John, Kate used the words "deaf and dumb" in Tracy's presence, he slapped her in front of Cukor and the actress, Ruth Gordon. "There is no such God damn thing," he shouted at Kate. She never used the expression again.

When Tracy wanted to spend time with his wife, his son, John, and his daughter, Susie, he would tell Kate to "go visit Claudette or one of your other gals. Why not a visit back home to your beloved doctor father?" And whenever Tracy returned to his home, he referred to it as "going to visit the folks on the hill."

Tracy was a devout Catholic, Kate a non-observing WASP. When he got around to asking Kate about her religious beliefs, she said, "Self-reliance is my God. You can have your Pope, your priests, and definitely your Catholic church. My parents taught me to distrust the Catholic church above all. I'd rather have been born Jewish than Catholic." Her words angered him.

They were both a study in similarities and contrasts. She was the eternal optimist, he the consistent pessimist. On screen he did as little as possible, whereas her acting was more theatrical. Both had wit and humor, and both hated sycophants who hung around big studios. Both of them had a bunker mentality about the press and detested publicity. For years, very little was known about their private lives, except by their most intimate friends.

He was more conservative politically than she was. Yet they were both Democrats and supported Roosevelt.

They shared a love of reading, the theater, and music which stimulated their intellectual curiosity. Neither one had much interest in watching films.

They discovered that both of them shared a love of painting. They called themselves "the two Sunday painters," and were seen driving to secluded spots along the southern California coastline where they would set up easels and paint until it was time for one of her picnic lunches.

Chester Erskine, a friend of both Tracy's and Kate's, and a writer-producer-director, once said, "Kate sometimes literally sits at Spence's feet looking up at him with admiration. She was also metaphorically at his feet. Aside from Dr. Hepburn, Spence was the only man she ever trusted, respected, and admired, although she knew his weaknesses better than anyone. He was her adored—*at times*—companion. He was also a trusted adviser, just like her father. If he didn't think she should accept a particular role, she always turned it down."

"It was some sort of love I guess," Cukor later told friends like Cary Grant in private. "The love was mainly on her part—not his. Instead of love, he developed a dependence on her that he could never shake. When she wasn't there, he went on alcoholic binges so severe that they were life-threatening. For all the self-confidence Spence portrayed on the screen, he was the complete opposite in private," Cukor said. "He was filled with self-doubt. Self-loathing might be more accurate. At times he would become a virtual basket case."

Kate could spend hours talking to Cukor about Tracy. She told him that "Spencer leads a life of crippling despair and stays up all night haunted by his demons. I've never known a man as deeply, even profoundly, troubled as he is. Often he blames himself for his son's deafness and sometimes uses that as an excuse to drink. But that was back around 1924 or some such time. He's had plenty of time to get over that. It's something more troubling, something deeper. He always looks so confident on the screen. Off the screen he's a total mess."

"With Jimmy Cagney and Pat O'Brien, Spencer has this persona of bluntness, even crudeness—definitely anti-intellectual," she said. "But that is a mask he wears. He's not like that at all. He's the most complex man I've ever known, except for Howard Hughes. Spencer's artistic brilliance comes through in every film he makes, but he doesn't even appreciate the fact that he's the greatest actor on earth."

***

Kate's close friends quickly divided into pro-Tracy camps or anti-Tracy camps, with Laura Harding weighing in strongly against him. "In time," as Cukor later said, "Spence and Laura realized that if they were going to keep Kate in their lives, they would have to learn to tolerate each other."

Although Garson Kanin knew all about the shadows in Kate's relationship with Tracy, he was the most supportive—at least publicly. In private, he had a lot more to say. To Cukor and others, he maintained that "Kate and Spence are good for each other. He anchors her on this earth since she has a tendency to be flighty. She's often unrealistic. Spence can kid her and make her see how wildly impractical many of her ideas are. If we can compare them to a boat, he is the anchor, she the sail."

Kate pictured the relationship with Tracy not comparable to a boat but to food. She claimed that she was the dessert "with lots of whipped cream. Spencer is the unadorned baked potato."

"Like hell," Lawler said when he heard that. "Kate is too tart to be a confection. If Tracy is the baked potato, then she's the chopped chives, the bacon bits, and the heady sour cream."

Although speaking candidly, perhaps over pillow talk with his new bride, Ruth Gordon, Kanin continued to support Tracy and Kate's relationship when talk of them came up at Hollywood parties, which it invariably did. "It's a relationship founded on mutual respect and a high regard for each other's talents. It's about exchanged generosity. A total lack of possessiveness. More than anything else, a gloriously shared sense of humor."

"What fantasy is that fucking Kanin talking about?" Anderson Lawler once asked. "When Kate hooked up with that selfish old Irish monster, she entered into the Valley of Hell's fire. I begged her almost weekly to dump that pile of shit and take charge of her life again. She never listened to me."

Lawler remained the severest critic of the Hepburn/Tracy affair, but not to her face. He told Cukor and others that "all Kate does is talk about what a man Tracy is. She didn't get a man when she hooked up with that one. Gary Cooper is a man. Except for his dick, even Clark Gable is a man. What Spencer Tracy is to Kate is both a father and a child surrogate—that's it, pure and simple."

From New York came another dissenting voice from the actress, Patricia Peardon, whom Kate had confided in since the *Jane Eyre* days. Peardon warned that "if you keep up this clandestine relationship with Tracy, you'll be a discarded mistress on Back Street. There are a lot of pitfalls here. You'll never wear a wedding band."

"That is the last thing I want to wear," Kate told her. "I'm free to live my own life. Spencer will have his affairs. But so will I."

Peardon never accepted the myth perpetuated about the great love affair of Tracy and Hepburn. "To me, he was just an old roué. Once when he was staying at Turtle Bay with Kate, I invited the two of them to go with me to the theater with my own date. The moment Tracy was alone with me, he propositioned me. So much for this grand love affair."

***

Mayer told Stevens that he liked the rushes of *Woman of the Year* and thought the teaming of Tracy and Hepburn was inspired. Mayer felt that Tracy and Hepburn caused "sparks to fly off the screen," and claimed that her exaggerated theatricality was a perfect foil for Tracy's masculine stubbornness and more prosaic outlook.

But Mayer said he was appalled at the ending as originally written by Lardner Jr. and Michael Kanin. Originally, the on-screen marriage of Tracy and Hepburn ended ambiguously, with the audience left to determine if they would remain together as a couple, with all their differences and disagreements intact. Mayer brought in a staff writer to provide a more schmaltzy ending, where Tracy ends up as the undisputed head of the family, with his "dutiful little housewife," as played by Kate, giving in to him, as symbolized by her preparation of his breakfast and her character's tacit agreement that Tracy had clearly won the battle of the sexes.

Stevens strenuously objected to the cliché-ridden new ending, thinking it "must have come from one of those Andy Hardy movies." But Mayer stood his ground, and insisted that his vision prevail. When Kate read the new ending, she shouted, "This is the worst piece of shit I've ever been called upon to act." Nonetheless, she had to go through with it because of her contractual obligations.

Although Tess Harding could advise some world leaders, Kate on screen can't prepare a simple breakfast for Tracy. She may be "woman of the year," but her eggs misbehave, bread pops out of her toaster like a jack-in-the-box, and she overboils coffee.

Mayer accurately believed that women all over America would feel superior to Kate in that they could prepare a decent breakfast for their husbands whereas she, in spite of her glamour and intellect, couldn't. Kate felt the scene was a blow to the women's liberation movement as advocated by Kit. In fact, she claimed that she was going to forbid Kit from seeing the movie. "I'd be too humiliated," Kate told Stevens. "Up to now, she's thought of me as an independent woman."

"Mayer's a bastard," Cukor said, "but he knew that Tracy had captured the heart of mid-America and that Kate's pictures never did. He felt that the breakfast scene would show Tracy putting Kate in her place, which was wearing an apron in the kitchen."

As Kate would later remark, "women's liberation in 1942 was about having the little wife of the house take a day off from baking brownies."

***

At one point early in her relationship with Tracy, Kate's role as a caretaker became severely overstretched. Dr. Hepburn became gravely ill in the East and Spencer had to be hospitalized in the West with a kidney ailment. Kate raced back and forth across the country to be at their bedsides—a week with Dr. Hepburn in Hartford, a week with Tracy in Beverly Hills. "She tended to them, supervised their care, consulted and even *advised* their doctors," said Patricia Peardon. "But mostly she cared for them and loved them. They had become the two most important men in her life."

Both men recovered. "This sounds really strange," Peardon said, "but I truly believe that this was the happiest time of Kate's life to have the two most important men in her life desperately needing her support. No other person in Tom Hepburn's life, nor in Tracy's—not even his wife—was quite the giver that Kate was. Once when I became desperately ill, she rushed to my bedside. Surely, there was no doctor in all the world with the skilled bedside manner of Katharine Hepburn. She was the tops!"

Cukor went so far as to call Kate "the ultimate caretaker—damn it, she should have been a nurse. Or, in Kate's case, a doctor."

He also felt that Kate thrilled at being Tracy's primary care-giver, and loved nursing him back to health. "But it was a downhill battle for her. Because of the years of heavy drinking, Tracy's health, even at the beginning of their relationship, was never good. I was astounded he lived for as long as he did."

***

After the release of *Woman of the Year*, Kate found herself more and more famous, and was constantly stalked by the press and besieged by autograph hounds. She eluded them both and only laughed when the Hollywood Women's Press Club began to consistently bestow on her its "Sour Apple Award" as "The Most Uncooperative Actress of the Year."

When the film editors at *Time* saw *Woman of the Year*, they declared that as a team, Hepburn and Tracy had turned "several batches of cinematic corn into passable moonshine."

Kate would receive her fourth Academy Award nomination, but suffered a bitter loss to the beautiful red-haired Greer Garson, who won for *Mrs. Miniver*. "I have to scrounge around and find scripts myself while Mayer gives all the best roles to his pet, Miss Garson."

After Garson's victory, Kate mocked Garson's nimble Irish tongue which ran on for more than thirty minutes, the longest acceptance speech ever at the Oscar ceremonies. Kate claimed to Cukor that she would have been far superior playing *Mrs. Miniver* that Greer Garson. When Tracy asked Kate about the film, she denied having seen it.

Since Bette Davis usually had high praise for Hepburn, Kate did call her and tell her that she should have won for *Now, Voyager.*

"What a liar I am," Kate later told her friends when she revealed the details of her call to Davis. "I was such a suck-up. I don't want to get on Davis' bad side like Crawford does."

For their original screenplay, the Oscars went to Ring Lardner Jr. and Michael Kanin.

Even though Kate didn't get the Oscar, *McCalls* magazine named her its own Woman of the Year, honoring her for her "beauty, grace, talent, and devotion. She is a raving individual," the magazine editors enigmatically claimed with no explanation as to what that really meant.

***

Over the years there has been much speculation about the exact sexual nature, if any, of the relationship between Katharine Hepburn and Spencer Tracy, with various points put forward, including, in the opinion of many, that it was strictly a platonic pairing.

"Kate's relationship with Spence was not about sex," Cukor later said to his confidants. "Believe me, I knew both of them intimately and their relationship was definitely not about sex. As the operator of every bordello in New York and Los Angeles knew from their gals, Spence had a penchant for oral sex performed on him. He was not known to reciprocate, as he found that act disgusting—at least with a woman. From what I've heard from countless actresses, he would sometimes crawl onto a woman in the missionary position. Like his pal, Clark Gable, Metro's two biggest stars were not great lovers."

Cukor also revealed that he thought the sexual part of Kate's relationship with Tracy lasted for only eighteen months even though they stayed together for years.

"After that, they found other relationships," Cukor claimed. "Hell, during their first eighteen months together, they both had other relationships going. Spence had Ingrid Bergman among others, and Kate had Colbert in the West and Laura Harding in the East."

"Instead of crawling in the sack all the time, Kate and Spence fulfilled each other on a professional and intellectual level—dare I use the S word, spiritual?" Cukor said.

Hedy Lamarr once said that Spencer Tracy was no sexual athlete. "Some of the most handsome and most virile men have made love to me," Lamarr confessed at a party in New York hosted by agent Jay Garon. "I would not consider Spencer Tracy among them."

Although he would continue to have affairs with women for the next fifteen years, Tracy in middle age was already suffering serious bouts of impotence, followed by a sudden sexual resurgence when he'd sober up, which would send him on the prowl.

His excessive drinking had led to liver and kidney ailments. While he was physically suffering, he would enter into long periods of melancholia.

Kate always cooked his dinner at her home, then took it to him. Sometimes when he was in a deep depression, he would not even let her come into his bedroom, demanding that she leave the food outside his door.

"There was a bond there," Cukor said, "even a fierce loyalty. When they stopped having sex with each other rather early in their relationship—probably around 1943—they remained good buddies to the end. It was like two males bonded at the hip."

"They not only slept in different beds, but under separate roofs," Cukor said. "Maybe that was the secret of their relationship. Had they been lovers in the traditional sense, such a so-called marriage as theirs might never have worked out."

Anderson Lawler claimed, "All of Hollywood—not the general public—soon learned that Kate and Spence were shacked up. In the Thirties, there had been much talk about Spence's fondness for handsome young men like George O'Brien and Lew Ayres. Of course, Kate's involvement with Jane Loring and

Laura Harding were corn for the gossip mill. Claudette Colbert hadn't come along yet. But when word got out about Kate and Tracy, those rumors more or less died down. It was years later before only the most insiderish people found out what was really going on. You might say that Tracy and Kate served as each other's beard."

Cukor, speaking intimately about Tracy with Kate, claimed that "I think there are two things that Spence never recovered from. His father, John, instilled in him a deep sense of religion, and he still carries this Catholic guilt with him. He told me that his father never recovered from his disappointment that his son, Spence, never became a priest, except on the screen, of course. Spence also views the acting profession as unworthy of him. It's all fantasy, make-believe—not a fit job for a real man."

"What Spencer Tracy can never do is come to terms with his own deep-rooted homosexuality," Cukor claimed to Kate. "If you continue to be involved with him, you'll find that he will disappear from time to time. When he does that, he's descending into what he calls 'my other life,' equating it with sin and debauchery. Yet, like the moth to the flame, he's drawn to it. Not only has he never come to terms with his sexuality, in my view, he never will."

Peardon queried Kate about rumors of Tracy's homosexuality. "I've seen no evidence myself," Kate said. "He seems a man for the ladies. However, he's getting friendlier with Cukor. They were never real friends before I met Spencer. Now he's the one who wants to visit Cukor. I think something's going on."

Peardon laughed. "Surely not between Cukor and Tracy?"

"Never that!" Kate said. "Perish the thought. If Spence is a homosexual, and I'm not completely convinced of that, he's making some sort of arrangement with Cukor. I'm not opposed to that. Maybe George can keep Spence from disappearing for weeks at a time to strange cities."

Kate had not been completely honest with Peardon. That same week she confided to Anderson Lawler that she suspected that Cukor was arranging handsome male prostitutes, usually out-of-work actors, to service both her favorite director and her favorite man.

"Nothing like a little commerce on the side," Lawler said. "That ugly, pot-bellied, thick-lipped Cukor buys only the best and freshest young men in Hollywood and has them delivered to his house. If your Spence wants to indulge, what's wrong with that? I mean, you're still shacked up with Claudette. Can't he have some fun on the side as well?"

"I guess," Kate said hesitantly. "Perhaps it's better this way than his going out with another woman."

Kate was years from mentioning her private life with Tracy in public, and she would never reveal any strong details, except with her most intimate friends. "He's the ideal man," she kept saying. "A man's man. Strong looking. A big sort of head with a boar's neck. A true man must have at least a seventeen inch neck. I represent the ideal American woman to his ideal American man. I needle him. I irritate him. And I try to get around him. Yet if he put a big paw out, he could squash me. The typical male and female in America can identify with our screen images."

Kate was merely talking for public consumption. When reading her remarks, Louis B. Mayer told his daughter, Irene Mayer Selznick, "The perfect American male and female. Don't make me laugh. My spies have kept me up to date. They're the ideal couple all right if you consider a lez and a cocksucker the ideal American couple."

In spite of Mayer's cruel remarks, which later got back to Kate, she continued to speak of Tracy as "the ideal man."

He was far from that, of course. When Kate finally broke her long silence after Tracy's death, and started to speak publicly and personally about him for the first time on the Dick Cavett show in 1973, she was more interested in creating a myth than she was in revealing the dark but true story of her tempestuous, troubled relationship.

***

Amazingly, after Kate scored two hits and an Oscar nomination, Louis B. Mayer had no good roles to offer her. "Anything hot seems to go to those sisters," she told Ruth Gordon. Kate was referring to Joan Fontaine and Olivia de Havilland. "Or else that Greer Garson hag," Kate added.

Ruth Gordon, whom Kate had always admired and even imitated as an actress, became her new best friend, at times closer than Constance Collier. Along with Kenneth MacKenna, Peardon, Cukor, and Lawler, Kate gained a new confidante whom she could trust. The tiny, outspoken Ruth Gordon had also been involved with the dreaded Jed Harris, having given him a son.

When Kate had learned of Gordon's romance and upcoming marriage to Garson Kanin, she told her, "You've come a long way since Jed Harris. Garson has his faults, but he'll make a great husband. You know, of course, you're his second choice. He was really after me." "I wish you hadn't told me that," Gordon chided her.

Kate privately joked to Cukor. "I hope her child with Harris won't become the *Son of Frankenstein.*"

Gordon was twelve years older than Kate, and since 1915 she had been one of the pre-eminent stage actresses of her day. Like Kate, Gordon had grown up in New England, the daughter of a retired sea captain. When Kate took Gordon sailing, she called both of them "two old Yankee salts."

In time, Kate nicknamed Gordon "Blossom," and could listen with fascination as she told of her adventures in the theater. "She knows everybody," Kate said to Cukor. "Alfred Lunt, Lynn Fontanne. Moss Hart. Booth Tarkington. The Barrymores. The Gish sisters. Thornton Wilder. George S. Kaufman.

Katharine Cornell. Dorothy Parker. W. Somerset Maugham. Noël Coward. Jeanne Eagels. Cole Porter. Theda Bara. Anita Loos. John Gielgud. Even George Bernard Shaw and Harpo Marx!"

Wanting—not needing—a job, Kate once again turned to the Theatre Guild and another play by Philip Barry, even though his heyday had come and gone.

Theresa Helburn of the Theatre Guild had written Kate that "no leading man worth his salt wants to play second fiddle to you. But come to New York, and we'll find you someone."

On one inspired morning, Kate asked Tracy to return to the stage with her in the play, *Without Love.* He flatly rejected her offer, claiming it was far too much work and he was comfortable staying in California.

What Tracy didn't tell Kate was that he was still deeply involved with Ingrid Bergman. As he told Gable, and others, "I don't want to leave Ingrid with that old man, Victor Fleming. "It's dangerous to compete for the same woman with your director," Gable confided in Tracy. "That was no trouble for the two of us when we were shooting *Gone With the Wind.* Neither of us could stand Vivien Leigh."

Unknown to either Tracy or Fleming, Ingrid was also having a secret affair with Humphrey Bogart during the making of *Casablanca.* Throughout her life she would deny that.

Before Kate left Hollywood for New York, Tracy had convinced her that "it's all over between Ingrid and me." In fact, they would never appear together on the screen after making *Dr. Jekyll and Mr. Hyde.*

But two years later, Anderson Lawler claimed that Tracy was discovered in the darkened rear of a restaurant in San Francisco in an intimate embrace with Bergman. Tracy unconvincingly insisted that he and the gorgeous star were discussing future film projects.

Fleming continued to maintain a "long-term interest in my wife," according to Petter Lindstrom, Bergman's increasingly estranged husband at the time. Six years after Fleming had directed Bergman in *Dr. Jekyll and Mr. Hyde*, Lindstrom discovered a romantic letter that Fleming had, shortly before its discovery by Lindstrom, written to his wife. In it, Fleming wrote that although he had been separated from her for six years, "six years is twice as long for me, for what I've lost is lost forever."

Before leaving for New York and her search for a leading man, Kate spent a "farewell weekend" with Claudette Colbert while Tracy was visiting Louise and his children. As Kate remembered it, the two women spent a lot of time discussing their ages. "The blasted Middle Ages," Kate said. "More like the Dark Ages for screen actresses," Colbert countered. Both women had fears about their future roles on the screen now that a new crop of World War II beauties had come along—not only Bergman, but Betty Grable, Rita Hayworth, Lana Turner, and Paulette Goddard.

No great soothsayers, both Kate and Colbert predicted the demise of their careers before the end of World War II.

***

Tracy and Clark Gable had been friends since they'd starred in MGM's *San Francisco* in 1936, neither actor making one of their "obligatory passes" at their co-star, Jeanette MacDonald.

Through Cukor, Tracy learned about Gable's homosexual past, when he'd been a male prostitute, renting himself out to such actors of the silent screen as Ramon Novarro, William Haines, and Rod La Rocque.

Many Hollywood insiders maintained that the real reason Gable insisted that David Selznick fire Cukor from *Gone With the Wind* was because the director knew of Gable's past as a struggling actor in Hollywood—that and the fact that Cukor often referred to him on the set as "My dear."

It is not known if Gable was aware of Tracy's homosexual tendencies. Perhaps he wasn't, because, along with fellow actor Robert Montgomery, Gable was always making anti-homosexual remarks in front of Tracy, calling many men "faggots," even if they weren't. Joan Crawford, who numbered dozens of homosexuals, including Haines, among her best friends, always said that she completely failed to teach Gable tolerance during their long love affair.

Tracy and Gable were great friends but at times, they had been rivals, as when they both had competed for the attention of Loretta Young. Gable told Carole Lombard, who told everybody else, "Tracy made the mistake of falling for Loretta. As for me, I only fucked her and gave her a kid, which neither of us wanted."

Kate had always had utter contempt for Gable, both as an actor and a man. She referred to him as "that arrogant prick." Although Kate felt that she and Errol Flynn could have made convincing lovers as Scarlett O'Hara and Rhett Butler in *Gone With the Wind*, she confided to Cukor that "Gable and I as lovers might have been laughed off the screen. Perhaps David Selznick was right about the lack of chemistry between us."

From the very beginning of her relationship with Tracy, Kate tried to lure him away from his "whiskey pals," as she called them. Those included Clark Gable at the top of the list, but also embraced Tracy's fellow friends, James Cagney and Pat O'Brien, both of whom came to be called "The Irish Mafia."

Kate had been furious when she learned that Gable sometimes strolled across the MGM lot to visit Tracy when he was also shooting a picture. "Only for a shot or two," Gable always said, as he brought along a bottle of whiskey, although at night he preferred big martinis.

When Tracy started seeing Kate, Gable told her, "When your boy turns ugly, I urge him to put the bottle away. Unlike me, Spence is one mean Irish drunk." He also warned her that she'd never be able to take Tracy out into polite company. "He's the sweetest guy you ever want to meet before he drinks.

391

A regular Dr. Jekyll. After a few drinks, it's strictly Mr. Hyde. He's been known to beat up on women, especially whores. There's no respectable whorehouse I can bring him to in Hollywood anymore. One night he's going to get drunk and knock your teeth out. You heard that first from me."

"Your friendship with Spencer sounds divinely inspirational, Mr. Gable," she said before turning and walking away from him.

Kate later told Cukor that she detested Gable, finding him "an evil companion" for Tracy. As for Kate, Gable always referred to her as "that stuck up lez Spence foolishly got involved with."

One afternoon Gable and Tracy started drinking at the Riviera Country Club in Los Angeles and ended up three days later in a hotel room in Tuscon, Arizona. A maid reported seeing them nude together in the same bed. In spite of the sexual suggestiveness of that, it is highly doubtful the men were having sex together. They were too drunk.

Mayer was able to locate them and called their hotel room. He got a barely coherent Tracy on the phone. Tracy was muttering something about having played a wild game of jacks for big stakes the night before. He claimed that they couldn't leave Tucson until each man came up with twenty-thousand dollars in cash to pay off the locals.

Mayer demanded to speak to Gable. "You can't," Tracy said. "Why not?" Mayer asked. "He's on his threesies," Tracy said before putting down the phone.

When Gable sobered up and was able to drive back to Los Angeles, Tracy continued drinking all the way. Gable virtually dragged his friend to Kate's doorstep. When she opened the door, she confronted these two disheveled box-office champions. "You sober him up!" Gable ordered Kate. "I can't."

Gable later told his friends that Kate uttered "every foul word I've ever heard and some I hadn't. And remember, I'm married to potty-mouthed Carole Lombard."

Kate chased Gable out of her garden with an umbrella.

When she sobered Tracy up, she read him the good news. Polls showed that he was now the number one box office champion in America, dethroning Gable as "The King." That afternoon Tracy wrote a note to Gable. "Dear Former King," was all he said.

Gable and Tracy continued to go off on their drinking binges in spite of Kate's protests. Tracy had been drinking with Gable when Lombard left on a plane tour of the Middle West to help sell war bonds.

Tracy told Kate that while Lombard was out of town, Gable was shacking up with Lana Turner.

On January 16, 1942, Cukor called Kate to tell her that the plane carrying Lombard, a TWA Skyliner, had crashed head-on into Table Rock Mountain, some thirty miles southwest of Las Vegas. "Carole, and everybody else aboard, were killed instantly. You've got to break the news to Spence."

Tracy attended the funeral. Kate, still feuding with Gable, did not. She also told Cukor that she didn't want to be photographed publicly with Tracy.

Due in New York, Kate called Kenneth MacKenna and told him she was leaving Tracy at the Beverly Hills Hotel in a stupor. She also phoned Cukor to tell him goodbye. "The Hepburn/Tracy affair is officially over. There's nothing I can do with him. John Ford went back to his wife. Why can't Spencer Tracy?"

Cukor's only comment was, "I noticed you gave yourself star billing in the Hepburn/Tracy affair."

***

Philip Barry told the press that "once again I've created a play with Katharine Hepburn in mind." That was an understatement. In his early drafts of *Without Love*, Kate herself was written on every page. Barry knew that without her name on the billboard, he had little chance of scoring a hit with his latest play.

Robert Sinclair, who had directed Kate in the stage version of *The Philadelphia Story,* had signed on as director. When he could find nobody else, Sinclair suggested to Kate that she consider a minor actor, Elliott Nugent, a blond, balding player sometimes called "a Charles Atlas reject." Nugent, seven years older than Kate, was a director, actor, screenwriter, and playwright—"and not any good at either of those professions," Sinclair later remarked when he had a chance to actually work with Nugent.

Interviewing Nugent over tea at her Turtle Bay townhouse, to which she'd invited Laura Harding, Kate was put off by Nugent's effeminate mannerisms. He put on his most smiling face for her, trying to conceal the fact that he was a manic depressive who virtually could not face the morning without several shots of whiskey.

"Insanity must have come over me," Kate told Sinclair a few weeks later. "I agreed to accept Nugent in the part. The man has no sex appeal. I think he's a homosexual."

Sinclair assured her that Nugent was married. "Like all other homosexuals," was Kate's response.

On their first day of rehearsals, the blandly debonair Nugent, with whiskey on his breath, had to act out a kissing scene with Kate. In the scene, Nugent stuck his tongue down Kate's throat. She backed away. "Maybe you're not gay after all," she told him in front of the cast. "Do you always deep-throat your female co-stars?" she asked him. "To get into the part, I do," he said. "Oh, what the hell," she said. "Let's get on with it."

In *Without Love*, Kate plays an attractive widow, Jamie Rowan, who allows Pat Jamieson, an Irish politician as played by Nugent, to share her large house in Washington, D.C. because of the wartime room shortage. For appearance's sake, Kate's character of Jamie proposes a "platonic" marriage, to which

Nugent's character agrees. The conclusion of the plot is predictable. The "without love" policy goes out of the marriage and is replaced by a real romance.

Right before the opening night of the road show at the McCarter Theatre in Princeton, New Jersey, on March 5, 1942, Kate received a call from Cukor. He warned her that Tracy was still drinking heavily in her absence. Even more ominously, he told her that their mutual friend was mixing bottles of whiskey with heavy dosages of barbiturates.

Nervous and agitated, Kate faced her first audience who'd bought tickets for *Without Love.* Because of her incredible fame, she was met with thunderous applause. "I think they were clapping for *The Philadelphia Story,*" Kate told Sinclair when the curtain came down. "Not this play."

"My wardrobe was better than I was in the play," Kate later recalled as she played to audiences in Providence and Cleveland. "The costumes by Valentina were hot-diggity." At one point Kate appeared on stage in silk pajamas dyed a flaming scarlet.

As the road show continued, Kate claimed that Barry never got the script right. As she called for more revisions, she could find no one who could be the play's doctor. When Kanin showed up to catch the play in Washington, D.C., she asked him what to do. "You and Nugent should change parts." Furious at his flippancy, she never spoke to him for another one and a half years.

It didn't help when he sent flowers backstage the next day to apologize. He enclosed a card in which he likened his flowers to the shape of "Queen Mab's Clitoris." Kate was not amused and continued her policy of having "no more to do with that vulgar rat."

As the road show continued, Kate discovered that Nugent was an even bigger alcoholic than Tracy. Night after night he went on stage half drunk. When she chastised him, he said, "I'm trying to make up for my lack of sexual charm as you so bluntly noted. Liquor makes me feel sexy." Amazingly, the Theatre Guild didn't fire Nugent.

To make up for his deficiency as an actor, Kate started to "overplay it," in the words of Lawrence Langner of the Guild. "She was trying to bring enough vitality to the stage for both of them."

Heading for an opening in her hometown of Hartford, Kate called her father. "There is some good news. I'm doing better box office business than Gargantua the Gorilla. But he's getting better reviews." The gorilla was traveling as part of a circus act, playing the same cities as Kate's *Without Love.*

***

Without warning, Tracy showed up drunk on the night of May 11, 1942, at the Nixon Theatre in Pittsburgh. He had checked into a different hotel from Kate's so as to "fool the wolf hounds of the press." Nonetheless, a reporter from the Pittsburgh press spotted him. Tracy, in a slurred voice, claimed that he wanted to catch a performance of *Without Love* in case Louis B. Mayer acquired the movie rights.

Backstage and unhappy about her performance that evening, Kate was further distressed to see Tracy drunk again. In her dressing room, she made black coffee and tried to sober him up.

When he was more or less coherent, he told her that *Without Love*, "in spite of all your fine acting," faced insurmountable odds. He strongly advised against taking the show to Broadway. "You'll be clobbered by the critics. Dump this turkey as soon as you can get out of it, and tell that Barry faggot to stick a dildo up his ass."

Later that night in a shared bed at Kate's hotel, Tracy begged her to forgive him "for my many failures." As she later told Patricia Peardon, Tracy won her heart again when he revealed to her that deep down "there is a fine man inside me if only I would let him come out."

"Poor Kate," said Lawrence Langner of the Guild. "She has to play to a drunken actor every night, Mr. Nugent, and now one backstage, Mr. Tracy."

Tracy had met with Mayer before coming East, and he told Kate that the MGM mogul was eager to star them as a team in another comedy. "He sees us as another Walter Pidgeon and Greer Garson, Mickey Rooney and Judy Garland, or William Powell and Myrna Loy. "Is Greer Garson the only female named you haven't slept with?" Kate asked. "Or have you made it with 'that other redhead' too?" He didn't answer her.

Even though Mayer was promoting their joint return in an MGM comedy, Kate was bitterly disappointed that Mayer had no script for them. Instead, Tracy brought along a script called *A Guy Named Joe*, a war story about a dead pilot who returns to earth. "I've got a great part in it," he told her. "And the woman's role?" she asked. "Is it right for me?" He told her that Mayer had already signed a contract to cast Irene Dunne in it, Kate's old rival from her RKO days.

Tracy said that he'd run into Ginger Rogers the other night. "With Rogers, that must have been a full head-on collision," she said sarcastically. "Ginger has made this discovery," Tracy said. "Van Johnson. He's a dancer. I've met him. He'd blond and sexy—just what the teenagers go for. He's got a boyish appeal that Tyrone Power and Errol Flynn never had."

"I'm sure that you, Miss Dunne, and that dynamic sexball, Van Johnson, will have a gay old time making this film," she said.

She told him that Cecil B. DeMille had originally offered her the starring role in *Reap the Wind*. "I was to play the part of a Southern belle pursued by both John Wayne and Ray Milland. At the last minute, DeMille pulled the plug on me the way Selznick did with Scarlett O'Hara. The role went to Paulette Goddard, Chaplin's whore. I've never met the bitch but I know that if I ever do I won't be able to stand her."

"I met Paulette the other night, and she's a really great kid," Tracy said. "You'll like her. She's divorcing Chaplin."

"Anderson Lawler told me that she'd never actually married the Little Tramp," Kate said. "Do you know when Selznick signed her, he intended to give her the role of Scarlett O'Hara?"

"I know nothing of the Miss Scarlett wars," he said. "But I do know that I told Paulette how to reach you. She desperately wants to talk to you."

"I can't imagine why."

The next morning in Pittsburgh, Kate kept Tracy away from the bottle to tell him about the latest script she'd received. Donald Ogden Stewart, fresh from his success in adapting *The Philadelphia Story*, had sent her the first draft of a play. It was based on I.A.R. Wylie's chilling Gothic thriller, *Keeper of the Flame.* Kate told Tracy that the screenplay eerily evoked Orson Welles' *Citizen Kane.* She claimed that she'd already talked to George Cukor who was eager to direct it.

Instead of Mayer's hoped-for Tracy and Hepburn comedy, *Keeper of the Flame* was heavy drama. It depicted the dangers of the Hitlerite fascist movement penetrating the United States. In some misguided way, Kate felt that she'd be helping the war effort, and keeping her promise to Eleanor Roosevelt, if she appeared in this anti-fascist film.

She told Tracy that her friend, Patricia Peardon, was urging her to do it. Peardon at the time was conducting a secret affair with Nelson Rockefeller, and she claimed that he frequently spoke of his own fears of possible Nazi excursions into America. At the time, Rockefeller was Roosevelt's Inter-American Affairs Chief.

Tracy read the screenplay and liked it, because he had a strong, meaty part. He'd play the role of a journalist, Steven O'Malley, a well-known correspondent back from Europe, who meets Kate's character of Christine Forrest, the widow of Robert V. Forrest, an American national hero said to have been loosely modeled on Charles Lindbergh. Tracy exposes her late husband as a "star-spangled fascist," and Kate for trying to protect his real identity from the American public.

After their Pittsburgh reunion, Kate agreed to return to Tracy when she got back to Hollywood. He had to go back at once to the West Coast to make *Torilla Flat,* with his old flame, Hedy Lamarr.

Kate disapproved of Tracy working with Lamarr again, and had plenty to say to her stage director, Sinclair. "Louis B. has cast an Austrian Nazi, Miss Hedy Lamarr, to play one of John Steinbeck's Mexican half-breeds in *Tortilla Flat* with Spencer. Mayer has obviously lost his mind."

***

Kate had never played her home town of Hartford. As *Without Love* limped through Wilmington, Delaware, and went on to Philadelphia and Boston, Kate prepared for her opening night in Hartford on April 28. All tickets had been sold out at the cavernous Bushnell Memorial Hall, which seated three-thousand five-hundred patrons. Touchy and on the edge, Kate arrived at the theater wondering if Nugent would go on drunk that night. She was also very irritable and unapproachable before facing hometown critics.

Theresa Helburn and Lawrence Langner of the Guild had urged Kate to cooperate with the local press, but she refused. When a photographer "came out of nowhere," as she later said, and snapped her picture, she became violently upset. She lunged toward the photographer, attacking him in her rage. She grabbed the camera from his hands and crushed it with her booted feet. Not stopping there, she recklessly clawed both sides of his face, causing a rush of blood to his cheeks.

A local policeman intervened and pulled "the tigress" (the cop's words) off the hapless cameraman.

Dr. Hepburn was summoned and treated the cameraman for surface wounds. He also agreed to pay him two-thousand dollars if he would not bring a lawsuit against his daughter—and, also, he promised to purchase an even better camera for him. The photographer agreed.

Dr. Hepburn even said he would pose for a picture with his wife, Kit, and his famous daughter after the curtain call. Even though Kate protested that she wouldn't do it, her father's will prevailed.

The next morning, Paulette Goddard called Kate at her family home, using the private number Tracy had given her.

Unknown to Kate at the time, the Motion Picture Costumers Local #705 had announced to the press that it would no longer be using rubber "falsies" on some of its "less endowed female stars." In the future, the union claimed, it would let the rubber go to the war effort and would start using fabric falsies on such stars as Paulette Goddard, Katharine Hepburn, Betty Hutton, and Hedy Lamarr. Goddard was enraged, urging Kate to join with Lamarr and Hutton in a law suit against the union. Kate politely listened to Goddard's rantings, then rudely slammed down the phone.

***

In New York, during her reunion with Luddy, Kate received a jolt. He served her with papers. In a divorce court in Hartford, he was suing her for desertion. When she protested that she'd already divorced him in the Yucatán, he claimed that his attorney feared that that divorce might not be recognized by U.S. courts.

"But what about Jack?" Kate demanded to know. "Where's Jack? I've got to talk to him."

"For me, Jack doesn't exist anymore," he told her. "I don't want you or

Laura to ever contact him again."

"Oh, I don't know about that..." She was hesitant, bewildered. "He's a good friend. But it's your choice, of course...oh, well."

Kate did not show up in court, but her father was there to testify that she was indeed a resident of Connecticut. It was only after he'd granted the divorce that Judge Patrick O'Sullivan learned that one Katharine H. Ludlow was indeed the famous screen star, Katharine Hepburn.

O'Sullivan seemed angered that he'd been misled. "Had I known who was getting a divorce, I would have demanded a court appearance from Miss Hepburn herself, even though I'm not terribly fond of her films."

Five days after the decree was granted, Luddy on September 18, 1942, applied for a marriage license. He told Kate he was marrying Elizabeth K. Albers, a young woman from Boston who was only twenty-four years old.

"Are you in love with her?" Kate asked.

"What does that matter?" he asked. "What matters is that I lead a normal life like I always intended to, even when we got married. I lost my way but have found it again."

"I *see*."

Back in Hollywood, Kate told her friends, "After practically living with us for years, Jack just disappeared from the radar screen one day."

She and Laura were never to learn of his whereabouts—or his eventual death.

His leaving left a sad vacuum in each of their hearts, and both women spoke lovingly of Jack for years.

As for Luddy, Kate would remain his "true friend" for the rest of his life. His death in 1979 from prostate cancer caused her great grief. "I never stopped loving him," she told Laura. "We just weren't meant to be man and wife."

***

While filming *Tortilla Flat*, Tracy took a suite at the Beverly Hills Hotel where he was to lodge until the end of the war.

Anderson Lawler had a close friend, Ralph Bladgeon, who worked as a grip on *Tortilla Flat*. Kate wanted to know what was happening on the set, and Lawler placed almost daily calls to her with all the latest gossip.

He claimed that Tracy, feeling miscast, was drinking more heavily than he'd ever been known to do while making a picture. "With all that alcohol, he's consuming chloral hydrate and all that good stuff."

Lawler said the picture had to be shut down for three days when Lamarr walked out. The blowup had come in a scene between Tracy and her. He had shouted at her in front of the cast. "You can't act, bitch, and you never could. All you're good at is giving great head!" Reduced to tears, Lamarr fled the set. Only the intervention of Louis B. Mayer had forced Lamarr to report back to work.

Lawler also claimed that the director, Victor Fleming, was still fighting Tracy over who, other than husband Petter Lindstrom, had "conjugal rights to visit Ingrid."

The next day, Lawler said that Tracy had become a sloppy drunk on the set, but somehow, with his great acting skill, managed to make himself camera ready when needed. "He's telling Victor Fleming and anyone who will listen that you have betrayed him."

"How in hell have I betrayed the bastard?" Kate asked.

Lawler told her that Tracy had been telling people that his wife, Louise, had been willing to give up her career and everything else in her life to become his wife and tend to his needs. "But then he says that when his deaf son, John, came along, followed by their daughter, Susie, that Louise turned from him," Lawler told her. "Tracy says that's why he runs off with other women. He never mentions other men, of course. I understand that he demands that a woman give up everything for him and concentrate only on his needs."

"That I will never do," Kate said.

"In front of several crew members," Lawler claimed, "Fleming told Tracy: 'If that is what you require, then you'd better drop Lamarr, Kate Hepburn, and our dear Miss Ingrid. Those cunts only know one word in the dictionary. That's *Me.*'"

On a sardonic note, Kate in years to come would entitle her tell-nothing autobiography *Me.*

"Fleming also told Tracy that you had failed to save another married drunk, John Ford," Lawler said to Kate. "He asked Tracy, 'What makes you think Hepburn can save an old drunk like you?'"

"What's he doing while I'm away?" Kate asked, perhaps not wanting to hear the answer.

"He's taken up with a woman I know quite well, having shared Gary Cooper with her," Lawler told Kate. "Paulette Goddard herself."

***

Back in Hollywood to film *Keeper of the Flame* with Tracy, the last of her real glamour girl roles, Kate continued to juggle the old "beaus" in her life and still found plenty of time, not only to nurse Tracy, but to carry on her friendship and love affair with Claudette Colbert. He was perfectly aware of the affair but never commented on it, good or bad. Kate did not pry into what Tracy called his "Twilight World," and he didn't want to look too closely into hers, fearing what he might discover.

Divorced from his turbulent marriage to Margaret Sullavan, Leland Hayward was still in Kate's life, but not as a lover. He halfway managed her career, although she let him know that she was really in charge. Leland told

Cukor that his failure to persuade Kate to marry him "was the biggest mistake of my life."

George Stevens, at least by letter, had not completely gone out of Kate's life either, and he kept her informed of his war activities. John Ford sent letters not only to Kate but to John Wayne and Ward Bond. In one letter to Wayne, he wrote: "The day will one day come when Kate and I will sail into the sunset together and awake one morning to see the bright green of the Irish coast before us. No one in Hollywood will ever hear of us again." Howard Hughes confided to Cary Grant that his failure to persuade Kate to walk down the aisle "was the most painful regret of my entire life and I've had a few regrets."

Kate rented a house in Malibu far from the eyes of the press. Most nights, she would drive Tracy out to her house for dinner, cooking the meal herself, and then return him to his suite at the Beverly Hills Hotel before midnight.

The shooting of *Keeper of the Flame* was a troubled production from the beginning. For reasons known only to herself, Kate battled Cukor and the play's scenarist, Donald Ogden Stewart, over the script. Even though she'd scored with Tracy as part of a romantic couple in *Woman of the Year,* she wanted the film script to follow more closely I.A.R. Wylie's novel. In the novel, Wylie portrayed the male character of Steven O'Malley, as portrayed by Tracy, as an "impotent eunuch" who played "sad love scenes." In front of the cast, Tracy ridiculed Kate's suggestions. "What are you trying to do? Impotent eunuch! Are you trying to cut off my balls in this film? I thought you liked my balls." She walked away in embarrassment.

Tracy consistently refused to listen to Kate's objections about the script. Also in the cast, Forrest Tucker later recalled, "Every time I heard her venture an opinion, he bluntly said, 'Who in hell asked you for your two cents?'"

In his frustration, Donald Ogden Stewart, the playwright, wrote to his wife. "Hepburn is God damned determined to see that there will be no active male in the story." The author also protested against Cukor's direction. "At the insistence of Gable, David Selznick took this fairy off *Gone With the Wind* because he can't direct a picture with any guts."

Although Tracy, Stewart, and Cukor viewed it as betrayal, Kate went over their heads and appealed directly to Louis B. Mayer, who was always in a bit of awe of her, because of her star power. He listened to and agreed to many of her changes in the script, ordering screenwriter Zöe Atkins to make some uncredited revisions. For Kate, this earned Stewart's undying animosity, though he never expressed his hostility directly to her face.

Although it wasn't meant as self-parody, Kate amazingly enters a frame in a white dress carrying calla lilies. That scene not only evoked her entrance in the Broadway flop, *The Lake,* but also a scene from the play-within-a-film in *Stage Door.* Her producer, Victor Saville, disliked her performance beginning the first week. He told Cukor he found her speeches "nothing but pedantic dialogue—and oh, those grand entrances, so phony and highfalutin'. She's playing the part like a movie queen instead of an actress."

The film had a strong cast of veteran actors, including Donald Meek, Howard Da Silva, and Blanche Yurka. But Saville thought the best role in the picture was that of Orion, a wiry little cornpone taxi driver played by Percy Kilbride. Kilbride would go on to achieve screen immortality opposite Marjorie Main as Ma and Pa Kettle in *The Egg and I*, co-starring Kate's former lover, Fred MacMurray, and her present lover, Claudette Colbert.

The one cast member Cukor devoted more attention to than either Kate or Tracy was a ruggedly handsome blond-haired young actor, Forrest Tucker. Tucker could be seen disappearing into Cukor's office during the lunch break. As Kate told Tracy, "George, like every other director in Hollywood, has installed the casting couch. He used to be against that. No more."

Lawler came onto the set on a day when Tracy had no scenes. He told Kate the reason for Cukor's attraction to Forrest Tucker. "He's one of the best-endowed men in Hollywood. Gary Cooper for length, Forrest Tucker for thickness—all the queens say that."

"Oh, Andy," she said, "You're such a size queen." The term was not in vogue at the time.

It was at the same lunch that Lawler asked Kate the question that had been on his mind ever since she started going with Tracy. "At least half of Hollywood is claiming that you and Tracy have a platonic relationship. What goes? You're my best friend and I truly want to know what goes on between the sheets."

Her response did not exactly set the record straight. "Sex is a force of life. You can't deny the thrill of riding high, wide, and handsome with someone you love. With Spencer, I'm confused about what he really wants. What I'll never know is exactly what he's thinking. Who he really wants to bed. Sometimes I think it's not me at all."

***

In the middle of filming, Mayer summoned Kate to his office and asked her if she could straighten out his "troubled singing sensation," young Judy Garland. Mayer had mistakenly assumed that Kate had sobered up Tracy, which she hadn't.

Kate learned about Judy's great admiration for her, and agreed to meet with her.

In the commissary, Kate was immediately touched by the singer's desperation and her admitted dependency on amphetamines and barbiturates.

Kate's immediate advice was to get rid of all the sycophants and doctors giving Judy all her pills. She wouldn't agree to that.

Judy also confided to Kate that, "I get my heart broken every day. I love this man. I love that man. But they don't love me back." Knowing of Kate's involvement with Tracy, Judy made a very confidential confession. "You don't know this but I too dated Spencer Tracy when I was only fifteen."

"I've heard," Kate said. "Weren't you a little young?"

"Not too young to get pregnant by Spencer," Judy confessed. "Mayer arranged for me to have an abortion. I mean, the American public isn't into seeing a pregnant Dorothy dancing down the Yellow Brick Road. I started dating Tracy again when I was eighteen, but he dumped me."

Later, Kate told Mayer that Judy would require a guardian on a twenty-four hour basis. "She needs so much help. She's sweet. She's adorable. But I have my hands full with Spencer."

Kate's intimate friendship would have to wait until 1946 when her husband, Vincente Minnelli, was directing Kate in *Undercurrent.*

That night Kate warned Tracy to stay away from Judy and angrily denounced him for seducing her at the age of fifteen. Tracy did not respond, as she later told Cukor. "With you, Judy will plunge much more quickly into Hell," Kate warned Tracy.

***

In spite of Kate's guardianship, Tracy continued to drink heavily during the making of *Keeper of the Flame.* She told Kenneth MacKenna that if Tracy were out of her sight for one minute, he'd slip off to one of his watering holes such as The Shamrock. The bar, which Tracy had once destroyed, had changed owners, and new management allowed Tracy to come back.

Enlisting the services of Pat O'Brien, Kate would drive around town and locate Tracy.

"She'd take him back to the Beverly Hills Hotel," O'Brien recalled. "She'd clean him up, make him some warm milk, put some clean pajamas on him, and tuck him into bed to sober up. Sometimes the ungrateful bastard would kick her out of his bedroom and lock the door behind him."

The staff, or even fellow guests at the hotel, would be astonished to find Kate sleeping outside his doorway, waiting for a summons from Tracy. "It was the sickest relationship I'd ever heard of," O'Brien said. "I love Spence dearly but he treated her like hell. The question remains, why did this fiercely independent woman put up with this outrage from a man? To my dying day, I'll never understand why Katie subjected herself to this kind of abuse."

Kenneth MacKenna ordered Kate to stop sleeping in "that God damn hallway. First, the press might get word of it." He later said to Cukor, "I love Kate too much to think of her as a guardian to Tracy's bedroom door, listening for him to turn the lock and let her back in. Or keeping her ear cocked for any sound of mayhem coming from inside those closed doors."

Sometimes, Lawler said, when Kate felt Tracy was asleep, she would bribe one of the maids or bellhops to let her into his bedroom. "Kate told me that

Tracy often soiled himself—those were her words—and that she would have to wash and clean him up before putting him back in the bed."

It was often six o'clock in the morning before Kate could be seen going back to her rented house in Malibu.

"She'd spend the night at the Beverly Hills Hotel," Lawler said. "Then on top of everything else, she had to get to the studio after a nearly sleepless night."

When Kate's friend and fellow actress Constance Collier arrived on the set to wish Kate well, she later reported she was horrified. "In Kate, Tracy found a slave. She drove him to the studio. She was his maid, nurse, cook, and bottle-washer. Andy Lawler told me she even wipes up his shit when he dirties himself. She's his confidante and professional adviser—not to mention nurse and psychiatrist. And God forbid, perhaps his lover, too, although I have serious doubts about that. When is Tracy ever sober?"

Laura Harding came west for a few days to see Kate and issued severe warnings that Kate would destroy her future career by searching for vehicles in which only Tracy and Kate could appear. "Naturally, Tracy will get the meatier roles, and you'll be reduced to playing housewives," Laura said. Claudette Colbert issued the same dire warnings. Every stage or screen role that Kate would be offered until Tracy's death would be considered by her on the basis of how it would affect their relationship.

"She turned down many great parts to be his nursemaid," Cukor said. "Even so, a few times in the future she struck out on her own and to hell with Spence. I admired Kate most when her independent streak came back. Spence actually made some of his greatest films without her. Fans seem to remember only the good Tracy/Hepburn movies. They made a disaster here and there, and certainly *Keeper of the Flame*, which I directed, leads the list."

Even though known as "a woman's director," Cukor cemented his bond with Tracy during the making of their ill-fated film. At that point, Lawler, who actually liked Cukor, was nonetheless calling the director "Tracy's pimp." Kate noticed that Cukor and Tracy often spent private evenings together without inviting her. She told Lawler, and he concurred, that those nights "had something to do with boys, don't they?" Lawler assured her that Cukor was known for paying the highest prices and obtaining the most beautiful male hustlers in Hollywood. "Hustlers consider him their dream date because of the hundred-dollar bills they get from Cukor in spite of his ghastly looks."

Back on the set after a night with Cukor, Tracy would never mention what he had done the previous evening.

Cukor, in spite of his fondness for Tracy and their shared interest in handsome young men, once asked Kate why she tolerated Tracy. "He is there for me," she said. "I feel I belong if not to him then with him. I want him to be happy. I fear for his safety. I want to make him comfortable. Actually, I've found my true calling in life. I like waiting on him. I like listening to him when he's sober. I like to talk to him. I like to feed him. I like to do things for him.

I fear irritating him. I know I bother him at times, and he gets really mad at me and runs elsewhere for love that I can't give him. When that love is with another woman, it's hard for me to adjust. I never felt more needed by anybody in my whole life than I have with Spencer. I know he loves me. He just doesn't know how to show it."

***

Often when Tracy wasn't with Cukor, or out drinking on his own, and when Kate was entertaining Colbert, Tracy was seen out on the town with Paulette Goddard. When Kate had come back to Hollywood, Tracy, knowing that she'd heard about his involvement with Goddard, had told her his fling with the actress was over. She knew it was a lie, just as he'd lied about his romance with Bergman being over. But she didn't challenge him.

It wasn't the gossipy Lawler but Bette Davis herself who called to report that she'd seen Tracy leaving the Hollywood Canteen with Goddard on his arm. Kate later told Cukor that Davis was a little too gleeful in reporting Tracy's indiscretion.

"As for me," Davis said, "in case you're interested, I ended up with John Garfield. That was only because Olivia de Havilland turned him down. Garfield raped me that night, and I insisted he do it again the next morning. At least the time he spent with me was denying Joan Crawford a good roll in the hay. He's fucking her too."

"Oh, Bette," was all Kate could say.

Davis may have beaten Lawler in informing Kate that her loving man was back with Goddard again, or perhaps had never left her. But Lawler called one morning to report what he called "a bombshell."

The previous evening at Ciro's, both a drunken Tracy and a drunken Goddard had arrived. "At one point in the evening, Goddard went under the table between Tracy's legs and was down there for at least twenty minutes," Lawler claimed. "It was obvious, certainly to judge from the expression on Tracy's face, that the bitch was performing fellatio on him. You know how fond our boy is of oral sex."

The Tracy/Goddard fellatio scene at Ciro's in time became a Hollywood legend, although some sources claimed that Goddard was performing her specialty on Anatole Litvak, the director who'd been married to Miriam Hopkins. In 1975 when Warren Beatty was filming *Shampoo*, he incorporated this fellatio scene into his movie.

The next week Lawler called her with even more startling news. "You'll never believe this," Lawler said. "I went to bed with Paulette Goddard last night myself. Up to now, the only woman I've ever fucked was Kay Francis, who is more lez inclined. I must have been really crazy. The only way I got through it was to imagine Gary Cooper naked."

404

To make matters even worse, Lawler told her that Goddard was worried about Tracy, fearing that he was getting only three hours of sleep a night because of his insomnia. "To quote her directly," Lawler said, "she told me 'between his heavy drinking and his lack of sleep, I feel Spence might lose his fucking mind—that is, if the hooch doesn't do him in first.'"

There was more. Lawler also told Kate that he'd run into Ginger Rogers and that she, too, had expressed much of the same concern as Goddard had about Tracy.

"The next time you see Miss Goddard and Miss Rogers, tell each of them to stick a milk bottle up her ass." Kate put down the phone and didn't accept Lawler's calls for at least another week, when she decided to forgive him.

***

Cukor finally ordered the final cut on *Keeper of the Flame* before going off to war himself. Shot by her husband's secretary to prevent her from exposing the dead man's fascist past, Kate dies as Tracy looks on. In the character of Christine Forrest, Kate urges Tracy to follow through with his revelations. In her best Bryn Mawr diction, she tells him, "Write your story. Don't spare Robert. Don't spare me." In subsequent releases, her dying speech was shortened.

It was *THE END* except it wasn't. There was the critical reaction and the poor box office. The first came from Louis B. Mayer, attending the opening of the picture at Radio City Music Hall in Manhattan. Seeing the film for the first time, he realized that the character of the fascist, Kate's late husband in the film, was too close to his dear friend, William Randolph Hearst, who had been accused of fascist leanings. In a rage, Mayer stormed out of Radio City Music Hall.

Fans, expecting another Tracy/Hepburn comedy, were severely disappointed. "Instead of an effervescent romantic comedy, we get all mucky guck and Gothic melodramatic," claimed critic Justin Hale. "Hepburn comes off as stiff, arty, and unconvincing. If any acting honors are to be awarded, they should go to Tracy who carries the film. Don't shell out your hard-earned twenty-five cents for this flop."

Kate was even accused of having too much concern for her cheekbones. One critic wrote, "She seems to be suffering from *Garbo-itis*, possibly because William Daniels, Garbo's favorite cameraman, photographed *Keeper of the Flame*. It's a classic case of one woman's glamour being another woman's poison."

Time magazine found it "a high point of significant failure" for Tracy and Hepburn.

Cukor himself later dismissed the film he himself had directed. "It was as artificial as the fake fir forests we used on the sound stage. The thunderstorms were created in the MGM prop room. The *faux* mansion was just that—didn't look real at all. The story line was pure hokey-pokey. Kate's part was just plain phony. She looked like something from Madame Tussaud's Waxworks."

Amazingly, her friendship with Cukor survived that critical blast.

***

Disappointed with *Keeper of the Flame*, Kate faced a dreadful showdown with the Theatre Guild. According to her contract, she was supposed to open *Without Love* on Broadway, even though Philip Barry had not conquered the play's main challenge of blending politics and romance. Tracy threatened that if Kate returned to New York, "I'll drown myself in booze."

To avoid calls from Theresa Helburn and Lawrence Langner from the Theatre Guild, Kate changed her telephone number several times. To Helburn's urgent wires, Kate responded in the form of a letter delivered through standard three-cent mail. In her letter, she stated her position, claiming she could not take the play to Broadway, and urging the Guild to find another female star. "Call Helen Hayes," Kate advised. "To go back to Broadway at this time and commit myself for a sixteen-week run would mean abandoning the man I love. That I can't do. Will not. *Cannot.* To do so would destroy me and Spencer too."

Getting no satisfaction, Theresa Helburn journeyed to Hollywood for a showdown with Kate held over tea at the Château Élysée. When her face-to-face meeting went badly, Helburn threatened to sue Kate. Even so, Kate refused to change her mind. "Spencer needs me at his side." When anger flared between the two of them, Kate threatened to retire not only from the stage but the screen as well.

"Come on, come on, dearest Kate," was Helburn's reasoned response to this bravura outburst of temperament.

At the end of their tense negotiation, Kate finally agreed to open *Without Love* on Broadway. Tracy promised to follow her to New York in ten days with his brother, Carroll Tracy. Both of them would check into the Waldorf-Astoria, a few blocks from Kate's Turtle Bay residence.

Kate went on to agree that Tracy could, every evening, come over for one of her home-cooked dinners after the curtain fell on *Without Love.*

Sometimes when Tracy drank too much, which was most of the time, he spoke of what a great woman his wife, Louise, was. He praised her for all the fine work she was doing to help deaf children, including their son John. Sometimes his self-flagellation about what a bad husband he was would continue into the early hours of the morning as Kate fell asleep on a sofa by her fireplace listening to him rant.

He did tell her a startling bit of casting information. Before filming *Dr. Jekyll and Mr. Hyde*, he had urged Mayer to cast Kate both as Jekyll's virginal fiancée and also the whore in the part. Mayer refused, wanting the roles to be divided between Ingrid Bergman and Lana Turner.

"Cast me as a whore?" Kate asked in astonishment. "I don't think I've played a whore before."

When Kate reported the news to Laura the next day, she was angered. "He wants to bring you down to his own level which is the gutter. He might play priests on the screen, but he is hardly one. He wants to cast you as his cheap mistress. If I were you, I'd pack my bags and leave. Since you're already home, kick him out instead."

Kate cried but could not take Laura's advice.

When Kate could not tolerate Tracy any more, and when her disappointment at the bad critical reception of *Without Love* disturbed her, she'd often take her car and drive around the wilds of Connecticut. She told fellow cast member Audrey Christie that she would just scream "until my throat is raw." In those days, primal scream therapy was not known.

Without Love had opened on Broadway at the St. James Theatre on November 10, 1942. In spite of the critics, including the "butcher of Broadway," Brooks Atkinson of *The New York Times*, the play did fairly good business for its one-hundred and thirteen performances, based on the star power of Katharine Hepburn's name.

Kate was anxious to get back to Hollywood and so was her co-star, the still insipid Elliott Nugent. He told her that he was going to the West Coast to direct *The Crystal Pal*. "Two of your Hollywood pals have passed on it," Nugent said. "Charles Boyer and Ginger Rogers. But Ray Milland accepted. Guess who's going to play the female lead?"

"Well, you've already told me that Rogers rejected it, so I must assume it's Paulette Goddard."

"It is!" Nugent said. "But of all the female stars in Hollywood, how did you come up with Paulette Goddard?"

"I guess I'm just lucky," she said, walking away from Nugent whose liquor-soggy breath evoked the hot air coming out of Tracy.

When Tracy wasn't with Kate, he often got into trouble. One night he went to the most glamorous night club in Manhattan, The Rainbow Room, on the sixty-fifth floor of Rockefeller Center. With its panoramic view, no other club epitomized the glamour of New York in the Forties.

Before his arrival at the bar, Tracy had consumed a powerful dose of the amphetamine Dexedrine, a drug that was very similar to what later became known as speed, hoping to combat his constantly occurring depressions. Carroll Tracy claimed that it "only made Spencer's sleepless nights more sleepless."

Carroll said he tried to intervene with Kate to get Tracy off the drug, but she refused, claiming that she'd checked with her father, and he said that it was all right for Tracy to take the drug. In fairness to Kate and Dr. Hepburn, the medical community at the time was not aware of how potentially damaging this drug's side effects could be.

At one point at the Rainbow Room, Tracy and his brother were already into their fourth round of drinks when a wounded soldier, William F. Perkins, of Clinton, Georgia, approached Tracy and tapped him on the shoulder. Tracy was Perkins' favorite actor, and the discharged soldier, still in uniform, wanted his autograph. Without even looking to see who it was, Tracy whirled around and delivered a devastating blow into the face of the soldier. He was knocked unconscious on the floor. Management called an ambulance and rushed the wounded man to a hospital, where it was discovered that he had a broken nose.

Back in Hollywood, Howard Strickling, publicity director for MGM, reached a long arm across the continent and managed to have MGM's New York offices keep the incident out of the paper. Much later, Strickling said, "If this had made frontpage headlines, it might have ruined Tracy's career. I could just see the headlines. DRAFT-DODGING TRACY K.O.'S WOUNDED G.I. To compound matters, the poor kid had just had his left leg amputated three months previously."

***

During the run of the play, Kate took time out for the war effort to film, without pay, *Stage Door Canteen*. A Sol Lesser production, it was shot in Manhattan and made for United Artists by the American Theatre Wing.

Staffed by volunteers, the real Stage Door Canteen, which provided the inspiration for the film, operated out of the basement of the 44th Street Theatre.

No fewer than sixty-five major stars, including Kate, contributed their talents to the production, hoping to boast morale among servicemen and women. Kate found herself playing opposite Cheryl Walker, a twenty-two-year old former Hollywood extra who had once been a stand-in for Claudette Colbert.

Stage Door Canteen marked the film debut of Katharine Cornell, who recited a scene from one of her biggest hits, *Romeo and Juliet*.

Other cast members included Tallulah Bankhead who warmly greeted Kate with, "I'd kiss you, dah-ling, but I'm just getting over the clap. *Again*." George Raft showed up and offered to take Kate back to his apartment and show her "my blacksnake." She declined. Even Tarzan (Johnny Weissmuller) offered her his studly services after the show. She turned him down, too, but accepted the offer from Gypsy Rose Lee to go with Alfred Lunt and Lynn Fontanne to see her famous strip act.

Kate shed tears of joy when the final curtain came down on *Without Love*. She vowed she'd never appear on the stage again, and for eight years held herself to that promise.

Tracy was heading back to Hollywood to film *A Guy Named Joe* with Van Johnson and Irene Dunne.

Kate, too, had signed to do another movie for MGM, which later turned out

408

to be one of the most disastrous career choices of her life.

Louis B. Mayer told her she'd have to "suck in your cheeks and slant your eyes" in her next film. Kate, after coming back big in *The Philadelphia Story* and *Woman of the Year*, had agreed to play a Chinese girl, Jade, in her next film, *Dragon Seed.*

It would lead to worldwide ridicule.

CHAPTER SIXTEEN

Kate knew that her designation as Jade Tan, a young Chinese girl, in the film adaptation of Pearl S. Buck's best selling novel, *Dragon Seed*, was absurd casting. But she told Tracy "it's my way of aiding the war effort," playing an enlightened peasant girl who dreams of "a New China" in the face of the Japanese invasion of her homeland. "Better that than a dead pilot who returns to earth." She was referring to Tracy's film, *A Guy Named Joe.*

In 1944, Louis B. Mayer was forging ahead with plans for *Dragon Seed,* wanting it to equal the success of the screen adaptation of *The Good Earth* in 1937, which had brought an Oscar to Luise Rainer. At first Mayer had considered casting Rainer again but a string of bad movies, following her win of two Oscars, had seriously dimmed her star power.

Then Mayer—at least in the words of *Dragon Seed* director, Jack Conway—"went insane with his casting." Mayer suggested Hedy Lamarr for the role of Jade but was talked out of it. Then he recommended his favorite red-haired Britisher, Greer Garson, for the role. "Mayer must have been drunk when he called me to cast Judy Garland as Jade," Conway later recalled. "I talked him out of that. I was the one who first suggested Katharine Hepburn. Our makeup artist, Jack Dawn, convinced me that because of the structure of Hepburn's face, with her cheekbones, that he could make her up convincingly as Jade. Even so, I was shocked when Hepburn actually accepted the role."

Other Caucasian actors were considered, including some whom Kate had worked with before: Fay Bainter, Donald Crisp, and her former lover, Van Heflin. Even Walter Pidgeon and Edward G. Robinson were recommended.

Mayer demanded "box office names" to ensure the success of the film. He also wanted to avoid "scenes of miscegenation"—that is, having Caucasian actors appear on the screen married to Orientals.

Conway couldn't round up enough Chinese Americans—thousands of them were involved in the war effort—so he selected "other racial groups" —his words—that included Filipinos and Mexicans for the minor roles, walk-ons, or extras. Chinese-American actors or Caucasians were selected to play the villainous Japanese invaders.

Even before the movie was shot, critics such as James Agee were ridiculing the casting of "such distinguished Chinese as Walter Huston, Aline MacMahon, Akim Tamiroff, Agnes Moorehead, and Turhan Bey." Amazingly, Agee didn't mention Kate on his list.

He saved his attack on Kate until he'd actually seen the movie. He wrote that it was hard for him to describe "how awful silly she looked in her shrewdly tailored Peck and Peckish pajamas."

Of the thirty-three actors with speaking roles, "only three actors were Oriental," Conway claimed.

The director said he had a problem distinguishing Japanese from Chinese. "All yellow men look alike to me. As for the women, I could never tell the difference between a Shanghai whore or a Tokyo Rose."

Once again, Kate was united with her old producer at RKO. Pandro S. Berman was now working for Louis B. Mayer. Berman told Kate that he was being besieged with calls from supporters of Chinese Nationalists and the Communists, both sides wanting to see their insignia on the uniforms of the Chinese battling the Japanese invaders. To solve the problem, Berman ordered that all badges and insignia be removed from the actors playing Chinese soldiers.

He also warned Kate that Jack Conway was suffering from tuberculosis and might not make it through the film.

Pearl Buck herself claimed that sections of California's San Fernando Valley closely evoked the Chinese countryside. At a cost of two million dollars, Berman ordered that a kind of Chinese Disneyland be created in the valley. The MGM production crew installed pipelines to flood the valley, creating rice paddies (actually barley was planted). Farms and even entire villages were erected and painted in the most minute detail. Kate was fascinated by all this, and showed up on location as the sets were being constructed. Before the film was shot, she was protesting to Berman that she, along with Wei F. Hsueh, should receive co-credit as technical adviser.

Whether true or not, the set decorator, Edwin B. Willis, reported that Kate often appeared early in the morning "with hammer in hand" to help construct the sets. Also receiving unwanted advice from Kate was the art director, Cedric Gibbons.

Whether she was needed or not, Kate insisted on driving every day to the location on a fifty-acre tract at Calabasas in the San Fernando Valley, a thirty-six mile run from Los Angeles.

Before the cameras rolled, Kate told Laura Harding that, "I know more about China, its history and its culture, than any expert in this country." She'd read everything about China she could.

Based on her recently acquired knowledge, she demanded that Berman call in Marguerite Roberts to rework the original script as conceived by Jane Murfin, who had proved such a disappointment to Kate in the ill-conceived 1934 film, *Spitfire.*

Because of his ill health, Kate befriended her director, Jack Conway, and helped "shoulder him from some of the stress of production," as she put it. Halfway through the film, however, Conway collapsed in her arms, and she ordered the crew to summon an ambulance.

412

He was off the picture. Berman replaced him with Harold Bucquet, and *Dragon Seed* ended up listing two directors in the credits. At first Kate was hostile to Bucquet, but she ended up liking him later. She requested that Mayer allow him to direct Tracy and her when they teamed once again in *Without Love.*

Ultimately, *Dragon Seed* would cost more than three-million dollars, "an outrageous budget," as Mayer put it.

One morning as Kate walked into Berman's office, she was astonished to see Jane Loring sitting behind the producer's desk.

***

One would loved to have had a voice recording to hear what Kate and her old flame had to say at their reunion. Kate quickly learned that Berman had hired Loring as his assistant on the film and not in her usual capacity as editor.

When members of the crew observed Loring and Kate on the set, they noted that Kate was cordial with her former lover but not overly friendly.

Art director Cedric Gibbons said, "I knew both women well, and I detected a slight chill in the air even when the sun was at noonday. In my opinion, Loring wanted to resume the relationship but Kate didn't seem willing. I guess you can't go back into an old love affair. Besides, Kate had Tracy to care for, and that was taking up every evening of her life." What Gibbons didn't know at the time was that Tracy also had Paulette Goddard and Kate had Claudette Colbert.

Ironically, the two lady loves in the lives of Hepburn and Tracy were co-starring together in the 1943 film, *So Proudly We Hailed.* At least two—sometimes three—nights a week, Kate listened patiently and even eagerly to Colbert's attacks on Paulette Goddard. Kate was still intensely jealous of Goddard's involvement with Tracy.

Colbert arrived at Kate's house one night holding a copy of *The Hollywood Reporter.* In an interview, Goddard said that she much preferred working with Veronica Lake, the third star of the film, "because Veronica and I are so much closer in age."

Colbert was born in 1903. Actually Goddard was born in 1905 so she wasn't that much older than Colbert. Lake wasn't born until 1919.

Colbert claimed that the picture was out of control, and that she was practically having to direct the film herself. "With Mark Sandrich in charge, what do you expect?" Kate asked. She still harbored bitter memories from having clashed with Sandrich when he directed *A Woman Rebels* in 1936.

Unknown to either Colbert or Kate at the time, Sandrich was dying and was no longer capable of supplying the energy he did when he directed Astaire and Rogers musicals.

In Miami, years later, Veronica Lake reported that there "was a constant cat-fight between Colbert and Goddard during the filming of *So Proudly We Hailed.*

"Before shooting began, I was supposed to be the bitch in the cast but Goddard and Colbert took those honors from me," Lake claimed. "Colbert was at Goddard's throat every minute, and Goddard fought back like a tigress. Even though she'd finally left Chaplin for Burgess Meredith, Goddard was still called 'Chaplin's whore' by Colbert. Goddard referred to Colbert as 'Marlene's lez girl friend.'" At the time, Goddard was unaware of Kate's romance with Colbert.

Goddard's hatred for Colbert remained strong for the rest of her life. The officers of the Lincoln Center Film Society in New York called Goddard in April of 1984, inviting her to be one of the hosts for a tribute to the long film career of Claudette Colbert. The staff at Lincoln Center was not aware of Goddard's long-time animosity toward Colbert, and wanted her to appear because she'd co-starred with Colbert in the famous World War II movie. After listening to their invitation, Goddard shouted back into the phone, "Tell that French dwarf to go fuck herself, which I'm sure she does regularly." She slammed down the phone.

One night when *So Proudly We Hailed* was still being shot, Colbert arrived at Kate's house with some startling news.

Veronica Lake had told Colbert that she'd heard it from Goddard herself—Tracy planned to dump Kate, divorce his wife, Louise, and marry Goddard, providing that Burgess Meredith could be shoved out of the picture.

Kate told Colbert that she didn't believe that. "I hear Miss Lake, with her peekaboo haircut, is actually insane," Kate said. "She must have been to have told you that. I happen to know who Spencer is in love with—and it's definitely not Paulette Goddard. Some women think that when a man uses them as a cheap piece of tail that that man is in love with them. Surely you know differently. Besides, I happen to know who Spencer *is* really in love with."

"You mean yourself, of course?" Colbert asked.

"Hell no!" Kate shouted. "He's in love with that teen idol Van Johnson."

***

Only that afternoon, Kate had received an angry phone call from her former rival at RKO, Irene Dunne, who was co-starring with Tracy in *A Guy Named Joe,* with Van Johnson playing the lead supporting role. Dunne got right to the point, as Kate later recalled to her former boss, Pandro Berman.

"I can't work with your soggy Irish drunkard," Dunne told Kate. "He needles me day and night. First, he attacks my wardrobe, then the way I wear my hair. He even makes fun of my bustline. He accuses me of being a Jew because of my longish nose. He told me this morning I can't satisfy a man in bed. He calls me and Cary Grant 'Hollywood's two pansies.' If you don't warn Tracy to stop this, I swear I'm going to Louis B. Mayer in the morning and tell him I'm off the picture."

414

Kate listened in silence. When Dunne stopped her ranting, Kate said, "I'll see what I can do."

Before ringing off, Dunne delivered her zinger. "Not only that, but that homosexual fool you live with is madly in love with Van Johnson. He follows Van around the set like a lovesick puppy."

At night, Kate saw more and more evidence that Dunne might be right. Tracy had even placed a glossy studio photograph of a beaming Johnson by his bedside.

Beginning with Van Johnson, Tracy began a series of unrequited crushes he'd develop on handsome leading men in pictures.

Cukor had told him that these men were unobtainable, and Tracy instinctively knew that. If Tracy wanted a young man like Van Johnson, he'd have to rent a hustler actor who resembled him. There is no evidence, however, that Tracy ever approached Johnson and made his desires known.

Having rushed prematurely into middle age, Tracy was graying at the temples and had a paunch. His face was often bloated. Although he could still attract women—and would do so for years to come—he found that in the body-conscious male homosexual world, he was viewed as a "john," which Cukor had to explain to him meant a paying customer.

Cukor later said that "Spencer constantly suffered from these crushes on handsome leading men, and used his lack of satisfaction in love as an excuse to continue his heavy drinking. He was definitely not Van's type, and Spencer would have embarrassed both of them had he pressed sex onto Van. I'm almost certain that Johnson would have turned him down."

Instead of with sex, Tracy expressed his love for Johnson by showing extreme loyalty at the sake of his own career.

Johnson was a great admirer of the acting style of Tracy and admitted to the film's director, Victor Fleming, that he was "sweating gumdrops" at the prospect of playing scenes with the more gifted older actor.

Two weeks into shooting of *A Guy Named Joe,* Johnson was driving with his longtime companion, Keenan Wynn, Evie Wynn (Keenan's wife at the time), and two servicemen—described as "extraordinarily handsome"—to see a special screening of the Tracy/Hepburn film, *Keeper of the Flame.*

Johnson had just steered his DeSoto convertible into the junction of Clarington Street and Venice Boulevard when another vehicle sped through a red light and crashed into their car, sending it rolling over.

Johnson's head stuck in the clamp in the middle of the windshield frame that locked the convertible hood when it was raised. Thrown to the curb, Johnson fractured his skull and suffered mammoth injuries to his face because of the shattering glass.

As later reported by the hospital, "practically the back of his head was peeled off. Fragments of bone had pierced his brain." Not only that, but an artery in his neck had been severed.

A Los Angeles policeman, Roger Flynn, rushed to the scene of the accident which had occurred in that city. However, he noticed that Johnson's body had been tossed across the municipal border into Culver City. The policeman told a hysterical Keenan Wynn that he could not come to Johnson's aid because he was outside of his jurisdiction. For forty-five minutes, Johnson lay bleeding to death until a Culver City ambulance could be summoned. He lost three quarts of blood.

At Hollywood Presbyterian Hospital, a surgeon closed up the bleeding artery and virtually sewed Johnson's scalp back on, before beginning the very delicate work of coping with the cavity in the once handsome actor's skull.

Glenn Clover, a hospital attendant, who saw Johnson wheeled in, later told the press that "he was almost decapitated."

Louis B. Mayer was called and told that Johnson was dead on arrival at the hospital.

On hearing the news, a grief-stricken Tracy rushed to the hospital and offered to give his own blood for the massive transfusions Johnson required.

As Johnson lay near death, Tracy met with both Louis B. Mayer and the director, Victor Fleming. Tracy was told that they were contacting both Peter Lawford and John Hodiak as potential replacements for Johnson.

At that point, Tracy became enraged and started screaming denunciations at both Fleming and Mayer.

Tracy threatened to walk off the picture. Amazingly, even though Mayer had briefly considered replacing Tracy himself, the mogul agreed to shut down the picture until Johnson recuperated. "*If,*" as Fleming said, "he recovers."

While Johnson was in a hospital bed, undergoing a series of painful and difficult operations, Tracy visited him almost daily, bringing flowers, candies, fruit, or books to read.

Kate confided her growing concern about Tracy's obsession with Johnson to both Anderson Lawler and Kenneth MacKenna. "Spencer is consumed with interest in Van's health. He talks about him day and night. If I try to divert him to another subject, he lashes out at me. Naturally, he uses Van's accident to drink even more heavily than before."

The accident occurred on March 30, 1943, and Johnson returned to the studio on June 28, against his doctor's orders. Tracy was by his side during the rest of the shoot, and came in to oversee the intricate makeup needed to make Johnson ready for the camera by concealing a deep gash in his skull and other scar tissue. When Johnson developed severe headaches in the afternoon, Tracy was at his side, with medication, in the same way that Kate administered to Tracy himself. Johnson's right arm was very weak following the accident.

Ward Bond, also appearing in the film, later said that he could "see Tracy massaging Van's arm for him, helping him regain his strength." Van tired easily, and shooting the film was difficult. When Van's headaches became too severe, and he grew weak and dizzy, Tracy would often demand that Fleming

416

shut down the picture. "As I wrote John Ford, Tracy was like a lioness protecting its cub," Bond recalled.

The film brought major stardom to Johnson, as wartime audiences flocked to see it. Johnson for decades thanked Tracy for believing in him and standing by him.

Other joint ventures for the two actors loomed in their future.

In a phone call to Laura Harding, Kate said, "Instead of Tracy/Hepburn movies, you're soon going to hear of Tracy/Johnson films."

***

In 1944, Jack Conway introduced Kate to her co-star, Turhan Bey, playing her husband, Lao Er, in *Dragon Seed*. Born in Vienna, he was of Turkish and Czech parentage. He became the leading purveyor of exotic foreigners in films of the Forties.

That night, Kate told Tracy and others that she was not impressed with Bey. She dismissed the star "as an actor in all those idiotic desert epics made over at Universal. A poor man's Valentino."

Bey was known as a ladies' man, but his male charm didn't impress Kate. Other glamorous women, however, succumbed to his exotic flash.

One day when Kate and Pandro Berman were watching rushes from *Dragon Seed*, Lana Turner arrived unannounced in the projection room. After the screening, Berman told Kate that the blonde-haired beauty often came to see the rushes of handsome leading men. If Turner liked what she saw on screen, she would call the actors for a date.

Kate had to wait until 1948 to learn about the conclusion of the Turhan Bey/Lana Turner romance. Kate had packed a picnic lunch and was taking it to Tracy on the set of MGM's *Cass Timberlane*, which co-starred Lana Turner. Encountering the star once again, Kate asked, "And, so, how did your romance with Turhan Bey turn out?"

Turner looked at her squarely and said, "I got the God damn clap!" With no further words to Kate, Turner walked on.

Kate found herself working once again with Aline MacMahon, one of the stars she'd played with at the Berkshire Playhouse in 1931. Kate "gave it my all" in playing Jade, hoping to win an Oscar like Luise Rainer did for *The Good Earth*. However, it was MacMahon who eventually won an Oscar nomination for playing Kate's forlorn Chinese mother. Kate told Berman that MacMahon "tried to infuse this silly movie with some dignity."

Kate also worked with Agnes Moorehead in *Dragon Seed*. Kate was familiar with Moorehead's work and respected her talent, claiming "Agnes can play anything from an intimidating mother to a spinster aunt." Moorehead had appeared as the mother in *Citizen Kane* in her 1941 movie debut, and Kate had admired Moorehead's performance in 1942 when she'd been nominated for best supporting actress for her portrayal of a spinster in Orson Welles' *Magnificent Ambersons.*

At one point Moorehead spoke to Kate and Jane Loring about how she objected to the labels applied to lesbians. She detested the word "dyke" and felt that "Sapphic" would be an improvement over "female homosexual. I feel women can have lesbian feelings without being homosexual," Moorehead told the two startled women. "Love should not have a sex."

"Give me time to ponder that," Kate said before walking away.

Kate was prepared to like Moorehead at the beginning of the shoot, but was avoiding her by the end of the filming, the co-director, Harold Bucquet, later claimed. "Moorehead fell hopelessly in love with Kate, but Kate did not feel the same way. This led to a certain tension on the set."

Colbert later reported that Moorehead also "developed a wild crush on me" when the two actresses were cast in the 1944 *Since You Went Away* for Selznick-United Artists.

The set one day was buzzing with news that Tracy was going to appear the next afternoon for lunch. He wanted to see Kate shoot a scene in which she prepares a ceremonial banquet for the Japanese, applying a generous amount of poison to their food to wipe out the invaders.

When Tracy showed up on the set, Kate herself had not seen him for five days. Nor could she locate him, even with Pat O'Brien's help. Anderson Lawler had told Kate that Tracy's romance with Goddard was officially over. "Goddard has been fucking my horse-dicked former boyfriend, Mr. Gary Cooper, hoping to get him to use his influence to get her cast in *For Whom the Bell Tolls.*"

Along with the ballerina, Vera Zorina, who also wanted a role in *For Whom the Bell Tolls,* Goddard lost out to another one of Tracy's girl friends, Ingrid Bergman, who had dumped Humphrey Bogart at the end of the shoot of *Casablanca.*

When Tracy came onto the set, he gave Kate no explanation as to where he'd been. He even had few words for veteran actor, Walter Huston, co-starring with Kate in the film. As director Bucquet later recalled, "Tracy had eyes only for the handsome young actor in the cast, Hurd Hatfield, much to Kate's annoyance."

Only the most insiderish people in Hollywood at the time knew about Tracy's fondness for extremely handsome, but unobtainable, young men. "Tall, blond, blue-eyed and well-built like Van Johnson, Hatfield was definitely Tracy's type," Bucquet said.

Making his screen debut in *Dragon Seed*, Hatfield was lean, smooth, and rather austere looking. He was in awe of both Tracy and Kate.

His makeup made him look somewhat more convincingly Chinese than the rest of the cast.

Years later he recalled that making *Dragon Seed* was a "personal night-

418

mare." In one scene he had to ride a buffalo while playing a flute. "I'd never even been on the back of a horse before. There stood the Oscar-winning Miss Katharine Hepburn watching me make a fool out of myself."

Hatfield claimed he was well aware that Tracy wanted to date him. "I respected him greatly as an actor but not as a potential bed partner," Hatfield recalled. "He was too old and not handsome enough for me. Errol Flynn, Robert Taylor, and Tyrone Power could make my heart flutter in those days, but certainly not those two pals, George Cukor and Spencer Tracy."

"In fact," Hatfield added, "I think I had the same taste in men as Tracy himself—Van Johnson for instance. Tracy gave me his phone number and asked me to call him, but I never did. In my heart, I just knew I could never get it up for Tracy, big box office star or not. All my life I've pursued male beauties, and Tracy didn't qualify. Back in those days, I wouldn't have gone to bed with Clark Gable either, even if he had asked me."

Not only did Hatfield reject Tracy, he infuriated Kate the next day by failing to muffle a snicker when she was forced to deliver this incredible line: "I don't want my baby teethed on Japanese bullets."

She didn't speak to him for the rest of the picture. However, her attitude softened the next year after Hatfield won the coveted role as the star of Oscar Wilde's *The Picture of Dorian Gray*. Hatfield claimed that he was "absolutely stunned" when Kate suddenly appeared on the set in the middle of the shoot.

"She came right up to me in front of the cast and crew and said, 'I hear you're marvelous in the part. Just splendid. Is that the truth?'"

Hatfield claimed that he was so stunned by her sudden appearance and her question that he had no ready answer for her. "When she saw how flustered I was, she said, 'Don't let me frighten you. I fly around on my broomstick only at night.'"

She invited him for tea in the commissary, and he joined her. "Over tea she poured her heart out to me. She said Tracy was in a bad way and drinking heavily," Hatfield said. "She claimed she was desperate to provide some joy in Tracy's life. 'Since he admires you so,' she told me, 'could you come over and see him one night? It would make him so happy.' Then she reached into her purse and gave me his private phone number, which Tracy himself had already given me. I never called. I was tempted to go by and see him, because I did admire him as an actor, but I was afraid he would proposition me and that I would only insult him by turning him down."

This is the only known incident where Kate was believed to have actually "pimped" for Tracy, the way their mutual friend Cukor did.

Near the end of Hatfield's career, Kate told her confidants that Hurd Hatfield is "only perfectly cast when he plays sex deviates."

***

Kate was so disappointed at the poor reception of *Dragon Seed* that she began to harass Tracy instead of him needling her.

Cue magazine found it "hard to accept Katharine Hepburn's New England twang and sharply Anglo-Saxon features" in the role of Jade. *Time* magazine labeled the film a "kind of slant-eyed *North Star*," a reference to a movie in which Kate's co-star in *Dragon Seed*, Walter Huston, had appeared.

The New York Post reviewer found that Kate's "memorable timbre defies all attempts at disguises," and yet another reviewer found Kate's interpretation of Jade "about as Chinese as Mary Queen of Scots."

Even its producer delivered a harsh judgment. Pandro Berman later said, "The film was laughably ill-conceived. What was Louis B. thinking?"

Once again Kate found her career, after two flare-ups, hurtling back to earth.

As Tracy continued to drink, her attacks on him became more pronounced. She couldn't criticize him for infidelity, lest he remind her of her ongoing affairs with Colbert in the West and Laura Harding in the East.

She began attacking him for drinking so heavily that he was not physically fit to serve in the military. She pointed out that such actors as James Stewart and Henry Fonda had enlisted. "Probably so they could sleep in the same bunk," Tracy quipped.

She pointed out that her former lover, John Ford, was in the military and that even Tyrone Power had joined. "Why did Howard Hughes let his boy do that?" Tracy shot back.

She noted that both Robert Montgomery and Garson Kanin were in the service—"even George Cukor."

"Homosexuals in the military," Tracy said. "We should write Roosevelt to do something about that."

"You're one to talk!" Kate said accusingly. "If gays aren't allowed in the military, that would leave you out."

Tracy was startled. As Kate later told Anderson Lawler, "That was the first time I had ever confronted him about his homosexuality. He went absolutely stark raving mad. I had touched a real sore point."

Kate claimed that Tracy struck her several times and knocked her down to the floor, causing bleeding. She told Lawler that she had run from him to escape his violence. Lawler said that he wasn't surprised. He knew that Tracy had beat up on women before, especially whores. "He's beaten up so many whores and so violently that there is no bordello that will take him in," Lawler wrote to Cukor. "It was just a matter of time before he turned on Kate. He's no longer sleeping with her—at least that's what she told me—but he's taken to striking her instead. I urged her to leave him. Amazingly, she went back to Mr. Hyde the very next day, nursing her bruises."

Actually, Lawler misstated the case. Kate did go back to Tracy. But in the wake of his violent attack on her, he disappeared. He was gone for about two weeks. Later she learned that he'd checked himself into the Hotel St. George on Clark Street in Brooklyn. It was discovered that he'd purchased two cases of Irish whiskey, then locked the door and put up the *do not disturb* sign. He'd then stripped off his clothes and had gotten into the bathtub where he'd remained for ten days and nights before emerging back into life again.

When Tracy finally arrived back in Hollywood, Kate was ready to end the relationship. He pleaded with her to keep him in her life, claiming that he had "irreparable heart damage," along with his failing kidneys and liver. He told her that a doctor in New York had informed him that he might have only months to live.

Feeling sympathy for him, Kate took him back. Even though she felt he was a "hopeless hypochondriac," as she described Tracy to her father, she felt he was still an ill man.

"There are serious ailments there but he also complains endlessly," Kate told her father. "If he gets the slightest headache or stomach upset, he views it as the onset of a heart attack or the beginning of cancer. The smallest physical upset can trigger another drinking binge."

"If you want my professional advice as a doctor, I'd say leave the bastard," Dr. Hepburn told her.

Even though it had set off a violent outrage in Tracy, Kate continued to glorify the exploits and heroic feats of others, such as John Ford, in the U.S. Navy. She talked constantly about Ford being one of the sixteen American B-25 medium-range bombers, commanded by Lt. Col. James H. Doolittle, who had raided Japanese military installations as a "pay back" for their surprise attack on Pearl Harbor. "She tried to keep him from drinking, yet was goading him to drink even more," Kenneth MacKenna later told George Cukor. "It was like she was fighting to save him yet driving him to drink at the same time."

Tracy's depression deepened when he reluctantly agreed to accompany Kate to the Hollywood Legion Stadium. There, hostile soldiers cat-called at him, yelling out the he was "chicken," "a coward," or a "shirker," for not being in the military.

Even though he'd just gotten back from a binge in Brooklyn, Tracy went on another drunken rampage almost immediately. Kate virtually had to strap him into bed again to get him sober. She kept him at her house until he had stopped drinking, and she felt that it was safe for him to go back to the Beverly Hills Hotel.

She drove over every morning to have breakfast with him. One Saturday morning they encountered Mary Ford, who was at the hotel to give a speech to a women's aid group.

Ignoring Kate completely, Mary told Tracy that John Ford had been wounded at the Battle of Midway. "Even with shrapnel wounds in Jack's body, he managed to film the Japanese attack." She looked at Tracy with contempt. "If there's one thing I can't stand, it's a God damn draft-dodger like you. Here you are safely ensconced in Hollywood at this luxury hotel, running around with this New England dyke and countless other women. Chasing tail while other men like Jack are risking their lives every day. You're not a real man at all."

Kate later told Kenneth MacKenna that in the wake of Mary's attack, she feared for Tracy's life. "I practically have to guard him day and night. He's threatening suicide."

Still, Kate continued to nag Tracy. When he started to play war heroes in movies, she would remind him that "Clark Gable, that shithead friend of yours, is flying dangerous missions over Germany. Hitler has a price on his head, promising to reward any Luftwaffe pilot who shoots Gable—or better yet—brings him to Hitler alive. What is Spencer Tracy doing? A war hero only in films. And all that's a fantasy—just make believe."

Lawler later claimed that Tracy once again bashed Kate's face in. He said that both MacKenna and himself had gotten a doctor to look at Kate's bruises. "We stood guard at her house that night in case Tracy came over in a drunken rage and tried to kill her."

Kenneth said that the very next day Kate was back at Tracy's side. "It became more than her friends could take. We loved her dearly. Hated Tracy."

As if inviting another bashing, Kate continued to ridicule Tracy for not doing enough for the war effort. To pacify her, he agreed to narrate Garson Kanin's documentary, *Ring of Steel*. Kate even got Tracy to volunteer to wash dishes at the Hollywood Canteen. But, even after he was doing that, she continued to mock him. "A dishwasher for the war effort!"

Finally, she got Tracy to agree to go on tour overseas to entertain the troops. Kate called Kanin and told her of Tracy's pledge, and asked Kanin to make all the necessary arrangements.

Before he was scheduled to leave California for New York, from whose port he would embark for overseas, Tracy again disappeared. Kate could find him nowhere. No one at his usual haunts, including The Shamrock, had seen him in days.

A mysterious letter arrived three weeks later with an anonymous tip. Tracy, the letter claimed, was in a mental ward in Chicago violently suffering from DTs. Kate immediately tracked him down and asked the hospital where he was a patient to hold him until she got to Chicago.

Rushing to Chicago, Kate confronted a defeated, beaten down old man, who had sobered up but under brutal conditions. She learned that he'd been given electrical shock treatments.

Because of her famous face and name, she got the hospital to release him in her custody, as if she were his wife, Louise.

On the train back West, and under heavy questioning, Tracy said he honestly couldn't remember how he got to Chicago.

***

Back in Hollywood, Tracy was making far more movies than Kate. He played a German anti-fascist in *The Seventh Cross*, produced by Pandro Berman and directed by Fred Zinnemann. Tracy's co-star was Signe Hasso, a popular Swedish actress of the early Forties. Hasso denied rumors that she'd had a brief affair with Tracy. "I didn't want the old drunk within twenty feet of me, much less in my bed."

Audiences would have a hard time accepting such an all American as Tracy playing a German.

Tracy's other co-stars in *The Seventh Cross* included the first-class acting team of Hume Cronyn and Jessica Tandy, who would later become close friends of both Kate and Tracy. "Tracy was getting through the filming of the movie with only two or three hours sleep, and was in a foul mood," Cronyn said. "When Kate came by one morning to check up on him, he was extremely abusive. He treated her with utter contempt and at one point he even accused me of wanting to go to bed with her."

Tracy was united in his next film, *Thirty Seconds Over Tokyo*, with his favorite, Van Johnson. Tracy got star billing in his role as Lt. Col. James H. Doolittle, but the fair-haired boy, Johnson, not fully recovered from his car crash, was clearly the star of the film.

Bobby-soxers adored Johnson, but the press nagged him about why there was no woman in his life. The actor's pat response was, "After making love all day in front of the camera, I haven't enough energy to keep it up at night." When he heard that, Tracy cackled. "I have trouble keeping it up at night myself."

Even though married to his wife, Evie, Keenan was spending most of his free time with Van Johnson. Rumors were rampant at the time about a *ménage á trois*, with Wynn depicted as Johnson's faithful pal and Evie as Johnson's "nurse" and confidante.

Since the object of Tracy's desire seemed fully occupied every night with Mr. and Mrs. Wynn, Tracy turned his attention to a young actor, Robert Walker, a handsome, rather soft-spoken man. He had met and married Jennifer Jones in 1939. But by the time he met Tracy, Walker's marriage was coming unglued. David Selznick, a much more powerful and alluring figure than Walker, had fallen for Jennifer Jones. Walker was drinking heavily throughout the filming of *Thirty Seconds Over Tokyo*. As Tracy told Fred Zinnemann, "Robert is more fucked up in the head than I am."

Walker and Tracy became instant drinking pals. "I knew he was gay but I had no problem with that," Walker later claimed. "He made a pass or two but I easily deflected them. If I were a homosexual—and I'm definitely not, as half the women in Hollywood can testify—I'd go for Robert Mitchum, not for an old goat like Tracy."

Walker was referring to another handsome young newcomer in Holywood.

Mitchum was appearing in a minor role in *Thirty Seconds Over Tokyo*, and would soon be co-starring with Kate in *Undercurrent.*

Both Tracy and Robert Walker remained drunk during most of the filming," said screenwriter Dalton Trumbo, who in the years ahead would be famously blacklisted.

***

Although not successful as a play, *Without Love* was purchased by Louis B. Mayer to star Kate. She persuaded Tracy to take the male lead. Lawrence Weingarten, the producer, told Mayer that the screenwriter, Donald Ogden Stewart, would iron out the problems with Philip Barry's script as he had done before with *The Philadelphia Story*. "Before we're through with this one," Weingarten predicted, "*Without Love* will attract larger audiences than the Philly thing." Since George Cukor was not available to direct, Kate recommended Harold Bucquet with whom she'd developed a good relationship during the ill-conceived *Dragon Seed.*

Instead of the Irish politician that Elliott Negent had played in the stage play, Tracy's role would be that of Pat Jamieson, a scientist. When Barry read Stewart's script, he went into a rage and kept Kate on the phone for almost an hour, screaming invectives into her ear. Nonetheless, in 1945, Weingarten ordered shooting to begin since *Without Love* did not have to have the original playwright's blessing.

In the film, as in the play, Kate, playing a rich widow, proposes a platonic marriage to Tracy's character. He accepts because he mistrusts romantic relationships. They are wed and predictably manage to fall in love, turning *Without Love* into *With Love*. Tracy plays a scientist who is trying to develop a new helmet for pilots who engage in high altitude flying, and Kate becomes his assistant.

Kate gave her blessing to the casting of the two supporting players, Keenan Wynn and Lucille Ball. When she encountered Wynn—not with Van Johnson this time—he told Kate that he specialized in failed Broadway productions.

"Fifteen flops in eight years," Wynn told her. He noted that she and Tracy had seen several of them and had come backstage on Broadway to greet the cast. "I think by the fifth flop, you guys had begun to recognize me. Oh, I remember you saying, 'the young character actor. You should be in films.' Well, here I am. In a film with the both of you."

"With your kind of luck, I know our picture will be a flop too," she said. "Mr. Jinx. At least I'll know who to blame."

Lucille Ball, whom Kate hadn't seen since she'd appeared with her in *Stage Door*, arrived on the set on the first date of shooting. It was in the afternoon. That morning, she told Kate, she'd filed for divorce from Desi Arnaz in the Domestic Relations Court in Santa Monica. "I told the judge it was mental cruelty," Lucille informed Kate. "But it's really his womanizing. How do you put up with Tracy screwing around?"

"Mr. Tracy is my dear friend," Kate rather coolly informed Ball. "He and I are not a sexual couple." At that time in her relationship with Tracy, Kate might have been speaking the truth.

During the shooting of *Without Love*, Kate was rather cold and distant to Ball until the actress fainted on the set. In those days, Ball experienced frequent fainting spells because of arrhythmia stemming from an adolescent heart ailment. Always the doctor, Kate rushed to her aid and opened a very tight blouse Ball wore so she could get more air.

Ball quickly recovered and was startled to find Kate fumbling with her blouse. Quick on the draw, Ball said, "Now you know. Mine are no bigger than yours. But when I was starving in New York, I once posed topless."

Standing up and slightly embarrassed, Kate countered, "And so did I. And I wasn't even starving."

Lucille Ball shone in her supporting role. She told the director, Bucquet, "Like E.F. Hutton, when Katie speaks, you listen—that is if you're smart. She even lectured me on how to brush my teeth properly and how to shell a pea. I don't think I had ever shelled a pea in my life." She seemed to regard Kate's authoritarian streak with an air of bemusement.

Almost from the beginning of filming, Kate took over, even objecting to the cushions used on the sofa in her living room in the film. The set decorator, Edwin B. Willis, threatened to quit several times during production. At one point, he told her, "Just looking at a photograph of you makes me tired."

Harold Bucquet found that the stars virtually directed themselves and wanted no interference from him. "All I had to do was tell them when I was ready to start the scene and to call 'Cut.'"

During the shooting, Bucquet called Kate into his office. It is not known exactly what her reaction was, but her director told her that he had been diagnosed as having cancer. A rigid Christian Scientist, he said that he had refused operations of any kind. She was told that it was doubtful if he would live for the duration of the shoot.

Kate hadn't learned much from Tracy's understated acting style in *Without Love*. Her highly mannered acting was as pronounced as ever, and to make matters worse, Donald Ogden Stewart inserted the phrase "By Gum!" into the script far too many times for believability.

Marion Herwood Keyes, the costumer, attired Kate in far too many polka dots and ostrich feathers, and should have assigned those floppy leghorn hats to Hedda Hopper instead. Arch, and playing the role rather girlishly, Kate comes across like a New England spinster. For the first time on screen, she became conscious of "my bad neck." She would spend the rest of her life covering that neck with scarves and high collars or even more disconcertingly, clutching at her throat.

When it opened, *Without Love* was a box office success, although, unlike *Holiday* and *Bringing Up Baby*, it has not withstood the test of time. Today it's regarded as the weakest of the Tracy/Hepburn comedies.

In revenues, *Without Love* fell far short of *Woman of the Year* but was a vast improvement over revenues generated by *Keeper of the Flame*. *Without Love* firmly established Tracy and Hepburn as a romantic team in the eyes of the movie-going public.

The film received only lukewarm reviews. Eileen Creelman of the *New York Sun*, always highly critical of Kate, found that *Without Love* "still seems like a waste of a fine actor's time." She was referring to Tracy. On the other hand, she claimed "Miss Hepburn caricatures her part." On one bit of casting, all the critics agreed: Lucille Ball and Keenan Wynn had launched themselves into major careers.

When filming on *Without Love* ended, rumors spread that the Tracy/Hepburn love affair had come to an end as well. She was seen nowhere, but he appeared at several nightclubs, drinking heavily. Instead of the big name stars he was often seen with, he began to show up at clubs with beautiful and very young starlets on his arm.

The Hollywood rumor mill went to work, and *Variety* reported that "Spencer Tracy and Katharine Hepburn were feuding. Their latest co-starring vehicle, *Without Love*, is aptly named." The columnist, Hedda Hopper, Kate's lifetime enemy, reported: "Katharine Hepburn's romance with a famous star is a thing of the past, though she won't admit it."

***

There is still a mystery surrounding Tracy's surprise visit to the White House in early April of 1945, just as World War II was entering its final stages. Even though Kate had enjoyed a well-publicized friendship with the Roosevelts, she had not been specifically invited. Despite that, she flew with Tracy to Washington anyway. In advance of his arrival, Tracy wired his acceptance of this strange and mysterious meeting with F.D.R.

While Tracy was escorted into the White House to meet with the President, Kate waited impatiently for an hour until he came outside again and got into the back seat of her limousine. As she told her friend, Patricia Peardon, also in Washington at the time, "Spencer was trembling and told me he needed a drink."

He claimed that the President told Tracy that he wanted him to make a morale-boosting tour overseas to entertain the troops.

As Tracy related to Kate, he said he told the President that he would try to entertain them, but that he thought "the boys really want to see Betty Grable— not me. I can, however, do a pretty good rendition of 'Pistol Packin' Mama.' A bit hammy, though." Tracy claimed that the President had laughed at that quip.

426

"Entertain the troops?" Kate said. "What's so secret about that?"

Tracy told her that the entertainment of the troops would actually be the beard for a covert mission FDR wanted to send him on. "I'm to be called back to the White House in two weeks. FDR is to give me a top secret message of the most vital importance. At that time, I'll be told who I have to deliver the message to, the when and where. But I won't be told what's in the message."

Tracy claimed that he had agreed to carry out the secret mission, and Kate was impressed and even thrilled with the espionage of it all.

A few days later, both Kate and Tracy were back in Hollywood when news came over the radio of the death of President Roosevelt of a hemorrhage in Warm Springs, Georgia, on April 12, 1945.

Tracy was never to learn what secret mission Roosevelt wanted him to perform. "He was haunted by it for years," Kate told Laura.

Both Tracy and Kate listened on the radio to playwright Robert Sherwood's moving tribute to the President which was broadcast around the world. Sherwood—standing six foot eight inches tall and called a "nine foot tower of gloom" by Noël Coward—had been a trusted confidant of Roosevelt. The winner of four Pulitzer Prizes, Sherwood often wrote speeches for FDR and had directed the overseas operations for the Office of War Information. Both Kate and Tracy had seen some of Sherwood's best plays, including *Waterloo Bridge, Idiot's Delight, Abe Lincoln in Illinois,* and *The Petrified Forest*, which had brought fame to the struggling actor, Humphrey Bogart.

Four weeks later, Kate and Tracy were amazed when he received a copy of a play, *The Rugged Path*, the first script penned by Sherwood in five years. Both Tracy and Kate read the play.

It dealt with a famous reporter fired for his antifascist articles. He then becomes a cook on a Navy destroyer and ends up getting killed in action.

Both of these skilled actors knew the weakness of the play, but they were eager for Tracy to star in it, Kate having more enthusiasm for his return to the stage than he did.

Tracy finally agreed to wire Sherwood his acceptance but only after Kate had promised to put her own career on hold and accompany him on his pre-Broadway tour. Without hesitation, she claimed that she'd do just that.

Kate headed East first in June of 1945, wanting to spend time with her family and to have a reunion with Laura Harding in New Jersey. Tracy, accompanied by his brother, Carroll, followed ten days later. It was announced to the press that Tracy would be returning to the stage after an absence of fifteen years.

After a week had gone by, Kate called Garson Kanin, recently discharged from the Army, and invited him to her Turtle Bay Manhattan residence for dinner. "I have decided to forgive him for his sin," she told Laura. Kate, of course, knew that she had to make peace with Kanin because Sherwood had selected him as the director of *The Rugged Path*.

Kate had her reunion with Kanin, and the two old comrades became fast friends once again. Shortly thereafter, she accompanied Kanin to the Waldorf Astoria for a reunion and reconciliation dinner with Tracy, where Kanin and Tracy renewed their friendship as well. Tracy's brother Carroll was also at the meal.

The rehearsals for *The Rugged Path* were a disaster, rivaling scenes from Kate's own pre-Broadway opening of *The Lake.*

In his affectionate memoir, *Tracy and Hepburn*, Kanin years from the date would write that Tracy was "imaginative, resourceful, and malleable" throughout the play.

Refuting her husband, and right in front of him, Ruth Gordon, at a dinner party in New York, claimed, "like hell Spencer was! He was nothing of the sort. Garson was just being kind to an old friend. Every night Garson came home in a rage and told me that Spencer was a God damn son-of-a-bitch and how he wanted to charge up on that stage countless times and heat him to a pulp."

Kanin told his wife, Ruth Gordon, and others, "it's impossible to work with Spencer. He absolutely refuses to take directions."

Off the booze for the first time in months, Tracy during rehearsals kept developing intense sweats. He started to vomit, once right on the stage. Kate stood by him, reminding him that she'd often thrown up before curtain time. "It's the actor's malady," she told him. "Totally expected since you haven't faced a live audience in so long."

During rehearsals with Tracy, Kanin later admitted that "my nerves collapsed. I was completely demoralized. When I caught Kate directing one of my actresses, Martha Sleeper, taking over my job, I screamed at Kate and denounced her like I've never denounced anyone in my life. I even called her a cunt. I later apologized, and she seemed to forgive me. I was coming unglued and she knew it. But compared to Spencer, I was the fucking Rock of Gibraltar. He appeared so strong and steadfast on the screen. But off the screen, he was a total mess. Although I liked him personally, he was the sickest person I have ever worked with in show business, and I've known Judy Garland, Errol Flynn, John Barrymore, and Frances Farmer."

Overhearing his attack on Kate, Tracy rushed to her defense. He plowed his fist into Kanin's face. Kanin ran from Tracy's presence and locked himself in a dressing room. In front of the rest of the cast, Tracy ran up to the door and tried to kick it in until the stage manager restrained him. In his memoir, Kanin left out the details of this violent incident.

Laura Harding attended every performance, telling her friends she was doing it to show her support for Kate and not because of Tracy. Laura claimed that as the show headed for its first trial opening in Providence, Rhode Island, the company was completely demoralized.

Patricia Peardon, who had sat in on several rehearsals, agreed with Laura. "The director and its star were hardly speaking, and Kate was being tested to her limits. Not one of her own stage appearances, including *The Lake,* had

428

caused her as much grief as Sherwood's *The Rugged Path*. The worst was yet to come."

***

When a break came in rehearsals, Kate drove Tracy to Fenwick to meet her family. He later commented on his impression of the Hepburns to Garson Kanin during rehearsals of *The Rugged Path*. "Talk, talk, talk, nonstop!" Tracy said. "I heard about statehood for Puerto Rico. Why abortions should be legalized. There was talk of the poor, the homeless, the hungry. Certainly I heard much about the downtrodden Negroes. Kate fitted right in. Madame Do-Gooder. She'll donate money for the committee to protect fireflies from getting trapped in Mason jars. She'll march in parades to protect the civil rights of child molesters. And, get this, the Hepburn clan members are bigger fruitcakes than she is. And I mean cakes that contain a lot of nuts, some of which can't be identified by botanists. The doctor believes in all the ultra-liberal causes, and Mama spends all her time trying to help Margaret Sanger protect young gals who are knocked up. But I found dust on the mantelpiece. She's out parading for abortions but can't even oversee dusting in her own living room. And I'm allergic to dust. They're basically hypocrites. In fact, when a poor old bum came onto their property, Dr. Hepburn chased the fool off with a shotgun."

After Tracy had gone, the Hepburn family review of him was equally as bad. "We just didn't like him," Kit told her friends. "First off, he's a married man. He should be back in California spending time with his wife who is helping all those deaf children. He should be with his own family. Another thing, he's an old Irish drunk. And Catholic. Don't forget that."

Dr. Hepburn claimed that he'd warned his daughter about going with married men, especially married men who were Catholics. "They have a system of beliefs—dictated by the Pope—that I find appalling. I also hear that Tracy is one of the biggest womanizers in Hollywood. Not only that. But a man prone to violence and, when crossed, one of the nastiest human beings that there is. He doesn't like to listen to debates of any kind, and he thinks he's found a slave in my daughter. I'm disappointed in Kate for hitching up with a man like Spencer Tracy. Why, he even plays tennis at Hyannis Port with that fascist, Joseph Kennedy. I also gave Tracy a physical examination in the library at Fenwick. The man was born in 1900, but he has the body of a man twenty years older. I told him if he doesn't stop drinking, he'll soon die. His kidneys, I think, are already about to go. God knows what abuse his poor liver has taken. Perhaps Kate will be attending his funeral soon and will then get on with her own life without carrying around such heavy baggage. Tracy also told me that he was impotent most of the time, so I know it's not sex that keeps her in bondage to this man."

Before the out-of-town opening of *The Rugged Path* in Providence, Rhode Island, in 1945, Tracy came down "with history's worst case of the flu."

When Kanin saw Tracy's condition before the Providence opening, he was told by Kate that he was running a temperature of one hundred and three degrees. "Spence was trembling with chills, sweating with fever, and throwing up in the wings," Kanin said. "I advised Kate to take him to the hospital. For reasons I still don't understand, since she was usually protective of Spence, she demanded that he go out there and face that audience. What could I do? Both of them had wills of steel. I ordered the stage manager to raise the curtain on time. It was one of the worst nights I remember from all my days in show business."

Kate later told Peardon that she feared if Tracy did not go on, the press would assume that he was too drunk to do so.

The out-of-town previews were a nightmare for Kate. Tracy and Kanin, though good friends, "fought like tigers" Kate told Patricia Peardon. "The bad reviews in Providence just devastated Spencer," Kate said. "Every day, sometimes three times a day, he threatens to quit."

In Boston, Tracy was still avoiding the bottle but his physical condition worsened. He entered a Boston hospital for treatment of a cold and sinus infection which came almost immediately after his recovery from the flu.

Louise Tracy, arriving from California, came to Boston to see the show. As Kate stayed locked in her hotel room, Louise took over the care and maintaining of Tracy. Kate was forced to sneak in for secretive visits when Louise had gone back to her hotel.

When doctors finally allowed Tracy to go on, "he was really too weak to perform," Peardon said. She'd come up to Boston from her summer home in Martha's Vineyard to catch the show.

After reading the bad reviews in Boston, Tracy informed Kanin that he was leaving the show. Tracy's contract allowed him to do so on a two-week notice, a generous concession to a stage star.

It was Kate who persuaded Tracy to take the show to Washington, DC, and then on to Broadway. In front of Peardon, she warned him, "if you pull out now, it will be far worse for your career than if you open on Broadway in a failure." In a cover story on Tracy in *Life* magazine, some of the behind-the-scenes conflicts of bringing *The Rugged Path* to Broadway were reported, an unusual, though not blatant, early "outing" of the Tracy/Hepburn relationship.

In Washington, in 1945, Tracy took a major political stand when he learned that the National Theatre would not permit Negroes, even if they were diplomatic representatives of foreign governments. Although called the National Theatre, it was actually owned privately and booked by the Shuberts. Negroes such as Paul Robeson or Ethel Waters could appear on the stage, but could not attend a performance.

Tracy had agreed to give a command performance for President Truman and his staff, including the Justices of the Supreme Court. When Tracy heard that wounded veterans from the nearby hospital were carefully screened as to their color, he refused to go on for the performance until that discrimination ended. Backed up forcefully by Kate, he stood his ground. "The end result was that Spencer Tracy and Katharine Hepburn almost single-handedly ended racial discrimination at the National Theatre," Kanin said.

But, in time, the battle to end segregation failed. Rather than integrating its audiences, the management of the National Theatre preferred to close it down permanently, and reopen it as a segregated movie house. When the new movie theater failed to attract an audience, the building was reconfigured yet again, this time as a legitimate theater with a nondiscrimination policy.

Kate's reaction was, "We must fight these battles one at a time until all theaters and movie houses in America end such restrictive policies."

In the summer of 1945, Tracy—but once again, not Kate—was invited to the White House for a reception given by President and Bess Truman for Robert Sherwood. Truman was hoping to sign up the playwright as a speechwriter for the articulation of some of his postwar policies. After some consideration, Sherwood turned the President down. "The man from Missouri is not my style," Sherwood later told both Kanin and Tracy.

Patricia Peardon, still involved with a member of the inner circle at the White House, also attended the Sherwood reception. "Perhaps the President and his wife didn't know of the close bond between Tracy and Kate," Peardon said. "If they did know, they may have felt that it was not proper to extend an invitation to an adulterous couple. I'm sure if Louise Tracy had been in Washington at the time, she would have been invited. Of course, Truman could have extended an invitation to Kate to come alone or with an escort."

Kanin blames President Truman for relaunching Tracy "as a boozer. The President stashed bourbon at the White House away from the bossy eyes of Bess. He invited Tracy, Sherwood, and some of the other cast members to go with him on a tour of the White House. Actually, we slipped into his private quarters, and a servant brought out the President's stash. By the time we returned to the reception, all of us, even Harry himself, was a little drunk. I'm glad he didn't have to order the dropping of any atomic bombs that day. I actually counted them. Spencer had six stiff drinks in a period of less than forty minutes."

"For the command performance in front of the President and the Justices of the Supreme Court," Kanin said, "Spence went on drunk but somehow got through the play. But the next four performances had to be cancelled while Kate struggled valiantly to sober him up so that he could complete the two-week engagement."

Kate and Tracy, accompanied by Peardon, drove north for the long dreaded

Broadway opening of *The Rugged Path*.

"Sherwood sure knew how to aptly title this play," Kate said.

***

The Rugged Path was scheduled to open on Broadway at the Plymouth Theater, an institution that retained a sentimental memory for Tracy. He'd appeared there in 1923 in a small part playing a detective in *A Royal Fandango*, which starred Ethel Barrymore. "I made a pass at Ethel," Tracy told Kanin. "The grand lady of the American theater gave me a grand slap on my face—and I can assure you it wasn't a stage slap."

At the theater, Kate again took charge as if she were the director. When Kanin came upon her, he almost didn't recognize her. She was down on her hands and knees scrubbing "this God damn filthy outhouse." She told Kanin that Tracy was staying with her at her Turtle Bay home "since I can't trust him to check into a hotel alone."

Later Kate told Peardon, "I have no life of my own. My career is in shambles. I have to look after him every minute of every day and through all his sleepless nights. Otherwise, he'll hit the bottle. What is it? Oh God what is it that's eating up Spencer's heart? He truly goes through the tortures of the damned every night of his life."

Peardon stood with Kate backstage on opening night in front of the New York's theater critics. "I thought she was the manager of a boxer," Peardon said. "Kate had thick towels stolen from the Waldorf Astoria, heavy medication, and a bottle of an unknown liquid she'd gotten from her father."

Kanin later said that Tracy got through the first act reasonably well but faltered during the rest of the play, forgetting his lines. He ad-libbed. "At one point he just seemed to be wandering aimlessly around the stage uncertain as to what to do. He moved toward the curtain to be near Kate. Concealed from the audience, she whispered his next move to him. Even so, he was a complete disaster."

Peardon recalled that the opening night audience gave him a standing ovation. "But that was because he was a bigtime movie star—not because he'd given a great performance."

Mr. and Mrs. Robert Sherwood gave a party after the show for Tracy. Tracy came with his brother, Carroll, not Kate. She showed up with Kanin and Ruth Gordon. Nervously, Kate and Tracy waited for the reviews. When they arrived at the party, they were disastrous for Sherwood but respectful of Tracy's acting skills. Tracy, gravely distressed at the reviews, even though he himself wasn't sentenced to the guillotine, left the party early. He refused all social engagements and interviews for the run of the play, which lasted another dreadfully tense ten weeks.

In spite of Kate's protestations, he started hitting the bottle again. Peardon claimed that Tracy was staggeringly drunk during his last ten performances. "I was shocked that both Kate and Garson Kanin allowed him to go on the stage in that condition. What were they thinking? I said nothing, of course. The reason I kept my friendship with Kate over the years was because I had learned to agree with her on everything."

Tracy was completely sober the night his son, John, flew into New York to see the play. "It was the high point of the show's run for Spencer," Kate told her friends. Tracy demanded that his son be seated in the front row, and Tracy slightly exaggerated his speeches so that John could read his lip movements.

The Rugged Path, one of the major disappointments in Sherwood's illustrious career, closed on January 19, 1946. It also marked the end of Tracy's career on the stage.

After the close of the play, Kate and Tracy refused to speak to Garson Kanin for another eighteen months.

***

In 1946, freed from the responsibilities associated with maneuvering Spencer Tracy through his disastrous run on Broadway, Kate, after almost a year of ignoring her own career, left him in the care of his brother Carroll in New York. Also leaving Laura Harding behind, but looking forward to a reunion with Claudette Colbert, she was returning to California for the debut of filming of *Undercurrent*, to be directed by Vincente Minnelli.

The episodes that follow go a long way toward explaining an intriguing gap in Tracy's life between the final disastrous performances of *The Rugged Path* and his mysterious resurfacing several weeks later in Hollywood.

Partly because of his fragile emotional state after the closing of *The Rugged Path*, 1946 was the first year since his signing with MGM that he did not appear in any films. In fact, he wouldn't return to the screen at all until more than a year later, when, in 1947, he would co-star with Kate in *The Sea of Grass*.

The moment Kate left town, Tracy went on one of the worst benders of his life. Two days later, in the hallway outside Tracy's suite at the Waldorf Astoria, a maid heard deranged shouting and the sounds of a violent struggle going on inside. Letting herself in with her pass key, she screamed when she saw what was happening. Tracy was attempting to throw his brother Carroll out the window. If he had succeeded, Carroll would have fallen several floors to his death.

The quick-thinking maid summoned security and struggled with Tracy until two men arrived to subdue him. In the process, Tracy struck the maid in the face, but she managed to divert him and consequently, may have saved Carroll's life.

Alert to Tracy's celebrity status, the staff at the Waldorf Astoria did not call the police, but instead managed to detain Tracy in their holding chamber until MGM officials in New York could be contacted. Within thirty minutes, five men from the MGM's New York office arrived at the hotel.

Just like in the movies, they had disguised themselves as paramedics. Tracy was put in a straitjacket and removed from the hotel on a stretcher into a waiting ambulance. If any guest of the hotel inquired, he or she was told that one of the hotel guests was suffering a heart attack.

Tracy was delivered to Doctor's Hospital on Manhattan's Upper East Side. Many celebrity patients in those days checked into this hospital because of its discretion. As Ruth Gordon once said, "It was known as a place where big names went to dry out." Today it would be likened to the Betty Ford Center.

MGM staff members persuaded the director of the hospital to register Tracy on the women's floor. The director agreed, entering Tracy under the name of "Louise S. Tracy."

It was later learned that this was the second known incident where Tracy had tried to kill his brother. In 1937, at the Beverly Wilshire hotel in Los Angeles, Tracy had also been caught trying to toss Carroll out a window.

That time, Whitey Hendrey, MGM's security chief at Culver City, had intervened and saved Carroll's life.

In a surprising coincidence, Hendrey was in New York on MGM business when the desperate call came in from the Waldorf-Astoria. It was Hendrey who once again covered up for Tracy, nimbly handling his admission into the women's ward at Doctor's Hospital.

The episode was later described by Garson Kanin to Victor Samrock, business manager of The Playwrights Company, producers of *The Rugged Path*. "Tracy had a total mental breakdown and nervous collapse," Kanin said. "He had to be kept in a straitjacket in a hospital ward." Years later, the scene would eerily evoke a similar incident that would occur in the life of a latter-day star, Marilyn Monroe.

"The guy was nuts," Kanin said. "Completely zonked-out. In outer space. Dangerous to other people and to himself. Not wanting to get killed, I avoided the hospital, although I knew he was there."

Even though Kate had virtually been designated by the Hollywood community as Tracy's official caretaker, she refused to take calls from Hendrey in New York at her new base in Los Angeles.

"Of course, she was working on *Undercurrent* and couldn't leave Hollywood unless she wanted to get sued, but I had always heard through my boss, Howard Strickling, about how Kate catered to Tracy and nursed him," Hendrey said. "But this time, when I finally talked to her on the MGM lot after I got back to Hollywood, she didn't seem interested at all. She told me that she was certain 'that Spencer has good care at the hospital, and I must wash my hands of him for the moment and get on with my life.' She didn't say that with any cruelty or venom. In some ways, she reminded me of a stern father who has kicked his child out on the street to fend for himself."

The actor, Don Taylor, who would go on to play Tracy's son-in-law in two films, *Father of the Bride* and *Father's Little Dividend*, confirmed Tracy's lock-up in the women's ward of Doctor's Hospital.

At the time of Tracy's admittance, Taylor was visiting his wife, Phyllis Avery, who was suffering from a gynecological ailment at the same hospital.

When Taylor was leaving his wife's sick room, he said he recognized several guys from the MGM publicity department, including Whitey Hendrey.

"I asked him, 'Whitey, what in hell's name are you doing in the women's ward? Knocked someone up?' Whitey told me 'to shut the fuck up.' He tried to even block my view. A group of men from MGM had surrounded a trolley which held a body. It was clearly Spencer Tracy. He was twisting and turning in a straitjacket like Harry Houdini trying to escape. As Tracy was being wheeled into a private room with a security guard at the door, Hendrey turned to me and said, 'If you want to work in Hollywood, you didn't see a God damn thing! Okay! Got that?'"

Later on, Taylor's wife, Phyllis, told him that "some asshole" managed to smuggle a bottle of Scotch to Tracy, which he consumed within less than an hour. "The word on the floor was that Tracy had gone into DTs again," Taylor said.

What caused this total breakdown which plunged Tracy into delirium tremens?

A tantalizing clue was provided by Patricia Peardon. "Before leaving New York, Kate had invited Luddy, Laura Harding, who was my own dear friend, and me to dinner at Turtle Bay. Over the course of the dinner, Kate said that she was seeing Spencer for one final time before heading back to California."

"'I've left him before,'" Peardon quoted Kate as saying. "'Then taken him back. But I deserve better in my own life. I've just been with Kit and my father. I told them I'm leaving Spencer for good this time. My father said he didn't raise his daughter to be a nursemaid to some old drunk and mop up his shit. It's not fair to me. I can't put up with it. I could do it for love. But, for reasons I can't tell any of you, I have recently found out in a very painful way that Spencer doesn't really love me.'"

Peardon said she was terribly intrigued to find out what Tracy had done to make Kate want to leave him forever.

"But when Kate didn't want to tell something, she never would," Peardon said.

The revelation that Kate had discovered about Tracy would apparently go with her to her grave.

"I was completely confused," Peardon later recalled. "To my knowledge, Kate knew the man's darkest secrets. What else was there to discover? She'd left Tracy before, but this time it seemed different. I had never seen such determination on her face. She thoroughly convinced me that night that she was going to get on with her life without all this excess baggage."

Heading back West and a new future in post-war Hollywood, Kate was on the verge of "a betrayed romance," the beginning of a new affair with a very handsome but rather sullen young actor, and the dawn of a great love with a beautiful singer who was even more emotionally disturbed than Spencer Tracy.

CHAPTER SEVENTEEN

Back in Hollywood, when Kate heard that John Ford had returned from the war, she made no attempt to call him. When she asked Ward Bond how Ford was, the actor told her that Ford had retreated, with a huge supply of Irish whiskey, to an upstairs bedroom of his house on Odin Avenue. "He plays the same Mexican revolutionary war song again and again and again, all day long," Bond said. "He must have seen me parking my car when I brought John Wayne for a visit. As we approached the front door, we felt hot liquid splattering down from above. We ran a few steps backward, and then looked up at the house. Jack, the old bastard, was pissing on us from upstairs."

"Then he's in good shape," Kate said. "At least his urinary tract is okay. My father would approve."

Bond claimed that he and Wayne weren't particularly offended by the pissing incident. Nor did they feel singled out for this liquid attack. "He routinely does that with anyone these days, male or female," Bond said.

Soon after, Ford contacted her with an offer to star in his next picture, *The Ghost and Mrs. Muir*, which would be his last film commitment to Darryl Zanuck at Fox. She carefully considered his offer, but within three weeks, after mulling it over, she wired him that she could not accept.

When the film was eventually made, Ford was not a part of its creative team. Kate's other director friend, Joseph Mankiewicz, became the director instead, casting Gene Tierney in the part originally intended for Kate. Tierney's co-star was Rex Harrison.

Upon her return to Hollywood, Kate made several attempts to contact Claudette Colbert, and was surprised when the French actress did not respond to her urgent messages.

When she invited Anderson Lawler to dinner, she asked him about Colbert's seclusion, since her gossipy friend knew everything.

"You mean, you haven't heard?" he asked her. "It's the talk of the underground. Claudette is carrying on a torrid affair with Joan Crawford. Haven't you seen the pictures of the cuddly duo that they've printed in the newspapers lately?"

"As a matter of fact, I haven't," she said.

"You were away too long," he chided her. "Beautiful actresses find other companions."

"But *Joan Crawford*? Claudette knows I detest Crawford. She's completely phony. Claudette is a dear and sensitive woman. What possible interest could she have in Crawford?"

"Some of my dearest women friends, like Kay Francis, tell me that Crawford delivers the best head in Hollywood."

Infuriated at what she felt was a betrayal, Kate smoked endless cigarettes that night, denouncing both Colbert and Crawford. "At one point," as Lawler later recalled, "she called them 'those dirty dyke bitches' and went on to ask, 'Why couldn't Claudette have taken up with some of my other favorites instead? Margaret Sullavan, Paulette Goddard, or Ginger Rogers. Anybody but Crawford!'"

Lawler remembered that Kate showed him to the door by around ten o'clock that night, saying that she wanted to retire. "She told me that she'd never speak to Claudette again."

But a few days later, when Kate called Lawler, she said that Colbert had come to her house and that they had made up.

"As painful as it was to go through, we really clarified our relationship," Kate told him. "Claudette made it abundantly clear that our time together was just that! When she was with me, she was with me, and when she wasn't with me, she was a free agent, involving herself with whatever man or woman she chose."

"She is, after all, a married woman, and you are bonded with Tracy, Laura Harding, and perhaps one or two others as well," he reminded her.

"You're exactly right! So is Claudette. I can be a selfish pig about these matters. I know that what's good for the goose is good for the gander. But I always thought I was the goose with a roving eye who always expected the gander to be true to me. I've come to realize how ridiculous and impossible I can be about this. But if I want my friendship with Claudette to survive, I must accept her on her own terms."

"Can you do that without becoming hysterically jealous?" he asked her.

"We'll see," she said. "I'm driving her to Palm Springs for a romantic weekend."

"Are you two lovebirds also taking along Joan Crawford for the ride?" he jokingly asked her.

"For once in my life, I know some Hollywood gossip you don't," she said. "Claudette has broken up with Crawford. *Finis.*"

"What caused the breakup?"

"Maybe Claudette got tired of Joan's Jungle Gardenia perfume."

"Get serious Kate," Lawler implored her. "Tell me the real reason."

"They broke up over a man. At a party Claudette was hosting, she introduced Crawford to Greg Bautzer. Do you know him?"

"He's Hollywood's most gorgeous attorney and the best lay in town," Lawler said. "I could go for him myself. Tall, tanned, muscular, and an ex-Navy pilot. Nine and a half inches. What's not to love?"

"Yes, but what Crawford didn't know was that Claudette was fooling

438

around with Mr. Bautzer herself. When Crawford moved in on him, Claudette got jealous."

"What does your boy Tracy think of Claudette?" he asked.

"When drunk, he calls her either 'Froggie' or 'Frenchie.' She's never been one of his favorites."

"I have reason to hate her too," he said. "Ever since my darling Gary Cooper placed Colbert across his knee and spanked her in *Bluebeard's Eighth Wife*, they've been having an ongoing affair of their own, slipping away every couple of months for a quickie. I think Colbert likes to get spanked."

"I didn't know that," she said. "But I'll try it on her this weekend. Before I ring off, I have one final word on Crawford. There's only one thing I approve of about the bitch. She takes as many showers a day as I do."

***

What happened during Kate's weekend with Colbert in 1946 would remain secret until 1955, when, fanned by the implications of blackmail surrounding it, it became one of the juicier and more notorious tales on the Hollywood cocktail party circuit.

In 1946, partly as a change of pace from her "usual" life in LA, Kate signed a one-month lease on a house in Palm Springs. It had three bedrooms and a swimming pool, renting in the booming postwar economy for the then-outrageous price of five-hundred dollars a month.

When Colbert and Kate arrived there together for the first time, they met Paul Krueger, a twenty-four-year old "houseboy," who had been assigned by the building's rental agent to cook for them, do their laundry, and tend to their needs.

Krueger, a handsome, blond, blue-eyed, and completely dissolute Hollywood wannabe, resembled the actor, Guy Madison, whose career had been launched in Colbert's famous World War II film, *Since You Went Away.*

As Krueger would eventually reveal in 1955, "I was more than a houseboy. I made money on the side by performing extra services after dark. Man or woman, it didn't matter to me. I preferred to service women, often older ones, but I wasn't adverse to going to bed with a man if the price was right. You'd be surprised how many men I seduced, even Charles Farrell, the mayor of Palm Springs."

In 1955, Krueger claimed that he would have been ready, willing, and able to inaugurate sex with either Colbert and/or Hepburn during that long-ago weekend in 1946. "But it soon became obvious that they didn't have any use for me. They were into each other."

"Hepburn, to my surprise, had no problem with nudity," Krueger later claimed. "She often walked around the house and pool area completely naked.

Colbert wasn't as blatant as Hepburn, usually wearing a modest cover-up."

Information about the Hepburn-Colbert weekend in Palm Springs might never have surfaced had Krueger, around Christmas of 1954, not run into trouble. Arrested and charged with stealing jewelry from two homes in which he was working as a houseboy, he suddenly needed money. As a means of paying for his legal defense, Krueger approached the editors of *Confidential* magazine with scandalous data, not only about Colbert and Hepburn, but about other weekenders to Palm Springs as well, Frank Sinatra among them.

At the time, *Confidential* was flourishing, thanks to the *exposés* it published about famous men and women. A typical story focused on tobacco heiress Doris Duke and her fondness for "Mandingo-like" black men.

Reportedly, and this was never verified, in 1955 the editors of *Confidential* offered Krueger five-thousand dollars for his sensational story about the "desert love nest" of Colbert and Hepburn that he had witnessed eight years before. Five-thousand dollars was considered near the top of the magazine's pay scale at the time; a huge amount of money that would be awarded only for the hottest and most scandal-soaked information.

Rumors about the impending *Confidential* exposé spread quickly through Hollywood, with a handful of local columnists vaguely referring to it in terms of impending doom for its players. The first rumors focused on Lana Turner and Ava Gardner, who were said to have shacked up together in a lavish Palm Springs house, cavorting in the nude. The protagonists within these vague but unfolding rumors were later changed to Marlene Dietrich and Greta Garbo, and then, later on, to Barbara Stanwyck and Joan Crawford.

Finally a columnist printed that one of the actresses involved in the clandestine lesbian love affair was also having an affair with a married man, an actor who was one of Hollywood's top box-office draws. At last the rumor factory got it right. Gossips finally, and accurately, nailed the two actresses as Colbert and Hepburn.

The article, originally conceived as a cover story for *Confidential,* never made it into print. Before the issue was run, someone "pulled the plug," and the story was buried in the magazine's archives, along with other such exposés, including one about the homosexuality of Rock Hudson.

To this day, it is not known why the story wasn't published. It was at first suggested that powerful studios intervened, but by the mid-Fifties studios were no longer protecting stars like they used to in the Thirties. Besides, Colbert and Hepburn were viewed more or less as "floating stars" at that point, negotiating their own deals from studio to studio. But mysteriously, the police charges against Krueger were eventually dropped.

Long after the dust settled on this scandal, the best guess about the *Confidential* episode is that Kate, with Colbert's tacit agreement, set up a meeting between *Confidential's* editors and attorney Greg Bautzer. It was rumored that Kate offered *Confidential* between fifteen-thousand and twenty-five-thousand dollars to "buy back" the exposé.

Gossip about the nude cavorting of Colbert and Hepburn was still a hot item until the early Sixties. But eventually, John Kennedy's assassination and the fall-out from the death of Marilyn Monroe gradually pushed the affair of these two fabled actresses to the side.

***

Louis B. Mayer had always encouraged the friendship between Kate with his attractive daughter, Irene Mayer Selznick. But apparently, he never became aware of the direction that friendship eventually took. Although the two women had known each other casually since the early Thirties, when David Selznick first brought Kate to Hollywood, they had not become intimate friends.

Their bond began in the East, not in Hollywood, when Irene had showed up at the Washington, D.C. opening of Robert Sherwood's *The Rugged Path*, starring Spencer Tracy.

While she was in Washington, Kate invited Irene for a drive out to Mount Vernon and lunch. Up to that point, Kate had seen Irene only when surrounded by other people. Once they were alone together, they found they could talk freely for hours, and that they shared many similar views. A camaraderie began to build between them. Irene's insights were so keen about the structure and staging of *The Rugged Path* that Kate told her that she was going to "repeat every word you've said to Spence-*suh*. He's eager for your insights." Irene later said that she was flattered that Tracy would even consider her opinions.

In later years, she claimed that Kate's enthusiasm for her ideas planted the idea about one day making an entry into legitimate theater as a producer.

Only the year before, Kate and Irene had bonded at a dinner party at Cukor's house. A friendship was brewing. In time, Irene would characterize it as "a lifelong conspiracy."

Even though all doors were open to her in Hollywood, Irene quickly learned through both Kate and Cary Grant how important it was to have Howard Hughes in your life. Both plane and rail tickets were in short supply in 1946. "If there was one thing that Howard was good at, it was arranging free transportation," Irene recalled. "I learned at the time that the friendship between Howard and Kate was still percolating, although it was certainly not a romance. From Hollywood, Kate insisted on returning to Connecticut and New York as frequently as possible, and Howard's money and influence made all that possible for her. It didn't cost her a cent, and she always traveled first class."

When Irene couldn't get a reservation for herself or her family for travel from Los Angeles to New York, and Cary Grant learned about her dilemma, he contacted Hughes, and all arrangements were taken care of.

To Irene's surprise, she began receiving, through Cary Grant, a series of personal messages from Howard Hughes. Just as Grant had previously tried to broker a romance between Kate and Hughes, he now tried to promote a relationship between Hughes and Irene.

At the time of Hughes' proposal, Irene, though estranged from her husband, David O. Selznick, had not yet divorced him. The divorce wouldn't come through until January of 1949, after nineteen years of a troubled marriage.

Grant told Irene that Hughes thought that she might make an ideal wife, and then arranged a date for Hughes and Irene at the "21" in New York.

"Howard came right to the point," Irene later told Kate. "A proposal of marriage. He claimed he really needed me. He phrased it by saying, 'Why should Cary have a woman and not me?'"

She said that Howard told her that he was very lonely, and once again claimed that his life's biggest mistake was his failure to convince Katharine Hepburn to marry him. Irene almost immediately refused Hughes' offer of marriage, although she maintained a friendship with him, as did Kate, for many years to come. Eventually, Hughes even offered her a job as a producer for RKO, which she also turned down.

As the years went by, George Cukor, Kenneth MacKenna, and Anderson Lawler each confirmed, individually, that a romance eventually developed between Irene and Kate. In New York, Kate's confidante, Patricia Peardon, also maintained that this was true.

Up to that point, Irene was known as a strictly heterosexual woman, though always (to use a modern-day term) "gay friendly," unlike her father, Louis B. Mayer.

Lawler speculated that Irene's relationship with Kate was her only known lesbian affair. "The two women just adored each other, and wanted to spend as much time with each other as they possibly could. Even though both women had full lives before they got involved, with lots of people crowding in on them, they still found plenty of time for each other. They would set aside entire days to be together."

Their love affair probably began when Kate would arrive at Irene's house loaded down with "lots of flowers, lots of towels, and a big picnic lunch." Kate would always announce that, "I've come to make a day of it." Spencer Tracy, Colbert, and her many other friends and commitments would be forgotten. Kate always said that "I want Irene just to myself."

In many ways Irene was far more practical than Kate. She was not given to Kate's "ways," which meant breaking into other people's homes. Irene jokingly told Cukor, "Before I met Kate I wasn't a housebreaker. Believe me!"

So persuasive was Kate that she actually got Irene to break into houses in the Hollywood Hills. "It was Kate's passion—not mine," Irene once told Tennessee Williams. "I was scared to death. But Kate convinced me how important it was to her, and I went along. Kate said that she was too afraid to break into the houses by herself. And she demanded that I be her accomplice. I was sort of under her spell in those days, and I played the absurd game. It's a wonder we weren't shot."

Long before anyone ever heard of the John Cheever short story, and the movie made from it, *The Swimmer*, starring Burt Lancaster, Irene and Kate were living out that fiction for real.

In the immediate post-war era, Kate devised a plan about how she and Irene could reach the surf at Malibu. They would literally swim their way there until they reached the coast, visiting one pool after another in the backyards of various homes along the way. "We simply invaded people's lawns and swam across their pool until we tired of that, at which time we headed on for a neighbor's pool," Irene told Tennessee.

He asked Irene if they were ever caught or evicted, or if any homeowner ever called the police.

"Amazingly not," Irene told him. "Sometimes the people were home. In all cases, everybody knew us. If they didn't know me, they certainly knew Kate. We were never made to feel unwelcome. Many of the homeowners were so honored to have two such famous Hollywood icons as Kate and me in their pools, that they offered coffee, cake, a drink, whatever. Once or twice one of the owners expressed surprise that we didn't have a pool of our own. In nearly every case, the owners told us that we'd be welcome back at any time to swim in their pools. We sometimes encountered men or women who worked for MGM, and they were only too willing to extend hospitality to the daughter of a powerful studio chief, and certainly to the great Katharine Hepburn herself. And I'm sure that after we jumped out of their pools and went to invade another pool nearby, these homeowners were completely bewildered at such odd behavior."

In her memoirs, *A Private Life*, Irene wrote, "An empty house and a sparkling pool had the effect on us of a formal invitation. We felt like Tom Sawyer and Huck Finn. For two people so passionate about privacy, this was a hell of a thing to do. Looking back, it seems to me that anything unconventional I ever did, I did with Kate. It wouldn't occur to *me* to ask a tugboat captain to give us a ride down the East River [in New York] and around the bay on a hot Sunday afternoon."

In those days, there were several small and discreet inns in Malibu where stars, usually with an illicit partner, went for some privacy. Kate and Irene preferred to stay at The Blue Jaybird, which changed its name frequently and which once ran into trouble with the authorities because of some licensing issue. The rule of the house was that if a star spotted a friend at the inn, he or she wasn't to acknowledge the other one. "Off-the-record meant off-the-record," Clark Gable once said. "Even if I ran into Gary Cooper there, I didn't know him. When we'd see each other the next week, we'd never even acknowledge that we had been in Malibu. The rule was so rigid that even if a man ran into his own wife, who was obviously sharing her bed with another man, nothing was ever said since the errant husband had a gal—or, in some cases, a boy—stashed in his room."

Kate never told her gay pals exactly who initiated the romance between Irene and herself, or exactly how it evolved.

"I assumed that their sexual relationship blossomed at that inn," Lawler said. "Kate had to be the aggressor. It was not an 'until-death-do-us part' type of love affair, since both Irene and Kate were involved with other people. But from the look on Kate's face when she spoke about Irene, I can only conclude it was a very special relationship. It went on for years—England, Montego Bay in Jamaica, New York. They became so close that in time Irene would invite Kate to live in her house at 1050 Summit Drive, since Kate never had a house of her own in California."

Where was Spencer Tracy during this clandestine affair?

Tracy always went back to see Louise and their daughter Susie on Friday night. Their son John had gotten married. Sometimes Tracy would stay over on Saturday night and return early Sunday morning.

He'd rented one of three guest cottages on Cukor's estate, where he would remain until the day he died—in fact, dying in that same cottage early one sleepless morning.

It was at the time he moved into the cottage that Cukor began to arrange "special entertainment," at a price, for Tracy. For a while, Tracy still kept his suite at the Beverly Hills Hotel.

As the months went by, Kate became more and more aware of the exact nature of this special entertainment. When she did, she never confronted Tracy with it, and in her own way seemed to approve. "It's what Spence wants and needs," she told Kenneth. "The man suffers so much. He's entitled to a little joy here and there."

***

Upon Tracy's return to the West Coast with his brother, Carroll, who presumably had forgiven him for his attempts on his life, a sober Spencer went looking for Kate. He found her in the hilltop aerie where the silent screen star, John Gilbert, got through many a drunken night during the height of his career. As Kate told Cukor, "Garbo used to drive up here as part of her affair with John Gilbert, right here in this house. Nowadays, Garbo comes to this house to see me, but only rarely."

The exact nature of the confrontation between Kate and Tracy will never be known, but Cukor always maintained that before they agreed to make *The Sea of Grass* together at MGM, they solidified the terms of their relationship for the future.

Cukor offered the most informed opinion of the agreement they reached with each other. "They virtually admitted that their affair was over," he said, "and I had been led to understand that they had not slept together as lovers since late in 1943. They, in essence, became what we called 'Sisters' back then. In fact, I've seen a note or two that Kate left for Spence in the cottage he rented from me. She signed it 'Sister Kate.'"

Kenneth MacKenna felt that Tracy and Kate agreed "to be there for each other" when called upon. Otherwise, they would be free to live their own lives and conduct their own affairs without any interference from the other.

To back up Kenneth's point of view, Tracy, shortly after his arrival in Hollywood, was seen out nearly every night at one club or another. Sharing his table was a string of starlets. "You could catch Tracy nightly at such clubs as the Trocadero or Ciro's," Gable once said. "Gary Cooper and Robert Taylor often ran into Tracy at the Mocambo, and Lana Turner remembers dancing with him at The Players. One night, Turner said, "Tracy was out with a starlet named Nancy Davis. I didn't think she was going anywhere in Hollywood. In those days, Little Miss Wide Eyed's phone number was passed along to a lot of fellows with a gleam in their eyes. I mean guys not important enough to call me."

Although Tracy had recently dried out, at great expense and pain to everyone around him, in Doctors Hospital in Manhattan, he was soon seen "slugging down the booze," as Gable said, "night after night in these joints."

Tracy was not necessarily bedding all the stars and starlets he was dating. Barbara Spainhour, who'd gone to Hollywood to break into films, said she met Tracy at Ciro's. "He slipped me his number, and asked me to call him even though he was with another gal. This I found a bit odd. In those days, the boy called the girl, not the other way around. Physically, Tracy didn't interest me at all. I wasn't into men who looked like my grandfather. I only went with him because I thought he would use his influence to get me a contract at MGM. There was never any sex with us. It just didn't come up, so to speak. I had three dates with him. At each of them, he kept drinking and drinking. Our evening would end when I would get someone from the club to help me put him into a taxi. I would take him to the Beverly Hills Hotel where two guys on the staff would haul him to his room on a baggage cart. Katharine Hepburn could have that flabby old drunk. Tracy did give me some advice, which I followed. He told me I didn't have an ounce of talent. He suggested I find some guy, get married, and go back to wherever in the hell I came from and settle down and have three kids. That is exactly what I did do."

Anderson Lawler had his own spin on the Hepburn/Tracy reunion. "I think that Tracy became many things in Kate's life—but not her lover. He became the older brother who was denied her by the suicide of her brother Tom. He became the cuddly father she always wanted but never had. Kate needed a father who would take her in his arms and hold her and cuddle with her. Dr. Hepburn was a bit too reserved for that. Kate was also the ultimate caretaker.

She liked waiting on sick people more than she did having a lover. Whenever I got sick, she was always at my bedside, tending to me. I know it sounds strange, but in addition to being a brother and a father, Tracy was also the son she'd never had or never would have. She looked after him the way a domineering and obsessive mother might focus on her son, especially when that mother-son relationship practically bordered on incest."

Kate's other confidante, Patricia Peardon, shed more light on the Tracy/Hepburn post-war romance, or lack of romance. "Kate lived in fear all her life that her lesbianism would be exposed," Peardon said. "The general public didn't know about her relationship with Tracy, but virtually everybody else—at least everybody who mattered—did know. As long as Hollywood, or the theatrical circuit in New York, thought that Kate was screwing Tracy, no one looked at who she was really having an affair with—namely Irene Mayer Selznick and Claudette Colbert, among others. In my view, and I'll go to my grave believing this, Kate and Tracy agreed to deceive the world. All I know is that when Tracy returned to Hollywood, and I used to visit Kate often on the coast, I heard that there were more handsome young men seen leaving Tracy's cottage than there were beautiful actresses. Of course, Cukor made all the arrangements. In fact, I think Cukor functioned something like the ladies-in-waiting did at the court of Catherine the Great in Russia, trying out the studs before passing them on to the queen. Cukor auditioned the guys first. If he was impressed, he booked them for another night with Tracy. Cukor and Tracy were the original dial-a-hustler duo in Hollywood. It was the talk of the town. Everybody knew what was going on back then, even Louella Parsons and Hedda Hopper. They just didn't put it in the newspapers. Tracy and Kate were, in fact, each other's beard, misleading the world until the two of them got too old to want to have sex anymore with anybody. Tracy retired from the sexual battlefields long before Kate did. His last known affair with a woman was with Grace Kelly, who liked to screw around with the stars of Hollywood's Golden Age even when they were gray haired, wearing a wig, and most definitely having to conceal their paunches on camera by wearing a girdle. Kate, being a far healthier and more vibrant sexual animal, would carry on a lot longer, of course."

***

Both Kate and Tracy had been impressed with the dramatic possibilities within Conrad Richter's novel, *The Sea of Grass*, and wanted to star in it. MGM had acquired the rights and had assigned Pandro S. Berman to produce it. He in turn hired the young Elia Kazan to direct it.

With Kate playing the role of Lutie Camera, and Tracy playing Colonel James Brewton, *The Sea of Grass* had a strong supporting cast, with Melvyn

446

Douglas, Phyllis Thaxter, Robert Walker, Edgar Buchanan, and Harry Carey. Walter Plunkett, who had designed so many of Kate's movie costumes at RKO, was back as her costumer, only now he was working for MGM.

Marguerite Roberts and Vincent Lawrence had been hired as scenarists to adapt Richter's novel. In the film, Tracy plays a cattle baron in New Mexico who owns a "Sea of Grass." The struggle deals with his fight with the homesteaders who want his fertile lands for farming.

Unhappy with Tracy's obsession with maintaining his land, Kate leaves him and heads for Denver where she has an affair with, and conceives a child with, her husband's worst enemy, the gloomy character played by Melvyn Douglas. She eventually gives birth to a son, whom Tracy accepts as his own after their reunion.

In time, Tracy tosses Kate off the ranch when she gives birth to another child, this one fathered by Tracy's character himself. This daughter was later portrayed in the film as a grown-up by Phyllis Thaxter. Eventually, Kate's son, as played by Robert Walker, grows up to be a nasty ne'-er-do-well and is killed by a posse. In old age the estranged Tracy reconciles with his wife, Kate, at the conclusion of this convoluted film.

It was inevitable that Tracy and Kazan would disagree over his directing. Kazan believed in the Stanislavsky method and had directed only one film, *A Tree Grows in Brooklyn.* Tracy grumbled repeatedly that Kazan's view of acting was "just a lot of high flown mumbo-jumbo."

Tracy acted from instinct; Kazan was concerned with introspection and psychological motivation.

Before filming began, Kate told Cukor, "My biggest job will be to keep Spencer and Kazan from coming to blows."

On their first meeting on the set, Kazan was alarmed at "the lard" around Tracy's middle as he struggled to get his plump body out of the back seat of a too small car. Kazan later said he felt Tracy "looked like an Irish burgher in the mercantile trade."

"I met Tracy on the day he was supposed to test ride the overfed horses," Kazan said to Tennessee Williams and the author of this biography years later. "I asked him if he wanted to mount. 'What the hell for?' Tracy asked. I remember him inviting me for lunch. When it and the many cocktails he consumed were finished, he literally crawled back into his car. So much for our overweight Western hero. I realized from the beginning that Tracy was no competition for Gary Cooper."

Kazan also said that he was a bit leery of directing Kate in her first Western. "A Bryn Mawr girl playing a cowgal. If she pulled that off, I thought she could make films with Roy Rogers, or at least with Gene Autry."

Kazan wanted to shoot on location, but Pandro Berman informed him that the movie was to be filmed in the studio in front of a rear projection. The "sea of grass" had already been shot.

"I wanted to photograph a land that stank of horseshit," Kazan claimed. "All we got were reels of almost manicured fields of grass blowing in the wind. It was all too pretty to be believed."

When Kazan met Kate, he found her "rather cool and overpowering. True Hollywood royalty. Completely miscast." The director confessed that he felt he'd walked "into the MGM paper shredder."

Kazan said he tried to direct Tracy but after one scene Kate would interrupt. "She'd run up to me and exclaim, 'Wasn't that wonderful? How does he do it? He's so true! He can't do anything false!' That didn't leave me much option to call for a retake."

"At least that was Kate's public face," Kazan said. "Often from his dressing room I could hear her bitter recriminations as she shouted at him in that distinctive voice. At least after making *The Sea of Grass*, I knew why Tracy drank. It wasn't his deaf son. It was not his Catholic guilt. It was because of Katharine Hepburn."

Kazan remembered that Jane Loring made several mysterious visits to the set to confer with Kate about the script. "I didn't really know who Loring was, but after she left, Hepburn demanded changes in the script. Loring also demanded to see rushes and attacked me for 'not watching Kate's neck.' I dreaded to see her come onto the set. So did Tracy. He detested Loring. Loring also told me to keep a 'baby spot' under Kate's neck at all times."

Both Pandro Berman and Louis B. Mayer had overruled Kazan when he'd wanted to cast unknown actors in the Tracy/Hepburn parts.

"I wanted an actor whose face looked like old leather," Kazan said. "Whereas Tracy's face looked like the inside of a melon, all soft and sweet. He did not like horses and they did not like him. He was plump, not a Western hero. He was completely miscast and was so lazy he practically fell asleep in front of the camera. As for Kate Hepburn, she was a decent person but every time she went to the bathroom to take a piss, she came out with a different gown on. None of her gowns looked like any woman had ever worn them. Mayer saw the rushes and even objected to her tears. 'They are too close to her nostrils,' Mayer said. 'It looks like the tears are coming out of her nose like snot.'"

Throughout most of the film, Tracy was ill during the day with stomach problems. "Like a dutiful slave, Hepburn attended to his every need," Kazan said. "Amazingly, when he said good-bye to Kate at night, he would miraculously recover for a round of nightclubs.'

During the filming, Tracy accepted an invitation to attend a party at the home of Irene Mayer Selznick. He showed up with Carole Landis, a World War II pinup with a lot of mediocre films to her credit. Eventually, in 1948, despondent over the breakup of her affair with Rex Harrison, she would commit suicide.

Irene later recalled that Tracy had arrived at the party drunk with Landis, also drunk. Kate had not wanted to be seen with Tracy, since Hedda Hopper would be there.

Only that day, the columnist had printed an item linking Tracy and Hepburn in the same paragraph, although it was not a romantic reference. Tracy, as Irene remembered, was furious to even be linked in the press in the same sentence with Kate. "I couldn't believe it," Irene said. "He actually kicked Hedda in her behind, sending her sprawling over my coffee table. She threatened to sue him but never did."

Although she detested Kazan, Kate looked with a kinder eye on the young, handsome, and psychologically troubled Robert Walker, who was playing her illegitimate son in *The Sea of Grass.* Walker's marriage to Jennifer Jones had ended two years before. Shortly after they began working together, Hepburn defined him as "a basket case."

Walker was drinking heavily throughout the production and kept urging Tracy to drink with him. "Normally, Kate would kick a man like Gable in the nuts if he offered Tracy a drink," Kazan said. "But in Walker's case, she forgave him again and again."

"Walker was seriously pissed off when Tracy wouldn't drink with him during the day," Kazan claimed.

Walker and Kate circled each other warily during the filming of *The Sea of Grass*, as he gave what *The New York Times* would eventually define as a performance that consisted of "no more than an ostentatious swagger and an occasionally overstudied leer."

Since Kate was trying to keep Walker away from Tracy, and away from his heavy drinking during their filming of *Sea of Grass*, her own friendship and involvement with the young actor had to wait until he was cast, in 1947, as her on-screen lover in *Song of Love*.

Kazan ultimately concluded that he had been "a God damn fool to make the film. I warned all future directors never to work with Hepburn and Tracy. What a pair! They ate up directors like a half of a grapefruit at breakfast—one segment after another. I had to check to see if I still had my two testicles at night."

Although expressed slightly differently, other directors had voiced the same sentiment about Kate as well.

Louis B. Mayer was so unhappy with *The Sea of Grass* that, although made in 1945, the film wasn't released until 1947.

Few films of that era were as misleadingly advertised:

RUGGED TRACY LIVING AS RUTHLESSLY AS HE RULED. ROMANTIC HEPBURN WHOSE INDISCRETION CAUSED A LIFETIME OF UNHAPPINESS! RECKLESS ROBERT WALKER BORN WITHOUT A NAME AND A RUTHLESS KILLER.

After *The Sea of Grass* was released, the film was denounced for its lame script. It was also attacked for Kazan's direction. Kate was once again criticized for overacting. Tracy's understated acting usually received praise, but in this case critics found it "resembling boredom." One reviewer said, "The best I can say about the picture is that Hepburn wears thirty gowns, not her usual pants." Another critic found it "a Western without action, not worthy of Hepburn and most definitely not worthy of Tracy." *Time* claimed it an "epically dreary film," and *The New Yorker* found Tracy "occasionally ludicrous," but conceded that Kate was "pert as a sparrow." Bosley Crowther in *The New York Times* found Kate's performance "distressingly pompous and false."

When Louise Tracy went to view *The Sea of Grass*, she told her friends, "Spencer let Hepburn steal the film from him, the same way he's letting her steal his life."

***

On the MGM lot, before the release of *The Sea of Grass*, production began on *Undercurrent.* Tracy had sat out the war in Hollywood, but other male stars were returning. Clark Gable came back to co-star with Greer Garson in the ill-conceived *Adventure.* Headlines blared: GABLE'S BACK AND GARSON'S GOT HIM.

The box office matinee idol, Robert Taylor, returned from the wars to co-star with Kate in the thriller, *Undercurrent,* which also starred a minor actor, Robert Mitchum, who had captivated Tracy when Mitchum played an even smaller role in *Thirty Seconds over Tokyo.*

Undercurrent would mark one of the low points of Kate's mercurial career, evocative of the time in the Thirties when she was labeled box office poison.

As Pandro Berman, *Undercurrent's* producer, said, "Finding a script for Kate is like one man servicing one hundred whores in one night. A possibility, but highly difficult."

Undercurrent also represented one of the low points of the film career of Robert Taylor, who had been honorably discharged from the Navy on November 5, 1945 as a Senior Grade Lieutenant

Taylor returned to civilian life to face a deteriorating marriage to Barbara Stanwyck, whose career was soaring. At the time, the players in the Taylor/Stanwyck union were regarded as "the poster boy and poster girl for a lavender marriage," in the words of Peter Lawford.

Both Stanwyck and Taylor were known as notorious bisexuals among Hollywood insiders, although their sexual proclivities would not generally be exposed until years later. When she started filming *Undercurrent* with Taylor, Kate was already aware of his sexual liaison with Howard Hughes.

Shortly after Taylor's return to Hollywood, he abruptly realized that roles he might once have been considered for were now being awarded to up-and-coming new stars like Peter Lawford, Cornel Wilde, Van Johnson, and a young Frank Sinatra.

Yet, in spite of the fact that few good roles emerged, he'd signed a sweet-heart contract with MGM for twenty years at four-thousand dollars a week.

When *Variety* published this news, Hollywood insiders were astounded. Many had predicted that Taylor, upon his discharge from the Navy, would never regain his pre-war fame.

Taylor would follow *Undercurrent* with a string of box office disappoint-ments. His career was rescued with the Biblical spectacle, the remake of *Quo Vadis?* in 1951. Following that were some sword-and-armor epics. By the time his long contract with Metro came to an end, his initial arrangement with Mayer was regarded as low pay for an actor of such fame. In fact, Taylor became known for holding the all-time record of being the lowest-paid star in history, but one with the longest-running movie contract.

Mayer was the first to note the physical change in Taylor after his return from the rigors of war. He was no longer the dazzling young beauty he was when he appeared opposite Garbo in *Camille* in 1937, when macho-looking photographs showing his hairy chest were spread across the front pages of movie magazines around the world.

Although Taylor had reached middle age, his hair was still jet black. But wearing the same moustache from the early Forties, with the same brilliantined hair, he seemed like an actor from a vanished era, even though he hadn't really been off the screen that long.

"So what do you think about appearing opposite Katie Hepburn in a movie?" Mayer asked him. "Don't know her," Taylor said. "I mean, I know who she is—that's it."

"You don't have to go to bed with her," Mayer said. "Just make this movie with her."

"That's God damn bad news," Taylor said. "I don't want to work with the dyke. I'm still recuperating from working with another man-eating dyke, Garbo, and that was nearly ten years ago. If I want a dyke, I can always go home to Barbara."

"It's a good part," Mayer said. "You get to play a villain, a real louse."

"Great!" Taylor took the script home and read it. He was horribly disap-pointed but showed up the next day to report for work.

From the first, Taylor infuriated Kate by bragging that MGM had, in addi-tion to a fat contract, given him a brand new twin-engine Beechcraft, an aircraft worth a least seventy-five thousand dollars.

The day he met Hepburn, he immediately complained that *Undercurrent* wasn't a fit vehicle for a comeback picture. He told her that "the only way I can forget this lousy script is to ride my motorcycle at high speed with Gary Cooper or else plan a hunting trip with Clark Gable up in Oregon. By the way, did you know that Clark always calls me 'Baby?'"

"Many women dream about becoming Gable's Baby," she said. "Men, too, I suppose."

"Hey, wait a minute!" Taylor said. "I didn't mean it that way. Don't get the wrong idea."

"I think I have the right idea."

"I'm more man than most of the actors in Hollywood," Taylor said.

"Why are you married to Barbara Stanwyck if that's true?"

"Why are you shacked up with Spencer Tracy?" Taylor asked. "Don't think I don't know what's going on between the two of you. You play the same little games that Barbara and I do."

"You know nothing about me, you bastard!" she said, slapping his face and heading immediately for her dressing room.

She called both Lawler and Kenneth MacKenna that day to report on her encounter with Taylor. "I just can't make a film with the shit. I just can't." Both of her friends urged her to ignore Taylor's remarks and fulfill her contract, which she only reluctantly agreed to do.

It was three days before she resumed speaking to Taylor. He was eager, he said, to finish *Undercurrent* so that he could go and hunt mountain lions in Mexico with Gary Cooper. "Coop has invited Ernest Hemingway to go with us."

"Maybe you'll have better luck with Papa than I did," she said to a slightly bewildered Taylor. "You're more his type."

***

The plot of *Undercurrent,* Kate's twenty-second film, was pure melodrama and not good melodrama at that. Kate was miscast as the innocent Ann Hamilton, the daughter of a college professor who falls in love with a wealthy industrialist, Alan Garroway, as played by Taylor.

When Kate is first glimpsed, she is a sort of dreamy-eyed bobbysoxer in a role that might have been better suited for Shirley Temple at the time.

In the film, Kate marries Taylor and tries to gain more sophistication and poise. Taylor tells her many stories about his mysterious brother, with the suggestion that he might be a psychopath. In the film, when Kate actually meets Mitchum, she finds him articulate and sensitive and even falls in love with him. Surprise of surprises. It turns out that Taylor is the actual psychopath.

Kate was pleased to be reunited with Edmund Gwenn, who once again played her father as he had in *Sylvia Scarlett*. Kate also had a reunion with her old friend, Marjorie Main, who provided comic relief in the film. Main told Kate that Taylor's marriage with her friend, Stanwyck, was virtually at an end.

The character actress also claimed that Taylor had fallen in love with an ex-Navy pilot, who he had stashed away in a home in West Hollywood and that Taylor was paying all his bills.

By the third day of shooting, Kate was clashing with Robert Taylor. She had a habit of walking around between scenes with her hair wrapped in a white towel. To mock her, Taylor began doing that too, parading mincingly around the set, imitating some of her worst mannerisms.

For the duration of the shoot, she told Kenneth MacKenna that she was going to speak to Taylor from now on only when the cameras were rolling.

She had nothing but complaints about Taylor's acting to the film's director Vincente Minnelli.

Minnelli only half listened to her, complaining to Pandro Berman that, "Hepburn makes me nervous. Never in my life have I met an actor as arrogantly self-assured as *that one.*"

A surprising choice by Mayer to direct this lurid melodrama, Minnelli was mainly known for slick musicals.

After only one week of working under Minnelli's direction, Kate went to Berman and asked him, "Why is Minnelli directing this film? It needs Alfred Hitchcock. Minnelli is Mayer's joke on us."

When word reached the director of Kate's disenchantment with him, he began to give her a hard time on the set. At one point, he exploded, denouncing her acting style and mannerisms. "This God damn part calls for Ingrid Bergman. Mayer sends me Katharine Hepburn. Even Judy could have played the part better." At the time, Minnelli was married to Judy Garland.

To retaliate for his outburst, Kate walked off the set four hours early and didn't report to work the next day until she was three hours late.

From the beginning, Minnelli had struck Kate as "an odd bird," as she expressed it to Berman. He always showed up on the set in a pair of pearl-gray slacks and a short-sleeved pink or yellow shirt. Unlike the male stars of the film, Minnelli was not a handsome face, with his drooping eyes and receding chin. Behind his back, the cast compared his look to that of a tiny dinosaur.

As he talked to Kate, she was acutely aware of his unconscious tic. His right eye, as if by clockwork, would click shut every three minutes. And he constantly pursed his lips as if he wanted to whistle, relaxing them again as no sound emerged. .

She had never worked with a director as effeminate as Minnelli. In an era long before the world ever heard of Michael Jackson, Minnelli showed up on the set often in full make-up—scarlet lipstick, black or sometimes purplish eye shadow, and lots of mascara.

"Why did Judy Garland marry a homosexual?" Kate asked Taylor on one of the days she was speaking to him.

"Why do you live with one as I do?" Taylor said.

Kate so resented his reference to Tracy that she decided to strike back at Taylor in a way that she knew would prick his vanity. "I've never seen but one of your pictures, and I don't think I'll see *Undercurrent* either. I did see *Camille.* But I didn't know you existed in that film. With Greta Garbo on the screen, who would look at Robert Taylor?"

Minnelli was so disturbing to her that she kept her business with him to the minimum. She was surprised one day when he knocked on her door at lunchtime and handed her a note.

After she'd shut the door, she quickly tore open the pink envelope. It was from Judy Garland.

"Please come by and see me any night next week," Garland wrote. "I'm desperate to see you. Vin won't be home at all next week. I want to show you my little baby daughter. Please, please don't disappoint me! It's a matter of life or death! Love, Judy."

***

Meeting the other male co-star of *Undercurrent*, Robert Mitchum, Kate was prepared to dislike him. She'd tired of Tracy raving about what good looks he had when he made *Thirty Seconds Over Tokyo* with Mitchum in a bit part.

When she was introduced, Mitchum wore a leather aviator jacket and a form-fitting turtleneck. As Kate later related to Lawler, she was immediately taken with his obvious virility which was in contrast to Taylor's rather fey quality.

The sleepy-lidded actor didn't seem too impressed with her. They merely shook hands and went on their way.

Later when Kenneth MacKenna—working in the MGM story department— dropped by to wish Kate luck, she told him, "That Mitchum is just some cheap flash actor but his body is built like a brick shithouse."

Kenneth reminded her that Mitchum had been nominated for an Oscar as best supporting actor for his role in *The Story of G.I. Joe.*

Both Kenneth and Anderson Lawler felt that Kate was obviously physically attracted to Mitchum but could not bring herself to admit that. Instead of loving him, she attacked him.

After her first scene with him, she told him, "You know you can't act. If you weren't so God damn good looking, you would never have been cast in this part. But you know how Minnelli is sexually attracted to types like you, or so I hear. I'm so tired of appearing with actors who have nothing to offer!"

To get even with her, Mitchum began to play a series of pranks and bawdy jokes on her. One day he showed up on the set with a large ceramic dildo, which had a hole in the head of the fake penis. He showed it to her and explained that it was used in a fertility festival in Portugal, where the young men go around asking the virgin girls of the village to drink from the dildo. To demonstrate, he drank from it in her presence. "I noticed you drink a lot of water," he said when he'd drained the last drop. "Here, drink from this." He poured water from the dildo and held it up to her mouth.

She backed away. "In your childish mind, you think all this is very funny,

454

don't you? I find it less than amusing."

In a close-up with Kate the next morning, she was overpowered by the smell of his breath, and bluntly told him so. Knowing he was to shoot an intimate scene with her that afternoon, he ordered a large sliced Bermuda onion and a big slab of Roquefort cheese for lunch. Not wanting to let him know he'd bested her, she bravely played out the scene with the foul-smelling actor.

In spite of his pranks, Kate found herself drawn to him and often could be seen walking casually by his dressing room. Mitchum always kept the door open. One time he emerged at the door in his underwear to greet her.

"I think Minnelli's directing style is lugubrious," he told her. "Now, you didn't think a dumb fuck like me would know what lugubrious means, did you?"

"Mr. Mitchum," she said, "you are full of surprises. I agree with you, though. Minnelli thinks he's creating another *Rebecca* or *Suspicion*. He's not."

The next day when she strolled by, he invited her inside his dressing room and closed the door. Seated across from her, he said, "You take all this artsy-fartsy moviemaking seriously, don't you? To me, it's just a paycheck."

"I noticed that you've been walking through this film with your eyes half closed," she said.

"So what? I'll make a hundred more films. All I have to do is tell RKO or Metro to send over their leading ladies. After I've finished with one, I'll close my eyes. When I open them again, I'll find yet another leading lady in my arms. I can get through my movie career by repeating that process endlessly."

"How enchanting, meeting an actor who takes his profession so seriously," she said.

"I'll fuck them off the screen if I have to," he said. "It doesn't matter what they look like. My stiff dick doesn't judge beauty pageants."

"I can assure you, Mr. Mitchum, that your stiff dick, as you put it, and I will not become all that chummy," she said, standing up to leave.

"Like you're getting it from Tracy," he said. "Don't kid a kidder."

Instead of slapping him, she spat in his face. He spat back at her before grabbing her and pressing her body against his.

With a certain kind of contained violence, she gave in to him since he'd accurately gauged that that was what she'd wanted to do all along.

As Mitchum would later tell it, and he repeated the story many times, "My God, I guess she hadn't had any lately. She was all over me. And once was not enough. The very next day at lunch, she showed up for more of my famous pounding."

Her love affair with Mitchum didn't make it to the end of the shoot. Unknown to Mitchum, Kate often showed up on the set on days she wasn't needed.

If she thought Robert Taylor's impersonation of her was cruel, she hadn't been prepared to see herself imitated in so deadly a fashion by Mitchum, her other male co-star. She was, in fact, aghast that so studly a man as Mitchum could even do such an accurate impersonation of a female. Yet all his friends knew that his impersonations of stars, ranging from Bette Davis to Charles Laughton, were good enough to get him bookings in a night club if he had wanted them.

Mitchum didn't know it, but Kate concealed herself and watched his devastating depiction of her at her most lockjaw affected. Still concealing herself, she turned in tears and left the set.

At the time he was co-starring in *Undercurrent*, Mitchum was shooting two pictures at once. He was also appearing with Greer Garson in *Desire*, a film directed by George Cukor.

Mitchum quickly added the director—"all puffy lips and lisping effeminacy"—to his repertoire of impressions. "But my take on Kate Hepburn was always the party favorite," he later claimed.

It didn't help the next day when Mitchum called her "Babe."

"Actually, you can call me Miss Hepburn," she told him.

"I forgot your name for a moment," he said. "Babe is actually a compliment. Usually, when I forget someone's name—either male or female—I call them Peter."

She never visited his dressing room ever again.

When *Undercurrent* was completed, Mitchum had "Kate Hepburn stories" to tell at every party. Even though married, he often bragged, "That Miss Hepburn was never fucked properly until I did the job for her."

Upon seeing the film, he preferred to call *Undercurrent* by his pet name of *Underdrawers*.

***

It was a Monday night when Kate drove up to the Minnelli house on Evanview Drive. Getting out of her car, she paused for a minute to take in the panoramic view of Beverly Hills and Hollywood at night. The lights were just coming on. From the beginning, she was rather awed by their pink stucco, Mediterranean style home.

When Kate arrived at Garland's house, the singer was no longer Dorothy in *The Wizard of Oz*. Nor was she any longer a part of the "dream team" with Mickey Rooney in those *Girl Crazy* pictures. She had blossomed into a beautiful young woman with the kind of bright wit that was for the most part lacking in Kate herself.

When Louis B. Mayer had first sent Kate to talk to Garland, hoping that Kate could straighten out his valuable star, Kate had found the prospect of channeling the young Garland too daunting for her, especially since she already had the spectacularly dysfunctional Tracy occupying much of her time and energy. But now, intrigued with the intricacies of another encounter with what she hoped was a more mature Garland, Kate felt adequate for the challenge.

Garland was no longer a child star. Along with newcomer Gene Kelly, she had already appeared in her first adult role, the 1942 *For Me and My Girl*. In 1944, her career skyrocketed after the release of *Meet Me in Saint Louis*, that delicious slice of nostalgia directed by Vincente Minnelli. He'd already directed Garland in the one dramatic film she made in the Forties, *The Clock,* released in 1946, in which she'd co-starred with Robert Walker.

Judy Garland had been born Frances Ethel Gumm on June 20, 1922, in Grand Rapids, Michigan. She was fifteen years younger than Kate, or, in Kate's words, "young enough to be my daughter had I been born in the days of Daniel Boone."

When Kate pulled her car into the Minnelli family's driveway, Garland was already into the second of her five ill-fated marriages. Garland's first marriage had been to the handsome David Rose on July 28, 1941. That marriage had ended in divorce. On June 15, 1945, Garland had married her director, Vincente Minnelli, at her mother's home, with the blessing of Louis B. Mayer, who gave the bride away.

After spending much of her honeymoon in New York searching with the obliging police for her lost poodle, Garland announced her intention to leave MGM and devote her career to singing on the Broadway stage.

That never happened. Back in Hollywood, she signed once again with MGM. At the time of Kate's visit, Garland was slated to once again be directed by her husband in *The Pirate* opposite Gene Kelly, a film that was eventually released in 1948.

Garland's daughter, Liza, was born March 12, 1946, at the Cedars of Lebanon Hospital, weighing six pounds, ten and a half ounces. Following the birth of her daughter, Garland became known as a devoted mother, "flowing with love," except for one thing. "I don't change diapers," she told the press.

When Kate was ushered into the living room, Garland was curled up on the sofa. It was obvious that she'd been crying. As Kate was later to tell her friends, Garland looked "more incredibly alive and more beautiful than I'd remembered."

Fresh faced, and without her usually heavy makeup and scarlet lipstick-slashed mouth, she had a pathetic, lonely, and almost shy quality to her. Yet, almost in contradiction, there was "something demonic about her," as Kate later told Anderson Lawler. "Without meaning to, she appeared incredibly demanding," Kate recalled. "She was like someone waiting to sweep you away into her own self-created whirlpool. I was captivated, but also a bit afraid of her. I tried to mask it with a certain indifference." Kate then admitted that she had uttered one of the most cliché-ridden lines she'd ever said. "How's married life treating you?" she asked Garland. "And motherhood?"

"Boy, do I have a story to tell," Garland said. "Later. First, how's Spence? Had life worked out different, I might have become a mother with him instead of with Vin."

Kate, as she was to tell her friends, was rather startled by how direct, even blunt, Garland was. Kate later said, "I vamped till ready by fumbling with my coat and excusing myself to go to the bathroom. My father always said that one should go take a good pee before a difficult conversation."

When Kate came back from the downstairs toilet, she finally had figured out what to say.

Having already learned of the Tracy/Garland affair, Kate had once told Cukor, "It's a shame that the kid wasn't born. With Judy for a mother, and Spencer for a father, it would probably have grown up to become the most talented kid in show business. The world's greatest actor and the world's greatest singer combined into one."

That the teenage Garland had decided to have the child aborted never presented any particularly thorny problem for Kate. After all, from the day she'd learned to understand what was said to her, Kate's mother, Kit, a close friend of birth control advocate Margaret Sanger, had strenuously advocated teenage abortion. And Kate herself, as she grew up, was a firm believer in aborting unwanted pregnancies.

Turning to Garland on the sofa once again, Kate lit a cigarette and studied the young woman closely. "If you and Spencer had decided to have the child in secret, I think I would have adopted the boy myself."

"What makes you think it would have been a boy?" Garland asked.

"It's a feeling I have."

Garland got up off the sofa and kissed Kate on both cheeks before leading her upstairs to the nursery. Kate was introduced to the nanny, Mrs. McFarlane, before being led to a baby's crib. In it rested the infant Liza Minnelli. Kate admired the child with its big brown eyes, dark hair, and long lashes. "That's Vincente's child all right. She looks more like him than you."

"The guys over at MGM, who make jokes about Vin's effeminate mannerisms, say that the birth was an immaculate conception," Garland said.

Kate was a bit startled by that and didn't know how to react. Leaving Liza with her nanny, Kate followed Garland back downstairs and into the living room. "I guess you had to have sex with your husband to produce such a lovely girl. Oh, my God, that is probably the most stupid remark I've ever made in my life."

"Surely you're not one of the people who think I don't have sex with my husband?" Garland asked.

"Actually, I've never thought about it before," Kate said. "I mean, some men who look obviously homosexual aren't, and some men who look incredibly manly are gay. I've been in Hollywood long enough to know that."

"You mean men like Spencer?" Garland asked.

458

"I'd rather not discuss that," Kate said, "although I feel a bond with you because both of us have known Spencer in bed. Except he never made me pregnant. I love him, but we have our own relationship and our own rules."

"That is why I wanted so desperately to see you," Garland said. "I want to know how you can continue to live with Spence and indulge him in his other pastimes."

"You mean his side affairs with Carole Landis, Goddard, *et al?*"

"No, I mean with boys on the side." Garland asked.

"It's nothing I've ever had to deal with directly," Kate said. "He's entitled to his privacy, and he respects my sometimes going off on my own to do God knows what."

"I think it's different when you're married," Garland said. "Right now I'm not with my husband and I don't expect him for another week. He's gone off with his true love, Gene Kelly."

"Perhaps they're just good friends," Kate said without any real conviction in her voice.

"You don't seem at all surprised by my revelation," Garland said. "I mean, about Vin and Gene."

"That's because I have a friend, Andy, who keeps me up to date on all the gossip. You may not know this, but the rumors about Kelly and your husband have even made it to the broom closet at MGM. Of course, all of those rumors may be just that—rumors."

"It's not mere gossip," Garland said. "The other night I came home unexpectedly. I was going to surprise Vin. I surprised him all right. Gene was fucking him. I'd call that more than just a friendship."

"What did you do?" Kate asked.

"I ran out of the house and didn't come back until midnight," Garland said. "When I finally came home, Vin had left me a note. He said that in the future, he would be sleeping alone in another room in the house. The next morning, he didn't mention Gene. He also didn't mention the incident and neither did I. He barely talked to me at all. He just kept his nose in a Hollywood trade paper—and that was that."

"Do you plan to divorce him?" Kate asked pointedly.

"I'm sure that's in our future," Garland said.

To break the tension, Kate asked Judy if she would walk out into the garden with her to enjoy the twilight.

As the two women strolled through the garden, Garland took her hand as if seeking comfort from her. When Kate re-created the enchantment on the phone with Anderson Lawler that night, she recalled that it was one of those incredibly beautiful evenings that occurred in the Forties back in Los Angeles when the air was much cleaner. "Suddenly, walking with Judy and holding her hand, I felt drawn to her as I never had before, although I had encountered her casually for years. I felt that she was pleading for my friendship."

Kate turned to Garland and looked deeply into her eyes. "You're no longer the little girl who met Spence when you were only fifteen. You've been in Hollywood too long. You must have known about Vincente before you married him."

"I turned a deaf ear to all those chorus boys at MGM who told me that Vin was gay when he was directing me in *Meet Me in St. Louis,*" Garland said. "I would turn to them and tell them, 'You're wrong about Vin. You're mistaking artistic flair for gayness.' I should have listened to them."

"Still, you forged ahead."

"Even before my wedding, two chorus boys, Frank Lot and Jimmie Schanker, both claimed that they had had a regular thing with my future groom. I remembered they called it 'a do.'"

Garland related the brief history of her relationship with Minnelli, claiming that he was "very passionate when he directed me in *The Clock.* Some lighting operators up high on the catwalk even spotted me going down on Vin in the dark shadows during a lunch break."

Sitting down on a wrought-iron bench, asking Kate to join her, Garland said, "I'm such a fool. I see but I don't want to see." She claimed that she had been invited, along with Minnelli, to a New Year's Eve party to ring in the New Year of 1945. "It was at the home of Jack and Mary Benny. When midnight came, everybody was kissing someone except Mary and me. I went looking for Vin. I found him in the Benny family library with Jack's tongue down his throat."

"Well," Kate said, "that should have provided a clue. All of us, including his wife, Mary, know all about Jack."

As the evening progressed, Garland told Kate about an encounter with Lena Horne, who said, "Vincente just loves making a woman look beautiful on the screen. He views it as his creation. He loves to dress women. Look at what he did for me, honeychild. That was your mama up there playing that sensuous seductress in *Cabin in the Sky.*"

Garland confessed that when she was dating Minnelli, trying to decide if she wanted to marry him, she was also secretly dating Orson Welles. "Orson told me, 'My dear child, Minnelli doesn't want to create a beautiful image of you on the screen, like your friend Lena talked about. *He sees himself as you!* Through you, he's living the illusion of what he passionately wants to be: A screen goddess like my own Rita Hayworth. Of course, all of us have our fantasies, especially me. I once had a dream in which I became Marlene Dietrich.'"

"You know how *I* am," Garland said, desperately clutching Kate's had. "I'm not very good with schedules." She said that one night she'd arranged dates with both Minnelli and Welles on the same evening. Because Minnelli arrived first, she went with him, later calling Welles from a restaurant and explaining and apologizing for her mistake. "He was very sweet about the whole thing,"

460

Garland said. "'You should have waited for me,' he told me. 'We could have had a three-way. I'd fuck you, then I'd fuck Minnelli, then I'd fuck you again. I'm sure I'd have had him panting for more of my noble tool.'"

I know Mayer put a lot of pressure on you to marry Vincente," Kate said to her. "He told me that himself. Mayer thinks that marriage to an older man will help stabilize you. From what you've just told me, it appears to be that marriage to such a man could drive a weak woman over the edge. That must have been hard to take, seeing the father of your newborn baby getting 'impregnated' by another man."

"But it's more than that," Garland said. "In my heart, I knew that Vin was enjoying the sex act more with Gene than he ever did with me. We have rotten sex. He has trouble maintaining an erection. When he does get one, I fear that he's not thinking about the woman under him, but that he's fantasizing about being fucked himself."

You do believe in telling it like it is," Kate said. "I'm amazed that you can talk so openly with me. Even though we've known each other for years, it was mostly sitting side by side and chatting while some MGM hairdresser did our hair. I find this sudden intimacy disturbing."

"Don't be disturbed," Garland said. "I'm like that with everybody. You are the mystery woman of MGM now that Garbo's retired. You hold in all your secrets, except perhaps for a close pal here and there—probably gay. Gay men are the only ones women can confide in."

"If Mayer thought that Vincente would straighten you out," Kate said, "who is he going to get to straighten out Kelly and Vincente? He'll find out about them one day. He always does. He's grooming Vincente to be his biggest musical director, and Kelly to be his biggest musical star. He'll want to keep both guys married, lest word get out about what they're really up to."

"There's more," Garland said. "Vin is also a drag queen. Do you know he sometimes tries to wear my discarded clothing? He gets Irene Gibbons over at MGM's costume department to alter some of my dresses. I caught him one night in our bedroom wearing my wedding gown. It's this smoky gray number with pink pearl beading. I tried to handle it with a joke. I said, 'Oh, Vin, take it off! It looked better on me.'"

Garland claimed that even when Minnelli took her to New York, he spent most of his time with his former lover, Lester Gaba. "He invited Gaba for dinner every night we were there. When those two were together, Vin paid me no attention at all. He had eyes only for Gaba. The remarkable thing was that the two of them looked so much alike that many people thought they were twins."

"Maybe Vincente isn't homosexual at all, but just a totally out-of-control narcissist," Kate said.

"He's gay all right," Garland claimed. "When Gaba came down to Grand Central to see us off, Vin was shedding more tears than a school of Greer Garsons."

As Garland led Kate back into the living room, since the evening was suddenly growing cold, she said that whenever Gene Kelly came near him, her husband behaved the same way he did with Gaba.

"They spend hours and hours together sitting like they're in a huddle," Garland said. "Even when I come into the room, they pay me no attention. Vin doesn't even seem to know I'm there. Those two don't need women to love them, much less wives. They have each other. I should have realized from the beginning what kind of man I was marrying. I've been made love to by men who really like women, and I've been made love to by men who don't. Believe me, Vin falls into the latter category. Gene Kelly can satisfy him in ways I can't."

"Kelly has the equipment, and we don't," Kate said. "Damn it, I've been stating the obvious all day."

Over a drink, Garland said that her husband could be sitting in the living room just staring into space and saying nothing to her. "But the moment Gene comes over, those big doe eyes of his light up and he comes alive for the first time all day."

Kate gave her some advice, as she did with all people she met. "Stick in there a little longer, especially since you've just given birth. You can still be with a man even though he sees other women on the side. Or, men as the case may be. Believe me, you're talking to an experienced person about that. I suggest you launch yourself into another affair." Kate rose from the sofa. "I really must be going. I'm having dinner with Spencer later. He's got stomach trouble tonight, and won't be on the town prowling. But tomorrow, I'll be by to see you promptly at seven a.m. I'm taking you for a long walk in the hills."

"I don't do that," Garland protested.

"Starting right now, if you want to be my friend, you'll begin by taking long walks with me every morning at seven."

"Is that the price I have to pay for a friendship with you?" Garland asked.

"That and more," Kate said, reaching for her coat. "I think we'll be friends. We have more in common that I'd thought at first."

"I just knew you'd become my most important woman friend," Garland said.

"What gave you such self-assurance?" Kate asked. "I don't extend friendship easily."

"Because I'm so vulnerable," Garland said. "Just look." In an amazing transformation of her facial muscles, she suddenly became the most pathetic creature in all the world. "How can you resist befriending someone who looks like me? I'm not a strong and independent woman like you. I can't survive alone."

As Garland stood up to show Kate out, a look of agonizing pain slashed across her face like the cut of a sharp razor. She screamed. Kate knew at once that her newly acquired friend was not pretending.

462

Garland fell to the floor where she rolled over several times in pain.

"Call Dr. Marc," she shouted to Kate. "His number's scribbled on the wall. By the phone in the kitchen."

Kate rushed into the kitchen, where she spotted the number and immediately dialed Dr. Marc's office. The doctor came on the phone and promised her he'd be at the Minnelli residence in less than half an hour. He assured Kate that his patient had these attacks frequently. "Don't be unduly alarmed. I know what to do."

Kate returned to the living room and tried to comfort Garland as much as she could until the doctor came, but there was nothing she could do but lift her back up onto the sofa. At one point, since Garland was sweating profusely, Kate went into the kitchen and came back with a wet towel which she applied to her forehead.

True to his word, Dr. Marc arrived and was let in by the nanny. He immediately injected some fluid into Garland's left arm. Once injected, Garland just seemed to drift off.

Before leaving, the doctor assured Kate that his patient would be all right, but asked Kate to remain with her for at least another two hours and call him if there was any change in her condition. Before leaving the house, he requested Kate's autograph.

Kate poured herself a stiff drink, then went and sat down in an armchair to watch over Garland. At one point, she got up and called Kenneth MacKenna to tell him what had just transpired between Garland and herself.

"There are worse stories I can tell you about Judy," Kenneth said. "I fear that for Judy, this is just the beginning. We've had self-destructive people at MGM before. Judy is just joining the club." Before ringing off, Kenneth warned Kate not to get too deeply involved with Garland. "I love Judy, but you deserve better than getting immersed in her crazy, mixed-up world. Keep me posted. I want to know about everything that's going on between the two of you."

Two hours later, when Garland still hadn't awakened, Kate went to find the nanny to tell her she was leaving.

Mrs. MacFarlane came into the living room and placed a blanket over Garland. She looked down at her protectively.

Before leaving, Kate said, "Seems to me as if you have *two* babies to take care of."

***

At seven o'clock the next morning, Kate had a very difficult time getting a drowsy Garland to arise from her bed. Kate had to enlist the help of Mrs. MacFarlane, who was engaged mainly with Liza since the child was screaming at the top of her lung capacity.

Driving Garland to a remote spot in the Hollywood Hills, Kate came to a stop near a belvedere where she stood holding Garland's hand as they took in the panoramic view.

After all the rapid talk and revelations of yesterday, Garland was strangely quiet. Kate enjoyed her company and even told her how beautiful she was in the morning light.

"Elizabeth Taylor is beautiful," Garland said. "Lana Turner is beautiful. Whenever I'm in a room with either of them, or especially both of them, no eyes look at me."

"Until you start to sing," Kate assured her. "Then you become the most beautiful woman who ever came into a room." She leaned over and gently kissed Garland on the lips.

Garland looked startled but kept on walking with Kate. "I dreamed about Mr. Gene Kelly last night," she said.

"I thought you would dream about me," Kate said, pretending that she was offended.

"You're my dream tonight," Garland assured her. "First off, I'm seriously pissed at Gene because the only time he invites me to his house is when he wants me to entertain his guests. Imagine getting the great Judy Garland to sing for free at your house."

"That's reality," Kate admonished her. "Get to the dream."

"In my dream I was married to Gene and we were embarking from Southampton on the *Titanic*," Garland said. "When it came time for me to get into a lifeboat, and leave Gene aboard the sinking ship, he grabbed Liza from my arms. Amazingly, he had dressed in my ball gown and had disguised himself as a woman. He was going to slip onto the lifeboat with my baby and he did. He left me on the sinking ship to be the girl singer for the band. In my dream, I was singing 'Nearer My God to Thee' and then I woke up screaming."

"A Freudian analyst would have fun with that," Kate said, guiding Garland to a bed of wildflowers that covered a hill. Kate said that she was enjoying the day so much that she wanted to spend hours in the hills and that they could return to her car later. "I've packed us the most delicious and nutritious picnic lunch."

"Instead of taking pills in the morning and lying in bed lamenting how bad everything is, you should get up and out and live, like we're doing today. I'll bet you haven't breathed fresh air since you left that farm in Kansas."

"You're probably right," Garland said. "I think I'm in Oz right now. Oz is Hollywood."

"We've both known that for a long time," Kate said. "*Me* even more than you."

***

464

It is not known when the friendship of Kate with Garland turned sexual. Usually candid with friends such as Cukor, Kate was extremely discreet about her seduction of Garland.

Anderson Lawler ventured forth with the best guess. "Their affair began sometime in 1946 and lasted through most of 1948—and maybe into 1949."

"Kate told me that when the owners were away, she cajoled Garland into breaking into a house with her," Lawler said. "Judy was apparently very nervous about doing that, but Kate could be extremely persuasive. I mean, she even got Irene Mayer Selznick to go house-breaking with her. My guess is that Kate seduced Judy in a stranger's bed. Without actually being there to witness it, I can just bet it was Kate who was the butch one, Judy playing the *femme*."

"Kate provided us with a lot of clues about Judy's mental condition at the time," Kenneth MacKenna later said. "Her daughter, Liza, had been born in March by cesarean section. Forever after, Judy always claimed that giving birth was one of the most traumatizing experiences of her life."

"Kate met her during one of her most vulnerable periods," Kenneth claimed. "At least in her life up until then. Judy was ripe for seduction when Kate came into her life. I knew that Judy was feeling worthless about herself, especially when she learned Minnelli had fallen big for Gene Kelly. When he wasn't with Gene, he was with various MGM chorus boys."

The birth of Liza was followed by one of the worst bouts of depression that Garland ever had. For many months, she not only avoided having sex with men, she was afraid to. She told Kate that the idea of ever getting penetrated by another man "is my worst living, breathing, fucking nightmare. I don't want to get pregnant again. My body was not made for birthin' babies." She, of course, was quoting from Butterfly McQueen's famous line in *Gone With the Wind*, which Garland had seen three times.

Her friend, Mickey Rooney, claimed that "Judy was self-indulgent and self-delusional—and in constant need of attention." Unknown to Rooney at the time, Kate was genuinely attempting to minister to Garland's needs.

For Kate, it became a losing battle, the way it was with Tracy. In spite of all the times she weaned him from the bottle, he always returned to liquor. In spite of Kate's repeatedly flushing Garland's pills down the toilet, Garland always managed to come up with new ones.

"I could never understand why Kate wanted to mess up her life with yet another emotionally crippled person," Kenneth MacKenna said. "Cukor, Andy, and I knew that there was some sexual attraction between those two. But it was so much more than that. In being the lonely bachelor woman that she was, Kate had had to give up a lot in life.

"She had already rejected the idea of having a loving husband like Luddy. Actually, Luddy isn't a good example, because he was gay. But Kate found many men in life who would have married her—and I don't mean weirdos like Howard Hughes. Frankly, they didn't come much sicker in Hollywood than Hughes. Regrettably, most of the men she loved were married, but she could have found someone suitable for marriage.

"Even if she had wanted a fulfilling relationship with a woman, she could have had that, too, with Laura Harding. But she spurned Laura when Laura began pushing Kate toward monogamy. In the end, good and steadfast Laura was Kate's sometime friend. Laura was always there, ready and waiting to share her bed with Kate. The tragedy is that Laura was a great and fine woman and richly deserved a truly satisfying relationship. I think that her life would have been far more rewarding if she'd never met Kate in the first place, and had found someone who would be at her side, enriching her life.

"Kate wanted to keep Laura in her life, at least on occasions, but she had this desire to mother things, and Laura was not the type of woman to be mothered. Kate loved challenges. That's where Tracy and Judy enter the picture. I think Kate loved to mother each of them more than she liked to have sex with them. So despite the many times Tracy and Judy disappointed Kate, she still felt that she—and she alone—could save them. Call it arrogance, or call it self-confidence gone astray, but Kate firmly believed that she could set the right example for both Tracy and Judy. Of course, Kate failed miserably in both cases. No one could save either Tracy or Judy.

"Kate never harmed either of those two. In fact, she helped them in many, many ways. But the one thing she couldn't do, and it was essential to saving both Tracy and Judy, was that Kate could not get either of them to help themselves.

"It is interesting to note that as much as Kate loved both Tracy and Judy, she never allowed them to suck her into their own nightmares. She was involved with them, and on the most intimate of terms, but she could always pull back from them at the last minute before being sucked into their vortexes.

"For Tracy and Judy, it was always Saturday night at the party. For Kate, it was always the sobering light of dawn on a bleak Monday morning. Kate could be self-delusional, but even so, she was a woman firmly anchored on this earth.

"In contrast, Judy and Tracy would face Monday morning and wonder whether they could get through another day without doing themselves in. Kate would wake up Monday morning and mull over where she was going to find the freshest vegetables for dinner that night," Kenneth concluded.

There is evidence that Kate never fully came to terms with the extent of Garland's tendency for self-destruction. "Kate believed that a few walks in the country and the extension of pure love and affection could pull Judy back from the edge of the cliff," Cukor claimed.

Mickey Rooney was more realistic about his dear friend. He said, "Judy was fighting pill addiction and doing everything in her soul to avoid a total nervous breakdown."

Cukor himself felt that Garland was forced back to work too soon after the birth of Liza. "She was weakened and traumatized both by the birth of Liza and by her realization that Minnelli loved Gene Kelly a hell of a lot more than he loved her."

Kate's worst critics, including Joan Crawford, felt that "Hepburn took advantage of the situation." That was Crawford's first reaction upon hearing rumors of a Garland/Hepburn affair. "Claudette, apparently, wasn't enough for our aristocrat from Connecticut." In fairness, Crawford admitted that Kate was not Garland's first lesbian affair. Crawford recalled that she knew that Betty Asher was seducing Garland at the time she made *The Wizard of Oz* in the late Thirties. "Everybody, with the possible exception of Louis B. Mayer, knew about the Garland/Asher affair. If he had ever found out that his Dorothy in *Oz* was indulging in lesbian sex, his left ball would have collapsed."

Asher, the beautiful daughter of a producer at Universal, worked for Howard Strickling in MGM's publicity department. Strickling called Asher "vice-president in charge of Judy Garland."

Unknown to Garland at the time, Asher was reporting everything that she did day and night to her boss, Strickling. When Garland learned of this spying, she justifiably felt that Asher—"my one true friend"—had betrayed her.

"I was confused back then," Garland later told Kate. "And I still am. One night it was Betty Asher. The next night the even more beautiful Tyrone Power. I never knew where Ty was on the three or four nights he didn't see me. With his wife, Annabella, perhaps, though often I learned he wasn't with her either."

"You should have called Howard Hughes at his Muirfield estate," Kate told Garland. "You probably would have found Ty there."

Crawford, who knew Garland only casually, said in later years that she felt Garland was basically heterosexual but enjoyed an occasional bout of female-to-female intimacy from time to time. "She was very experimental and very loving in those days," Crawford claimed. "She was in such desperate need of love that anyone—male or female—who got close to her could end up making love to her. Amazingly, she seduced more homosexual men in her day than did Spencer Tracy himself."

Almost daily, Kate struggled with Garland to wean her from her pill addiction. For Kate, that was as successful as her losing battle to wean Tracy from the bottle.

Garland told Kate that she was afraid she'd get fat if she gave up the pills. "I can balloon and balloon fast," she said. "Dexedrine keeps me slim."

"But there's a downside," Kate ventured to say. "Dexadrine also makes you highly nervous, very irritable, and almost impossible to live with. I've confirmed this with my father. He's a doctor and knows about such things."

"Mayer wants me to look sylphlike on the screen," Garland said.

Kate came up with a startling idea. "Why don't you give up the screen and become a concert singer? You could get bookings all over the country.

Abandon the pills and eat anything you want. Singers don't have to be thin—in fact, some of the world's best singers are fat. You could become known as 'the little Kate Smith.'" She stopped for a minute. "My God, if I hadn't gotten my husband to change his name, and if I'd followed the conventional patterns of married women, I'd be known today as Kate Smith myself."

"I did give up pills one time," Garland claimed. "I was walking along the East River in Manhattan with Vin on our honeymoon. Like you, he was urging me to give up the pills. I reached into my handbag, took out the pills, and tossed them into those murky waters. 'I'll never take them again,' I vowed to him. He became very emotional and even cried with joy at my vow. Of course, the next day I went out and found another doctor who prescribed more pills for me. Actually, I get most of my pills through the dispensary at Metro. There's a doctor there who's very generous with me. He's an addict himself and understands my need for them. When he cracks down on me, I get close friends to get their own doctors to prescribe pills for them, and then they turn their cache over to me."

Kate thought this was horrible, and she warned Garland that she could destroy "a God-given talent."

Sometimes Garland would break out in cold sweats and would desperately call Kate in the middle of the night. Whenever that happened, Kate would arise from her bed and drive over to Garland's house to help her.

"For several months," Lawler said, "Kate tended to Judy even more that she tended to Tracy. After Tracy got back from touring in *The Rugged Path*, he would sometimes go for days without actually seeing Kate. They always spoke on the phone. A few affairs with women on the side, plus a supply of boys from Cukor, were keeping Tracy occupied in those days. Kate was carrying on with both Judy and Miss Colbert, with occasional arrivals of Laura Harding from the East, so she was kept fairly busy too. I don't think she was involved with any men at the time. The thing with Robert Mitchum could be tossed off as a quick roll in the hay."

Sometimes Garland would get a migraine that would last for days. Kate would try every remedy she knew, often to no avail, to help her friend get over those crippling headaches.

If not a migraine, it was some other ailment plaguing Garland. At least once a week, Kate was summoned to Garland's house when her left arm—never her right one—or her left or right leg would become numb. To provide some welcome relief, Kate often massaged the limb for more than an hour or so at a time. After that she would go into the kitchen and cook some nourishing food for her stricken friend. Garland would often turn down the plate offered. "I prefer a diet of pills," she'd tell Kate.

Kate told Cukor that Garland would often stand nude looking at herself in the mirror, especially at her breasts. "They each point in a different direction," Garland said. "Directors, to my embarrassment and humiliation, often point

468

this out to me and order wardrobe to tape them so the nipples don't shoot out east and west."

Kate often called Dr. Hepburn in Connecticut and had long talks with him about Garland's condition. She reported to her father that Garland's hands trembled so much that she couldn't even apply lipstick and especially mascara to her face. "It's not because I'm drunk or on medication," Garland said. "All the Gumm women have trembling hands. It's genetic."

Even on the MGM lot, Kate would sometimes be summoned by Minnelli himself to help his wife. "I can't do anything with her," he'd tell Kate.

Going into Garland's dressing room, Kate often found the singer huddled in a corner in a fetal position. "I can't face the camera," Garland said on one such occasion. "It feels like when I go out there, I'm naked! Completely exposed to the world. Without wearing a stitch of clothing!"

"Kate would sometimes comfort Judy in her arms," Minnelli later confessed. "I couldn't do that for Judy. But Kate could."

Lawler felt that in time, Kate began to view Garland more as a daughter than as a female lover. "I think at some point their relationship ceased to be sexual. Judy was back to men again, carrying on affairs with Yul Brynner and the like. Later Kate became the most reliable female friend in Judy's life. When Judy tried to commit suicide in 1950, Kate was the first person at her bedside."

"In 1961, Kate practically held Judy together when we were making *Judgment at Nuremberg,*" claimed Kenneth MacKenna, who was also in the film playing a judge.

"Although Judy would sometimes lash out at Kate, and one time, or so I've heard, actually attacked her physically, there was genuine love between the two women," Cukor claimed. "Kate was the forever scolding but also forgiving mother, and Judy was the always erring, always inconsiderate, but also loving daughter. Judy knew that she could pull any stunt, and Kate would forgive her. And so their relationship went on and on. If Kate didn't really love Judy, she would have walked away from her years before. At least throughout the rest of the Forties, Kate put up with as much from Judy as she did from Spence. Thanks to her self-assumed duties as a nurse, Kate would probably have been brilliant in an on-screen interpretation of Florence Nightingale."

***

Kate usually cooked dinner for Tracy and drove her meal over to his cottage on the grounds of George Cukor's estate. There, she'd reheat the food for him. But once, when she had spent the afternoon at his cottage, she decided around four o'clock to cook his favorite dish: Irish lamb stew with lots of potatoes, onions, and carrots.

Since she liked to go to bed by nine-thirty in the evening, she always left early, leaving Tracy alone with his insomnia, wandering through the cottage, reading his detective stories, and drinking endless pots of black coffee, which did little to put him to sleep.

That evening, around seven-thirty, as they were eating in the dining room, there was the faint sound of a small explosion originating in the kitchen. Suddenly, all the lights went out. Excusing herself, she checked the kitchen to see if anything there was on fire. She hastily found some candles and lit them, then she found a flashlight and examined the fuse box but could see nothing wrong. Back in the living room, she called out to an inebriated Tracy that she was going up the hill to Cukor's house to see if anyone there could investigate their loss of power. Nearby, she could see electric lights illuminated, so she knew it was not a global power failure.

Walking up the hill, she heard a wild party going on in the main house of the Cukor estate. All of Cukor's friends knew that, depending on his mood and the venue at hand, evenings at his house were often wildly varied. Some of his parties were strictly for A-list Hollywood stars, directors, and producers, sometimes including Garbo herself, Joan Crawford, Pandro S. Berman, and Gary Cooper.

On other nights, Cukor staged either intimate dinners for a few gay friends and some select hustlers to entertain them, or else he threw what he called "stag parties" for his gay guests, along with the cream of the hustler colony. Through Lawler, Kate had learned that Cukor hated the word, "hustler," preferring to call his sex industry entertainers "out-of-work actors." Cukor was known to favor very handsome, virile young men, never anyone effeminate. For reasons known best to himself, he preferred his "gay-for-pay" actors to be, or at least pretend to be, primarily straight. As he often stated to his gay friends, "Making love to a homosexual is just not as thrilling as making love to a straight man."

Moving toward his house across his rear lawn, Kate spotted nearly a dozen young nude men either swimming or lounging beside the pool. Several fully dressed older men were clustered around the bar drinking and smoking.

Ignoring the nude swimmers, Kate barged on by and demanded that the bartender bring Cukor to her at once.

As she waited the few minutes it took to summon Cukor, a young, naked swimmer put a towel around his magnificent physique and came up to her. "You're my favorite actress, Miss Hepburn," he said. "I'm Derek Harris. My father met you one time. He's the director, Lawson Harris. My mother's an actress, too. Dolores Johnson. Just bit parts, so perhaps you've never heard of her."

"Young man, I don't know your parents, and I hope they don't know you're here at George's house tonight," Kate said. "I'm glad you admire my work."

"I want to break into films too," he said. "I was already cast with your friend, Miss Colbert, in her picture, *Since You Went Away.* I'm sure you saw it.

My part was so small I guess you didn't notice me."

"I saw it. It was a big homefront tearjerker," she said. "Actually Claudette herself took me to see it. Forgive me, but I don't recall you in the film. I do remember this rather stiff-jawed but incredibly beautiful young man. What was his name? I have a hard time remembering the names of the little boys populating pictures these days."

"Guy Madison," he quickly added.

"Yes, that's our boy," she said. "Until I saw you, I thought he was the most beautiful male animal ever to step in front of a camera. Now, I must say you have him beat by a country mile. If good looks is what it takes to make it in pictures, I predict you'll be a big star. But don't get the wrong idea. You're definitely not my type!"

"I'm sorry to hear that," Harris said, feigning disappointment.

"How did you meet our friend George?" she asked. "Is the question too intrusive?"

"He gave me a small part in *I'll be Seeing You.* Did you see it?"

"You mean the one where Ginger Rogers was type cast as a convict released from a state penitentiary?" she said sarcastically.

"That's the one!" he said. "Your friend, Joseph Cotton, was in it. He spoke most highly of you."

"That's nice," she said. "I hope Ginger kept her man-eating paws off you, and that you didn't molest Shirley Temple."

"I was a good boy—at least until I met Cukor," Harris said. "He corrupted me."

She surveyed the scene by the pool. "So I see. You're getting ahead in Hollywood just the way I did it. I fucked every producer, male star, and director there was. Sometimes even Mayer himself calls me into his office to service him."

Although obviously said in jest and with a smile, Kate spoke those words with such conviction that it took Harris a moment to register the impact of her remarks. Coming from Kate, such a statement hit him like a shock wave.

"You must be joking," Harris finally said, regaining his composure.

From the shadows of the party came the voice of a soggy Anderson Lawler, sprawled out on a chaise longue. "Kate, darling, I heard every word you said to this trick. You should be ashamed for praising his male beauty so much. Every man at this party has already done that. You'll spoil him and ruin him for us fellows."

"Andy," Kate said, "I figured you'd be here."

At that point, Cukor rushed up to her. "Kate, you weren't supposed to come tonight. This one is just for the boys."

Kate explained the emergency that was happening in the cottage's kitchen. "Oh, hell, there's nothing I can do about it now," Cukor said. "I hate being a landlord. Why don't you tell Spence to read by candlelight tonight. Abe

Lincoln managed to educate himself that way, and I'm sure Spence can get by for the night. Or else drive him over to your house up on the mountain. You guys can sit out and watch the full moon. The stars are out tonight, each of them radiant. Now, I have to go."

Cukor kissed her on both cheeks. She could easily tell that he'd been drinking heavily.

Lawler rose on wobbly legs and kissed her good night, too. She looked back to say goodbye to Derek Harris but he'd disappeared.

As she was heading back across the grounds to Tracy's cottage, the now partially dressed young man ran after her, easily catching up with her. Barefoot, Harris had slipped into a pair of tight blue jeans and a form-fitting white T-shirt. "Wait up!" he called to her. "I might be of some help. I'm a pretty good handyman. In fact, I was going down to see Spence later tonight myself."

"Spence, is it?" She was skeptical.

"*You* know," he said, indicating that she must be well aware of the situation around Cukor's estate. "He's advising me about my acting career."

"That's more than he's ever done for me. He tells me to remember my lines and not bump into the furniture."

At the cottage, Kate called ahead to warn Tracy that a young man was accompanying her.

"It's Derek," called the dashingly handsome California boy who looked about twenty years old.

"Derek Sullavan Harris in the flesh," Tracy called back. "You're welcome! So, you've met Katie?"

Tracy looked embarrassed as Harris walked into the cottage as if he owned the place and went immediately into the kitchen to investigate the problem.

Kate sat silently with Tracy as he finished his Irish stew. He did not tell her how he knew Derek Harris. Nor did she enquire. He demanded that she bring him a Scotch. In the kitchen she found Harris with a flashlight investigating the switchbox. She poured Tracy a meager Scotch and returned to join him in the dining room. "You make a pretty good Irish stew, but nothing like my mother made."

Suddenly, the lights came on. "You did it, boy!" Tracy called out to Harris in the kitchen.

The young man came out beaming. "I'm sorry Spence," he said. "I know I wasn't due until nine."

"That's fine," Tracy said, looking the boy up and down. "Kate, would you give me a quick kiss and call me late tomorrow morning?"

"Yes, I know," she said. "I'll gather up my things."

She stood at the doorway, looking back at the two men. "Derek here tells me you're giving him acting lessons."

"His biggest acting challenge is to pretend he likes spending an evening with a broken down old man like me."

472

At those words, she turned and hastily departed from the cottage and the grounds, heading back to the privacy of her own home.

Lawler had gone to search for her. He found her sobbing, and offered to drive her back home. During the drive back, she told him what had happened in the cottage between Derek Harris, Tracy, and herself.

***

Kate's exposure to Tracy's secret life didn't alienate her from him. If anything, it helped them form a closer bond in their friendship. Each of them became more relaxed with each other and more comfortable with their respective peccadillos. They began to confide in each other and to laugh and share more of their private moments away from each other.

Tracy told Cukor, "Now that I know that Kate knows everything, I have less guilt about what I'm doing."

"Don't worry about it," Cukor told him. "While I'm keeping you entertained with my bag of tricks, Kate is having a gay old time with her girlfriends. But you claimed Judy Garland's cherry long before Kate ever did."

In 1949, through Anderson Lawler, Kate learned that Derek Harris had changed his name to "John Derek" and that he'd gotten his first big break in films. He was going to appear opposite Humphrey Bogart in the film, *Knock on Any Door*. When the movie was released, Tracy insisted that Kate drive him to see it at a remote theater in Pasadena, since they didn't want to be seen together in any of the movie houses of Hollywood.

In the decades ahead, John Derek became better known for marrying famous and beautiful women than he was for his mainly lackluster films. After photographing his wife, Ursula Andress, for a spread in *Playboy*, he divorced her to marry Linda Evans, whom he'd directed in *Childish Things*. Eventually tossing her aside as well, he became captivated by a sixteen-year-old, Mary Cathleen Collins. Under the name "Bo Derek," she was slated to become "my greatest creation." Because of her success in the 1979 comedy, "10," John Derek became famous around the world as her Svengali-like mentor.

Kate later told Lawler, "I guess pretty boys in Hollywood have to get their start somehow. It's the same with women. I never had to do it, but sleeping your way to the top seems to be an acceptable way of getting ahead in this town. Take Lucille Ball, for instance. And I hear Nancy Davis is doing the same thing but without much luck."

Derek Harris (aka John Derek, who died at his ranch in California on May 22, 1998) became one of maybe one-hundred to one-hundred and fifty young actors whom Tracy "auditioned" between 1946 and the early 1960s, usually with Kate's tacit approval if not outright endorsement.

Four or five of these "casting couch" young actors later became household names. Once or twice, the same magazine, *Confidential,* that had threatened Kate and Colbert with exposure also threatened to expose Cukor and Tracy. It is not known why the staff at *Confidential* didn't, since they had all the data and documentation they needed for such coverage.

Even Lawler, who seemed to know everything, didn't know how—or even if—the magazine was bought off. Amazingly, Kate's affair with Tracy wasn't exposed during either the Forties or the Fifties. Neither was the more incendiary news about her lesbian activities and his homosexual dalliances. Tracy's gayness was such a closely guarded secret that when *Variety* "outed" him as late as the 21st century, the news of his homosexuality, although well known to the elite members of the Hollywood community, came as a shock to the general public.

Only one of Tracy's hired boy friends, "Chad Cummings" (his real name isn't known) officially outed Tracy and a host of other stars in an unpublished manuscript sent in the late 1970s to the literary agent, Jay Garon, in New York. A decade later, Garon was partially responsible for launching the career of best-selling author John Grisham.

Garon ran the best-known independent literary agency in New York, and had known Cummings back when Garon called himself "Cukor's boy" in Hollywood. Although Cukor quickly tired of Garon, Garon was initially hired to have sex with Cukor, and eventually evolved into a sort of errand boy and house boy. Garon cleverly managed to remain within the Cukor household partly because of his incredible talent for securing handsome and virile young men for Cukor and, on occasion, for Tracy as well.

After Garon's attorney vetted Cummings' manuscript, the agent was advised not to submit it for publication. The very real and very viable fear at the time was that, because of its incendiary material, many stars—both male and female—would sue its publisher for libel.

The six-foot, two-hundred pound, muscular, blond-haired Cummings was from Austin, Texas. Within months of his arrival in Hollywood, he was categorized as one of Tinsel Town's most highly paid and most sought after hustlers, known for his striking looks and generous endowment. He preferred to advertise himself in gay magazines as "a sweet Southerner…extremely charming and very sensual." Cummings claimed that even by the late Forties he was pulling in one-hundred dollars per liaison. He said that he serviced both male and female stars, including Joan Crawford and on one occasion, even an aging Mae West.

"I was making one-hundred big ones per lay when some guys were lucky to get a ten spot," Cummings wrote in his manuscript. "Cukor launched me into the business. You'd be surprised the doors I knocked on in Hollywood. Some really big stars. Some of the least likely and so-called straightest guys in Hollywood used my talents. Being actors and being experimental, these guys

474

wanted to try anything once, and I was known as the best. Even George Montgomery—he was once married to Dinah Shore—booked me for one night of love."

In a chapter within the manuscript submitted to Jay Garon, Cummings revealed some of the details of his involvement with Tracy. Cummings wrote that of all of his clients, he remembered Spencer Tracy the best of all. "I have never known a man more repulsed by his own sexuality. I dreaded when I had to go see him. I brought great joy to most of my clients, especially the repressed ones. But with Tracy, I felt terrible. It was obvious that he hated himself for what he was doing."

Cummings recalled that from the time of his first visit to Tracy's cottage, he had been warned what to expect: "Tracy's fondness for oral sex on both men and women was well-known in Hollywood."

In his manuscript, Cummings claimed that Tracy was very awkward "about getting down to business. I had to take the lead or else I would have been there all night."

"He didn't even show me to the bedroom that I heard he shared with Kate Hepburn," Cummings said. "We did it right there in the living room."

Cummings revealed that at no point did Tracy remove his own clothing. "I was standing up as he fellated me. I could tell he'd done this many times before. He was quite good at it, and went after me like he'd been deprived for a very long time."

The hustler claimed that "the bad part came in at the end of the act. He swallowed but then seemed so revolted by what he'd done that he excused himself and went into his bathroom. I could hear him gagging. It sounded like he was forcing himself to vomit. I think he wanted it but didn't want it."

Although Cummings said he was rather put off by Tracy, he returned again and again to his cottage. "When I needed help in buying a car, he lent me five-hundred dollars. Of course, I had no intention of paying him back, and I'm sure Tracy didn't expect me to pay him back either."

"After several visits, Tracy never called me again," Cummings said. "I guess he found other guys. Cukor continued to call me and use my services up until 1952. Then, because of a misunderstanding with a client (I was falsely accused of stealing three-hundred dollars off one of his Cukor's drunken friends) I lost his business too.

In time, Cummings drifted to New York and formed one of the most successful "dial-a-hustler" services in that city. Garon often used his services, not only for himself, but as a reward to certain editors for buying manuscripts from him. Cummings and the agency he headed always insisted on hiring handsome young men who could service both male and female clients.

By the late 1980s, Cummings had made enough money to retire.

He died in Sarasota, Florida, of AIDS in 1992.

When *Undercurrent* opened in New York in 1946, it was the first of Kate's films not to play at Radio City Music Hall. The moment critics saw the film, there was almost universal agreement that Kate was horribly miscast as the wife of the psychopath, as played by Robert Taylor.

Manny Farber, writing in *The New Republic,* found *Undercurrent* "a waste of high-priced Hollywood talent." *Time* summed it up as an "indigestible plot, full of false leads and unkept promises."

After the first week of opening, Kate knew she'd made another flop. That's why she was more eager than ever when Clarence Brown showed up with a script that Louis B. Mayer himself had approved. It was called *Song of Love,* and Kate was to headline a cast that would include Paul Henreid and Robert Walker. Brown told her that he had been designated as both director and producer, and that Mayer had ordered him "to come up with a blockbuster."

Kate knew that she wouldn't be able to coast much longer on the success of *The Philadelphia Story* and *Woman of the Year.*

Back to making bad pictures again, her career in the Forties reached its lowest point when she was improbably miscast as pianist Clara Wieck Schumann in *Song of Love.*

Garson Kanin told her, "Go to Louis B. Mayer and tell him to take this picture and shove it up his ass."

"I'm sure Mayer knows what's best for me," she said. "He's always been honorable to me. And I've got my friendship with Irene to consider."

"Great reasons for making another turkey," Kanin said, sarcastically.

"I want to stick with MGM," she said. "The MGM staff in Chicago is marvelous when you have to change trains there." She actually said that.

Even though, during the course of her career, she'd made an inordinate number of terrible films, Kate had never lost her hard-core audience. That audience tended to include relatively sophisticated, mostly middle-aged men and women, for the most part college educated, and centered largely in the East, especially in New York, Hartford, and Boston. Almost no adolescent boy growing up in the Forties took his gum-chewing date to see a Katharine Hepburn movie.

As one movie-goer, Ralph Baywood, told a newspaper in Des Moines, "Hepburn reminds me of the teacher who taught me English lit. I flunked out." In the same newspaper, an older reader, Mabel Stroud, claimed, "I'm sometimes put off by her fluttering all over the place. Unlike Tracy, she's really pretentious at times, even deadly so, but so far, I've never missed a Kate Hepburn movie even if I have to go alone. My boyfriend prefers Lana Turner but Ann Sheridan is his favorite."

Still viewed as his prestige star, and proud of Irene's friendship with Kate, Louis B. Mayer continued to treat Kate "like the Queen of MGM."

"She insisted that all her films be shot on closed sets," Kenneth said. "Mayer didn't insist that she sit for photographs or provide interviews. Whenever she was to make another picture at MGM, Kate always sent word to our publicity department, 'If you want to get along with me, keep the God damn sons of the press off my ass. If you don't, I'll make your life absolute hell!'"

During this period, Kate was being announced for roles that she would never make. These included the Elizabeth Goudge novel, *Green Dolphin Street*, which would be made in 1947 into an MGM movie with Lana Turner. Kate was also set to play the title role in John B. Marquand's *B.F.'s Daughter*, a role that eventually went to Barbara Stanwyck instead.

Ironically, her former lover, Van Heflin, had signed to star in both of the above-mentioned films. Thinking he'd be cast opposite her, he wanted to repair their friendship. Partly for practical reasons, he'd decided to forgive her for her failure to recommend him as her co-star in the film version of *The Philadelphia Story* in which he'd wanted to repeat the role he'd originally developed with her on stage.

He suddenly came back into her life, and they were even photographed together during one of her rare visits to a night club. In the snapshot, she seems to be looking off into space.

As she later told Lawler, "I think my affair with Van began again on a Sunday morning—at least that's when we got together—but by the time the cannon had shot for the last time around midnight that Sunday, we both knew that things were over between us. And we didn't need mere words to confirm that."

More personally damaging than a string of bad pictures were harmful rumors about Kate's affair with a married man, whispered asides about her lesbianism, and Kate's left-wing politics. Political controversy like that brought her unfavorable gossip and threatened her career. By the late 1940s, as America moved deeper into its fears of Communist sabotage from within, some of the stars who had worked with Kate, especially Robert Taylor and Adolphe Menjou, were spreading the word that she was a "pinko." Louis B. Mayer, reading in the newspapers growing numbers of comments about Kate's alleged "pink sympathies," was increasingly horrified." The Hollywood witch hunts were just beginning, and would eventually lead to the destruction of many notable careers.

The worst was yet to come. Edward G. Robinson called and said he was too sick to make an important speech and asked Kate to go on in his place the following night. The speech was about censorship in Hollywood films. Without knowing all the details, Kate agreed to go on in his place. She told Robinson, "I'm sure that if you weren't ill, you'd be speaking out for the right principles."

During the war years, Kate had escaped political fallout for her so-called left-wing politics, mainly because of her friendship with the Roosevelts and contributions to the war effort that included patriotic radio broadcasts and her appearance in the morale-boosting *Stage Door Canteen.*

Perhaps angered that Truman had invited Tracy to the White House and not her, Kate refused to back the sitting President when he was running for office against Governor Thomas Dewey of New York. Tracy remained with Truman, but Kate announced that she was backing the Progressive ticket and endorsing the left-winger, Henry Wallace, instead.

Wallace's attack on Truman's "get tough" policy toward the Soviet Union had cost him his position as Secretary of Commerce under the Truman administration. Wallace was also under investigation from the increasingly powerful Committee on Un-American Activities (HUAC), in which a rising young politician from California, Congressman Richard M. Nixon, was coming into prominence. Nixon called Wallace "a Communist dupe."

Wallace had been barred from addressing a rally at the Hollywood Bowl in May of 1947. Filling in for Edward G. Robinson, Kate agreed to speak at an anti-censorship rally at the Los Angeles Gilmore Auditorium. She even persuaded a rather unpoliticized Judy Garland to address the audience as well.

Kate later regretted her decision, claiming that her first big mistake was in her choice of clothing. "At first I was going to wear white," she later recalled. "But then I thought I'd look like the Dove of Peace. So I decided to wear a red Valentina dress. Red, of all colors. Believe me, it wasn't deliberate. I just wasn't thinking. When my enemies, including Miss Hedda Hopper, whose politics were to the right of Attila the Hun, heard of my choice of colors the next day, it was as if I had endorsed Josef Stalin for president instead of Wallace. Even though my ancestors had sailed over on the *Mayflower* and I'd never joined any group in my life, I suddenly became part of the Communist conspiracy to overthrow the American government. Actually, I'd written Eleanor Roosevelt, urging her to run for President against Truman, but she ever so gently turned me down."

Kate had seen how powerful J. Parnell Thomas's HUAC committee was. Thomas, the chairman and chief investigator, had been responsible in part for destroying the careers of such friends as screen writer Donald Ogden Stewart. Stewart, in fact, had been blacklisted because of the anti-Fascist—and allegedly pro-socialist—statements he'd made when writing the screenplay for the Tracy/Hepburn film, *Keeper of the Flame.*

Witnesses at the auditorium that night reported that Kate's voice grew shrill as she warmed up to her attack. She launched into an assault on "super patriots who call themselves the Motion Picture Alliance for the Preservation of American Ideals."

"For myself," she shouted, "I want no part of their ideals or those of Mr. Thomas."

In her impassioned speech before twenty-thousand people, Kate personally attacked Thomas for engaging in a "smear campaign against the motion picture industry. The artist since the beginning of time has always expressed the aspirations and dreams of the people. Silence the artist and you have silenced the most articulate voice the people have."

Even little Judy Garland got up on the podium, although no one expected her at a political rally. She, too, attacked HUAC as the "Un-American Committee," and urged the audience to write their congressmen, protesting "Mr. Thomas's kicking the living daylights out of the Bill of Rights."

Anti-Hepburn forces rallied the next day. Louis B. Mayer called Kate in to explain why she'd made such an incendiary speech. She told him, "In my heart, I had to stand up for my beliefs like my mother, Kit, has done all her life. I wanted Kit to be proud of me."

Since Kate had already been cast in *Song of Love*, and since he had legally contracted her for the role, Mayer went ahead with the production despite the negative implications of Kate's designation as a "pinko." But although he didn't inform her immediately, the studio chief, in the months ahead was "unable to find any worthy scripts" for her.

More to the right in his politics than Kate, Tracy did not attend the rally, nor did he join Kate in any of her political protests. When asked what he thought about actors going into politics, he said, "Remember who shot Lincoln?"

After the speech, in spite of Mayer's protests, Kate joined in with hundreds of other actors, along with writers, directors, and non-studio producers, including David O. Selznick, John Ford, Bogart, and George Stevens, to launch the Committee for the First Amendment, hoping to combat the unfavorable portrait of the film industry rising out of the bad publicity of the HUAC hearings.

Tracy's name surfaced a few times at the HUAC hearings, but references to him did not harm his career. The movie-going public just didn't believe that Tracy was part of any Communist conspiracy to overthrow the American government.

Kate stood by and watched the careers of such actors as John Garfield and Larry Parks destroyed. Amazingly, in spite of all her left-wing activities, she was never called before the committee, although almost daily she rehearsed what she'd say if she did receive such a subpoena.

Her name was mentioned several times and always unfavorably at the hearings. She sat by her radio in Los Angeles and heard directors Sam Wood and Leo McCarey testify that they knew "for a fact" that she had helped raise nearly ninety thousand dollars for "a very special political party, and we're not talking the Boy Scouts of America." The directors did not name the party.

Traveling between New York and Washington, Patricia Peardon called Kate with an alarming report. Perhaps over "pillow talk" with Nelson Rockefeller, Peardon had learned that J. Edgar Hoover of the F.B.I. had amassed a dossier on both Tracy and Kate that "would stretch around a city block and then some." Hoover, according to Peardon, was making noises that he was about to destroy the careers of both Tracy and Kate herself.

***

J. Edgar Hoover, for reasons known only to himself, had long been fascinated by the private lives of Katharine Hepburn and Spencer Tracy, Tracy even more than Kate.

A closeted and cross-dressing homosexual himself, Hoover was particularly fascinated by Tracy's gay life and the actor's patronage of male hustlers.

He ordered his agents to dig up all the material they could find on both Kate and Tracy. Eventually, he accumulated massive documentation on Kate's lesbian affairs, especially with Laura Harding.

After Kate's speech attacking HUAC, Hoover became more determined than ever to expose both Kate and Tracy, not only for what he alleged was their Communist leanings, but their private lives as well.

As he told his associates, "Just wait and see what happens when America learns that its self-styled most ideal couple are really a faggot and a dyke."

Meeting with Richard Nixon, Hoover unveiled what he was doing to help the HUAC committee members. At the end of their conversation, Hoover dropped his "bombshell" about Hepburn and Tracy.

Although Hoover thought that he'd be applauded by Nixon for his efforts, the young congressman was horrified about the Hepburn/Tracy file Hoover revealed to him, but for reasons that the FBI chief had not anticipated.

"For the very precise reason that Tracy and Hepburn are America's most ideal couple is why you have to burn this file," Nixon warned Hoover. "It will kick back on all of us and all the work we're doing to clean out the Commies. Hepburn and Tracy are too much of an entrenched institution by now. Besides, all these revelations about gay stuff would be too much. There are homosexuals working everywhere."

Perhaps Nixon was sending a subtle signal to Hoover when he delivered his final zinger. "There are even gay people working for the FBI!"

The conclusion of the dialogue between Nixon and Hoover isn't known. Nixon spoke several times about their confrontation later; Hoover never did.

However, Hoover must have gotten the message because he destroyed most of the Hepburn/Tracy file, leaving only some minor and relatively unimportant details, such as press clippings about Kate's speech in Los Angeles.

As Nixon later told his cronies, "I personally saved the career of Tracy and Hepburn. They may never know that, but they should always be in my debt. I kept that fag from blowing the whistle on America's favorite box-office love birds."

Nixon even quoted himself, "Drag Tracy and Hepburn through the mud and you'll trigger a backlash."

When Joseph Mankiewicz years later heard about the Nixon/Hoover meeting, he weighed in his own assessment. "If the American public had learned that Father Flanagan was cheating on his sainted wife, Louise, with a Byrn Mawr lesbian, it would have triggered a nation-wide scandal. It would even have undermined the film industry. Besides, it would definitely have killed Spence's image to learn that he had beat up whores in bordellos and rented male hustlers. His having an extramarital affair with Hepburn would have been the least shocking revelation. Could you see Tracy being convincing as Elizabeth Taylor's dad in *Father of the Bride* if the public knew that he was a closeted cocksucker in his private life?"

When Harry Truman learned of Hoover's file on Hepburn and Tracy, he more or less agreed with Nixon, perhaps the only time these two political enemies ever agreed on anything. "Let it lay," Truman advised Hoover. "Don't touch that with a ten-foot pole. You say you're going after Communists—that's enough. Don't start seeking out homosexuals, much less lesbians, or else we'll go back to burning people at the stake in America, like they did in Salem."

Throughout his life Nixon remained image-conscious. In 1956 when he was running for vice president on a ticket with Eisenhower, his media advisor was Edward A. Rogers, who arranged for him to appear on a televised question-and-answer session at Cornell University. Facing a barrage of some of the toughest questions of his career, Nixon appeared in total control as he answered his attackers.

Yet afterwards, when Nixon boarded the campaign plane with Rogers, he yelled at him. "You son of a bitch! You put me on with those fucking, asshole, liberal sons of bitches. You tried to destroy me in front of thirty million people!" Completely losing control, Nixon physically attacked Rogers, pounding his face until two newspapermen restrained the vice president.

That same year, 1956, Nixon wrote a joint letter to Hepburn and Tracy, seeking their support for his election campaign with Eisenhower. "I think you owe me a favor," he said. "It is important that we carry California and if you can get some of your many friends and admirers to support us, it might help in what could shape up to be a close race."

It is presumed that at this point, Nixon knew that both Hepburn and Tracy had become fully aware of his efforts to have Hoover destroy their FBI files. He sent the message in the form of a typewritten personal letter, and arranged for it to be hand-delivered to Kate at her home.

Kate, as she told Cukor, was startled. "I don't think I had ever received a letter addressed to 'Miss Katharine Hepburn and Mr. Spencer Tracy' before. Did you notice he put my name first? Smart man."

That very afternoon Kate wrote back to Nixon. Tracy chose not to respond.

"I heard what you did to help maintain my privacy, and I guess in my way I'll always be grateful for that. However, I must also be true to my convictions, and I believe that my parents would disown me if I offered my support in any way to a Republican vice-presidential candidate. Mr. Tracy shares my convictions."

Kate signed her note to the White House as: THE LADY IN RED.

CHAPTER EIGHTEEN

Clarence Brown, Greta Garbo's favorite director—the New Englander and the Swedish star made seven films together—began directing Kate in *Song of Love* on a Monday morning in 1947. The ill-fated movie would mark the lowest point in Kate's career.

It was the sudsy, largely invented story of two real musicians, Robert and Clara Schumann. Kate was cast as the brilliant pianist wed to the struggling and unappreciated composer by whom she bears seven children.

The emotionally disturbed Robert Walker, suffering the throes of his failed relationship with Jennifer Jones, was improbably miscast as the young Johannes Brahms who comes to live and study with the Schumanns. He ultimately falls in love with Kate's character of Clara, but she turns him down. He departs with a broken heart. Walker had also played Jerome Kern in the 1946 *Till the Clouds Roll By*, with such stars as Judy Garland. In his previous film, *The Sea of Grass,* Walker had played Hepburn's son—not her suitor.

The plot thickens in *Song of Love*. Robert Schumann, as played by Paul Henreid, is tormented by his lack of success. While conducting his Cantata from *Faust*, he suffers a mental breakdown and is sent to an asylum where he dies.

Making a comeback on the concert stage, Clara, thanks to her brilliant piano playing, brings her husband's splendid music to an appreciative audience.

Weeks before shooting began on the film, Kate threw herself into the role almost with a kind of violence.

Brown assured Kate that her piano playing could be faked. "Nonsense!" she told her director. "I'm not going to pound away at some God damn silent keyboard. I'm going to play a real piano. I'll lead in with the first few bars and then you can switch to Artur Rubinstein's music."

Kate meant that. She studied for weeks with Laura Dubman, a protégée of Rubinstein's. Dubman was astounded at her progress.

At the piano, Kate preferred the clawlike eighteenth-century style of piano playing. When Rubinstein came onto the set to hear Kate play, he said, "If I hadn't seen it, I wouldn't have believed it! That woman is incredible!" After hearing a recording of Kate leading off with the number and his coming in as the camera moves away from her hands, the maestro said, "Where she ends and I begin, only I in the whole world can tell the difference."

***

On the first day of shooting, Kate met her handsome, debonair co-star Paul Henreid, who at the time was best known to American audiences as the suave continental who lit two cigarettes at once for Bette Davis is *Now, Voyager.* Kate had also been intrigued by his performance in *Casablanca*, where he played the Resistance leader, Victor Lazlo, who gets the girl, Ingrid Bergman, from Humphrey Bogart.

Growing up with the aristocrats of pre-World War I Vienna in the last days of the Austro-Hungarian Empire, Henreid impressed Kate as a man with a certain charm and integrity.

Although married to Lisl, his wife since 1936, Henreid's reputation as a ladies' man had preceded him to the set. In fact, he was to entitle his 1984 autobiography, *Ladies Man.*

The day he met Kate, he handed her a letter. "My beloved wife received this only this morning. Please read it!"

"I don't normally read other people's mail," she said. "No, that's not true. I sometimes break into other people's houses and always read the letters they have in the top drawer of their desks."

He looked startled, thinking she was joking. "Go on, please, read it."

Kate took out the letter from the already opened envelope and read it:

"Dear Mrs. Henreid, You don't know me but I'm writing this for your own good because you should know. Even before shooting begins, your husband has been slipping onto the set to make passionate love to Katherine (sic) Hepburn. She does not respect marriage vows. I'm sure you know she's living with a married man, Spencer Tracy, and that she has seduced many other married men—for instance, John Ford, who has a loyal wife, Mary, much admired in the Hollywood community. I cannot give my name, but know that I am employed at MGM. The other day I went by Hepburn's dressing room, and I could hear these two lovebirds. She was demanding that he perform an abnormal act on her. Something definitely against Mother Nature. What action you want to take against this wanton bitch and your husband is entirely your business. I never interfere in anybody else's business. It's not my way. Both Hepburn and Henreid will burn in hell, but perhaps you will devise some suitable punishment for them before THAT GREAT DAY!!! Anonymous."

Kate folded up the letter and returned it to him. "My, we *are* getting right down to it, aren't we now?"

The actor seemed amused. "Lisl and I get these letters all the time. Only last week Lisl got a letter claiming 'your husband is having an affair with Zsa Zsa Gabor.' And, the stories spread about dear Hedy Lamarr and me are legendary. Hedy's a bad actress and has a most peculiar outlook on life, but I still have a warm feeling for her. I develop these warm feelings for all my leading ladies."

"Please don't include me as one of your leading ladies," she said. "I'm no one's leading lady. I'm the star of this picture. You are, in fact, my leading man."

"Thank you," he said. He reached into his pocket and pulled out two cigarettes, lighting both of them for her. He handed her one. At first reluctant to take it, she finally did.

"I lipped it a little before passing it on," he said.

"What a quaint custom!" she said. "Doesn't sound Viennese to me."

"I'm learning all sorts of new American customs," he said. "Actually Bogie taught me that one."

"Fine, I'll take that up with him if I ever meet this Bogie. It seems that everybody in Hollywood knows him. He's even a dear friend of Spencer Tracy's, and has been since the Stone Age. I haven't met the devil yet. I hear he drinks."

"Merely a cocktail before dinner, I'm sure," he said.

The next day, Henreid showed up with another letter sent to Lisl. "Read this one," he said. "It was so good I saved it."

Opening the letter, she found it printed in block letters. "Your husband and Ida Lupino were together last Tuesday. They finished work at two p.m. and they were in Paul's dressing room until six! Although his dressing room is on the second story, I have a way of peeking in and I watched them. After fucking on his sofa, they decided the floor was better. I watched as they rolled around completely naked in every known position capable between a man and a woman. Some positions were unknown to me and my wife. After he had climaxed in her, he went down on her and sucked out his own semen. Your friend...who is trying to save your marriage."

Folding the letter, she handed it to him rather stiffly. "I think this is the last letter of yours I'll read. If this is some seduction technique that you Viennese use, it will not work on me. I think these letters are disgusting. I thought you had some manners and some breeding. I can see that I was wrong about you. Frankly, I suspect that you are the author of these letters, and I don't think I want to have anything to do with you off the set."

After lunch, Brown dismissed Henreid because he wasn't needed for the afternoon. Kate retired to her dressing room at four o'clock with her old friends from previous films, Walter Plunkett, Cedric Gibbons, and Edwin B. Willis. She'd invited the members of the crew for afternoon tea in her dressing room, having grown tired of her luncheon picnics.

In the middle of tea, there was a knock on her door. Gibbons got up to answer it. Without an invitation, Hedy Lamarr walked in. "I'm looking for Paul," she said.

To Kate's astonishment, Lamarr carried a laundry bag with her. Kate resented the intrusion and had no reason to like Hedy Lamarr, primarily because of her past association with Tracy.

"Your Mr. Henreid has gone for the day," Kate said coldly. "How may we assist you? I hope that's not a laundry bag you're carrying. Fortunately, I don't take in laundry on the side."

"I take my laundry over to the house of Paul and Lisl," she said. "But I don't have time to go over today. That's why I'm dropping it off at the studio. They have the most wonderful girl—her name is Laura—who does laundry more exquisitely than any woman in Hollywood. I take my most delicate lingerie to her. I've tried to hire her for twice what Paul and Lisl pay her, but she refuses to leave them."

"A loyal servant indeed," Plunkett said. "I should hire her to work in our costume department at three times the salary."

"Leave your laundry in the corner there," Kate said, "and I'll give it to Paul tomorrow."

Without an invitation, Lamarr sat down in the one vacant chair. "I hope you don't mind, but I would like some tea too."

"By all means," Kate said. "You're most welcome." She then proceeded to give her guests a five-minute lecture on the proper way to pour tea.

"If I ever get invited to Buckingham Palace, I'll know how to instruct the Queen," Lamarr said.

Edwin Willis admired Lamarr's stunning diamond bracelet. "I got it in Vienna by devious means," she said. "I was married to Fritz Mandl. He's a multi-millionaire. He loaded me down with a vast king's ransom in precious jewels. But he would let me wear them only for special occasions. One night he invited me to the opera. I demanded that he let me wear all my most valuable pieces. I wore so much jewelry I looked like a Christmas tree. In the middle of the performance, I excused myself and told Fritz I was sick. He stayed on to see the finish of the opera after arranging for me to be driven home. Once at home, I packed my furs and gowns and fled in the middle of the night, jewels and all. It was a long road but here I am in Hollywood."

"As we can plainly see," Kate said, seemingly impatient that Lamarr had upstaged her tea. "But I must kick everybody out now since I'm going home."

At the door, Lamarr paused and looked back at Kate and the crew members. "I'm still mad at Paul. He said he was going to use his influence to get me cast in *Casablanca*. After *Algiers*, I would have been the most natural choice for the role, and I'm sure everybody in this dressing room agrees with me. Only I could have played Ilsa the way she should have been acted."

"At least we agree on one point," Kate said. "I too think Bergman, a sort of clodhopper, was wrong for the part. But I always tell everybody that the role should have gone to Ann Sheridan. Good day, Miss Lamarr!"

***

The next morning, in a most unusual move, Tracy dropped by the set. Thinking the two men would dislike each other intensely, Kate introduced him

486

to Henreid, having resumed speaking to him after those letters.

"Is she behaving herself?" Tracy asked.

"Oh, yes, Mr. Tracy," Henreid said.

"Spence to you."

"Spence. She's being wonderful. I especially like it when she disappears for a few minutes in the middle of a scene. She goes back into her dressing room and emerges smelling like a rose."

"It's not a rose exactly," Kate interrupted. "More like Jungle Gardenia. I figured Crawford does all right with that perfume, so why not me? I put just a little bit on my nose, a little bit around the corners of my mouth."

"Absolutely delectable," Henreid said.

"Can't stand the smell myself," Tracy countered. He turned to her. "Have you learned your lines?" Then he looked at Henreid. "Is she bumping into the furniture?"

"Yes, dear," she said. "I know all my lines and Paul's lines, too. So far, I haven't bumped into one piece of furniture."

"Remember what I told you," Tracy said. "Say the lines loud and clear. Don't grin and make faces—just say the words. And don't flutter about the set like you're about to lay eggs. Come on to the set like you've already dumped your load for the day."

Henreid was shocked that Tracy talked this way to Kate, but he only smiled.

"Yes, Spencer," she said demurely, "I'll do as you say."

As Henreid was to recall, "I just couldn't believe it. Before Spence arrived, I thought I was talking to the single most independent woman in films, with the exception of Garbo. But Garbo had retired. In the presence of Tracy, Kate became like a child. That's right. He treated her like a kid. She was the slightly naughty daughter, and he was the wizened old gray-haired papa."

Amazingly, and in spite of Kate's prediction to Clarence Brown, Henreid and Tracy became the best of buddies. The friendship was based largely on the fact that, in Henreid, Tracy found a chess-player to match his own skills.

Tracy started dropping by the set on a regular basis to play chess with Henreid when he was not otherwise engaged in front of the cameras.

Their chess-playing became so vital to Tracy that he often invited Henreid to his cottage on Cukor's estate, where their games continued late into the night.

Kate would prepare dinner for both actors before retreating around nine o'clock in the evening. Sometimes she would go up to Cukor's for a talk and a nightcap since she was left out of all the action whenever Tracy and Henreid got together.

When Tracy wasn't around, Henreid devoted all his attention to Kate. She warned him that "Spence might be developing a little crush on you, but it's completely harmless. He won't carry it to any sort of conclusion."

"I admire his talent as an actor, but that's as far as it goes," Henreid said. "We're just good friends."

"And I'm sure that's how it will remain," she said. "Now come over to my dressing room and let's go over our lines. I've seen some of the rushes. That shit, Clarence Brown, isn't doing for me what he did for Garbo. Just between you and me, I swear he's trying to sabotage this picture and our careers."

Henreid later said that he thought Kate was taking him to her dressing room to seduce him but nothing like that happened, at least not then.

"She meant what she said," Henreid recalled. "We really did rehearse our lines."

Henreid in 1969 said "it was hard for me to understand exactly, but I felt I was in some sort of competition. That I was the party favor, as you people say over here, in some game between Kate and Spence. They seemed engaged in a private war with each other, and somehow I was the bounty awaiting the winner. When the three of us were together, they vied for my attention. It made me uncomfortable. At the time, I didn't understand the dynamics of their relationship. I still don't."

Henreid was speaking privately about Kate and Tracy after he'd reunited with Kate that year to make *The Madwoman of Chaillot*. "For Kate, it was a reunion with her former lovers—namely Charles Boyer and *moi*. At the time, she had eyes only for the very handsome John Gavin, but I think their relationship was confined to his admiring her as a fine but aging actress. Richard Chamberlain was in the film too, but I think he was involved with some young man at the time. Yul Brynner was also in the film. Having long ago broken up with Judy Garland and Marlene Dietrich, among countless others, he was dating—of all people—Sal Mineo. As for Danny Kaye, he was still in love with Kate's old friend, Larry Olivier. Only Edith Evans, cast as the other madwoman, was, like Caesar's wife, above reproach."

"I really got to know Kate only after *Song of Love* was completed," Henreid remembered. "She stood by me when I ran afoul of the HUAC anti-American committee, and I'll always be grateful to her for her loyalty in those dark times when my career as an actor was being destroyed."

To Cukor, along with her pals Anderson Lawler and Kenneth MacKenna, Kate confided again and again her admiration for Henreid as the filming of *Song of Love* progressed. "At first I thought he was some continental smoothie, dancing the soft-shoe around all his leading women with an intent to seduce. I'd heard what a womanizer he is. To some extent, his reputation is deserved. But there is the soul of an artist there. He's a very caring and sensitive man. He's not the prettiest boy in Hollywood—no John Derek—but there is an incredibly seductive quality about Paul. It's easy to understand why so many intelligent, sensitive, and artistic women fall for him. I only grew impatient with him when he seduced both Judy Garland and Claudette Colbert. I think he was moving too much onto my turf there."

When Henreid sent Kate a copy of his autobiography in 1984, she read these words: "For some reason, probably because I was so often cast as a foreign lover, I was always suspected of having affairs with my leading ladies. The truth is, I never did. I liked many of them tremendously, and others I disliked, but the type of woman who always appealed to me was one I had to take care of, someone who had a streak of vulnerability. Stars are not vulnerable women. To get to the top, you must have an aggressive nature."

After reading his book, she sat down and wrote Henreid a letter, which she shared with Patricia Peardon before mailing.

In it, she wrote:

"Dear Paul,
A lovely sentiment in your book—about not seducing your leading ladies—and in your heart I'm sure you were honest and truthful and pure to your wife, Lisl. I completely agree that an autobiography is the last form of media in which one would want to tell the truth. If I ever get around to writing one—and I don't think I shall in spite of repeated offers—I will not tell one iota of truth. But—in your case—as one who knows—or knew—you so well, here's my best guess of the leading ladies you slept with—Michele Morgan, Bette Davis, Merle Oberon, Ida Lupino, Hedy Lamarr, and at least ten others who come to mind. I can only assume that you, along with Humphrey Bogart, slept with Ingrid Bergman during the making of *Casablanca*. Every man sleeps with Bergman, even Victor Fleming and—dare I say it—Spencer Tracy. Before I end my list of your seductions, let's not leave out the most important name of all: KATHARINE HOUGHTON HEPBURN.
Love, Kate.
P.S. Old age is a pisser!!!"

***

Tracy had been fond of the handsome but tormented Robert Walker when they'd starred in *The Sea of Grass*, but Kate tried her best to keep the two heavy drinkers apart, fearing that Walker would entice Tracy into consuming even more alcohol than his excessive daily intake.

On the set of *Song of Love*, Walker played her lover instead of her son. Ironically, the roles were reversed. In real life, he almost became the son she never had.

From the first day she'd talked privately with him, she liked his candid appraisals. He held up a copy of the script and said, "This crap must have been assembled overnight on the backs of old pianola rolls."

Only a few years before, she'd known of this talented man as part of the "dream duo of wartime Hollywood" during his ill-fated marriage to Jennifer Jones before David O. Selznick stole her away. As a couple, Robert Walker and Jennifer Jones ranked up there at the top of the "cuddly twosomes" list along with Jane Wyman and Ronald Reagan.

Kate already knew, through Anderson Lawler, that Selznick's Svengali-like obsession with Jones not only had destroyed her marriage to Walker, but was also ruining Walker's life.

At first Kate surmised that it was the loss of Jones that was driving him to drink. Later she concluded to her friends that "anything could drive him to drink, like accidentally running over a dog on the highway."

Over tea one afternoon on the set of *Song of Love*, Walker opened up to Kate and became very confessional. Even though expressly forbidden to drink liquor while a picture was being shot, the young actor had been drinking since ten o'clock that morning. He told Kate, "my personal life has been completely wrecked by Selznick's insane obsession for my wife. How can I fight a man as powerful as he is?"

There was an appealing quality about Walker that day that touched her heart. She later spoke to Irene Mayer Selznick, who knew almost as much about her husband's obsession with Jennifer Jones as did Walker himself. "I feel there's a quality of the little boy lost there," Kate said to Irene.

Other of Walker's female co-stars had voiced their concern. June Allyson said, "Whenever I look back on Robert Walker, I almost cry. I wish I could have helped him." Unlike Allyson, Kate decided that she could do something in his life.

Beginning the afternoon she invited Walker for tea, Kate, who defined Walker as a more compulsive and self-destructive alcoholic even than Tracy, moved into the actor's life. Claudette Colbert shared many of Kate's grave concerns for the troubled star, since Colbert had befriended and starred with the young actor in *Since You Went Away.* "I sensed Jennifer's distress when we made the film together," Colbert said to Kate. "I particularly felt sorry for both Bob and Jennifer when they were forced to play poignant love scenes together in the wake of their failed marriage. It must have been extremely difficult for them. This forced intimacy. Throughout the entire shooting, Jennifer seemed in a state of mild hysteria. She not only had Robert Walker there, but David Selznick himself was constantly hovering over her. Selznick's courtship of Jennifer seemed neurotic at best. Maybe he was more sinister. I think the jealous fool wanted to destroy Bob."

Kate individually contacted Walker's friends, asking them for any insight they might have as to what demons were haunting the actor other than his ongoing love for Jennifer Jones. "I never in all these years have discovered Spencer's demons," Kate told Cukor. "But I thought I might find out what's driving Bob into an early grave with his excessive drinking."

Keenan Wynn, who was known to be a close friend of Walker's, had appeared with Kate in *Without Love*. When Kate encountered him on the MGM lot, she stopped to ask him about his friend, as if Wynn held the secret that might cure Walker.

490

Wynn told her that he'd noted a major change in Walker ever since he'd appeared in *Since You Went Away*. "I'm one of his closest friends, and I always thought of Bob as a happy-go-lucky guy. But I noticed that as the months went by, he was growing more and more morose. His downhill run started when he first learned that Selznick was moving in on his wife. He also feared that his two sons would be taken away from him and that he'd never be allowed to see them again. As the melancholy increased, so did the drinking. Bob's become just a shadow of himself. I think Selznick was heartless to have brought Bob and his estranged wife together to play intimate love scenes. It was almost like Selznick was gloating with the message, 'She's my girl now—not yours.'"

Sometimes after she'd put a drunken Tracy to bed, Kate would drive over to Walker's apartment. For hours she'd sit with Walker and try to keep him from drinking.

"He drinks so much—a bottle a day, maybe two," she told Wynn. "He then goes and throws it all up so he can drink some more. It's all I can do to get him to eat. I think he's killing himself. Sooner than later."

On some nights Kate would let Walker vent his rage. He was still furious over his arrest on the night of August 20, 1946, when he'd been drinking heavily and had caused an accident with his new Chrysler on Santa Monica Boulevard, sideswiping a bakery truck and ripping off its fender. He'd fled the scene of the accident but was later apprehended, making headlines—WALKER, ACTOR, ADMITS HIT-RUN.

Judge Cecil B. Holland had sentenced Walker to one-hundred and eighty days in jail but had suspended the sentence on conditions, one of which was that he was not to touch liquor during his probationary period. Walker was appalled when the judge told him, "You have a bright future as an actor, but you are getting into some bad habits. You owe it to your public to straighten yourself out."

Kate would sit patiently listening to Walker rant about this scene with the judge. "I don't owe a God damn thing to my public," Walker would shout at Kate. "I don't owe the public for my sons. My public doesn't own me. Fuck the God damn public. Fuck everybody!"

Kate believed that it was good to let Walker vent all his rage and hostility. She felt that by getting it out of his system, he would ultimately free himself of his inner demons.

As she told Clarence Brown, Walker was "hating every day on the set of *Song of Love*," and she begged him not to be so harsh in his direction or ridicule the young actor's performances before the camera.

This intervention on Kate's part didn't help matters at all. If anything, Brown became even less tolerant of Walker and more demanding.

As Walker had already told Kate, he knew he was miscast in the role. "I feel I'm fighting a losing battle," he told Kate, "and Brown is only making it worse."

The actor instinctively knew what was coming from his critics, including an attack by Bosley Crowther in *The New York Times*. That critic, a few months later, found Walker's "solemn posturing as Brahms, well, it's good for a guffaw." Other critics also were equally hostile and demeaning. At the end of the shooting, deeply disillusioned with his talents, MGM sent roles that once might have been intended for Walker to either Van Johnson or Peter Lawford instead.

A most peculiar relationship developed between Kate and Walker, a bonding heretofore unknown in the annals of Hollywood reporting. It is believed that Kate's relationship with Walker was more mother-and-son than man and woman. But there were sexual overtones.

Clarence Brown remembered coming to the door of her dressing room during the shooting of *Song of Love*. "I called out to her but there was no answer. I had some important script changes. Since the door was partially opened, I stepped inside and was going to leave the revisions on her vanity. What I saw shocked me, and I think the picture will live in my head forever, like a movie I directed. Kate was sitting in a chair with her breasts exposed. Bob was actually suckling her left breast like he was an infant in the nursery draining his mother's milk from her. When I looked into Kate's eyes, I saw the most hostile glare I've ever seen one human being cast at another. I dropped the script on the floor and fled from the room, shutting the door."

"When Bob and Kate came back onto the set after lunch, not one word was exchanged between us about the incident," Brown said. "I'm like Garbo in that I believe some things should remain unspoken."

***

A similar incident was reported by the writer, Jim Henaghan, who at one time was married to the dancer and actress, Gwen Verdon. For the last six years of Walker's life, Henaghan was his most intimate friend and confidant, leading to speculation—rumors only—that the two men were lovers.

One afternoon in 1981, long after Walker's death, Henaghan, at his apartment in Century City, California, spoke confidentially about his controversial relationship with Walker.

"Bob and I used to play this silly, stupid game," Henaghan said. "Even now, I hesitate to speak of it because it reveals too much about our own relationship. Bob was quite a womanizer in those days. Judy Garland. Ava Gardner. Hedy Lamarr. I don't know about June Allyson. Then there were the lesser names, like that model and writer, Florence Prichett, which ended in such bitterness. Many gays also came on to Bob because he was handsome and got a little careless when he was drunk. I know he was picked up by men some nights, but I'd bet that he was too drunk to perform. Then there was that weird connection between him and Farley Granger when they made *Strangers on a Train* for Alfred Hitchcock. But I don't want to go into that. Bob was definitely straight—you have my word on that."

Henaghan at that point in his life had a tendency to wander conversationally. He was brought back to the exact nature of this game he had mentioned between Walker and himself. He said that on certain nights when Walker planned to seduce a Hollywood beauty, he would "tell me to come over and see for myself. Bob kept a ladder outside his building. I could climb this ladder and look into his bedroom on the second floor. He always kept the shade up and a light on. When I climbed the ladder up to the window, I could see everything going on inside the bedroom. Bob always said he performed better with a woman when he knew I was overseeing it like a director might. Once, when I dropped in to spend the night drinking with him like I often did, no one answered his bell. I went around to the side of the building and saw his bedroom light on. I thought at the time he had forgotten to call me. I climbed the ladder and peered into the window. What I saw that night almost made me fall off the ladder. Instead of Ava Gardner, it was Katharine Hepburn in bed with him. Bob was completely nude. Hepburn was propped up on pillows. She was still in her clothing but her blouse was open. Bob was sucking one of her breasts like a baby might do with its mama. I looked at the scene with such astonishment that I embarrassed myself for witnessing such a thing. I'd been expecting to see Bob pounding Gardner, and I got this instead. I came back down the ladder as fast and as quietly as I could. I never mentioned to Bob what I'd seen, and he never brought it up to me. He was so lost in his own world that I don't think he even knew that I was at the window. Sometimes it's better not to know what your friends are really like."

In the months ahead, Kate formed a bond with Henaghan after they'd been more formally introduced. In those days, you didn't know Walker without knowing Henaghan. Kate came to trust Henaghan when she saw for herself how protective he was of the actor. They bonded. "Look after Bob when I'm not around," Kate instructed Henaghan.

"Kate and I jokingly referred to ourselves as 'The Protective Friends of Robert Walker, Inc.,'" Henaghan said.

It was during the time of Walker's enforced idleness from MGM, following *Song of Love,* that Kate noticed that, in spite of her help, he was growing more and more morose. Both Henaghan and Kate reported that Walker could spend entire days in his apartment just listening to records and drinking. Both of his friends were alarmed that Walker, already dead drunk when he left his apartment at night, would go out bar-hopping. He always insisted on driving himself from bar to bar, regardless of how much he'd had to drink.

Kate told Henaghan that she was astounded one day when Walker revealed that he'd been having an on-again, off-again affair with Judy Garland since 1945. Apparently, according to Henaghan, it had begun when Vincente Minnelli had directed the two of them in the MGM film, *The Clock.* But despite Henaghan's long friendship with Kate, Henaghan, even as late as 1981, was unaware of Kate's own involvement with Garland.

Lawler later said that Kate had refused to talk to him about her reaction upon learning about the Garland/Walker affair. "I can only imagine all her conflicting emotions," Lawler said. "She was, if not in love, then at least sexually attracted to, and deeply protective of, Garland. Now, her 'son'—that's what Walker was to her, not her lover—was carrying on with the very same woman Kate was enchanted with. It must have really stirred up her emotions. That's why she couldn't talk about it. I also felt at the time that Kate was growing increasingly disenchanted with Colbert. Their lesbian affair was entering its final stages. Of course, there was Tracy in the background...that Tracy was always lurking somewhere. Those two didn't have much of a life together. When he was home, he was drunk. He had his hustlers sent down the hill by Cukor, and he had his cook and nursemaid in Kate. When he was sober enough to go to a nightclub, it was with some other woman, never with Kate. First, Kate didn't go to nightclubs, and she and Tracy were determined never to be photographed together—except on the screen—if they could help it. So what was left for Kate? At that point, she was only speaking to Garbo on the phone. Although it was about to enter an exciting new phase, her love life was virtually over at that point, except for a minor fling with Paul Henreid. Kate had an excessive amount of time on her hands, and she often spent that time dealing with Garland and Walker, the two hopeless and helpless little bluebirds she'd adopted."

***

At the box office, *Song of Love* fared poorly, both with its critics and with the general public. Even before the film's release, the president of the American Legion called Mayer to inform him that his then powerful organization was going to boycott the film "because of Hepburn's pinko leanings. Don't ever cast Hepburn in another movie, or you'll be sorry you did. That goes for Tracy, too. The old drunk is also a pinko!"

The Baltimore Sun pronounced *Song of Love* "a muted musical raspberry in B minor." In the *New York Times*, Bosley Crowther interpreted Kate's performance as "one of her familiarly agonized jobs—a compound of soulful expressions, fluttered hands, and prideful lifts of the head." The critic also claimed that *Song of Love* was "reminiscent of the *Phantom of the Opera* on a night out."

***

One of the great mysteries in post-war Hollywood casting involved why Claudette Colbert dropped out of the cast of *State of the Union* at the last minute, just before the beginning of filming.

It was a Friday afternoon on October 9, 1947, and she was scheduled to begin shooting the following Monday morning opposite Spencer Tracy, with whom she'd last appeared on the screen in *Boom Town* in 1940 with co-stars Clark Gable and Hedy Lamarr.

For his appearance in the film, Tracy was to get one-hundred and seventy-five thousand dollars, Colbert even more—two-hundred thousand dollars.

Three weeks previously, Capra had driven up to Tracy's cottage on Cukor's estate and presented the script to him. He read it that night, and called Capra the following morning, saying that he would play the lead role of Grant Matthews, a Republican presidential candidate who throws the nomination rather than betray his ideals.

Scenarists Anthony Veiller and Myles Connolly had concocted a film script from the Pulitzer Prize-winning play by Howard Lindsay and Russel Crouse, which had opened on Broadway.

Even before she read the film script, Kate was already familiar with the play, having turned it down before Ruth Hussey, opposite Ralph Bellamy, was cast in it for the Broadway run. Before that, both Helen Hayes and Kate's nemesis, Margaret Sullavan, had also passed on the role.

Originally, Hayes claimed that she'd been intrigued by this story of a presidential candidate, a sort of Wendell Willkie type, carrying on an extramarital affair before he rediscovers his love for his wife after being forced to campaign with her.

Since Willkie was having marital troubles before his run against Roosevelt in 1940, it was widely assumed that the playwrights had been inspired by this politician's woes. In the end, Hayes turned the play down because she felt that the role of the wife was "too mousy a character."

Bellamy and Hussey, however, made a success of the play, and Capra purchased the rights to it in January of 1947 for Liberty Films, a corporation he'd formed with Samuel Briskin,. William ("Billy") Wyler, and Kate's former lover, George Stevens.

Liberty's first film had been *It's a Wonderful Life,* starring Kate's old beau, Jimmy Stewart.

At first, Capra saw it as a film to reunite his famous co-stars, the Oscar-winning team of Claudette Colbert and Clark Gable. MGM, however, refused to make Gable available. MGM, which had agreed to release the film, envisioned it as a vehicle for Gary Cooper and Claudette Colbert. Since he'd had trouble with Colbert before, Capra rethought his choice, wanting to cast Maureen O'Hara instead. She turned him down on September 11, 1947.

When Cooper, too, showed no interest, Capra made a decision to approach Tracy, and to team him with Colbert in spite of his reservations about her.

Until they started working together on the script at Colbert's home, Tracy had expressed nothing but contempt for Colbert. When he'd signed to do the role, Tracy told Kate, "You won't believe this, but I've agreed to appear with Froggie on the screen again after vowing that I wouldn't. She knows how to play only one part. Herself."

Tracy had once told Cukor that Colbert had never gotten over winning the Oscar for *It Happened One Night.* "She's always the same on the screen. No variety to her. I think it wasn't Kate who ran the gamut of emotions from A to B. It's Colbert. You know, of course, that Rex Harrison refers to her as 'the French Dwarf.'"

Initially, Kate had been delighted to see her dear friends and lovers, Tracy and Colbert, getting along so famously and working creatively together. At first, she hovered over them as if supervising them like a nervous chaperone.

But, eventually, she drifted away out of sheer boredom, as she later told Lawler. At the time, Kate preferred to spend some of her evenings with Robert Walker, Judy Garland, and to an increasing degree, Paul Henreid when he could slip away from his wife, Lisl.

"I found that Claudette and Spencer liked to spend too much time talking shop," Kate told Cukor. "I didn't have much shop to talk about. In fact, I was out of work." She admitted that she began to grow slightly jealous of the fact that her lovers had a creative project to work on, whereas no film or stage roles had materialized for her. "I get offers," Kate said, "but everything is so hopeless."

At this point, the story grows murky. Only four people in Hollywood—Dr. Joel Pressman; his wife, Claudette Colbert; Tracy; and Kate herself know exactly what happened that Thursday night preceding Colbert's withdrawal from the cast of *State of the Union.*

Neither of the participants ever revealed exactly what took place. Kate, who outlived the other three, refused to give a full explanation to even her closest confidants.

In New York, Patricia Peardon claimed that Kate one night suggested to her what happened, but only in a vague way.

Peardon recalled the event like this: "Dr. Pressman returned home unexpectedly and I think he found his wife in bed with Tracy. The two had never liked each other, but I guess a lady like Colbert was entitled to change her mind. I suspect that Pressman called Kate later in the evening and told her what he'd discovered. Unknown to Pressman, Kate was also having an affair with his wife, so Kate must have been placed in a most awkward situation. The whole episode could have been made into a soap opera.

"Whatever Pressman told Kate, he said something that made her drive over in the middle of the night to the house that Colbert shared with her husband. By the time Kate got there, the doctor had already kicked Tracy out.

"We'll never know what words Pressman and Colbert exchanged with Kate. But, from what I gathered, the shit hit the fan. Not only did Pressman discover Tracy screwing his wife, but he learned about Kate's own sexual involvement with Colbert too. Pressman also became aware of Colbert's other affairs, including the one with Joan Crawford. The evening ended violently.

496

"Pressman, from what I gather, struck his wife in the head, injuring her badly. She'd fallen against the fireplace and was bleeding. When Kate pleaded with Pressman to provide medical care for his wife, he refused and stormed out of the house.

"Kate herself picked up Colbert and got her into a car and drove her to the nearest hospital, where she registered under an assumed name.

"That's my best shot on what I think happened from what little bit I could get out of Kate," Peardon concluded.

***

Quite possibly, Peardon's analysis of the event was right: A cover-up began almost immediately.

Although Colbert was struck down by Pressman, Kate had rushed to her aid. But, the next day, when it became apparent that Colbert had not been seriously injured, Kate vowed never to speak to Colbert ever again.

Throughout the course of her affair with Colbert, neither actress had ever made any vows of fidelity to the other.

"But I think it was just too much when Kate learned that Colbert was in bed with Tracy," Peardon said. "Kate could hardly accept Joan Crawford as Colbert's lover, but not Tracy. That involved moving in too close to the bone. It would almost be the equivalent of Kate betraying Colbert by sleeping with Pressman behind her back. At any rate," Peardon remembered, "that long-enduring relationship between Colbert and Kate ended on that night. Pressman and Colbert resumed living together, and Kate ultimately forgave Tracy, once again, for his indiscretion. I think she could forgive him for sleeping with any woman, with the possible exceptions of Margaret Sullavan and Ginger Rogers. But Colbert was just the final straw. As happens in so many of these cases, the man was forgiven, and the woman was blamed."

There is a postscript to this rundown of the Hepburn/Colbert affair.

Although the friendship between Hepburn and Colbert was never repaired, the two actresses retained some professional links. In 1969, it was announced to the press that Colbert would appear in the London production of Kate's award-winning Broadway show, *Coco*.

And although soon afterwards Colbert bowed out of the role, she went to see Kate perform in the show three times, although never going backstage to greet her old friend.

In the 1960s, Bennett Cerf, the chief of Random House, in an act that was unknown at the time to most of his editors, approached his "pal," Claudette Colbert, with a proposal to write her memoirs.

Obviously indicating to her that he knew a lot more than he pretended, he said, "and you must devote a chapter—even two or three chapters—to Miss Hepburn."

You must be kidding!" she told Cerf.

Years later, when Colbert was living in Barbados, long after the death of Dr. Pressman from cancer, and after the more recent deaths of Colbert's mother and brother, the author of this biography encountered Colbert at a dinner party. When asked if she would ever consider a return to the screen, Colbert said, "I still get offered scripts, believe it or not. Usually the roles involve playing somebody's mother as I did in *Parrish,* or else a murderous lesbian."

When asked about Katharine Hepburn, she looked puzzled. "Didn't she make *The African Queen* with Bogart?"

***

Since the real story about why Colbert bowed out of *State of the Union* couldn't be publicized, and since it was such a prominent picture, a scenario had to be invented. Frank Capra himself contributed an apocryphal story that made the rounds.

He claimed that Colbert arrived at his office late one Friday afternoon, with shooting set to begin on Monday, and informed him that her doctor (actually, her husband) and her agent (actually her brother) claimed that she couldn't work after five o'clock. According to this tale, Colbert said that she had just learned that the director was planning to run the production of the film on some evenings until as late as eight or nine o'clock. She was supposed, according to the face-saving tale invented by Capra, to have said that her face grew tired by the late afternoon and began to sag—"and doesn't photograph at all well after 5 o'clock."

At the moment she was supposed to have been saying and doing this, Colbert was actually in the hospital. It was true that her face wouldn't have photographed well at five o'clock in the afternoon, or during that period, even at five o'clock in the morning, either. Her famous face was bruised and her blacked right eye was swollen shut.

According to the story he told MGM, Capra said that he had refused to grant Colbert the working concession of a five-o'clock cutoff to her work day. He also said that he had demanded that she return, at once, her entire wardrobe to MGM. It had cost the film's producers fifteen-thousand dollars, and it had been specifically designed by one of MGM's chief costumers, Irene Gibbons. "In essence," Capra said, "I fired her." He also maintained that Colbert "had thrown a fit and had barged, screaming, from his office, threatening a lawsuit."

Actually, Colbert had called Capra from the hospital, asking him to visit her there. There, beside her bedside, Capra heard her highly sanitized version of the events of the previous night. Colbert claimed that she was forced to retire from the picture. It was she who suggested that he call Kate and offer her the role instead.

Capra claimed that that was exactly what he eventually did. What he did-

498

n't reveal, however, was that on that very night, he made a last desperate attempt to get Greer Garson for the role. In later years, he couldn't remember if Garson had another commitment, or if she rejected the part merely because she didn't like it.

Because, thanks to her political leanings, Kate had been "semi-blacklisted" by MGM, Capra was extremely reluctant to cast her in any film with a political message, fearing fall-out from the far right.

He later confessed that it was only his desperation that forced him to place a late-night call to Tracy to inform him that Colbert was no longer part of the cast of *State of the Union*. (Ironically, at the time, Tracy knew a hell of a lot more about what had happened with Colbert than Capra did.)

Even so, Capra reported that Tracy appeared surprised that Colbert had walked. Supposedly, Tracy said, "I've got a bag of bones sitting next to me. She'll jump at the part. She's been helping me rehearse. Kinda stops you, Frank, you dago bastard. Kate's a real theater nut, you know. She might go for it just for the hell of it."

Then Tracy, according to Capra, put Kate on the phone. "Just tell me what time I'm to show up on Monday morning, Mr. Capra." Kate said, "and tell me what I'm supposed to wear. I'll try to get Irene to adjust Claudette's wardrobe for me. I've worked with Irene before, and she knows my size better than I do myself."

Apparently, it was true, as reported, that Kate agreed to the role without talk of salary or contracts.

By Monday morning, rumors were rampant all over Hollywood as to the real reason Colbert had bowed out of the picture. The story that seemed to gain the most credibility had Colbert calling Capra and telling him that she'd broken her ankle and couldn't work.

That tale was eerily evocative of the painful back injury that had led to Colbert's withdrawal from *All About Eve* in 1950, her intended role going instead to Bette Davis, a loss that Colbert regretted for the rest of her life.

The casting of Kate as Mary Matthews in *State of the Union* brought an immediate reaction. Mayer had wanted to keep Kate dangling until some of the red menace scare had died down, and until her name was no longer being heard in those committee hearings in Washington.

Both Tracy and Kate appeared on the set Monday morning to greet Capra. "As I told you," Tracy said to Capra, "Kate's not been hamming it up lately, and I was sure she'd go for it. Let's get to work!"

Right-wingers throughout the country, upon learning of the casting of Tracy and Hepburn, sent letters of protests to both MGM and Liberty Films, and especially to Frank Capra.

Ralph Lawrence, president of Clean Films for Clean Living the American Way, wired Capra: "Katherine (sic) Hepburn is a card-carrying Communist. She believes in the overthrow of the American government. She's attacked marriage. She advocates abortion. She is a known harlot. If you go ahead with this movie, I assure you that groups such as ours, composed of God-fearing people, will not only boycott the film, but will stage protest marches at any theater that shows this filthy red propaganda."

Capra showed Kate and Tracy the threatening telegram.

"What do you want us to do, you dago bastard?" Tracy asked.

"Are you afraid to go ahead with two card-carrying communists like us?" Kate said, looking over at Tracy. "The only thing pinko about Spencer is his nose, from drinking too much."

"Here's what I'm going to do," Capra said. "Get in front of the camera and start acting. My only advice to the two of you, especially you, Spence, is to remember your lines and don't bump into the furniture."

***

The surprise casting of a young Angela Lansbury proved to be "a stroke of genius" for Capra. Lansbury had already received Oscar nominations for *Gaslight* and *The Picture of Dorian Gray,* but she truly came into her own as an actress in *State of the Union,* delivering an unsentimentalized, yet movingly sympathetic, portrait of her character of Kay Thorndyke. In the film, she plays the mistress of Tracy's character, a right-wing newspaper publisher who pushes him to run for president on the Republican ticket.

Although rivals on film, Kate and Lansbury got along well together, and the younger actress later publicly thanked Kate for her support.

In the film, Van Johnson, by then fully recovered from his automobile accident, was cast as Spike McManus, a disillusioned, smart-talking columnist vaguely reminiscent of Drew Pearson. Johnson depicted a wise-cracking reporter whose cynicism is a mask for his idealistic principles.

Aware of Tracy's long-ago crush on the handsome blond actor, Kate carefully observed the two of them together on the set. Later, she told Cukor, "I think Spencer has completely recovered from his bout of unrequited love for Van Johnson. Spencer's heart has obviously strayed elsewhere—oh, but where?"

Unlike the conflicts she'd had with her previous directors, Kate worked well with Frank Capra, who she admired. Tracy referred to Kate and Capra as "the mutual admiration society."

Capra said, "There are women and there are women and then there is Kate. There are actresses and there are actresses and then there is Hepburn. Unlike Colbert, there is no clock-watching about Kate, no humbug, no sham temperament."

She returned Capra's flattery, finding him "a funny, totally concentrated, imaginative, and warm creature who felt violently, loved to laugh, and could

500

lead an audience to water and make them drink."

In the old days, Kate might have demanded that many of her lines be rewritten. But under Capra's direction, she even delivered such lines as, "Grant [a reference to Tracy's character] likes to get up on the mountain and slap the hurricanes down."

For his part, Tracy seemed content with many of his scene-stealing lines, such as his memorable parting words, "here and now, I withdraw as a candidate for any office—not because I'm honest, but because I'm dishonest. I want to apologize to all the good, sincere people who put their faith in me."

There were many women in the industry that Kate didn't like, notably Margaret Sullavan and Ginger Rogers. Among male actors, one in particular topped what she referred to as her "shitlist."

He was Adolphe Menjou.

***

Menjou was left out of what he called "the lovefeast" that was transpiring nearly every day on the set during the filming of *State of the Union.* Playing the villain, Jim Conover, Menjou was cast as a sleazy, conniving, behind-the-scenes politician.

Kate had appeared opposite Menjou in both *Morning Glory* and *Stage Door.* She'd disliked him in the Thirties. On the set of *State of the Union,* she positively loathed him.

The right-wing actor had appeared before HUAC, and he had named names of every person in Hollywood that he thought had "pinko leanings."

Although he had never specifically named Tracy or Hepburn in his testimony, Menjou was the uncrowned leader of the pro-Senator Joseph McCarthy clique in Hollywood. Of Kate, he said, "Scratch a do-gooder like Kate, and she'll yell *Pravda.*"

When Tracy heard Menjou's remark, he responded, "Scratch Hepburn, and what you get is an ass full of buckshot."

Kate was amused when a columnist with moderate political views wrote an unflattering reference to Menjou's behavior before the witch-hunting committee in Washington. Menjou had just published his autobiography which he titled *It Took Nine Tailors,* a reference to his preference for "bespoke" tailored suits. Thanks to the glee with which he rattled off the names of alleged communist sympathizers in front of the committee, the reporter—after hearing Menjou "naming names and then naming some more"—suggested that Menjou retitle his book *It Took Nine Tailors and a Helluva Big Mouth.*

Commanding the kind of attention that only she could muster, Kate read the columnist's account to some of the crew. Menjou, who at the time was standing only thirty feet away, clearly heard her.

Veteran actor Lewis Stone was cast in *State of the Union* as Sam Thorndyke. In spite of a long and distinguished acting career, he was known primarily at the time for playing the wise and lecturing old dad to Mickey Rooney's *Andy Hardy*. Stone was often seen talking privately to Menjou. The long-faced, gray-since-youth Stone referred unflatteringly to Kate as "that Tracy camp follower."

In Stone, Menjou found a kindred spirit. Menjou referred to Kate as both a hypocrite and a phony. "She pretends to be some monument to morality, but she's the mistress of a married man," Menjou was fond of saying. "She unashamedly insults everybody with impunity while slavishly knicking under to some old drunk's tyrannical whim. The old drunk, in case anybody wants to know, is a woman-beater and a sodomite."

The press was eager to provoke a feud between left-wing Kate and right-wing Menjou. To prevent that, Capra demanded a closed set. No real feud ever developed between the two actors, although Kate rarely spoke to Menjou unless the cameras were recording.

Because the script called for Kate to face Menjou in confrontational situations, she was able to vent her spleen against the actor in front of the world at large. One reviewer would later notice that when confronting Menjou, Kate's "eyes narrowed into slits and her voice became as abrasive as sandpiper."

During the course of one particularly exasperating day, Kate angrily confronted Menjou off-camera.

"The American patriot." she said, mockingly, "Is that why you invest all your money in Canadian bonds? By the way, did anyone ever tell you that that old-fashioned moustache of yours evokes a stage villain from the days of Queen Victoria?" Ignoring her, Menjou walked away.

She spoke to him off-camera later in the day, when she'd just performed a scene with Menjou and Capra had just yelled, "Cut!" Kate asked Menjou, "Must you deliver every sentence as if there is an exclamation point at the end?"

Near the end of the shoot, Kate told Capra, "if there was ever a man I wanted to hit in the face with a baseball bat, it's your boy, Menjou!" Even so, the film concluded without violence.

Years later, in 1957, Cukor invited Kate to go with him to see Menjou in *Paths of Glory* in which the aging actor played a foolish and self-serving French general who betrays the courage of his men, and then abandons them for execution before a firing squad Coming out of the movie theater, Kate turned to Cukor and said, "Type casting!"

Hearing of the actor's death in 1963, Cukor remarked, "The late, unlamented Adolphe Menjou."

***

Tame by today's standards, *State of the Union* in 1948 was viewed as "dangerous" in some right-wing quarters, since its plot led to a revelation of corruption at the highest levels of political life in America. Many of its sharpest jibes were aimed at President Harry Truman himself.

To the surprise of the press, Truman himself agreed to attend the Washington première of the picture on April 7, 1948. Capra accompanied the president to the show at Loew's Capital Theater in front of one-thousand six hundred other guests.

Truman liked the film and even ordered that it be shown at private screenings aboard the presidential yacht. In retrospect, Truman's endorsement of *State of the Union,* along with Nixon's earlier intervention in the Hepburn-Tracy affair, did much to squash rumors of Kate being "the lady in red."

The film also impressed a future president, Ronald Reagan, who saw *State of the Union* four times. He even stole one of Tracy's lines in the film, making it his own during his campaign for New Hampshire during the Republican Primary before the national elections of 1980. In the film, the producer of Tracy's radio and TV show tried to cut Tracy off in midspeech, in response to which Tracy snaps, "I'm paying for this broadcast." In a parallel situation, when his microphone was about to be cut off by a supporter of George Bush, Sr., Reagan declared, "I'm paying for this microphone."

Capra was so impressed with Kate's performance in *State of the Union* that he offered her the lead in *A Woman of Distinction* with Ray Milland as her co-star. Although Kate was eager to star in that picture, Capra eventually sold the rights to Columbia. Rosalind Russell was cast in Kate's hoped-for role, and the picture was released in 1950.

Like most political dramas of the Forties, *State of the Union* was not a major financial success. Capra himself admitted that the film did "only respectable business at the box office." Nevertheless, it was not the fiasco that *The Sea of Grass* was for Tracy and Kate, but it did restore some of their lost prestige with distributors.

Kate told both Tracy and Cukor, "What we need is a wonderful comedy to put us over the top again, something like *Woman of the Year.* Only better!"

Even as she spoke, her on-again, off-again friends, Ruth Gordon and Garson Kanin, that talented married team, were hard at work on the next Tracy/Hepburn picture.

Both Tracy and Kate were livid when they read that Adolphe Menjou had denounced *State of the Union,* the film in which he had co-starred, calling it "nothing more than a dirty Communist plot."

The film, when it was released in Britain as *The World and His Wife,* didn't arouse any stir at all, because it dealt with American, not British, politics.

In the States, Lee Mortimer, Hollywood columnist for Hearst's *New York Mirror*, found that *State of the Union* was an "indictment against this country, its customs, manners, morals, and economic and political systems." He also said that the words "put in the mouths of Tracy and Miss Hepburn would not seem out of place in *Izvestia*."

President Harry Truman, weeks later, admitted to his cronies that even though he liked the picture, "Bess didn't take to it at all."

Time found that "Hepburn's affectation of talking like a woman simultaneously trying to stay a loose dental brace sharply limits her range of expression." However, that same magazine found that Angela Lansbury "as the adderish lady publisher sinks a fine fang."

Howard Barnes, in *The New York Herald-Tribune*, found Kate's performance "restrained, persuasive, and altogether delightful."

After the release of the film, Kate was saddened to see Tracy hitting the bottle again. She was growing tired of his company, finding being with him both unrewarding and unfulfilling. She was slipping away most nights to be with the more vital Paul Henreid, when he wasn't with his wife, and her favorite couple, Judy Garland and Robert Walker, whom she sometimes saw at the same time, but more often, separately.

Walker's pal, Jim Henaghan, reported that once, when he was invited over for dinner to join his friend and Kate, he was surprised to see Walker walking around in the nude while Kate prepared dinner in her kitchen. "I don't think they'd had sex," Henaghan said. "Bob later told me that when he was around Kate, he wanted to be like a new-born babe, and infants popping out of the womb aren't clothed." Henaghan reported that Kate got through the dinner and hardly seemed aware of Walker's nudity. "Although she was fully clothed herself, she just accepted his nudity as the most natural thing on earth. Personally, I was very embarrassed. As for myself, I often didn't want women I was having sex with to see me in the nude. That's why I usually made love in the dark."

***

Although she'd turned down the co-starring role in *Edward, My Son*, Kate agreed to fly to London on a separate plane to join Tracy during part of the filming. The story was set in Britain, and the studio decided to film it at an authentic locale instead of trying to re-create the sets on a Hollywood sound stage. Tracy had accepted an invitation to stay at Notley Abbey, the home of Vivien Leigh and Laurence Olivier. For appearances' sake, Kate booked a suite in London at Claridge's.

Privately, Kate had told Cukor, who had signed to direct *Edward, My Son*, that the role of the alcoholic wife was not for her. Consequently, he cast Deborah Kerr in the part instead. Kate also told Cukor that he'd badly miscast Tracy as the ruthless, self-made British millionaire.

Most days, while Tracy was on the set filming, Kate hung out at the British Museum and in curio shops, but mainly she poked around London, discovering its secret alleys and hidden mews. Tracy had warned her not to break into any houses, and she only reluctantly had agreed.

Each night, when he returned from the set, Tracy was growing more and more despondent, realizing after only the first week of shooting, that he was wrong for the role of a pompous rags-to-riches British tycoon. Robert Morley had written the play, and it had been a big hit in London, with the portly actor/writer himself as the star.

Kate spent her first week in London at Claridge's, but accepted a weekend invitation to visit Notley Abbey and the Oliviers. The drive was less than fifty miles from London. She'd seen the Oliviers on and off for a number of years, their friendship developing casually after she'd been maid of honor at their hasty wedding. Kate had long ago forgiven Leigh for taking the role of Scarlett O'Hara in *Gone With the Wind.*

When Kate arrived with Tracy on a Friday night, their reunion with the Oliviers had been triumphant. Olivier was now Sir Laurence, as he'd recently been knighted. Olivier and "Lady Olivier" made a stunningly handsome couple and seemed very much in love.

Leigh was the perfect hostess, having filled the drafty old mansion with flowers and having ordered the staff to keep the fireplaces blazing because oil was still in short supply in post-war England.

It was so cold for a Californian like Tracy that he didn't even take off his overcoat. Kate didn't mind the cold—in fact, welcomed "the bracing air of the place."

Wisely assuming that Tracy and Kate no longer slept together, Leigh had assigned different bedchambers to her honored guests.

Tracy drank too much on their first dinner together, and staggered off to bed early to read detective stories. Kate followed shortly afterward.

About an hour later, she heard Leigh screaming at Olivier. She couldn't make out all the words, but Kate quickly realized that something was seriously wrong with the marriage.

She had forgotten that Lord and Lady Oliver were the world's greatest theatrical couple. That "perfect evening" and the "perfect couple" had been staged for Kate's benefit and for Tracy. But it had been just that—a stage play. They were perfect for the roles.

But what Kate heard that night might have made Leigh and Olivier the ideal stars for Edward Albee's *Who's Afraid of Virginia Wolff?,* a play that wouldn't be written till long in the future.

The following morning, Olivier and Leigh hardly spoke to each other. Leigh directed her conversation at Kate, and Olivier concentrated on Tracy. Olivier had arranged for them to attend a special screening of *Hamlet* in London. Neither Kate nor Tracy had seen the film, since they rarely attended movie theaters—and never together. Olivier had just recently won the Oscar as best actor for his portrayal of *Hamlet,* and the film had won the Oscar for best picture.

Tracy complained about the shortage of hot water in England, and Kate countered that she loved it, having taken cold showers all her life. As Tracy headed for the studio and Olivier left for a luncheon in London, Leigh invited Kate for a walk along the banks of the murky and fast-flowing Thames.

Leigh had bundled herself up heavily. When Kate suggested biking or a game of tennis later in the day, Leigh had to refuse. It was only then that Kate became aware that Leigh, in spite of the beauty of her porcelain skin, was a woman in physical torment. As the Thames rushed by, Leigh confessed that she was very seriously ill, having recently suffered one of her worst attacks of tuberculosis.

She said that she felt very debilitated and could only hold herself together for two or three hours at a time before she had to retreat to her bed.

Ever the caretaker, Kate offered to help, but Leigh said that there was nothing she could do. As the days went by, Kate began to realize—and she confided this to both Cukor and to Tracy—that Leigh was not only physically ill but mentally ill as well, suffering from some undiagnosed form of manic-depression.

In a confidential moment one night when they were alone in his library, Olivier confessed to Kate that Leigh had run, two weeks previously, screaming into the night from Notley. "When I caught up with her, I found her completely nude. She scratched at my face, and threatened to kill me. I had to use brute force to get her back into the house before she died of pneumonia."

Kate had already noted the rapid mood swings in Leigh. One night at Notley Abbey, she'd be the perfect hostess, telling them about how the manor had been endowed by Henry V himself. Her charm, wit, and beauty glowed by the open fireplaces. On other evenings, she came to dinner morose and melancholy, wearing no makeup and appearing in a sloppy dress, unlike the well-tailored gowns she wore most evenings.

Regardless of Leigh's condition, Oliver was always charming, ignoring his wife when she was quiet, sullen, or withdrawn, and including her in the conversation when she was her "normal" self. Mostly, Olivier concentrated his attention on Tracy, wanting to talk more about acting styles than his reluctant guest did.

One weekend at Notley, a handsome and charming Welshman, the young actor, Richard Burton, had been invited as a houseguest. He arrived slightly drunk, but Kate was used to soggy actors.

Olivier had been introduced to Burton when he was appearing at the Shakespeare Memorial Theatre at Stratford-upon-Avon, along with such established actors as John Gielgud, Michael Redgrave, and Peggy Ashcroft, and such emerging talent as Paul Scofield and Albert Finney. Olivier had been enchanted with Burton from their first meeting.

Kate found Burton "robust and very masculine," as she later reported to Cukor. "He seemed filled with an inner fire. He's unpretentious and I love his frankness."

After a dinner in which Burton heaped lavish praise on Tracy's acting, the quartet retired from the dining room for more drinking. Kate preferred to sip a sherry instead of Scotch.

Despondent over his miscast role in *Edward, My Son,* Tracy, with great effort, rose from an overstuffed armchair and announced his retreat upstairs to his cold bedchamber. Leigh had her maid deliver him a hot water bottle.

Kate, too, turned in early, leaving Lord and Lady Olivier in the living room talking to Burton. She felt largely excluded from all this gossip about the British theatre. As she was leaving, Burton was entertaining his hosts with a story about how John Gielgud had made a pass at him the first night they'd met.

An hour later, as Kate was propped up in bed reading, she heard Olivier come up the steps. He must have seen her light on from under the door, as he called out "good night" to her. He shared the room next to her. She was mildly perturbed that she could hear virtually every sound coming from his room, as the walls seemed paper-thin.

Unable to sleep, she got up an hour later and went downstairs to get some water. She was only mildly surprised to see Burton on the sofa with Leigh. "It looked like he was going for her tonsils," she told Cukor the next day. "He was all over her."

Later in the evening, as she was to report, she heard double footsteps coming up the stairs. She figured that Lord and Lady Olivier had long ago worked out their frequent changes of sexual partners, in much the same way that she and Tracy had.

Kate just assumed that the randy young actor had retired to bed with Leigh for the rest of the night. She fell asleep, but was awakened around two o'clock that morning. From the sound of voices next door, Burton was entering Lord Olivier's bedroom. Burton still seemed slightly drunk, and was talking in a loud voice.

Olivier tried to get him to speak more softly. The two men were talking with great animation, and at one point, they got into an argument. It was quickly settled. Then, in a loud voice, Burton called out, "That, my dear Sir Laurence, is what we call a 'blunt instrument' in Wales." It was designed to give the greatest of pleasure to man, woman, or beast in the field."

There were no more voices, although Kate heard the sounds of rhythmic squeaking coming from the bedsprings. It seemed that Burton was the lover in charge of the action, Olivier the willing recipient.

As Kate would later recount to Cukor, "Those Welsh boys have stamina. As a houseguest, I must say that Burton believes in sharing his favors with his hosts."

"Surely you've known for years that Larry is gay," Cukor said. "I'll let you in on a secret. All English actors are gay. That's why they're better than American actors. English actors are more in touch with both their male and female sides."

***

Although Tracy stayed at Notley Abbey, Kate preferred to continue living at Claridge's in London, visiting him and the Oliviers only on the weekends. She saw much more of Cukor, however.

At one point, Cukor came up with the idea of having Kate play the minor role of the secretary in *Edward, My Son,* although he warned her that she'd have to take third billing to Tracy and Deborah Kerr. Kate wisely turned down his offer, the role eventually going to Leueen MacGrath.

Cukor had installed himself on the top floor of the Savoy Hotel, with a panoramic view of the River Thames and Waterloo Bridge. He very candidly told Kate that he planned to seduce each of the King's Guards at Buckingham Palace. In those days, gay men wanting to make contact with one of the guards could meet them in Belgravia at the now-defunct Duke of Wellington Pub. The Royal Guards received such low wages that many of them supplemented their income by hustling on the side.

Cukor, often with his gay London friends from the theater, would make contact with the guardsmen at the pub. He told Kate that he gave them a "preliminary audition," asking all "the vital questions" before bringing them back to the Savoy.

"You've got to bathe them before bedding them," he said to Kate. "There's a lack of hot water in this country, and they do need a scrub-down. All that uncut meat can get a bit gamey. I hope the Queen stands downwind when she and the King review the guards."

Kate pretended that she didn't know what he meant, and quickly changed the subject.

Even though not in the film herself, Kate frequently showed up on the set hoping to keep Tracy from drinking. On some occasions, he didn't drink during shooting, but Cukor told her that Tracy was drinking every day, although not enough so that he looked drunk on camera.

Both Tracy and Kate seemed to resent all the attention that Cukor was paying to Deborah Kerr. Kate had long ago despaired of hearing what a great actress Kerr would eventually become.

One night, Cukor invited Kate for dinner at his suite at the Savoy. The director told her that she'd be joined by a few close friends. Arriving late at his suite, she discovered that the party was deep into its pre-dinner drinks. In the living room of the suite, Kate immediately spotted Alfred Hitchcock and his

508

wife, Alma, Lady Juliet Duff, and the director, John Farrow.

In the largest armchair of all sat a stunningly beautiful Ingrid Bergman in a beaded white dress. Upon seeing her, Kate brusquely left the suite without saying hello or goodbye to the other guests.

The following day on the set, Cukor chastised her for her rudeness, assuring her that Bergman was a "dear, dear girl."

That same afternoon, Bergman herself arrived on the set for a visit with her former flame, Tracy. Spotting Kate, she walked on by. Since Kate remained lurking on the set, watching, from afar, Bergman's every move, Bergman gave Tracy only a chaste kiss on his cheek.

Perhaps nervous that Kate was there, she cut short her visit after wishing Tracy luck with his role in *Edward, My Son.*

An hour or so later, Kate overheard Tracy talking to Gilbert Lockhead, a member of the London press corps. "Ingrid Bergman is the greatest actress I've ever worked with." Seeing Kate, Tracy hastily added, *"except one."*

To make up for her rudeness at Cukor's party, Kate accepted yet another invitation from Cukor for dinner in his suite. He promised to introduce her to a special guest, who Cukor promised her would be fascinating.

The surprise of the evening turned out to be a twenty-three-year-old, extraordinarily handsome blond, blue-eyed young man, Ronald Fernburn. He was a telephone operator at the Savoy, and had helped Cukor place several emergency calls to the States. In those days, it was very difficult to get an overseas line.

It was obvious to Kate that Cukor was quite taken with the young man and had even gone so far as to promise him a screen career.

"George wanted to return the favor for my getting through on all those calls to the States," Fernburn told Kate. "He asked me what I wanted. I said more than money, and even more than a new suit of clothes, I wanted autographed photographs of Joan Crawford and Barbara Stanwyck. Amazingly, one day George comes down to the lobby of the hotel—and guess what he's got?"

"Young man," Kate said, getting up and taking a piece of hotel stationery from Cukor's desk. She quickly scribbled her name on the sheet of paper and handed it to Fernburn. "Here is *my* autograph. Hang on to it! It'll be very valuable one day, and will fetch a lot of money when autograph seekers will no longer know who Crawford and Stanwyck are."

The next day, Kate ran into her old friend, Noël Coward. He told her that the King and Queen had wanted to invite Tracy and her for tea at Buckingham Palace. But the playwright went on to sadly inform her that "it is out of the question. Her Majesty didn't feel that it would be proper. A married man and his mistress. She told me to tell you—'perhaps some other time,' but she did send her regards."

When Kate arrived at Notley Abbey one Friday afternoon, Tracy had already left the set and was deep into a bottle of Irish whiskey. The moment she walked in the door, Tracy shouted at her, "Tell your lousy friend to go fuck himself."

"You mean, George?" she asked.

No, George is always getting fucked in spite of his looks. I'm referring to that second-rate asshole, Donald Ogden Stewart. I loved his screenplay. Great part for me!" Tracy was obviously being sarcastic. "My character is ruthless. I commit arson. I goad two people into committing suicide. I may harbor incestuous feelings for my dead son, and I drive my wife to drink. A great role for Spencer Tracy! There's sure to be another Oscar in my future."

"Where are our hosts?" Kate asked, trying to change the subject.

"Larry has run off to London with his Fancy, Mr. Richard Burton, after fighting all week with Vivien. She's locked in her room and may need you to go on a suicide watch for the whole weekend. Only last Wednesday, a constable came by here with two very angry parents. It seems that Vivien had seduced their sixteen-year-old son, and they were talking about taking her to court. Fortunately, Larry was here, and he managed to calm them down with an offer of five-hundred pounds. That's a pretty good fee for a sixteen-year-old's stud services."

"It sounds like this weekend will be a lot of fun."

After a dreary weekend, Kate returned to London to find a message waiting for her at Claridge's. It was from Irene Mayer Selznick, who had arrived in London.

In the days ahead, Irene divided her time between Kate and Cukor, for whom she served as a "beard" whenever he was invited to the theater or to an A-list gathering of his straight admirers.

***

During the time Irene was in London, Kate no longer spent time on the set of *Edward, My Son* as the unofficial caretaker to Tracy. Instead she spent her days exploring London with Irene, often attending matinees at West End theatres. Evenings were sometimes spent in Irene's suite at the Savoy. The staff reported that Kate could often be seen using the service elevator, departing from the hotel at five o'clock in the morning.

By the end of filming in 1949, both Kate and Tracy knew they had been right about their dim assessment of *Edward, My Son*. It was slated to be a dismal flop. When many critics saw it, it was pronounced as one of the weakest Spencer Tracy movies since the mid-Thirties.

Kate left a drunken Tracy at Notley Abbey and began planning a flight back to the States for a visit to her friends in New York and her family in Connecticut.

After thanking the Oliviers and spending time alone with Tracy, Kate was

510

driven back to London by a chauffeur. Cukor came by Claridge's to see her off. He told her that he'd accepted an invitation to visit the homosexual author, W. Somerset Maugham, on the French Riviera. "He's promised me a daily diet of Grade-A French beef." Cukor went on to say that after his vacation, he was going to rush back to Hollywood to help his old friend, Billie Burke. "She hasn't made a film since 1946, and she's completely run out of money and girl friends." Kate asked to be remembered to her co-star in *A Bill of Divorcement*. Kate also added, "While you're helping Billie, please try to line up another comedy for Spencer and me. We desperately need another good picture."

"I'll see what I can do," Cukor said, "but it's a very different Hollywood we're returning to."

***

Cukor was right.

There were no roles waiting for either Tracy or Kate in Hollywood. Instead of worrying about a future Tracy/Hepburn role, Metro-Goldwyn-Mayer was concerned about its own survival.

Television was beginning to make inroads into America's once-favorite pastime of going to the movies, and the studio had ended its fiscal year of 1948 with a loss of about seven-million dollars.

It was also managing its way through an anti-monopoly suit. MGM, along with several other major studios, had been ordered by the Supreme Court to divest itself of its heretofore profitable theater chains.

Film production was down, and pink slips were going out to many employees. Some of the stars who had been major names in prior years could still be seen walking, sometimes aimlessly, around the studios. The days of many of them were numbered.

Upon Kate's return to Hollywood, Judy Garland called. She told Kate, "Papa Mayer and that paternal system at MGM is over. Life is going to get very dim for us little chickens, the lowly contract players. The studio isn't taking any shit from anybody anymore. Just to let you know how bad things are, Mayer is even selling off his race horses. Soon, there won't be any long-term contracts. Everybody in Hollywood will be free-lancing."

"We can't wallow in nostalgia," Kate cautioned her. "Whatever it is out there, we've got to get on with it!"

Back in Hollywood, after having sampled, by his own reckoning, a dozen Provençal boys, Cukor echoed Garland's sentiments to Kate. He told her that MGM had slipped to fourth place in box office receipts, having been topped by Paramount, Warner Brothers, and 20th Century Fox.

"Even Margaret O'Brien is making bad pictures," Cukor said. "Don't waste your money on seeing her in *Tenth Avenue Angel*. Margaret was an adorable little girl, but she's going to be a disaster as a grown-up actress. Mark my words."

As Kate moved deeper into 1949, she resumed seeing Garland privately, finding her still warm and loving. Kate asked her about Frank Sinatra's latest picture, *The Kissing Bandit.* In response, Garland advised her to "Skip it! Frank is much better kissing in bed than he is on the screen."

"So you've been kissing Sinatra?" Kate asked. "Whatever happened to Robert Walker?"

"Robert *who?*" Garland asked.

On the subject of MGM's declining revenues, Kate made a sarcastic judgement to Garland. "I could have saved the studio by changing the ending of *Sea of Grass.* When my character got pregnant out of wedlock, and then gave birth to a illegitimate son, I should have died as moral punishment. Then the picture would have been a big hit."

Paul Henreid brought Kate up to date on the Red Scare, which he said was threatening more and more media-related careers, even his own. He told her that MGM was planning a re-release of Garbo's 1939 *Ninotchka* and Hedy Lamarr's 1940 *Comrade X* to prove that it had been among the first studios to ridicule Communism.

Without any suitable roles, Kate embarked on one of the most socially visible roles of her Hollywood life. Perhaps as a means of working out her frustrations, she turned to what she referred to as "violent exercise," especially tennis. And the demands of her sexual side were being deftly handled by her newest love, Paul Henreid himself.

On the tennis courts at the Beverly Hills Hotel, Kate could be found almost every morning playing with Bill Tilden, the former Wimbledon champion. In disgrace because of child molestation charges, he was on the staff, working as tennis pro, of the luxury hotel.

William Tatem Tilden II was the pre-eminent tennis player in the world during the first quarter of the 20th century. He'd even appeared in silent pictures, bringing a wholesome, all-American quality to his roles. His mother, Selina Tilden, doted on her son, and called him "June" until he was eighteen.

The author, Vladimir Nabokov, was the first to note Big Bill's interest in adolescent boys. Seeing the player surrounded on the court by three fourteen-year-old boys, Nabokov told Kate one morning, "Looks to me like Big Bill's got himself a harem of ball boys."

"I get it!" she said angrily. Well aware of Big Bill's interest in young boys, Kate never condemned him. The same position was adopted by Charlie Chaplin, who was also a friend of Big Bill's. Of course, Chaplin could not afford to condemn, since he, too, pursued an interest in underaged sex kittens.

Nabokov ended up immortalizing Big Bill in a strange kind of way. He appeared as Ned Litam—that's "Ma Tilden" spelled backwards—in *Lolita,* Nabokov's brilliant novel of an April-and-December romance.

Big Bill's name ultimately became "Stumpfinger" when the tip of his middle finger became infected and had to be amputated. Kate noted, however, that his tennis playing was still as good as ever following the operation.

Caught masturbating a young boy by the Beverly Hills police on November 23, 1946, Tilden was in disgrace. He was sentenced by a judge to the equivalent of a minimum-security prison.

After his release, he was convicted again, this time for propositioning a boy at a Beverly Hills junior high school, and subsequently served time on a chain gang.

Released for the second time, Tilden never got into trouble again. But he found that his former pupils had deserted him. These included, among others, Errol Flynn, who also maintained a vivid interest in sex with teenagers. Both Tallulah Bankhead and Tracy himself, although not the world's greatest tennis players, had been among Tilden's pupils. Alone among his celebrity friends from yesterday, Kate maintained her loyalty to Tilden even after his return from prison.

But after playing with him for at least six months, she too drifted off. "Not for moral reasons," she told Anderson Lawler. "I felt that he'd taught me all that he could."

Nonetheless, she was saddened to read about his death, which occurred on June 5, 1953. He'd died of a heart attack, and was found penniless in a seedy apartment in Los Angeles.

In the summer of 1949, Kate rented a cottage in the small oceanside resort of Trancas, California, immediately next door to her close friends, Chester and Sally Erskine. Tracy was often a secret visitor. She would cook private dinners, even entertaining the likes of Judy Garland and Vincente Minnelli. Arriving drunk, Robert Walker was a sometimes guest, too. And whenever he could get away from his wife, Paul Henreid would show up at her door as well. She also entertained Lawrence Weingarten, who, unknown to her at the time, would eventually produce the next Tracy/Hepburn film.

Scripts continued to pour in for Kate. Rarely were they firm offers from studios. Most often, they were from struggling screenwriter wannabes, hoping that with Kate's endorsement, financial backing for their scenarios would follow.

Over the next few months, Kate developed the unusual habit of driving over to see a bedridden Ethel Barrymore every morning. Because of the grand lady's failing eyesight, Kate read the scripts of the day to Miss Barrymore. In every case, the aging *grande dame* advised against accepting the role, finding none of the scripts worthy of Kate.

Kate also read some of her scripts to "Funny Girl" Fanny Brice, who was at the time living temporarily in Hollywood. Kate trusted the female comic's shrewd sense of show business. Like Miss Barrymore, however, Brice too nixed all the scripts.

"I don't think any script sent to me at that time was ever filmed." Kate later told Patricia Peardon during one of her brief returns to the East Coast for a visit with her family in Connecticut and a reunion in New York with Laura Harding and Luddy.

Back in California, Kate found Tracy drunk in Cukor's cottage. He hadn't bathed or shaved since she'd been gone. After scrubbing him down and giving him a shave, she tried to sober him up, but succeeded only in getting him to nominally cut back on his consumption of liquor.

During his more lucid moments, he told he that he was delighted that Dore Schary was gradually easing Louis B. Mayer out of the chief power position at MGM. Tracy had known Schary for years, and he told Kate that Schary was "bright, idealistic, and liberal." Tracy predicted that when Schary eventually took over MGM, far better scripts would be offered to them, both as individuals and as an acting duet. He compared Schary's upcoming takeover of the studio as equivalent to Roosevelt's New Deal in the 1930s.

"How I wish that Spencer's optimism—unusual for one such as him—had turned out to be true," Kate later told Kenneth MacKenna.

In the beginning, at least, there were hopeful signs.

Kate and Tracy as a team were about to be offered one of their most memorable film scripts.

But first, an old friendship had to be repaired.

***

I've fallen in love," Kate announced to a startled Anderson Lawler, upon waking him up early one Saturday morning.

"And I have, too," Lawler said. "With Derek Harris. But he's too much into women. Strictly rough trade."

"C'mon, you silly thing," Kate chastised him. "I'm really in love for the first time in my life."

"Male or female?"

"A man, you stupid goose. I don't fall in love with women. They fall in love with me. I'm in love with Paul Henreid."

"Why Henried? He's married."

"Aren't they all?" She then proceeded to bring her trusted friend up to date on the new twists and turns her relationship with Henreid had taken since her return from London. She told him that she fully expected that within a few weeks, the actor was going to ask his wife for a divorce so that he could marry her.

In the throes of love, Kate saw in Henreid the type of man she felt she wanted to be with at all times, except when she wanted to entertain a woman on the side.

514

"He's not the arrogant, smug, continental I thought at first," she said, "but a cultured, caring, and sensitive man. He doesn't crawl off until I'm completely satisfied."

Even though once again forced to lead a love life in secret, the way she had with Tracy, Kate nonetheless began to slip secretively around Hollywood for appearances with Henreid at various private homes for dinner. Under no circumstances did Henreid want his wife to know he was having an affair with Kate.

She was most impressed with Henreid's choice of friends, especially with Charles Chaplin, whom she admired as an actor, figuring the comic to be a genius.

Some of Henreid's friends were also intimates of Kate's. She was astonished that he was close to Judy Garland, although Henreid detested Vincente Minnelli.

Kate had a reunion with actors she'd known in the Thirties, including her unfulfilled romances with Fredric March and Lew Ayres.

Minor actors such as Paul Stewart and Hugh Marlowe were also among Henreid's closest friends. She had a reunion with Franchot Tone again, and was surprised at how talkative Gary Cooper could be at private gatherings, a striking contrast to his image on the screen as a man of very few words.

Hollywood liberals and intellectuals such as Paul Muni and Edward G. Robinson were also among Henreid's trusted friends.

Most often, the subject of their conversations during these dinners in 1950 concerned the rising threat to their careers based on the vague suspicion of communist sympathies, even though none of the actors mentioned above was ever a "Red Menace."

Amazingly, during those days of Red Hysteria some segments of the American population sincerely believed that Gary Cooper, a super-patriot, was "red." Cooper himself effectively dispelled that idea when he appeared before HUAC in Washington, D.C. in the late 1940s. Even John Wayne and Irene Dunne testified before the committee.

Kate watched in horror as her friend, Ring Lardner, Jr., was named one of the "Hollywood Ten," and declared guilty of contempt of Congress for refusing to "name names." He was jailed.

The only bright news came when Kate learned that the chairman of HUAC, J. Parnell Thomas, whom she loathed, had been convicted of taking kickbacks arranged through his staff and sentenced to jail. Ironically, Thomas's jail sentence came almost simultaneously with those of Lardner, Jr., and another member of the Hollywood Ten, Lester Cole.

Kate was pleased to see that Judy Garland and even Claudette Colbert, with whom she was estranged, had joined director John Huston in a radio broadcast protesting this infringement of the First Amendment.

Henreid invited Kate to fly with him and with a group of other actors to

Washington. They planned to appear before HUAC and denounce the committee for infringing on First Amendment rights. Howard Hughes made a TWA plane available for the transport from California to Washington of such stars as Humphrey Bogart, Lauren Bacall, Evelyn Keyes, Danny Kaye, Sterling Hayden, and others. Fredric March and Hugh Marlowe also agreed to go, along with John Huston himself.

After making a strong stand in defense of the accused Hollywood Ten before the HUAC committee in Washington, Bogie later recanted his position after he reached Chicago and feared a detrimental "fall-out" effect on his own career. His "turncoat" interview earned him the lifelong animosity of some of the more liberal and courageous actors in the entourage. "If I ever run into Spencer's dear friend, Mr. Bogart, I'm going to smack him in the nose," Kate threatened.

For some reason, and Kate never revealed why, she cancelled plans to fly to Washington with Henreid and the others, thus delaying her eventual meeting with both John Huston and Bogie.

Back in Hollywood, Kate had dinner with both Henreid and March, her co-star from *Mary of Scotland.* Enough time had elapsed that by now March could laugh at his comeuppance when she'd placed an unripened banana into her panties just before he tried to feel her up.

She was saddened to see March falsely accused of communist activities, and stood by for the next ten years, watching as he spent nearly a million dollars on legal fees in the fight against his blacklisting.

Amazingly, in 1950, when other actors were losing long-term contracts, and in spite of his left-wing political views, Henreid was offered a seven-year contract with MGM that would have paid him one-hundred and fifty thousand dollars a year. Kate denounced him for his stupidity when he turned down the offer.

Henreid had told Kate that his contract said he could not be suspended for any reason except for committing adultery. "I guess they're trying to tell you something," Kate responded. "Now come to bed."

Later, Henreid regretted that he didn't listen to Kate, for he too found himself blacklisted and unable to find work. "You should have accepted the God damn contract when the going was good," Kate said.

Kate remained supportive and loving of Henreid, until he told her that he wanted to end their affair and return to his wife's loving arms.

"He no longer calls," she said, sobbing, to Lawler. "I've fallen for him. We could have had a grand life together. He doesn't drink very much. He's intelligent. We could have played in films together. Or on the stage. Traveled to Europe. It would have been the life I always dreamed about with someone but never had."

"When the going gets tough, those louses go back to their spouses." Lawler warned her.

"And so they do," Kate said. "Paul Henreid is my last love affair. I'm getting too old for this type of thing. It hurts too much at my age to be carrying on like a schoolgirl. Call it my last romance."

It took only about a month before Kate was on the phone with Lawler again, proclaiming that she'd fallen in love again. Only this time, it was with a woman.

***

Garson Kanin and his author/actress wife, Ruth Gordon, were writing a script called *Man and Wife* whose name was later changed to *Adam's Rib*. It was the story of a couple, both members of which were attorneys, who take opposite sides in a court case.

Kate was cast as Amanda Bonner, a militant feminist, defending a dumb blonde, as played by Judy Holliday. In the film, Holliday, playing the role of Doris Attinger, shoots her two-timing husband, Warren Attinger (as played by Tom Ewell). Warren has been caught in the arms of "the other woman," Beryle Craighn, as played by Jean Hagen. Tracy stars as the prosecuting attorney, Adam Bonner. David Wayne provides support as a good-looking but closeted homosexual, Kip Lurie, and Hope Emerson, playing the role of Olympia La Pere supplies comic relief. George Cukor had signed to direct the film, with Lawrence Weingarten as producer.

Tracy and Kanin hadn't spoken since their falling out, when Kanin had directed his old friend in the disastrous experience *The Rugged Path*. In the meantime, Kanin had reached the peak of his career, having earned a huge success on Broadway in 1946 with his script of *Born Yesterday,* starring Judy Holliday, a role that that same actress would later revive in the screen version, for which she would win an Oscar in 1950.

In the hopes of ending their feud, and realizing that he would be the one to break the ice, Kanin called Tracy during one of his trips to California. Kanin invited both Tracy and Hepburn to dinner at Chasen's. Tracy accepted, but Kate refused. "Garson knows I don't dine out in public."

Kate remembered, however, that after their dinner ended, both of the men came to her house and all three of them talked until dawn. "The broken friendship has been repaired," she told Cukor the following morning.

After MGM had paid the Kanins one-hundred-and seventy-five thousand dollars for their script, *Adam's Rib* went into production in the spring of 1949.

Much of the film was shot in New York, near the corner of Lexington Avenue and East 52nd Street. Kate could walk over to the set from her Turtle Bay residence.

Noticing how nervous she was, Kate immediately befriended Judy Holliday. Encouraging the young actress, Kate gave her moral support. In time, Kate's extreme care with Holliday worked, and the blonde actress delivered a brilliant performance.

During one long (and frankly, somewhat tedious) scene where Kate, in the role of Holliday's attorney, was interviewing her at a table, Kate insisted that Cukor and his cameras focus for the most part on Holliday throughout the scene.

Tracy had already concluded that Kate was so charmed and mesmerized by Holliday that she was "giving her the picture on a silver platter with a knife to cut us up with after she's finished off the fat bird we're feeding her."

The seven-minute scene, staged at a conference table between Holliday and Kate, played better back in 1949 than it holds up today. Most of it, in complete contrast to what Kate might have demanded in other pictures, was shot over Kate's shoulder, with the camera focusing almost entirely on Holliday.

"I've never heard of such kindness from a reigning star," Weingarten said after seeing the way Cukor, based on Kate's rigid instruction, was shooting the film. "Can you imagine Joan Crawford or Bette Davis, certainly not Lana Turner, doing that for a newcomer? It was incredible."

At one point, Weingarten ventured forth with the idea of giving Kate top billing over Tracy. When he heard that, Tracy shouted him down. "I'll never take second billing to that bag of bones." Then he threatened to walk off the picture unless Weingarten retreated from his position.

During the friendship that developed between Kate and Judy Holliday, Judy confided that she desperately wanted the role of Billie Dawn in the upcoming screen adaptation of Garson Kanin's *Born Yesterday*. It didn't seem like a particularly outrageous request, since Holliday, simultaneous with her filming in New York of *Adam's Rib,* was playing the same role, to huge acclaim, on the Broadway stage.

But ironically, despite Holliday's success in the original Broadway version of *Born Yesterday,* she was not the automatic choice for the same role in the screen version. Harry Cohn, head of Columbia, had referred to Holliday as "the fat Jewish broad" and wouldn't even let her test for the screen version. Consequently, Kate, prevailing upon her friendship with Cukor, the designated director for *Born Yesterday,* began a program of serious politicking to ensure Holliday the role in the movie version.

Cukor, after some investigation, told her that Harry Cohn had originally wanted to turn the film version of *Born Yesterday* into a starring vehicle for Rita Hayworth. "But now," Cukor reported, "Cohn is ranting about 'the dumb cow marrying some Arab with a big dick and an even bigger wallet.'" If not Hayworth, Cohn was reported as preferring Lucille Ball, Alice Faye, or Barbara Stanwyck for the role.

As a footnote to Hollywood history, Cohn approved a screen test of the unknown starlet, Marilyn Monroe, but didn't even bother to look at the result of the blonde bombshell's tests. "I had her in my office, though," he told Cukor. "Great fucking piece of pussy and what a cocksucker! But I didn't think she can carry a picture like *Born Yesterday,* for which I paid one-million God damn fucking dollars—and you'd better believe it."

After hearing that, Kate began defining *Adam's Rib* as "the most elaborate screen test in Hollywood history." She knew that if Holliday was brilliant in her part in that film, and if she received critical acclaim, Cohn would relent and cast her as Billie Dawn in *Born Yesterday.* And that is precisely what happened.

***

For six short weeks of her life, Katharine Hepburn became absolutely mesmerized by "the dumb blonde" in *Adam's Rib.* From the time of her first meeting with Holliday, playing the role of the quintessentially blue-collar New York girl, Kate realized at once that Holliday, in spite of the role she played, was no dumb blonde.

Actually, Holliday had an genius-level IQ of 172, far greater than that of virtually any other actress of her day. In addition to her sharp wit, she was also brilliant, funny, and on occasion, poignant. What intitially attracted Kate to her was a look of vulnerability that Kate had also sensed in another actress, Judy Garland.

"Behind all that wit and grace, and that heart-winning smile, I sense doom in her," Kate told Patricia Peardon in New York. "It's almost like there is fun and gaiety on the surface, like you might have at a wonderful, sunny picnic. But lurking somewhere on the distant horizon is an ominous black cloud. I don't know what it is. But there's something there, and it's altogether frightening."

Completely unlike the role she immortalized—that of Billie Dawn in *Born Yesterday*—Holliday had emerged into life in the Russian-Jewish immigrant world of New York City during the Twenties and Thirties. In that troubled but highly intellectual brewing pot, she quickly became politically conscious at an early age.

By the time she was twelve years old, she had opinions that were, if not Marxist, definitely left-wing liberal. Her enemies would later characterize her as a "card-carrying communist" in the way they did with Kate herself.

Kate found none of Holliday's political opinions particularly frightening, and agreed with her about most issues.

As work progressed on *Adam's Rib,* Kate told Cukor, "Behind that Billie Dawn façade, I sense a real tragedy brewing in Judy. She has the capacity to be hurt deeply by life. It's like she hasn't built up a protective shell like the tortoise. She's all raw and vulnerable, waiting for someone to devour her. But I also feel such courage and spirit in her that I predict she'll triumph in a way that's different from other actresses. I can't put my finger on it. She's an original, I suppose. She has the potential to become the next Fanny Brice for the second half of the 20th century. She makes you want to love her, but she can also make you want to cry."

"It sounds like you're falling in love," was Cukor's jaded pronouncement.

Holliday liked both men and women and, before her marriage to the clarinet player, David Oppenheim, she had been involved in a long-term lesbian relationship with her best friend, Yetta Cohn.

During the shooting of *Adam's Rib,* in New York, Holliday and Kate became almost inseparable. The blonde-haired younger actress, taking time off from her husband, began to acquaint Kate with a side of New York that she'd never seen before.

Holliday later recalled that Kate found almost anything, regardless of how trivial, "fascinating." Holliday succeeded where almost no one had before— she actually got Kate to go to public restaurants. They tended to be small, out-of-the-way places, far off the tourist circuit. Kate later told Luddy that she was surprised that no one recognized her; or, if they did spot her, they didn't' come over and hound her for autographs.

Kate even followed Holliday not only to her favorite haunts, but to places where Holliday had lived before, including an apartment at 226 West 58th Street, where she'd shared the high-ceilinged, skylit quarters with Yetta Cohn. "We paid fifty-seven dollars a month rent," Holliday said. "A lot of money to scrape together every month. We weren't rich like you Hepburns."

"We were never rich," Kate said. Only well-off and well-stuffed."

It was through Holliday that Kate truly discovered Greenwich Village, although she'd been walking through it for most of her life. Kate took Holliday by the house where she'd found her brother, Tom, hanging by the neck so very long ago. Even so, Holliday remembered Kate standing there and weeping at the site.

Although Kate had spent most of her life deliberately misleading the public about her private life, she found in Holliday an open, honest person, so unlike herself.

Holliday made Kate laugh when she spoke of her early, failed attempts at dating men. "They wanted a dumb blonde but got me instead. I was never one to pretend that some man was fascinating when he wasn't. I only acted dumb on the stage. If a man said something stupid to me, I challenged him. If he keeps saying dumb things to me, I often get up, tell him he's a crashing bore, and leave the table at whatever restaurant or nightclub we're at."

On the subject of dating, she told Kate, "I went out mostly with boy who would take me to Broadway shows instead of parties. Symphony concerts and recitals instead of dances. I was more interested in writing poetry than passing love notes, and I preferred listening to Bach more than dancing to Benny Goodman. I must have been obnoxious."

Kate applauded that attitude, but confessed that she hadn't always been that honest with men. "Many times, I've applauded what John Ford, and especially Spencer, said to me, even though their observations were hardly earth-shaking. Deep down, in spite of what I pretend, I suspect there lurks a courtesan in Katharine Hepburn. Maybe I'll play Madame du Barry one day."

Holliday, even though married, seemed to have no problem with her homosexual feelings. She told Kate that most of her friends in the theater were "double-gaited," or at least had been during some period of their lives. "Even many of my friends who later get married—male or female—often have had a brush with homosexuality when they're young."

"Well, it seems to me that you've grown up in what the right wing calls 'the free-thinking artistic melting pot' of New York City," Kate said.

The relationship between Kate and Holliday grew so intense that Kate invited Holliday to a number of what Michael Jackson would have referred to as "sleepovers" at her Turtle Bay residence.

***

If there was one thing Holliday loved far more than sex, it was food. All of her life she struggled with a fear of getting too fat. She'd originally turned down her role in *Adam's Rib* because Garson Kanin had a description of her character as fat. Kate prevailed on her successfully to get her to change her mind and accept the role.

Holliday told Kate that she loved "to cook and then I love to eat what I've cooked. If I get the role in *Born Yesterday*, I know I'll have to diet for months. Out there in Hollywood they don't let a girl eat." She was always amazed that Kate could eat large portions and never gain a pound. "You are truly amazing. I just look at a bowl of pasta going by to another table and immediately put on five hard-to-lose pounds."

Holliday said that when she was trying to get started in show business, she wasn't stuffed like Kate growing up. "I never went on charity because I felt a lot of people in New York needed it more than I did. But I learned to survive. I'd go out with my theater friends like Betty Comden and Adolph Green. We all went Dutch back then. They'd order big steak dinners that cost one dollar and fifty cents. Who had that kind of money? I'd order a five-cent cup of coffee. As the waiter was clearing off the plates, I'd ask him to put the leftovers in a bag for my dog. Except, I had no dog. When I got home, I devoured what was in that doggie bag."

Holliday said that some of her friends thought she was in the money because she was always seen about town wearing an expensive mink coat. "I found a shop owner who gave me the coat on a wear-now, pay-later installment plan. But one night I gave this big party in this small apartment in the Village. Someone at the party stole my mink coat, and I had to work and pay it off anyway while seen about town in a bargain basement coat from Klein's."

Peardon was a frequent visitor at Turtle Bay in those days, and she claimed that Holliday and Kate, even though they'd known each other for such a short time, were like survivors of a long-standing relationship.

"They were so different, but so comfortable in each other's presence,"

Peardon said. "Sometimes when not running around, they liked to sit by the fireplace and read scripts, never saying a word. But there was some silent communication between them. I thought they were falling deeply in love. I adored Kate and wanted her to be happy, and I was also delighted that Kate was breaking away from Tracy and letting him stew in his own juices at the Waldorf-Astoria. If Judy were free for the night, Kate had no time for her old drunk."

But by the time Harry Cohn finally agreed to cast Holliday in *Born Yesterday*, and she was off to Hollywood to make the film with co-stars Broderick Crawford and William Holden, her affair with Kate came to an abrupt end.

"When it's over, it's over," Kate said to Peardon. "I wanted to go on with it, but she didn't. I think that Judy is basically drawn to women as companions, but for sex, she prefers men."

"Are you heartbroken?" Peardon asked.

"Not at all," Kate said. "I don't think relationships should be judged by their longevity but by their intensity at the time. We'll remain friends."

And so they were, heeding Holliday's own philosophy: "Lovers have a right to betray you. Friends do not!"

During the making of *Born Yesterday*, Holliday spoke frequently to Kate. She shared Kate's disdain for Hollywood parties.

"The social life in Hollywood is deadly," Holliday said. "Go to a party and you always meet the same people there, talking about the same thing—motion pictures. The urgent topic of conversation is, 'Are you on your way up or down, on the inside or outside?' You're weighed the second you enter a room. You can almost see their minds busily working. 'What's she wearing? What did her last picture gross? Who did she come with?' If you don't happen to conform, you're hounded."

When Holliday saw the first preview of *Adam's Rib*, she called Kate. "One critic said that I started as a moron in *Kiss Them For Me*, and I worked up to becoming an imbecile in *Adam's Rib*. What I want to know is, where does a girl go from being an imbecile? Maybe, if I'm lucky, I can graduate up to playing an idiot or a cretin."

Holliday was always grateful for Kate's support in launching her film career in *Adam's Rib*. When Holliday was nominated for an Oscar in 1950 as best actress for her role in *Born Yesterday*, Kate called her to congratulate her for her entry into what was called "the stiffest actress competition in history." Those words came from film writer David Shipman.

Holliday was up against Gloria Swanson in *Sunset Boulevard* and Bette Davis in *All About Eve*. Both of these strong contenders were playing actresses in their greatest roles. Perhaps they cancelled each other out, paving the way for a "third runner up" like Holliday, who actually emerged from the competition with the most votes.

Kate was always ready to give her advice about her film career. In fact,

Kate gave Holliday better advice than she often heeded in her own career. Foolishly, Holliday would often listen attentively to Kate, but not follow her wisdom.

When Holliday was offered the lead in the film version of *Gentlemen Prefer Blondes*, Kate urged her take it. But Holliday decided not to. "It may sound old-fashioned, but I've seen Carol Channing play the part magnificently on Broadway. The role, I feel, is made for her. I can't take it away from the one woman who deserves it. I once fought for the privilege of doing the movie counterpart of an original stage role I created. Now that the shoe is on the other foot, I still haven't changed my mind about that principle."

Channing, of course, lost the part to Marilyn Monroe, who immortalized the role and herself.

Kate stood by Holliday, giving her moral support when she was called before the Senate Internal Security Committee—the Senate's counterpart to the HUAC committee that had already proven so dangerous—to answer questions about her alleged Communist ties one year after winning the Academy Award.

At the hearings, Holliday used her dumb blonde image to her advantage, skirting a couple of dangerous questions where she could have implicated others. In her subtle way, like Billie Dawn in *Born Yesterday,* she was cleared of any "wrong-doing," but the stigma of the scandal kept her name on a blacklist of actors who weren't allowed to work in television.

Holliday found little work in the two years that followed her Oscar win. She later told Kate that in the weeks following her appearance before the Senate Committee, she received nearly two-hundred death threats from around the country.

Holliday died on June 7, 1965, from breast cancer. Kate did not come to the funeral but sent the largest wreath of flowers. She signed it: IN LOVING MEMORY OF A DEAR, DEAR FRIEND WHO COULD LIGHT THE DARKEST NIGHT. KATHARINE HOUGHTON HEPBURN.

In her only public pronouncement about Judy Holliday, Kate said: "She looked like a Renoir. Judy is one of the people I miss the most, of all my friends, who have passed away in the near or distant past. Her death affected me deeply; I felt as though she was a sister to me, though we weren't terribly close. But when we talked, it was so comfortable, so amusing in a lovely way— I just loved her. I'm sorry we didn't work together another time."

***

During the filming of *Adam's Rib*, Tracy and Kate sensed they had a hit on their hands, and they were right. *Adam's Rib* became the biggest battle-of-the-sexes comedy of the Forties. Rather daringly, it advocated a woman's right— as expressed by attorney Amanda, played by Kate—to take a few compulsive potshots at a philandering husband.

The film was a hit in spite of *Time* finding it "more absurd than comical." Most of the actors, including Tracy and Kate, received good reviews. The only sour note was the almost universal criticism of the film's theme song, "Farewell, Amanda," written by none other than Cole Porter. It was and still is, considered one of the worst theme songs ever written for a major film. *Time* suggested that Porter "must have written it while waiting for a bus."

Adam's Rib rescued the sagging box office receipts of MGM, and brought renewed prestige to the acting team of Tracy and Hepburn. The Kanin-Gordon screenplay was nominated for an Oscar but did not win.

***

At the end of filming, Tracy became increasingly hostile to Kate, as he resumed his heavy drinking. At one point, he ordered her from his cottage and told her that if she returned, he'd "give you a boot in your bony butt." He told Cukor that he was tired of Kate and her nagging, interfering ways. "Sometimes when I hear the sound of that out-of-control voice, my whole body cringes. I encourage her to smoke more since that lowers her voice register."

One day, Tracy claimed that he'd found an adoring woman, one who understood him, respected him, and gave in to him on any issue. "It's the woman I've been looking for all my life and never found. Believe it or not, it's someone I've known for years but had never thought of in that special way before—that is, until now. Hell, I was even a friend of her mother's."

"Who might this goddess of virtue be?" Cukor asked him.

"Nancy Davis."

***

Kate was very depressed when her name appeared on June 8, 1949, on the House Un-American Activities Committee list of "Communist appeasers." Keeping company with Kate on this list was Pearl Buck, presumably because she'd written *The Good Earth* and Kate's own *Dragon Seed*. Also on that list, as a surprise, was Maurice Chevalier, one of the most died-in-the-wool reactionaries in French show business. Lena Horne's name was also on the list, possibly because she married a white man. Sinatra denounced the list as "the product of liars."

In spite of the success of *Adam's Rib*, it was a low point in Kate's life and her relationship with Tracy.

Without being officially fired, Kate's days at MGM had virtually come to an end. She went to the studio and packed up her possessions and left within two hours without looking back.

No one, certainly not Louis B. Mayer or Dore Schary, escorted her to the gate.

She would return to MGM to make one final film to fulfill her contract. The film would be *Pat and Mike*, teaming her again with Cukor, Tracy, Lawrence Weingarten, Ruth Gordon, and Garson Kanin.

But as Kate was later to recall, "That was just a swan song. My career at MGM more or less ended when I walked out the door after *Adam's Rib* was in the can."

Kate had come to the mid-point of her life, and her insecurities about aging arose. "As you get older," she said to Weingarten, "it becomes more humiliating because you've got less to sell. Certainly not youth and beauty. Let Gloria Swanson carry on with this glamorous granny stuff. I also don't believe in all this fabulous after forty crap. It's pure bunk! I'm getting old."

Later, she called Cukor and said, "Spencer has all but given up. He'll end up one day all alone with the bottle. I won't be there for him."

At the time of that assessment of Tracy, she was unaware that he was finding renewed vigor through his involvement with starlet Nancy Davis.

Cukor told Anderson Lawler that in spite of Tracy's brief fling with Davis, his longtime friend was "enjoying the comforts left to the damned—a bottle of whiskey. He's lost his health. He's no longer king of the box office. He looks like shit. He's a walking tub of suet. His kidneys are shot. He sucks off hustlers but will never admit he's gay. And for some reason, he's still a big enough name that he can get a date on Saturday night, if only with Nancy Davis."

Kate complained to Kenneth MacKenna and Anderson Lawler that she was finding life with Tracy on a day-to-day basis "too claustrophobic for my tastes." She claimed that, "I want to break free again—perhaps forever."

In New York, she'd told her friends much the same story, including her newly acquired friend, Judy Holliday.

The other Judy in her life, Garland, was seeing Kate at that point very infrequently.

"My love affair with Spencer Tracy is officially over," she said in a phone call to Patricia Peardon. "I'm not saying that we won't make up. We've broken up and then made up countless times. This time it's different. If we ever reconnect in the future, it'll be like the coming together of Bette Davis and Miriam Hopkins in that old movie, *Old Acquaintance.* Yes, that's what Spencer and I will be. Old acquaintances!"

Driving over to Cukor's, Kate was shaking violently and nervously. She was smoking countless cigarettes and, unusual for her, had lost her appetite. She told him, "Sitting around Hollywood waiting for a good script, which might never emerge, is slowly killing me. I'm at the peak of my power as an actress, and I want to put those powers to work while I still have them. At my age, you know that my days as an actress are coming to an end, unless I want to vie with Constance Collier for parts. I want some breakthrough in my life. I want to take on a real challenge."

She revealed to him that she knew what that challenge was going to be.

William Shakespeare.

In spite of all her previous denials that she'd never appear in a work by the Bard, Kate had signed with her old friends at the Theatre Guild to play Rosalind in *As You Like It*. She would take the play to Broadway.

That night Kate informed a drunken Tracy of her decision. Not only that, she did the unthinkable. For the first time in her life, she asked him to seek professional help.

As she later told Cukor, "Spencer went into the worst rage of his life. Those words—coming from me—were more than he could take. He exploded. He started throwing anything breakable in his cottage. When he tossed a porcelain vase of flowers at me—flowers I had just brought over—and almost hit my head, I fled."

Fearing serious injury from such violence, Kate had run up the hill for safety at Cukor's house.

She begged him to call an ambulance and to help her in getting Tracy committed to a sanatorium.

"Louise Tracy—not you—should be the one doing that," he cautioned her.

Cukor poured her a drink and took her into his library, where he possessively put his arm around her. "You live in an expanding universe. I fear Spence's world is shrinking. You must leave him and soon before he completely destroys you. He's almost destroyed himself. He's only the shell of the man I used to know."

The next morning around six o'clock, Kate drove up to Tracy's cottage. She did not go inside but left him a note in his mailbox. She'd earlier shared that goodbye note with Cukor.

"Spencer,
Time to goose the career again. Yes, Shakespeare. Don't laugh—it's a challenge. A way to stay fresh. One must not be found rotting one day in the steamy California sun.
Much love,
Farewell, Amanda."

***

Even though she'd left Hollywood and Tracy, Kate was still eager for news of Tracy as she began rehearsals for *As You Like It*. She frequently called Kenneth MacKenna, Cukor, and especially Anderson Lawler, for news. Although Cukor was the most informed about the Davis/Tracy affair, it was Lawler who revealed the details to Kate. She was immediately furious.

In New York, Patricia Peardon said it "ignited a fuse in Kate's soul, and I don't know why. Kate was aware that Tracy had had a number of affairs with other women during their long friendship. She also knew that he'd seduced twenty times the number of men as women. But the mere mention of Nancy Davis and Tracy made her explode."

When Kate called Cukor for an explanation as to what was going on between Nancy and Tracy, the director said, and this is a much-publicized quote, "Spence is a big name and Nancy will date anybody with a big name in Hollywood. She likes to associate with important people. She's practically worked her magic skill on every executive at MGM, most of them Jewish. In fact, if I had a nickel for every Jew Nancy was under, I'd be rich."

At the time that Tracy began to be seen on the town with Nancy, the actress was no stranger to Kate. Tracy had been a friend of the Davis family ever since he'd appeared with Nancy's actress mother, Edith Luckett Davis, in the 1927 hit stage play, *The Baby Cyclone*, with George M. Cohan.

Tracy had often used the Davises' family home for drying out time following one of his long-drawn-out boozing binges.

Kate first encountered a very young Nancy when she'd showed up to watch Tracy during rehearsals for *The Rugged Path*. Tracy had introduced "this cute little starlet" [his words to Kate], claiming he was an old friend of the family. Until then, Kate had been courteous but rather aloof from Nancy.

"I wasn't impressed with her," Kate later recalled to their director, Garson Kanin. "I figure she's a bit young to be attracted to Spencer's girlish figure, so I don't expect undue competition here."

At Tracy's urging, Kate began to see Nancy when she moved to New York and took an apartment near Kate's Turtle Bay townhouse. Kate remembered Nancy as dropping in "all too frequently and often unannounced."

Tracy told Kate that he wanted her to give the young hopeful some tips about how to become a successful film actress. Instead of encouraging Nancy, Kate did just the opposite. In fact, Kate went out of her way to discourage Nancy from pursuing a show business career. Once she even wrote a long letter to Nancy. In the letter, later revealed by Nancy, Kate warned her of "how God damn awful the acting profession really is." Kate claimed that Nancy's mother, Edith Luckett Davis, might have given young Nancy a false impression of show business. "Perhaps you think it's all too glamorous, and it's all about socializing with rich and famous stars." Nancy had told Kate that her mother had designated Alla Nazimova, once the queen of MGM, a lesbian and a strident egomaniac, as her godmother.

Kate wrote, "Most people who dream of being actresses end up waiting tables or else are found at the switchboard."

When Kate told Tracy what she'd done, he was furious. As if to prove Kate wrong, he arranged a date in New York between Nancy and his old friend, Clark Gable, in spite of the difference in their ages. Independent of Tracy, Gable went on to ask Nancy Davis out an additional two times. Gable later told Tracy, who in turn passed the word on to Kate, that "I scored a home run on each date."

"Nancy Davis won't be the only actress who tries to sleep her way to the top," Kate said, somewhat smugly. "Some of us other actresses got by on talent alone."

Tracy derided her, "I don't think many studio chiefs are itching to go to bed with your bag of bones."

Ignoring Kate's advice, Nancy headed for Hollywood where she continued to call Kate to report on her progressing film career. Kate told Lawler, "All Nancy Davis is doing is progressing from one bed to another."

From the beginning, Tracy, wanting to pay back old hospitality favors from the Davis family, introduced Nancy to Benjamin Thau, vice president of Loew's and head of casting for Metro-Goldwyn-Mayer. Soon Kate was hearing stories about the romance—or at least the sex—going on between the fifty-year-old Thau and the younger Nancy, then only twenty-eight. Even at that young age, she was considered old for a starlet. Most studios didn't sign starlets who were over twenty-five.

Thau's receptionist once reported to the author Laurence Leamer that she had "standing orders" every Saturday morning to usher Nancy immediately into his office. The receptionist also revealed that "after every Nancy visit I found used rubbers in the wastebasket." Since she wasn't the maid, she must have specifically looked for this evidence.

Before he died at the Motion Picture and Television Hospital in 1983, Thau himself claimed that Nancy "became known around town for performing oral sex. She would even perform it in the offices of MGM executives, particularly the married ones. That's why she got a contract at MGM—not because of her looks or talent. We wanted another Ava, another Lana, in those days."

When Kate heard these stories from Lawler, she was furious and at one time threatened not to be at home if Nancy called again. She didn't keep her vow and continued to speak to Nancy, mainly to pacify Tracy, who insisted that Kate "be nice to my discovery."

Tracy even went so far as to tell Dore Schary, in Kate's presence, that he predicted Nancy Davis was going to be a big star. "The Forties are over," Tracy said. "Ava, Lana, and especially Betty Grable, represent that era. In the Fifties a cleaner cut woman like Nancy will be called for." At Tracy's urging, Schary agreed to give Nancy a screen test.

Tracy even drove Kate over to George Cukor's house and, after some cajoling, got him to agree to direct the test with the actor, Howard Keel, who soon was to become a big name MGM musical comedy star.

Gottfried Reinhardt, a producer at MGM, was awed at the effort Tracy expended in launching Nancy's career. "I never noticed him doing anything for Kate Hepburn. She had to get by on her own. But for Nancy, Tracy demanded only the best. Not only Cukor, he even got the best cameraman in the business, George Folsey. Nancy Burns Sydney, a top drama coach, rehearsed Nancy, and

Tracy got the best makeup and wardrobe. How could she lose? All she had to do was show up on the day of the test and not upchuck on camera." Reinhardt told this to Kate, who found it terribly amusing.

Upon seeing the test, Schary was less enthusiastic than before, but claimed that Nancy would be suitable for "those girl-next-door parts in some B release."

Kate encountered Pandro S. Berman, who told her that "Nancy's only hope is to marry well. She doesn't have the looks or talent to make it as a star."

"My sentiments exactly," Kate shot back.

Nancy dated Tracy for only a few months, mainly, Kate told Cukor, as a means of being seen around town on the arm of a big star. Thau claimed that during the late Forties, Nancy began to compile a list of eligible stars, directors, and producers as marriage candidates. "She went only for the big ones, no struggling out-of-work actor for her."

"Apparently, at some point, she ruled Tracy out," Thau said, "because he was already married and had this strange relationship with Kate Hepburn that no one could figure out."

"She admitted to me one night that Ronald Reagan was at the top of her list," Thau claimed. At that time, Reagan was breaking down and weeping openly in the wake of his divorce from a bigger star, Jane Wyman. He was also the president of the Screen Actors Guild and a B picture star at Warner Brothers.

One night when Tracy asked her about Reagan, Nancy said, "If only I could figure out a way to rescue him from the clutches of Doris Day."

Tracy encountered Reagan a few times and always tried to avoid him. He called Reagan a "Red baiter," and claimed that he was always "looking for a pinko in every wood pile."

When Tracy stopped seeing Nancy, he told Cukor, "Miss Nancy is laying a trap for Ronnie boy. Who cares? Those two deserve each other. I just hope Ronnie baby goes in for oral sex like I do. If he does, he'll be happy as a pig in shit."

***

When Kate headed East to perform in *As You Like It,* she knew she was leaving Tracy in bad shape. She was also concerned about her "son," Robert Walker. His life seemed to be growing more turbulent by the day.

After his divorce from Jennifer Jones and his break-up with Judy Garland, he had embarked on an ill-fated marriage with Barbara Ford, the daughter of Kate's former lover, John Ford.

During the few short months of their marriage, Kate was once again in constant contact with John Ford, as he lamented his daughter's bad choice for a husband. Kate, however, in the wake of her violent encounter with her arch enemy, Mary Ford, never went to the Ford house again. Sometimes on the same night she'd listen patiently to Ford, and shortly after it ended, she'd get an inebriated late night call from Walker, waking her up to tell her about his own marriage difficulties with Barbara.

Of the Barbara Ford/Robert Walker marriage, Kate told Kenneth MacKenna, "I can't think of two worse candidates for marriage, even if I put my mind to it."

"I can think of two people even more ill suited," Kenneth said.

"Name them!"

"Katharine Hepburn and Spencer Tracy."

Kate put the phone down and because of his impertinence, didn't speak to Kenneth for a week or two.

On October 22, 1948, Walker had been arrested on a charge of drunken driving. A picture of him at the time of his arrest was flashed around the world, even appearing in *Life* magazine. In the photograph, Walker is obviously drunk, his right hand balled into a threatening fist and his face contorted with rage. "I feel Bob is crying out for the world to save him," Kate at the time had told Irene Mayer Selznick when she saw the published photograph.

After his arrest on the drunk and disorderly charge, Dore Schary at MGM warned Walker that he had two choices—either quit films or else undergo psychiatric treatment at the Menninger Clinic in Kansas, where stars often went to "dry out."

Walker opted for the clinic where he spent seven months in rehabilitation. Eager to see how he was responding to treatment, Kate remained in constant touch. The moment he stepped off the plane upon his return from Kansas, the press mobbed him. Walker announced, "I'm able to work again—eager to live."

Kate was upset when Walker began dating Nancy Davis again after his return from Kansas. Soon after his release, he returned to his self-destructive habits, including the consumption of inordinate amounts of alcohol.

When she wasn't dating Tracy, Nancy could often be found at Walker's home in the Pacific Palisades. She played surrogate mother when Jennifer Jones sent their two children, Bobby and Michael, over to visit their father.

Joe Naar, a friend of Walker's, and Peter Lawford claimed that one day they went to visit Walker unexpectedly without calling. "We walked in to find Nancy nude in the living room," Lawford said. "She quickly raced toward the bathroom and reappeared wrapped in a large bath towel. She seemed terribly embarrassed. But not that embarrassed. She started dating Bob *and* me, sometimes at the same time."

Lawford later claimed that Nancy invited both Walker and him to drive with her to visit her parents in Arizona. "Nancy kept both of us entertained orally during the trip there," Lawford said. "First, Bob drove and I got into the back seat with Nancy. Then I drove and Bob got into the back seat. We were two exhausted men by the time we reached the Arizona state line."

Nancy Davis, later Nancy Reagan, would later comment on her friendship with Kate. The then First Lady claimed that they remained friends until Tracy's death. "After that," according to Nancy, "the friendship ended, although I made several attempts to revive it."

Tracy obviously had forced Kate to be nice to Nancy. When he was no longer around, Kate could be as rude as she wanted.

Nancy recalled that once she phoned Kate one afternoon and that she came onto the phone. Nancy quotes Kate as having said, "I'm terribly busy. Besides, I don't know what we'd have to talk about. After all, you're a staunch Republican, and I'm a staunch Democrat."

Regardless of how contemptuously Kate acted toward Nancy, she was still eager to pick up the slightest bit of gossip about Nancy. Kate had come to regard Nancy as her nemesis, placing her on her self-described "shit list" immediately alongside such bigger stars as Margaret Sullavan and Ginger Rogers.

In dismay, Kate watched as Nancy continued to pursue rich and powerful men, even after she'd become First Lady. "Personally, I think Nancy wanted Frank Sinatra more that she wanted Reagan," Kate told Laura Harding and Patricia Peardon. "Sinatra told me that himself," Kate said. "But he also told me that Nancy has fat legs. Not his type at all." Kate used to chuckle when she related that tidbit of gossip.

Kate was especially delighted when Patricia Peardon told her a "delicious tidbit" that she had heard when President Reagan and First Lady Nancy were being entertained at Buckingham Palace in London.

The Queen herself was reportedly perturbed when she spotted Nancy Reagan breaking with protocol and linking her arm with that of Prince Philip, Peardon's former "beau."

Apparently, Nancy's reputation had preceded her to England, and the Queen seemed jealous, especially since the press had reported only that afternoon that the First Lady dressed with more style and flair than she did.

Thinking she was not being overheard, the Queen said to an aide, "That woman!" She looked again at Prince Philip whose arm was linked with Nancy's. "Who on earth does she think she is?"

***

Evoking her 1932 appearance in *The Warrior's Husband*, Kate once again put on what she called "a leg show" playing Rosalind in Shakespeare's *As You Like It*. Accustomed to seeing her either in pants or in long formal gowns on the screen, audiences were thrilled to see a lot of flesh and to know that Kate in middle age "still has a smacking pair of gams, right up there with Betty Grable," as described by Michael Benthall, who staged the play.

Langner of the Theatre Guild once told the cast that "Katharine Hepburn still has the most attractive legs in the United States."

Kate demanded that Michael Benthall be imported from England to direct.

531

A disciple of Tyrone Guthrie, he immediately impressed her. She found him "lyrically romantic, evoking a painting by Watteau. He speaks of hooting owls in the moonlight, nights right out of *Macbeth*, blizzards on haunted evenings, and oak trees that can withstand the mightiest lightning."

"You sound like you're falling in love," Langner told her. "If so, you're out of luck."

Kate also demanded that Constance Collier, her old and dear friend, work with her to perfect the longest woman's part ever written by Shakespeare, a vehicle for such former stars as Lily Langtry and Sarah Siddons. At the age of seventy-one, Collier was just as flamboyant and sharp-tongued as ever. She was still one of the *grande dames* of English theater.

Collier agreed to work with Kate for the entire run of the play, and never missed one of Kate's performances, helping the following day to improve her acting skills.

Theresa Helburn, the other Guild director, was less impressed with Benthall than Kate was. She found him "a bit flamboyant, perhaps too delicate, overly fancy." But Kate defended Benthall at every turn.

Before Benthall was hired, Kate had an awkward moment. Diplomatically, she had to turn down Cukor who wanted to direct *As You Like It*. Kate told Helburn, "I want to get away from George, Spencer, and Hollywood for a few months. Not take Hollywood on the road with me."

Kate herself was the unofficial producer, director, and even the casting consultant, agreeing on the handsome actor William Prince, as her co-star. She told her Theatre Guild friends, Langner and Helburn, that "Prince looks quite knightly in a pair of the tightest green tights I've ever seen on any actor. If his crotch is padded, it doesn't matter, so long as it doesn't slip on opening night."

***

During Kate's absence from Hollywood, Tracy had been cast in *Malaya*, a film that co-starred Kate's former beau, Jimmy Stewart. The all-star cast also included Valentina Cortesa, Sydney Greenstreet, John Hodiak, Gilbert Roland, and Lionel Barrymore. It was only mildly successful.

On the road, theater critics were praising Kate's physical beauty but pointing out that she was miscast as Rosalind. *As You Like It* was increasingly becoming known as "Hepburn's folly." Quoting an old Arab proverb, Kate said, "The dogs bark, but the caravan moves on." She noted with smugness that every theater she played was packed to the rafters, as her performance broke all previous attendance records for *As You Like It*.

After *Malaya* wrapped, Tracy flew to Cleveland, where Kate was performing, for a reconciliation. He arrived drunk and testy, Collier later confided to Cukor. Although drunk, Tracy in Kate's suite, and in the presence of Collier, agreed to give up booze if she'd take him back. Kate reminded him that he'd made that promise to her many times before and had never kept it.

"Their reunion lasted all of two hours," Collier later said. She said that Kate ordered him from her suite. "I went to the manager and booked a separate suite for the staggering actor."

When Tracy woke up around noon the next day, he went again to Kate's suite, only to find her gone. She'd left a note with the reception staff, claiming that she and Collier would be away for the rest of the day. She suggested that if Tracy wanted to see her, he could attend her performance that night.

Afraid of making the front-page edition if he went to the theater, Tracy left her a goodbye note and flew on to New York. Once there, he headed for his favorite hotel in Brooklyn where he ordered twelve big bottles of Irish whiskey. Pulling off all his clothes, he plopped his corpulent body into a claw-footed bathtub for many days and nights of boozing.

After its initial road tour, *As You Like It* opened at the Cort Theatre in Manhattan on January 26, 1950, where it would run for one-hundred and forty-five performances. Collier claimed that Kate charged "onto the stage like a fire-horse in a pair of tights."

In the role of Rosalind, Kate was once again playing a cross dresser as she had in *Sylvia Scarlett.*

Brooks Atkinson of *The New York Times* was on her case, claiming that "Katharine Hepburn's electric and refined personality is miscast in a rustic role." *Life* magazine noted Kate's return to Broadway after an absence of seven years, claiming that "her gams are as good as her iambics—those legs are eloquent."

An ailing Kit Hepburn came down from Hartford to see Kate in the play on opening night and approved of her daughter's performance. Kit had never liked Kate in the movies but felt that Shakespeare was quite suitable for her famous daughter.

Kate found her mother as devoted to birth control as ever. Unknown to Kate at the time, *As You Like It* would be the last performance on stage or screen that Kit would ever see of her daughter. She was soon to die.

Tracy was still in New York. Forgetting his promise to give up drinking, or unable to commit to his vow, he appeared several times at Kate's Turtle Bay townhouse, hoping for a reconciliation.

Patricia Peardon was seeing Kate every day at that time, and Constance Collier was residing in Kate's house. They were witnesses to the many bitter fights between Kate and Tracy. At one point, Peardon said, Tracy accused Kate of sleeping with Robert Walker.

"You want that young drunk instead of this old drunk," Tracy shouted at her. She then confronted him for the first time about his affair with Nancy Davis. Tracy denied the affair, claiming that his feelings for Nancy were only paternalistic.

"Paternalistic, is it?" Kate shouted back at him. "I'd call it incest then."

Tracy staggered out the door.

Peardon said Tracy always came back the next day. Without a job, he continued to drink heavily at his suite at the Waldorf-Astoria.

Kate confided in Peardon that she was delighted to learn that Tracy was flying back to film *Father of the Bride* with Joan Bennett and Elizabeth Taylor. Kate said that she had been offered the role of Tracy's wife in the film, but had found the part "hopelessly weak for me."

Even news about Tracy going back to work triggered another argument between them. "I'm sure you and Joan Bennett, that bitch, will take up where you left off in the Thirties," Kate said mockingly to Tracy. "And it's almost certain that you'll have an affair with young Miss Elizabeth Taylor. Aren't aging old farts like you always attracted to jailbait?"

"Tracy was furious at Kate," Peardon claimed. "He looked like he wanted to strike her but thought better of it. On his way out the door, he called back to Kate in the harshest, meanest tone I'd ever heard him use on or off the screen. "I'll go back to Nancy. At least she knows how to give head. Something I could never teach you to do. I'm through with you, bitch. You're more dyke than woman anyway."

"And that was their goodbye," Peardon said. "Kate ran to her bedroom in tears, and I thought that was the end of that. It was time that the partnership of Spencer Tracy and Katharine Hepburn ended. I could see how bad they were for each other. I predicted to everybody I knew in the theater that they'd never get back together again. How wrong I was!"

***

After a final road show of the play, following the New York opening, Kate returned with Constance Collier to Los Angeles. Both women were exhausted one afternoon as they sat in Kate's living room doing a post-mortem on *As You Like It*. Kate had not even bothered to contact Tracy upon her return.

The doorbell rang, and Kate asked Collier to go and see who it was, no doubt expecting Tracy's arrival at her doorstep.

Kate was not expecting visitors and had recently changed her phone number so that no one could get in touch with her except a half-dozen trusted friends.

Collier was gone for a while and returned in about five minutes. "A Mr. *Humphrey Bogart* and a Mr. *John Huston* are standing out in the foyer with a script in their hands. I told them you're not seeing anyone, but *those two* are very persistent. Perhaps you should see them."

"No, I'm not up to seeing anyone," Kate said. "Send them away. I'm still mad at Bogie for chickening out in front of that so-called Un-American Committee in Washington. As for Huston, I don't do his kind of picture."

"All right, I'll tell them," Collier said reluctantly. This time she was gone for at least fifteen minutes.

Kate by this time had strolled out into the garden.

When Collier came out of the house, she said, "I've sent them on their way. They left this script for you to read."

"Leave it on the glass table over there," Kate instructed. "I want to sit here and have a much deserved rest. After that God damn tour, I'm near death."

When Collier went into the kitchen to make some tea for them, Kate glanced only briefly at the title of the script.

"You remember, of course, strawberry jam to sweeten the tea," Kate called to Collier in the kitchen.

"How very barbaric!" Collier called back to her. "Thank God Her Majesty is not having tea with us today."

"You mean, George Cukor, don't you dear?"

When Collier came back to join Kate at the table, she pushed the script over to her actress friend. "Be a dear and read it first and tell me if it's any good. It's called *The African Queen*. Isn't that amusing? I have a mind to call Huston and Bogie right now and give them a piece of my mind. Tell them that Katharine Hepburn hasn't sunk so low in life that she has to perform before the camera in black face in a jungle epic." She smiled only slightly to suggest she might be joking. "*The African Queen.* What a shitty title. How very gay! That Huston is such a phony. Clark Gable himself told me that Huston couldn't hit a tin can with a peashooter but likes to give the impression he can hunt elephants. I smell flop written all over it. Anyway, read it for me, my darling. I want to walk in the garden."

A few minutes later, as the sun began its descent over the Hollywood Hills, Kate called back to her aging friend.

"Oh, Constance, come here! The calla lilies are in bloom again. Such a strange flower!"

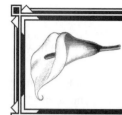

Katharine the Great
will be Continued

Katharine the Great: A Cast of Thousands

My interest in Katharine Hepburn began with an argument between my parents, my father insisting that he wanted to go and see *The Grapes of Wrath,* my mother demanding to be taken to see *The Philadelphia Story.* We had two movie houses in the small town, deep in the heart of Appalachia, where I grew up, and each of the films was playing that day.

Mother won the argument. Hepburn had been her favorite actress ever since she'd seen her in *Little Woman.* She never missed a Hepburn movie, and even as an adult, continued to keep a scrapbook of movie reviews and press clippings. From that scrapbook of yellowing clippings lay the origins of this biography.

In time, I became as addicted to movies as my mother, and I too started my own scrapbooks. I clipped magazines and newspapers for Hepburn stories, but began to build up my own dossier on my particular favorites—notably Joan Crawford, Clark Gable, Spencer Tracy, Bette Davis, Cary Grant, and Judy Garland, among many others.

Shortly after my father was killed at an early age, we moved to Miami Beach, which was experiencing its Golden Age. Mother got a job working as "The Girl Friday" (a politically incorrect term often used during that era) for the great Sophie Tucker.

Suddenly, movie stars were no longer assigned to fading scrapbooks. I was actually getting to meet the stars in person. All the big names arrived in Miami Beach in those days, and it was considered almost obligatory to call on Sophie, "the last of the Red Hot Mamas." At Sophie's, I was overhearing the most personal of conversations between Judy Garland and Sophie. Frank Sinatra came to call, as did Lena Horne, Martha Raye, Bing Crosby, Betty Grable, Victor Mature, Lana Turner (an off-the-record weekend), and even Ronald Reagan.

Like the boy hero of James Leo Herlihy's novel *All Fall Down,* I began to keep a journal in which I wrote down everything of interest that I overheard that day. As my journal soon revealed, those stars I heard talking weren't at all like the heroes and heroines they were playing on the screen. They were real people with real problems—alcoholism, lovers who betrayed, career disappointments, money problems. Before I started hanging out at Sophie's, I used to think that all movie stars were rich. Then I started hearing about the awesome Internal Revenue Service that could come and take your home and possessions even if you were a movie star.

My flirtatious and beautiful brunette-haired mother, with a figure far shapelier than that of many starlets on the screen, had recently met a ruggedly handsome movie star named Richard Widmark. My mother never told me exactly where or how, or under what circumstances they had met, but later on, he got her a job working on the set of a film he was making called *Slattery's Hurricane.*

My biggest thrill in life came when I was actually taken onto my first movie set. Sophie was Miss Show Business, but her milieu tended toward cabarets and night club acts. The set of *Slattery's Hurricane,* at least for me, was the real thing.

On the set, Mother become friends with Linda Darnell and was even designing a white bathing suit for her. Miss Darnell drank a lot, and had a hard time appearing sober on film. The other star of the film, Veronica Lake, befriended me. We'd slip off together to Big Mike's for a juicy hamburger. Miss Lake said that Mike made the best hamburgers in the world, and I agreed. Every day, she'd buy me one.

One day when I was in Veronica's dressing room, her co-star, Linda Darnell came by for a chatty visit. They weren't really needed on the set that afternoon, and they began to talk and drink a bit. The subject of Howard Hughes came up, and soon, they began to "compare notes" about him.

That night, I wrote down everything they had said about Howard Hughes. He sounded fascinating, and I decided I should keep a journal on him, too. At the time, though, I don't think I knew the difference between Hughes and Charles Lindbergh. All I knew was that both of them had made historic flights.

Several years later, while enrolled at the University of Miami, I began to work for a gossip columnist (who shall go nameless). He was too drunk most of the time to make the rounds of the fabulous parties and entertainment events to which he was invited. For very little money, he hired me to go in his place. My job involved taking notes and gathering material for his column, which would run the following morning in *The Miami Herald.*

I thought I had arrived in Heaven when I found myself hanging out with movie stars, and in some cases, learning their most closely guarded secrets. On a few occasions, I formed friendships. In those days, we never wrote anything unfavorable about the stars. Instead, we produced only image-conscious or myth-generating texts. Consequently, movie stars assumed that they had a kind of inbuilt protection, feeling more or less safe around me, even though they knew that I was a reporter.

Gradually, all my movie star illusions began to collapse. I began to see up close that that woman who played a saint on the screen might actually be shacking up with various adulterous lovers on the side. Those macho men who made love to Betty Grable or Lana Turner on the screen would sometimes, in private, invite a young kid like me to go to bed with them instead. Nothing was as it had originally seemed.

When commissioned by *The Miami Herald* to open a news bureau in Key West, Florida, I got a call on the first night from the port's reigning *duenna,* Miss Jessie Porter Newton. She invited me over to meet her house guest and a noted playwright. The house guest turned out to be Robert Frost and the noted playwright was Tennessee Williams.

I found Frost "a bit chilly" (pun intended), but Tennessee and I became friends for life. Through him, I continued to meet the stars. Everybody came to Key West in those days, many hoping to be cast in one of his films. Warren Beatty showed up, wanting to play the role of the gigolo in *The Roman Spring of Mrs. Stone;* and Gloria Swanson showed up to lobby for the lead role of the fading actress in *Sweet Bird of Youth.*

One night, Tennessee's longtime companion, and eventually my close friend Frankie Merlo, invited me over to dinner. On the patio of the Williams-Merlo home sat Paul Newman and Geraldine Page. And so it went, "as time goes by."

In New York, London, Miami, New Orleans, Paris, and Los Angeles, Tennessee began to introduce me around. I suddenly knew stars on a first-name basis. For a movie-star crazy kid, I had arrived in Valhalla.

Back at my home in Key West, I was introduced to Stanley Haggart, a creative talent 27 years older than myself whose career and social life had been active in Hollywood during its formative years. He had designed the sets for a play called *Crazy October,* which had been written by James Leo Herlihy, and which was starring Tallulah Bankhead. Stanley introduced me to Tallulah later that night, at dinner. From the time of that first dinner, Tallulah and I bonded, and as our lives progressed, I visited her frequently until the day she died. Tallulah told me stories about everybody, including Katharine Hepburn and Humphrey Bogart. Of course, I recorded them all.

When Stanley Haggart invited me to New York to manage his television studio, the "yes" came out of my throat before he had completed the question. Within the year, I found myself not only interviewing or hanging out with movie stars, but actually hiring them for television commercials. In those days, before the advent of "realistic" casting policies set in, stars, some of them big-time, were hired to endorse products.

Although I'd met her before, Joan Crawford suddenly came back into my life. She got us the job of designing sets for Pepsi-Cola commercials. Even more than with Tallulah, I bonded with this magnificent woman, and would go anywhere she invited me any time.

She knew everything worth knowing about Hollywood, and over the years told me volumes, including stories about Katharine Hepburn whom she did not altogether admire. She'd even had an affair with one of my favorite actors, Spencer Tracy. I was a bit startled that she referred to him as "an old drunk."

In Stanley, I had found a fellow journal writer like myself. He had picked up the habit from his mother, Maria Jane Haggart, who had arrived in Hollywood in 1910 when the town had a full-time population of only four-thousand people. She'd begun her own journals many years before.

During Stanley's formative years, he lived with his mother in a house immediately next door to the Hollywood columnist, Adela Rogers St. Johns. The Haggart mother-son team, both of whom were rigorously addicted to their journals and scrapbooks, recorded virtually everything they heard, saw, felt, and smelled. And what they didn't know already, they learned from Adela.

Thanks to Stanley, I realized that I wasn't alone in writing journals, especially when he introduced me to his journal-writing friend, Anaïs Nin. She knew Gore Vidal, who had stories to tell about Jacqueline Kennedy. She was also friends with Truman Capote, who had stories to tell about everybody.

As I moved deeper and deeper into the worlds of Broadway and Hollywood, I found that virtually everybody I met had at least one Katharine Hepburn story. My journals on Miss Hepburn grew longer and longer as I met and dined with both her friends and enemies. Gradually, I began to meet people who knew her, worked with her, loved her, or hated her—it ran the gamut from A to Z, (to alter Dorothy Parker's quip a bit).

Stanley had been a close friend of Hepburn's husband, Luddy, and his longtime companion, Jack Clark. Stanley also knew both Laura Harding and Hepburn, and had once lived in the house shared by Cary Grant and Randolph Scott. Howard Hughes was a frequent visitor. Stanley was the first person to ever tell me that Hepburn was a lesbian and Spencer Tracy was a homosexual. In fairness, he should have called them bisexuals.

A great deal of the material about Luddy, Jack Clark, Laura Harding, Cary Grant, Howard Hughes, and Randolph Scott was drawn from Stanley's Hollywood Journals of the 1930s and 1940s.

Without material supplied by Stanley, I could never have written this biography.

In time, I too became friends with friends of Hepburn—notably Garson Kanin and his wife, Ruth Gordon, who knew everything about Hepburn and Tracy, but who never recorded all that they actually knew.

I also owe the deepest debt of gratitude to two of Stanley's closest friends, relationships that went back to the late 1920s.

One of the best sources of material for this book was Kenneth MacKenna, who contributed vast amounts to Stanley's unpublished *Hollywood Journals.* MacKenna was among Hepburn's top three male confidants. Their relationship began on the stage and led to his "deflowering" her, as she so colorfully put it. In an ironic twist, MacKenna was also the best pal and confidant of the century's greatest male film star as well, Humphrey Bogart. MacKenna married Bogie's second wife, actress Mary Philips. An actor himself, MacKenna later became story editor at Metro-Goldwyn-Mayer. His last appearance on the screen was when he played the role of a judge, alongside Spencer

Tracy, in *Judgment at Nuremberg*.

If actor Anderson Lawler had never existed, there might never have been a book of such intimacy about Hepburn. Along with Kenneth MacKenna and George Cukor, this red-haired Virginian became Hepburn's most intimate confidant. As she put it, "Andy is the only person in Hollywood I can have girl talk with." A former lover of Gary Cooper, the homosexual actor was, for three decades, the best-informed source about Hollywood "After Dark" that existed in Tinsel Town.

A compulsive gossip, he was no keeper of her secrets, however, and once attempted his own memoirs which—at least at the time—could not be published because of libel issues. Stanley Haggart, who helped Lawler type his memoirs, claimed, "They were the most explosive in the history of Hollywood. Andy spared no one, and seemed to take special delight in revealing the bedroom secrets of Hepburn, Cukor, Tracy, Tallulah, and Gary Cooper. He was especially revealing about Cary Grant, Howard Hughes, and Randolph Scott. His stories about young Gable alone were worth the price of admission."

Eventually, I dated the actress, Patricia Peardon. She was Hepburn's closest female confidante, and was also the best friend of Hepburn's longtime companion, Laura Harding. Patricia and I once planned to write a book about Hepburn "but only after she dies." Ironically, Hepburn outlived Patricia, and the book was never written.

I came to know Kate's other best friend, George Cukor, as did my closest friend at the time, James Leo Herlihy (author of the book, *Midnight Cowboy,* on which the film was later based). Cukor invited us to many of his dinners and private parties, where a sort of reluctant guest, Spencer Tracy, would sometimes make an appearance. Tracy lived in a cottage on the grounds. From the first, I realized that Tracy in person was hardly the man he portrayed on the screen.

As Jamie Herlihy would say, "You couldn't talk with Cukor for more than four minutes before he'd bring up a Kate Hepburn story." Although he was kind in his recitation of those stories, Cukor was also realistic about her foibles. His Hepburn stories, in my view, were the best in Hollywood. Naturally, I recorded them.

But the man who really knew the inside story on Cukor was Jay Garon. Long after he'd left the services of Cukor, he became New York's leading independent literary agent, launching the career of, among others, author John Grisham.

After Cukor's death, Jay and I talked about writing a real behind-the-scenes Hollywood biography of Cukor, his life and times. Jay, thanks to his having been an intimate member of the Cukor household, was privy to the most intimate secrets in the Cukor/Tracy relationship. But, like so many other proposed books, the biography never got off the ground, even though the stories Garon provided for it were among the richest I've ever heard.

In all, I ended up collecting enough material on Hepburn (and also on Tracy) to fill at least a dozen volumes. This biography contains just some of the pre-selected highlights of that vast dossier I've collected over the decades on Hepburn.

In a few hundred cases, I've known or met people who knew Hepburn well, often fellow co-workers at RKO, MGM, and other studios. Everybody who came in touch with Hepburn had a story to tell about her. Somehow, her every utterance or action was viewed as something to comment on or to repeat to others.

Over the years, when I personally didn't gather the comments myself, a long list of people helped provide me with quotable quotes.

Regrettably, many of the people who helped me never lived to see this book published, since Hepburn virtually outlived most of her contemporaries.

Therefore, with gratitude and in loving memory of past and present friends, I want to thank Howard Bennett, Frances Pellman, George Brunner, Felix St. Johns, Betty Kelly, Fred Bronston, Geoffrey Walker, Daniel Walker, Marie St. Just, David Johnston, Woodrow Martin, and especially my longtime associate, Margaret Bellman. Special thanks also go to my chief researcher, Monica Dunn, bull-dogged in her pursuit of Hepburn data, regardless of how minor. I'd also like to thank Lisa Keeter for her help in the preparation of this manuscript.

Here is the round-up of the "usual suspects"—both living and dead—whose opinions, comments, stories, and anecdotes were used in the preparation of this biography. Some of these "suspects" provided only a paragraph; others supplied more lengthy material about Hepburn.

The list is too long to thank everybody, but I'm appreciative nonetheless.

I want to express heartfelt thanks to the following, including many who died before I ever got to meet them. Thankfully, their impressions and stories about Hepburn were recorded either in personal interviews or left as stored oral memories, either with me, or their friends and confidants.

Here goes:

I'd like to express my thanks to members of Laura Harding's family, none of whom was more charming and insightful than Emily King.

Thanks go to various police officers of long ago in both New York and Hartford, including Peter O'Rourke and John Taylor, for the light they shed on the mysterious death of Tom Hepburn, Kate's older brother. These law enforcement officials spoke both on and off the record over the years. Thanks also go to Dr. Bradford Cody and Dr. Juan Gonzales, and to Tom's godmother, attorney Mary Towle, and her friend, Bertha Rambaugh, for their opinions and revelations. The long-departed staff of *The Hartford Courant* also provided information, even if some of it was informed speculation.

A great debt is owed to Bradford Fenton, a New England journalist, who provided much information. In time, he collected so much data about the family that he was once going to write his own book, which, had it been published, would have been entitled *The Hepburns of Connecticut.* Fenton often spoke with Dr. Thomas Hepburn about his famous daughter.

Estelle Davis and Geoffrey Bonnard supplied a great deal of the information that led to the insertion of comments by Dr. and Mrs. Thomas Hepburn. Bonnard and Davis, long-time residents of Connecticut, were intimate friends of Kate's parents for decades. The Hepburns often discussed their famous daughter with Davis and Bonnard.

Jill Davids furnished schoolgirl revelations about Kate and her gym teacher, Cathy Watson. Connecticut Yankees Tom Skippers and Barry Moorehead provided sketchy, but helpful, opinions about the mysterious Tracy Walker, object of Tom Hepburn's affection.

Gratitude is extended to many residents of Hartford, including Phil Kilmore, who once provided information about Hartford and the Hepburn family at the time Kate was growing up. Birth control advocate Margaret Sanger's oral and published comments over the years about her friend and fellow activist, Kit Hepburn, were also useful.

Allie Barbour's memories and recollections of growing up with Kate were extremely revealing, as were the insights of Allie's former companion, Robert Post.

Many classmates of Kate's at Bryn Mawr, including in particular Hepburn's closest friend there Alice Palache, shared their memories of the future screen diva.

The famous sculptor, Robert J. McKnight, seemed honored to have been Hepburn's "first beau" (as she called him) and was doubly honored to have enticed her to pose nude for him.

Theater manager Edwin Knopf had bittersweet memories of Hepburn's attempt to break into the theater, as did her school friend, Elizabeth Rhett.

Among the administration at Bryn Mawr, Helen Manning had no good marks to put on Hepburn's report card, but offered useful insights into the character of one of Kate's "beaus," H. Phelps Putnam, a celebrated poet of his day.

Mary Boland, a famous stage star of her day, remembered vivid details about working with Hepburn, but assured her interviewers that she was not a member of the Katharine Hepburn fan club.

For tales about the infamous Tony's Speakeasy in New York, thanks go to boxing champion Jack Dempsey for his memories of the saloon. I also thank him for his tales about Polly Adler's famous bordello on West 54th Street. America's most infamous madam also provided information about Kate's sole visit to her house, accompanied by Dorothy Parker and Robert Benchley.

Many friends of both Dorothy Barney and J. Barclay Harding shared memories as well. They were the parents of Laura Harding, Hepburn's longtime companion and one of the great loves of her life.

The *grande dame* of voice coaches, Frances Robinson-Duff, also freely shared memories of her former pupils, Katharine Hepburn and Laura Harding. (In those days, Laura, too, wanted to be an actress.)

Producer Arthur Hopkins offered wonderful stories about the theater, particularly about his involvement with Hepburn. Hepburn always claimed that the actress, Hope Williams, was her role model. As for Williams' point of view about Hepburn, many of her comments are still unprintable. Actress Barbara White supplied data about the rivalry of Hope Williams and Hepburn during the run of the stage play, *Holiday.*

The always witty and insightful Noël Coward could (and frequently did) "dine out" on Hepburn's stories.

In their roles as the writers of many of her scripts, including many that were written exclusively for her, Philip Barry and Donald Ogden Stewart were closer to Kate than many other writers. But their friendships with her were troubled, as they revealed.

Many people in the theater have commented and told stories about Hepburn's first ventures onto the stage, notably Lawrence Marston, who directed the play, *Death Takes a Holiday.* Its producer, Lee Schubert, also added anecdotes, as did cast members Florence Golden and James Dale. Russian-born director Rouben Mamoulian told fascinating stories of working with Kate and the turbulent Alla Nazimova in *A Month in the Country,* as did Alexander Kirkland, Eunice Stoddard, and Hortense Alden. Kirkland also provided his memories of Hepburn in the play *The Admirable Crichton.*

No one provided more data about Hepburn's often troubled relationship with the Theatre Guild than Theresa Helburn and Lawrence Langner, her producers. Although they both expressed love for Hepburn, they painted a "warts-and-all" portrait.

Actress Edith Barrett had no kind words for either Laura Harding or Hepburn in recalling the play *A Romantic Young Lady* at the Berkshire Playhouse.

Thanks go to Anaïs Nin, the late diarist, for introducing me to Djuana Barnes at her Greenwich Village apartment. Mercedes de Acosta, a dear, dear friend whom I encountered late in her life, supplied volumes about many theatrical luminaries, including her own involvement with Hepburn.

Actors Richard Hale, Osgood Perkins (father of Tony Perkins), and George Coulouris had lots of memories—none of them good—about Laura Harding and Hepburn from when they appeared in Stockbridge, Massachusetts.

A less than flattering view of Hepburn was expressed by veteran actress Jane Cowl during the time they acted together in the play *Art and Mrs. Bottle.* Actress Joyce Carey was even more helpful.

Julian Anhalt provided data about Hepburn's venture into summer stock with the Ivoryton Playhouse in Connecticut. Late in his life, veteran actor Henry Hull had much to say about working with Hepburn, also at Ivoryton, but we didn't believe a word of his highly exaggerated "seductions" of Hepburn.

Mixed and confusing stories were sounded about Hepburn's ill-fated appearance with Leslie Howard in Philip Barry's *The Animal Kingdom.* Various versions of what actually happened were later recited by producer Gilbert Miller and actors Frederick Forrester and Ilka Chase. Even Leslie Howard himself had comments, but none of them very revealing. The details about "that night" between Howard and Hepburn will never be known, although actor Walter Abel provided the best scenario. Howard once told Cukor that he was horrified at the idea of playing Ashley Wilkes opposite Hepburn's Scarlett O'Hara in *Gone With the Wind.* As it eventually worked out, he didn't have to, of course.

The best friend of Humphrey Bogart, Bill Brady, Jr., who was to die a tragic death in a fire, told a troubling story about Hepburn and his own actress wife, Katherine Alexander.

Many eyewitnesses have weighed in on Hepburn's appearance in *The Warrior's Husband* on Broadway, including producer Harry Moss, and actors Alan Campbell and British-born Colin Keith-Johnston. Stage manager Phyllis Seaton also knew a lot.

Much of the material on Alan Campbell himself (husband of Dorothy Parker) was supplied by his intimate friend, Stanley Haggart, especially the revelations about "Luddy" (Hepburn's husband) and his link to Campbell.

To Ralph Nieves, longtime friend and confidant of Leland Hayward, I owe the bulk of my data on this producer and super agent. Nieves wrote the unpublished biography *Agent and Lover to the Stars,* which was "too hot to handle" by publishers in its day.

Many moons ago, an aging Adolph Zukor contributed one delicious tidbit about his encounter with Hepburn and Laura Harding, whom he met in Albuquerque during their first trip West.

Myron Selznick, brother of David O. Selznik, contributed many anecdotes to this biography. As Leland's partner, he was "co-agent" for the aspiring Hepburn.

No producer in Hollywood ever supplied more data about Hepburn's days at RKO and at MGM during the 1930s and 1940s than did the quite wonderful and charming Pandro S. Berman, to whom we owe a huge debt.

But sometimes it's "the little people" (as Swanson's Norma Desmond might say) that also furnish interesting details—Jo Ann St. Auger, hairdresser to the stars, makeup artist

Mel Burns, and even RKO's doctor, San Hirschfeld.

John Barrymore's soggy brain was most charitable when he tried to set the record straight on whether he did or did not seduce Hepburn during their co-starring roles in *A Bill of Divorcement.*

Good witch Billie Burke was most insightful about Hepburn and Adolphe Menjou in the 1930s, but her memory became foggy in revelations about herself and Dorothy Arzner. In other words, she didn't "out" herself. Others, such as George Cukor, did that for her.

The comments over the years from gossip maven Louella Parsons would fill a book, but another columnist (in addition to the previously mentioned Adela Rogers St. Johns) was even more helpful. Stanley Haggart was once a leg man for Hedda Hopper, a declared enemy of Katharine Hepburn. Even though she couldn't publish much of the material Stanley gathered for her at the time, she fervently wanted to know what was going on anyway.

David Manners, an actor in *A Bill of Divorcement,* shared his memories about Hepburn's first time in front of the camera. Laura Harding's longtime friend Carlton Burke, had an amusing story about Hepburn's first encounter with Mary Pickford.

I am particularly grateful for the information that Stanley Haggart provided about his dear friend, the very talented Nancy Hamilton, and her brief affair with Hepburn. Hamilton herself contributed some quotes about her own post-Hepburn career.

Thanks go to A. Aubrey Walker, journalist, for his report about an astonishing interview that Hepburn gave aboard the *S.S. Paris* as it was anchored in New York harbor. An acknowledgement is also made to Sara Hamilton of *Photoplay* magazine for providing information that didn't make it into any of her printed stories. _

George Cukor supplied much of the information about the Garbo/Hepburn relationship, and Mercedes de Acosta spoke about it as well. Kenneth MacKenna also reported on the mysterious Swede who became his friend during her days at MGM.

The ill-fated actress, Lilyan Tashman, was also very vocal and revealing about Garbo before Tashman's tragic death at a young age from a brain tumor. Actress Barbara Barondess and Director Rouben Mamoulian also contributed data about Garbo, the making of *Queen Christina,* and Hepburn.

No one helped more in revealing details about the private life of Laura Harding than three of her closest confidantes: Margaret Brent, Kitty Bowden, and Irene Ellis. Many of the quotes attributed directly to Laura were revealed by these three remarkable women, who had known Laura and the Harding family since the 1920s.

The bizarre story about Hepburn and Harding, and their illegal entry into Ramon Novarro's house, was transmitted by Novarro to the gossipy William Haines, who told Joan Crawford, Carole Lombard, and "the rest of Hollywood."

Walter Wanger provided rich data on Hollywood, as did director William Welman. Laura Harding's friend, polo-playing Fred Johnson, told a fascinating story about the time Harding and Hepburn called on Mary Pickford and Douglas Fairbanks, Sr. at Pickfair.

Los Angeles detective Roger Pearl provided an interesting glimpse into Fairbank's habit of taking his dinner guests on a post-brandy tour of the ghettos of Los Angeles, visiting, in squad cars, scenes of crimes shortly after they were committed.

Scriptwriter Zoë Atkins and director Dorothy Arzner had much to tell about working with Hepburn on *Christopher Strong.* They were less than candid about themselves, although their "sewing circle" girl friends, including the Junoesque Jobyna Howland, have had much to say about both of them.

Walter Plunkett, Hepburn's sometimes costumer at both RKO and MGM, provided many Hepburn stories—both "dressed" and "undressed."

"The Prince Charming of Hollywood," Douglas Fairbanks, Jr., has also shared his memories of Hepburn, both on and off the record.

A very sourpuss version of Hepburn was reported by Adolphe Menjou, who appeared in three pictures with Kate, including *Morning Glory.* Director Lowell Sherman weighed in with his impressions of directing Hepburn in *Morning Glory.*

In the early 1930s, Martin Sheehan and Greg Douglas, homosexual lovers who evolved into Elissa Landi's close confidants, provided very insiderish information about the Landi/Hepburn affair that briefly scandalized Hollywood.

Johanna Madsen, Hepburn's longtime cook and housekeeper, later in her life, provided amazing information about what was really going on both at Hepburn's private homes as well as what was happening during Hepburn's sojourn with Howard Hughes at his Muirfield estate. Johanna never managed to get her own badly written but very revealing "book of recollections" published.

Hugh Gregory contributed much valuable information about his on-again, off-again friend, Margaret Sullavan, Hepburn's nemesis.

Little Women memories were drawn from the writing team of Victor Heerman and Sarah Y. Mason, as well as from actress Jean Parker.

Joan Bennett's somewhat bitter memories about working with Hepburn on *Little Women* were also tapped, as were her much more favorable recollections of Tracy, which managed to be both affectionate and gruesome at the same time.

For her wit, humor, and insights about Hollywood, Marjorie Main deserves an Oscar. Toward the end of her life, when she had nothing to lose, this irresistible old buzzard, who appeared with Hepburn in *Undercurrent,* had many tales to tell, not only about Robert Taylor, but about Barbara Stanwyck, Robert Mitchum, Cary Grant, Billie Burke, Spring Byington, Agnes Moorehead, and Dorothy Arzner. When Main made *The Egg and I* with Claudette Colbert, the two actresses became very friendly. Main knew many of the intimate details about the Hepburn/Colbert affair.

After her death in 1975, Main's best buddy, Carl Malone, published the hilarious "Did You Know Ma Kettle was a Dyke?" which was distributed in mimeographed form in Greenwich Village during the summer of 1978.

Only bitter pills emerged from John Cromwell, who directed Hepburn in *Spitfire,* and from her co-stars in that film, Robert Young and Ralph Bellamy, both actors claiming that they would never want to work with her again.

Many theater people, both cast and crew, contributed to the portrait of producer Jed Harris, "The Vampire of Broadway." An assistant to Harris, and Hepburn's friend, Jimmy Schure, provided many of the most gruesome details.

Special gratitude is extended to Isabella Stevenson, who later became the doyenne of the Tony Awards, for introducing me to fifteen people in the 1960s and early 1970s, who collectively contributed an entire volume of information about the dreaded Jed Harris. Most of these theatrical people spoke—since Harris was alive at the time—on condition of anonymity. Ruth Gordon and Helen Hayes, however, were particularly outspoken, not only about Harris but about his treatment of Hepburn.

Jean Dalrymple was a major contributor. She told wicked stories about Harris, whom she had dated briefly, and his treatment of her actor clients, Cary Grant and James Cagney.

Jo Mielziner (brother of Kenneth MacKenna), Blanche Bates, and Frances Starr provided data about Hepburn's ill-fated appearance in *The Lake,* as did Tony Miner. Actor Colin Clive was most revealing about working with Hepburn in the film, *Christopher Strong,* and the stage play, *The Lake.* Writer Ben Hecht also provided information and is quoted directly.

Some of Harris' own comments were used directly when he conducted his own autopsy on *The Lake.*

Leopold Stokowski spoke several times about his own encounters with Laura Harding and Hepburn.

A special tribute goes to scholar Fredric Ballman for letting me use some of his own extensive thesis research into the private lives of Eleanor and Franklin Roosevelt. As a journalist, I met Mrs. Roosevelt late in her life, and on some occasions, I was her escort to various political and social functions. At no time did the subject of Katharine Hepburn ever come up. Ballman and Patricia Peardon were my main sources for describing the intimate link between the First Lady and Hepburn.

548

The one actress who was never reluctant to talk about Hepburn, whether asked to or not, was Margaret Sullavan, who loathed her. Surprisingly, she had nothing but good things to say about Jed Harris. (Apparently, she was the only person in the world who did.)

Another Hepburn nemesis, Ginger Rogers, was far less outspoken about Hepburn, but still devastating in her appraisals. However, she'd end every revelation with the admonition, "Don't print that!"

In Key West, my friend, Gregory Hemingway, related to me his father's many memories of Marlene Dietrich and, to a lesser extent, tales about his father's brief involvement with Hepburn.

Over the years, Irene Mayer Selznick revealed much about Hepburn to her friends and confidants, including Tennessee Williams, although she was never completely candid about her own intimacies with Hepburn.

Thanks go to Mexican journalist Diego Sanchez for the reports he filed on Kate's Mexican divorce from Luddy.

Stanley Ridges, the British character actor, found Hepburn "sadistic" to work with, viewing her somewhat like "a female Jed Harris."

Actor John Beal co-starred with Hepburn in *The Little Minister* and *Break of Hearts,* both flops. He blamed both Hepburn movies for derailing what might have become a promising film career.

With different escorts, Paulette Goddard and Franchot Tone arrived at the opening night of the Broadway play *Midgie Purvis,* starring Tallulah Bankhead. Later that night, Tallulah invited both of them to her townhouse, and extended the same invitation to Stanley Haggart, James Leo Herlihy, and myself.

It was a memorable evening, as Tallulah, Tone, and Goddard told wicked and very personal stories, with Tallulah directing the traffic. At one point in the evening, Hepburn's name came up. Each of the stars spoke about their own startling encounters with Hepburn, sparing few details for such an appreciative audience as us.

Francis Lederer, one of Stanley Haggart's best friends, was an avowed enemy of Hepburn's. As the years went by, and in conversations with him, he never lost his bitterness toward her and their ill-fated attempt to make *Break of Hearts* before he was fired. The starring role was awarded to Charles Boyer. Boyer himself would discuss Hepburn, but never with references to his sexual relationship with her. Others close to the scene were only too willing to talk about Boyer and Hepburn, however.

I'm grateful for the many reporters who have investigated the private life of Charles Boyer, especially Robin Hansberry.

Thanks also to actress Una Merkel, who was the protagonist in a single brief encounter with Spencer Tracy—but what an encounter it was!

More than a dozen former employees at RKO contributed information about the Jane Loring/Hepburn romantic link, including friends such as Robert De Grasse and Van Nest Polglase who worked with Kate on *Alice Adams,* among many others of her films. William Hamilton and Carroll Clark had much to say about the relationship, and Edward Killy also got his word in too.

A few lines in this biography came from Irene Dunne, not exactly an admirer of Hepburn.

Makeup artist Mel Burns, already mentioned, kept popping up as a fountain of information about many of Hepburn's films, as did RKO writers Anthony Veiller and Jane Murfin. Philip Moeller provided much useful material about the making of *Break of Hearts.*

Director Richard Wallace had nothing but anti-Hepburn stories to tell after having worked with her on *The Little Minister.*

For the public and private life of Fred MacMurray, Patricia Clary and Robbin Coons, who knew the actor well, shared their information with me.

For George Stevens, and in particular his relationship with Hepburn, the late Hollywood scholar Don Forrest was a beacon in the night. He seemed to know about every time Stevens went to the bathroom.

Betty Grable's comments about both her lover, Stevens, and his relationship with Hepburn were also amusing.

Many thanks to lovely Hattie McDaniel, in the late 1940s, who provided stories about Hepburn, Tallulah, *Gone With the Wind,* and Hollywood "as seen from the maid's perspective."

Over a lobster dinner along the Maine coast, Bette Davis shared her memories of Kate. It was obvious that she both admired her and was jealous of her at the same time.

Thanks to Jeb Burnhill, a airplane mechanic in St. Louis, for contributing a quote about a strange Hepburn/Leland Hayward stopover in his town.

Henry Cable at RKO strongly expressed his views about Hepburn's antagonism—even violence—toward the press and how difficult that made their work for the men and women in the publicity department.

Brian Aherne shared his memories of Hepburn, Howard Hughes, Cary Grant, and George Cukor during the making of their doomed *Sylvia Scarlett.* He also confessed, "I played the role like a sodomite."

John Ford never talked publicly about his affair with Hepburn, and she actually went so far as to deny that it ever happened. Ward Bond, John Wayne, and countless others, however, including members of the Hepburn family, knew that their favorite daughter was lying. Additionally, Mary Ford had plenty to say throughout the years about her husband's involvement with Hepburn—nothing favorable, of course.

Cliff Reid was particularly helpful in contributing vast lore about his boss, John Ford.

Carole Lombard "dined out" in the 1930s on stories about both her own encounter and Hepburn's encounters with Fredric March.

The photographer, Joseph H. August, is cited for his behind-the-scenes report on the filming of *Mary of Scotland.*

My files on Cary Grant and Howard Hughes are as extensive, if not more so, than my dossier on Hepburn. From an early age, I have been collecting data about both Grant and Hughes from the hundreds of people who knew them, loved them (there weren't many of those), or hated them.

A Woman Rebels was one of Hepburn's worst films. Actor Herbert Marshall and director Mark Sandrich always regretted having made the picture with her. Actors Donald Crisp and Elizabeth Allan also had tales to tell for having worked on *A Woman Rebels.*

Van Heflin, rather discreetly, has gone on record about his work with Hepburn in both *A Woman Rebels* and on the stage with her in *The Philadelphia Story.* About a dozen other sources about Heflin were used, including Frederick C. Othman, former reporter for the *Hollywood Citizen-News.*

Sometimes, reporters who had had "close encounters," some of them violent, with Hepburn, lived to tell their stories, notably Philip Davis, a reporter in Connecticut who was physically assaulted, and Phyllis Sheldon, who provided a devastating appraisal._

RKO employees over the years were always a good source of information, including David Abel and Henry Berman, who knew a lot about the details of the Hepburn/Ginger Rogers encounters.

Hepburn's "gang of girls," including her stand-in, Eve March, and her secretary, Emily Perkins, were also privy to many of Hepburn's most closely guarded secrets.

Actresses Fay Bainter and Bonita Granville provided stories about events that occurred during the shooting of *Quality Street.*

Helen Jerome was a source of rage about having worked with Hepburn on the stage play, *Jane Eyre.* Once again, Tony Miner is thanked, although his recollections of *Jane Eyre* were much more favorable than Jerome's. We've even used information from Harry Weinstein, of Sons Funeral Home, in Connecticut, who functioned briefly as

Hepburn's chauffeur.

George S. Kaufman's comments about Hepburn were useful, and Patricia Peardon furnished much of the information about Hepburn's involvement with Howard Hughes during the run of *Jane Eyre.*

Minor sources include Chicago-based reporter Johanton Elder, and even the Cook County (Illinois) clerk, Michael J. Flynn.

In bits and pieces, staff members at Howard Hughes' Muirfield mansion leaked information to the press. These included Louis Prysing, Ranghild Prysing, and Richard Dreher, plus housekeeper Beatrice Dowler's account of a dinner prepared for Bugsy Siegel and hosted by Hepburn. Glen Odekirk supplied much of the information about Hughes' history-making flight around the world.

Everybody, it seems, has offered recollections of the film *Stage Door,* including its director, Gregory La Cava, as well as Lucille Ball, Eve Arden, Gail Patrick, Jack Carson, Ann Miller, and the dreaded Adolphe Menjou. The kindest and most loving stories were told by veteran actress Constance Collier, who became Hepburn's lifelong friend.

Howard Hawks made many candid remarks about directing Hepburn and Cary Grant in *Bringing up Baby.* The comedian, Walter Carlett, shared his experiences about teaching Hepburn to play screwball comedy. Veteran actress May Robson shared her memories of Hepburn and Grant as well. Phyllis Brooks spoke of her courtship with Cary Grant during the making of that film.

Police Surgeon C.E. Cornwell reported Cary Grant's attempted suicide in 1934.

Marlene Dietrich herself provided information about her eastbound train ride with Hepburn after both stars had been labeled "box office poison."

Even author John O'Hara contributed his devastating impressions about Hepburn.

During and after the filming of *Holiday* at Columbia, studio chief Harry Cohn made many disparaging remarks about Hepburn and George Cukor, especially their sexual preferences. He reserved his most devastating comment for the struggling Marilyn Monroe.

Actress Margot Grahame's "sighting" of what she saw going on in a parking lot between Randolph Scott and Cary Grant was cited in this biography.

Information about Lew Ayres was provided by a number of confidential sources, many of whom did not want to be named, although Clarence Huskins and Barry Stiller have accumulated an impressive dossier of off-screen Lew Ayres stories. Also, Ginger Rogers over the years became increasingly outspoken about the details of her marriage to Ayres.

Makeup artist Richard Moseley and Robert Ridley reported on the Errol Flynn/Hepburn photographs in period costumes when they'd hoped to be cast as Rhett Butler and Scarlett O'Hara in *Gone With the Wind.*

"Red" Hammond, a house guest at Fenwick, in Connecticut, spoke several times about what went on when the hurricane of 1938 blew the Hepburn home into the air.

Many, many sources contributed to this biography's description of the stage play *The Philadelphia Story* and its later evolution into a film. Philip Barry had much to say about it in the Forties, as did Robert Sinclair, who did the staging. Helburn and Langner of the Theatre Guild have also weighed in.

Several sources contributed to revelations about Hepburn's relationship with Joseph Cotten, including Agnes Moorehead, Orson Welles, and John Houseman, among other friends and confidants. Members of the play's cast have also made comments, including Leonore Lonergan, Vera Allen, Don Tobin, Forrest Orr, Frank Fenton, and Shirley Booth.

Pilot George Briggs, who flew Hepburn to Hyde Park for a meeting with President Roosevelt, once gave an interview about this famous trip.

Joseph Mankiewicz, when he was no longer friendly with Hepburn following their disastrous work together on *Suddenly, Last Summer,* was amazingly frank about her in his later years. He described what was really going on behind the scenes during the film he had produced, *The Philadelphia Story.* He also set the record straight about what Hepburn and Tracy really said to each other during their first meeting.

Two old friends of Henry Fonda and James Stewart from the 1930s spoke about the intimate relationship that existed between the two actors. Broderick Crawford, encountered by the author unexpectedly in Barcelona as he was wandering around alone and with nothing to do, had many a tale to tell. Josh Logan was particularly revealing about the Fonda/Stewart relationship when he directed James Leo Herlihy's play, *Blue Denim,* on Broadway.

Burgess Meredith provided much of the personal information about James Stewart during the time they roomed together.

Garson Kanin furnished much of the data about the wedding of Vivien Leigh and Laurence Oliver, where Hepburn was the maid of honor.

Actor Pat O'Brien supplied information about his lifelong pal, Spencer Tracy, and director Victor Fleming also had plenty to say about Tracy. Sean MacArthur, owner of the now-defunct Shamrock Bar, provided details about Tracy and his binges.

Bogie himself has sounded off about what he heard Hepburn say about his *Casablanca* co-star Ingrid Bergman. The ailing Swedish star made several candid revelations when we visited her at her vacation retreat on a remote island off the west coast of Sweden, but asked that they not be published during her lifetime. For lunch, she served a gigantic boiled beet and a loaf of freshly baked Swedish rye bread. Wryly, and very accurately, she predicted that *The New York Times,* upon learning of her impending death, would lead off with a headline: CO-STAR OF CASABLANCA DIES.

Over the years, Petter Lindstrom has spoken of his wife, Ingrid Bergman, and her involvements with both Tracy and Victor Fleming.

The usual gang—Stevens, Mankiewicz, Cedric Gibbons, and Edwin B. Willis—have gone on the record about the making of *Woman of the Year,* as have actors Fay Bainter, William Bendix, and Reginald Owen.

Some of the recollections of Chester Erskine were used. The writer-director-producer was a friend to both Hepburn and Tracy.

Jay Garon's former client, Hedy Lamarr, has also sounded off on Spencer Tracy and Hepburn too.

Many of the remarks Gable said about Tracy and his relationship with Hepburn were reported to his friends, and from there, widely bruited around Hollywood.

Actor Elliott Nugent revealed "my life in purgatory" during the run of the play *Without Love,* and Robert Sinclair, its director, also provided insights into behind-the-scenes struggles.

Comments by Judge Patrick O'Sullivan have been published. They were made at the time of the "final" Hepburn-Ludlow divorce in Connecticut.

Actor Forrest Tucker provided some memories (many of them a bit coy) about the filming of *Keeper of the Flame* with Hepburn and Cukor. Some of those comments were delivered in a sauna on 49th Street in New York City, when he was in town supporting Barry Goldwater for president.

Victor Saville, producer of *Keeper of the Flame,* is also thanked.

Over the years, we have accumulated as much information about Judy Garland as we have on Hepburn herself. The information used in this biography on the Hepburn/Garland relationship came from friends, enemies, co-workers, and former MGM employees. The same people had many comments about the ill-fated marriage of Garland to Vincente Minnelli. Hepburn provided details of her relationship with Garland to George Cukor, Kenneth MacKenna, and Anderson Lawler.

Although she never became a close friend, I had numerous friendly encounters with Judy Garland in New York, California, Florida, and London. Once, we encountered her in New York, wandering virtually penniless and homeless, after having made millions for MGM.

Georgia-born soldier William F. Perkins reported his attack from Tracy in New York's Rainbow Room.

Howard Strickling, publicity director of MGM, spent much of his career keeping the Hepburn/Tracy association out of the press. But in private, he often spoke candidly to friends about this ill-matched duo.

Cheryl Walker, Johnny Weissmuller, George Raft, and Sol Lesser have all spoken about Hepburn's appearance in *Stage Door Canteen.*

Dragon Seed comments and data—both publicly and privately uttered—were culled from Jack Conway, Jack Dawn, Walter Huston, Aline MacMahon, Akim Tamiroff, Agnes Moorehead, and Turhan Bey—and in addition, Lana Turner, who did not appear in the film.

Critic James Agee also had plenty to say about *Dragon Seed,* as did Pearl S. Buck, Edwin B. Willis, Wei F.H. Hsueh, Cedric Gibbons, Marguerite Roberts, and Jane Murfin.

In Miami, Veronica Lake had comments about both Paulette Goddard and Claudette Colbert. An official at the Lincoln Film Society reported Goddard's reaction to an invitation.

Van Johnson spoke many times of the loyalty that Tracy showed him early in his career, and fellow co-star Irene Dunne had several acid comments about Tracy.

Roger Flynn, a Los Angeles policeman, supplied many of the details of Van Johnson's near decapitation in a car accident, as did Keenan Wynn, Johnson's close companion. Glen Clover, a hospital attendant, supplied other details.

In Long Island, the handsome actor, Hurd Hatfield, once gave me enough behind-the-scenes information to fill a book unto itself.

A very special thanks to Hume Cronyn and Jessica Tandy for sharing, during a visit I made to their home, their memories of Hepburn and Tracy.

Lawrence Weingarten, who produced the Tracy/Hepburn films *Without Love* and *Adam's Rib,* provided much information about each of the actor's individual foibles.

Whitey Hendry, of MGM's security division, provided data about Tracy's first attempt on the life of his brother, Carroll Tracy, and Tracy's confinement in a New York hospital. Actor Don Taylor also supplied data about his official sighting of Tracy in a mental ward.

Keenan Wynn also supplied information about the film *Without Love,* as did Lucille Ball.

Playwright Robert Sherwood has expressed his views on *The Rugged Path,* a play in which Tracy (disastrously) starred.

Paul Krueger's revelations about a weekend in Palm Springs shared by Claudette Colbert and Hepburn once had Hollywood gossips buzzing.

Irene Mayer Selznick's revelations to Tennessee Williams were not only about Hepburn but about Howard Hughes, George Cukor, and Cary Grant, among others.

Barbara Spainhour is typical of the many starlets who reported on their dates with Tracy in the late 1940s.

Many actors shared memories of making *The Sea of Grass* with Hepburn and Tracy, including Melvyn Douglas, Phyllis Thaxter, Edgar Buchanan, and Harry Carey.

Much of the information about Robert Walker, other than comments made by the actor himself, came from Walker's close friend and confidant, the writer Jim Henaghan.

Elia Kazan often spoke about his failed attempt to direct Hepburn and Tracy in *The Sea of Grass.*

Peter Lawford contributed much of the information about Robert Taylor.

Tayor spoke to several friends, including Clark Gable, about his return-from-the-war meeting with Louis B. Mayer, just before his filming of *Undercurrent* with Hepburn.

Many of Vincente Minnelli's comments on directing Hepburn in *Undercurrent* were reported directly to Pandro S. Berman, who later commented on them, as he did on Hepburn's relationship with Judy Garland.

Robert Mitchum spoke with a kind of contempt to many of his acquaintances in Hollywood about his brief affair with Hepburn. In those days, reporters heard what Mitchum said, but didn't report it, as it was against the journalistic style of the 1940s to do so.

Lena Horne has spoken out publicly about Vincente Minnelli, as did Orson Welles.

Whereas Mickey Rooney's comments on Judy Garland have been widely distributed, Joan Crawford's remarks about Garland are far more intriguing.

It was through the unpublished manuscript that the hustler, Chad Cummings, submitted to literary agent Jay Garon that I learned the intimate details between Tracy and his "rent boys."

Anderson Lawler reported on how Derek Harris (better known as John Derek) launched his Hollywood career.

Adolphe Menjou spoke out against Kate when he was co-starring with her in *State of the Union* and called her a "card-carrying communist," but not to her face.

To dozens of scholars, but in particular to Dennis Wademann, Eric Broker, and Felix Hammer, I am extremely grateful for the years of their lives they devoted to investigating Richard Nixon, J. Edgar Hoover, and J. Parnell Thomas's HUAC committee, and for their generosity in letting me see part of their hard-earned research.

Clarence Brown provided information about his direction of Hepburn in *Song of Love*, and offered insights into the Garbo/Hepburn friendship. About the same film, Artur Rubinstein and his *protégée*, Laura Dubman, provided comments about Hepburn's piano playing.

Paul Henreid, in later years, shed light on his relationship with Hepburn during the making of *Song of Love*. However, he denied that he was the author of the mysterious letters he presented to Hepburn, as she had accused him of being at the time.

June Allyson and Keenan Wynn have both spoken on the record about their respective friendships with Robert Walker.

Frank Capra provided comments about the intrigue surrounding his film, *State of the Union*, and why Claudette Cobert withdrew from the cast at the last possible moment.

Claudette Colbert, in Barbados, was a fountain of information about the Golden Days of Hollywood, but not at all helpful about her private relationship with Hepburn. After our first meeting at a dinner party, she invited me back on all of my subsequent annual trips to Barbados, and provided data galore about everybody else in Hollywood, including Spencer Tracy and Clark Gable. In all of our meetings, however, she steadfastly refused to divulge intimate details about Hepburn.

Fortunately, Colbert's friends were more outspoken, especially Larry Bremmer, who spent a good part of his life learning everything there was to know about Colbert—his favorite movie star—and her private life. Lawler, Cukor, and Kenneth MacKenna provided additional details about the Colbert/Hepburn affair, as reported directly to them by Hepburn herself.

Angela Lansbury, during the filming of *All Fall Down*, reported many favorable remarks about Hepburn to its writer, James Leo Herlihy.

Harry S. Truman, in 1959, in Key West, Florida, confirmed to me (then bureau chief of *The Miami Herald)* that *State of the Union* had remained his all-time favorite film.

I am particularly grateful for Robert Bossley's unpublished memoirs, *Life with the Oliviers at Notley Abbey*, which was submitted in 1978 to New York literary agent, Jay Garon, but never published. I was allowed to use certain material from this manuscript.

Author Vladimir Nabokov spoke out frequently about Hepburn's relationship with controversial tennis player, Bill Tilden.

Many sources contributed to information about the relationship between Hepburn and Judy Holliday, none more so than her good friend, actor Tom Ewell. In Key West, Florida, I spent many evenings with Tom when he was working in his last film, *The Last Resort,* which was based on my novel, *Butterflies in Heat.* He spoke at length about the Hepburn/Holliday affair. Additionally, during the making of *Adam's Rib,* he became Holliday's friend and confidant, remaining so for the rest of her life.

Benjamin Thau, head of casting at MGM, spoke candidly about his affair with Nancy Davis, as well as about her affairs with other men, including Spencer Tracy. Additionally, Nancy Davis Reagan herself has spoken out publicly about some of the more discreet aspects of her relationship with Tracy and Hepburn.

Dore Schary also has contributed information about starlet Nancy, as did Gottfried Reinhardt, producer at MGM.

Comments were also made by cameraman George Folsey and voice coach Nancy Burns Sydney, who helped produce Nancy's screen test for MGM.

Joe Naar, a friend of Robert Walker, and Peter Lawford also contributed highly personal and intimate information about Nancy Davis.

Michael Benthall's memories of staging the play *As You Like It,* which starred Hepburn, were also drawn upon.

William Prince, her co-star in *As You Like It,* contributed his impressions of Hepburn and the production itself, as did Theatre Guild producers Langner and Helburn.

I'd like to drink a belated toast to all the other people not named who have helped me over the years in providing rare information for my behind-the-scenes journals on Hollywood and Broadway.

Many of these people are no longer with us, but their memories linger on. Others who knew and worked with Hepburn are still around, some barely hanging onto life at this point.

To all of them, congratulations for having been involved, if only in a minor way, in the life of that remarkable piece of work known as Katharine Hepburn.

An American original.

Darwin Porter
New York City
February, 2004

INDEX*

A Month in the Country 46
A Woman Rebels 413
Adam's Rib 517, 519
Adler, Polly 28
*Admirable Crichton, Th*e 51
Agee, James 411
Aherne, Brian 206
Akins, Zoë 103-105, 109, 111, 112
Albers, Elizabeth K. 398
Alexander, Katherine 71, 72
Alice Adams 191, 193, 194, 200
Alice Sit-by-the-Fire 59
All About Eve 499
Allyson, June 490
Andress, Ursula 473
Anhalt, Julian 56
Animal Kingdom, The 60
Arden, Eve 293, 294
Arnaz, Desi 424
Arzner, Dorothy 85, 105, 109, 112
As You Like It 526, 531, 532, 533
Asher, Betty 467
Astaire, Fred 260
Atkinson, Brooks 138, 272
Avery, Phyllis 435
Ayres, Lew 226, 292, 316, 317, 318, 319
B.F.'s Daughter 477
Bacall, Lauren 516
Bachelor and the Bobby-Soxer, The 300
Ball, Lucille 261, 293, 424-426, 518
Bankhead, Tallulah 37, 38, 103, 106, 127, 163, 172, 179, 197, 211, 320, 334, 342, 347, 408
Barbour, Allie 10, 14
Barnes, Djuana 47
Barnes, Howard 504
Barondess, Barbara 97
Barry, Philip 56, 59, 328, 333, 335, 345, 390, 393, 394, 406, 424
Barrymore, Ethel 432, 513
Barrymore, John 79, 82, 83, 118
Bates, Blanche 145

Bautzer, Greg 438
Bayly, Nancy Bell 215
Beal, John 176, 181
Bellamy, Ralph 134
Benchley, Robert 28, 29, 152
Bendix, William 376
Beatty, Warren 404
Bennett, Constance 112, 128, 129, 182, 282
Bennett, Joan 128, 181, 534
Benny, Jack 460
Benny, Mary 460
Benthall, Michael 531, 532
Berg, A. Scott 6
Bergman, Ingrid 231, 380, 387, 390, 418, 453, 509
Berkshire Playhouse, The 50
Berman, Pandro S. 78, 85, 112, 135, 174, 178, 183, 194, 205, 210, 224, 258, 262, 281, 319, 412, 420, 446, 447, 529
Bey, Turhan 417
Big Pond, The 33, 34
Bill of Divorcement, A 69, 81, 89, 93
Bogart, Humphrey 390, 418, 473, 485, 516
Boland, Mary 25, 26
Bond, Ward 416, 437
Born Yesterday 517, 518
Bow, Clara 124
"Box Office Poison" 301, 314
Boyer, Charles 100, 183, 185-189, 190, 191
Brady, Bill Jr. 59
Brandt, Harry 301
Break of Hearts 180, 183, 187, 190
Brice, Fanny 211, 513
Brice, Herbert 42
Bride the Sun Shines On, The 71
Bringing Up Baby 297
Briskin, Samuel 495
Brooke, Clifford 54
Brooks, Louise 124

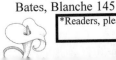
*Readers, please note: The people acknowledged in "A Cast of Thousands," begin-ning on page 537 are not included within this index

561

Brooks, Phyllis 299, 314, 315
Brown, Clarence 476, 483, 492
Brunner, Yul 488
Bryn Mawr 8- 14
Buchanan, Sidney 313
Buck, Pearl S. 411, 412
Bucquet, Harold 413, 424, 425
Burke, Billie 73, 74, 85, 106, 511
Burke, Carlton 84
Burns, Mel 179, 302
Burton, Richard 506, 507, 510
Byington, Spring 129, 130
Cabin in the Sky 460
Cagney, James 140, 378, 391
Camille 453
Campbell, Alan 64, 69, 151
Capra, Frank 495, 498, 499, 500, 503
Carey, Joyce 55
Carson, Jack 291, 298
Catlett, Walter 299
Cavett, Dick 389
Celeste, Madame Olga 297
Cerf, Bennett 497
Channing, Carol 523
Chaplin, Charles 414, 512
Chevalier, Maurice 186, 524
Christopher Strong 109, 110, 112
Claire, Ina 141
Clark, Jack 16, 19, 21, 90, 92, 115, 398
Clover, Glenn 416
Cody, Dr. Bradford 3
Cohn, Harry 312, 314, 518, 519, 522
Cohn, Yetta 520
Colbert, Claudette 123, 342, 348-352, 355, 381, 387, 390, 399, 401, 403, 413, 414, 418, 437-439, 446, 467, 488, 490, 494-499, 515
Collier, Constance 294, 295, 403, 532-534
Collier, John 204
Colman, Ronald 361, 362
Comrade X 512
Confidential Magazine 440, 474
Connolly, Myles 495
Conway, Jack 411, 412
Cooper, Gary 342, 418, 439, 495, 515
Cooper, Merian C. 134

Cornell, Katharine 91, 408
Cotten, Joseph 333-336, 343
Coughlin, Charles 154
Coward, Noël 55, 137-139, 151, 354-356, 427, 509
Cowl, Jane 54, 55
Cradle Song, The 15
Crawford, Cheryl 46
Crawford, Joan 119, 264, 391, 437, 467, 474, 509
Creelman, Eileen 426
Cromwell, John 134, 135
Cronyn, Hume 423
Crouse, Russel 495
Cukor, George 69, 70, 74, 78- 82, 102, 126, 168, 200, 205, 206, 211, 234, 248, 314, 319, 345, 350, 358, 359, 377, 381, 383, 387, 388, 391, 400, 403, 406, 415, 442, 446, 470-475, 511, 518, 525, 527
Cummings, Chad 474, 475
Cummings, Constance 54
Czarina, The 25
Dalrymple, Jean 139, 140
Daniels, William 405
Dark Victory 172, 173
Davenport, Doris (aka Doris Jordan) 332
Davids, Jill 6
Davies, Marion 300
Davis, Bette 174, 189, 200, 226, 347, 386, 404, 522
Davis, Nancy 445, 524-528, 530-534
Davis, Philip 256
Dawn, Jack 411
Day, Doris 529
De Acosta, Mercedes 48, 50, 55, 95, 163
De Grasse, Robert 195
de Havilland, Olivia 347, 404
de la Falaise de Coudraye, Le Marquis Henri 129
Death Takes a Holiday 45, 46
Dee, Francis 98
DeMille, Cecil B. 395
Derek, Bo (Mary Cathleen Collins) 473
Derek, John (aka Derek Harris) 470, 471- 473
Desire 456
Di Frasso, Countess Dorothy 101, 103,

287

Dietrich, Marlene 124, 158, 161-163, 171, 205, 304-306, 347, 352, 440, 460

Dix, Dorothy 171

Doctor's Hospital (Manhattan) 434

Douglas, Melvyn 447

Dr. Jekyll and Mr. Hyde 380, 406

Dragon Seed 409, 411, 413, 417-420

Dreher, Richard 283, 284

Dubman, Laura 483

Duke of Wellington Pub 508

Duke, Doris 205

Dunne, Irene 282, 395, 414

Edward, My Son 504, 507, 508, 510

Elizabeth II, Queen 531

Elizabeth, Empress of Austria (Sissi) 122

Ellis, Havelock 12

Erskine, Chester 382, 513

Erskine, Sally 513

Esmond, Jill 120

Evans, Linda 473

Fairbanks, Douglas Jr. 117-119, 257

Fairbanks, Douglas Sr. 101, 119

Farrell, Charles 439

Father of the Bride 534

Faye, Alice 518

Feeney, John 244, 245

Fenton, Frank 335

Fenwick 332

Ferber, Edna 204

Fernburn, Ronald 509

Fiddler, Jimmie 131

Finishing School 36

Fleming, Victor 372, 399, 415, 416

Flynn, Errol 205, 319, 326, 328, 343, 347

Flynn, Roger 416

Folsey, George 528

Fonda, Henry 125, 151, 351, 363, 420

Fontaine, Joan 262, 263, 268, 347

Fontanne, Lynn 408

For Me and My Girl 457

For Whom the Bell Tolls 418

Ford, Barbara 529

Ford, John 226-233, 236, 237, 242, 243, 284, 298, 377, 399, 420, 421, 437, 529

Ford, Mary McBride Smith 237, 238, 240, 241, 243, 244, 247, 248 421

Francis, Kay 86

Franz-Josef, Emperor of Austria & Hungary 120

French Without Tears 304

Front Page, The 370

Furness, Betty 212

Gaba, Lester 461

Gable, Clark 340, 343, 376, 379, 391, 392, 400, 422, 451, 495, 527

Gaoler's Wench, The 141

Garbo, Greta 87, 94-96, 111, 124, 173, 189, 346, 405, 440, 451, 453

Gardner, Ava 440, 492

Garfield, John 404, 479

Garland, Judy 371, 401, 402, 411, 453-469, 478, 479, 488, 492, 494, 515, 525

Garlinghouse, Caroline 7

Garson, Greer 386, 411, 450, 456, 499

Garon, Jay 387, 474, 475

Gavin, John 488

Gentlemen Prefer Blondes 523

Gerrard, Henry 177

Gibbons, Cedric 350, 412, 485

Gibbons, Irene 498

Gibbs, Lola 108

Gielgud, Sir John 507

Gilman, Charlotte Perkins 9

Goldman, Emma 9

Goddard, Paulette 319, 395-399, 404-407, 413, 414, 418

Golden, Robert 378

Gone With the Wind 319, 320, 329, 332, 391, 400

Gonzales, Dr. Juan 3

Gordon, Max 279

Gordon, Ruth 117, 139, 142, 389, 428, 517

Goulding, Edmund 174

Grable, Betty 195

Graham, Sheilah 381

Grahame, Margot 315

Granger, Farley 492

Grant, Cary 131, 140, 205, 206, 209, 211-213, 268, 285, 297, 299, 300, 303, 315, 325, 354, 355, 358, 414, 441

Green Bay Tree, The 137
Green Dolphin Street 477
Grisham, John 474
Guy Named Joe, A 395
Gwenn, Edmund 452
Gwynn, Edith 212
Haggart, Stanley Mills 90, 91, 354
Haines, William 99, 347, 391
Hale, Justin 405
Hamilton, Nancy 91, 92, 93
Harding, Ann 282
Harding, J. Barclay 32
Harding, J. Horace 43
Harding, Laura 31, 32, 39, 43, 49, 52, 53, 64, 65, 75, 81, 87, 92, 97, 99, 115, 122, 125, 127, 131, 153, 169, 170, 178, 179, 184, 201, 224, 238, 239, 321, 365, 368, 383, 403, 407, 428, 435, 466, 480
Harlow, Jean 294, 339
Harris, Jed 111, 124, 137 140-150, 155, 156, 181, 389
Harris, Lawson 470
Harris, Leland 107
Harris, Mildred 146
Harrison, Rex 448
Harsh, Judge Fresh 362
Hasso, Signe 423
Hatfield, Hurd 418, 419
Hawes, Elizabeth 76
Hawks, Howard 297, 298, 300
Hayden, Sterling 516
Hayes, Helen 142, 146, 224, 225, 495
Hayward, Leland 65, 66, 70, 76, 89, 104, 107, 108, 110, 119, 123-125, 156, 157, 165-168, 172, 174, 177, 178, 180, 183, 199, 201-203, 212, 249, 261, 292, 308, 357, 373, 379, 399
Hayworth, Rita 518
Hearst, William Randolph 300, 405
Heerman, Victor 125, 133, 175, 180
Heflin, Van 250, 254, 255, 334, 336, 343, 477
Helburn, Theresa 173, 269, 390, 397, 406
Hemingway, Ernest 158-165, 170, 171, 452
Hemingway, Gregory 164

Henaghan, Jim 492, 493, 504
Hendrey, Whitey 434, 435
Henreid, Lisl 489
Henreid, Paul 483, 484, 487, 514, 516
Hepburn, Dick 310, 331
Hepburn, James, Earl of Bothwell 8
Hepburn, Kit 3, 7-9, 116, 154, 203, 242, 309, 429, 533
Hepburn, Margaret (Peg) 156
Hepburn, Marion 156
Hepburn, Richard 156
Hepburn, Robert (Bob) 156
Hepburn, Sewell 5
Hepburn, the Rev. Sewell Snowdon 8
Hepburn, the Rev. Sewell Stavely 39
Hepburn, Dr. Thomas 3, 4, 8, 9, 12, 14, 45, 116, 167, 168, 202, 203, 241, 247, 267, 309, 385, 397, 421, 429
Hepburn, Tom 1, 4-7, 42, 302
Hickok, Lorena 366
Hitler, Adolf 422
Hodiak, John 416
Hoey, Dennis 269
Holiday 36, 308, 313
Holland, Judge Cecil B. 491
Holliday, Judy 517-521, 523
Hollywood Women's Press Club 386
Hoover, J. Edgar 480
Hopkins, Arthur 35, 41, 42
Hopkins, Miriam 124
Hopper, Hedda 194, 350, 371, 426, 446, 449, 478
Horn, Frank 207
Horne, Lena 460, 524
Houghton, Alfred Augustus 3, 7
Houghton, Amory Bigelow 7
Howard, Leslie 57, 58, 60
Howland, Jobyna 105, 111
Hsueh, Wei F. 412
HUAC (House Un-American Activities Committee) 488, 501, 515, 516, 523, 524
Hudson, Rock 440
Hughes, Allene Gano 216-219
Hughes, Howard 207, 209, 210, 212, 213, 215, 218-221, 267, 269, 270-283, 285, 286, 299, 301, 308, 309, 317, 321-

326, 329, 346-348, 420, 442, 466, 467, 516

Hull, Henry 56

Hume, Benita 361

Hurricane of 1938, The 329, 330

Huston, John 515, 516

Huston, Walter 418

Hutton, Barbara 301

It Took Nine Tailors (autobiography of Adolphe Menjou) 501

It's a Wonderful Life 495

Ivoryton Playhouse 56

Jane Eyre 268, 270, 279

Jerome, Helen 271, 272

Johnson, Dolores 470

Johnson, Van 395, 414-417, 423, 500

Jones, Jennifer 423, 483, 489, 490, 530

Kanin, Garson 310, 312, 360-363, 369, 377, 383, 384, 394, 420, 422, 427-430, 433, 434, 517

Kanin, Michael 369, 386

Kaufman, George S. 142, 291

Kaufman, The Rev. Charles E. 154

Kaye, Danny 488, 516

Kazan, Elia 446-449

Keel, Howard 528

Keenan, Evie 423

Keenan, Wynn 423

Keeper of the Flame 396, 399, 400, 402, 403, 405, 478

Kelly, Gene 457, 459, 461, 462, 464-467

Kennedy, Joseph 78, 129

Kerr, Deborah 508

Keyes, Evelyn 516

Keyes, Marion Herwood 425

Kilbride, Percy 401

Kirkland, Alexander 51

Knock on Any Door 473

Knopf, Alfred 25

Knopf, Edwin 25, 34

Krueger, Paul 439, 440

La Cava, Gregory 288-296

La Rocque, Rod 391

Lake, The 145, 151, 155

Lake, Veronica 413, 414

Lamarr, Hedy 359, 372, 387, 396, 398, 411, 485, 486, 492

Lamour, Dorothy 315

Landi, Elissa 68, 111, 120-123

Landis, Carole 448

Langer, Ralph 285

Langner, Lawrence 269, 394-397, 406

Lansbury, Angela 500

Lardner, Ring Jr. 369, 386, 515

Lawford, Peter 416, 450, 530

Lawler, Anderson 103, 127, 185, 345, 383, 384, 387, 437, 442, 459, 465, 471, 494

Lawrence, Ralph 499

Lederer, Francis 181-183, 186

Lee, Gypsy Rose 408

Leigh, Vivien 332, 359-362, 505-507, 510

Levy, Benn W. 54

Lewis, Sinclair 369

Liberty Films 495, 499

Lincoln Center Film Society 414

Lindsay, Howard 495

Lindstrom, Petter 390, 399

Little Minister, The 175-178

Little Women 123, 126, 133

Litvak, Anatole 404

Logan, Joshua 352

Lombard, Carole 231, 232, 352, 392

Loring, Jane 183-185, 195-197, 201, 202, 210, 221, 230, 231, 247, 250, 259, 262, 413, 448

Lortel, Lucille 375

Lowe, Edmund 102

Lunt, Alfred 408

MacArthur, Sean 379

MacFarlane, Mrs. 463

MacKenna, Kenneth 26, 33, 54, 74, 86, 119, 345, 402, 442

MacMahon, Aline 51, 417

MacMurray, Fred 194-196, 401

Mädchen in Uniform 111

Madsen, Johanna 284

Madwoman of Chaillot 488

Main, Marjorie 130, 132, 401

Malaya 532

Mamoulian, Rouben 46, 97

Mandl, Fritz 486

Mankiewicz, Joseph 353, 372-375, 380,

437, 481

Manning, Helen Taft 14, 23

Marc, Dr. 463

March, Fredric 231, 232, 516

Markey, Gene 128

Marlow, Hugh 516

Marshall, Herbert 250, 252

Mary of Scotland 212, 223-225, 229, 230, 236, 248, 249

Mason, Sarah Y. 125, 133, 175, 180

Maugham, W. Somerset 511

Mayer, Louis B. 173, 343, 372, 373, 379, 384, 385, 389, 395, 398, 400-406, 411, 416, 442, 448, 449, 451, 453, 456, 457, 461, 467, 476, 477, 479, 494, 499, 511, 514, 524

McCall's "Woman of the Year" Contest 386

McCarey, Leo 479

McCarthy, Senator Joseph 501

McCrea, Joel 98, 318

McDaniel, Hattie 198, 332

McKnight, Robert J. 15, 26, 365

McLaglen, Victor 229

Me (Katharine Hepburn's autobiography) 5, 10, 380, 399

Meet Me in Saint Louis 457

Menjou, Adolphe 289, 290, 477, 501-503

Menken, Helen 224

Meredith, Burgess 414

Merkel, Una 182

Messenger, Lillie 68

Meyer, Gabriel 216

Mielziner, Jo 145

Miller, Ann 294

Miller, Gilbert 57, 59

Minnelli, Liza 457, 458, 463, 464

Mineo, Sal 488

Miner, Tony 145, 146, 268

Minnelli, Vincente 453-455, 457, 459-461, 465, 468, 493

Mitchum, Robert 454, 455, 456

Moeller, Philip 180, 182, 184, 188

Monroe, Marilyn 518

Montgomery, George 475

Montgomery, Robert 420

Moorehead, Agnes 417, 418

Morley, Robert 505

Morning Glory 117, 129

Morro Castle, S.S. 170

Mortimer, Lee 504

Moseley, Richard 327

Moses, Harry 60, 63, 64

Motion Picture Costumers Local #705 397

Mourning Becomes Electra 173

Mrs. Grant 361, 363

Naar, Joe 530

Nabokov, Vladimir 512

National Theater, The (Washington, D.C.) 430, 431

Nazimova, Alla 46-48, 50, 527

Newhill, Charles 148, 256, 324

Newton-Brainard family, the 10

Ninotchka 512

Nissa (the Brazilian leopard) 297

Nixon, Richard M. 478, 480, 481

Notley Abbey 504, 506, 508, 509

Novarro, Ramon 99, 391

Now, Voyager 484

Nugent, Elliott 393, 397

O'Brien, George 234

O'Brien, Pat 379, 391, 402

Odekirk, Glen 288

Odets, Clifford 355

O'Hara, John 312

O'Hara, Maureen 495

Oliver, Edna Mae 129

Olivier, Laurence 120, 121, 138, 141, 356, 360-362, 505-507

O'Neill, Eugene 173

Oppenheim, David 520

O'Rourke, Peter 3

O'Sullivan, Judge Patrick 398

Paley, Natasha 207

Pankhurst, Emmaline 9

Park, Marion Edwards 16

Parker, Dorothy 28, 65, 151, 204, 269, 336

Parks, Larry 479

Parsons, Louella 446

Paterson, Pat 186, 188, 190

Patrick, Gail 293

566

Peardon, Patricia 269, 272, 341, 367, 368, 384, 385, 388, 396, 428, 430-432, 435, 442, 446, 480, 496, 522
Perkins, Emily 270
Perkins, Osgood 50
Perkins, William F. 408
Philadelphia Story, The 328, 332, 333, 335, 337, 341, 342, 350, 365, 366, 369
Philip of Windsor, Duke of Edinburgh 531
Pickford, Mary 84, 101, 119
Pirate, The 457
Plough and the Stars, The 377
Plunkett, Walter 126, 128, 177, 447, 485
Polly Adler's bordello 28
Porter, Cole 524
Post, Robert 10
Powell, Selina Lloyd 8
Power, Tyrone 420, 467
Pressman, Dr. Joel 348, 496, 497
Prince, William 532
Pritchett, Florence 492
Private Life, A (The Autobiography of Irene Mayer Selznick) 443
Prysing, Louis 282
Putnam, H. Phelps 22-24, 27
Quality Street 258, 261, 266
Quo Vadis? 451
Raft, George 287, 408
Rainbow Room, The 407
Rainer, Luise 309
Rambaugh, Bertha 2
Reagan, Ronald 174, 489, 503, 529, 531
Reid, Cliff 235
Reinhardt, Gottfriedt 528
Ridges, Stanley 172
Ridley, Robert 327
Ring of Steel 422
Roberts, Marguerite 412
Robinson, Edward G. 477
Robinson-Duff, Frances 30, 33, 52
Robson, May 298, 299
Rockefeller, Nelson 396, 480
Rogers, Edward A. 481
Rogers, Ginger 80, 177, 196, 203, 222, 223-226, 251, 260, 263, 282, 289, 291, 292, 294, 296, 312, 347, 366, 395, 405

Romantic Young Lady, A 51
Rooney, Mickey 465, 466
Roosevelt, Eleanor 149, 339-341, 344, 366-368, 396, 478
Roosevelt, Franklin D. 148, 337, 338, 340, 367, 426, 427
Rose, David 457
Royal Fandango, A 432
Rubinstein, Artur 483
Rugged Path, The 427, 428, 430, 433
Rumbold, Lord Hugo 105, 111
Russell, Rosalind 503
Sagan, Leontine 105, 111
Sandrich, Mark 250-252, 413
Sanger, Margaret 9, 154, 429, 458
Saville, Victor 400
Schary, Dore 514, 524, 528, 530
Schubert, J.J. 35
Schure, Jimmy 138
Scott, Randolph 131, 300, 315, 355
Sea of Grass, The 433, 446, 448, 449, 450, 489
Selznick, David O. 69, 70, 78-80, 89, 168, 319, 332, 391, 400, 423, 442, 489-491
Selznick, Irene Mayer 11, 70, 168, 169, 441-443, 446, 448, 465, 490, 510
Selznick, Myron 66, 76, 89, 155
Seventh Cross, The 423
Shaw, George Bernard 369
Shearer, Norma 253, 357
Sheldon, Phyllis 257
Sherman, Lowell 117
Sherwood, Robert 427, 431, 432
Shields, Jimmie 347
Siegel, Bugsy 286, 287
Sign of the Cross 123
Sinatra, Frank 512, 531
Since You Went Away 418, 490, 491
Sinclair, Robert 393
Sleeper, Martha 428
Smith, C. Aubrey 118
Smith, Gertrude Clemson 22
Smith, Kate 468
Smith, Lewis I. 22
Smith, Ludlow Ogden (Luddy) 17, 20, 21, 24, 38-42, 51, 69, 72, 90, 92, 143,

144, 151, 157, 168-170, 172, 204, 307, 327, 348, 381, 397, 398, 435
So Proudly We Hailed 413
Song of Love 476, 479, 483, 489, 494
Spainhour, Barbara 445
Spencer, John 433
Spitfire 133, 134, 135, 136, 137
St. Johns, Adela Rogers 353
Stage Door 204, 288, 292, 296, 400
Stage Door Canteen 408, 478
Stanwyck, Barbara 264, 450-452, 509, 518
Starr, Frances 145
State of the Union 86, 494, 496, 498, 499, 501, 503
Steele, Suzanne 152, 153, 155-158
Stein, Gertrude 159, 160
Stevens, George 191, 193-199, 202, 221, 222, 259-262, 266, 267, 315, 370, 376, 378, 385, 400, 495
Stewart, Donald Ogden 313, 314, 345, 396, 400, 424, 425, 478, 510
Stewart, James 351, 352, 354, 355, 356, 357, 358, 359, 363, 364, 420, 532
Stiefel, Milton 56
Stokowski, Leopold 71, 148
Stone, Lewis 502
Strickling, Howard 408, 467
Suicide Attempt (Cary Grant's) 303
Suicide Attempt (Hepburn's) 302
Sullavan, Margaret 124, 146, 149, 150, 151, 175, 177, 186, 193, 202, 204, 213, 222, 249, 288, 351, 352, 357, 363, 399, 495
Swanson, Gloria 522
Swing Time 260
Sydney, Nancy Burns 528
Sylvia Scarlett 205, 210, 211, 452
Symon, Burk 60
Tandy, Jessica 423
Tashman, Lilyan 102
Taylor, Don 434
Taylor, John 3
Taylor, Laurette 59
Taylor, Robert 450-453, 476, 477
Temple, Shirley 300
Tenth Avenue Angel 511

Thalberg, Irving 253
Thau, Benjamin 528
Thaxter, Phyllis 447
The Egg and I 401
The Good Earth 411
The Lake 111, 400
Theatre Guild, The 406
These Days 35
Thirty Seconds over Tokyo 423, 450
Thomas, J. Parnell 478, 479, 515
Thompson, Dorothy 369
Three Came Unarmed 97
Tierney, Gene 437
Tilden, "Big Bill" 512, 513
Tobin, Dan 335
Tone, Franchot 258, 263-266, 311
Torch Bearers, The 51
Tortilla Flat 396
Towle, Mary 1, 2, 65
Tracy, Carroll 406, 407, 427, 433, 444
Tracy, John 382, 399, 406
Tracy, Louise Treadwell 320, 382, 399, 406, 430, 444, 450
Tracy, Spencer 57, 182, 231, 305, 311, 343, 360, 370-388, 391-395, 398, 400-404, 408, 414-422, 424, 427-450, 455, 458, 466, 468, 472, 474, 475, 479, 480, 487, 494-496, 499, 509, 514, 522, 524-526, 532, 533
Tracy, Susie 399
Truman, Harry S. 431, 478, 481, 503, 504
Trumbo, Dalton 424
Truth About Blayds, The 14
Tucker, Forrest 400, 401
Turner, Lana 392, 417, 440, 445
Two-Faced Woman 129
Undercurrent 450-452, 476
Valentino, Rudolph 99
Van Dyke, Woody 352
Veiller, Anthony 495
Virtuous Sin, The 86
Waldorf-Astoria, The 433
Walker, Cheryl 408
Walker, Robert 423, 449, 457, 483, 489, 490-494, 504, 512, 529, 530, 533
Walker, Tracy 6

Walker, Virginia 298
Wallace, Henry 478
Wallace, Richard 176, 177
Wanger, Walter 99
Warrior's Husband, The 60, 63, 64
Watson, Cathy 6
Wayne, John 437
Weingarten, Lawrence 424
Weinstein, Harry 269
Weissmuller, Johnny 408
Welles, Orson 460
Welman, William 100
West, Mae 132, 133, 474
Whalen, Grover 322, 325
Willkie, Wendell 495
Williams, Hope 36, 37, 41, 44, 45, 60, 106
Williams, Tennessee 447
Willis, Edwin B. 412, 425, 485
Winterset 261
Without Love 390, 393, 395, 396, 406, 408, 424, 426
Woman in the Moone, The 24
Woman of Distinction, A 503
Woman of the Year 378, 385
Woman Rebels, A 250, 257
Wood, Sam 479
Wyler, William 193, 495
Wylie, I.A.R. 400
Wyman, Jane 489, 529
Wynn, Evie 415
Wynn, Keenan 415, 416, 424, 426, 490
Young, Loretta 320, 353, 391
Young, Robert 134
Ziegfeld, Florenz 73, 85
Zorina, Vera 418
Zukor, Adolph 75

If you've enjoyed this book from

Please consider these other fine works by
Darwin Porter
from the

The Secret Life of
HUMPHREY BOGART;
The Early Years (1899-1931)
by Darwin Porter

When it was released in June of 2003, this book ignited a firestorm of media controversy that spilled immediately from the tabloids into mainstream newspapers, magazines, and talk shows.

This is one of the best, most controversial, and most revealing books about the Movie Stars of the Golden Age ever written.

The Secret Life of
Humphrey Bogart
The Early Years
(1899 - 1931)
Darwin Porter

This myth-shattering biography gives a controversial CLOSEUP of a young, hot and horny Bogart pre-Casablanca, pre-Bacall, pre-African Queen. Revealing for the first time what was under the trench coat of history's most famous movie star

from The Georgia Literary Association
ISBN 0966-8030-5-1
528 pages, plus 64 photos and an index. $16.95

"Humphrey Bogart was one of Hollywood's most celebrated lovers, his romance with Lauren Bacall hailed as one of the greatest love stories of the 20th century. But before they met, he was a drug-taking womanizer, racking up a string of failed marriages and broken relationships with some of the world's most beautiful women. In this extraordinary biography, drawing on a wealth of previously unseen material, veteran showbusiness writer Darwin Porter, author of Hollywood's Silent Closet, reveals the truth about Bogart's shady past."

As reported by London's **Mail on Sunday** in June of 2003

Hollywood's
by Darwin Porter
Silent Closet

AN ANTHOLOGY OF STAR-STUDDED SCANDAL
FROM THE HEYDAY OF SILENT FILMS

Compiled from hundreds of interviews with survivors of the Silent Screen, this is the most intimate and most erotic novel ever written about sex, murder, blackmail, and degradation in early Hollywood.

Quirky but brilliant, it's a well-crafted compilation of Hollywood gossip that was recited, years later, to celebrity interviewer Darwin Porter.

If you believe, like Truman Capote, that "the artful presentation of gossip will become the literature of the 21st century," then you will LOVE this book. Irreverent and juicy, it's the most shocking overview of behind-the-scenes Hollywood scandal ever published. "Langorously decadent."

ISBN 0966-8030-2-7 746 pages, 60 photos $24.95
www.GeorgiaLit.com